PANAMA

THE WHOLE STORY

KEVIN BUCKLEY

SIMON & SCHUSTER
New York   London   Toronto   Sydney   Tokyo   Singapore

Simon & Schuster
Simon & Schuster Building
Rockefeller Center
1230 Avenue of the Americas
New York, New York 10020

DESIGNED BY BARBARA MARKS
Manufactured in the United States of America

10 9 8 7 6 5 4 3 2 1

Library of Congress Cataloging-in-Publication Data

Buckley, Kevin.
    Panama : the whole story / Kevin Buckley.
        p.   cm.
    Includes bibliographical references and index.
    1. Panama—Politics and government—1981–
    2. Panama—History—American invasion, 1989—
    Causes. 3. Panama—Foreign relations—United
    States. 4. United States—Foreign relations—Panama.
    I. Title.
    F1567.B83   1991
    972.8705'3—dc20   91-2727
                                                   CIP

    ISBN 0-671-72794-X

Acknowledgments

"PANAMA DESK" was the nickname for the project among a very small group of people whose hard work helped me to write this book and whom I want to thank. Their contributions included research, fact-checking, steady attention to the events of the story, and a shared fascination with the strange turns events often took. Rebecca Chace was present when "Panama Desk" was born, and every page and note of this book is graced by her diligence and intelligence. Her meticulously assembled "timeline" of events was the basic path of the story. Michael Preston followed in her path. Without him, many parts of the story might have remained obscure.

Others who were at one time or another members of "Panama Desk": John Therese, Laurence Heath, Sarah V. Chace, Silvana Paternostro, Kate Doyle, the Rev. George Kuhn, Tito Mesa, Matt Schudel, Barbara E. McMullen, John F. McMullen, Lenny Glynn, Peter Andrews, Kitty D'Alessio, John Stockwell, Hannah Kaiser, Robert G. Kaiser, Larry Collins, Martie Proffitt, Nicholas C. Proffitt, Bernard Berkowitz, Dr. Lewis Sorley, Arthur T. Hadley, and Peter Emerson.

At Simon & Schuster, my thanks for the extraordinary efforts of Alice Mayhew and George Hodgman on my behalf. I also want to thank Adelle-Marie Stan, Lydia Buechler, Jane Herman, and Steve Messina for all their assistance. I am indebted to the Simon & Schuster legal department, especially Eric Rayman, Emily R. Remes, and Felice Einhorn.

I am grateful to Jonathan Black, Peter Moore, Reg Potterton, Amanda Urban, David Hollander, William F. Wisneski, and Richard Waltzer for all their counsel and assistance.

In Panama, I want to thank a number of people who helped me in very different ways. It occurs to me that these people would probably never assemble in one place except on this page: the Spadafora family; Jose de Jesus ("Chuchu") Martinez; Queenie Altamirano and her family; Willie K. Friar; Michele Labrut; the staff of the Continental Hotel, and especially its indefatigable telephone operators; Alonso O. Fernandez, Jr., and his family; David Amado; the Reverend Xavier Villanueva; Monsignor Sebastian Laboa; Fred Sill; Elba Guardia; Roberto Arias, Jr., and his family; Louis Martinz; and Gerasimos "Gerry" Kanelopulos and his family. In fact, Gerry's internationally famous Argosy bookstore in Panama City might be the only other single place these individuals might assemble.

For Gail

Contents

Contents

Cast of Characters

IN PANAMA:

ARNULFO ARIAS: Four times elected president of Panama and never completed a term. Died in 1988.

RICARDO ARIAS CALDERON: Elected vice president of Panama, 1989.

NICOLAS ARDITO BARLETTA: President of Panama, 1984–85.

JOSE BLANDON: Former political adviser to Noriega; a key witness in the 1988 indictments of Noriega.

ARTHUR DAVIS: American ambassador to Panama, 1986–89.

ERIC ARTURO DELVALLE: President of Panama, 1985–88; attempted to fire Noriega and was himself fired in February 1988; supported by the U.S. government until 1989.

COL. ROBERTO DIAZ HERRERA: Officer of the Panama Defense Forces (PDF) who retired in June 1987 and made shocking statements about Noriega and corruption within the PDF.

GUILLERMO ENDARA: Elected president of Panama, 1989.

GUILLERMO "BILLY" FORD: Elected vice president of Panama, 1989.

MAJ. MOISES GIROLDI: PDF officer who attempted coup against Noriega in October 1989; killed when coup collapsed.

MIKE HARARI: "Former" member of Israeli intelligence; political adviser to and business partner of Noriega.

COL. EDUARDO HERRERA-HASSAN: PDF officer recruited by the Reagan administration to lead a coup in 1988 and subsequently an exile in Miami. In 1991, Herrera-Hassan was in a Panamanian jail.

MONSIGNOR SEBASTIAN LABOA: The papal nuncio in Panama City.

GABRIEL LEWIS: Former Panamanian ambassador to the United States; opposition member and lobbyist in Washington, D.C.

LOUIS MARTINZ: Opposition member; former editor of opposition paper *YA!*; press secretary for Arnulfo Arias and press secretary for President Guillermo Endara.

GEN. MANUEL ANTONIO NORIEGA: Until 1983, head of G-2 (Intelligence) of the PDF; commander of the PDF, 1983–89.

GUILLERMO SANCHEZ BORBON: Columnist for the opposition paper *La Prensa*.

HUGO SPADAFORA: Guerrilla fighter and Noriega opponent; murdered on September 13, 1985.

WINSTON SPADAFORA: Hugo's brother, an attorney and member of the opposition; took up the cause of justice for Hugo after his murder.

GEN. MAX THURMAN: Commander, SOUTHCOM, September 1989–October 1990.

OMAR TORRIJOS: Charismatic military dictator of Panama, 1968–81; negotiated the 1978 Panama Canal treaties; killed in a plane crash in 1981.

GEN. FRED WOERNER: Commander, SOUTHCOM, June 1987–September 1989.

IN WASHINGTON:

ELLIOTT ABRAMS: assistant secretary of state for inter-American affairs under President Ronald Reagan, 1985–89.

GEORGE BUSH: President of the United States.

WILLIAM CASEY: Director of the CIA during the Reagan administration.

GREG CRAIG: Congressional aide to Senator Edward Kennedy; worked with Deborah DeMoss.

DEBORAH DEMOSS: Senator Jesse Helms's congressional aide.

JOEL MCCLEARY: American political analyst who annoyed Noriega with blunt criticism.

LT. COL. OLIVER NORTH: White House aide whom Noriega mesmerized and used.

NESTOR SANCHEZ: CIA officer and later an influential consultant at the Department of Defense.

Introduction

IN early September 1987, I went to interview Gen. Manuel Antonio Noriega in his office at the Comandancia, the white, five-story concrete building where the Panamanian Defense Forces were headquartered. The ground rules for our meeting prohibited questions about the political crisis that had exploded in Panama that summer. Also specifically forbidden were questions from me about the accusations that Noriega was a murderer, a sadist, a cocaine trafficker, a practitioner of voodoo, a spy for Cuba, and a secret U.S. ally in the Contra underworld.

The rules were fine by me. Noriega had denied all the accusations against him in the past and rarely said anything interesting in public about his own real work. I just wanted Noriega to talk about himself. We met under cordial circumstances even though one of his most outspoken enemies had helped me get to see him. She simply called one of her very good friends, who was also an intimate of Noriega and who came along that afternoon. Panama City was a very cosmopolitan place and a very small town.

When I entered his office he stood and almost posed for just a moment behind his desk. Behind him was a vast framed map of the world, one of the biggest produced by the National Geo-

13

graphic Society. Then he came forward, a broad smile on his famous pitted face, and shook my hand. We all took seats around a large glass coffee table. At the far end of the room was a conference table surrounded by heavily padded executive swivel chairs done up in camouflage fabric.

Noriega did not remain seated for long; he was soon on his feet again, getting a book from the shelves to show me. It was a collection of Salvador Dali's work. Noriega said Dali was his favorite painter because of "his satiric view, his mockery of humanity."

Noriega enjoyed showing me around the office and was especially proud of the huge collection of miniature frogs that adorned his bookcases. The frog, *sapo* in Spanish, was the mascot of the intelligence unit Noriega had commanded for many years. "Sapo" was also the nickname for all of Noriega's reputedly innumerable secret agents.

He invited me to look over his desk, which, he volunteered, was made of Chinese rosewood. There were several phones, many scattered folders, and a notepad. Under the glass he had placed small color photographs of Pope Pius XII and Pope John XXIII and between them the business card of Washington journalist John McLaughlin, who had interviewed Noriega and whom Noriega said he greatly admired. "Is very honest," he said, trying his hesitant English. "Was exactly all my expressions. No change anything."

The other prominent feature in the room was a large painting near his desk. In delicate lines and pale hues it portrayed two young women. They seemed to be huddled together, hovering on the edge of tears. We stood back and examined it silently. I asked Noriega what he saw in their faces. "Wonder," he said and beamed. His face was transfigured. He looked up, as if he were a wonderstruck, innocent lad.

He made it clear that he had no quarrel with the American people. He told me he admired "the formation of the United States people, the arrival of the pilgrims, their struggle for freedom against a foreign power."

Maj. Edgardo Lopez, the PDF press officer, looked at me and smiled. "You get the point?" Lopez asked. Everyone laughed.

He told me that he wanted to emulate Simon Bolivar and make Panama what Corinth was in ancient times, a bridge and a center of civilization. Noriega also wanted to get it across to me that he was a real stud. He said he tried to find time for lunch with his secretaries as often as possible. They were, he told me with a man-to-man little wink, "very good-looking."

His interests certainly included the occult and religion. "All religions have one origin, one point of departure," he said. "They are born out of man's incapacity to understand what surrounds him . . . the need to believe in something . . . the need to believe."

He said he was a solid family man who liked to go home after work and watch television. One of the aides suggested that he watched "Miami Vice" and Noriega said "No, no" and wagged his finger. He wanted it to be absolutely clear that it was a joke and that "Miami Vice" was a bit risqué for his simple tastes.

Noriega was the picture of confidence that afternoon. We agreed to another meeting, but it was put off and put off and I never saw him again. I did return to Noriega's office, however—in January 1990, after the Just Cause invasion. I poked through the debris that covered the floor. The room had been emptied of all its furniture and fixtures except for the huge wall map. Noriega, who said he had been "double-crossed," was in an underground, windowless cell in Miami at the center of an extremely complicated legal proceeding. A civilian government was trying to pick up the pieces after the U.S. invasion, the largest U.S. military action since the war in Vietnam, which had driven Noriega from power.

This book explains how and why those events took place and what Panama was like before and after the invasion.

It explains, for example, how powerful Americans, including Oliver North, went to that same office in the Comandancia to seek Noriega's help just a few years before U.S. troops went there to carry away Noriega's files. It explains why Noriega was happy after each of his meetings with George Bush, one in Washington in 1976 and one in Panama in 1983. It explains Noriega's central role in some of the most important foreign policy initiatives of the Reagan-Bush administration and explains his knowledge about important, still officially unexplained, aspects of the Iran-Contra scandal. It explains the uniquely close ties that existed between the United States and Panama, ties that produced feelings of love and hate and led to the single bloodiest episode in Panamanian history.

I chose to begin the narrative with the events of Friday, September 13, 1985. I made that decision because Panamanians now invariably cite the murder that occurred that day as the historic event that began the chain of events that ended with Noriega's downfall.

In preparing the account I have listened to hundreds and hundreds of stories from Panamanians, Americans, and others. I was not surprised that I heard different stories. Many of the people hated each other, and one man whom Noriega had reportedly vowed to kill was a frequent visitor to my apartment in Manhattan. Some people shared secrets with me and told me the truth, no matter how improbable it may have sounded when I first heard it and no matter how risky it was for them to tell me. On other occasions, people looked me in the eye and told lies, which I detected as I checked information with other people and other sources. I read the transcripts of Senate testimony and a variety of documents, both public and private, and closely followed the often excellent media coverage of events. All this helped me assess the importance of certain events, no matter how much or how little treatment they received in the media. I have done my best to gather all this evidence into a single, true story, the whole story of Noriega, the United States, and Panama as best and as concisely I could tell it. What remains untold will not be known until the public has access to the secret histories of the time and until public officials fully account for their actions.

1

Friday the Thirteenth

A GHOST haunted Panama in 1985, a ghost named Omar Torrijos. Torrijos had run the country from 1968 until his mysterious death in a 1981 plane crash. At the time of his death, Torrijos was still trying to figure out his own political stance and Panama's future. Already, he had changed history by negotiating the controversial treaties that guaranteed the eventual transfer of the Panama Canal from the United States to Panama.

Torrijos was passionate, sentimental, callous, charismatic, provincial, and cosmopolitan. A party-lover, he was drunk most of the time. This made him repugnant to many Panamanians. For others it was an endearing foible. He was able to bedazzle people as diverse as John Wayne, Graham Greene, and Jimmy Carter, all of whom were among his closest friends. His protégés, who ran Panama with him, were just as varied.

On September 13, 1985, three of these protégés were drawn into a strange circle of events. By the end of the day, one of the men would be dead, his headless corpse stuffed in a mailbag. Another would be heading for a fall.

Manuel Antonio Noriega, Hugo Spadafora, and Nicolas Ardito Barletta all had reason to claim Omar Torrijos as a mentor.

17

Each believed he had U.S. support for his endeavors. All would be proven wrong.

Gen. Manuel Antonio Noriega, whom Torrijos had called "my gangster," once directed all of Torrijos's internal and external intelligence gathering. Now, since gaining control of Panama's military, he was the single most powerful man in Panama. On September 13, he happened to be in Paris at the Nikko Hotel for what an aide called "business and pleasure." The trip was not unusual. Noriega traveled constantly, checking in with friends and associates.

Noriega was, at this time, a central figure in two top secret actions—the U.S. Contra campaign in Nicaragua and the Medellín Cartel's drug trafficking activities. Pablo Escobar, one of the cartel leaders, and Oliver North, a U.S. Marine lieutenant colonel assigned to the National Security Council (NSC), had recently been to see him—as supplicants.

Still, Noriega was anxious and somewhat jumpy that morning, never far from the phone. He was apparently expecting a call from Panama where rumors were bubbling. Nicolas Barletta, his handpicked president, was floundering. And Hugo Spadafora, who had vowed to expose Noriega, was coming back to Panama after a period of exile. Noriega's phone conversations may have been about Barletta or Spadafora. Or they may have been about both. Noriega knew how to keep secrets.

If ever a man had found the right job, it was Noriega. He was an instinctive intelligence agent, relentlessly gathering, analyzing, and saving information. Panama City cafe gossips dubbed him "Peeping Tony." By 1985, Noriega had *sapos* (the Spanish word for toads), or agents, throughout the netherworld of intelligence services.

For nearly twenty years he had been an "asset" of the Central Intelligence Agency (CIA) and, over the years, had appeared to enjoy warm friendships with some influential CIA officials including, since 1981, CIA director William Casey.

By 1985, Noriega also enjoyed high standing with those members of the U.S. government who were making policy in his region. But U.S.-Noriega relations hadn't always been so cordial. In 1971, American law enforcement officials had rated Noriega one of the world's most significant narco-traffickers and had proposed his assassination. His CIA contacts, however, saved him. These same men were now supervising the Agency's efforts in Nicaragua.

Noriega was starstruck; in conversations, he loved to drop the names of his powerful friends, often mentioning Casey and Nestor Sanchez, a retired CIA man who now worked on Latin affairs at the Pentagon. Noriega also liked to talk about his strong relationship with George Bush. As directors of their respective intelligence services, Bush and Noriega had lunched together in late 1976 at the Panamanian embassy on McGill Terrace in Washington. In 1983, Noriega had greeted Bush when the vice president visited Panama.

Noriega made it easy for friends to operate in Panama. The U.S. Southern Command (SOUTHCOM), a network of U.S. bases inside the country, was second only to Honduras as a center of Contra military support, especially in intelligence gathering and analysis. Noriega allowed SOUTHCOM to operate without impediment, and other U.S. operations received the same cooperation. Since the 1970s, Noriega had received a steady stream of grateful letters from Drug Enforcement Agency (DEA) officials for his help in busting drug traffickers. Panama City was one of the most successful of all DEA offices.

In the late afternoon or early evening of September 13, Noriega took a call from Maj. Luis Cordoba, an old friend from G-2 days. (There were many branches and departments within the Panamanian Defense Forces [PDF], but the most famous, or notorious, was G-2, the intelligence office, headed by Noriega since 1970.) Cordoba was the PDF commander for Chiriqui province, on the border with Costa Rica. Their conversation was brief and cryptic. "We have the rabid dog," Cordoba told his boss. "You know what to do with a dog that has rabies," Noriega replied.

———

Nicolas Ardito Barletta, the president of the Republic of Panama, had political problems that seemed insurmountable. But he thought that Friday, September 13, would be one of the most auspicious days of his eleven months in office. He looked forward to becoming the first president of Panama to travel through the Panama Canal in a ceremony celebrating a multimillion-dollar plan to improve the canal.

Despite this pomp, Barletta was the butt of jokes inside Panama, a man with many old friends but no real political allies. He had lost the May 1984 election to the popular Arnulfo Arias, head of one of Panama's most respected families. But Noriega had Barletta "declared" the winner anyway, and Barletta quickly earned the nickname "Fraudito," a sobriquet first bestowed by Guillermo Sanchez Borbon, the popular columnist for the newspaper *La Prensa*. The United States blessed the fixed election without delay. U.S. policymakers despised and feared Arias because of his independence and because in his own way he was every bit as charismatic as Torrijos. Before 1984, Arias, who was born in austere surroundings in 1901, had been elected president four times: in 1940, 1948, 1964, and 1968. Early on in each term he was thrown out. His enemies were the oligarchs, who feared his populism. They controlled the National Guard, which provided the muscle. In each case, the U.S. embassy cheered on Arias's usurpers. Instead of spending sixteen years in the presidency, he spent a little more than two, and in 1968, when Torrijos overthrew him, the interval between inauguration and ouster was only eleven days. Arias would have made it more difficult for Americans to operate in Panama.

Barletta had one mission as president: to revive Panama's sagging economy. But his only hope was new bank loans, which had to be approved by the International Monetary Fund (IMF) and the World Bank. When no loans were made during Barletta's first year in office, the president had to explain how complicated the loan process was. Few had the patience to hear him out. The consensus was that he would be out of office by October 11, the anniversary of his inauguration.

Barletta, however, felt secure, and with good reason: He was "underwritten" by President Ronald Reagan's administration, a force more powerful than political ridicule. Washington had proclaimed Barletta's administration a successful example of the Reagan doctrine, the return of democratic rule and the retirement of the military from politics.

Barletta's relations with Noriega were formal. During August, they had met for only four hours. Barletta had explained his long-term economic strategy; Noriega had reaffirmed his support for the return of democracy. The next day, Noriega surprised Barletta when he and a group of his officers turned up at the president's office to celebrate Barletta's forty-seventh birthday. It wasn't as if Noriega had a habit of dropping by.

To Noriega, Barletta was a convenient accessory in a settled policy picture. Unless he raised a fuss about something, he was easier to keep than to get rid of: Military coups were not popular in Washington, and on September 13 there was a widespread assumption that no Panamanian could disturb the United States and survive. Noriega, however, did not bother to hide his contempt for Barletta. "I know everything the president does," he had boasted to reporters. "I even know which moment he pees."

———

Dr. Hugo Spadafora—physician, guerrilla fighter, former Torrijos government official, and inveterate maverick—was traveling on September 13.

Spadafora, Torrijos's old favorite, had announced that he was returning to Panama from exile in Costa Rica to tell the whole dirty Noriega story, that Noriega had become immensely rich by selling Panama and its services to anyone who could pay. The doctor intended to explain that Noriega was known in the netherworld of Latin America as "The Caribbean Prostitute." He said his information was a "bomb" strong enough to drive Noriega from power. If all else failed, Spadafora said, he would resort to guerrilla warfare to rid Panama of Noriega.

There was nothing new about Spadafora's claims. Other individuals and institutions knew as much as he did or more. Noriega and his activities had been the subject of several White House–level reports over the years. But Spadafora threatened to document his charges in articles and radio talks. No one had dared that.

Spadafora's departure from Costa Rica was a signal that his offensive had begun. He was a formidable opponent—glamorous and charismatic with friends in all parts of Panama, from Noriega's G-2 offices to *La Prensa*. He was effortlessly, unconsciously macho with a Roman hero's look. Spadafora was popular with men who sat around the cafes of Panama City talking politics, men who admired his instincts for surviving ambushes. Women said they would volunteer to live with him in the jungle. Even Noriega, whose own face was ridged and pitted from smallpox and acne, had at one time been taken with Spadafora. "I want his face," Noriega, in his cups, had once said of the doctor. On another occasion, a tipsy Noriega, edging closer to Spadafora on a banquette, had been brusquely shoved away. Noriega denied that his hand had brushed his rival's crotch. "I was only trying to get his attention," he insisted.

Hugo, one of Carmelo "Don Melo" Spadafora's twelve children, had grown up in Chitre, a small town 157 miles west of Panama City. Don Melo, a carpenter, was also a revered local politician and Hugo had spent his childhood listening to political conversations around the table. He also read a lot and enjoyed the outdoors. His childhood was a typical middle-class life in the "interior," as all parts of Panama except Panama City are known.

At eleven, Spadafora left Chitre to attend Panama City's Instituto Nacional, the country's best public high school. He was a very good student, but his most important lessons were political.

When Panamanian school kids of Spadafora's generation visited the famous Panama Canal, they learned that their very country was a U.S. invention, dreamed up because the Americans wanted to build a canal across the isthmus. Colombia, of which Panama was still a province at the time, was being difficult and the United States needed a compliant government.

Students like Spadafora learned that on November 3, 1903, a band of Panamanian entrepreneurs and a French businessman, reassured by support from Washington and a U.S. gunboat offshore, declared Panama a republic. The United States instantly recognized the new government, and a treaty granting it the right to build and maintain a canal was quickly signed. The treaty also created the Canal Zone, a strip of land five miles on either side of the waterway that was always to be part of the United States. Not a single Panamanian signed the treaty, a fact that young Hugo Spadafora never forgot.

When Spadafora was young, the Zone, where the Americans lived, was a Norman Rockwell world, tropical style. Some Zonians, as is common with colonial types, assumed the attributes and attitudes of home in exaggerated form, and the most vocal Zonians were also the most jingoistic and racist. "Zonians thought all Panamanians were Mexicans," a Panamanian oligarch said with some disdain.

After high school, Hugo left Panama and the Zonians, moving to Italy to study medicine at the University of Bologna. The intensely political atmosphere there exhilarated him. In January 1964, he organized a demonstration to call attention to the bloody flag riots in Panama, which had erupted when angry students from the Instituto Nacional marched to the flagpole in front of the Canal Zone's Balboa High School demanding to fly the Panamanian flag along with the Stars and Stripes.

Dr. Spadafora traveled widely and in 1966 and 1967 served as a combat medic with guerrillas fighting to end colonial rule in Portuguese Guinea in West Africa. They triumphed, renamed the country Guinea-Bissau, and named a street in Bissau, the capital, after Spadafora.

By the time Spadafora returned to Panama, Omar Torrijos had seized control from Arias, and Spadafora joined a loose network of young men and women who talked about raising arms against him. Most were cafe revolutionaries, and they dubbed Spadafora "Dr. Zhivago," a salute to his romantic revolutionary style. When the police arrested Spadafora, he was brought face-to-face with Torrijos, and the two men instantly hit it off. Spadafora became one of Torrijos's first important protégés, serving out the sentence for his alleged antigovernment subversion productively, in the wilds of Darien province, laying groundwork for the expansion of government medical services. By 1978, when the new Panama Canal treaties were signed, he was vice minister of health and could take much of the credit for the greatly improved health delivery system in Panama.

On September 13, Spadafora began the day in Costa Rica where he had been living for several years. He awakened just after dawn in San José, did yoga, showered, breakfasted, and left his house at nine. He carried a light canvas bag containing several copies of a memoir he had written in 1980, and a notebook in which he constantly recorded the raw material of Panamanian history. After a short hop by plane from San José to an airport just inside Costa Rica, Spadafora took a taxi to Paso Canoa, a village that straddles the Costa Rica–Panama border.

Paso Canoa is the sort of place where nonchalance seems rehearsed, where strangers attract the attention of sullen men in studied mufti. Thickets of orange, banana, and coconut trees grow amid the low, tin-roofed shops and cafes. Some of the small passenger buses at the open-air terminal are new and sleek, but there are still saddled horses hitched to wooden posts outside the town's groceries, barber shops, clinics, jewelry and dry-goods stores, and bars.

One senses the presence of contraband and intrigue in the broiling, humid heat. Los Mellos, a three-tabled tropical greasy spoon where Spadafora finished a plate of rabbit stew just before noon, was, like everything else in Paso Canoa, just a short stroll from the headquarters of the PDF's 5th Military District, a whitewashed compound with a towering radio antenna. The compound, a bank, and a customs-immigration building were set right on the borderline.

After he paid for his lunch, Spadafora said good-bye to Los Mellos's proprietor, his friend Ivan Garcia (nicknamed "El Guapo," which translates somewhere between "Hunk" and

"Gutsy"), and gave him a copy of his book. Then he climbed aboard the Toyota Coaster minibus to start the long west-east journey along the isthmus. The first stop was David, the capital of Chiriqui province, about two hours away. There he would transfer to another bus for the eight-hour trip to Panama City. The next day he would pick up his wife, Ariadne, when she arrived by plane from Costa Rica.

Hugo Spadafora's bus had a new passenger when it pulled out from Paso Canoa. The man wore sunglasses, and carried no luggage. His name was Francisco Eliecer Gonzalez, but because of his surliness and because he was believed to be a martial arts aficionado, he was known around the border town as "Bruce Lee." He was a sergeant in G-2.

At the PDF checkpoint at Jacu, two miles away, the guard inspected the passengers' papers and told Spadafora to get off the bus. "Bruce Lee" followed him. Spadafora skimmed a newspaper while he waited; as he got back on the bus, Spadafora ignored the guard's mutterings about "the great Hugo Spadafora." Eight miles later, at a wooden shed at the side of the two-lane Pan-American Highway, Spadafora was told again to disembark to have his papers checked. This stop lasted just a few minutes. Then the green and white minibus rolled on.

———

The confrontation between Spadafora and Noriega really began in 1978, the year that the treaties were passed. Torrijos had been in power for a decade and, now that he had made history with the treaties, he occasionally hinted he would retire. Competition to succeed him was fierce, and Noriega considered Spadafora a rival, even though he was a civilian.

Those were heady days; the U.S. presence in Panama appeared to be in retreat. The Canal Zone had ceased to exist, and the days of the Zonians were numbered. The transfer, or "reversion," of Canal Zone land, buildings, a railroad, and all kinds of equipment and treasure to the military was scheduled. Meanwhile, U.S. military aid to the National Guard increased.

Around this time, Torrijos gave Spadafora command of a brigade of some three hundred Panamanian volunteers who went to Nicaragua to join the Sandinistas' fight against the dictator Anastasio Somoza. (Noriega directed the supply system, finding pilots and arms dealers and setting up schedules, using small airfields that were dotted throughout Panama and new ones that were appearing in the region.) Once again, Spadafora distinguished himself in combat. Not long after Spadafora arrived, Somoza called a press conference to announce that he was dead. But on July 19, 1979, when the rebels took over Managua, Spadafora was there, triumphant.

By this time, Spadafora had grave doubts about the integrity of the Sandinistas. He himself took up arms against them, and for a while worked with Eden Pastora, the legendary Commander Zero, who had also defected from the Sandinista camp. When they had a falling out, Spadafora went to live and fight with the Miskito Indians on the east coast. Along the way, he learned more and more about the web of politics and crime in the region.

During the 1980s, wars broke out in Nicaragua, El Salvador, Guatemala, and Colombia and there was sporadic violence in several nearby countries. Noriega helped the flow of arms to many of these combatants. Through his control of "end-user" certificates (the documents required for the sale and shipment of most weapons), it was easy for him to make Panama a weapons supply hub. Cargoes from all over the world could enter Panama—and then go wherever Noriega wanted. He helped the Contras, but he also shipped arms to the rebels in El Salvador who opposed the U.S.-backed government. His stance was always the profitable one.

Weapons cost money, and selling, or helping in the sale of, cocaine produced the enormous revenues that produced the weapons. So Noriega made Panama crucial to the cocaine business, by far the most successful enterprise in the region.

Spadafora and Noriega were both denizens of this clandestine netherworld populated by pilots, smugglers, arms salesmen, intelligence agents, and the occasional journalist. They were all at home in Panama, and Spadafora was outraged that Noriega, without Torrijos's knowledge, had stepped up his narco-trafficking and become a war profiteer.

In due course, Spadafora went to Torrijos with his accusations, but Torrijos had no immediate reaction. Later, Spadafora came to believe that Noriega was plotting to kill Torrijos and seize control of Panama himself.

He confronted Torrijos, who brought Noriega and Spadafora together in his office. Noriega leaped from his chair when Spadafora entered and greeted him, smiling.

"Comandante!" Noriega exclaimed.

"Bullshit," Spadafora replied, refusing Noriega's hand. Six months later Torrijos was dead.

———

By September 13, 1985, as he set out for Panama, Spadafora knew the stakes were higher than ever. *Sapos* always harassed him on his trips home, and his friends had persuaded him to buy a .45 automatic. There were attacks against him in the government press, including a cartoon with the caption, "The head of the traitor will fall."

Noriega had been threatening Spadafora for years. An intermediary once told him that Noriega had "judged and sentenced" him. Once, Noriega had sent Spadafora a message that said he could "die any day from a fish bone." Another time, a Noriega emissary had told Spadafora's first wife that her husband was "on the edge of the grave." But after all the years of attempted intimidation, Spadafora had become complacent.

"I am tired of Noriega playing a cat-and-mouse game," Spadafora told a radio interviewer in 1982. "I do not have a vocation to be a mouse, and I have decided to let him know that I am also chasing him . . . with the weapon of truth. I am on his heels on the drug issue and I . . . ." The electricity in the radio studio had suddenly gone off.

———

Now, as the bus carrying Hugo Spadafora to Panama City stopped alongside the square in the pleasant little town of Concepción, "Bruce Lee" motioned to Spadafora. "Come with me," he said, lifting Spadafora's bag from the rack. As Spadafora got off the bus he showed his ID to the conductor and said, "So you will know who I am. I'm Dr. Hugo Spadafora." The conductor asked if he was staying in Concepción. When Spadafora replied, "I'm being detained by this member of the Defense Forces," the conductor asked him for the $1.20 fare.

Spadafora and the PDF sergeant stood on the sidewalk outside a department store called Almacende Esperanza, the Store of Hope. It faced the town square, an empty place about the size of a New York City block with a bandstand in the middle and almond trees shading quiet, dusty crisscrossed paths. When Omar Vega Miranda, another PDF sergeant, appeared, the two *sapos* and Spadafora walked toward the local PDF headquarters about three blocks away.

When Spadafora failed to meet his wife at the airport, one of his sisters telephoned Sanchez Borbon at *La Prensa*. The journalist tried to reassure her, but he began making inquiries. Sanchez Borbon had a very effective network of sources, which had come to be after he had facetiously announced its existence in a column. Immediately after that, information began to pour into his office from all sorts of people who wanted to be part of his network.

On Sunday, September 15, *La Prensa* reported on page one that Hugo Spadafora was missing, perhaps under arrest. Later that day, his family was relieved to hear that he had been seen on Friday in Paso Canoa. Sanchez Borbon was not so optimistic. He felt his first pang of dread that evening when G-2 headquarters in Panama City angrily denied they had arrested Spadafora and accused *La Prensa* of slander. Sanchez Borbon thought the communiqué was "hysterical" and feared the worst.

On Monday, September 16, Spadafora's brother Winston, an attorney, and Don Melo were preparing to file a writ of habeas corpus with the PDF when they received a phone call from Costa Rica. Two old friends from his Nicaraguan campaigns had identified Spadafora's decapitated body, which had been dumped on a riverbank inside the Costa Rican border in a U.S. mailbag.

His killers' method was symbolic. Most Panamanians know the story of Vasco Nunez de Balboa, the Spanish explorer who was the first European to gaze at the Pacific Ocean (in 1513) and whose likeness appears on Panamanian coins. Balboa was accused of sedition by a Spanish administrator and beheaded. A bullet between his eyes would have silenced Spadafora but would not have carried the correct message. His murderers had announced that they were capable of anything against any traitor.

As Sanchez Borbon later pieced the story together, Spadafora had died perhaps seven hours after he had left the bus in the Concepción town square. His agony began in the local PDF headquarters, but as the day wore on his tormentors took him to a succession of small towns on and near the Pacific coast—places like Alanje, Canto Gallo, Santo Tomas, and Estero Rico. During those hours they repeatedly rammed a large stick or pole up his rectum, beat his genitals until they were gargantually swollen, shoved sharpened objects under his fingernails, broke several ribs, and probably, before anything else, severed—with professional skill—several muscles in his thighs so he could not close his legs.

The autopsy showed he was still breathing when finally, in the town of Corozo (according to Sanchez Borbon's investigation), a PDF cook sat astride him and slowly killed him by severing his head. Then, or perhaps before (the Spadafora family hopes one day to determine this in a trial in Panama), the murderers carved on his shoulder, two inches high "F-8," the designation for an unofficial and brutal paramilitary strong-arm squad, apparently composed of *sapos*.

———

At a press conference on Tuesday, September 17, Don Melo tearfully described his son's horrible torture and mutilation and denounced Noriega. As family members traveled to Costa Rica to claim Hugo's body, President Barletta telephoned Don Melo in Costa Rica, offering condolences and promising an investigation. He followed the call with a handwritten letter reiterating the pledge. Barletta said that Noriega would supervise the police work. He was just the man for the job, Barletta added, without irony, though he could hardly have been unaware of Noriega's probable role in the murder.

Not long after, Barletta received a call at home. It was Don Melo. He was calling to thank the president and to repeat his belief that Noriega had ordered his son killed. Hugo had always kept his father informed about everything. Don Melo had no doubts about who had given the order. Barletta said there would be an investigation.

The Spadafora family flew into Panama City with Hugo's body on the morning of Thursday, September 19. From there they traveled about four hours by car to Chitre for a funeral mass at the Cathedral of St. John the Baptist, the baroque edifice in the center of the tropical town. After the funeral, a large, surging crowd followed the coffin to a cemetery several hundred yards away on the edge of town. "Bury him deep," said Don Melo, who had been carving his own tombstone that summer from a granite boulder.

One of the pallbearers was Jose "Pepe" Pretto, a friend since Spadafora's days in Darien province and now a garage and car wash owner in Panama City. Pretto noted that the crowd was riddled with *sapos*. One of them, Favio, known for his shiny shoes, asked Pretto lots of questions and tried to edge in to get his hands near the coffin as it was lowered into the ground.

Pretto had last seen his old friend just a month before, at his own house in Panama City. That night Spadafora had been talking about the sudden death of Torrijos at the end of July 1981, just at the point when Noriega had begun consolidating his power.

———

Noriega telephoned Barletta that Sunday, September 22, from Paris. He planned to remain there until departing for New York, where both men would take part in festivities marking the fortieth anniversary of the United Nations. Noriega told Barletta, "Stick to the PDF, Nicky."

In Paris, Noriega kept his own counsel and never, according to a member of his intimate entourage, even mentioned Spadafora. But this person also recalled that Noriega flew into a cursing rage during a phone call from Panama after the news of the murder hit the press. The widespread public revulsion at the news of the murder apparently surprised Noriega.

On Monday, September 23, at 3:00 P.M., Winston Spadafora and other family members occupied the U.N. offices in Panama City and declared a twenty-four-hour fast. Don Melo, hospitalized in Chitre with heart trouble, was not present.

After a day of hunger, Winston announced he would continue his fast at home but reiterated that he would not eat until there was justice for Hugo. Arnulfo Arias went to Don Melo's bedside to offer moral support. The visit signified a bridge between Arnulfo's devoted followers and the Torrijos followers who had initially accepted Noriega but were now turning against him.

On Tuesday morning, September 24, the PDF announced that the Spadafora murder had taken place in Costa Rica, meaning it occurred outside official PDF jurisdiction. The case was closed. Sanchez Borbon then reported in *La Prensa* that Spadafora had been tortured and decapitated at a garrison near a small Panamanian town called Corozo, very close to the Costa Rican border. The columnist later learned that the murderers had buried Spadafora's head outside the barracks, but a dog had tried to scratch away the soil. The murderers had shot the dog and taken Spadafora's head away.

Also on Tuesday, Barletta left for New York. In addition to participating in the U.N. festivities, he was scheduled to deliver a major speech on Latin American debt at the U.N. Before he left, Barletta said that the attorney general would be able to announce the members of the investigative commission by the next day. Both of his vice presidents, Eric Arturo "Tuturo" Delvalle and

Roderick Esquivel, were at the airport to see him off. As the three men stood together for the photographers, Barletta murmured, "Remember, the family that prays together, stays together."

Delvalle was part of Barletta's safety net. A Delvalle presidency was unthinkable. He was a *rabiblanco* (a derisive term for Panama's upper, whiter classes) who represented everything the military regime ostensibly opposed. He was further compromised by rumors that his place on the ticket was owed to a reported million-dollar campaign contribution to the Revolutionary Democratic party (PRD), the government's political party. He was also a prominent, if not exactly popular, member of Panama City's Jewish community, known mainly for his interest in the racehorses he raised. "Tuturo is only happy when he smells horse shit" was a common remark.

As Barletta settled back for the flight to Miami and then New York, he seemed the picture of power, traveling with his entourage. One of the passengers was Gabriel Lewis, the ambassador to Washington while the treaties were negotiated and probably one of the best-liked Panamanians in Congress and the State Department. He owned Contadora Island, a resort where the Shah of Iran had stayed during his last journey. Also aboard were Dame Margot Fonteyn and her husband, Roberto "Tito" Arias (Arnulfo's nephew), a diplomat paralyzed since 1964 when he was shot on a Panama City street by a political rival.

At the airport in Miami, Barletta called his chief of staff to make sure that the commission would be announced that afternoon.

On Wednesday, September 25, Sanchez Borbon's column reported that after the killers had dumped Spadafora's body, they had driven their bloody PDF vehicles to a banana washing station equipped with high-pressure scouring hoses. The station was located in Balsa, just inside Costa Rica. Readers could only wonder what other details Sanchez Borbon knew and to whom he was talking.

New York meteorologists were sounding early warnings of Hurricane Gloria as Noriega arrived in the city and checked into a suite at the Helmsley Palace Hotel on Madison Avenue. The hotel, Noriega's New York favorite, was just a short stroll from the Waldorf Towers, where Barletta was holding nonstop meetings and waiting for Noriega's call. Noriega had arranged earlier for

Jose Blandon, his principal civilian intelligence analyst from Panama, to meet him in New York. He told Blandon that Spadafora had deserved to die, but that he was not involved in the murder. The culprit, Noriega told Blandon, was Maj. Luis Cordoba.

Noriega spent much of his time on the telephone as he gathered information from Panama and Washington. Sometimes he simply listened and sometimes he outlined his plans, testing on several callers his determination to return to Panama and settle the question of Barletta's future, which was causing unrest within the PDF. Noriega's most important calls that day were to CIA friends, including (or so he encouraged his friends to believe) William Casey. His manner was subdued. As the day progressed, Noriega's initial jitteriness eased. No one, it appeared, had challenged his plans, which at this point were to sack Barletta and prevent an investigation of the Spadafora murder.

By early evening, Noriega and his friends were in the air again, on their way back to Panama to start actions against Barletta before the storm closed in. He had not even bothered to call Barletta.

———

Still in New York, Barletta learned that the Spadafora commission had not been announced as scheduled. As he prepared for a television interview he tried to find out what was going on. His vice presidents were no help. Esquivel was a nonentity and Delvalle could not be found. Moments later there was a call from Panama; Barletta disappeared to take it. It was Delvalle calling from PDF headquarters.

As the television crew waited, Mrs. Barletta and Mrs. George Shultz, wife of the U.S. secretary of state, arrived at the suite.

After a while, Barletta reappeared. He knew that Delvalle's presence at PDF headquarters meant trouble—especially in light of the fact that the special commission had not been announced. He made no reference to the call and went in to do what he did best: explain the international debt problem.

In Panama, Col. Roberto Diaz Herrera had had a busy day. A cousin of the late Torrijos, Diaz Herrera was Noriega's second in command. He had met with Delvalle at PDF headquarters and he had commenced a coup against Noriega that had already collapsed by the time Barletta spoke to Delvalle. Diaz Herrera had ordered the commander of Battalion 2000, one of the few PDF units with any semblance of infantry training, into Panama City, explaining they might be needed to quell unrest. But the battalion had not budged. Diaz Herrera had shown his hand—and had it slapped.

By late Wednesday, Noriega was back at his headquarters, listening to Diaz Herrera's transparently fictitious account of the coup attempt. Diaz Herrera told Noriega that he had discovered a plot by Barletta against him and had been compelled to ask for reinforcements to thwart Barletta. Noriega remained silent, taking it all in. He knew pretty much what he was going to do.

━━━━━

Early on Thursday, September 26, Barletta talked to the former Secretary of State Henry Kissinger and visited the editorial boards of the *New York Times* and the *Wall Street Journal*. Then he went to the U.N., where he greeted his old friend Secretary of State George Shultz. Shultz had taught Barletta economics at the University of Chicago and had (despite overwhelming evidence on the fraudulence of the election) attended Barletta's inauguration in October 1984. The two men put their signatures on more documents pertaining to the future of the canal, then Barletta addressed the General Assembly, stressing the need for IMF and World Bank support in solving the debt crisis. The speech was well received. In the early afternoon he held a press conference but most of the questions were about coup rumors in Panama. Barletta laughed them away.

Shortly after the press conference, Barletta's foreign minister passed him a terse message from the PDF urging him to return home quickly. The message referred to problems between the military and the president. Barletta called Col. Marcos Justines, a key PDF officer. "Come now or later in the afternoon," Justines said. "We have to talk to you."

At six o'clock that evening Barletta joined his foreign minister and the rest of his entourage for a reception at the Harley Hotel on 42nd Street, but attendance was off. Hurricane Gloria was on her way. Barletta, smiling, betrayed no sign of his troubled afternoon.

Under normal circumstances, Barletta could easily have spent the night in New York and taken stock of the situation early the next morning. But the hurricane forced a quick decision. After some discreet farewells, he left for the airport, but takeoff was delayed.

One of the first Panamanians on board the plane had a nasty surprise: "F-8" had been painted on one of the windows near her seat. The bomb squad completed its work around 2:00 A.M. and takeoff came quickly after.

Barletta intended to head home upon arrival in Panama City. He had a shower in mind, after which he would go to his office and receive the military officers who wanted to see him. It had been an exhausting and triumphant week. Very quickly, however, he reconsidered his plans. Perhaps it would be better for him to go directly to PDF headquarters. He telephoned Noriega, who apologized for not meeting him in New York. Noriega then invited Barletta down to PDF headquarters that morning. Noriega was genial.

At 10:00 A.M., Noriega and his cronies greeted him in Noriega's office. The officers were polite but blunt. Barletta, they said, had to go.

Barletta tried to hold firm. He demanded to know why.

The officers mentioned subversion. They said new measures were necessary.

Barletta asked them to explain what they had in mind. Diaz Herrera tried to respond but Noriega was quiet. Hours passed. For a while, Barletta was left alone in the room. When the officers returned, they asked if he would close *La Prensa* and call off the Spadafora commission. When he declined one told him, "You see, you are too damn democratic."

———

"They're toppling Barletta," the urgent voice on the telephone had told a sleepy Guillermo Sanchez Borbon earlier that morning.

"Why are you bothering me at this hour?" Sanchez Borbon asked. It was 7:30 A.M. Tips that Barletta was out were routine. The caller described plans to put Delvalle in power, insisting that Sanchez Borbon's life was in danger.

Sanchez Borbon said that was nothing new.

"Yes, but now you are in much more danger."

Around 11:30, Sanchez Borbon arrived at the Continental Hotel. *La Prensa* had Winston Spadafora's hunger strike, now in its fourth day, on the front page. Glancing up from his paper, Sanchez Borbon greeted a friend of Noriega's who told him that Barletta was out without any doubt. Sanchez Borbon called his paper and was told the report was false.

Not much later, he was strolling home when someone beckoned to him. The stranger whispered a warning: twenty *sapos* were waiting to arrest him at his home. Later, he discovered that a member of Barletta's staff who had been fired while the president was at PDF headquarters said that on his last trip home in a government car, the driver had shown him a photograph of Sanchez Borbon. This particular driver (a G-2 agent like all the others) said that hundreds of the photographs had been distributed to his fellow *sapos*. Their orders were to kill him on sight.

Sanchez Borbon decided the time had come. Monsignor Sebastian Laboa, the papal nuncio in Panama, greeted the columnist at the door of his residence down the hill from the Holiday Inn in the Paitilla neighborhood and showed him to a tidy room on the second floor. The air conditioner and television were both broken, but he was safe from Noriega's *sapos*—at least for a while.

———

About noon, Barletta learned that Elliott Abrams had called. The U.S. assistant secretary of state for inter-American affairs had left a Washington number. Sitting in Noriega's office, Barletta dialed the number and asked for Abrams.

"Listen, we're supporting you, you hear. Hang tough," Abrams said.

Barletta chose his words very carefully, certain the conversation was monitored. "That's exactly what I'm doing. Do something about it—hanging tough."

For Barletta, the call was crucial. After speaking to Abrams, Barletta felt reassured. Abrams had told him in plain English that he still had U.S. support. He led Barletta to believe that Washington was in his corner and would save his presidency. Barletta would now play for time, survive, wait for help, hang tough. He had not slept much. He hadn't eaten. He eyed the officers' trays of food as he listened to their denunciations.

But nothing else happened in Washington, except that Pentagon official Nestor Sanchez telephoned his old friend Noriega. Barletta heard Noriega, at his desk at about 5:00 P.M., saying, "Yes, Nestor, yes, Nestor, we have to keep it constitutional."

About a half hour later, Barletta demanded an audience with senior officers. Barletta did his best and, for what it was worth, proved yet again that he could speak eloquently. The officers listened silently but Diaz Herrera denounced Barletta as a traitor.

The president asked for some paper and to be left alone. At 6:00, trying to stay awake and to buy yet more time, he wrote a letter to the Panamanian people. He knew he could not say that he had resigned. Instead, he wrote out a statement saying that he was taking a leave of absence from office. Perhaps that would pacify the PDF and give Abrams more time to come through with help.

"The television says you resigned," his wife said anxiously when Barletta telephoned her at 9:30.

"That's not so," he replied. He hung up and headed for the door. "You better not try," Diaz Herrera told him.

Barletta was left alone again. One officer, as he exited, ordered Barletta to sign the letter.

Diaz Herrera reappeared minutes later and warned Barletta to be cautious, reminding him that his family could be in danger.

———

Throughout the city, people talked of Barletta's imminent "decapitation."

Vice President Delvalle would not take the oath of office until he had seen a copy of Barletta's resignation. At midnight, fourteen hours after he'd arrived at PDF headquarters, Barletta decided to sign. There might be bloodshed if he continued to try to buy time.

After he signed the letter, Barletta turned to Noriega. "Remember my words," he said. "You will be sorry for what you do." He turned and walked out.

Barletta drove directly to the presidential palace and telephoned Fernando Eleta, the owner of Channel 4. He wanted to make a live television announcement. Eleta admired Barletta's guts and quickly granted the request.

As cabinet ministers arrived at the palace, Barletta tried to organize a denunciation of the coup. He insisted that the entire cabinet appear behind him during his TV appearance because, according to the constitution, the cabinet had to accept or reject a request for a presidential leave of absence. While he waited, he requested that his letter be brought to him. Surprisingly, his request was granted. The PDF seemed suddenly obliging. He soon found out why: His TV statement would be taped.

A few minutes before 3:00 A.M. Barletta read his letter of "separation from power" to a television camera, adding a veiled message that should have been a clear signal of duress. "Something has been said that is not true," Barletta said. "It is said that this situation arose because of differences in economic policies."

The legislative assembly reconvened soon after Barletta's tape was broadcast. There was a hurried reading of the "letter of separation." All discussion was prohibited. Several legislators attempted to explain the reasons for their votes but were refused. A "resignation" was unanimously accepted.

Just before 4:00 A.M. Delvalle, wearing the red, white, and blue presidential sash, stood before the assembly as the chief justice of the Panamanian Supreme Court administered the oath of office. Then Delvalle addressed the legislators and television audience: "The incidents that have culminated with my presence before you . . . are not the product, like some would like to believe, of plots filled with personal ambition . . . in due time, history will judge my actions in this hour of difficulty."

On Sunday, Barletta's close friends talked him out of denouncing his "resignation."

2

Casey, North, and Noriega

EVERYTHING was different by October 1985. With Barletta gone, Noriega, who had always preferred to act quietly in the background, was forced out into the open. Suddenly, there was no one to deflect attention away from him; he was the visible leader of Panama. Then, too, the Spadafora business was out of hand. Noriega simply had not expected the public outcry. And the publicity surrounding Spadafora's death was troubling to him for a reason that went far beyond public opinion. During a state visit to Peru the previous August, Noriega had slipped away to the city of Cuzco for a six-hour summit with the leaders of the Medellín Cartel. The Colombians had told him that Spadafora was a problem and he should solve it. Now here it was October and the problem was anything but solved. Everyone was still talking about the murder. Noriega was useful to the cartel and his other "customers" only if he was "low profile." A notorious Noriega was bad for the cocaine industry and anyone else who used the services he provided, whether that be money laundering or providing training facilities for the Contras.

In Washington, the Spadafora episode had created what one angry State Department official called "a public stench" that undercut the administration's public support for democracy in the region and, indirectly, its rationale for backing the Contras. Noriega hoped that he still had more to offer Washington than he had to fear, but it was too early to tell.

Noriega's cool started to crack a little—in small ways. He lost his taste for macabre humor. The first week of October, at a dinner party, an eager-to-please government official exclaimed, "I see it," as he lifted the white linen table cloth. "There's Spadafora's head. His head is under the table." The general was not amused.

Noriega took out his tension on Marcela Tason, his long-time private secretary who held the rank of captain in the PDF. He had always treated her politely, respectfully. Now he shouted at her often—for imagined transgressions—although he usually apologized later. Tason kept his schedules and knew all about Noriega's life. She knew, for example, when he was home with his wife, Felicidad, and their teenage daughters, and when he was with his mistress, Vicky Amado, an advertising executive with two teenage daughters.

As October rolled on, Winston Spadafora continued to fast and receive a steady stream of visitors. Then a new spectacle began. A group of women, often ten but sometimes forty or fifty, gathered in the noon sun each day to pray the rosary outside Spadafora's house. Soon they were praying in larger numbers, always at noon, in the shelter of a one-hundred-year-old mahogany tree on the sidewalk outside the attorney general's office.

One of these women was Rosario Arias Galindo, the sixty-five-year-old niece of Arnulfo Arias, a proud woman still protesting Torrijos's seizure of her three newspapers in 1969. She and her friends marched, praying, demanding an investigation of Spadafora's murder.

One day a squad showed up with power tools and removed the tree, the women's shelter from sun and rain. "We got so mad," Mrs. Galindo recalled. "But two days later we planted another mahogany tree and every day we came to water it and pray. We kept on praying. The idea was to spread the news. We wanted to draw attention to what had happened. There was plenty of traffic there on Avenue Peru, and when people asked what we were doing we said we were trying to get justice for Hugo Spadafora. After a while some people began carrying umbrellas, black umbrellas that said 'Justicia' or 'Spadafora' in white letters."

After nineteen days and a promise from church figures to carry on his crusade, Winston Spadafora ended his hunger strike.

The Spadaforas were making other plans. Winston was even thinking about taking his brother's case to Washington. While he was recuperating from his fast, two of his brothers and a sister chained themselves to the flagpole in the courtyard of the nunciature, where Guillermo Sanchez Borbon had found refuge. They remained for three days and three nights while friends like "Pepe" Pretto and Monsignor Sebastian Laboa, the papal nuncio, arranged for food and blankets. Afterward, they joined a human chain reaching from the papal embassy all the way down Balboa Avenue along the bay to within shouting distance of Delvalle's office. PDF police barred the protestors on the end from delivering a letter to the president.

Noriega was more concerned about another problem—right next door. Cesar Rodriguez was an old Noriega ally. His hero was Tony Montana, the big-spending drug dealer in Brian DePalma's movie *Scarface*. Montana was "my kind of guy," Rodriguez would tell the beauties he squired around. Like Montana, Rodriguez lived in discotheques, drove fast cars, and had, according to one woman, "more champagne than most people have water."

Then he bought a house—for $1.2 million—right next door to Noriega's own house in Golf Heights. Golf Heights was one of Panama City's most expensive neighborhoods and certainly its most respectable. Noriega was furious.

The general telephoned his former pal and told him to stay the hell out of his neighborhood. "Noriega told him that he would like to run for president in the 1989 election and said that as general and future president of the country, he had to care for his image," said Jose Blandon, Noriega's intelligence chief. Noriega told Maj. Luis Del Cid that if Rodriguez continued to flaunt his wealth and call attention to his former association with Noriega, he would end up like Spadafora.

Rodriguez sold the first house and bought a bigger one a few blocks away. He made jabs at Noriega a part of his repertoire at such discos as Bacchus and Magic, bragging to friends (and using one of Noriega's favorite idioms) that Noriega was afraid to "screw with" him. He knew enough about Noriega and the drug business to put the general in jail, he said. He had the evidence in bank vaults around the world. And there were people, like Floyd Carlton, who knew he was telling the truth.

Rodriguez and Carlton were both stalwart members of the pilot fraternity, the men who knew all about Noriega's clandestine operations. They had both known Hugo Spadafora very well, and his death had particularly terrified Carlton, a childhood friend. Hugo had often called Carlton searching for details; they had even spoken on the telephone a short time before Hugo's murder. Carlton had told Spadafora about flights he and Noriega had made. Spadafora had told Carlton that neither he nor Cesar Rodriguez would be hurt in the exposé he planned.

Among the stories that Carlton told Spadafora was the tale of the 1980 flight when he and Rodriguez delivered weapons and ammunition from a remote Costa Rican airfield to the rebels fighting against the U.S.-backed government in El Salvador. U.S. officials knew that Noriega was working against U.S. policy, but they chose to ignore the matter. Still, Noriega didn't want it to become an issue. One night, after he finished his delivery, Carlton had to return to rescue Rodriguez, who had crashed inside El Salvador. Since the plane could be traced back to Noriega, Carlton was to rescue Rodriguez and destroy the plane.

Carlton found Rodriguez trapped in the cockpit with two broken legs. With the sound of Salvadoran helicopters in his ears, Carlton smashed the windshield with a rifle butt and dragged Rodriguez out of the explosive-packed wreck. He could smell the fumes of the extra fuel load that Rodriguez had risked carrying because he was anxious to return to Panama for Father's Day. Rodriguez had doubted that the guerrillas would provide the fuel they had promised.

Carlton realized that if he destroyed the plane as ordered, both he and Rodriguez could die in the fireball. So he abandoned the wreck and dragged his crippled friend to his nearby Piper Seneca. Carlton and Rodriguez made their getaway at tree-top level as the Salvadoran helicopters approached. As soon as Rodriguez was in a hospital, Carlton called Noriega, whose first question was whether the plane had been blown up. Carlton lied and Noriega arranged for both men to go into hiding. But the general soon found out that Carlton had lied and excoriated him.

When his rage subsided, Noriega assured Carlton that they were back in business. Carlton flew charters and sold airplanes from Paitilla airport, a strip lined by hangars for small jets, tourist-industry passenger planes, and an administration building. In 1983, a Medellín Cartel representative approached Carlton and asked him to pass on a proposition to Noriega, who exploded at Carlton for even talking to the man without permission. Within a week or two, however, Noriega was friendly again and Carlton became the intermediary between Noriega and the Medellín Car-

tel, a not very complicated piece of business. The cartel flew scheduled flights and paid Noriega for the unrestricted use of airfields
inside Panama.

Not long after Carlton took the job, he went on vacation and
returned to find Noriega "very displeased." The Medellín people
had added a drug flight without paying him. "The people who
were waiting for the plane carrying the drugs were captured,"
Carlton recalled, "and they were severely tortured, and they had
limbs fractured, and this cost those individuals a lot of money. . . .
And that is why I said before, nothing could be done in Panama
without Noriega's approval—that is, if you want to be successful."

Carlton, unlike Rodriguez, kept quiet about his stories after
Spadafora's murder. But eventually he decided that if he was go-
ing to survive, he had to talk—and he decided to talk to the DEA.
A meeting was arranged.

At the appointed hour, a nondescript sedan with two DEA
agents swung into the driveway of the Holiday Inn in Panama
City. Carlton got in and demanded to know if they knew who he
was. He reminded them that he had tried before to talk to them
and he said he could give them information about money laundering, drugs, weapons, assassinations, and corruption in general.
He wanted nothing in return except protection for his family. The
agents were curious. They listened. Then Carlton said something
that upset the two agents: He mentioned Noriega's involvement.
The mood in the car changed. Carlton became very nervous and
the meeting ended quickly. Afterward, Carlton tried to reach them
but they never returned his call.

Carlton may have underestimated Noriega's popularity at the
DEA. The general frequently provided tips to DEA agents that
usually led to arrests and cocaine seizures. Noriega's critics said
that he simply used the DEA to weed out individuals who did not
cooperate with him, or people picked at random, to flaunt his
power. "Noriega used the DEA as his enforcer," observed Roberto Eisenmann, the publisher of *La Prensa*. So it was plausible that
the agents had told Noriega about the meeting.

Eventually, Carlton was arrested in Costa Rica, but he survived to provide evidence against Noriega. His friend Cesar Rodriguez was less fortunate.

Cesar kept up his public denunciations of Noriega, and in
March 1986, still defiant, flew to Medellín, the "Orchid City,"
where he checked into the Nutibara Hotel. With him was Ruben

Paredes, Jr., a business partner and son of one of the PDF generals whom Noriega had brushed aside on his way to becoming commander in chief. Both men vanished two days later and were eventually found dead. Cause of death: the "Medellín necktie," a symbol that the victim had talked. The men's throats were slit open, and their tongues were pulled out through the holes. There were no suspects.

On November 8, Don Melo Spadafora collapsed from a heart attack just as he was about to address a meeting. He died shortly afterward and was buried in the same grave as Hugo. Don Melo had almost finished carving the headstone he would share with his son. A friend added this inscription: "Here Rest the Bodies of Two Heroic Souls—Where the Father Is the Head of the Son and the Son Is the Heart of the Father."

By the end of the month, Winston Spadafora was in Miami talking to Roberto Eisenmann, who was spending the 1985–86 academic year as a Nieman Fellow at Harvard. Eisenmann traveled frequently to Washington and Miami and kept in close touch with his newspaper, which had just printed a letter (obtained by Sanchez Borbon) that gave vivid details about Spadafora's murder. Sanchez Borbon (who had left the nunciature after Noriega had guaranteed his safety to the nuncio) had offered the letter to the authorities, but they had ignored him. Then, when it appeared in La Prensa, "all hell broke loose." At their meeting, Eisenmann tried to encourage Spadafora but also warned him about what he might expect in Washington. Hardly anyone there wanted to talk about Panama, Eisenmann said.

He was right. That winter, Winston Spadafora went to the U.S. capital to seek justice. With his cousin Alfonso Gonzalez, he trekked from one congressional office to another, from human rights group to editorial offices. He was received politely and sympathetically—especially when people saw the photos of his brother's corpse. (When it came time to open the brown manila envelope, Winston always left the room.) But his reception on Capitol Hill was generally discouraging.

A visit with Deborah DeMoss, an aide to Senator Jesse Helms of North Carolina and a specialist on Latin America, did little to raise his spirits. DeMoss was well known on Capitol Hill for her ferocious devotion to Helms's causes, including his passionate opposition to the Panama Canal treaties. Spadafora, however, found her cool. Shortly after leaving her office, Spadafora, still weak from his hunger strike, flew home.

DeMoss, deeply moved by Winston's photos, was more interested in the death of Hugo Spadafora than she had let on. She also thought something was about to happen. "I knew then that things were going to break in Panama," she said. "At that point it was not emotional. I didn't know him. . . . It was a political reaction."

"Que milagro" ("What a miracle"), Winston Spadafora replied the next day when DeMoss telephoned him in Miami to say that Helms wanted to do something. She was already at work on a draft of an amendment that her boss planned to tack onto a foreign aid bill. It was the first small encouragement he had been given.

Five days later, on Tuesday, December 10, Helms submitted an amendment to cut off financial assistance to Panama until there was justice for Spadafora. The Helms amendment was defeated in committee by a vote of 19–2. "People were bewildered," DeMoss recalled. "They thought it was just some Helms nut kick, trying to get back the canal, or get revenge on Panama."

A week before Christmas, the Panamanian attorney general summoned Sanchez Borbon to his office. He wanted to know who had written the letter with the purported details of the murder, where this person was, and how the columnist had obtained the letter. Sanchez Borbon replied that he ought to be more interested in the questions raised in the letter than in who wrote it. He told the attorney general truthfully that he did not know who had written the letter and that he had burned the original.

At the same moment, Winston Spadafora, his family, and a few close friends were making a 157-mile pilgrimage from Chitre to Panama City—the latest in a series of long demonstrations that symbolized Hugo's unfinished journey. People cheered them along the way and on Christmas Eve hundreds of friends met them at the Bridge of the Americas that spans the canal. They walked into the city and camped out at the National Cathedral until the doors opened for midnight mass.

One week later the attorney general officially closed the investigation.

By December, Noriega was relaxing, having survived the crisis. Business with the cartel was proceeding and the Spadafora demonstrations had not ignited wider protest. Noriega was confident that his Washington friends could protect him, as they always had, from Winston Spadafora's challenge.

Indeed, that December, Noriega received confirmation that despite the murder and the coup his license to operate with and for the U.S. government had been renewed. There had been three important encounters with U.S. officials that tense autumn, all involving U.S. support for the Contras in Nicaragua. Despite Noriega's apprehension, each had gone well. Events in Panama were scarcely mentioned.

In fact, those meetings were part of a series going as far back as 1983, meetings that accelerated in frequency with the Reagan administration's growing obsession with supporting the Contras.

In June 1985, Oliver North had hosted Noriega and Jose Blandon aboard a yacht in Balboa harbor. North told the two Panamanians that he needed their help. It was against U.S. law to train Contras with U.S. funds. Nor could American bases be used as Contra training sites. Could Contras be trained on PDF bases? Of course, Noriega said. Could Contra leaders visit Panama? Of course, Noriega replied. An hour and a quarter later, Noriega and Blandon left. The next October, North, Noriega, and Blandon met again in Noriega's office at the Comandancia. It was their first meeting since the Spadafora murder. Noriega wondered how North would use the murder and the Barletta coup. He anticipated that North would make him pay for whatever support he could provide in Washington. But Noriega seized the initiative by offering North a specific plan to help the U.S. government in Nicaragua.

Noriega told North there were terrorist units within the PDF, though they were officially described as "counter-terror" forces. He offered to send them into Nicaragua to help attack the Sandinistas. North reminded Noriega and Blandon of the outraged public reaction to the U.S. mining of Nicaraguan harbors and said he did not have the authority to accept the offer. He would, however, relay it to his superiors. When Noriega and Blandon brought up Panamanian political and economic problems, North told them he would see if he could help.

Noriega was somewhat relieved, but he knew that North was a flunky. He was worried again when CIA director William Casey summoned him to a meeting at Langley headquarters on November 1.

Casey noticed that Noriega was nervous as he launched into

a complaint about Panama's making it easy for Castro to skirt the U.S. trade embargo. It was a predictable complaint, an old joke, like a father razzing a grown son about his haircut. Casey may even have been trying to put his visitor at ease. He said nothing designed to upset Noriega, nothing about murder or presidential coups; he focused on U.S. policy in Central America. When Noriega left his office, Casey felt that his visitor had been reassured. Noriega's confidence was further bolstered after a lunch with several CIA staffers at a restaurant in the Virginia countryside.

Two week later, Casey sent Noriega a signal that reaffirmed Noriega's relationship with the U.S. government. In mid-November 1985, the CIA station chief in Panama told Ambassador Edward Everett Briggs that he had received a message from Casey for Noriega in which Casey clarified a point or two about the discussion the two men had about U.S. foreign policy in the region. The incident was a measure of how the administration did business with Noriega. Casey had cleared his message with Elliott Abrams, which meant that a State Department official had agreed to the exclusion of the U.S. ambassador, to say nothing of the State Department, in a matter of state, and allowed one intelligence chief to deal directly with another. Briggs was a bystander.

A month later, in mid-December, Noriega was informed of another meeting and once again was apprehensive. Briggs and Abrams would be present, along with SOUTHCOM commander Gen. John Galvin and Vice Adm. John Poindexter, who had succeeded Robert "Bud" McFarlane just ten days earlier as national security adviser. Some of the general's loudest enemies in Washington were former or current members of the NSC, and they had been lobbying Poindexter to dump Noriega. Their case was simple: He was a squalid, disloyal criminal of dubious value. Spadafora's murder confirmed it.

Noriega and Captain Moises Cortizo, his interpreter (a West Point graduate), were waiting on a couch in the conference room at Howard Air Force Base when the U.S. delegation arrived. They joked about how Noriega could afford a Lincoln Continental on his official salary. Elliott Abrams, just six months into his job, had not met the general before and was taken aback by his ugliness enough to comment about it.

This meeting was singular in one respect. Poindexter actually talked about Panama, and he also brought up some unpleasant subjects. He said that the United States felt that Noriega was stepping outside his military role, taking on a political one and in general becoming conspicuous. He mentioned drug trafficking, money laundering, and human rights abuses. His tone was matter-of-fact as he noted that there were strong indications that PDF corruption could be traced to Noriega. Spadafora's name was not mentioned, but Poindexter's reference to PDF "brutality" was understood. Abrams recalled that Poindexter had told Noriega "to clean up your act," adding that the general was beginning to "stand out more and more like a sore thumb."

Noriega's response was a little speech he often delivered to Americans, changing the emphasis to suit the occasion. First, he denied all the charges, saying that the PDF was no more corrupt than any other part of the government. Then he began a succinct history of Panama.

The uniformed services, he said, had always been the country's only source of social infrastructure. The people relied upon the PDF to maintain roads and bridges and keep Panama running. For half an hour Noriega outlined a history of the United States in Panama, a history of the two countries' symbiotic relationship. His narration suggested that he had always done what the United States had expected him to do.

No one chose to pursue the charges against Noriega after that. The meeting was over. Poindexter had omitted any threat of U.S. action in the event of continuing problems. There was no "or else."

Briggs, who listened in silence, despised Noriega and made no secret of his feelings in his cables to Foggy Bottom. (Six days later, he flew to Washington and briefed a number of officials, including Vice President George Bush, about the situation as he saw it in Panama.)

Noriega was elated after the meeting. He had his license back. He understood that Poindexter had had no choice but to recite the grievances, but it seemed to Noriega that he had recited exactly the charges that the White House was planning to overlook.

By the time the Panamanian attorney general officially closed the Spadafora case, the United States had taken exactly two punitive actions against Panama: The State Department had temporarily diverted $14 million in aid from Panama to Guatemala and the Pentagon had canceled a scheduled performance by the U.S. Air Force Thunderbirds, a precision flying unit, over Panama City.

Noriega was pleased. The Americans knew what he had done

but there had been no punishment. As far as he was concerned, the Americans were his accomplices now.

But Deborah DeMoss, certain that Noriega's dirty secrets were destined to be revealed, had declared war on Noriega. On January 5, 1986, after a flight from Florida, she recognized Kaizer Bazan, the new Panamanian ambassador to the United States, at the luggage claim area at Washington's Dulles Airport. Bazan was a West Point graduate and veteran politico.

He struck up a conversation with DeMoss, who with her black hair and olive skin, was often mistaken for a Latin.

"So, you're waiting for your luggage?" he asked the young woman. They agreed it was taking a long time.

"You're the new ambassador from Panama, aren't you?" she asked.

"How did you know . . .?"

"I guessed," she said to the amazed Bazan.

"Who are you?" he asked.

DeMoss paused, but only briefly. "I'm Deborah DeMoss, Senator Helms's assistant," she replied.

Bazan, maintaining his composure, introduced DeMoss to his wife and a colleague as the conveyor belt began throwing luggage onto the carousel. Bazan offered DeMoss a ride to her Watergate apartment in his chauffeur-driven limousine and on the way invited her to dinner the next night at Tiberio's, a flashy Washington power spot. The following night, as waiters hovered, Ambassador Bazan proposed that she and Helms meet President Delvalle, a wonderful man.

"So what?" asked DeMoss. "The point here is Noriega," she said. "No one wants to meet Delvalle. Let Noriega come up, bring Noriega here. We want to talk to him about Hugo Spadafora, drugs, Cuba. Delvalle has got nothing to do with it. Delvalle is not the issue; he has nothing to do with it. I know who runs the ports, customs, the railroad. . . ."

She warned Bazan not to try to defend what he could not defend. She told him not to bother coming to Congress to defend Noriega. "Don't even try."

By January 23, Winston Spadafora and his cousin Alfonso Gonzalez were once again in Helms's office. This time the senator looked at the photographs Winston could never bring himself to look at. Helms threw them down on the table and froze. There was a silence at the table.

"I'm going to do something, right away. We will hold hearings on Panama. I promise you I will make this a presidential issue," Helms said.

———

On February 18, the Panamanian attorney general summoned Guillermo Sanchez Borbon to his office and informed him that he was being sued for libel by a PDF member he had identified as one of the group who took Spadafora into custody. A technicality of Panama's legal system permitted the attorney general to put Sanchez Borbon in jail after a brief and perfunctory court appearance. It touched off a diplomatic shoving match between the United States and Panama.

Sanchez Borbon's friends began making telephone calls, rallying support for his release. One reached Ambassador Briggs just as he was about to make his farewell call on President Delvalle. The ambassador personally protested to the president, pointing out the harm it was doing to Panama's reputation. *La Prensa* put up $5,000 bail money and within three and a half hours Sanchez Borbon, the only person still investigating the Spadafora murder, was back at his desk.

Briggs had argued that Sanchez Borbon's jailing would become an issue at the confirmation hearings of his successor, Arthur Davis, scheduled for the next day. Davis was a Colorado businessman with many Republican friends, including Ronald Reagan and Jesse Helms. In his previous, and first, diplomatic posting in Paraguay, he had surprised everyone by openly challenging dictator Alfredo Stroessner on human rights questions. Davis's nomination, firmly backed by Helms, was already a rebuke to Noriega.

At his hearing, Davis had told the senators that he hoped reports of PDF narco-trafficking would be investigated. He said that the sooner Panama returned to genuine civilian democracy the better, and that the investigation of the Spadafora murder should be reopened. Rogelio Novey, a Panamanian and international diplomat who worked for the Organization of American States (OAS) and who despised Noriega, turned up. He noticed that there was not a single journalist from any country in the hearing room. Novey took careful notes and, when the hearing was over, telephoned *La Prensa* and dictated the explosive remarks to a reporter. That night, Novey hosted Ambassador Bazan for dinner and they talked about problems in Panama. The next day Davis was page-one news in Panama.

Noriega, still smarting from Briggs's intervention on behalf of Sanchez Borbon, dispatched Alonso Abadia, his foreign minister, to Washington "to satisfy our national dignity." Abadia got an hour and a half of Secretary of State George Shultz's time and a statement asserting that the United States "had no intentions of interfering in any way in Panama's internal affairs." Noriega, and his friends in Washington, were able to generate sufficient heat that Davis's remarks went through an unusual "clarification" process. The United States stopped just short of an apology. When it was over, Noriega could afford to gloat. It had been a scuffle but he had made a point.

━━━━━━

Joel McCleary had no idea that the report he submitted to Noriega that winter would one day threaten his survival. McCleary was a political consultant, one of many Noriega employed from time to time. He had been on the general's payroll for several years. Noriega respected McCleary because the energetic, articulate young American was smart and not only understood but enjoyed the intrigue of Panamanian politics.

McCleary had excellent if unusual credentials. A Harvard graduate, class of 1971, he became a certified insider at the Carter White House and treasurer of the Democratic National Committee. Hamilton Jordan, Carter's chief troubleshooter, recognized McCleary's political acumen (in domestic U.S. politics and international affairs) and often sent him as the White House liaison on congressional junkets around the world, where he made many friends. By 1986, he was established as a political consultant and was familiar with political intrigue from Tokyo to Buenos Aires. The more lurid and convoluted the situation the more he liked it—an unusual trait for a devout Buddhist and a close friend of the Dalai Lama. Noriega, who sometimes called himself a Buddhist, was fascinated with McCleary's religion. Both men had always understood that McCleary's first responsibility was to tell Noriega the realities of his political situation.

The document McCleary prepared was political intelligence of the highest order. It presented a clear and balanced description of all the circumstances Noriega faced. McCleary paid great attention to the state of the general's relationship with Washington. It presented findings, or "perceptions," likely to please Noriega— "There is no viable alternative to the current government"—and others that were less sanguine—"The military is corrupt, involved with drugs, out of touch with the 'people,' brutal and unable to make Panama work." McCleary identified the Spadafora murder as a major problem that he said must be investigated. The murderers must go to jail.

The document was distributed to a few people, including Mike Harari, the legendary Israeli intelligence agent who had become Noriega's best and most trusted friend. Harari had extraordinary clout in Panama and was known as "Mr. Sixty Percent," a reference to the commission he charged on business deals brokered through Noriega. Noriega's veteran political analyst Jose Blandon also received a copy. The document warned these men that Noriega did not have an open-ended free pass in Washington, and that Noriega was mistaken if he believed that one segment of the U.S. government (headed by William Casey and including Nestor Sanchez and Oliver North) could guarantee his protection indefinitely, especially if he continued to behave in a way that made it difficult for his allies to justify him.

There was an irony in Noriega's reaction. The champion in the world of intelligence had received a report that impartial judges would rate as superb analysis. It certainly merited a *verificado*, the "verified" stamp that was reserved for the real thing in Noriega's G-2 office. But Noriega bristled when he read McCleary's analysis. He told a close PDF associate that McCleary had written as if he were a teacher scolding a pupil. The general decided that maybe McCleary was trying to screw with him.

McCleary's verdict was unacceptable, unthinkable. Noriega continued to believe that the United States would need him forever. He threw the report away and began to distance himself from McCleary.

————

By the time Jesse Helms had fulfilled his promise to Winston Spadafora by convening his hearings on Panama (in March, April, and May), it was clear that there were two Panamas: the real-world place, and the "simulated" nation described by U.S. officials. Helms's hearings revealed both—and displayed the State Department's continuing support for Noriega.

Much of the testimony involved the PDF that U.S. officials described as a highly trained, well-equipped military and social action institution that held Panama together (while rigorously obeying civilian law). That was only the beginning of the distortions.

When Elliott Abrams described Panama one might have thought he was talking about England. "We have never lacked a sympathetic hearing for our views from Panama's government," Abrams said. "Also, and importantly, Panama has not tried to involve our bilateral treaty relationship in other issues. There has been no dispute concerning U.S. military bases in Panama. In a region where we have too many problems, the virtual absence of difficulty about our most significant military bases is notable and beneficial to us."

In Abrams's view, Panama was a staunch ally in the war on drugs and something of a beacon of enlightenment. "In the matters of controlling the production or trafficking in drugs or precursor chemicals," he said, "we have received excellent cooperation from Panama's civil and law enforcement authorities. . . . Panama is one of the most open societies in the hemisphere, with pluralistic social and economic institutions, a free enterprise economy. There is general freedom to express political dissent and the legal rights of individuals are generally respected. . . ."

Helms challenged Abrams and Abrams fought back, doggedly making the case for the powers that were in Panama. Under the senator's pressure, Abrams admitted that the PDF was very powerful. "They intervene a lot in the affairs of the government, and the degree of military interference is simply inconsistent with the kind of control by an elected government that you would have to have, I think, before you would be willing to call it a democracy."

Helms was skeptical but Abrams hung tough. Panama, he insisted, had a civilian government, albeit "a civilian government with military interference in areas of interest to the military." The transcript noted "laughter" but made no mention of a reply from Abrams when Helms asked for a list of areas controlled by the PDF but then changed his mind: "Well," he said, "I think I could save both of us time by asking you to identify those activities that the Defense Forces do not operate and control."

Abrams's remarks were particularly disappointing to the Spadaforas and their friends. Abrams appeared to accept the findings of Panamanian authorities that there was insufficient evidence connecting the crime to the PDF. He made his remarks despite abundant evidence to the contrary, evidence available to him and other officials. He told Helms that the photos of Spadafora's corpse had been described to him, but that he had deliberately avoided looking at them.

———

The hearings buoyed Noriega's confidence. Helms was virtually alone in the Congress in his interest in Panama. American journalists displayed no particular interest. And on the heels of joint maneuvers between the U.S. Army and the PDF (codenamed "Kindle Liberty") there was more good news. On April 17, 1986, the Pentagon announced an increase in U.S. military aid to Panama—from $8.4 million in 1986 to $14.6 million in 1987.

Noriega was soon feeling downright cocky and, in May, when Deborah DeMoss visited Panama with an air force colonel on liaison duty with the Senate and another Senate staffer, he decided to have some fun. His task was made easier by a background report on DeMoss and her colleagues that had been prepared for him and Blandon by the CIA. The documents were stamped "classified."

First, Noriega instructed Kaizer Bazan at the last minute to cancel the schedule he and DeMoss had worked out for her stay. Government press photographers ambushed the weary Americans when they walked into the diplomatic reception lounge at the civilian airport. Photographers leapt from behind potted plants in all corners of the room, blinding the travelers with popping flashbulbs. The three instinctively shielded their faces or turned away, gasping. Appearing in the newspapers over the next few days, the pictures made the American officials look like criminals on the jailhouse steps, hiding their faces from public view. They were the perfect accompaniment for stories describing them as Helms's spies who had come to take back the canal and overthrow the government.

There were stories that DeMoss danced late into the night and slept with all sorts of people as part of her intrigues. One account reported that the air force officer made a practice of recruiting agents at beaches to foment wars. *Sapos* and photographers followed the group everywhere. Each day they printed their schedule with the names of the Panamanians they were seeing. Some of the information was accurate, most of it was fabricated. By the time they left, Noriega had demonstrated that he could mock and humiliate U.S. citizens, even U.S. Senate staffers, and get away with it.

In May 1986, two people who had never set foot in Panama entered the drama. One was Howard Simons, former managing editor of the *Washington Post*, who had played a leading role in the paper's Watergate coverage. Since 1984, he had been curator of the Nieman Foundation, which provides journalists from around the world with a year of study at Harvard. Simons had listened carefully to Roberto Eisenmann and realized that Panama was a great story waiting to be told. But when Simons tried to interest several Washington journalists in what he had learned, he found they were not interested.

Near the end of the academic year, Simons gave up on all the major news-gathering organizations and decided to call a free-lancer, his old friend Seymour M. Hersh, one of the best reporters in the United States, in the hope he would show some interest. Sy Hersh had written about the My Lai massacre, the CIA's illegal domestic spying program, and the shooting down of the Korean airliner—among many other ground-breaking stories. He had some of the best sources in the world—and protected their anonymity zealously. Hersh was smart and stubborn, a maverick who never played the Washington press corps game of reporting a leak designed to test, advance, or kill a policy.

Simons was mistaken about Hersh's free-lancing. That very morning, he had officially rejoined the staff of the Washington bureau of the *New York Times*. Just a week before, someone else had mentioned to him the fascinating and all-but-ignored Helms hearings. Hersh eagerly agreed to talk to Eisenmann. From that moment on, Noriega and Hersh were on a collision course.

Hersh and Eisenmann met on May 22, 1986. Afterward, Eisenmann sent Hersh a note on Nieman Foundation stationery. "I don't want to sound dramatic, but two million freedom-loving Panamanians could be depending on your success in breaking this cover-up and support of a terrible man. Best regards, Roberto. I'll be in touch." Eisenmann, by this time, had decided to stay in the United States when the academic year was complete. He had received credible reports that he would be killed if he returned to Panama.

On June 11, Noriega was at Fort McNair in Washington for a meeting of the Inter-American Defense Board (IADB). Wearing one of his dressiest uniforms, he placed a medal on a ribbon around the neck of an American general. The ceremonies were designed to underscore the close bonds between parts of the U.S. military and Noriega.

But there was tension in the air. Noriega was refusing phone calls from Seymour Hersh, who was putting the finishing touches on his Panama story. Some of the questions Noriega's press office back in Panama were getting were very alarming. Who was this Hersh, Noriega wanted to know.

He began to find out that evening, when the first editions of the June 12 *New York Times* hit the streets. He left Washington in a hurry the next day. There were enough allegations in the *Times* to make Noriega frightened that he might be arrested.

Hersh's story asserted that what he was revealing was already known inside the White House. That information included charges that Noriega was, in short, a murdering, election-fixing, narco-trafficking CIA agent of long standing and a double agent for Cuban intelligence. Hersh made it clear that a great variety of sources, including many U.S. intelligence agents, had answered his questions.

In Panama City there was jubilation in some quarters as *La Prensa* reprinted Hersh in Spanish. Noriega's foes pointed out that there was nothing new in the Hersh report. All the stories had long been known in Panama City. But now U.S. officials, officials who said they had documentation, were talking to the American press.

3

Mystical Guerrilla Warfare

NORIEGA saw the Hersh articles as a sneak attack by a person or persons inside the Reagan-Bush administration. Someone had opened a trap door under his feet and he had been formally transformed into a traitor. His enemies were preparing the public for his demise. To Noriega, it was the beginning of the demonization process that his enemies within the administration and the bureaucracy were using to prepare the public for his ejection. He had seen it happen before to close friends of the United States—most recently Ferdinand Marcos, who had fled Manila just four months earlier. For years, the Philippine president had been a war hero and then a staunch ally in the U.S. press. Then they had repainted him as a despot and thief.

But, Noriega wondered, why him, why now, and why so fast? He suspected that he had somehow come to be seen as a liability in the U.S. Contra-support game. The Contras were an obsession; even a hint of disloyalty to their cause was enough to doom him. He made up his mind to strike back.

He was, as it happens, wrong, but his mistake was understandable. The idea of an independent reporter such as Hersh was unimaginable to Noriega. He could not believe that the U.S. government would allow a newspaper to print such information unless it wanted it public. For all his contact with Americans over the years, Noriega had almost no sense of how the United States really worked.

Contrary to his perception, he was not then in trouble. One might even have said he was at the crest of his worth to the administration. But his mistake about the Hersh reporting, which provoked him to risk severing an extremely important U.S. connection, was the first of a series of blunders. He failed to understand that the U.S. bureaucracy had its own trap doors—and that U.S. domestic political life, from which he had always been shielded by anonymity, could be volatile. There were dangers within his own country, within his own PDF, that were easy to spot and to counter. But for all his guile, Noriega ignored his political advisers, such as Blandon. He was too much of a tough guy. The result: He started to create problems for himself. Within a year, he would be in serious trouble from which he would not escape.

That evening he went to the Presidencia, the Moorish-Spanish edifice on the waterfront that houses the president's office and residence. Known as the Palace of the Herons because of the birds inside its atrium, tiled courtyard, and fountain, the Presidencia was a perfect setting for intrigue. Its corridors twisted around a honeycomb of offices.

That night, President Delvalle played host to an impromptu gathering of government ministers, friends, cronies, and hangers-on. All were seeking information and consolation. Most regarded the *New York Times* as the voice of the U.S. government, and Hersh's story as a challenge to Noriega's existence and the government. They compared the story to an invasion.

Noriega—seemingly nonchalant, gregarious, dressed in a sport jacket, a drink in hand—reassured his circle. "There are two kinds of gringos," he said. "There are the gringos we all know, and then there are the gringeros. Those are the Panamanians who crawl for the gringos"; Noriega said that the *Times*'s preposterous charges were the invention of Panamanian gringeros in cahoots with a New York newspaper. It was supposed to soothe fears, but the gathering was dismal and discouraging. Delvalle's friends felt that the president had failed them, and Delvalle fawned on Noriega and gossiped the evening away.

Delvalle made no protest, even when the Jews were dragged into Noriega's face-saving scenario. The gringero story gave way to an even more elaborate rumor that was constructed to explain the Hersh fiasco. According to this concoction, Hersh and Roberto Eisenmann (two Jews, it was noted—one of whom worked for a Jewish newspaper) had met in the lobby of the Plaza Hotel in New York. Money (either $1,000 or $10,000) had changed hands. In one version, Hersh gave Eisenmann money for information. In another, Eisenmann gave Hersh both the information and cash as payment for running the stories. Noriega's friends were not familiar with the protocols of American corruption. The Plaza rumor quickly became one of the most popular *bolas*, at least in government circles.

The morning after, June 13, 1986, brought another shocker from Hersh. In his second article, he reported that U.S. officials had considered murdering Noriega in 1972 because of his narcotrafficking activities. It is unlikely that Noriega had known about the murder plan in such detail. To be sure, the term used in the Bureau of Narcotics and Dangerous Drugs (BNDD) document unearthed by Hersh referred to Noriega's "total and complete immobilization." To Noriega, its mention in the *Times* was alarming, a sign that his murder had been soberly discussed in Washington. Noriega decided, on no evidence, that the source of the stories was Oliver North.

To Noriega and his entourage, North was a figure of fun. "Even when he's listening to you he's not paying attention," said Blandon, who sat in on North-Noriega talks. Noriega knew that North regularly leaked stories to reporters in Washington—and that he would do anything if he thought there was short-term gain for the Contras. To Noriega, North had always seemed untrustworthy and gullible. Over the years, he had observed the colonel as he created crises and melodramas, and had listened to his delusional talk about nonexistent Contra armies. Noriega didn't think North could do anything right, though many thought North relished the relationship. "To North, Noriega was a spymaster, an operator, a man who made things happen. He worshiped him like a schoolboy," according to an American who observed the relationship. "To North, Noriega was like Brando up the river in *Apocalypse Now*. No rules." But Noriega had decided North was to blame and he was going to get even.

Two of North's Contra-related schemes were boiling over that day. The first, in Costa Rica, involved a muddy patch of ground at a place called Santa Elena where the renovation of an airstrip (to be used in support of Contra activities) had been started in 1985. The Udall Research Corporation had managed construction. Udall, Lake Resources, and NRAF, Inc., were all businesses set up by North or his associates and all were registered in Panama. Noriega had been as helpful as he could. His own lawyer, Juan Castillero of Quijano Associates in Panama City, had drawn up the papers for Udall. Noriega had little direct connection with the operation of the project. His interest in it was based entirely on what he could learn from it. Noriega had access, if he wanted it, to the private records of any company set up in Panama, and Udall was a keyhole for him through which he could learn what North and his friends were doing with their money.

The crisis had begun on June 9 when an airplane loaded with ammunition had sunk into the mire at Santa Elena. It was a political embarrassment: Oscar Arias, Costa Rica's president, had expressly forbidden the United States to use the strip for Contra support flights when he was inaugurated in May 1986. Noriega knew that Santa Elena offered an opportunity to embarrass North.

The *Pia Vesta*, another North scheme, interested Noriega even more. The *Pia Vesta*, a Danish freighter, was a floating ruse developed by North in collaboration with Noriega. It was steaming toward Panama, laden with 1,500 82-KF rifles, 1,500 rocket-propelled grenade launchers, thousands of rounds of ammunition, and 32 military vehicles. All the material had been loaded in Europe, but Noriega had doctored the *Pia Vesta*'s documents to create the illusion that the cargo had been picked up in Nicaragua.

According to North's plan, Contra patrol boats would seize the ship on the high seas, just before it reached its ostensible destination, the Salvadoran rebels. The plan was designed to accomplish two goals: The Contras would get tons of weaponry, and North would make a powerful political point, proving that the Sandinistas were, in fact, supplying arms to the rebels in El Salvador. Anyone who investigated the *Pia Vesta* would find paper trails leading in all directions: intrigues in Florida, Peru, France, even South Africa. Noriega had created cover stories within cover stories all designed to bolster North's trick. After three months of planning, success was a few days away. Then Noriega acted.

On June 14, PDF patrol boats approached the ship as it steamed into Panama Canal waters. Their presence in those waters was a serious and unprecedented violation of the new treaties. The PDF seized the *Pia Vesta* and took it to one of its moorings near the Pacific entrance to the canal, where it remained. Its cargo, however, was commandeered by the PDF. The trucks became fixtures on Panama City streets where they were dubbed "Pia Vestas."

The attack was a message to North—and whoever else might be tempted to screw with Noriega: He could scuttle Contra operations when he chose. Hit Noriega, he would hit back.

———

"The U.S. is like a monkey on a chain," Noriega used to say. "All you do is play the music, and the monkey performs." Noriega assumed that this crisis in his usually calm relations with the United States would pass if he played Contra music. It didn't occur to him that the drug issue—his narco-trafficking activities and Medellín Cartel associations—could provoke a shift in public opinion that even his best Washington friends couldn't override. He didn't count on the American public's revulsion with drugs and those whom the *New York Times* accused of helping to make them available. He was too confident that North and Casey wanted to continue operations as much as he did. He may have been right. "Casey and North both got off on Noriega," remembered one Noriega confidant who knew them all. "Noriega gave them a thrill." He was as squalid as they came and it was just that quality that attracted Casey and North to him.

Rogues and rascals like Noriega have always been part of intelligence legends. By Casey's time, the preference for flashy amoral foreign agents had intensified. Depravity was a definite plus on a potential agent's résumé, especially if it worked in favor of the Contras.

Noriega was not wrong to consider the U.S. Contra obsession in his assessment of the war he was now waging with Washington. The story of Barry Seal was a constant reminder to him of the damage North's Contra zeal could wreak. Seal was an American pilot and part of the Central American pilot fraternity that included Floyd Carlton and the late Cesar Rodriguez. Seal had been caught in a drug operation by the DEA and made a deal by which he became an undercover agent. On June 25, 1984, Seal had managed to take an extraordinary photograph at an airport outside Managua. What he had photographed was Pablo Escobar, one of the principals in the Medellín Cartel, and several Sandinista officials loading cocaine onto a Fairchild C-123K Provider. Seal had orchestrated the whole purchase as a "sting" that would put them all in jail. At extraordinary risk to his own life, he managed to get out of Nicaragua with this photograph.

But the photograph never got to court. Instead, three weeks later, it appeared in U.S. newspapers, courtesy of Oliver North, who wanted to publicize the link between the Sandinistas and the cartel and influence a congressional vote on Contra aid. Publication of the photo destroyed the DEA's undercover operation and the cartel put out a contract on Seal—offering $500,000 for him dead and $1 million if he were brought back to Medellín alive. Escobar and Jorge Ochoa, another target of Seal's operations, remained at large. In March 1986, Ronald Reagan used Seal's photo in a televised appeal for Contra aid. By then, Barry Seal was dead—machine-gunned in Baton Rouge, Louisiana, a month earlier. All this was followed closely in Panama. The lesson was clear: Contras matter; drugs aren't a factor.

By late August, Noriega had decided to kiss and make up with North. A representative of Noriega met with North and put forth an extraordinary proposition. Noriega wanted his image cleaned up. He also wanted a resumption of military sales (suspended by the Pentagon in the wake of Sy Hersh's stories). That was all he wanted. In return, he would assassinate the entire Sandinista leadership. He was offering nearly a dozen heads. (These talks were carried out in great secrecy. They did not become part of the public record until North's trial in 1989.)

The offer was unacceptable, North quickly told Noriega's go-between. It was against the law. Undeterred, Noriega's representative said that Noriega might perform other services inside Nicaragua, services not explicitly forbidden by U.S. law. Sabotage, for example, had been successful in the past. Just the year before a Panamanian team had sabotaged a Sandinista arsenal. That caught North's attention. He remembered the incident with some pleasure.

In Washington, North and Poindexter discussed Noriega's offer. There was no question that he could be helpful. Poindexter told North to continue discussions. Project Democracy, North's Contra operations, could foot the bill, North pointed out. A month later, in late September, North and Noriega met in London and came to terms. Noriega promised to take immediate action against the Sandinistas and proposed a menu—an oil refinery, an airport, and a cargo facility. North reported the good news to Poindexter. It was some of the last good news those men heard while in government service.

In early September, consternation was growing in Costa Rica over the Santa Elena airstrip. North and his men ignored Arias's orders and continued to make "secret" repairs. They were caught again. The Costa Rican minister of public security scheduled a press conference on September 6 to proclaim that the field was closed. It had become a matter of national pride, to say nothing of national security, for the Costa Ricans. The Arias government wanted to let the world know that North and his friends could not casually force Costa Rica into a war.

North tried to pressure Arias. He wanted the U.S. ambassador to threaten to cancel Arias's scheduled meeting with Reagan and an $80 million U.S. aid package, but he got nowhere. So North wrote Poindexter a memo, boasting to his boss that he himself had telephoned Arias to threaten him with an aid cutoff. There had been no such phone call, but in the uproar over Santa Elena, Elliott Abrams did threaten Arias with cancellation of the Reagan visit. On September 25, Costa Rica closed the airstrip, saying that it had been used to supply the Contras and for drugs.

North's world began to crumble. As part of his deal with Noriega, he went to John Lawn of the DEA in early October to seek his help in rehabilitating Noriega's reputation. But his visit to Lawn was a joke: North seemed to have forgotten what had happened to Barry Seal and the DEA's major drug investigation. Lawn had not. He told North to leave his office.

On October 5, a Sandinista soldier shot down a Contra re-supply plane and Eugene Hasenfus, the only surviving crew member, was captured. The plane was the same one Barry Seal had once owned, the same plane he had used, and photographed, in his sting. Now it was flying ammunition for the Contras. Intelligence agents noted the curious fact that ammunition on the plane matched rifles that had been aboard the *Pia Vesta*. The copious records aboard the plane—dubbed "The Flying Filing Cabinet"—included the phone numbers of many Americans.

The crash began to bring North's secret supply systems into public view. In November, he (and Poindexter) were thrown out of the White House as what came to be called the Iran-Contra scandal erupted. Most of it was old news to Noriega, who knew far more than the American public ever learned.

THE HOME FRONT

Guillermo Sanchez Borbon had taken a long vacation after his brush with prison in February 1986 when U.S. intervention had saved his skin. He had returned in May and quickly set about reopening his investigation of the Spadafora murder. Several of his columns mocked the attorney general and pointedly advised him to investigate a government propagandist who could shed light on the planning of the murder. The propagandist, a hack journalist of small reputation, sued Sanchez Borbon for libel. On July 9, the attorney general ordered Sanchez Borbon to appear in court the next day to face a second libel charge. Because of a technicality in Panamanian law (at the discretion of the court a person accused of libel twice can be incarcerated immediately, a convenience for government officials who wanted to squelch criticism), Sanchez Borbon had to face the possibility that he would proceed directly from the court appearance to prison.

This charge had been brought by Carlos Nunez, who had written vitriolic attacks on Spadafora in the months before the murder. One had been accompanied by a menacing cartoon with a reference to chopping off the head of the traitor. Sanchez Borbon contended that Nunez never wrote anything except what his bosses told him to write. He urged the attorney general, in print, to ask Nunez who had given him his instructions. Nunez's attacks on Spadafora were, he said, "the political and moral preparation for murder," a term Leon Trotsky had used to describe the press vilification that had preceded his murder.

Attorney General Carlos Villalaz refused to meet Sanchez Borbon. Instead, he deputized a fat and bullying district attorney named Manuel Jose Calvo to deal with the columnist. In short order, Sanchez Borbon dubbed Calvo "Memellena," the name for a cheap gelatinous pudding of little nutritional value. The name stuck—just as "Fraudito" had stuck to Barletta after the fraudulent 1984 election.

Noriega was stepping up his harassment of opponents, what *La Prensa* called "legal terrorism." The next target was Radio Mundial, a small but lively station operated by Miguel Antonio Bernal, a law professor and veteran opponent of the military. Villalaz shut down the station and dragged Bernal into court on July 9. The charge was libel. Bernal was jailed and his friends were beaten by the PDF at the attorney general's office. He went into "academic asylum" at the university when he got out on bail.

Sanchez Borbon had no way of knowing what the court would decide about him if and when he showed up for his scheduled appearance the next day, July 10. So, first, he went to a friend's house with the intention of staying there in hiding. Then he realized that the PDF would search for him and "beat the shit" out of anyone who had helped him. While his friend Bernal was in court, Sanchez Borbon returned to *La Prensa* to figure out what to do next. While there, he received through an intermediary a message from a government official who described his situation bluntly: He was a marked man. If he went to court he would go to jail where he would spend at least five years. Then again, he might not last that long.

In fact, Sanchez Borbon could not know how long he would last even at *La Prensa*. The newspaper offices were on a well-traveled avenue near open fields. To stay in the building was dangerous, but so was leaving. "Noriega has gone crazy," Sanchez Borbon told his colleagues. "I knew what was in store for me. If I go to jail, I'll not get out alive. They'll put me in a cell with maniacs or kill me while 'escaping.' This country has become a nightmare."

Sanchez Borbon wrote a last column and decided to leave the country. Ricardo Arias Calderon, leader of the Christian Democrat party, volunteered for the hazardous task of driving him, past PDF surveillance, to the Venezuelan embassy. Four days later, with diplomatic protection, Sanchez Borbon was on his way to Caracas, Venezuela, and three months later he arrived in Miami where he continued his column for *La Prensa*. The Spadafora investigation was closed again. And this time there was no American or Panamanian protest.

———

On Tuesday, July 8, the morning before Sanchez Borbon had gone into hiding, Berta Mitrotti had awakened from a sound sleep, startled to find herself alone in bed. Her husband, Serafin, always came home. Within minutes she and her three sons (Serafin, Jr., twenty-eight, Jaime, twenty-six, and Luigi, twenty-four) and one daughter, twenty-two-year-old Dilia, had started to search. It was the beginning of an ordeal for the Mitrotti family that terrified the thousands of Panamanians who had believed they could remain aloof from Panamanian politics.

Until very recently, Serafin Mitrotti had remained on the sidelines. A well-to-do, upper-middle-class entrepreneur, he owned a photo laboratory and traveled around Latin America selling a variety of Panamanian merchandise. If he—and the thousands of middle-class people like him—had formed a party they might have been called "Babbittistas." Free market–oriented, civic minded, they had pledged their allegiance not to any political party but to the Rotary, Kiwanis, and Lions clubs. Mitrotti had just been reelected president of one of the several Rotaries in Panama City when he disappeared. All the civic organizations discouraged, if not prohibited, political involvement by their members—a regulation Mitrotti had always been happy to comply with. He and his friends tended to keep their distance from people like Bernal and others in the small "opposition." Middle-class businessmen over the years had usually been protected by whatever government was in power.

But Mitrotti had recently become more active. When the civic organizations, fed up with Noriega and his effect on business, had banded together to establish the Committee for the Redemption of Moral Values, Mitrotti had been elected president. The committee's charter was vague—and emphatically apolitical (to honor the rules of the participating organizations). But the group had an unspoken political agenda. By 1986, it was clear that there were two economies in Panama; one was composed of the old businesses run by the "Babbittistas," and the other was run by Noriega and the PDF. Noriega was muscling out the Babbittistas and expanding his own business empire in all directions, creating a new commercial elite composed of his accomplices. Noriega's extended family, the PDF, government employees, were the beneficiaries of "reverted" Canal Zone properties and were involved in everything from smuggling computers and shrimp, to black market steroids, to property development.

Eduardo Vallarino, president of the Business Executive Association of Panama and chairman of the National Caucus of Private Enterprises (CoNEP), described the situation. "You could be in business provided your activity did not compete with any of the regime's favorites. You also had to pay your 'dues' to the proper officials, and you didn't oppose the system politically in an open fashion." Vallarino said that those favored by the regime were granted immunity to deal in contraband or default on government contracts. Those who didn't "play ball" were subject to harassment, trumped-up court proceedings, the delay of permits, and, in some extreme cases, bankruptcy or government appropriation of their businesses. Otilia Koster, a human rights activist, described it: "Panama used to be an open whorehouse but now it's an exclusive whorehouse." Mitrotti's committee was the first tentative step by the middle class to tidy the whorehouse.

The Mitrotti family knew only that Serafin had left his house Monday afternoon because he had Rotary business. He had taken a taxi. On Tuesday morning, family members telephoned every hospital in Panama City and every law enforcement agency, assuming there had been an accident. The three sons went in person to a homicide office where they got what Berta described as "the first official word." A PDF detective contemptuously told Jaime that his father was probably with a woman.

On Wednesday, with only the vaguest of explanations, PDF police swooped down on Mitrotti's office and the pleasant Mitrotti house. The family protested the exhaustive search of Serafin's papers. A policeman said they were looking for clues.

On Thursday morning, Col. Nivaldo Madrinan, a close Noriega ally, telephoned Berta Mitrotti. In a flat tone he told her that her three sons, but not herself nor her daughter, should come to his office at the National Department of Investigation (DENI, a branch of the PDF commonly described as the FBI of Panama) immediately. He had good news, and bad news.

Later that day, Madrinan clutched a folder that the Mitrotti sons could see contained photographs and said matter-of-factly that the good news was that the PDF had found Serafin Mitrotti. The bad news was that he was dead. He was not absolutely sure of the identity of the corpse, he said, and the photos of it were too terrible for anyone to see. The Mitrottis would have to go to Penonome Hospital, 93 miles west of Panama City, to identify the body.

The three young men were terrified. While Madrinan was talking, Jaime tried not to stare at the officer's diamond ring. It looked exactly like his father's. He told his brothers about it as they hurried home. By the time they got there the government radio station was broadcasting the news that Serafin Mitrotti had been found dead. According to the report, his body had been discovered in a small motel in Anton, a resort town 81 miles west of Panama City. It was slight consolation that "news" on that particular station was often false.

The Mitrottis and some friends, including a doctor, set out for Penonome. They had hired a funeral manager to come along with a hearse. On the way they stopped at a motel whose Chinese proprietor had been quoted in the radio story. The proprietor said he had rented a room to a man and thought no more of it until the following day when a strange smell caught his attention. He had called the authorities. He did not want to talk about it—and only reluctantly showed the Mitrottis and their friends the room where the corpse had been found. It was bare, as if it had been sterilized. There was no furniture and nothing on the scrubbed walls and floors. They moved on to Penonome.

It was decided that the doctor would identify the body. When he emerged from the hospital mortuary, he said that it was indeed

Serafin Mitrotti. The corpse was very bloody and the doctor wanted it cleaned up before the dead man's sons were brought in. Even after the cleaning, the violence was obvious. There were cuts all around his head, almost in a circle, like a hatband; his nose was smashed and there were cuts on the elbows, arms, wrists, and both sides of the neck. The cuts on both wrists had all but severed the hands. His sons all noticed the sand in their father's toenails. The Mitrottis learned that there had been an autopsy and an official investigation the day before. The cause of death was officially suicide and the case was closed.

Later that same Thursday, a priest viewed the body and immediately gave his permission for a Catholic burial, which would have been impossible if suicide had been a real possibility. The funeral took place at the El Carmen cathedral the next day before a huge, stunned crowd. Descriptions of the body circulated. Most mourners knew about the ring on Madrinan's finger.

Several hours after the funeral the Mitrotti sons sat in the busy El Tambal restaurant waiting for Madrinan, who had demanded to meet with them. He arrived in his light brown PDF colonel's uniform. His hands were shaking and he gulped back a double scotch. "You are talking too much," he said, as he put the ring on the table. "You are playing with my honor and nobody does that," he said. "Take it," he ordered and made each of the sons look at the ring. "If you say it is not mine, you will have personal problems. You will have trouble with me. Now you have seen it. Now you understand my position." Madrinan put the ring back on his finger and left the restaurant.

At home, Dilia Mitrotti answered the phone and burst into tears after an anonymous caller threatened the death of another Mitrotti. The next morning another caller delivered the same message. On Monday morning, Madrinan called Berta at 8:00 A.M.

He demanded that she make a public announcement saying that the ring was his ring. She refused, reminding Madrinan that her husband's ring had vanished. Very shortly afterward, despite the closed investigation, four different prosecutors telephoned to order the entire Mitrotti family into their offices.

It soon turned out that the prosecutors were attempting to implicate the dead man in drug trafficking. They pointed out that his photo laboratory required imported chemicals, the same chemicals required for cocaine processing. They also pointed out Serafin's frequent visits to South America. Mitrotti's friends and associates would have dismissed the notion of drug dealing as quickly as the priest who saw Serafin's body had ruled out suicide.

The Mitrottis sat through their ordeal stoically. One prosecutor falsely accused Jaime of having a drug problem and said he was to blame for his father's suicide. In another room, another prosecutor advanced another theory to Berta: The sand in her husband's toenails was evidence that he had met with a gangster at a certain beach resort where a deal had gone wrong. He then turned to Dilia and sweetly expressed his sympathy, explaining that he had to ask questions to prepare a thorough report. Then, abruptly, he became scornful and came up with yet another theory about Serafin's death. He told Dilia that her father had also met a prostitute at the beach, and she had threatened to embarrass him. That was why he had committed suicide. "I told him he better stop saying things like that because there are very few women like me who trust their husbands one hundred percent," Berta Mitrotti said.

Late Wednesday afternoon, a prosecutor told Berta that their work was completed and gave her a shopping bag that he said contained her husband's clothes. Berta recognized nothing. By Thursday, the government papers were hinting that Mitrotti was a drug dealer. The Mitrottis, however, had begun running a large ad in *La Prensa* that chronicled—like a message to friends—what they knew and what had happened to them. The paid ad asked for the support of Panamanians and God.

By 10:00 A.M. Thursday, Berta, at her desk at the family's photo business, received another call from a prosecutor ordering her to report to his office. She refused. The prosecutor yelled that he was sending two police officers to arrest her. Send them, she said. Berta Mitrotti was already angry. Suddenly, a young man who she knew had worked for the government in the past turned up at her office. He said he had come to express sympathy. She was suspicious when he offered to call Attorney General Villalaz and ask for help for her. He grabbed the phone and punched the number.

On the phone, Villalaz told Berta Mitrotti that he would not tolerate the conduct she described from any of his prosecutors. Could she come to his office that afternoon at two? Villalaz assured her that when she saw the official reports, she would agree that Serafin had committed suicide. She went. At the meeting, Villalaz picked up the reports as quickly as he had put them down, but Berta managed to see that some of the pages were blank.

"What do you want from us?" Berta asked. Villalaz offered a deal. The attorney general said that if Berta Mitrotti pulled her ad from *La Prensa*, he would see to it that the press campaign against the family ceased. "You will have to deal with the consequences," he said when Berta refused.

At 5:00 P.M. Thursday, the family left the attorney general's office. After a quick dinner, they were home by seven. By that time, government radio and television news broadcasts were reporting that the Mitrottis had just held a press conference announcing their acceptance of the suicide finding. Immediately, Berta and two friends went to see Archbishop Marcos McGrath, who then telephoned Villalaz. Villalaz said it was impossible, there could not have been such a report. Berta, on the extension, said, "Listen, it's a pity that you are such a servile worm." Berta went back to see Villalaz, and he again insisted that there had been a mistake—but there was no retraction of the report. Before Berta left Villalaz's office, a crowd of reporters and photographers had gathered on the sidewalk where the women still said the rosary every day at noon. "You better stop them," the attorney general said to Berta, pointing at the reporters.

DIAZ HERRERA

That autumn of 1986, Noriega began to make another big mistake—very slowly—and he would not recover from the consequences. The mistake was to ignore and scorn his second in command, Col. Roberto Diaz Herrera, the man who had tried to mount a coup against him in September 1985. Noriega had known that Diaz Herrera had been behind the plan he had blamed on Barletta. He also knew that Diaz Herrera knew that he knew. Yet Noriega had continued to let Diaz Herrera's claim stand. Silence was a psychological device of torture.

By that autumn, Diaz Herrera had grown restless. He had heard rumors that Noriega had wanted to retire him involuntarily in 1987. Through intermediaries, Diaz Herrera proposed that if he had to retire he wanted to be ambassador to Japan, a very lucrative post. Also through intermediaries, Noriega told him to forget it. The general had a more modest retirement package in mind. Noriega refused to discuss these issues face-to-face even though the two men saw each other often around the Comandancia. Noriega just wanted to sidestep the whole issue. He hated confrontations—and did not think it was important whether Diaz

Herrera was happy or unhappy. He had squeezed Diaz Herrera out of any serious responsibilities. He kept him around the Comandancia, where he was regarded as a has-been. The most important factor in his rise within the ranks, after all, had been the fact that he was a cousin of Torrijos.

Diaz Herrera now had to face the prospect of powerless civilian life as a pensioner. He knew that Noriega, a master of cat and mouse, might decide at any minute to take horrible revenge on him for his attempted coup in 1985. For Diaz Herrera, it was deeply alarming.

Jose de Jesus "Chuchu" Martinez, the poet, philosopher, reveler, and former Torrijos bodyguard about whom Graham Greene had affectionately written in *Getting to Know the General*, knew both men very well. Since Torrijos's death, Chuchu had devoted his energies to collecting and publishing Torrijos's speeches. He was the keeper of the flame. Now he watched the interplay between Noriega and Diaz Herrera with great interest. To Chuchu, it was very simple. "Noriega's biggest mistake was in underestimating how crazy Diaz Herrera was," he said.

Even after Torrijos's death, Diaz Herrera had maintained ambitions for the top. According to an agreement that he, Noriega, and other officers signed seven months after Torrijos's death, Noriega was supposed to retire in the summer of 1987 and Diaz Herrera was to assume command. The agreement, called the "Secret Torrijos Plan," was a timetable for the settlement of Torrijos's political estate. It was to be honored unless "unexpected events" ("death, physical or mental incapacity, or free and voluntary resignations") intervened.

Noriega had broken the agreement shortly after he had taken command in August 1983. Diaz Herrera had happily cooperated with him in betraying their fellow officer Ruben Paredes, Jr., who after his voluntary retirement from uniform was to be the PRD candidate for president in 1984. But Noriega made other plans the moment Paredes left the PDF and demonstrated that when one was out of uniform in Panama one was out of power. Noriega preferred Barletta, and so did U.S. policymakers. Paredes, furious that he had been tricked so easily, and trying to retaliate, broke the military's strict code of silence and accused Noriega of treason. Diaz Herrera scorned Paredes and declared, "We don't wash our dirty linen in public."

But Diaz Herrera had plenty of dirty linen himself. He was a multimillionaire whose most noticeable revenue source was the sale of Panamanian visas to desperate Cubans hoping to make their way to the United States. The going price was "whatever you've got," often more than $20,000 per visa. Diaz Herrera also handled some of the PDF's "political" chores. This often meant arranging the delivery of thousands of government workers to rallies, a task at which he excelled. Otherwise, he was an outsider at the Comandancia. At five foot four, he was one inch shorter than Noriega. His nickname was "The Midget." He was also the whitest of all his colleagues, a distinction he enjoyed and used in his climb up Panama's social ladder. Diaz Herrera adopted the ways of the elite, mimicking their tastes and prejudices. He scorned things he considered lower class—for example, the occult practices in which Noriega and many of his fellow officers dabbled. Noriega had been a student of mysticism and the supernatural for many years, a pursuit in no way uncommon in Panama. For Diaz Herrera, it was all beneath him, a practice of the darker people. His fellow officers regarded him as an ineffectual, pretentious, social-climbing hypocrite. No wonder Noriega had no worries about humiliating Diaz Herrera.

Diaz Herrera took tranquilizers. Sometimes he locked himself in his office and wept, for hours on end. In October, watched over by a Noriega *sapo*, he went on a vacation and embarked on a strange campaign that eventually changed his life and jolted Noriega.

On October 14, Diaz Herrera flew to Buenos Aires with his wife, Maigualida, on a Panamanian Air Force 727. They took a suite in the Sheraton for a week and very quickly found themselves in the middle of some intriguing new ideas. An Argentinian folk singer named Piero, an old friend, brought Indra Devi, a frail, elderly, white-haired woman in a sari, to their hotel suite on their second evening in town. By midnight, Diaz Herrera was standing in the middle of the hotel room, his arms outstretched. Indra Devi used an apple slice and some white bread to explain *prana*—the idea that all objects have positive or negative energy. The apple from the room service tray was pure and had positive, good energy, but the white bread—and Maigualida's cigarette—were impure and had negative energy. The Diaz Herreras were impressed.

The old woman told them of her spiritual mentor, Satya Sai Baba, a holy man with a vast following in southern India who had many disciples around the world. "His powers are beyond comprehension," the woman told the Diaz Herreras. "He can stop rainbows; heal the sick; materialize all kinds of objects; read the past, present, and future of everyone; and transform himself into any human or nonhuman form. He can even be in two places at once." Sai Baba had always been special. Even in grammar school his classmates often asked him to make candy materialize from empty bags—an easy matter for an avatar.

Over the next few days the Diaz Herreras visited Indra Devi and met a friend of hers, a psychic from California named Shama Calhoum. Calhoum was an extraordinary-looking woman—according to Diaz Herrera the most exotic woman he had ever seen. Her feline eyes, steady gaze, and heavy brows evoked ancient Egypt. Chuchu Martinez, who had met her when she became a regular visitor to Panama, recalled that she had "the face of an angelic child—and the body of a voluptuous woman." To Diaz Herrera she was "La Gringa," and when he and Maigualida encountered her again at a dinner party a few days later, he was happy to have his future read.

La Gringa told the colonel to stare at her "third eye," in her forehead between her other eyes. "Fix your eyes on that spot for a few minutes so I can take a look at your aura, your magnetic camp," she said. The woman stared at Diaz Herrera and the air around him and then told him and the spellbound guests what she had found:

"You have a big mission in life. A big cause is calling for your help. I can't see very clearly what it is, but it involves many people, thousands, tens of thousands, maybe millions." She paused. "I see a war, a big war. You will get involved in a big fight. There's nothing you can do about it, it's clearly in your future. It's a fight that will demand your entire energy. Don't expect to win in the short run. You should be prepared to be seen by the world as having lost the fight, even if you will win it in the long run. Don't worry, you'll be all right in the end. Have faith, a lot of faith. You will appear to have lost the fight at first, but you will win in the end."

There were no specifics, but Diaz Herrera said he knew she was talking about his relationship with Noriega. He also realized that he had never before considered a pitched battle with the commander in chief. In the 727 on the way back to Panama, Diaz Herrera studied *Sai Baba, the Holy Man and the Psychiatrist* by Samuel H. Sandweiss, M.D., a present from Indra Devi. Diaz Herrera read and reread an exhortation from the holy man. "You must dive deep into the sea to get the pearls. What good is it to dabble among the waves near the surface, and swear that the sea has no pearls in it and that all the tales about them are false? So also, if you must realize the full fruit of this Avatar, dive deep and get immersed in Sai Baba."

People began to notice a change in Diaz Herrera. For one thing, there was the matter of his hands. The colonel sometimes walked around PDF headquarters with his arms outstretched, like a sleepwalker. He had a ready explanation. He said that his palms faced up when he was feeling good energy and down when the vibes were bad. Sometimes he sat at his desk staring straight ahead. "A little session of meditation wouldn't hurt you," he shouted back at some fellow officers who were staring at him. They were more convinced than ever that he was crazy.

Not long afterward, the first in a series of visitors that included a nutritionist, a masseuse and relaxation expert from Miami, occult practitioners, a seer, and various dabblers in the supernatural turned up in Panama. They usually stayed in suites at the Continental Hotel, all at government expense, as Diaz Herrera's guests; it was a privilege of his rank in the PDF. And they were often at the Diaz Herreras' dinner table, where they conducted lively discussions of relaxation techniques and ways of fighting stress. Just as Noriega divided the world into winners and losers, Diaz Herrera now divided it into positive and negative energy, so he began to say.

In February 1987, Diaz Herrera invited Shama Calhoum—La Gringa—down to Panama. Once installed at the Continental she visited the Comandancia and asked for a black and white photo of the man in the photo on his office wall. It was, of course, Noriega. She also wanted a photo of Omar Torrijos.

"Noriega is your enemy," she told Diaz Herrera. "He is the man I was talking about in Buenos Aires. He is evil and he will do anything in his power to destroy you. The big war we talked about is now clear to me. It's between you and him. It will start soon. I don't know when, but soon." She was, however, optimistic. Good was on his side. La Gringa delved into Diaz Herrera's previous incarnations. He was intrigued to hear that someone named Alexander Pushkin somehow figured in his past and was thrilled when he looked up Pushkin in his encyclopedia: The nineteenth-century Russian writer was an idealist—a man who believed in principle.

La Gringa made three trips to Panama during the spring of 1987. On one trip, at the recommendation of Diaz Herrera, she visited Coiba, a picturesque Panamanian island in the Pacific where

Panama's largest and most brutal prison is located. Diaz Herrera called ahead to tell the prison warden, Cap. Mario Del Cid, that he would appreciate any courtesies he and his staff could provide. That night the psychic from California and the Panamanian prison warden (who, like his brother Maj. Luis Del Cid, was a close friend of Noriega) drank, dined, and talked about the occult world.

In April, Diaz Herrera installed Indra Devi in his mother-in-law's house immediately next door. The holy woman became highly visible in Panama City and even appeared on television news programs. At one dinner she read a passage from Sai Baba that Diaz Herrera found particularly apt. "In our country, there is a peculiar method of trapping monkeys. This process consists of bringing a big pot with a small mouth and keeping some material which is attractive to the monkey inside the pot. The monkey will put its hand inside the pot and catch hold of a handful of the material. It will then not be able to pull out its hand from within the pot. It will imagine that someone inside the pot is holding its hand. No one is holding the monkey. The monkey has trapped itself, because it has taken in its hand such a lot of material. The moment it lets the material in its hand go, it will be free." Indra Devi drew the lesson: "The moment you give up the pleasures and detach yourself, you will be free."

Indra Devi stayed into May, by which time a psychic battle of some sort was definitely shaping up. Diaz Herrera had stopped drinking and eating red meat, and he looked more and more gaunt. Before she departed, Indra Devi provided him with a mantra whose repetition would shield him in the impending battle: "Rama, Rama, Rama." The mantra had been transmitted to Ms. Devi directly from Sai Baba; it was as if he were on the phone. By staring into the stone of her ring she could communicate with the holy man in India.

Not long afterward, La Gringa returned; according to Diaz Herrera, she related to him the questions asked by Captain Del Cid pertaining to spiritual matters when she had dined with him on the prison island months before. Diaz Herrera expressed distress. He worried that Noriega was trying to steal his psychic secret weapon.

Was Diaz Herrera under the influence of his occult friends or was he using them? In his book *Panama, Much More Than Noriega*, he suggests the second explanation. He calls his behavior after the vacation in Buenos Aires a "smokescreen," part of a deliberate campaign to strike back at Noriega. (In later interviews, he insisted he had had a real conversion.) He had hoped to scare Noriega with a demonstration of psychic firepower that would addle him and somehow—Diaz Herrera is not clear exactly how—enable him to prevail over the general. He describes his approach as "mystical guerrilla warfare." "I harbored . . . the idea of creating a true 'nuclear bomb' in the terrain of esotericism, with clearly predefined objectives."

He hoped to scare Noriega, who was susceptible to all things mystical, with his new powers. And according to his book, it was working. "Alarmed, Noriega found out immediately. My new spirituality increased this preoccupation of Noriega day by day. A couple of very visible slogans in my office, of esoteric style, confused him even more." Diaz Herrera believed he was putting on a dazzling display of his own kind of voodoo. "My interest was that Noriega know my steps," he wrote.

By late May, Diaz Herrera's retirement package was not looking good. The story inside the PDF was that Noriega would offer Diaz Herrera diplomatic posting to the Vatican and $1 million. It was a double Noriega insult. The sum was contemptuously small and the Vatican offer was a sneering allusion to Diaz Herrera's newfound beliefs.

On May 25, 1987, Noriega—after much prompting by his aides—invited Diaz Herrera to his office for a courtesy chat. It was a strained encounter because Noriega intended to go through with all of his plans. He usually avoided seeing someone he was treating badly, because he never knew what to say. The moment Diaz Herrera entered his office, Noriega inquired about his health; the man had become noticeably emaciated. ("Never before had I been so healthy," Diaz Herrera stressed in his book. "I had great vitality and a well-balanced state of mind.") Diaz Herrera suggested that his precise retirement date—the only decision he had been allowed in the whole business—be set for thirty days hence. Meanwhile he would go on vacation. Fine, fine, said Noriega and the encounter ended.

Leaving the office, a bitter Diaz Herrera paused at the door to address Noriega and some other officers who were paying little attention. "I hope Justines [Col. Marcos Justines, who was to replace him] helps you as much as I did," Diaz Herrera said. "Besides, remember that the 1989 elections have to be won as well." It was a reminder that he had hosted the Electoral Tribunal in his house when they had faked the returns in 1984.

The very next day, Diaz Herrera sent Noriega a handprinted note, written in bold capital letters across the top of their 1982 secret agreement. "Tony, This paper—which, for me, more than historical, could be considered histrionic, or hysterical—I return to you to keep, or tear up. Cordially, Roberto."

A few days later, Diaz Herrera and his wife seemed the picture of serenity—dining out at Las Bovedas (The Dungeons), a trendy spot in the old part of the city. He was wearing white trousers and a pastel-colored shirt. The restaurant, one of the most cosmopolitan in Panama City, was situated in what had once been giant cells where prisoners had been left to drown in the incoming tides.

———

On June 2, 1987, Noriega signed the papers making Diaz Herrera's resignation from the PDF official. Once again, Diaz Herrera heard about his fate through intermediaries, and he craved a face-to-face encounter. When Diaz Herrera went to his office on June 4 to say good-bye to his staff and clean out his personal belongings, he was obviously distressed but determined to talk to Noriega. After an impassioned request for an interview, he waited with Maigualida and their two sons and daughter, having decided to bring his family as protection against whatever Noriega might try. But Noriega ignored him; word came back that the general was not available. Diaz Herrera took his pictures of Sai Baba and his "Rama, Rama, Rama" slogan off the wall. He distributed some photos of himself to his staff and headed home. "From that moment on," he said, "together, we were to begin the most heroic family odyssey recorded in the annals of Panamanian history."

Diaz Herrera and Noriega were the only PDF officers who lived in the traditionally upper-class, or *rabiblanco*, Golf Heights enclave of Panama City. As they drove past Noriega's house, Diaz Herrera and his wife noticed Felicidad Noriega's driver lounging near a car just inside the front gate, a sure sign that the unofficial First Lady of Panama was at home. Minutes later, at her husband's request, Maigualida was on the phone, asking to speak to Mrs. Noriega, hoping to elicit her help in arranging a meeting between their husbands. The maid put her on hold. When the maid returned she said that Mrs. Noriega was not available.

Diaz Herrera wrote another note. "Tony, You want to declare a world war on me. We have known each other for many years. I know Lorena, Sandra, and Taiz [the Noriega daughters], and you know my children. I don't want this war, but I'm not going to run away from it. You are avoiding me. I need to talk to you. Call me. Roberto." His guard delivered the note to the Noriega household and was back in a few minutes. As the day wore on several reporters telephoned and Diaz Herrera gave some interviews. Noriega did not call back.

That June there were duties more important to Felicidad Noriega than returning Maigualida's phone calls. Both she and her husband were engrossed in their daughter's wedding. The Noriegas' middle daughter, twenty-two-year-old Sandra, was engaged to the son of a military heavyweight from the Dominican Republic. The wedding, scheduled for July 11, 1987, the Noriegas agreed, would combine opulence with dignity. It would "say something" and would perhaps be covered by *HOLA*, the *People* magazine of the Spanish-speaking world (one of Felicidad's favorite bits of reading material). By early June, the preparations were making news across the capital. The guest list totaled four thousand.

Each guest received an invitation that included a bottle of pink champagne with a commemorative label especially prepared by Moet & Chandon. Also included was a Baccarat crystal goblet with the young couple's initials. Noriega had rented a twenty-story hotel for the foreign guests and had spread the word around PDF headquarters that he planned to dispatch the PDF 727 to ferry the bridegroom's party in from Santo Domingo. The ceremony would be at the cathedral in the old part of the city and the reception would be held at the enormous Atlapa convention center.

On Friday, June 5, 1987, Noriega made more news, announcing that he would remain commander in chief for another five years.

Diaz Herrera sent a messenger to *La Prensa* with the transcript of an interview he had previously given to a television reporter. The covering note to editor Winston Robles informed him that Diaz Herrera wanted the entire interview in Saturday's paper. Robles read the questions and answers and decided to pass.

In the middle of the afternoon on Saturday, Diaz Herrera telephoned Robles and accused him of cowardice. Why else would he refuse to run the interview, Diaz Herrera wanted to know. Firmly and contemptuously Robles told him that he was not afraid of anything that Diaz Herrera said. He told Diaz Herrera that if he ever uttered anything interesting he would put it in the paper—but that time had not yet arrived. Diaz Herrera told Robles that if he sent a reporter he would provide some amazing disclosures.

There was no reason to expect that he would fulfill his pledge, but as a precaution, Robles instructed news editor Alfredo Jimenez to dispatch staff reporter Jose Quintero and a staff photographer, who happened to be the editor's son, Aurelio Jimenez. "Call me if he says anything," the editor called out as they left the office.

It was two and a half hours before Jimenez felt that he could break away for a call to his father. He had not wanted to break the extraordinary spell that Diaz Herrera appeared to be under. "He's saying something," the young man said. "We've got something big."

Diaz Herrera had been talking about the 1984 election and how it had been fixed. He had explained in detail just how the Electoral Tribunal had altered the results. He had bragged about his role in forcing Barletta to resign, saying that he had been "the hardest president to take out." Barletta had resisted for eighteen hours but he, Diaz Herrera, had "twisted his arm." For emphasis, Diaz Herrera mimicked the gesture of arm twisting, seeming to enjoy the memory.

He talked well into Saturday evening, taunting the journalists, saying their newspaper would never run what he was saying about the election. Meanwhile, *La Prensa* staffers were remaking page one.

By 1:00 A.M. Sunday, the first editions were being printed and word of the interview was spreading through the city. Jimenez happily escorted a Reuters correspondent who had shown up at *La Prensa* to Diaz Herrera's house—and listened as Diaz Herrera repeated everything he had said earlier. When the two journalists headed for the door, Diaz Herrera abruptly pulled a gun on them. "Get down on your knees or I'll shoot you," Diaz Herrera barked. Jimenez tried to be soothing and firm. Be calm—and put the gun away, he suggested. They stayed until after daybreak—hostages against a possible raid on the house that Diaz Herrera had begun to fear. Diaz Herrera apologized when he saw them out the door.

Panama was about to explode.

4

The Long White Summer

DIAZ HERRERA was considered irrelevant in Washington. Noriega had represented him to his contacts as an untrustworthy leftist, and Diaz Herrera hadn't helped his own cause. His only contact with Ambassador Davis had been a telephone call inquiring about tango lessons. He had heard that Davis was thinking of organizing tango classes (a joke the ambassador had made at a diplomatic reception), and he was interested in signing up.

That call came not long before Diaz Herrera had given his interview to *La Prensa* during the last days of quiet in Panama. Now, by early June, Noriega was the only game in town as far as the United States was concerned, at least publicly. But his relationships with some prominent U.S. officials were increasingly frosty. Ambassador Davis had never concealed his opposition to Noriega's policies.

"General, I want to tell you one thing which I hope will help our relationship," Davis told Noriega during their first meeting. "I was not sent as a judge. I was sent as Ronald Reagan's representative. I'm not here to throw you out of office. If anything happens to you, that's a Panamanian decision. Not mine."

"I've worked with the U.S.," Noriega told him. "If you talk to your people up there [in Washington] you'll find that we've had a very fine relationship. I look forward to our two militaries, as well as our two nations, working together." This was Noriega's standard reply to the gringos. He wanted them to know that he was "a valued, trusted ally," as one U.S. military officer put it.

Later, the dialogue between Davis and Noriega loosened up. "You say that you would accept the will of the people," Davis said when Noriega endorsed free and open elections in May 1989. "What if Arnulfo Arias wins?"

"We would never allow Arnulfo Arias to be president."

"What about Arias Calderon?"

"He couldn't win."

"What if he did?"

"He'd have to work with the PDF," Noriega replied. Davis mentioned that a free election "doesn't work that way." Noriega laughed.

On one occasion Noriega asked Davis what a U.S. congressman might have on his mind. "He will ask you if you killed Spadafora," Davis said.

Noriega told him he had nothing to do with the murder.

———

On Saturday, June 6, 1987, Gen. Fred Woerner took over as commander in chief of SOUTHCOM. Woerner had held senior staff jobs in Panama for a total of four years and knew many of the PDF officers, including Noriega. Woerner was a practical, honest, by-the-book man and his job was clear. All indications were that the Reagan administration was content with the status quo in Panama.

Woerner said that Noriega was "the antithesis of every professional value I had." But he knew that the two of them would have to cooperate. On that Saturday, however, Woerner "wanted to dispel any thought that I was in Noriega's or anyone else's hip pocket." He decided to use the change of command ceremony to make clear his opinion.

In his speech, Woerner praised the U.S. military for its professionalism and commitment to civilian rule. It seemed to many in the audience to amount to a rebuke of Noriega, whom he did not mention by name and who sat, sullen, in the audience. Noriega skipped the reception.

Mayin Correa, a leading voice in the opposition who hosted a radio interview program on KW Continente, a station owned by her family, had been part of the press gallery that day at SOUTH-COM.

At the reception afterward, two U.S. military men with long service in Panama approached her. One was Col. Al Cornell of the army and the other was Col. Matt Farias of the air force.

"We have a message for you," Farias said.

"Who from?" Correa asked.

"General Noriega," Farias said. "He wants to have a secret meeting with you—and Madrinan will arrange the meeting." Madrinan was still wearing Mitrotti's ring.

"Why?" Correa asked. "I don't want to murder anyone, so there is no need for Madrinan. And if Noriega wants to talk politics we do it openly."

But Correa agreed to think about the "message" and the three agreed to have lunch at the officers' club at Howard Air Force Base on Monday.

Noriega knew that if Correa kept the date, he could exploit the act of the meeting to discredit the opposition. But there was a more important reason behind the exercise. By using two colonels (with reputations as intelligence officers) as messenger boys, Noriega was reminding Correa and the rest of the opposition of his bond with the Americans who mattered. Arthur Davis and Woerner could say whatever they wanted, but those who counted in the U.S. government were on his side.

Later that day, after talking it over with family and friends, Correa decided to agree to meet with Noriega—with certain stipulations. The meeting would take place at the papal nuncio's residence with a guest list that included as many Noriega opponents as she could round up.

Sundays in Panama are sleepy. All but a few stores are shuttered. On Sunday, June 7, most Panamanians listened to their radios, and especially to Mayin Correa, who was broadcasting the Diaz Herrera interview in *La Prensa*. Diaz Herrera was expanding on several themes. Now he was saying that Noriega had murdered Torrijos by placing a bomb aboard his airplane.

All day, people were speculating about the interview. It was the first time a PDF insider had broken ranks, let alone made the sort of accusations Diaz Herrera was making. He admitted to reporters that he himself was corrupt. He said that his house had been paid for with money he had extorted from Cubans for visas. He asked other PDF officers to follow his example and come clean.

On Sunday evening, Winston Spadafora and his wife went to

mass at the Church of Christo Rey, whose pastor was the Reverend Xavier Villanueva, a Spaniard Somoza had deported from Nicaragua in 1972. His dictators had changed but his sarcastic sermons had not. He mentioned Hugo's soul at mass every day.

After mass, Winston and his wife and some friends went to dinner at the Galaxie, a bustling steak house in downtown Panama City. They talked about what they could do in response to the Diaz Herrera news, quickly came to a decision, and drove straight to Golf Heights. A very nervous PDF guard (one of the few retirement perquisites Diaz Herrera still enjoyed) opened the heavy steel security barrier and admitted them.

"Who killed my brother?" Winston asked, as soon as he entered the house. Then he and Diaz Herrera went into another room and stayed there alone for an hour. When they emerged, Winston told his friends that they had to record Diaz Herrera's statements. He had confirmed all the important details in Sanchez Borbon's reports.

Winston also decided that they had to protect Diaz Herrera as well as themselves. It was certain that Noriega would silence his former colleague before long. The telephone lines from his house had already been cut—except, they discovered, for a single phone in the basement bedroom. Spadafora and Diaz Herrera passed the phone back and forth, each calling friends to action. Winston was successful. Over the next hours an extraordinary procession of political and religious figures and scores of journalists poured into the house to provide a shield for Diaz Herrera and to show solidarity with Spadafora.

Diaz Herrera told them that he was fed up, and that he wanted to clean up the PDF. He said that he would enlist the support of his former colleagues. But the fact was that most had refused to take his calls. One had told him, "You are a traitor."

Around midnight, Winston reached Jose "Pepe" Pretto, Hugo's close friend, who had been a pallbearer at the funeral. Pretto and his family had spent the day in the country, but they were at Diaz Herrera's house within the hour, picking up Father Villanueva on the way.

As the night wore on, priests, nuns, a bishop, and even some politicians crowded into the room with the phone as Maigualida came and went, praying out loud and clutching a Bible. Weapons and ammunition clips suddenly materialized. If Noriega wanted to rid himself of almost everyone who opposed him, they were all in that house.

When the guards changed at 2:00 A.M., Diaz Herrera told the new guards that they were under arrest and they almost eagerly handed over their weapons. As far as they were concerned, he was still the PDF's second in command. Another detachment was expected at 4:00 A.M., and Diaz Herrera cradled a machine gun as he strolled from gate to house and room to room.

Diaz Herrera entrusted one of his favorite weapons to Pretto. It was a Peruvian-made automatic rifle, a gift from Fidel Castro. The stock was inscribed "To Roberto from Fidel." At 4:00 A.M., Pretto pointed it at the newly arrived guards, told them to lay down their own weapons, get back on their bus, and leave. Diaz Herrera stood at his side. This was the first time since the 1968 coup that any Panamanian civilian had raised a weapon against the military. The surprised guards were only too happy to comply. When dawn came, fears of a raid lessened, at least for the moment.

Mayin Correa had decided to skip Monday's lunch with the American colonels. Instead, she stayed on the radio, booming out Diaz Herrera's news and denouncing Noriega. She told her listeners that if they felt the way she did they should come down to Via Espana in the banking district where her station was.

Louis Martinz realized that Panamanian history was changing when he gazed down at Via Espana from the balcony of his family's real estate company office. He had been Arnulfo Arias's chief of protocol for his eleven days in the presidency in 1968 and then spent nearly a decade in exile after the Torrijos coup. In June 1979, Martinz founded *YA!* (*NOW!* in Spanish), the first newspaper established with the intention of opposing the military regime. (*La Prensa* was founded about a year later.) Under Martinz, the paper combined the style of a racy tabloid with coverage and support of antigovernment activities such as teachers' strikes. Just before Christmas 1984, however, a friend of Noriega's blatantly expropriated the paper and the government-controlled courts backed him up. The paper was soon renamed and became pro-Noriega. Martinz listened to Correa on his portable radio and watched the crowd swell. He said that either Correa or Noriega was going to have to leave Panama and hurried downstairs to join the crowd.

Most of the demonstrators—chanting "Down with Noriega"—were milling about in a vacant lot between Correa's station and the Banco Nacional. Suddenly, Harari-trained PDF units charged the crowd, firing tear gas, and swinging heavily weighted rubber hoses. People scattered. Martinz and others took shelter in a clothing store with a steel shutter. Later, he ventured down the street, but a phalanx of riot police, the "Dobermans," charged toward him. Just as he reached the clothing store the steel gate crashed down onto the sidewalk. Martinz banged on the gate as a riot policeman with a Darth Vader helmet and visor ran toward him, brandishing a rubber hose that could fracture a skull. Martinz stopped pounding on the gate and spoke to him. "Can you imagine? They shut it down on me." The cop, oddly enough, raced on.

The action ebbed and flowed all day as the damp air grew bitter with tear gas. In the afternoon, Martinz turned a corner and found his good friend and fellow "Arnulfista" Guillermo Endara sprinting toward him. The lawyer, usually immobile, weighed well over two hundred pounds. Endara had just escaped a band of Dobermans who appeared around the corner as he caught sight of Martinz. The two took off again, finally reaching a hotel coffee shop where they talked about the future.

———

Diaz Herrera alternated between coma and panic. Maigualida, backed by her mother, who lived next door, begged him to expel Spadafora and all the others. But Spadafora and Pretto argued that their interests were now intertwined. They said they could all help each other if they remained united. So the "guests" stayed, spilling out into the garden and down the lawn to the cabana and swimming pool. Diaz Herrera described the mood as *rifa*, or lottery time, "the moment when everything's up in the air . . . you just make some desperate move because nobody knows what the hell is going on."

By Tuesday the house was a tourist attraction and political shrine. Cars passed by in slow, bumper-to-bumper procession, clogging streets and traffic for miles around. Diaz Herrera, flanked by bodyguards, greeted the caravans and distributed copies of a handwritten diatribe against Noriega. "You know what I'm saying is true," one said. Another warned Noriega, "Your days are numbered."

Throughout the city there were violent clashes and some women began waving white handkerchiefs, a gesture that became the symbol of the protest during the long white summer.

On Tuesday night, June 9, the Mitrotti contingent of middle-class business people made history. Most of those who assembled at the Chamber of Commerce were members of the Rotary, Kiwanis, Lions, and other civic clubs and had been members of Mitrotti's Committee for the Redemption of Moral Values. That

night, at the beginning of "people power" in Panama, they created the National Civic Crusade, an umbrella group for a variety
of medical organizations, labor unions, teachers, students, and
churches. Their mission was to "make things decent again," and
they intended to do so through public protest.

The political landscape had changed. The "opposition" had
multiplied. In fact, by June 1987, it seemed endless.

On Tuesday night, Diaz Herrera reiterated his charge that
Noriega had murdered Torrijos and added details. He said that
Noriega had acted at the request of the CIA, and he gave American names but no proof at all. Nevertheless this accusation made
it possible for anti-American Panamanians to turn on Noriega
without betraying the memory of Torrijos.

Noriega appeared on television to accuse Diaz Herrera of
"high treason," and one of his press officers said Diaz Herrera was
suffering from "a serious state of paranoia." Noriega seemed to
threaten attack and then back off. At one point, he seemed to
vanish from public view. It seemed as if he realized he was no
match for Diaz Herrera.

"I am a criminal," Diaz Herrera cried. "I admit it before God
and the international press. But I also know that I can't take my
millions to heaven. I am ready to go to jail for my crimes, but I
think Noriega should go with me." He appealed to the PDF.
"There are people there who are nauseated with what has happened in the PDF. There are men there who will . . . resolve
things internally." He also resumed his "mystical guerrilla warfare," now on a world stage. He put up an altar at his house for Sai
Baba and had yet another mystic friend with Hindu connections
wear the robes of an Indian priest and wander about singing Indian
mantras to the priests and nuns.

The "guests" remained at the Diaz Herrera home for weeks.
There were lines for the bathrooms. Prayer rugs appeared on the
lawn along with a shiny, gold-colored plaque with the symbols of
major religions surrounding a lotus flower. The plaque rested
against Diaz Herrera's foot during interviews. He told reporters
that satanism was loose in Panama and that "there are people concentrating their mental powers to try to crush me." His struggle
with Noriega was "mind against mind and spirit against spirit."

Sometimes he remained silent for long periods. Sometimes he
spoke phrases no one could understand. Occasionally he would
extend his arms in front of him. "Associates advise visitors that
when he feels positive vibrations, his palms face upward; he turns

his palms down if questioning becomes too aggressive," Steven Kinzer reported in the *New York Times*. "I have no doubt that he, not I, is in command of everything," Diaz Herrera said, speaking of Sai Baba, the Indian holy man. Sai Baba was shielding him from the "strong negative impulses" of his enemies. "I have confessed, and it would be best for Panama if General Noriega also confesses. . . . Our war is psychic, mystical, and religious."

The visitors came and went, bringing new rumors and take-out food from McDonald's and Kentucky Fried Chicken. Other associates who explained the colonel's beliefs about "vibrations" offered reporters soft drinks, scotch, and bathing suits.

Later, in his book, Diaz Herrera said that the display was all a ruse to bewilder Noriega, who, he claimed, "grew very uneasy. He was immobilized for some time by the uncertainty of whether we really had direct help from Hindu mystics."

The occupants of the house were often terrified, especially at night. One day, early on, helicopters hovered over the house and an attack seemed imminent. Father Villanueva offered mass in a hallway and explained that anyone could receive communion without making a confession—"no questions asked." Eventually, Winston Spadafora and the others emerged from the house and joined the street protestors, though Pepe Pretto, his life in danger, fled to the nunciature.

———

Strange things began to happen. Some Panamanians whose power had been in eclipse returned to the fore. Gabriel Lewis, a short, nimble man with a gravelly voice, had been Torrijos's ambassador to the United States in the 1970s. A savvy political analyst, he was ostensibly a friend of the government since he had been an intimate of Torrijos. But his relations with Noriega were cool. He had decided that Noriega was finished.

On Friday, June 12, Lewis told some of his American embassy contacts and Panamanian friends that they should try to create a dialogue with Noriega. He said they should not try to corner him, but look for a way out for the general. "I am sure they picked that up," Lewis said, "because then I got a call from Carlos Duque." (Duque, a Noriega crony, was entrusted with running Transit SA in Colon, an enterprise whose sole function was to charge colossal fees on all goods that passed through its duty-free gates.) Lewis could correctly assume that Noriega was behind whatever Duque said.

"Maybe things are getting out of hand," Duque said. "We have to look for an intelligent solution to this crisis. I wonder if you can put a group of people from the opposition together so that they can talk to us."

"Sure, I'm more than willing to do this," Lewis replied from a phone at the Banco del Isthmo, where his brother was chairman. He started for home as soon as he hung up. Moments after he left, the PDF swept down and trashed the bank. The PDF slashed paintings on the walls and carted everyone away in three military trucks. Yelling obscenities, they beat everyone in their path. One secretary was forced to fondle a soldier's genitals.

Moments later, Noriega called Lewis. "Look, General," Lewis said, "they have attacked the bank. This is intolerable."

"I didn't know anything about it," Noriega said. "The reason for my call is because I am interested in that dialogue that Duque talked about."

"Look, General, I'm going to put aside my personal feelings about what happened in the bank—that's very upsetting—let's sit down and talk it over," Lewis said. "But let me tell you before we do anything, it is about time that you start thinking about making yourself a sacrifice, because the way things are you're going to end up ruling a country that is in ashes. So you have to find a way out that's best for your country, your family, and yourself." Lewis insisted that Noriega send someone who could negotiate seriously and Noriega assented to all of Lewis's suggestions.

Almost immediately, through intermediaries, Noriega tried to undo the agreements he had just made with Lewis. He wanted a different representative and a different venue. But by that afternoon, two "teams" were assembled at Lewis's home. Negotiations quickly became bitter, especially when Lewis said that Noriega should step down. "There were unpleasantries," Lewis said. The Noriega team departed with a promise to stay in touch. But as it happened, Lewis never heard from them again.

At 6:30 P.M., shortly after the meeting had broken up, Ambassador Davis arrived at Lewis's house. Noriega had put Ricardo Arias Calderon under house arrest. Arias Calderon, the leader of the Christian Democrats, would have been a vice president if the 1984 elections had not been fixed by Noriega. Davis had gone to visit the menaced politician and many Panamanians believed that the visit was meant to show U.S. support for his cause. That same day, Davis's daughter Susan had joined opposition figures at a crowded mass at El Carmen cathedral as heavily armed soldiers surrounded the church.

Davis wanted to send Noriega an informal message—that powerful people in Washington might get angry if he continued to arrest people and harass the opposition media. Davis and Lewis decided to telephone Noriega together. He was unavailable, but one of his officers threw their message back at the two men. "Are you telling me that Ronald Reagan is menacing us?" the PDF officer demanded. Lewis told him not to be "stupid," but said that there were U.S. senators who were outraged that the PDF had jailed people just for waving white handkerchiefs.

"It's about time you people talked to Noriega and tell him he's got to leave. Talk to your other colleagues," Lewis said.

"I will, I will," the PDF officer replied. "Who do you want released?"

"Everybody," Lewis replied. "We'll wait for your call."

The two men waited and waited. Finally, at about 11:00 P.M., Davis went home. Just minutes later, the PDF officer called Lewis. "I want you to know that I am here with all the colonels—all of us except General Noriega—and we all have decided you are an enemy of the institution. From now on, you're on your own."

"I get your message," Lewis replied, "but what about the people in jail?"

"That's none of your business," the PDF officer replied and hung up.

Lewis made two phone calls to friends. President Oscar Arias of Costa Rica assured him that he could have Costa Rican diplomatic protection and would be welcome in San José. Senator Edward M. Kennedy made it a three-way conversation. "Look, Noriega, I know you're listening to all the conversations of Gabriel. If anything happens to my friend Gabriel Lewis, you're going to pay dearly. This is Ted Kennedy and I repeat, if anything happens to my friend Gabriel Lewis you will pay dearly."

Lewis and his family departed for Costa Rica and then Washington, where he set up a branch of the National Civic Crusade, the umbrella group for all the *civilistas* that had been formed at the Chamber of Commerce on June 9. The Connecticut Avenue office became the center of all anti-Noriega lobbying efforts in Washington. Lewis told friends that it would be a difficult struggle, and that only one of the two, he or Noriega, would survive.

Very quickly, the outlines of Noriega's response to the growing unrest became apparent—and his tactics had the Harari imprint. His troops displayed enormous force but emphasized nonlethal scare tactics and selective savage beatings. Noriega also deliberately spread rumors, and one of the most effective was his own invention: Everyone who went to jail could assume that he or she would be raped by an AIDS carrier. "We Create the Fear" was a slogan that Noriega invented and plastered on the walls of his PDF headquarters. He also put up photos of the PDF's "enemies." Eisenmann and Arias Calderon were the most prominent.

Noriega was invisible to the public, but he worked carefully to maintain the constituencies whose support he most needed. None was more important than the PDF, his power base. He had the loyalty—and the fear—of his top commanders and worked to maintain both.

He also had to pay attention to his friends in Washington. There were plenty of personal contacts between PDF officers and U.S. Army officers in Panama, and for Noriega himself, Washington was just a phone call away. He learned how he could make it easier for his friends to help him. He learned that if he appeared flexible and reasonable, he would be easier to defend.

But on June 26, Noriega got a shock. The U.S. Senate passed, by an 84–2 vote, a resolution demanding that he step down while Diaz Herrera's charges were investigated. The Senate had come a long way, thanks to the combined efforts of Helms, Kennedy, their aides, and a few others. Diaz Herrera's accusations and Gabriel Lewis's skillful lobbying had also helped make Noriega a villain and a popular political target. In response to the vote, the Panamanian legislative assembly, at Noriega's behest, voted to declare Davis persona non grata. The foreign minister also recalled Panama's ambassador from Washington.

Noriega wanted to maintain his American friendships, but the Senate vote had insulted him. He played his hand badly, throwing his weight into an anti-Yanqui campaign. Noriega's decision revealed the shortcomings of his political imagination. To be sure, anti-American rhetoric had often been popular in Panama, but in 1987 the protestors were not all anti–United States and they wanted that to be clearly understood. In fact, a strange phenomenon took place that summer. Angry students raced about the city tearing down anti-gringo posters that the government had begun putting up when the crisis started.

On Tuesday, June 30, toward midday, several hundred Panamanians gathered on a quiet downtown street. They were all government employees, ranging from office workers and G-2 *sapos* to eight cabinet members and their wives. The leaders denounced "U.S. intervention in Panamanian affairs," and mocked the *civilistas* as U.S. puppets and traitors. After an hour or so someone started shouting about the U.S. embassy and immediately the crowd began walking. The cabinet wives marched slowly in their spiked heels.

The U.S. embassy, white stucco and red tile, already had the look of a set in a B-movie. Its gleaming facade was freshly spotted with rusty paint stains from an attack the night before. As the crowd approached the handsome building chanting "Yankee Go Home," trucks loaded with their supplies followed. One carried sandwiches and crates of a brand of beer sold legally only in the SOUTHCOM PX. Another carried rocks, paint, and little plastic baggies. At the appropriate signal, the crowd went to work. For nearly an hour they chanted denunciations and flung paint-filled baggies and rocks, smashing embassy windows. The action ebbed and surged. The crowd shattered car windows in the parking lot behind the embassy and went on to the consulate building and the Amador-Washington library, where they broke more windows. The government media, which for much of the summer was the only media, hailed the spontaneous response to U.S. "aggression."

In Washington, Panama had returned to the headlines. The crisis offered opportunities for bold moral stands and no one needed a moral cause more than Elliott Abrams, the man who had defended Noriega just a year earlier when Jesse Helms had pressed him about the PDF.

Abrams was in big trouble with Congress in June 1987 because of what many members considered his lack of truthfulness in testimony about administration support for the Contras. It was as if lawmakers had discovered that Pinocchio was in charge of Latin American policy at the State Department. On June 14, as Panama began to make headlines, 129 House Democrats and several senators had demanded Abrams's resignation. Abrams had openly scorned Congress on the Contra issue.

"As far as Congress is concerned, Elliott is a man without a mission," said Senator Christopher Dodd, of Connecticut, who refused to let Abrams testify to his subcommittee on Western Hemisphere and Peace Corps Affairs. He said there was no reason to believe anything Abrams said. "His time is up," Dodd said. "There is a price to pay for misleading Congress." Elliott Abrams needed a reputation rehabilitation and Noriega might be useful. He was an odious villain who appeared mortally wounded.

According to his colleagues, George Shultz was outraged when he heard that a government mob had attacked the embassy. He unleashed an eager Abrams to sound a new theme and to suggest that U.S. policy was finally going to change. Abrams's forum was a speech to the World Affairs Council in Washington. Reporters were briefed that the speech was a milestone; it was pointed out, for example, that Abrams had used the word *corruption* when describing Noriega's activities. The aides explained that "corruption" really meant narco-trafficking—and that no administration official had ever raised that charge before. (In fact, Abrams called upon the PDF to "remove their institution from politics, end any appearance of corruption, and modernize their forces to carry out their large and important military tasks.")

Given everything, Abrams's complaints were a far cry from his comments to Helms in April 1986—even though there had been no substantive change in Panama except exposure. The aides made clear that the speech was by far the harshest official U.S. attack on the Noriega regime. Noriega, an aide said, was an "obstacle" to democracy, a doomed man. Elliott Abrams wanted credit for the kill.

Other officials were eager to follow Abrams's lead. In an attempt to underscore the U.S. charge that Noriega's government was behind the attack on the embassy, the State Department sent the Panamanian government a bill for $106,000 to repair the damages caused by the mob. The gesture lost some of its punch when Noriega paid the piddling sum, as if to say, "So what?"

The U.S. government also suspended some $25.5 million in military aid. "We're not going to restore the aid if they're still tear-gassing people in the streets," said a State Department officer. Another disclosure from officials to reporters dramatized the tough new line from Foggy Bottom. The Panamanian government, it turned out, had placed an order with an American tear-gas manufacturer that, in compliance with the law, made a routine request for U.S. government approval before shipping the canisters to the PDF. The U.S. government forbade the shipment. A *Wall Street Journal* reporter wrote that "Panama's corrupt military dictator, General Manuel Antonio Noriega, appears to be nearing the end of his days in power. The Reagan administration, once again, must seek the delicate balance between interfering in another nation's affairs and helping to prod it toward democracy."

But it turned out that the military aid had been only technically "suspended." The United States had already given Panama $20 million in economic aid and $6 million in military aid by this time. And the administration had not changed its request for a total of $33 million in military assistance for the fiscal year beginning in October.

For all the talk at policy-planning meetings that summer, the meetings usually ended in inertia—which meant more of the status quo. The meetings brought together representatives from the State Department, the Defense Department, the CIA, and occasionally other agencies to thrash out what could be done about Panama. The best informed individuals tended to be people who had worked with Noriega in the past, or who represented agencies that wanted to continue to enjoy the access he provided. It was useless to talk about getting rid of Noriega, they maintained. Only killing him would get him out of power. It was a valid point. But no one was willing to go on the record with a recommendation to kill Noriega, and the White House remained aloof from the entire policy debate. There was no discernible political cost for inaction.

———

Noriega decided to take action against his domestic opponents. On July 2, around 7:00 A.M., seventy heavily armed Dobermans appeared in front of Mansion Dante, a two-story department store known as the Bloomingdale's of Panama City. The store and the Jaguar dealership next door belonged to Roberto Eisenmann, the publisher of *La Prensa* who was still in exile but considering a return to Panama. His family and colleagues had already installed Lexan, a brand of bullet-proof glass, in his ground-floor office at the store. (Eisenmann's wife was a sister of President Delvalle and one of the Mansion Dante employees was Delvalle's niece.)

Toward noon, as business went on as usual, the PDF soldiers drifted away. Almost immediately, however, a gang of paramilitaries in civilian clothes showed up and began breaking windows, firing automatic weapons, and setting fires. Some employees fled to Eisenmann's office. Through the Lexan they saw crowds gathering to watch the blazing building where they were trapped by the arsonists milling about outside with their weapons. Then the terrified employees saw the paramilitaries point their guns at them and take aim. The bullets, some of them brightly glowing tracers, came toward the Lexan window and caromed wildly away. Eventually the hostages escaped.

The Delvalles were terrified when they heard about the assault. Mariela Delvalle, the First Lady of Panama, approached the site by car but withdrew without her niece. Then President Delvalle himself drove up and shouldered his way through the crowd to collect the terrified young woman. It was probably the most courageous action Delvalle had ever taken.

By sundown, with Mansion Dante a smoldering ruin (the fire department put in a perfunctory appearance after the arsonists departed), the Crusade announced plans for their largest demonstration yet. It would take place in eight days on Friday, July 10, the eve of the Noriega wedding. The leaders announced they were inviting the entire country to attend their celebration and there was good reason to believe that huge crowds would show up. The almost daily demonstrations were evidence of the superb, high-tech communications techniques developed by Crusade leaders. They used call-waiting and call-forwarding, copying machines and fax machines. They distributed flyers to boutique counters and supermarket shelves with announcements about who should be where and when.

The Crusade leaders seemed to imagine that they were running a marketing campaign to demonstrate that each and every part of the country hated Noriega. One day, doctors would be in the streets; the next day lawyers, then schoolteachers. The demographics were broad. One group, composed entirely of several hundred blacks, marched behind a banner inscribed "The *Rabiblancos* of San Miguelito" to parody Noriega's claim of representing the poor. The banner referred to Noriega's rhetoric about his "enemies," the United States and their traditional collaborators, the *rabiblancos* of the white business elite.

On Noriega's orders. Delvalle appeared on television to forbid all demonstrations. There was more than a hint that waving a white handkerchief had become a capital offense. Schools, banks, and government buildings were shut down. Very soon, Noriega's *sapos* found Crusade flyers calling for a massive, jeering crowd outside Atlapa, the giant convention center where the Noriega

wedding reception was to be held. Noriega realized that his enemies were trying to ruin his daughter's wedding plans.

On Monday and Tuesday, July 6 and 7, Noriega's *sapos,*
messengers now, started passing out new wedding invitations to
a select few. Everything was done quietly. The small ceremony
took place in a chapel inside a PDF compound on Wednesday, July
8, three days ahead of schedule. Afterward, some four hundred
guests arrived at the heavily guarded Noriega home in Golf
Heights for a somber reception.

"They'll pay for humiliating my little Sandra," Noriega said,
over and over again as he moved through the reception crowd. He
wore an iridescent silk tuxedo that shimmered, as one guest recalled, like an oil slick. He drank heavily and repeated his oath.
"They'll pay, they'll pay for humiliating my little girl."

On Thursday night, Noriega dispatched his *sapos* to harass
opposition leaders, many of whom were changing residences every night. He publicly warned Davis that he would be responsible
for any violence on Friday. The implicit message was: The gringos
were behind the demonstrations and they could call them off if
they wanted to. If they didn't, he had no choice but to strike
back—hard.

At headquarters, Noriega told his commanders it was time to
use force but warned them not to kill anybody.

Louis Martinz had been in and out of street skirmishes with the
PDF almost every day. On July 4, five Dobermans attacked him
while he stood in front of the McDonald's on Via Espana. He was
still bandaged from that beating when he took to the streets on July
10. That day, as he and friends chanted "Justicia," a group of Dobermans fired tear gas directly at them. They were then clubbed,
punched, and thrown into a small police truck. A policeman tore off
Martinz's watch, a ring, and a gold crucifix he wore on a chain
around his neck. Martinz had been to jail before, but this time was
different. Even before he got there he had several broken ribs and
chipped teeth. "At least I was among friends. There's never a dull
moment here in the twilight zone," Martinz said.

Martinz and the others went through La Preventiva, the name
for the "reception room" at La Modelo prison. Regular inmates
were set loose on the arrivals with license to rough them up and
steal whatever the arresting officers had missed. Then, each new
arrival was photographed, usually naked, before passing into the
crowded, filthy cells.

Martinz encountered a short man with intense eyes.

"Hello, I'm Dr. Watts and I'm innocent," the inmate said. Dr. Watts had been convicted of murdering his wife. Martinz's newspaper had covered the trial.

"You were terrific for circulation," Martinz said, as Dr. Watts hurried away to treat some badly beaten prisoners.

The day came to be known as Black Friday. Thousands of Panamanians earned new and powerful "war stories" in what was an extraordinary display of "people power." Wherever there were crowds, there were Dobermans and other PDF units. The police firing birdshot and tear gas wherever they saw white—at balconies of high-rise apartment buildings and through the stained glass of churches. Huey helicopters flew between high-rise apartment buildings and drove terrified, handkerchief-waving residents off the balconies of their lavish, Miami-style buildings. Police ran among the tables of sidewalk restaurants, flailing at people with rubber hoses and nightsticks. Demonstrators filled the air with white confetti (many downtown offices had paper shredders) and waved white from every corner. They set up barricades of trash (and the very occasional private car) and poured through side streets into the main boulevards chanting, "Pineapple Face. Pineapple Face," a reference to Noriega's skin.

Crowds streamed along Via Espana toward El Carmen cathedral. On their way, many of the marchers paused to shake their fists and shout curses at the seventh floor of the Continental Hotel, where, according to rumor, the G-2 had established their forward tactical post. Ildefonso Riande, the hotel's nominal owner, was a close friend and business associate of Noriega, a man Noriega trusted enough to let him handle his mistress's business affairs. What better hotel could the G-2 choose?

By nightfall, some six hundred demonstrators were undergoing their initiation to La Modelo. But scattered crowds remained throughout the city as bonfires blazed. Toward sundown two men broke off from a cluster of people near El Carmen and sauntered toward the Continental. People carrying banners and wearing baseball caps with the word *justicia* on them were not the hotel's usual clients, and they were stared at as they approached. But the crowd parted and a few applauded as they entered the breezy open-air lobby. When they reached the seventh floor and the G-2 room, there were cheers, slaps on the back, and general bonhomie among the *sapos* in the room. Their colleagues' duty that day had been to observe and foment trouble. They had reason to cheer. The *sapos* had battered and stunned a crowd of several hundred thousand—and there had not been a single fatality. There were no possible martyrs. After nearly six weeks of demonstrations and clashes, the death toll in Panama remained zero.

Five days later, La Modelo's doors swung open, freeing nearly all of the six hundred arrested protestors. Most were black and Indian, but they were now comrades in arms with the *rabiblancos* and other middle-class prisoners. With the released inmates came a blast of Noriega's psychological warfare in the form of horror stories—most of which involved the specter of rape by AIDS carriers. Noriega's motto of the summer—"We Create the Fear"— was working. Louis Martinz remarked on the reaction of his fellow inmates to the filth, threats, and violence of La Modelo. "Knowing that you could be going back there has got to make some people think twice before protesting again," he said.

The violence had also boiled over into the American population. Bruce Quinn, an executive with the Panama Canal Commission, remembered that "people were calling in and saying they were being shot at. People were in their apartments and the Dobermans were firing up, right at them. They started asking, about then, when is the U.S. government going to rid us of this individual." Quinn established a Hot Line telephone service that Americans, or anyone, could call for information. Suddenly, the Panamanians and the dwindling number of American Zonians, once antagonistic, were in the struggle together.

After Black Friday, the government newspaper *Critica* wrote a mocking commentary on the *civilistas*, saying that too many grandmothers were out waving white handkerchiefs when they should be home with their grandchildren. To be sure, there were women of all ages in the streets. "Noriega said something to the effect that there were only 5,000 demonstrators," Quinn said. "Well, he forgot to say that 4,800 of them were women. Noriega never understood the power of a woman."

Mayin Correa had issued the first call to protest, and from that first day women had always been in the forefront. One of the most vigorous and defiant organizers was Rosario Arias Galindo, the former newspaper owner who had said the rosary for Hugo Spadafora even after the PDF cut down the mahogany tree that sheltered her and her friends. The attack on grandmothers angered her and she retaliated with an essay in *La Prensa* called "The Revolt of the Grandmothers" that immediately became famous. "I said that grandmothers were fighting so much because we had lived in a democracy and we could compare it with what we have now. Of course I was sorry that I couldn't give more time to my grandchildren, but I thought at this time that this was more important to my grandchildren than reading stories to them."

Despite the presence of blacks, Indians, and women from all classes, the most visible Crusade members were fancy-pants male Yuppies. They got noticed a lot by the international press. "Eduardo Vallarino, an opposition leader who is now in hiding," wrote Charles Lane in *Newsweek*, "is president of the local Harvard Club. Antigovernment businessmen send clandestine communiqués by fax machine, and so many BMWs, Hondas, and Mercedeses show up at opposition rallies that they resemble pregame traffic at the Yale Bowl."

The summer's events had elements of an insurrection and a fiesta. "Make Honesty Fashionable Again" read one red-and-white lapel pin. "I ♥ Sedition" was also popular. Loathing for Noriega exploded in odd places—even on a television game show. Contestants on the live show had to choose between a large box and a small box—both of which, they were told, concealed valuable prizes. One contestant chose the large box, and the show's host, who seemed to have received a signal from the wings, had to restrain him from lifting it. Did he want to reconsider his choice? No, the man said, and reached for the large box again. Remember, the host said, small boxes often have valuable contents. I want whatever's under the big box, the guest said. He lifted it and found one very small pineapple. The response was a thunderclap of laughter and several minutes of wild cheering and handkerchief waving.

Then there was the ice cube assault—the only recorded case of violence against a government figure. It took place at the new home of the Union Club, across the bay from the old city and old club premises. The new club had wide and breezy tropical verandas and a luxurious dining room and bar with dark wood, polished brass, doors with windows like portholes, and comfortable leather chairs. It was in this bar that some vociferous members of the opposition, who were celebrating a wedding, became infuriated at the sight of President Delvalle. The merrymakers began chanting slogans, challenged Delvalle's manhood, and demanded his resignation. "Murderer's puppet," they yelled as the president of Panama grabbed the band's microphone and began to reply. He was forced to flee when the crowd pelted him with ice cubes, tapping their glasses with heavy silver spoons.

Why shouldn't Noriega just retire—and enjoy his millions? That was one idea heard over and over in Panama around this time; everyone assumed the general was finished. But Noriega could not have retired; he would have been murdered by the Medellín Cartel. In power, Noriega was useful to them. Out of power, he was dangerous; he knew too much. Staying in power and staying alive were the same for Noriega.

In late July, the cartel sent Noriega a miniature coffin to make their feelings clear. According to one account, it was an elaborately carved piece of fine wood etched with Noriega's distinctive initials: MAN. Other people said it was made of plywood, the size of a shoe box with a hinged top. Inside was a videocassette that proved that someone had been able to get very close to all three of his daughters without any trouble. "Noriega realized he was up against something much more formidable, more powerful than the U.S. government," a U.S. official said.

Diaz Herrera remained free, and as talkative as ever. Every day, he distributed his message to those who drove by. As July wore on, the opposition leaders were busy elsewhere and Diaz Herrera announced that he wanted a special commission to investigate his charges against Noriega. Then, with his advisers telling him he could delay no longer, Noriega made his move.

Late on Sunday night, July 26, staffers at *La Prensa, Extra*, and *El Siglo*, busy closing the next day's papers, looked up to see thirty plainclothes G-2 agents and uniformed PDF soldiers, heavily armed, fan out through their offices. They told everyone to go home immediately and no one tried to resist. When a reporter telephoned the news desk at *La Prensa* several hours later a man answered and told the reporter he had the wrong number. There was no telling how long the opposition papers would be closed this time. The government announced that the state of emergency, which had been imposed and lifted several times, was back in effect.

Just after dawn on July 27, a PDF Huey helicopter, hovering just a few feet above Diaz Herrera's house, shattered the dewy stillness of Golf Heights. The crew dropped tear-gas canisters and stun grenades, and fired clip after clip of machine-gun bullets. A raiding party knocked down the door of the Diaz Herrera house just a few minutes later. Official estimates by the PDF and SOUTHCOM say the raid lasted between seven and fifteen minutes. There is no question that it was brief and effective—"a classic Israeli operation," an American general said. Diaz Herrera, his family, and entourage—forty-five people in all—were taken away in PDF vehicles.

A photo of a morose Diaz Herrera soon appeared in a government paper. He was being interrogated and, officials said, could face charges of sedition. Without a free press, rumors spread quickly. Diaz Herrera, according to the stories, was being displayed at one PDF base after another as a cautionary symbol. He was confined to a wheelchair, immobilized by medication or torture. He had become a vegetable.

Diaz Herrera's lawyer took a habeas corpus motion all the way to the Panamanian Supreme Court, where it was rejected after a brief pause to suggest it had been considered. Just a few days later, Diaz Herrera—in a statement issued from an undisclosed location—repudiated all his charges. He said that the Spadafora family and opposition political leaders had put him up to it. "I'd like to add that this declaration is made in complete liberty with the desire to take corrective measure in front of third persons and with the concern to obtain a normalization of my private life and that of my family," the statement said. It included special mention of the Spadafora murder. "I gave that news but I do not confirm or ratify what I said because I based it on what the Spadafora family pointed out. This event is not clear to me since I have no proof of it." A short while later, Maigualida and the children went to Caracas. Diaz Herrera himself followed in December.

Noriega made a rare public appearance during Diaz Herrera's incarceration. Foreign reporters yelled questions. "Can you tell us please, General, what is the condition of Colonel Diaz Herrera's health?" one shouted.

Noriega was hurrying past but he paused and smiled at the reporter. "You should start worrying about your own health," he said, and continued on. Indeed, as August began, even as the Crusade announced plans for a demonstration called the Great White March (to be held on August 6), Noriega appeared more and more confident.

Two days before the event, *sapos* arrived in a midnight rainstorm at Crusade headquarters and carted away boxes of papers. The crowd yelled "Murderers" and "Justice." A few hours later a government official said he had discovered "flyers posing a threat to state security." Six more Crusade leaders went into hiding. By dawn on Thursday, the day of the demonstration, tension in the city was high.

That morning, a Panamanian investment banker, strolling toward his office near the Chamber of Commerce, saw several government pickup trucks skid to a stop. Men in civilian clothes removed heavy containers from the back and lugged them across the sidewalk to the front door of the building. The stench reached the banker's nostrils even before he saw what they were splattering on the building. It was the debris of a slaughterhouse—red, purple, and black; shiny and stinking; the rotting guts of livestock. The banker knew instantly what he had witnessed. "It was basic Brazilian voodoo," he said. "If you want to destroy a family or a group, you throw animal guts at their doorway. Noriega was using every possible force on earth to stay in power."

By late afternoon, it was said that the entire population was in the streets. Most crowded into the broad intersection in front of El Carmen cathedral. Close to a half-million people turned out at one time or another during the day.

At one point, as if a secret had been passed, the crowd's attention turned to the statue between the cathedral spires a hundred feet above. A cluster of white balloons had sailed into the sky and snagged on the wrought-iron halo attachments of the Savior and Mary. The balloons danced in the breeze, waving at the crowds. "Que milagro, que milagro," "What a miracle, what a miracle," people gasped. People swayed and wept and chanted, "Justicia." After several minutes the balloons broke free and descended gently into the crowd.

Shortly afterward, the crowd dispersed. "That was their best chance, the damned fools," a woman who was in the crowd said later, with disgust. "I started shouting, 'Let's go and get Noriega. Let's go to the Comandancia. Demand his head, for Christ sakes.' But they just wanted to congratulate themselves and talk about miracles. They wanted everything done for them. They deserve what they got."

When Noriega had been in trouble before, he had wanted Jose Blandon at his side. Blandon was a good negotiator. In 1984, for example, the cartel had issued a contract to kill Noriega because the Colombians believed he had stolen $5 million from them. Blandon helped orchestrate a peace parley in Havana, supervised by Fidel Castro, that saved Noriega's life. Blandon had university degrees in agriculture and economics. Noriega respected him but he was not a hard-drinking crony.

No one knew everything Noriega knew, but Blandon knew most of it. He had watched the summer's events unfold from New York, where he was consul, and was dismayed at Noriega's handling of things. As far as he could tell, Noriega had no plan and was just drifting. In early August 1987, U.S. newspapers had carried stories that a federal grand jury in Miami was investigating Noriega's drug involvement. The DEA in Miami and the FBI and Customs Bureau in Tampa were also gathering evidence. Blandon realized that Noriega could be indicted—and knew that this would make him a pariah to even his most loyal U.S. friends.

Blandon headed for Panama to discuss things with Noriega. He decided to see the general even before he checked into his hotel and told the driver who had picked him up to go straight to the Comandancia. There was a crisis after all. Blandon found Noriega slightly tipsy at a boisterous, boozy party with a few cronies. His words to Blandon were, in effect, Don't worry, have a drink, say hello, we can talk tomorrow. Noriega's attitude confirmed Blandon's sense that his boss was drifting. He was in more trouble than ever before and didn't seem to know it.

That night, as Blandon stepped into the elevator at the Marriott, a woman passenger recognized him and recoiled in disgust. That had never happened before; Panama had changed. Confirmation came shortly afterward when Blandon's twenty-year-old son, Jose Jr., a university student, stopped by his father's hotel room. The young man had been a conspicuous figure in the summer's anti-Noriega demonstrations.

Blandon's son accused him of supporting a shameful regime. The father listened. He wanted his son's approval very much. No sooner had the son departed than Blandon's mother called him. She told him just as bluntly that the country was being torn apart. Do something, she told him.

The next day, Noriega listened as Blandon told him he was in serious trouble. Noriega could probably cling to power but would have more problems; the indictments, if they came, would be disastrous. He could, however, probably head them off. Blandon said that Noriega had to take steps to ensure the continuation of the PDF. Blandon stressed that now was the time to start taking action. If he waited, he would have to make more concessions.

On Wednesday, August 12, Noriega celebrated his fourth

anniversary as commander in chief. For the first time, he hinted vaguely at a negotiated settlement of the crisis. The code words in his speech were "a Panamanian solution." Noriega seemed to have heard Blandon's warning. Two days later, Blandon and Noriega sat down again for three hours and talked about the issues, the personalities, the stakes. Blandon departed Panama shortly afterward with a blank check to talk to people in the United States to see if he could cut a deal.

5

Admiral Murphy Pays a Call
AUGUST 1987–DECEMBER 1987

WHILE Blandon prepared to meet State Department officials, relations between Noriega and Washington remained chilly. Noriega and General Woerner, for example, still had not met in public since the day Woerner took command.

In mid-September, Noriega journeyed to Mexico City for Independence Day festivities during which he received a medal from the Mexican government, presented as a token of friendship and admiration for a fellow Latin American.

Pro-Noriega demonstrations had materialized in time to be captured by the cameras for the international press. The troubles in Panama seemed far away. At one point, Noriega saw an opportunity to improve the public perception of his relationship with Woerner. He joined Woerner and his wife on a small balcony overlooking the festivities. There was hardly room for all three and Noriega and Woerner stood shoulder to shoulder.

"Turn around," Gennie Woerner whispered to her husband. "They're trying to get a picture of you." She had spotted a photographer just below them, pointing his thirty-inch telescopic lens up at the balcony. Noriega was primed but Woerner suddenly shifted his position. When the photographer tried a second time, Woerner shifted again at the last second. No one spoke. Finally, Noriega left the balcony. The message was clear.

Later, Woerner's sedan was racing to the airport with motorcycle escorts. Suddenly, a small car approached with a huge Panamanian flag waving from the passenger window. Woerner watched as his astonished police escort forced the car onto the exit ramp, and they continued, speeding straight to the airport tarmac. The man with the flag was waiting there. "To this day," Woerner says, "I have no idea how he ever got there. He was there waving the Panamanian flag. He was someone from the embassy, I am convinced, that was told to show me that Noriega was everywhere."

———

Back in Panama, Noriega learned that Blandon had succeeded in opening tentative discussions with the State Department, offering the same basic quid pro quo that he and Noriega had agreed upon earlier. Noriega would agree to step down but only if the administration assured him that he would never be indicted for narco-trafficking.

From the beginning of the talks, there was one fundamental issue: Noriega's silence about his "cooperation" with the United States over the years. There was no denying that Noriega had been of service to the United States in any number of ways, many less public than his cooperation with the DEA. Intelligence officials said he served as a "back channel" between Richard Nixon and Fidel Castro. Who knew what else he might have done? The question was never dealt with. U.S. officials knew that Noriega might sing "songs we don't want to hear," as Oliver North had said, in reference to another shady Contra supporter. From their point of view it was best to forget the past.

Noriega, however, missed no opportunity to bring it up among friends. If he had committed crimes, he pointed out, he had committed them with U.S. knowledge. It would have been impossible for the Americans to have missed them. As far as Noriega was concerned, they had always been part of his résumé.

In early October, Noriega spent several hours with reporter Lally Weymouth, daughter of Katharine Graham, owner of *Newsweek* and the *Washington Post*. The result was a four-column headline in the *Washington Post*'s "Outlook" section: "Why is Elliott

Abrams Picking on Panama's Noriega?" Noriega, Weymouth reported, was bitter.

"When the Americans need something, they picture it very nicely and say you're a hero, but when they don't need you anymore, they forget you," he said. "We are going to make a list of those the U.S. betrayed." He mentioned, among others, the Shah of Iran and Marcos. "You can erase me," he told Weymouth. "But there are another two guys behind me. Ten years ago, I wasn't here," he said.

Noriega stressed that he had been particularly helpful to the United States with Cuba. Omar Torrijos, he said, had dispatched him in the early 1970s to obtain the release of a U.S. serviceman whom the Cubans had been holding. Noriega also described an October 1983 phone call from George Bush, just hours before the Grenada invasion. According to Noriega, Bush told him to tell Castro not to interfere. "Bush is my friend," Noriega told Weymouth. "I hope he becomes president."

Noriega blamed all his problems on Jesse Helms, who wanted the canal back, and Elliott Abrams. "Elliott definitely has his own strategy to save himself from his own problems," Noriega told Weymouth, adding that unspecified Americans had said Abrams's attacks were meant to "ingratiate" himself with Congress.

Just a few days after the interview, Noriega gave Blandon the go-ahead to open a dialogue with Gabriel Lewis, his sworn enemy since June. Lewis was respected by nearly everyone in Washington. Noriega, however, could hardly expect any kindness from Lewis, who also distrusted Blandon.

Both Blandon and Lewis, however, trusted Joel McCleary and had maintained close contact since his consulting contract with Noriega had expired. In early October, the three men ate Chinese take-out food in Lewis's house in Washington's Foxhall Road neighborhood and talked frankly. They had problems with each other, but they were Panamanians, for whom grudges can be perishable items. (Ambassador Davis liked to say that the national motto of Panama should be "Let's Make a Deal." He could tell the joke to Panamanians with no offense meant, nor taken.)

McCleary said they needed a plan to jump start the U.S. policy-making apparatus. He saw no consensus on Panama in Washington. This worked to Noriega's benefit. As the meeting continued, it became clear that the three men did not know how to go about driving Noriega from power. No one did.

In late October, McCleary met Blandon and Lewis again—

this time in New York. There was still no plan, but McCleary extracted a consensus about what had to be done and how to do it. When the Panamanians went on their way, McCleary went to work. Just before dawn, he finished a preliminary draft of "The Blandon Plan," which he faxed to Lewis, who had returned to Washington.

Several hours later, Lewis called. He was enthusiastic about the plan, which he had just delivered to the State Department—as if to say, "Here is your policy." The outline of the plan—which called for free elections, an independent media, and U.S. aid for the reborn civilian democracy—was to be distributed to other officials throughout the bureaucracy. "If I had known it was going to the National Security Council I would have used my SpellCheck," McCleary said.

Blandon received a copy of McCleary's document and prepared a slightly amended paraphrase that, for example, omitted McCleary's suggestions about how to persuade Noriega to accept the plan. Blandon sent the basic summary to Noriega, who instructed Blandon to proceed. The plan's single most dramatic component, couched in diplomatic language, was the decapitation of the PDF. Noriega was to retire no later than April 1988. Before then he was to have ordered the retirement of six top PDF officers, known as "The Gang of Six." These men were to receive lucrative diplomatic postings and were to be guaranteed immunity from prosecution in Panama. That was a controversial issue. Many Noriega opponents were leery of giving these men amnesty.

Blandon, Lewis, and McCleary all agreed about the best way to convince Noriega to leave. They proposed that Nestor Sanchez be immediately recruited to tell Noriega that the time had come for a political solution. He must be tough, they said, as only such a good personal friend can be. They wanted him to tell Noriega that he had to make a deal. They knew he trusted Nestor.

The question was whether Noriega could actually be trusted to retire. Some opposition members would never buy it and Blandon had no illusions. "To lie, for Noriega, is part of his work," he said. But he was convinced that Noriega had to step down and that was what he told him.

Almost immediately, Noriega sent for retired U.S. Navy admiral Daniel J. Murphy, a man he had met in December 1983 when Murphy was chief of staff to then Vice President Bush. Murphy had also been Bush's deputy at the CIA and had served him on the Southern Florida Task Force. In 1985, he had left government service and entered the "risk-analysis" business in Washington. By 1987, he was an international lobbyist, president of Murphy & Demory, a firm with clients, associates, and partners in many parts of the world.

Murphy answered the summons quickly and his early November visit to Panama was a major development in Noriega's eyes. He saw Murphy as Bush's man and a representative of the intelligence community. Everything about Murphy suggested this.

Noriega was ecstatic when he learned that Murphy had Washington friends who wanted to help him. Like everyone else, Murphy told Noriega that he had to leave, but the date he mentioned was comfortably far off in the future, 1989. Noriega decided the heat was off. He could make reassuring noises with promises to step down and assurances of reform. But he assumed that this would close the episode and that "business" would return to normal.

When Murphy's trip came to light months later, he was reluctant to talk about it. Some time later, he testified under oath about his relations with Noriega, saying twice that he had not met with the general before 1987. Finally, a senator's prompting reminded him of the 1983 meeting he and Bush had held with Noriega. Murphy said his November 1987 trip (and a less momentous visit in August 1987) were strictly private business.

Murphy said the meeting was unimportant. "I went down as a businessman," he said later. "I'm a businessman. I'm trying to make a dollar. I've got a new firm. I'm trying to move along." He said he went to Panama to talk about what had to be done to make the nation a good risk for investment. He told Noriega that reforms were essential. These reforms included his departure by the date he specified.

He denied negotiating with Noriega or contradicting U.S. government policy. He did not deny having met with U.S. officials before and after his trips, and said these officials included Richard Armitage at the Pentagon; Elliott Abrams at State; and Donald Gregg, Bush's chief of staff.

The meetings, according to Murphy, were briefings to clarify U.S. policy. He was not told to say anything. He briefed the officials on his conversations; there was no discussion. Murphy testified that Noriega listened to him but said he left Panama still thinking it a bad investment risk.

Whatever happened, Noriega was relieved after Murphy's

visit. Murphy's schedule gave him thirteen more months in power than the Blandon Plan. And an option to renew was implied, he believed, if Panama stabilized. Murphy also spared Noriega the task of retiring his six top commanders. He repeated the old refrain about U.S. desires for an apolitical military but left it at that.

Blandon says that Noriega called him very soon after Murphy left. He told him that there was obviously another scenario for Panama in Washington, a scenario very different from the one they had been discussing. Blandon promised Noriega that he would investigate, but, not surprisingly, Noriega wanted to believe Murphy.

Blandon says that Murphy presented himself to Noriega as an emissary of Bush, Shultz, Gen. Colin Powell, the president's national security adviser, and the entire NSC. According to Blandon, Murphy told Noriega that if he launched reforms and announced a retirement date (to be announced later, if necessary) the joint United States–Panama military maneuvers scheduled for January 1988 would be held. The U.S. Defense Department would still align itself with his military. Murphy told Noriega bluntly, according to Blandon, that he could expect better treatment from a Bush presidency and added that he could help Panama get money from Japan—aid and investment that would be needed in the event of a cutoff of funds by the United States.

Murphy's traveling companion in Panama was Tongsun Park, the Korean businessman who had been at the center of the Koreagate scandal of the 1970s. Park was friendly with Noriega and worked as a paid intermediary for a number of Japanese firms that wanted to buy property or open hotels or businesses in Panama. Japan watched developments in Panama very closely and Noriega visited Japan frequently. Except for Peru, Japan was the only country in the world whose economy still depended on the Panama Canal.

Blandon understood why Noriega interpreted Murphy as an official—if utterly deniable—messenger. Murphy and Park (and two aides) were the only passengers on a 707 Park had borrowed from a friend in Miami named Sarkis Soghenalian. Soghenalian, an arms "coordinator," was Iraq's main supplier during its war with Iran and an occasional "asset" of American intelligence.

Blandon brought up the possibility of a policy war in Washington. He said that Abrams and other U.S. officials denied that Murphy was an official representative. Blandon said that his plan was the real plan and reiterated that it was ultimately best for Noriega and all concerned. Noriega finally told Blandon to pursue the original plan.

As Murphy later made clear, U.S. officials, if they knew nothing else, if they had ordered no specific communication, were aware of Murphy's visit. All would have known what it would mean to Noriega. Yet no effort was made to cancel the trip and no attempt was made to enlighten Noriega.

On November 22, Blandon—at Noriega's direction—broadcast a radio speech and PDF officers were ordered to listen. In the speech, Blandon said that he was working on a "political solution" to Panama's situation, a solution that would include the opposition. Noriega's approval of the speech reassured Blandon: He thought Noriega was cleverly preparing the PDF for negotiations—and implementation of the plan.

———

On November 17, Deborah DeMoss, Greg Craig (a Kennedy aide), and four other Senate aides flew to Panama to find out firsthand what was happening. They symbolized the extraordinary senatorial coalition that had built up against Noriega. DeMoss, suffering from the flu, refused to bow out of the trip, but when she landed in Panama she went directly to Gorgas Hospital.

The government press called them intruders and mocked DeMoss's illness. The writer said that Panama hated her so much it had made her sick. But in Gorgas Hospital, DeMoss was a celebrity and hero. A stream of Panamanian doctors and nurses came to her bedside to thank her and encourage efforts against Noriega. In the evenings, the other aides visited their ailing comrade and discussed what they had done and seen. The visit was proving to be eventful.

One evening, they attended a party at Gabriel Lewis's house, hosted by one of his sons. A crowd of the sort that had stoned the U.S. embassy also turned up, chanting slogans about Panamanian sovereignty and American intervention. Very quickly, a second, much larger crowd had materialized, waving white handkerchiefs and denouncing Noriega.

The aides got a similar show when they went to see and photograph the boarded-up *La Prensa* building. Drivers slowed down and honked their horns. Handkerchiefs waved. The PDF guards looked nervous and menacing. One soldier tore a camera from an aide's hands and threatened to destroy it. Violence seemed imminent. When the aides left, the PDF tailed them.

———

Noriega wouldn't commit to an interview but arrangements were made for the group to show up at PDF headquarters at a certain hour. DeMoss left the hospital for the occasion. In the car she asked Col. Al Cornell, the U.S. attaché who had, with another colonel, conveyed Noriega's invitation to Mayin Correa in June 1987, for his assessment of a series of PDF officers she named. Cornell was uniformly laudatory. "Great guy," he said, or "West Point grad," or "speaks good English," or "studied in the U.S."

"Wait a minute, Colonel," DeMoss said. "I don't want to know who speaks English. I don't want to know who went to school at West Point. I don't want to know who's visited the United States. Tell us about these people for heaven's sakes! Are they thugs? Are they drug traffickers? Are they clean guys? Are they professional military?" she demanded.

"They're nice guys," Cornell replied. "They're not so bad. They help me out a lot. They cooperate with me." DeMoss thought Cornell "incredibly naive, and not very smart either."

The group joined seven PDF officers who were waiting at a big wooden table in an office down the hall from Noriega's. Noriega was missing but had arranged some theater. Police chief Col. Leonidas Macias invited DeMoss to sit beside him. A tape recorder was conspicuous. When the staffers started questioning Macias, it became clear that the meeting was a stunt.

Macias kept whispering to DeMoss while she tried to follow the questioning. He flirted with her, making little jokes and suggesting that a girl like Deborah would not be interested in all the serious talk.

Then Macias jumped up to make an impassioned speech about democracy, thumping a copy of the Panamanian constitution, declaring that "if President Delvalle today asked Noriega to step aside, Noriega would step aside." Another colonel rose to orate further about Noriega, patriotism, and his own loyalty.

Back in Washington, the aides succeeded in canceling the joint maneuvers scheduled for January 1988. Greg Craig spearheaded the effort and, with Kennedy pulling strings, managed to arrange the announcement by 5:00 P.M. the day of their return.

During the following months, Noriega followed Blandon's

negotiations closely. On December 7, Blandon went to the State Department for a meeting with Abrams and two other officials. For him, this was the "best moment." He believed that his plan was becoming U.S. policy though no one made any promises about avoiding indictments—Noriega's one condition. Blandon sent a full report to Noriega.

Two days later, Noriega sent his reply: "I recommend that you be careful, cautious, conceptual in setting forth the issues," he wrote. "The document, the discussion, must be kept under your strict control, so that it does not appear as a formula of understanding on the part of the government." Noriega praised Blandon's work as "valuable, well ordered" and promised him that when "we develop or create other points I will send them to you."

Noriega acted like a man about to take a step, but he wanted to be careful. He stressed the importance of atmospherics to Blandon. His departure from power should not resemble the "Japanese empire in World War II, signing its capitulation on the decks of the Missouri."

Blandon eagerly went ahead. "You guys are so reasonable," he exclaimed during a meeting in Miami where he described the plan to Ricardo Arias Calderon, Roberto Eisenmann, and other opposition figures. It was no surprise. These men had insisted for years that Noriega had to go. Blandon convinced the opposition leaders that he knew what he was talking about, and that he might even have some leverage himself on Noriega. It was possible that he could use incriminating evidence against him.

Roberto Eisenmann never believed that Noriega would negotiate seriously and also doubted that the Reagan administration would take action unless domestic politics made it unavoidable. Eisenmann was even more dubious after a conversation alone with Blandon.

"We should sit down and discuss a constituent assembly," Blandon said.

"If Noriega falls down today, when do we call for constituent assembly elections?" Eisenmann replied.

"No, I'm not talking about elections. We can't have an election. We have to name a constituent assembly and I think the PRD should have a third."

"You know we've just been through twenty years of autocracy. We're talking about a democracy, and you're talking about a named assembly. I mean what the hell is that?" Eisenmann said.

"You just don't understand power," Blandon said.

"You just don't understand democracy," Eisenmann replied.

On December 12, Joel McCleary was in Tokyo, following Blandon's progress with great interest. His Japanese friends—policymakers and businessmen—looked at him doubtfully when he mentioned negotiations to get rid of Noriega. They asked him if he really knew what was going on, was he in synch with U.S. policy? They mentioned the Murphy visit and said that they considered the "Murphy Plan" to be operative U.S. policy.

McCleary was stunned. "We often go to the Far East to attain enlightenment. This time for me it was not about the Buddha but about U.S. foreign policy. I had a satori experience, an awakening experience. A satori experience is a sudden turnaround of consciousness—you ain't the same afterward. When they told me about Murphy, I realized that the U.S. government had been playing with Jose Blandon, and playing with all the others all the time. Murphy was the real message."

McCleary told Blandon and Lewis about his fears, but they waved him away. Both men had the assurances of people they knew and trusted in the U.S. government; the "Blandon Plan" was operative.

"The only people who understood all this were the Japanese," McCleary said, and now so did he. "They look at things dispassionately. They look at the budgets of the Department of Defense and the CIA and then the State Department budget. The State Department to them is a policy think tank with very few resources. The CIA and DoD are empires." McCleary and the Japanese believed that Murphy was an instrument of those organizations of which he was an alumnus.

On December 21, McCleary's pessimism was proven right. Noriega telephoned Blandon in New York; his tone was abusive. He shouted that he had just discovered Blandon's secret negotiations, which he denied knowing about. "What is this plan? I've never heard of it," Noriega yelled.

"Don't talk to me like a sergeant," Blandon replied. Noriega sounded scared to him. He suspected that the Gang of Six themselves were probably with Noriega. "Call me back when you can talk," Blandon said. But he never spoke to Noriega again.

It was time for another message to Noriega and this time Richard Armitage was the bearer. Armitage, an assistant secretary of defense, had been involved with Panama policy for months, and Armitage and Noriega had gotten along well in the past.

Ambassador Davis looked forward to the visit. He had just learned, from State officials, of an historic consensus between State and Defense. Everyone now agreed that Noriega had to go. He was more trouble in office than out. Everyone also agreed that Noriega should be informed of the unanimous decision. Armitage, with Davis at his side, was to tell Noriega that he had to face the fact that no one would speak on his behalf anymore. Nor would anyone try to impede any effort to remove him. This was it. Noriega was fired, with no appeal.

When Davis greeted Armitage at Howard Air Force Base on December 30, the ambassador showed him these instructions, instructions that he had believed identical to those Armitage had been given. "Sorry, I don't have that," Armitage told Davis.

"What the hell are you down here for?" Davis asked.

Davis queried the State Department. He learned that "somebody at DoD canceled the agreed statement and gave [Armitage] a watered-down version of what he should say."

"Christ, you're here now; we might as well go ahead with the meeting," Davis said. Then Davis, Armitage, and Bob Pastorino, another Pentagon official, went to see Noriega at the Comandancia. They all sat around a big table. The mother of Miss Panama acted as translator. Armitage stated the traditional U.S. concerns. When his statements were described soon afterward to Washington reporters, they seemed to indicate a stern message from the Pentagon to Noriega.

But Armitage never asked Noriega to leave. He, Noriega, and some aides shared almost two bottles of Old Parr scotch and told stories. "After a few drinks, they all wanted to be friends," Davis said. "They all wanted to be buddies." Davis declined the drink offers. He was there on official U.S. business and he could see a major victory for Noriega taking shape as the afternoon wore on.

"There were some friendly things said at that meeting that infuriated me," Davis said. "I did not want to make any goddamn toast but naturally the other three guys said, "Aw, just have a little bit," so I took a little wine glass and held it up in a toast and I sipped the scotch."

Hours later, Noriega embraced his American friends and said

farewell. "When we went out [Noriega] played it perfectly," Davis said. "He had all his officers and some of the gals in the office. And he wanted to send some cigars back to Nestor Sanchez and he came out with four boxes and he said, 'Will you give this to Nestor?' And he gave one to Bob, one to [Armitage], and then he turned to me and I stared at him and he just put the box down. He did not offer me the box."

6

Indicted

ON Saturday, January 9, 1988, Panama took to the streets. By late afternoon there were thousands gathered downtown celebrating. Word had spread that Noriega had left Panama. "Don't come back," the crowds chanted.

He had left, earlier that afternoon, on a PDF plane to Santo Domingo in the Dominican Republic. He did not travel incognito; one traveler saw him and phoned Panamanian friends in Washington. The news spread like wildfire. Noriega, it was reported, had checked into a hotel.

As the day wore on there were more rumors. No one bothered to inquire as to how long Noriega planned to stay in Santo Domingo. People ignored the fact that he was always traveling. Nor did they seem to remember that some of the worst recent crimes, most notably the Spadafora murder, had taken place when Noriega was out of town.

Shortly after nightfall, the PDF waded into the crowds on the streets, firing tear gas and automatic weapons. The jubilance evaporated quickly.

Noriega returned to Panama on Sunday. "It was a trap I set to test their honesty," he said, apropos the trip. He referred to the

PDF, government employees, and businessmen whom he counted as allies. No one broke ranks.

In fact, he had visited his daughter Sandra and her in-laws, including her husband's father, a retired military officer. The public had misread his journey.

Noriega prepared for a new round in the war of words with the United States. Background briefings in Washington had portrayed his boozy afternoon with Armitage as another "message meeting": Word was out that Noriega had been chastised and told to pay heed and pack his bags. Armitage was seen as a figure of doom, not a conveyor of Cuban cigars. He was described as a brawny Vietnam vet and the implication seemed to be that he might have roughed up Noriega if the general had not paid attention.

This particular "spin" on the story was useful in Washington and Panama. The administration could say that it was maintaining pressure on Noriega. Noriega could say he was resisting it. "I am not a peon of the United States, and this commander will never compromise national sovereignty," Noriega said after the Armitage trip made news in the U.S. papers.

Jose Blandon, waiting in Miami after the blow-up with Noriega, had not given up hope that the general would retire. He had refused Noriega's summons to return to Panama and was waiting for some sort of clarification of his position. Noriega provided it in early January when he publicly denounced Blandon as a "traitor." Blandon got his son Jose Jr., a vocal opposition member, out of Panama. He was a natural target.

On the Sunday he returned from Santo Domingo, Noriega dispatched two PRD men to talk to Blandon, who responded bluntly: "I give you three days. If you are not willing to discuss this problem with me, then I am going to play my card. Then I will understand that we are at war." Noriega would surely understand that Blandon's "card" was knowledge of incriminating information about him. Noriega did not know that Blandon had already been subpoenaed to testify to grand juries in Miami and Tampa, beginning January 28.

Four days later, Noriega sent his reply. "Why don't you return to Panama?" he asked.

Just a day or two later, Blandon got a phone call from his younger son, Raul, who had always avoided politics and Panama City. Young Raul, who had severe emotional and physical problems, lived on a farm outside the capital where he was well looked after. He kept a small menagerie of barnyard animals.

"Daddy, Daddy," the boy sobbed. Blandon tried to calm him as the boy tried to explain the events of the day at the farm. Several goons had turned up. Some had held the boy and made him watch as others killed his beloved animals before his eyes. They left the carcasses.

Blandon was in danger—but he was also dangerous. Despite intensive investigations, the Florida federal prosecutors still had not been able to assemble enough information to indict Noriega. They lacked a witness like Blandon, someone who was not a convicted narco-trafficker himself (as nearly all their witnesses were) and had firsthand documented knowledge of Noriega's crimes. Just a few days before his January 28 appearance before the grand jury, Blandon had given Noriega one last chance, in the columns of the *New York Times*. In an interview with Elaine Sciolino he sent what seemed like an ultimatum: "I have a lot of information about Noriega, probably more information on his arms trafficking, drug trafficking and the internal problems of the Defense Forces than anyone else," Blandon said. He said he had evidence that would confirm the charges that Noriega was connected to the murder of Spadafora. "I don't want to be forced to use it. But if there is not any political solution, I will use it." The sine qua non of any political solution, Blandon said, was Noriega's departure from power. Blandon was still pushing his plan.

"It's a generous plan, because it says we're going to forgive him, and it's the best deal he's going to get," Blandon said. "He can kill me, that's the risk. But he can't kill what I know. I'm not a military man. I'm a politician. And I don't feel loyalty to Noriega. I feel loyalty to my country. I've told him since 1984, 'You have a lot of problems.' "

Staffers from two Senate subcommittees were now as eager as the Miami and Tampa district attorneys to see Blandon. Deborah DeMoss flew to Miami, listened carefully, and pronounced him credible.

Blandon's testimony, DeMoss hoped, might finally spur the inert administration into action. She and Blandon, unlikely allies just months before, became friendly. He told her that around the time of her visit to Panama, his office had received CIA material to help fuel press attacks against her and the other aides. This disclosure, and others like it, produced a quick reaction: Key intelligence officials set out to discredit Blandon as a liar and covert

Castro ally. His credibility—accepted by two Florida prosecutors and senators as diverse as Helms and Kennedy—eventually became an issue.

Panama press conferences began to multiply. Senator Alfonse D'Amato of New York, co-chairman of the Senate Caucus on International Narcotics Control, told reporters that Noriega had created a "total criminal empire probably as large as any that may exist in the world." D'Amato quickly made it known that he had ordered around-the-clock bodyguards from the U.S. Marshals Service for Blandon and his family.

———

On February 3, Blandon got a telephone call from a trusted Noriega messenger.

"Don't do anything until you discuss it with the general," the man said. "We are ready to discuss things with you."

"Why don't you come to Washington?" Blandon asked him.

"No, another country," the man said, and suggested Costa Rica.

"Let me think about it," Blandon said. "I'll call you back."

Blandon called a trusted PDF friend. He learned that if he went to Costa Rica he would be met by Col. Nivaldo Madrinan. The friend didn't say whether the policeman was still wearing the Mitrotti ring.

Blandon immediately telephoned Noriega's emissary to say he would definitely be in Costa Rica the next weekend. In fact, Blandon made plans to stay in Washington.

In Miami, on February 4, Noriega was formally indicted on thirteen counts of narco-trafficking and racketeering. Incidents cited came from as far back as 1981 and were as recent as 1987. "In plain language," said Leon Kellner, the Miami district attorney, "[Noriega] utilized his position to sell the country of Panama to drug traffickers." The indictments echoed Hugo Spadafora's charges.

Early February was a pivotal moment in U.S. politics. All the barometers of the voting public confirmed that, for the first time, most Americans believed drugs a greater threat than communism. Noriega had become the ugly symbol of the reigning evil. He didn't realize what had hit him. He didn't sense what the indictments meant to American voters.

The prosecutors had spoken to State and White House officials before they announced the indictments and the administration had persuaded them not to indict the entire PDF as a criminal enterprise under the Racketeer-Influenced and Corrupt Organizations (RICO) statutes. But that was all they could do. When accused of meddling in foreign affairs, the prosecutors stood firm. "We got involved with indicting people in foreign policy," said Richard Gregorie, a Miami prosecutor, "when the people who were making foreign policy began dealing with dope dealers."

Noriega lacked the political imagination to see how constrained his friends were. If they had tried to block the indictments in 1988, they would have run the risk of being accused of obstructing justice. Still, until February 1988, Noriega's defenders held to the party line, saying that his crimes were rumors, and that there was no evidence against Noriega. The indictments, however, stamped Noriega guilty in the public's mind. Testimony from Blandon and Floyd Carlton before the Senate subcommittee on narcotics and terrorism confirmed the impression. The headlines of early February 1988 made it impossible for the military and intelligence officials who had once wined and dined Noriega to speak up on his behalf.

The indictments were not, as most Panamanians took them to be, a declaration of war by the administration, but they complicated administration calculations. Why would Noriega agree to leave Panama if he faced capture by U.S. law enforcement agencies? Dropping the indictments was impossible to contemplate from a political point of view.

———

Gen. Fred Woerner saw Noriega shortly after the indictments were announced. "He couldn't believe it," Woerner said. "He said, 'What are you doing?' He thought he was double-crossed. He was genuinely hurt by that. As an individual he felt betrayed."

In public, a defiant Noriega said the indictments were "strictly a political act aimed at frightening me and other nationalistic Latin American leaders who dare to criticize the United States." He hired some American lawyers and began jabbing back, denying all charges and announcing that he had ordered his attorney general to find out whether Lewis, Blandon, and others might be indicted in Panama for slander. His lawyers condemned what they called "indictment diplomacy." One said that he had seen some of Noriega's archives, and that they were "political dynamite."

The day after the indictments, Noriega gave what came to be known in Panama as "the Chinese restaurant speech." This impromptu oration came at a meeting organized by some civilian politicians. It was held at a Chinese restaurant that Noriega, a devotee of Chinese food, particularly liked. At the meeting, Noriega told a long story about why the United States was attacking him. He struck a Latin David pose—and his Goliath was Adm. John Poindexter. According to Noriega's story, Poindexter had, in a December 1985 meeting, all but commanded Noriega to make Panama a jumping-off place for a U.S. invasion of Nicaragua. Noriega had resolutely refused to betray his Latin American brothers. Poindexter and other officials had been so enraged that they had started this political campaign against him.

The battle accelerated. Two nights later, Noriega appeared on "60 Minutes" with Mike Wallace, in tight close-up. He called Blandon a "Benedict Arnold" and said, "He who fights gets indicted." He offered a shorter version of "the Chinese restaurant speech," again blaming a vindictive U.S. government for the indictments. He scoffed at the accusations, producing letters of praise from the DEA. Why, he asked, if there was so much evidence, had he not been indicted before?

When Wallace asked Noriega what his annual salary was, Noriega seemed unable to comprehend the question. "Break, break, break," he ordered, trying to stop the cameras while he figured out what Wallace was getting at. In fact, Noriega had no idea that his annual legal income from the PDF was approximately $50,000.

Over the next few days, Noriega continued his offensive, condemning the United States for slandering him and Panama and demanding the departure of all U.S. troops. At a heavily guarded and nationally televised meeting in Santiago, the birthplace of Torrijos, he said that the crisis was "a problem for Panamanians, and we don't want manipulations by anyone from up north. We do not want the interference of any foreign power or the influence of any proconsul, because this is a people emerging from colonialism."

Things had not worked out as Tuturo Delvalle had hoped when he took the presidency. The indictments made his life even more miserable. He hated crises.

To lose money as president of Panama was unprecedented (except in the case of thrice-deposed Arnulfo Arias). But Delvalle was doing exactly that, and it was not a distinction that he—or his proud family—wanted in the history books. Tuturo made much of his wealth from sugar. From the late summer of 1987 on, however, there had been a suspension of the U.S. sugar quota. The legislation was particularly damaging for Delvalle, as it was intended to be. The aim was to sow dissension in the Noriega camp.

Nevertheless, as far as anyone could tell, Delvalle was as subservient with Noriega as ever, and he remained despised and unpopular in Panama. To the opposition, Delvalle was a cur. Just a few months after drunken revelers had driven him from the Union Club with ice cubes, two dozen members of his own synagogue congregation turned their backs to him at Yom Kippur services. There were prayers for the dead—and Hugo Spadafora's name was mentioned five times.

In private, Delvalle criticized Noriega and said he was doing everything he could to improve the situation. Did people think his job was easy? he would ask. He said he had implored Noriega to be less repressive.

Family and friends urged him to take action to avoid disgrace. He didn't want to go down as the most cowardly president in Panamanian history, they said.

Delvalle visited the nunciature on several occasions during the summer and autumn of 1987. Sipping one brandy after another and occasionally sobbing, he told the nuncio his problems. Hugo Spadafora's friend Pepe Pretto (who had taken refuge there from the PDF in July 1987) heard it all as he sat outside his room on the second floor, the same room Guillermo Sanchez Borbon had occupied, near the stairwell. To Pretto, who escaped to the United States later in 1987, Delvalle's anguish was mere self-pity.

As president, Delvalle had never been more than a sycophantic figurehead. Shortly after he took office from Barletta, he led a procession from the Presidencia to the Comandancia to pay homage to Noriega.

He also did Noriega's dirty work—without hesitation. "He signed the orders that allowed the army to kick the crap out of us," said Pierre Leignadier, vice president of the Chamber of Commerce. "On [Delvalle's] authority they shot us with birdshot, they gassed us, and they beat women and children. They did terrible things to people and even imprisoned some without charging them. Delvalle signed those orders and after the demonstrations were over, he publicly congratulated Noriega for restoring order."

"I always liked him," said Elliott Abrams. "I found him very personable and I liked him and I liked his wife. . . . We had a good relationship. But I thought of him as a weak man. I thought of him as a man who would never take on Noriega. I thought of him as kind of a playboy businessman, more interested in horses. Fate had thrust him into this job."

Delvalle was venal and trivial. After the indictments, when he talked to friends about his pain and anguish, many doubted that he felt guilty about his presidential performance. He harbored, they suspected, not a yearning for justice but a yearning for the sound of ice cubes in his glass and the camaraderie of his horse-breeding pals. He longed for easy hours.

On the night before the indictments were officially announced, Ambassador Davis decided to pay a call on the president. "I reminded him of the fact that he always said publicly and privately if Noriega ever got indicted for drugs or charged for drugs, he'd remove him from office," Davis said. "He said, 'Yes, well, I've been thinking of that,' and I said, 'Well, they're coming out tomorrow. You better get something ready.'"

In the first days after the indictments were announced, Delvalle assured his angry family, his contemptuous friends, and Ambassador Davis that he would honor his word. Just give him time, he said, let him speak to Noriega in private.

Delvalle clung to the hope that the indictments would force Noriega from power and get him off the hook. He seemed to believe that they were only the first in a series of steps planned by the U.S. government to rid Panama of Noriega.

Delvalle told Davis that he was trying to persuade Noriega that the indictments had created an intolerable situation. "The country can't have this hanging over its head, the chief being a drug trafficker," Delvalle claimed he told Noriega. He said that he told Noriega that he had to step aside if the crisis was to have any satisfactory conclusion. According to Delvalle, Noriega listened, his face blank.

In January 1988, Delvalle had traveled to Miami on a number of occasions, ostensibly to see his dentist but also to see U.S. officials. The Americans and the president of Panama had "exchanged views." On February 17, Delvalle went to Miami again, this time to meet with Elliott Abrams, and introduced a new idea: If Noriega were to step down, he asked, was it possible for the indictments to be erased? Abrams listened and made no commitments.

Delvalle raised another explosive subject, the possibility that he might sack Noriega. He told Abrams that he was thinking about going to Washington and taking that step in a speech to the Organization of American States (OAS).

"I told him that was a very bad idea," Abrams said. "It seemed to me that doing anything from outside Panama was a bad idea. The OAS was not a useful forum, I thought. And I urged him not to do that, and to go back to Panama. Not to do that meaning not to go to the OAS and fire Noriega."

According to Abrams, he did not believe Delvalle would ever fire Noriega. He says he reported this to George Shultz.

A few weeks after the Miami meeting, according to Abrams, Delvalle fired Noriega. In fact, it was no more than five days later that Delvalle took that very step, though he still hesitated to make it "official."

Wearing the presidential sash around his chest, Delvalle sat at a desk at the nunciature before a background contrived to resemble his own office. He stared straight ahead into a video camera. "There is no other alternative," Delvalle said, "but the use of the powers that the constitution gives me, to separate General Noriega from his high command and to entrust the leadership of the institution to the current chief of staff, Col. Marcos Justines." Delvalle said that he had asked Noriega to step aside while the charges against him were investigated. When Noriega refused, Delvalle said he had to fire him "to allow justice to continue an impartial course without pressures of any kind."

Then he took the cassette and continued to worry.

Four or five more days passed—Delvalle's "Hamlet period," as an American official called it. During this time, Delvalle continued to talk to Noriega about resignation. Noriega thought nothing of yelling at Delvalle when the mood struck, and he finally refused even to see his president when Delvalle asked for an appointment. Noriega was not thinking about resigning.

Delvalle waited, hoped, and squirmed as the people close to him urged action. During the interval, Delvalle's Florida conversation with Abrams hit the papers. "State Dept. Aide Hints at a Deal If Noriega Quits," read a *New York Times* headline. Gradually, a fuller description of the meeting and its consequences began to emerge. John K. Russell, a spokesman at the Justice Department, said that Abrams had told officials there that "he would seek to have the indictments dropped against Noriega if he left the country. We told him we would be against the idea."

On Thursday, February 25, the nuncio telephoned Ambassador Davis. He was concerned that Delvalle would hold on to his tape forever. "You know, [Delvalle] said he is going to do it at noon. I'm afraid if he doesn't do it at noon he won't do it at all," the nuncio said. The fear was justified. Delvalle remained silent through the noon television news broadcasts. In mid-afternoon, Ambassador Davis went to see him.

"What do you think I should do?" Delvalle asked Davis.

"Well, Mr. President, that's your decision," Davis told him. "You've got your reputation with the papal nuncio, with your family, and others. And now the word has gone around. You've either got to do it, or go on the air and make a statement on it anyway." Davis told him that he had to take some action—even if he just promised to get to the bottom of the charges against Noriega. "While I was there," Davis continued, "he called his son and said, 'Eric, get the word out and tell them to go on the air.'"

That afternoon at 5:00 p.m., Delvalle suddenly appeared on Panama City television screens just as the news was beginning. The tape played as planned; the firing was announced. As the people of Panama heard his announcement, Delvalle himself waited in the nunciature. He decided shortly afterward to return home.

People had poured into the streets. They were honking horns and waving flags and white handkerchiefs. They all believed that something important had actually happened. But unless Delvalle's declaration was followed by action from the United States—a military operation was a popular option among Panamanians—it would mean nothing.

The celebration lasted no more than half an hour. The PDF were soon out in force, and one after another the cheers were silenced by PDF tear gas.

Within hours of Delvalle's speech, Colonel Justines—the man Delvalle had named as Noriega's successor—said the president had acted "under pressure from the United States. I think it was a grave error."

Justines was as surprised by Delvalle's action as anyone else. Some said Delvalle never warned Justines at all. Others claimed he called Justines at ten minutes before five. According to this story, Justines had told him without hesitation that he was making a serious mistake.

So did the rest of the PDF. "None of us wants to be commander," said Colonel Macias, the chief of police. "Our commander is staying. The president is going. We all support Noriega."

Washington sent words. "We understand that President Delvalle today dismissed General Noriega from his position as commander of the Panama Defense Forces," said White House spokesman Marlin Fitzwater. "At this time we want to reiterate our unqualified support for civilian constitutional rule in Panama. There is but one legitimate, sovereign authority in Panama and that is the Panamanian people exercising their democratic right to vote and elect their leadership in a free society."

Gen. Fred Woerner watched in amazement. "What a hero to get," he said later, referring to Delvalle. "He becomes a U.S. hero. My God, how easily we forgot the role he played in removing Barletta and the fact that Barletta had gained office by a dishonest count to begin with."

Woerner thought U.S. policy was taking a strange path, which he traced: "The U.S. supports the fraudulent election of Barletta. The U.S. condemns the fraudulent removal of Barletta by Delvalle. The U.S. recognizes the legitimacy of Delvalle only when he is removed by Noriega." Woerner wondered where "policy" might lurch next.

In the hours after the announcement, Delvalle's ranch-style house became a magnet for members of the opposition, journalists, priests, and diplomats. What was going to happen next? That was the question. "Nothing" was the answer. Or so it appeared as the evening wore on and drink trays appeared. Delvalle mingled with his guests while the riot police kept watch outside.

Noriega shut down the media. Within hours, stations not carrying PDF loyalty pledges were broadcasting continuous music. Everyone was waiting for the United States to intervene. But Washington policymakers were also waiting. Later it became clear that many believed that Delvalle's action would touch off a popular uprising.

Delvalle was relaxed. "I have old friends who have come back to me," he said, referring to the opposition members who had come to his house. "I am very calm because I have had to make a very difficult decision having to do with a person with whom I have worked for nearly two years with a great deal of respect and consideration."

As that odd evening wore on, guests realized that only two of the five telephone lines in Delvalle's house were working. New arrivals brought the news of the press shutdown. "I'm staying as long as I am wanted," Ambassador Davis told a reporter. "My presence here is to show my support for the government, because we always have supported the civilian government and we are going to continue doing so."

There was talk that Delvalle would seek refuge in the nunciature, but he denied it. "I am still the president of Panama and I don't see why I have to leave my home," Delvalle said. "I will fight it out here because there is no reason why I should be removed. The international community will react strongly against the Panama Defense Forces. . . ."

Noriega called a meeting of the national assembly. By 1:00 A.M. Friday, just eight hours after the tape had appeared on television, the assembly had voted to sack Delvalle and replace him with Manuel Solis Palma, the education minister. Solis Palma accepted with the same speed Delvalle had demonstrated twenty-nine months earlier.

7

Noriega Strikes Back

FEBRUARY 1988–MAY 1988

ON Friday, February 26, President Delvalle appointed Gabriel Lewis Panama's roving ambassador and Jose Blandon ambassador to the U.N. He gave both permission to act in his name as they saw fit. As far as he was concerned, he now had done what he could. Others had to get to work. The night before, Noriega's allies in the national assembly had accused Delvalle of conspiring "to permit the U.S. government to intervene in the internal affairs of Panama."

Delvalle awaited the intervention. Noriega, determined not to repeat old mistakes, set out to prevent Delvalle from making his house a dissident headquarters as Diaz Herrera had done. PDF roadblocks sealed off the neighborhood. Police turned Ambassador Davis away when he and a visiting U.S. congressman tried to visit.

At dawn Saturday, Delvalle left his house by the back door and climbed over a low fence to his neighbor's garden. From there he made his way to a waiting car and a hideout where friends were waiting. Quickly, he telephoned his wife, Mariela, to say he was safe. At about 6:30 A.M., four men—two civilians, two in uniform—banged on his door and told Mariela that her husband must leave Panama by noon. The family was obviously in danger.

A few hours later, Susan Davis and a Panamanian friend pulled up at the Delvalles' in a jeep. The ambassador's daughter told reporters and the PDF guards at the gate that Mrs. Delvalle would make a statement soon. Minutes later, the two emerged from the house carrying two large bundles of clothes which concealed the tiny First Lady of Panama. The three then rushed to the U.S. ambassador's residence, where eleven refugees had settled in by the afternoon. The group included Delvalle's daughter, servants, and Gabriel Lewis's three sons. Their presence at the residence reflected the ambassador's personal, unofficial decision.

The ambassador's residence was large (17,000 square feet, according to Davis, a veteran real estate man) but the refugees were still crowded. There were other complications: Two of the guests were in the midst of a divorce.

President Delvalle waited at a friend's house not far from a U.S. base. "I am going to stay here and stick it out," he told ABC television, which had no trouble finding him. It was obvious that Noriega could seize him any time he wanted.

According to Noriega's spokesman, no one was looking for Delvalle. He was not charged with anything and was free to return to his house whenever he wanted. He wasn't the president anymore but was free to join Barletta and the other "formers" in comfortable retirement. The presidents sacked by the military were known as the "Kleenex presidents." All were disposable.

Delvalle and Reagan both issued statements rejecting the idea of military action. But very shortly afterward, Delvalle changed his tune, seeming to ask for an invasion. "All imaginable pressures," he said, "no matter how dramatic they may seem, should be taken if we want to have a democracy in Panama." Many Panamanians, who believed wrongly that they were watching a scenario unfold, anticipated the arrival of U.S. troops.

———

Gabriel Lewis now represented the man he called the legal president of Panama. But Lewis wasn't Delvalle's only public supporter; the opposition cause was now one of Washington's most popular. Praise for Delvalle flowed from the White House, State Department, and Congress, and Lewis set about exploiting the circumstances.

Because of Washington's ostensible support, many Panamanians now felt they could intensify the anti-Noriega campaign.

They were determined to transform Washington's signals into action.

On the day Delvalle had gone into hiding, Gabriel Lewis hired Washington lawyer William D. Rogers to represent the Delvalle government. Rogers, a partner at the powerful firm of Arnold & Porter, knew the issues and the personalities. He and Gabriel Lewis had been friends since the treaty negotiations in the 1970s. Rogers had managed the Alliance for Progress for President Kennedy and served as assistant secretary of state for interAmerican relations and under-secretary of state for economic affairs in the Ford administration. He was astute, trusted, and bipartisan. Very quickly, he and Delvalle's supporters drew up a plan. They were confident that their scenario, which required prompt White House action, would be effective.

What followed were the first shots in what was envisioned as a short and brutal economic war aimed at the quick destruction of Panama's economy. According to the plan, the economy would be resuscitated with U.S. help after Noriega lost control.

Rogers's first task was to cut off Panama's cash. On March 1, Juan Sosa, Panama's U.S. ambassador, who had cast his lot with Delvalle, told the press that the Noriega regime had no diplomatic or financial legitimacy.

Rogers decided his next move would be to bolster Delvalle's claim to legitimacy in court. With a team of twenty lawyers, he drafted a presidential proclamation that Delvalle approved over the phone and Sosa read at a press conference. It asserted the constitutionality of the Delvalle presidency and denounced what it claimed was the illegality of the Noriega regime. The proclamation ran in its entirety in the *Wall Street Journal*.

Rogers then moved quickly to seize control of the Panamanian government's U.S. bank accounts. Close to $40 million in cash was at stake and Noriega needed it to meet the government and PDF payrolls. Over the signature of Ambassador Sosa, letters went out to ten banks in Boston, New York, and Miami. They were informed that business with the Republic of Panama should be conducted through him. Noriega's representatives, he said, had no claim to the money.

Panama's economy began to crumble. On March 4, Panamanian banks closed and remained closed until April 18, when they reopened with limited services. There were sporadic strikes and many shops and businesses also closed.

The scenario now called for a series of blows to finish off the

Noriega regime. Only the Reagan administration itself could order U.S. companies and individuals to withhold tax payments and other fees owed to Panama. Only the administration had the power to seal all economic escape routes. It could, for example, declare a total trade embargo or take steps to cut the flow of around $120 million monthly from SOUTHCOM, the Panama Canal Commission, and other offices into the Panamanian economy immediately. It could dispatch a messenger of doom to Noriega—perhaps Nestor Sanchez or Daniel Murphy—to kiss Noriega good-bye.

But nothing, beyond gestures, happened. The State Department said that it regarded Delvalle as the president and Elliott Abrams gave him—and the opposition's financial maneuvers—full support. "If the government of President Delvalle says to American banks, 'Don't pay money to Noriega,' then all those banks are going to come to the State Department and say, 'Who's got the authority here? Noriega or Delvalle?' We're going to answer that question: Delvalle is president of Panama," said Abrams.

But there was still no consensus within the administration. In one conclave, according to Abrams, CIA director William Webster, ignoring Delvalle, suggested that the United States could get along very well with the man Noriega had put in office. "Panama's new president, Solis Palma, is not a bad fellow. . . . He is a typical upper-class Panamanian. He's not some kind of leftist or something," Webster said.

"What do you mean 'Panama's new president'?" a State Department representative asked. "Panama's president has not changed. There has been no election in Panama. We recognize President Delvalle. [Solis Palma] is not Panama's new president."

Abrams wanted a "command decision" from Reagan to resolve the situation. "You just had endless pulling and hauling and a refusal by the president to settle this dispute," he said.

Reagan had shown himself capable of action earlier in a bitter battle between the State and Defense departments. In the days after Delvalle's dismissal of Noriega, there was the question of whether General Woerner should continue to meet with Noriega. George Shultz wanted to end all contact, but Defense Secretary Frank Carlucci maintained that private conversations would serve to better inform everyone in Washington. Shultz countered that Noriega was no longer commander in chief, and if he wasn't commander in chief, why should Woerner see him?

The judgment came quickly. "[Reagan] ruled in favor of

Shultz and I had a gag put on me," said Woerner. "There was no communiqué to Noriega on this at all. I just stopped talking to him and his attempts to talk to me just tapered off."

On March 11, Reagan finally took punitive economic action, diverting monthly payments from the Panama Canal Commission to Noriega into an escrow account. He also stripped Panama of all trade preferences previously guaranteed under the Generalized System of Preference and the Caribbean Basin Initiative. The presidential action seemed mighty indeed—or at least that was the intended spin on the story. In fact, monthly payments ran to only $6.5 million and the March bill had already been paid. The action did not hurt Noriega.

Eleven days had passed since the first shot in the economic war, and according to the plan, the economy was supposed to be dead. But it was still only dying and the people were suffering from the fallout.

Noriega was in trouble, if not completely finished. He was almost out of cash and another PDF payday was approaching. By mid-March, he had failed to pay 140,000 government workers. Many, including electrical workers, went on strike. To help, the government began to distribute "dignity bags," $16 worth of grocery staples, available at a slight discount, to government employees. They had little effect. There was intermittent street warfare; barricades were burned. People believed that Noriega's end was near. In Washington, there was talk of tougher economic sanctions as George Shultz appealed to the PDF to sack Noriega.

Noriega, however, had already laid the groundwork for a fight. In early March, he had dispatched his trusted colleague Maj. Augusto Villalaz, the PDF's senior pilot (he had flown Hugo Spadafora to Darien province in 1969), to Cuba where, courtesy of Fidel Castro, he picked up sixteen tons of weapons. Noriega had placed the weapons in secret caches around Panama City and the countryside. He was prepared.

It was a smart move; there was turmoil inside the PDF. Beginning around March 10, some twenty officers planned a coup against Noriega, led by none other than Col. Leonidas Macias, the chief of police who had harassed Deborah DeMoss and who had been among Noriega's most outspoken defenders. Another co-conspirator was Major Villalaz himself.

Noriega learned of the conspiracy very shortly after it was hatched, thanks to his extraordinary network of *sapos*. They learned that the actual move was scheduled for Wednesday, March 16.

On that day striking electrical workers barricaded the streets and new strikes flared. Dockworkers, teachers, even doctors who had gone unpaid walked out. Power cuts silenced radio and television, garbage dumpsters burned on street corners. Looting was sporadic. Apprehension and anticipation grew: Perhaps Noriega was gone, or dead. Rumors of gunfire inside the Comandancia filled the city. It was said that there were many corpses.

Noriega watched as if he had written the script. At 6:30 A.M. on March 16, Macias and the others assigned to seize Noriega walked into a trap. Noriega loyalists ushered some of the plotters into a weapons room with vault-like doors that were slammed shut. Later, Noriega posed for the press on a broad outdoor staircase under his office—smiling and laughing, safe and secure with PDF loyalists. "They were kisses," he shouted to questions about the gunfire and blew some more to the crowd.

In a communiqué that day, Noriega said that most of the PDF members involved in the coup attempt attended "specialization courses in different military installations in the United States, where they were influenced and involved in the betrayal of their oath to the Institution and the Fatherland."

Macias was one of those captured, but Major Villalaz and a few others managed to reach U.S. bases. Villalaz made headlines almost immediately with the news of Noriega's secret arms caches in Panama City—and the fact that they came from Castro.

The PDF, on which Noriega depended for survival, had withstood an unprecedented trauma. Noriega quickly moved to make repairs, making it clear that the organization had entered a new era. He also took action against the conspirators. Reprisals inside the military had been rare in Panama's past. Now the traitors' families told stories of brutal interrogation and macabre torture at the Coiba Island prison where the rebels were being held. Some guards, it was reported, wrapped the prisoners in U.S. flags before beating them.

In Panama City, Noriega handed out 104 promotions to the loyalists and fired some officers he had come to distrust. Increasingly, he made loyalty and complicity the only standards. The defection of old friends such as Macias made everyone suspicious of everyone else. It had never been this way before.

Noriega revealed his intentions in odd ways. One day after the coup attempt, he gathered his remaining general staff in his office and called for a hen. In one account Noriega tore her head off with his hands. In another he bit it off and spit it out, smiling.

Noriega moved aggressively against his domestic opponents. On Wednesday, March 23, hundreds of mourners had crowded the Christo Rey church to hear Father Villanueva condemn Noriega at the funeral of Alcibiades Vasquez Ojo, a young man killed by PDF birdshot, the fourth such fatality since June 1987. It was a rare slip-up by the well-trained police, who were under strict orders to prevent fatalities—and therefore headlines.

Just before the 11:00 mass the following Sunday, Noriega's *sapos* assaulted a woman distributing anti-Noriega leaflets outside the church, smashed car windows, fired pistols, and roughed up journalists. Father Villanueva instructed his congregation to pray and sing louder to drown out the gunfire.

The international press, having returned to Panama in force, were headquartered at the Marriott, where opposition politicians and *civilistas* also gathered. One day, as an opposition organizer finished preparations for a press conference, the PDF charged into the hotel, beating and arresting Panamanians and foreign journalists and seizing the journalists' files and gear.

In early April, reporter Lally Weymouth returned to Panama and found Noriega jumpy. He was no longer talking about friendship with the United States, as he had six months earlier, and he resented interview attempts. "Sitting at a table with one of his cabinet ministers, a top military aide and a visiting reporter, he rings a gold bell and orders tea only for himself. In addition to drinking tea, he paces around the room, appearing unable or unwilling to concentrate or to sit still," Weymouth wrote.

In one encounter, in Noriega's office, she found him in camouflage fatigues with a girlfriend, acting like a "caged tiger." Weymouth asked him when he was leaving and Noriega replied, "I am leaving. I've got to go." Weymouth asked again, when?

"At what time?" Noriega snapped, rising from his chair. "At what minute? Please! This is a Panamanian problem, not an American problem. The State Department wants to create a Vietnam in Panama, to have U.S. troops confront the Panamanians. It's not Reagan—it's the State Department. If that happens, American mothers are going to see their sons fighting in a nation without necessity."

When Weymouth mentioned the domestic opposition, Noriega grew louder and more "visibly angry." He again recalled the many services he had provided the United States and told Weymouth that he had assisted in the capture of gangster Meyer Lansky, a fugitive in Israel and Argentina before he was seized.

Weymouth asked if he felt the CIA and his friends had betrayed him. "Between countries you have no friendship, only convenience," he said.

When Weymouth returned to the subject of his departure, Noriega was not as testy. "Everything in life is being born and then you disappear. It's also the law of institutions. You go up, you perform, and when everything is ready . . . For me, it is very easy to wash my hands and be tranquil. The problem is my country's dignity."

Noriega began an extraordinary comeback in the last week of March, just as Elliott Abrams declared that he was "hanging on by his fingernails." Even the president had been gloating about his downfall. Reagan had said the Dominican Republic was "not far enough" when discussions arose about asylum for the general.

They were too confident and chose not to take any of the powerful steps (a complete trade embargo, for example) that might have pushed Noriega over the edge. There was talk, but only talk, about "sanctions," a word with ambiguous meanings. There was also discussion of a plan to forbid Americans and American companies in Panama to pay taxes or other fees, including utility bills.

Treasury Department officials opposed the plan, arguing that such measures jeopardized all U.S. foreign investment. They said that sanctions at this point, so long after the cash crisis had started, would be particularly counterproductive and would further damage the already collapsing mainstream economy without hurting Noriega. Moreover, Noriega could make life very difficult and dangerous for Americans who obeyed the regulations. Americans and Panamanian businessmen in the opposition echoed these arguments. They could see that the proposed sanctions—if they were ever declared—would be purely symbolic. They did not want to be symbols.

The president himself was detached and apparently amused by the spectacle. At the Gridiron dinner on March 26, Reagan brought down the house when he mentioned complaints about infrequent press conferences. He asked his audience who they thought had been giving Delvalle tips about hiding.

Noriega, however, was dead serious, listening to the advice of a team of talented economists, including Minister of Commerce Mario Rognoni, an articulate spokesman who had become a regular on ABC's "Nightline." The specialists pointed out to him that, despite the tough talk, the United States was still pouring millions of dollars a month into the economy. U.S. policy, as usual, was long on bombast and short on action. Rognoni and the others proved themselves every bit as skilled at economic warfare as their opponents in Washington. They observed how the people reacted to the cash crisis, adopted their own tactics, and managed to increase the cash supply greatly by creating a new, negotiable currency. The currency was the government paycheck, and its transformation into a supplemental cash supply happened almost by accident.

When the economic crisis had begun, the government had demanded cash for utility bills, taxes, and other government payments. But they quickly assured all government employees that their paychecks were acceptable in all government transactions, and even at markets, dry cleaners, and other establishments that catered exclusively to the PDF.

Markets sprang up spontaneously on sidewalks outside certain government offices, especially branches of IRHE (the government-controlled utility), where people had to pay their bills. A few middle-class *civilistas* approached government workers and offered to buy their paychecks with cash. Then, after these *civilistas* had paid their utility bills by submitting the signed-over paychecks, they boasted that they had outsmarted the government. They had, they told friends, given money directly to the lower-middle-class government workers—and a worthless piece of paper to the government. For a very short time, buying government paychecks became a political fad. Some Panamanians even tried to buy the checks in volume until they were stopped. In other words, certain Noriega opponents had actually invested in his virtually worthless and easy-to-print government paychecks.

At the same time, a popular string of grocery stores began accepting the paychecks as currency. Even more significantly, several U.S. companies operating in Panama told their employees that they would cash the paychecks. Very quickly, the government began paying employees with multiple checks, which paralleled the dollar currency. Thus a person earning $100 might receive ten $10 checks, or even a hundred $1 checks.

Also in late March, Noriega got some good news. Three American companies with large operations in Panama (Texaco, Eastern Airlines, and Chiriqui Land Co., a United Brands subsidiary) made early tax payments of $3 million to Noriega. The cash itself was welcome but so was the gesture. The American executives voted for their own survival, but their decision was also a powerful verification of the continuing reality of the Noriega regime. Shultz, Abrams, and Ambassador Davis might claim that Noriega was finished. But in the real world, it was still impossible not to "recognize" Noriega.

In political terms, Noriega challenged and perhaps surpassed Muammar Qaddafi in international villainy. His continued presence in power was the political equivalent of defeat in the war on drugs. And despite the political embarrassment, there was no indication that the Reagan administration would ever resolve its ambivalent feelings about Noriega. There were many reasons. There were any number of issues where the State and Defense departments were at loggerheads and Reagan chose not to take presidential action. And in the overall scheme of things, Panama was not that important. The canal was still operating and U.S. bases performed their functions. Everything else was ultimately irrelevant.

On April 8, despite warnings, Reagan made the move that American and Panamanian businessmen and Treasury Department officials had most feared. He announced that the United States would impose economic sanctions on Panama. Reagan's aides portrayed the announcement as resolute action, and to a large extent that was the way the story played in the media. After all, there were all the trappings of dramatic action. Reagan issued an Executive Order and invoked the International Emergency Economic Powers Act (IEEPA), which certainly suggested it was urgent business.

But sanctions had become a Washington-style mantra, as ineffective as Diaz Herrera's "Rama, Rama, Rama" chant. And these particular sanctions lacked teeth. They seemed to have been chosen for their lack of value. To the Panamanian opposition, it was now clear that Noriega was low on the administration's list of priorities. Enforcement of the sanctions, for example, fell to the Office of Foreign Assets Control (OFAC) at the Treasury Department. The person at OFAC assigned to the Panama case was the same person who enforced the sanctions against Nicaragua. The administration's economic "war" against Noriega could not possibly succeed, waged as it was by a single individual with other responsibilities. Treasury Department officials who had argued against the sanctions did not disguise their distaste for the project. They pointed out that Reagan's emergency order made the U.S.

Treasury Department the equivalent of Delvalle's tax collector.

Finally, on April 29, the Treasury Department made an announcement. The regulations designed to implement the presidential sanctions were still not ready though the exemptions to those regulations were. The spokesperson announced a long list.

Thanks to the exemptions announced and those that came later, Noriega was able to get about half of what otherwise would have been denied to him. On May 10, the regulations were finally ready, but there was more hesitation. The sanctions finally became effective on June 3, 1988.

By then, the mainstream Panamanian economy was in a deep depression. Between February and June, Panama's overall economic activity fell by 50 percent, bringing it to a lower level than the U.S. economy had reached during the Depression. Some industries, like construction, were all but wiped out. Half-finished skyscrapers became ghostly fixtures on the Panama City skyline. Unemployment was 40 percent and climbing.

An American official summarized events this way: "We have ruined a healthy capitalist economy, weakened the pro-American middle class, and created the conditions in Panama for growing Communist influence. You've got to give yourself credit: That's a hell of an achievement for diplomacy."

Communists had always been rare in Panama, a fact that made the official's remark all the more damning. Fighting Communist influence in the region had been a U.S. preoccupation for decades. And it had been Noriega's helpfulness in those battles that had made him so important to the United States in the first place.

In late March and early April, Delvalle—the tired puppet on whom the State Department based its "policy"—was making noise, threatening to resign. "What good is it to be the legitimate president of Panama if he can't even walk on the street?" a friend asked. Angry and frustrated, Delvalle wanted the United States to invade Panama. According to friends, he had expected the United States to send an international force, in the manner of the Grenada invasion, to restore him to power. There had never been a firm promise, but he felt let down.

In Panama, the government papers mocked Delvalle. One story said that he traveled disguised as a woman. Delvalle himself told an interviewer that he moved among half a dozen safe houses, always at night and always hiding in the backseats of cars. In Washington, Ambassador Sosa told reporters that Delvalle, as president, granted the United States the right to take "any action" to remove Noriega. Sosa's personal preference was a commando raid.

Congressional pressure for action was strong with Senator Alfonse D'Amato still weighing in as one of Noriega's most vocal enemies in the Senate. After a stormy phone conversation in the last week of March, Secretary of Defense Frank Carlucci wrote the senator a letter, saying he had "been reflecting on your emotion-charged telephone call." D'Amato had, Carlucci wrote, "charged that I and the Joint Chiefs of Staff are 'cowards' and that we are 'supporting a drug dealer.' I hope you can indicate to me that you, in fact, did not mean [the charges] as stated."

D'Amato issued a statement saying, "I did not call Carlucci a coward. My recollection of the conversation was that [I said] the inaction would be perceived as cowardly." Later, D'Amato released a letter to Carlucci that stated, "I certainly do not believe that the Joint Chiefs of Staff are cowards. There is no doubt, however, that the lack of U.S. action in Panama has made us appear weak in many people's eyes."

It was in this political climate that Elliott Abrams suggested for the first time that U.S. military forces be used to oust Noriega. Abrams suggested a commando raid to pluck Noriega up and deliver him to justice in the United States. He also proposed that two U.S. combat brigades, totalling 6,000 soldiers, be sent to Panama. Their mission—as far as his description went—would be to surround the U.S. base where Delvalle would stay after he emerged from hiding. The presence of the brigades would demonstrate that the United States backed Delvalle. Abrams said his two-pronged plan would solve the problem.

But the Pentagon raised practical issues. There were 46,000 U.S. citizens (6,000 of them military dependents) living in or near the capital. Shouldn't those Americans be relocated before the shooting started? Adm. John Howe, an aide to Adm. William Crowe, chairman of the Joint Chiefs of Staff, pointed out the danger of hostage-taking by the PDF. He suggested that military dependents living in the city be moved to the bases.

"Tell us about that," Abrams said. "It's not a crazy idea. How long is it going to take?"

Howe replied that he would have an answer at the next weekly meeting, and he reported then that the evacuation would take six months. All the commercial moving companies were booked solid. He had checked.

Abrams thought Howe's answer "unbelievable" and was outraged at the Pentagon's attitude. "They were just throwing in the kitchen sink in an effort to tell you that you couldn't confront Noriega," he stated. "They were stonewalling, they were not saying no. They were doing it the way the Pentagon always does it. One understands this, that from a PR point of view, they don't want to do anything that is unpopular. And one understands that they are the guys that have to send out the telegrams that say, 'Your son was killed.' So one has to give them that. On the other hand, the way they do that is with these ludicrous arguments. They stonewall. They don't say, 'We will not do this. Let's go to the president and let's fight it out.' They just set impossible preconditions."

Abrams cited the "Vietnam syndrome" and concluded that the Pentagon was afraid of a fight. "They would say, 'What if the PDF attacks the bases? What if he makes it impossible to function? What if they put traffic lights and traffic checks and ID checks in seventy different places? We have 10,000 soldiers in Panama. A certain percentage of them get drunk every night. What if they start making trouble? They can make life impossible. On a second level they can attack. They can shoot at you, they can attack the bases physically.' "

But Abrams had no answer to the questions or, in the opinion of the Pentagon officers, any real plan beyond picking a fight and trusting that it would end somehow with Noriega gone. Any of Abrams's ideas would almost inevitably produce casualties, and those flag-draped coffins on the nightly news would propel the confrontation to a more severe and unmanageable level. Americans could be evacuated very quickly, as Howe well knew, but he also knew that an evacuation might prompt Noriega to take hostages.

While Abrams tried to prove he was the toughest man in Washington, the military men were painting him as the dumbest. "They've got some ideas that would make your hair stand on end," a Defense Department official told the *Wall Street Journal* after a White House meeting where Abrams, backed by Shultz, had outlined his ideas. Leaks from anonymous Pentagon officials proliferated. Two of the kinder descriptions of Abrams's plans that got into print were "harebrained" and "cockamamy."

Quite apart from the inevitable bloodshed, and the possibility that Noriega might survive anything short of a full invasion, there were base treaties with the Philippines, Turkey, Greece, and Spain to consider. All would have to be renegotiated in the future. If the United States used its Panama bases to attack the host country's government, these negotiations would be even more difficult.

As for the commando raid plan, many officers were contemptuous of its Rambo-ism, to say nothing of its illegality. "Kidnapping is a crime," one officer asserted. "Under what international law would you have us do that?" Abrams accused the Pentagon of "engaging in dangerously irresponsible behavior" by leaking his plans.

The Pentagon officers thought it imperative to maintain a media offensive against Abrams's schemes lest the White House carelessly approve one. But Abrams's inability to reply to any of their questions led them to believe that he was just playing politics anyway.

Abrams had been eager to claim the praise when it appeared that Noriega would be driven from power. But his ineptitude had helped Noriega survive. Now he was trying to shift blame for Noriega's continued presence onto the military by insisting that the solution was military action. The issue was the lack of military action. At the Pentagon, his machinations were transparent. Abrams fit a Washington tradition long feared by the military: the "field marshal," a civilian policymaker of minimal competence who enthused about violence.

White House policymakers knew they were not scaring Noriega with occasional references to "the military option," as officials usually called it. "I kept telling them you cannot bluff Noriega," Woerner said. He believed such "posturing" dangerous. "You have to be prepared to intervene militarily if your posturing is to be credible and effective. And since I didn't believe in military intervention for this issue at that stage of the game, I believed that the posturing was not productive."

Even so, the talk in Washington got tougher. On March 29, Marlin Fitzwater had said the United States was "willing to take a look at all the hard options." In real life, U.S. actions had made U.S. citizens more vulnerable. More and more Americans were being harassed by the PDF.

Reagan had ruled out military action firmly, yet the political pressures finally led to the dispatch of some 1,300 more troops on April 1. Among them were 500 M.P.s, 300 marines, a helicopter squadron, 150 airmen, and 6 police dogs with 12 handlers. Their mission was to protect U.S. citizens. But since they were assigned amid war whoops and talk of "hard options," their assignment to Panama inflamed tensions and made life even more dangerous for Americans.

The troops arrived on Wednesday, April 6. Less than a week later, the first American died. Cpl. Ricardo Villahermosa, USMC, twenty-five, from Santurce, Puerto Rico, was killed by another marine in a seven-shot crossfire between two parts of the same patrol. The marines had been searching for a possible intruder in the heavy jungle that surrounded a giant fuel tank farm near Howard Air Force Base.

The next night, nearly a hundred marines fired automatic weapons, mortars, and illumination flares for two hours in dense jungle near another tank farm a few miles away. The marines insisted they had seen furtive figures in dark uniforms, but there was some doubt about whether there was actually anyone there at all. No casualties were reported. "It shows that they are even afraid of palm trees," Noriega joked. He told an Austrian television interviewer that he hoped the Americans went on killing each other. A SOUTHCOM information officer, pressed to account for what had happened, said, "At this point in time, we don't categorically rule anything out."

A few days later, Panamanian and American papers were filled with accounts of the slapstick encounter between U.S. forces and a nest of "Africanized" or "killer" bees. The U.S. forces destroyed the bees but not before they had put eight GIs and two marines in the hospital. The government papers said it was proof that even the insects of Panama were against the U.S. military pressure. Talk of commando raids ebbed.

———

As time went on, Noriega grew stronger, in large part by defying American predictions of his doom. "The psychology and the momentum were changing," Elliott Abrams said, when describing the administration's relations with Panama in April 1988. "It looked as if, unbelievably enough, Noriega was going to beat the gringos. They didn't, oddly enough, run Panama anymore."

Noriega had understood that for some time. Now events—and Abrams—had given him a chance to prove it. But the stronger Noriega grew, the more imperative his departure for the United States became. He was a failure for the administration and could continue to cause embarrassment.

During April, Noriega and his associates began hinting to journalists that he would soon release some information to embarrass the Reagan administration. He wanted to hint about what he knew and how talkative he could be, so he instructed subordinates to tease journalists with promises of information. Nothing concrete was ever forthcoming.

Still, the promises drew attention to Noriega's legendary archives, his life's work. Included were old black and white movies, audio- and videotapes, photographs and documents from his lifetime as an intelligence agent. He had used the best surveillance and eavesdropping equipment available. Any meeting, any encounter, any tryst where he had access was recorded on video- or audiocassette. Bush's 1983 meeting with Noriega had probably been recorded. Oliver North's request, in Noriega's office, for help with the Contras was also doubtless on file.

Noriega had everything from the financial records of the Panamanian front companies used by North and Maj. Gen. Richard Secord (USAF, Ret.), North's partner in the secret Contra supply operation, to recordings of "everybody's orgasms, and all their orgasms" (as a woman who kept company with him in the early 1980s said). What stories Noriega could tell. But could he blackmail important U.S. officials? He wanted them to believe that he could. A circumspect former CIA officer thought before answering that question, and said: "Blackmail? No. Leverage? Yes." And Blandon commented that Noriega had the power to make "a headline a day" in the U.S. papers.

Noriega's potential talkativeness added pressure to the talks that had been taking place since March between State Department officials, Noriega representatives, and sometimes Noriega himself.

The United States took a tough negotiating position based on three main points: Noriega had to step down and leave Panama; there was no chance of dropping the indictments; and the PDF would withdraw from political life under the supervision of President Delvalle.

Washington officials said that the purpose of the talks was to introduce Noriega to the real world. The challenge was to convince him that his time was up. U.S. negotiators reminded him that if there had been one coup attempt there could be another: He might die in the next one. On the other hand, he could leave now, with his money. Just leave. They didn't understand how Noriega could fail to grasp the obvious. Abrams seemed irked by Noriega's obtuseness. "The only way this crisis is going to end is when Noriega leaves."

The talks floundered but the Panamanians and American officials remained in touch. The administration was obviously not trying to reduce tensions; the Americans wanted more confrontation. "I don't want to rule anything out, because I want Noriega to have some sleepless nights," said Abrams.

During one day-long negotiating session, the U.S. team brought along a psychiatrist to observe Noriega, who sat hunched and silent. He appeared to be scared. After a short lunch break, he returned visibly angry, aggressive, insulting, and obstreperous. Some officials thought his postbreak behavior was the result of lunchtime snorting, but though he drank copiously, Noriega used cocaine sparingly.

The mood swing was typical. U.S. officials were well aware that Noriega loved the negotiating process because it gave him a chance to play-act and to sow confusion among his adversaries. It was foolish to expect him to take the negotiations seriously. During this time he sometimes gave machete-waving speeches and appeared on television in front of posters proclaiming "Get Out Yankee Dogs."

Noriega also pretended to launch plans with the papal nuncio and other foreign diplomats. He spoke about going to Spain, whose government might offer asylum if the United States promised not to seek extradition. But he wanted to be able to return to Panama as soon and as often as possible with immunity from prosecution. He wanted also to be able to name his successor in the PDF before he retired. And he wanted to make sure that his president, Solis Palma, would not be replaced. "This proposal is like getting the fox out of the hen house, then giving him quarters next door," said Marlin Fitzwater in late March.

On April 28, Noriega won the right to live next door to the hen house. The administration agreed that if Noriega retired he could stay in Panama, and Solis Palma could remain as president. "Our policy is that General Noriega must go, which means leave power. We've talked about that a number of times. We have said we prefer him to leave Panama, but the policy issue is to leave power," said Fitzwater.

Now the task became an attempt to persuade Noriega to resign. The process was still called negotiation, but it was increasingly a one-sided affair. Washington offered what Noriega had already proposed. The Panamanian opposition had again become irrelevant.

"They panicked in the United States," said Gabriel Lewis. "The U.S. should consult us before closing a deal about the fate of our country."

The decision to allow Noriega to remain in Panama dismayed Shultz, who went to the White House to protest to the president. Reagan, who had specifically instructed the negotiators to make the concession, listened intently to his secretary of state's protests and promptly changed his mind. Of course Noriega had to leave Panama, Reagan told Shultz. "The president, being the president, was surprised to discover what his own people were saying," said a State Department official.

Noriega immediately pressed for more concessions. He wanted the proposed sanctions (still not in effect) lifted and demanded that the United States make reparations for the damage its policies had inflicted on Panama's economy. He wanted a big say in any new government. He wanted the U.S. troop presence in Panama reduced. And if he was going to retire, he wanted a lavish ceremony on August 12, the anniversary of his becoming commander in chief. Then he would hand the command of the PDF to whomever he wanted. All these demands were now on the table, together with his most important request: He demanded that the Reagan administration drop the indictments against him. All other matters were secondary.

For the Reagan administration, the situation was simple to assess. If Reagan dropped the indictments, he and his administration could expect to be accused of hypocrisy. But if the indictments were dropped, it was almost certain, they believed, that Noriega would quit.

On May 11, the White House announced that Reagan would move to erase the indictments if Noriega stepped down. This was the only "command decision" (Elliott Abrams's term) that Reagan made on Panama during all the time he was president.

As expected, there were questions. Why was the administration so willing to tamper with American justice for Noriega? Why were they so eager to get rid of him? Was this an example of the war on drugs? There were editorials, speeches in Congress, press conferences.

Noriega had forced an extraordinary concession from his opponent and given absolutely nothing in return, and the United

States had no choice but to continue the process. Just three days after the White House announcement about the indictments, Noriega put new ideas on the table. He wanted to be able to run for president in 1989. He wanted guarantees that the next administration in Washington would honor the promises made by the Reagan administration. One of Noriega's lawyers floated a story that Noriega might receive a presidential pardon from Reagan.

For Noriega, the negotiations were a way to jeer at his enemies and demonstrate to his fellow PDF officers that he, and they, had nothing to fear from the United States. He had the gringos begging—an unprecedented achievement in Panama. One day he announced that the talks had collapsed. "Everything fell apart, everything fell apart," he told reporters. Then he resumed the talks with no further explanation.

After much discussion, Noriega finally agreed on May 24 to leave Panama—but he would depart only after an August 12 retirement ceremony. He wanted to return to Panama at Christmastime 1988 for a visit and then come back full time after the May 1989 presidential election. It was still possible that Noriega could be a candidate in that election. In any case, with Solis Palma remaining in the presidency, Noriega would maintain control over all the electoral machinery. Delvalle, according to the negotiated settlement, would remain in hiding. U.S. officials were optimistic that Noriega would agree to the package for the simple reason that he had dictated it. Noriega had committed to little more than a leave of absence, a holiday from power.

The U.S. negotiators began to work with a self-imposed May 25 deadline for signing the agreement that would govern Noriega's departure. That was the day when Reagan and Shultz were to begin their journey to Moscow, and a rendezvous with Mikhail Gorbachev. The administration wanted the Panama problem settled.

Sometimes Noriega sat in on the continuing talks—and sometimes he didn't. But he took them all very casually. Rognoni, the minister of commerce and economic wizard, was amused at all the attention the Washington press was giving the reported Noriega "deal." "There is no deal," he told any journalist who inquired.

On May 25, the negotiators said they were close to calling in the photographers for the signing. They were close enough that Shultz decided to delay his departure for three exasperating hours. Then there was a snag in Panama. Noriega said yes to everything but balked when the U.S. negotiators began to be specific about his public statement. They wanted him to announce his retirement. No, said Noriega, he had never promised a public statement. He would promise that he would follow the terms of the agreement, but it would have to be their secret. The Americans protested. Noriega was adamant. The terms were fine, but a public statement was out of the question. And the statement, of course, was the only point that counted in the United States.

Still in Washington, cooling his heels, Shultz angrily announced that all U.S. offers had been removed from the table, and departed for the summit with Noriega still in power.

Cindy Adams of the *New York Post* watched Noriega close-up in his hour of triumph. He told her he was pleased at "being a pain in the rear" of the United States. "My only business with the U.S. has been supplying information." He asked Adams to pass along a message to Senator D'Amato in the pages of the *Post*. He invited him to come down to Panama so they could meet "*mano a mano.*"

"Women kneel at his shiny patent boots," Adams observed at a public meeting of over 1,000 women. "They snap photos of and with him, bend over him while he's seated, whisper in his ear. The supra-nationalist has *cojones* and power is the ultimate aphrodisiac." Noriega told Adams that he wanted Clint Eastwood to play him in the movies. "He is very macho," Noriega said. "He doesn't take xxxx from anybody. Clint Eastwood is a man who, if you mess with him, he'll kick your ass." He told her he was reading Don Regan's book. "I am not like Reagan, with his astrologers. I rely on my own thinking. But I do study my daily horoscope in the paper. And I read the Bible. I align with King Solomon."

8

Bush, Noriega, and Friends

NORIEGA'S comeback embarrassed the Reagan administration but posed special problems for Vice President Bush. Candidate George Bush was lagging in the presidential polls and had the most to lose. He had been Reagan's de facto drug czar as director of the Miami/South Florida Task Force during Noriega's rise. If he pleaded ignorance of Noriega's crimes, he would look ineffective. If he admitted knowing, then he would have to explain why he did nothing to stop Noriega.

So far, Bush had avoided getting tangled in the Iran-Contra scandal, which still loomed as a campaign issue. Bush's story—that he knew nothing of Oliver North's secret activities until the autumn of 1986—was wearing thin by May. Bush knew and worked closely with many people who knew about North's activities, but he remained ignorant, or so he said, even after his chief of staff was fully briefed on North. "Given all the evidence that was piling up," a former CIA officer joked, "Bush faced two choices. He could think about going to jail, or he could run for president."

Bush's crisis began with the February indictments against Noriega. Only a few days earlier, reports of Daniel Murphy's November visit to Noriega (the meeting Noriega interpreted as reassurance from Bush) had made the papers. Still, Murphy and Bush vowed they knew nothing of Noriega's narco-trafficking until the indictments.

Senator Robert Dole of Kansas, Bush's rival for the 1988 Republican nomination, ridiculed their claims. "We knew about [Noriega's drug connection] when we were debating the Panama Canal Treaty ten years ago," Dole said. "The fact is many of us talked about it on the Senate floor. . . ." He challenged Bush to explain. "Frankly, a big part of the problem we're having," said Dole, "is that we've been sending mixed messages to Noriega for years. People have been playing footsie with this guy—people who knew, or by virtue of their jobs and résumés ought to have known, that he was up to his eyeballs in dirty drugs and anti-American politics." Dole claimed that Daniel Murphy carried a message of support from George Bush to Noriega.

———

Bush and Noriega had actually met only twice. The first time was December 1976 in Washington when Bush was director of the CIA and Noriega headed Panamanian intelligence. The topic was a series of Panamanian bombings aimed at Zonians opposed to a new canal treaty. The explosives used were available to the Panamanian military and Noriega, the prime suspects. Noriega, however, denied involvement and the talk ended.

A remarkable subject apparently went unmentioned. Earlier in 1976, Noriega had hit the jackpot in a successful operation against the U.S. National Security Agency (NSA) in Panama. In his haul of tapes and transcripts from the NSA facility, Noriega had acquired the entire list of telephones and radios throughout Latin America upon which the NSA eavesdropped. Not only was he able to learn which of his own radio and telephone links were U.S. targets, he could sell the list from Cuba to Patagonia.

It had been easy. Noriega had simply bribed six U.S. sergeants ("The Singing Sergeants," they were dubbed by U.S. counterintelligence) who worked for the NSA. Almost as soon as the leak was discovered, however, the six sergeants were granted immunity from prosecution, possibly a Bush-approved decision. Lew Allen, Jr., NSA director, argued that the six sergeants should be openly prosecuted to discourage other bribes. If the case threw Noriega's "operations" into the spotlight, so be it, Allen said.

Bush, however, said he could not overrule the mysterious immunity grant—a legal position open to some debate. Why did it look as if Bush was protecting an "asset" who had pulled off one of the largest intelligence thefts against the United States in recent history? When Bush sat down to lunch with Noriega in December 1976, he still had not informed the Justice Department of the Singing Sergeants' crime despite a law requiring the CIA director to share his knowledge of any crimes with the attorney general.

Bush's second meeting with Noriega was also confusing. In December 1983, Bush stopped off in Panama after the inauguration of Raul Alfonsin in Argentina. Noriega, accompanied by Panama's then-president Ricardo de la Espriella and Colonel Diaz Herrera, met Bush during a refueling stopover. "What I talked to the Panamanians about," Bush said, "was doing what they could to get their banks out of laundering any money . . . for the narcotics traffic." Others remembered differently.

Donald Gregg, Bush's chief of staff who was present at the meeting (along with Daniel Murphy), said that de la Espriella surprised Bush by citing newspaper stories describing Panama as a money-laundering center. De la Espriella had wanted to deny the stories. "I wasn't aware of them," Bush said, according to Gregg. "If I had been, I would have raised them with you."

The record gets more muddied. In December 1985, three months after Spadafora's murder and Barletta's ouster, Ambassador Everett Ellis Briggs flew to Washington to discuss Panama with Bush. Briggs was well informed about Noriega and deeply regretted Barletta's departure. By the time of the meeting, he had already sent a series of detailed cables to Washington. "They were extremely strong," a former official said. "They said the United States should take action against this man, that this was a man who had a history of all these things: drug dealing, gun running, technology transfer, and now he's murdered one of his opponents and nobody seems to be interested."

Briggs briefed a congressional delegation around the same time. "Briggs said there were a lot of allegations that Noriega was involved with drugs, but that they hadn't been able to get evidence," said a member of the delegation who had attended the briefing. "It was kind of like Al Capone: Everyone knew he was doing illegal things but nobody could get enough to take him off the streets and put him in jail. That was what Briggs was portraying."

Col. Samuel Watson III, a Bush aide, prepared a memo setting the agenda for the December 16 meeting between Bush and Briggs. According to the memo, the meeting was called to "discuss U.S. relations with Panama and narcotics matters." One section included this passage: "There have been disturbing events in Panama of late and Ambassador Briggs, a long-term observer of the scene, will be in a good position to interpret them [for] you. Of particular interest will be: political developments following the resignation of President Barletta—drug interdiction."

There seems to be little doubt that George Bush was well briefed on Noriega's activities. Several former government officials, most notably Norman O. Bailey, an economist who had served on the NSC, made it clear that Noriega's crimes were well known to top U.S. officials, and long before the spring of 1988. "Available to me as an officer of the NSC, and available to any authorized official of the U.S. government," he said, "is a plethora of human intelligence, electronic intercepts, and satellite and overflight photography that, taken together, constitute not just a smoking gun but rather a twenty-two-cannon barrage of evidence" that Noriega was a narco-trafficker and at least a prime suspect in the Spadafora murder.

Bailey said that "clear and incontrovertible evidence was at best ignored, and at worst hidden and denied, by many different agencies and departments." According to Bailey, "the only possible reason or excuse for being ignorant of it would be because the person involved did not want to know or to find out, or willfully ignored the overwhelming evidence."

Bailey cited two specific editions of the National Intelligence Daily (NID), a top secret intelligence report available to high government officials. Both NIDs, Bailey said, reported meetings between Noriega and leaders of the Medellín cocaine cartel.

In 1983, there had been a meeting in Panama. The Colombians and Noriega struck a deal whereby Noriega would permit them to open a processing plant in Panama. Another agenda item was the cartel's plan to ask the Colombian government for immunity from prosecution in return for a payment of $11 billion, the amount of Colombia's foreign debt. To be sure, the cartel would have plenty left over. The amount of money they laundered inside Panama at that point was hundreds of millions of dollars a month.

"The second meeting," Bailey said, again citing an NID, "took place in the summer of 1985 in Cuzco, Peru, and involved Noriega and drug traffickers from Peru, Bolivia, and Colombia. Noriega was reported to have been present . . . and to have been told by the drug traffickers to get rid of Hugo Spadafora."

From Noriega's point of view, his 1983 meeting with Bush showed that he had been a loyal U.S. ally. It also confirmed that the administration's commitment to Panamanian democracy in 1988 was very new. At the time of the 1983 meeting, Noriega had been commander in chief for only four months, but he had already demonstrated that, contrary to the spirit of the treaties, he was not taking the military out of politics.

In November 1983, Noriega had bribed and coerced the legislative assembly to pass Law 20, which for all practical purposes was the death certificate for Panamanian democracy. Law 20 gathered virtually every government agency, many of which had been under civilian control, under PDF control. It also served as the underpinning for Noriega's increasingly powerful criminal empire. Bush hadn't complained.

According to Noriega, what Bush had done was ask indirectly for his help with the Contras. According to Blandon, Noriega reported immediately that Bush spent most of the time talking about the U.S. commitment to democracy in Nicaragua. Noriega and Blandon both read Bush the same way: He was asking for help in Nicaragua.

Noriega and Blandon decided to act. Noriega quickly confirmed that the SOUTHCOM bases could operate without interference and even reputedly made a cash contribution to the Contra effort.

Noriega and Blandon knew that the May 1984 election would be a good test of the U.S. attitude. U.S. embassy officials seemed to have a very different priority than what Bush had seemed to suggest; they told opposition leaders that the United States was committed to a free election—even if Arias won again.

Noriega and everyone else knew that if Arias became president he would try to dismantle the PDF, as he had always promised. It was most unlikely that the United States would have the same ease of operation in Panama under an Arias regime.

Every reliable poll predicted an Arias victory, especially over Barletta, whom Noriega had handpicked and who was very popular in Washington. To keep Arias out, Noriega would have to fix things. If the administration looked the other way, it would confirm Noriega's reading of the Bush visit. The election of May 1984 that saw Barletta ascend, with Noriega's help, to the presidency seemed to verify the general's reading of George Bush.

Two months after Bush's visit, Noriega fired President Ricardo de la Espriella, making a bitter enemy of the former president. Still, de la Espriella's account of the 1983 meeting corroborates Noriega's story. There was, de la Espriella says, no overt request for help with the Contras. But he does recall that Bush devoted almost the entire half hour to his concerns about Nicaragua. According to de la Espriella, Panama was hardly mentioned, if it was mentioned at all.

Not long afterward, Noriega increased his support for the Contras. Not long after that, he became involved with Oliver North.

According to Blandon, he and Noriega always assumed that Bush was well informed about North's Contra supply system. They knew he was close to some who were directly involved— such as Felix Rodriguez, the Cuban-born CIA veteran who, with the help of Donald Gregg, got a job as an adviser to the Salvadoran air force in 1984. Rodriguez instructed air force personnel at Ilopango in helicopter tactics he and Gregg had developed in the countryside near Saigon when they first became friends in the late 1960s.

In September 1985, Oliver North invited Rodriguez to join his network and Rodriguez began overseeing Ilopango aircraft and crews that flew supplies to the Contras. During this time, he and Gregg spoke on the phone several times a week. In May 1986, Rodriguez visited Washington and met with Gregg and Bush. According to the memo prepared by Colonel Watson, the subject was El Salvador and "resupply of the Contras."

On August 8, 1986, Rodriguez returned to Washington, met with Gregg and Watson, and, according to all three men, told Gregg and Watson for the first time about North's secret supply system. All three insisted that until that day Rodriguez had kept his work with North secret from them. North had very recently brought Richard Secord into his operations. Rodriguez did not trust Secord and associated him with former CIA agent Edwin Wilson, who had been convicted of selling explosives to Libya. As it happened, North and Secord had set up several Panamanian front companies with the help of one of Noriega's attorneys.

Gregg's summary of the briefing began with the word: "Secord." Despite having just learned the astounding news that a marine officer at the White House had set up a secret and illegal supply system in Central America, Gregg did not tell Bush what he had learned, or so Gregg testified.

Rodriguez's operation came to an end on October 5, 1986, when the cargo plane that the late Barry Seal had used for shipping drugs took off from Ilopango with Eugene Hasenfus and the others and a cargo of weapons. When Rodriguez realized that the plane had been shot down, his first phone call was to Gregg's office where he spoke to Colonel Watson. Still, no one told Bush.

━━━

Throughout the 1988 campaign, presidential candidate George Bush stuck to his story that he did not know Noriega was involved in drugs until the indictments. He continued to deny knowing anything about North's activities until the whole story became public in November 1986.

Noriega had "gone bad," according to Bush. "There are a lot of people around the world who don't pass the perfection saliva test," Bush said. "But in terms of did we know he was smuggling drugs—no." (Technically speaking, Noriega probably never smuggled drugs, but he did allow drug smugglers to use Panama.) Bush refused to discuss any of his actions as CIA director, saying that he had taken an oath that forbade him from talking. But he said he most certainly had not known about Noriega's drug involvement during that time. Despite the early challenge from Dole, Bush escaped serious scrutiny by the other candidates and the press.

By early May, when another reporter asked him if he had known about Noriega's drug involvement when he was CIA director, Bush was bolder than ever: "In terms of drugs, absolutely not," Bush replied. "And nobody with any sense of decency in the political arena has alleged I have. And they had better not, because it's not true. And if they say it's true, let's see the evidence. You have to defend yourself in life and that kind of charge coming out of the Democrats—I hear it from some of the liberal McGovern types around Mr. Dukakis and Jackson—that there is some connection there—what is it? Let them be man enough to stand up to my face and tell me."

He grew more emphatic in early May. On May 2, he told high school students in Vandalia, Ohio, that "when it became demonstrably clear that Noriega was involved in drugs we moved against him, with an indictment." In other words, Bush asserted that he and others in the administration deliberately "brought Noriega to justice" as he put it. In fact, the administration's only involvement in the indictment process was to persuade prosecu-

tors to drop plans to indict the entire PDF under the RICO statutes. Bush's claim undoubtedly surprised federal prosecutors who
had felt administration pressure to stop "interfering in foreign
affairs." The claim was also ambiguous. Shortly after taking partial credit for bringing about the indictments, Bush returned to his
original assertion that until the indictments he himself had not
even heard any rumors that Noriega was a narco-trafficker. "Not
that I was ever aware of," Bush told a reporter on May 5.

The indictments themselves reflected only a tiny fraction of
what was known, or alleged, about Noriega within the administration. Indeed, it was quite possible that the administration had
evidence—such as the NIDs cited by Norman Bailey—that would
help prosecutors convict Noriega. Unfortunately for the prosecutors, Noriega probably had a better chance of seeing that evidence
than they did.

On May 8, the *New York Times* carried a story that directly
challenged Bush's credibility. ("Seeming Contradiction" was one
tier of the headline.) *Times* reporters had learned about the Briggs-
Bush meeting in December 1985. According to their sources (identified as two former State Department officials, and one former
White House official, all three anonymous), Briggs had painted a
complete and accurate picture of Noriega to Bush and told him
about the narco-trafficking connection. The story reported the
Briggs cables of 1985 and the well-known facts behind Briggs's
distaste for Noriega. If Briggs had told Bush about Noriega's drug
involvement, then Bush was lying when he said he knew nothing
until 1988.

The Sunday morning that the story appeared, Donald Gregg
telephoned Briggs in Tegucigalpa, Honduras, where Briggs was
stationed as ambassador. Gregg urged Briggs to have a press conference and simply "tell the truth." That afternoon, Briggs chose
his words very carefully. "I could not have briefed the vice president on Noriega's drug-running, drug-smuggling, or money-
laundering activities because we simply did not have evidence of
those activities at that time, and so any statement to the effect that
I did brief him on such matters at that time simply is not true," he
said.

Within a single day, however, Briggs's memory clouded. On
Monday, in response to further questions, Briggs said through a
spokesperson that he could not remember if drugs had been discussed when he talked to Bush about Hugo Spadafora and Barletta. It seemed a likely possibility.

No one, it seemed, could remember exactly what happened. Craig Fuller, a Bush staffer who was listed as a participant on the briefing memo, could not even recall if he had attended. No one could remember much, but no one definitely remembered Briggs telling Bush that Noriega was a drug trafficker. "I don't recall specifically whether they were or not," Colonel Watson replied, under oath, when asked if drugs had been discussed. "I could make that assumption, but I will not state it as a certainty." Watson's lawyer intervened when his client was asked what Briggs had told Bush about narcotics. He said that Watson did not have to answer on grounds of executive privilege.

A few days later (May 13), when the *Times* reported Briggs's briefing of the congressional delegation, Bush's credibility was reeling.

Yet the vice president stuck to his story. On May 24, Bush said, "I can tell you [Briggs] did not go into the fact that Noriega was involved in narcotics, as he himself has said," Bush declared. (Briggs's memory was still problematic.) "To imply . . . that the man is lying when he said he didn't talk to me about Mr. Noriega's involvement in drugs—I'm sorry, I just don't agree with that. I've said it's not true, he's said it's not true, and people who weren't at the meeting, for reasons of their own [are] questioning the veracity of me and him, and I don't understand it, and I wish they'd stop writing the stuff, especially when these people are unwilling to have their names put on the story. I find that a little bit offensive, but I know how it works."

Bush's problems worsened on May 11 when Reagan offered to rescind the indictments if Noriega stepped down. Bush, as usual, agreed publicly with Reagan, but the decision was tantamount to political suicide.

In the midst of the attacks that followed, there was another bombshell. On May 16, *Newsweek* and ABC's "World News Tonight" broke stories about North's secret Contra supply network. The stories jeopardized Gregg's credibility and therefore threatened Bush. They also introduced another figure from the shadow world of Latin American intrigues to the public at large.

Richard Brenneke was a pilot and arms broker who claimed to have worked for the CIA over the years. In the previous weeks he had told his story to ABC's investigators, *Newsweek*'s reporters, and, under oath, to Senate staffers. It went like this: In 1983, Pesakh Ben-Or, a Mossad agent in Guatemala, tried to recruit Brenneke to shop for arms in Eastern Europe. The deal was part of a major project in which American and Israeli covert operators would supply arms to the Contras in Nicaragua. The Israeli assured Brenneke that the project had the highest U.S. blessing. When Brenneke demanded proof, Ben-Or gave him Donald Gregg's number in Washington. Reassured by Gregg, Brenneke, according to his sworn testimony, went ahead.

Very quickly he discovered that the Medellín Cartel had put up the money and airplanes to buy and fly the weapons. In return for the service to the Contras, the cartel was able to fly cocaine cargoes into the United States. In the middle of 1985, he said, he flew one of the cocaine shipments from Colombia right into Amarillo, Texas. This was around the time that his son was becoming a cocaine addict.

Brenneke called Gregg. He wanted him to know what was going on and to share his misgivings. "You do what you were assigned to do," Gregg responded, according to Brenneke. "Don't question the decisions of your betters. You are not to worry about or concern yourself with the movement of drugs. That's not your business, it's none of your business, just do what you were hired to do."

Bush was in Seattle on the campaign trail when the story broke. "It's not even news; it's old, tired, I'd hate to think politically motivated material. It has been looked at and you get sick and tired of saying, 'I've told the truth,' " he said.

The White House helped deflect the Brenneke story. Press secretary Marlin Fitzwater attempted to smear Brenneke on May 17. "Wasn't he on trial?" Fitzwater asked. "I challenge you to look up his court case in New York. He introduced all of this evidence as part of his trial in New York. It was considered by the jury, considered by the courts, and rejected." Not a word of that was true. Brenneke had never been on trial anywhere, and his evidence about Gregg (which included phone logs and other documents) had never been considered by any jury or court.

Around this time, a Bush aide succinctly described the price Bush was paying for his loyalty to the administration: "George Bush can't make a speech these days with any credibility about drugs if we're dealing with the drug kingpin of the world," the aide said.

In Los Angeles on Thursday, May 19, Bush said: "Drug dealers are domestic terrorists, killing kids and cops, and they should be treated as such. I won't bargain with terrorists, and I won't bargain with drug dealers either, whether they're on U.S. or foreign soil." The speech made news. The Reagan administration was unquestionably bargaining with Noriega, whom they called a drug dealer. Just eight days earlier, Reagan had decided to drop the charges if Noriega stepped down. Since then, the criticism had been scathing and bipartisan. Did the Bush speech signal that the vice president disagreed with Reagan on the Noriega negotiations? Bush had never disagreed with Reagan on anything since they had been inaugurated in 1981. If he did disagree on Panama, it was a first—and big news.

By Thursday, his aides confided to reporters that Bush felt he had to challenge Reagan publicly. On Friday, his office made it official: Bush did not want to negotiate with Noriega. Over the next five days, until the talks collapsed, there was talk of furious debate inside the administration. James Baker argued Bush's case. The spin to Bush stories now was that he was making his bid to "be his own man."

Reagan was apparently unaware of the split and not familiar with the negotiations that were causing such commotion. "I can see why the vice president said what he said," Reagan told reporters, "because the impression has been given . . . based on rumors and news leaks and so forth, that we are in negotiations somehow with a participant in their drug trade and all."

By June, Panama dropped from the headlines and, for all practical purposes, from the 1988 presidential campaign. Just as Noriega had made an extraordinary comeback that spring so, too, did George Bush. Bush transformed his political identity vis-à-vis Noriega from that of a man who had much to fear from Noriega because of their past associations to one of Noriega's most dedicated foes. Bush supporters argued that if Noriega had "Bush by the balls" as he claimed and knew so much, why was he not talking about what he knew? It was easy to attack Noriega's credibility ("To lie, for Noriega, is part of his work," as Blandon had commented), and his teasing about what he knew backfired, or so it seemed. He never produced even the smallest sample of "political dynamite," as one of his lawyers called his files. Reporters grew impatient and skeptical.

No one asked Noriega why he dangled the prospect of sensational information and then never revealed any. He might have answered that it was even better to have a president by the balls.

9

Open Season on Americans

BY the summer of 1988, U.S. initiatives against Noriega, such as they were, had all failed and the Panamanians who had cast their lot with the Americans were confounded. Their disillusionment quickly became a problem for the Reagan administration.

One of the most problematic was Col. Eduardo Herrera-Hassan, a man the United States had recruited to lead the coup against Noriega it was alternately planning and postponing. Herrera-Hassan was ready and had definite ideas about how to proceed; but not all of them squared with the plans made by the United States.

Herrera-Hassan's involvement with the United States had begun very shortly after the attempted coup of March 16, 1988. Around that time, William Walker, a senior State Department official, turned up in Tel Aviv and asked Herrera-Hassan, who was then Panama's ambassador to Israel, if he was interested in joining an effort to oust Noriega. Walker stressed that speed and secrecy were essential. Herrera-Hassan agreed on the spot to discuss the matter further in Washington.

By this time, Herrera-Hassan had been in Israel since 1985, first as military attaché and then as ambassador. Despite his title, for all practical purposes, he was in exile. He and Noriega had been antagonists since the mid-1970s when, in a casual remark, Torrijos dubbed Herrera-Hassan (a distant relative who shared his rural, lower-middle-class background) "the right guy" to succeed him as military commander. The story got around and the jealous and ambitious Noriega (already nicknamed "my gangster" by Torrijos) immediately declared bureaucratic war on Herrera-Hassan. Their hostility had increased over the years.

Herrera-Hassan, like Noriega and other PDF officers, had attended special training courses run by the U.S. Army at such places as Fort Benning and Fort Bragg. In fact, he looked like an idealized American colonel and tended to make a very good impression on U.S. officials. He was lean and trim, with a flat stomach. The sleeves on his fatigues were rolled to his biceps in just the right manner for an infantry officer. "He looked and acted like a soldier," said one U.S. officer with long experience in Panama.

Herrera-Hassan was as famous for honesty as Noriega was for corruption. A politician who openly disliked him said, "He hardly touched the benefits that were available to him." He lived modestly in Israel with his wife and four children. His family in Panama, which included a brother in the PDF, had never shown signs of the riches prized by the families of most high-ranking PDF officers. He was, it appeared, a straight shooter, blunt, verging on indiscretion. A European diplomat observed that Herrera-Hassan "had enough guts to make an effort and enough charisma to sell it."

Noriega sent him to Israel because it was the safest way to tune him out of the picture. Mike Harari kept an eye on him and, to be sure, Herrera-Hassan kept an eye on Harari. He came to understand Harari's importance to Noriega as a friend and business partner in great detail. He recognized Harari's influence, and he and Harari became enemies. This further estranged Noriega and Herrera-Hassan.

On July 10, 1987, at the height of the *civilista* protests, Herrera-Hassan was visiting in Panama. Noriega pressed him into service, ordering him, he says, to brutalize the street demonstrators. According to Herrera-Hassan, he disobeyed the orders. He tried, he said, to keep the troops in his sector under control. When he saw innocent *civilistas* rounded up, he ordered their release. Some of his troops chased demonstrators into the National Sanctuary, shooting tear gas. He was, it appeared, responsible, but witnesses corroborated his story that he tried to show restraint, even sympathy for the demonstrators. After all, somewhere in the crowd was his own mother, an ardent *civilista* and Christian Democrat. She had often urged her son to sit down and talk with Ricardo Arias Calderon.

At the end of the day that came to be called Black Friday, Noriega announced on television that Herrera-Hassan had been in charge, and that he had ordered the PDF to savage anyone with a white handkerchief. The trick helped establish Herrera-Hassan as the Bull Connor of the PDF.

Afterward, Herrera-Hassan returned to Israel and seemed content to wait out the crisis, living quietly. Then William Walker arrived.

According to Panamanian opposition members, strange events were taking place in Washington even as the two, traveling in plain view on a commercial flight, approached the city. According to sources, Walker had a very specific role in mind for Herrera-Hassan, a role that the interagency committee appeared to have endorsed but which Walker had not yet disclosed to Herrera-Hassan. Walker said he felt compelled to wait until his colleagues were present to discuss it.

There was, however, a snag: By the time the men reached Washington, the plan, whatever it was, was "no longer viable," as one member of the opposition said with some sarcasm. An American officer scoffs at this. "There was never any plan, ever, no plan at all," he said, with just as much sarcasm.

Herrera-Hassan quickly sensed that something was wrong, but he agreed to attend the meeting scheduled for the next day and checked into a hotel, the Keybridge Marriott in Roslyn, Virginia, just across the Potomac from Georgetown. Roslyn, a "national security" suburb, is home to many privately owned consulting firms staffed by former military and intelligence officials. The Keybridge Marriott is a popular meeting place for these officials; they like doing business in its comfortable dining room. Some intelligence agents even boast of special, secret rates. Statistically speaking, there was probably more chance that Herrera-Hassan would be recognized by someone passing through the Keybridge Marriott than at any other hotel in the United States.

The next day, March 29, Walker escorted Herrera-Hassan from the hotel to a conference room just down the hall from Elliott Abrams's office at State. At the meeting, Walker shared the chair with Dr. Anthony Gray, a Pentagon official and associate of Nestor Sanchez. Also present were several other civilian and military officers, all with very high security clearances, and three of the PDF officers who had escaped during the coup attempt thirteen days earlier. One of them was Noriega's former pilot, Maj. Augusto Villalaz.

Herrera-Hassan spoke forcefully. "It was obvious to me that he could make things happen," one of the Americans later recalled. Even though Herrera-Hassan had been away from Panama, except for brief visits, for several years, he briskly and incisively reviewed the PDF officer corps, providing thumbnail biographies and unequivocal judgments on whether or not the twenty or thirty men he mentioned would join a coup. Major Villalaz, with fresher experience, corroborated Herrera-Hassan's assessments. "If you goddamn gringos are going to get serious and show some real resolve we can work together," Herrera-Hassan said. "But we need you to let us know that you're not playing games." He did not elucidate further, and no one asked him how the United States could make such a demonstration.

The meeting lasted an hour and produced a single decision: Herrera-Hassan would verify that the officers he mentioned would join a coup effort. There was no discussion of how the United States would prove it meant business.

The Panamanians, especially Villalaz, were disappointed. Herrera-Hassan had a few more meetings—"the tour" as one Panamanian put it—and was on his way back to Israel in a few days. The other Panamanians went to more meetings where U.S. officials quizzed them for information about Noriega's vulnerabilities. The officials even flew in the mistress of one exiled officer in Venezuela. She was questioned closely about the people around Noriega and how the United States might help foment trouble for him.

The meetings had one clear result: Herrera-Hassan's days in Israel were soon numbered. It became obvious that Noriega knew Herrera-Hassan had consorted with Americans. It was hard to imagine how he could have avoided finding out.

Within a few weeks, Herrera-Hassan found himself involved in an apparently trivial but bitter argument with Mike Harari. At issue was a Panamanian embassy car that Herrera-Hassan had sold because he needed cash (not forthcoming from Panama City) to pay embassy expenses. Harari, technically only a consul, challenged Herrera-Hassan's authority, claimed the car belonged to him, and demanded the money. When Herrera-Hassan refused, Harari told him he was fired—fired as ambassador and fired from the PDF. Harari was happy to act as Noriega's hatchet man.

Herrera-Hassan came to the United States and joined the ranks of exiles. "Our greatest dreams for Herrera-Hassan were just before our initial encounter," an American officer said. "After that it was all downhill."

The Panamanians grew more disillusioned. They were convinced that the United States would never really act. By June, Herrera-Hassan had moved into place as the so-called military half of the Delvalle government, but the opposition was still despondent. They sensed Noriega's triumph.

Later in June, a PDF traffic policeman flagged down an American soldier and his eighteen-year-old wife traveling on a highway just outside Panama City. The Panamanian, clutching a gun, ordered the Americans out of the car and proceeded to punch and pistol-whip both. Then the Panamanian locked the GI in the trunk of the car and proceeded to rape the wife. Later, the victims were able to provide enough information for the PDF to begin a so-called investigation. But there was no real investigation. The PDF simply ignored American inquiries about what was being done.

Not long afterward, more American protests followed when a group of PDF soldiers roughed up the pregnant wife of a GI. But American demands for an investigation were greeted by more PDF sneering. Later, when some Panamanians soldiers stopped an air force enlisted woman, also pregnant, and slapped her around, it seemed like open season on U.S. civilians and military personnel. SOUTHCOM began a list of harassment incidents that grew into the hundreds very quickly as the summer turned to autumn. The list itemized broken fingers; loosened teeth; abrasions from billy clubs, rubber hoses, and pistols; strip searches; long detentions; robberies and "fondlings" (as the report put it) of female military personnel.

Noriega tightened visa regulations for U.S. travelers entering Panama. Entry visas had always been formalities for Americans landing in Panama. Now PDF immigration officials advised airlines that passengers without the difficult-to-obtain visas would not be allowed to enter the country.

This discouraged journalists from coming to Panama and embarrassed U.S. government personnel, many of whom traveled in and out of Panama frequently.

Noriega's bullying stemmed from his very clear perception that the Reagan administration was bound and determined to forget he ever existed. He wanted the Americans to know that he knew he had won. The harassment was also designed to show his fellow officers that there was a new day in Panama. If they stuck by him, he boasted, they had nothing to fear from the United States. The United States was afraid of him. "Look at them," he said one day at a boozy gathering at the Comandancia. "Nothing but a bunch of AIDS-infested faggots."

———

Gen. Fred Woerner's orders that summer confirmed Noriega's assessment of the situation. To be sure, Woerner, who traveled to Washington every few weeks, never received anything in writing in regard to policy. (One of the reasons he was commander was that he did not need to have things explained to him.) But Woerner listened carefully to the chairman of the Joint Chiefs of Staff and the secretary of defense as well as other Pentagon policymakers. He paid attention to State Department officials and tried to intuit the mood on Capitol Hill. He knew how to read the signals.

In April, when the administration had been feeling the pressure to act militarily against Noriega, Woerner put his troops on alert, increased patrols, and generally assumed a reasonable facsimile of a confrontational pose. He had done this even though he believed the posturing was dangerous.

In May, during the so-called negotiations with Noriega, Woerner's job had been to create the impression of decreased hostility or, in military parlance, a "drawdown." Woerner had to make sure that his troops avoided any risk of conflict with the PDF.

Woerner understood his orders very clearly and realized that he had to cope as best he could with very conflicting pressures. He could not strike back against PDF harassment despite his responsibility for the safety of his troops, despite the fact that the PDF harassment of Americans was increasing.

"Before the elections, as we started to get into active campaigning, the word was out: Put Panama on the back burner," Woerner said. A drawdown "reduced the possibility of conflict that would have brought Panama back into the news again." He stresses that the objective was to "keep it out of the news." The message was absolutely clear. "It came not through uniformed military channels but through civilian Department of Defense channels and was reinforced by State," he said.

The policy worked. Panama stayed out of the papers, and in

public Woerner gave no indication of his personal misgivings about the drawdown. In his view (as he said later), his orders were "based blatantly on partisan politics and no other single consideration." The administration did not want to embarrass presidential candidate George Bush. In other words, as Woerner saw it, U.S. domestic politics now governed the administration's behavior in Panama. To Woerner, the administration's policy was "contrary to the interests of the U.S. . . . What we did . . .," Woerner says, was "put in jeopardy the attainment of U.S. policy objectives for a domestic, political, partisan objective."

Woerner says now that Panama could have only become an embarrassing campaign issue. There was no possible positive spin for Bush no matter how it played for a variety of reasons: the failure of U.S. policy, Bush's CIA linkage, the alleged possibility of collusion between Bush and Noriega, Noriega's drug activity and the U.S. failure to do anything about it.

━━━━━

The Panamanian opposition understood the American actions just as clearly as Noriega and Woerner. Delvalle was particularly disappointed and, with the backing of other opposition leaders (in exile and in Panama), threatened to resign from the presidency. It was a dangerous move; Delvalle was probably the opposition's greatest asset at this point. On the other hand, they had nothing to lose.

An angry Delvalle was an obvious threat. If he publicly accused the Reagan administration of betrayal, he could make Panama a campaign bombshell. His threats alarmed White House staffers who moved quickly to defuse the mercurial Panamanian.

The result was a presidential "finding" that commissioned a covert operation, to be managed by the CIA, to foment a coup against Noriega. Herrera-Hassan was to take charge of the Panamanian side of the operation. He and his handpicked band of exiles were to conduct "nonlethal" sabotage, distribute leaflets, and break into PDF radio and telephone communications with anti-Noriega messages. He would be given a budget of $1.3 million— funds that were to be drawn from the Panama government's frozen accounts over which Delvalle had gained legal control. Elliott Abrams was named as custodian, or overseer, of the funds.

The plan emphasized psychological warfare, directed mainly inside the PDF, and reflected administration policy in a number of ways: it was showy and the weapons were words; it was safe, almost undetectable; and there was little chance anyone would be injured. It also stood no chance of actually unseating Noriega.

The CIA position was that if the administration wanted to get rid of Noriega they would have to "play hardball," a euphemism for killing him, by either assassination or invasion. But the finding steered clear of this option despite the fact that the CIA was charged with managing the plan.

With the finding "in progress," White House staffers decided that Delvalle merited a personal phone call from Reagan, a rare event at the White House. Considerable planning and rehearsal were required. On July 15, Delvalle visited his dentist (still in hiding, he was allowed to travel to the United States by U.S. government aircraft from Howard Air Force base). Reagan telephoned Delvalle at the dentist's office; he said that he had signed a secret presidential finding for a covert operation against Noriega. Reagan assured Delvalle that he still opposed Noriega and sketched in the broad outlines of the proposed covert action. He said that Herrera-Hassan was in charge. The phone call worked. Delvalle would remain quiet.

Word of the call spread but with Congress in recess it took eleven days to progress to the next step in the "finding" process. On Tuesday, July 26, a CIA officer went to Capitol Hill to conduct a secret briefing for the Senate Select Committee on Intelligence. The subject was what the "finding" would actually entail.

There was tension in the room as the CIA officer laid out the Panama plan and stated that Noriega's death was not the expressed purpose of the coup but was a possibility. Not all the tension stemmed from the actual plan: Two members of the committee, David Boren, an Oklahoma Democrat, and William Cohen, a Maine Republican, were backing a bill that would require the administration to inform congressional watchdogs forty-eight hours before the start of any covert operation. Administration and CIA representatives opposed the bill.

On the day of the briefing, Joe Pichirallo and Lou Cannon of the *Washington Post* discovered sources (strictly anonymous) within the administration who confirmed that Reagan had signed the finding. Through the course of the day, they put together a story about the administration's new effort to remove Noriega from power. The story cited sources from the administration and Congress.

The story appeared July 27. After it broke, White House

officials told reporters (from elsewhere than the *Post*) that committee members and staff who had been at the secret briefing had exposed national secrets and seriously hampered efforts to get rid of Noriega. They said that the Senate blabbermouths began leaking the plan almost the instant the secret briefing was adjourned. Now, they asked, could such people be trusted to contain themselves for forty-eight hours? How could anyone seriously consider the Boren/Cohen bill?

When a reporter asked Reagan at a photo opportunity that day if "congressional leaking" made him angry, he responded: "I'm usually angry at Congress, yes." The statement added presidential weight to an adroit political maneuver. The administration had, in one day, created the impression that it was trying to take action against Noriega and had also found scapegoats for the eventual failure of the action. They also discredited the bill Boren and Cohen were backing.

Boren and Cohen held a joint news conference on July 28. They accused the administration of the obvious. "I think the matter was handled in such a way as to set up members of Congress to make them appear as the source of the leak," Cohen said. "I think it was a set-up deal . . . I am offended by it."

Both Boren and Cohen pointed out that the *Post* reporter called their offices well before the afternoon briefing and that the Reagan telephone call to Delvalle, reported accurately by the *Post*, had not even been mentioned to them at the briefing. "Someone, somewhere, obviously in the executive branch . . . put this information out even before we got it," Boren said. "We talk loudly and carry a small stick . . . what has been done obviously has failed."

Senators Helms and Kennedy and a few other legislators kept trying to ask questions about Panama, but the administration was determined to keep the subject out of the papers. The experience of two other legislators confirmed this. Senator John Kerry of Massachusetts and another Democrat, Congressman Bill Alexander of Arkansas, ordered the General Accounting Office (GAO) to prepare a report on how foreign policy and knowledge of drug trafficking by foreign leaders were connected. Panama was to be used as the "case study." This was the only recourse they could find to stimulate some debate on Panama policy. In response, the White House took the extraordinary step of ordering the CIA, the Defense Department, and the State Department not to cooperate with the GAO investigators.

Later in the summer, an invitation to a Pentagon party included a joke invitation to a farewell party for Noriega. The card carried a large red "POSTPONED" stamp. "Due to circumstances beyond Elliott Abrams's control the farewell party has been indefinitely postponed," the card said.

———

Herrera-Hassan got the picture. He knew that the administration's "psywar" tactics were just theatrics without military action. But whenever Herrera-Hassan brought up new plans (including a commando raid against Noriega) that involved possible fatalities on either side, they were rejected. Many Panamanians felt that the CIA kept Noriega in power by saying that the only way to get rid of him was assassination, which was against the law. Frustration was high.

Herrera-Hassan realized that if he was going to supplant Noriega he needed firepower, which he wasn't going to get from the United States.

Herrera-Hassan also paid a courtesy call on Dr. Arnulfo Arias at his small bungalow in Coconut Grove, Florida, in July. If there was another election in Panama, Arias remained the obvious opposition candidate. He was eighty-six but still vigorous. Even if he chose not to run, his blessings were essential for anyone who wanted to speak for the opposition. Herrera-Hassan acknowledged Arias's power and asked for his moral support, which the old man promised.

On Wednesday, August 10, just five days short of his eighty-seventh birthday (he was two years older than the Republic of Panama), Arias died of a heart attack while watching the CNN midday news. All scenarios for Panama's future became null and void. Arias's death also created an embarrassing political problem for Noriega. His fifth anniversary as commander in chief was just two days away and he planned a triumphant ceremony—with saturation coverage by the government-controlled press. Noriega wasn't sure how to handle the ceremony in light of Arias's death.

Just hours after Arias died, his family in Coconut Grove announced that they would remain in Miami with the body until Noriega had completed his ceremony. The corpse would return to Panama at dusk on Saturday; the hearse would proceed directly from the airport to the cathedral. The public was invited to pay their respects on Sunday. On Monday, there would be an outdoor mass on the cathedral esplanade at noon. At 1:00 P.M., the procession would depart for the Garden of Peace cemetery, a twenty-minute drive away.

Noriega's ceremony, held at a PDF base immediately adjacent to SOUTHCOM, was a dismal, dispirited affair. The small celebration was a clear reflection of Noriega's power base. PDF officers, government employees, and his cronies made up the crowd.

Noriega did not rise to the occasion. "Welcome to the territory of Panama in the Canal Zone," Noriega shouted, shaking his fist in the direction of the U.S. headquarters. "Welcome until you march."

A few hours later, right on schedule, Arias's hearse turned into Via Espana on its way to the cathedral. The river of mourners lining the street was vast and hushed. Many held flickering candles and wept as the hearse inched forward. Hundreds of thousands of people turned out. Arias's body reached the cathedral toward midnight, five hours after the hearse left the airport.

The cathedral doors opened early Sunday. Hundreds of thousands of Panamanians filed past the casket until late at night. On Monday, the crowds packed the cathedral square. All morning rain drenched the city, but shortly before noon the sun came out just as it had in 1978 when Arias returned from exile. At that time, the rain poured until his small plane approached Paitilla airport. By the time Arias appeared, the sun was shining. "You're half saint, half witch," an old woman had cried.

At 1:00 P.M., the casket was put aboard a gleaming red fire truck, the traditional funeral hearse for Panamanian dignitaries. Church bells tolled and flowers rained from balconies in the cathedral neighborhood. Seven hours later, after passing through what appeared to be the entire population of Panama, Arnulfo was interred in the soggy Garden of Peace cemetery. A priest said prayers as clods of earth fell upon the casket. He told the mourners that they were burying the true president of Panama.

On December 11, 1988, President Delvalle, who had renewed his threats of resignation, had a fifteen-minute meeting in the Oval Office with Reagan and Bush. Administration officials had found an effective way to mollify Delvalle when he acted up. They let him travel to the United States, where he saw friends, shopped for horses, and talked to U.S. officials. He particularly liked the presidential-level bodyguard force the United States assigned to him. "They make me feel like I'm a real president," Delvalle gushed to a Panamanian friend.

But Delvalle wasn't completely swayed. He was blunt with

the president and president-elect, saying that economic sanctions had been a disaster. He told them that only U.S. military force would get rid of Noriega.

Afterward, through a spokesman, Bush said, "There must be no misunderstanding about our policy. Our policy will be that Noriega must go." But in one of his last interviews as president, Ronald Reagan acknowledged the clear possibility that Noriega would still be in power in 1999, when Panama assumed sole control of the canal. It seemed a safe bet now as the Christmas season approached and Noriega began his celebration.

In the old days, Americans who lived in the Zone had placed their most lavish manger scene on the grounds of a police station, long since taken over by the PDF. For Christmas 1988, the PDF erected a different scene with an Uncle Sam cut-out pouring money into the throat of a Delvalle look-alike. Ambassador Davis was portrayed shooting and killing Santa Claus. Parents did not take their children to see it.

10

The Election

BUSH had dealt himself a difficult hand. Bush the candidate had saved his political campaign in May 1988 by adamantly refusing to make any deal with Noriega. He stated unequivocally that Noriega had to leave power and stand trial. This pledge now prevented President Bush from negotiating Noriega out of power without great political cost. In the event of a showdown, Bush would have to use military force.

Bush also had to contend with Delvalle, whose term as president of Panama ended on September 1, 1989. Until then he remained a threat—as he had made clear in the December 1988 meeting when he complained about sanctions and virtually invited Reagan and Bush to invade. Bush, however, had reaffirmed the U.S. commitment to sanctions as a sign of toughness and determination. This, not surprisingly, disappointed Delvalle.

Bush had to mollify him. He had to convince him that he would not let Panama drop from his agenda. In early February 1989, Bush informed Delvalle and other opposition leaders that he had signed his own secret finding allocating $10 million to help the opposition in the May 1989 election. This finding would stress communications and psychological warfare assistance and the CIA was to supervise the effort.

Bush publicly challenged Noriega to allow a free and open election, an irony for everyone who remembered Noriega fixing the 1984 election with the blessings of the Reagan–Bush administration. Bush also declared that the upcoming election should be free of tampering and secret influence of the sort he had funded with his finding.

Bush proposed that international observers monitor the elections, and he named Jimmy Carter to head an international team and serve as his personal observer. Carter was a folk hero in Panama because he had negotiated the canal treaties. Respect for his statesmanship also extended throughout much of Latin America. Bush, expecting trouble, needed someone to help deflect it from the White House door.

▄▄▄▄

On February 17, 1989, Gen. Fred Woerner addressed American and Panamanian businessmen at a regional meeting of the Chamber of Commerce in Panama City. Just a few days earlier, some of the businessmen had pleaded with Ambassador Davis and his deputy chief of mission John Maisto to remove the economic sanctions that had been in place since the middle of 1988. The supplicants were all Panamanians—*civilistas* and "Babbitistas," members of Kiwanis and the Young Presidents Organization. They laid out proof that the U.S. sanctions had ravaged all parts of the Panamanian economy, except those vital to Noriega's power. Davis and Maisto had been forced to defend the policy.

Woerner knew he was walking into a minefield. He wanted to be candid but was still under strict instructions to avoid making headlines.

In his prepared remarks, Woerner made little mention of Panama. But later, in the question-and-answer period, the first speaker was an American businessman who asked if the Bush administration would change U.S. policy toward Panama. The questioner's tone had a sarcastic edge. Woerner, fearing that Panama would monopolize the remaining time, brought up the May election. "I believe," he said, "that we should be seriously debating and deciding now what our actions are to be on May 8 given a variety of scenarios. We ought to know what we plan to do in the event of a reasonably honest election, a grossly dishonest election, a postponed election, or any other possible outcome." This was the sort of advice he routinely provided to Washington.

"We are frankly ill prepared to do that now," he continued,

"because, as you well know, we have a vacuum in Washington in the absence of an appointment of an assistant secretary of state for Latin American affairs. Until we get that position filled and the debate can commence, I offer you little hope of an articulated policy," Woerner said. There were no more questions about Panama and Woerner went about his business.

On February 24, the *New York Times* reported, "General Sees Lack of Panama Policy." Elaine Sciolino's story from Washington quoted parts of Woerner's answer, most notably his mention of a "vacuum" in Washington. It placed his remarks in the wider context of unfilled positions and stalled policies throughout the administration nearly a month after inauguration. It was correct in concept and in all details but erred, according to Woerner, in suggesting that he had thrown down a gauntlet, an intention that was inconsistent with Woerner's conduct over three decades in the military, and which he denied. To be sure, Woerner could have resorted to boilerplate about the "policy review process." His bluntness was probably a measure of his own frustration. Woerner had simply told the truth to a roomful of people who could not be fooled about what was really going on. The trouble, for Woerner as it turned out, was that what was obvious in Panama was unmentionable in Washington.

"The phone starts ringing off the hook," Woerner recalled. " 'What did you say? The president is furious. What did you say?' " Woerner sent a tape and transcript of all his remarks to Washington immediately. "They listened to it," Woerner said. "Conclusion: no problem." Or so he was told.

Not long afterward, Woerner and Admiral Crowe, chairman of the Joint Chiefs of Staff, met at the White House with Brent Scowcroft, the national security adviser. Crowe, who knew Woerner's position and respected his work, adamantly opposed U.S. military action in Panama. He believed that U.S. military force should be used exclusively to defend strategic interests.

"Fred, will you stay a minute?" Scowcroft asked as Woerner and Crowe were leaving. Crowe lingered in the corridor as Woerner returned to Scowcroft's office.

"I want you to know the president was very angry with your speech," Scowcroft said.

"Do you know what I said?" Woerner asked. He was somewhat angry himself.

"Yes, what you said was true, but you shouldn't have said it," Scowcroft said.

"I apologize. I did not consider it indiscreet or [want] to cause the president any embarrassment. . . . I did not criticize the president. I described a condition which everybody acknowledges," Woerner said.

"Just be careful and it's all over and just be careful," Scowcroft said.

"You can be assured that I will be careful. I'm not talking to anybody right now," Woerner said. The general tried to laugh off the presidential chastisement.

Woerner, rejoining Crowe, could see that the admiral was perturbed. "Fred, did he talk to you about your speech?" Crowe asked.

"Yes sir, he did," Woerner said.

"Damn it, it's agreed that was a closed issue. He should not have mentioned it," Crowe said.

Woerner was also in trouble back in Panama. U.S. civilians, military personnel, and their families were angry about the policy that permitted Noriega to threaten and humiliate them on an almost daily basis. Just after Woerner's exchange with Scowcroft, armed PDF "Transito" troops under the command of Maj. Luis Cordoba (one of the "Gang of Six" and the prime suspect in the murder of Hugo Spadafora) ordered twenty-one U.S. school buses, traveling in a loose convoy after a school event, to the side of the road. They charged that the buses lacked the proper license plates. Inside were hundreds of U.S. schoolchildren, many under twelve. After hours of wrangling, the PDF finally allowed the buses to move on.

As the election approached, the turmoil grew but the opposition forces produced neither a new political party nor a leader. Still, there was widespread consensus that the opposition could use the campaign to reignite rallies and denounce Noriega. The bickering leaders of the political parties, meeting at a ranch for a weekend, produced an amended version of the 1984 opposition slate. (Arias was dead and Carlos Rodriguez, one of the vice presidential candidates, was an exile in Miami.)

In Panama, one votes for a president and two virtually co-equal vice presidents. For president, the opposition chose Arnulfo Arias's closest confidant and protégé, Guillermo Endara, a fifty-two-year-old lawyer who specialized in labor negotiations, divorce, and corporate work. This was his first candidacy. "I remember," Endara said, "Dr. Arias always saying to me and to others that responsibilities for the country were things that came up on oneself by force of destiny, sort of, although we're not orientalists, a sort of a karma. You don't seek the karma, you have the karma." It was clear that Endara, who shared the mystic rhetoric of so many Panamanian politicians, was not the product of political packaging. Shy and retiring, he weighed over 250 pounds and smiled frequently. His expression seemed at odds with his dismal prospects.

Guillermo "Billy" Ford, one of the opposition's two vice presidential candidates, came from the National Liberal Republican Movement (MOLIRENA) party. (In Panama, the various parties were almost identical on the issues.) Ford was a *rabiblanco* who had never achieved great business success but who was well liked. He was a wise-cracking, slangy raconteur, a flirt with white hair, a deeply lined face, and a voice made raspy by scotch and cigarettes.

The other vice presidential candidate was Ricardo Arias Calderon, leader of the Christian Democrat party whose grass-roots organization in Panama was widespread and committed. A philosophy professor and devout Catholic, he was durable, dedicated, and grim. Torrijos had ordered him investigated in the 1970s and had found absolutely no dirt. "Such a man is very dangerous," Torrijos had said.

A slight hitch occurred when Arias Calderon balked at appearing on the same ticket with Endara and Ford. He called them "lightweights," a term that was singularly inappropriate for Endara, a fact Ford pointed out. After forty-eight hours, Arias Calderon gave in and the somewhat idiosyncratic coalition lurched into action.

The platform consisted of a single plank: If elected they would retire Noriega. To be sure, they also spoke about how they would then root out the corruption that had ruined the country, but Noriega was the issue. When someone raised the question of amnesty for Noriega and his closest accomplices if he stepped down, the troika agreed immediately that all crimes should be investigated by a reformed judicial system, and that there would be no amnesty for any guilty PDF officer. "If we talk about amnesty for the PDF killers, who will tell Winston Spadafora or Berta Mitrotti?" one of the candidates asked.

The candidates, funded mainly by friends and families as well as various Latin American political parties, said later that they were unaware that George Bush had also kicked in $10 million and commissioned the CIA to help them. This is not to say that the candidates did not knowingly accept assistance from the U.S. government. A U.S. embassy officer insisted that Endara use a telephone voice scrambling device when he learned that the candidate and others often telephoned Miami and Washington to discuss plans with Panamanian exiles. Endara was bemused by the gadgetry and often asked Louis Martinz for the use of his house—and telephone—when he and the others wanted to meet and talk to their friends in the United States.

Endara said that if they had to use such gear, they should also use code names and enter the spirit of the affair. He suggested "El Gordo" (The Fat One) for himself because it was easy to remember. His interlocutor in the United States was "El Flaco" or "The Thin One."

Noriega didn't bother with code names. He gave the election very little attention, a big mistake. Noriega's handpicked ticket was even more unlikely than the opposition line-up:

Carlos Duque, the morose, unhealthy-looking presidential candidate, was even fatter than Endara. A long-standing Noriega business crony, Duque ran Transit SA, one of the general's most lucrative enterprises. For the vice presidential slots, Noriega chose his brother-in-law, Maj. Ramon Sieiro, Felicidad's younger sibling, and Aquilino Boyd. The latter was a figure of fun in Panamanian political circles. "Here Lies the Future President of Panama," his tombstone would say, according to a popular Panama City joke that mocked his obvious, ferocious ambition to be president, an ambition he first declared when he was a tiny child. Rich, with a full shock of black hair, he qualified as an oligarch, since one of his forebears, a Founding Father of Panama, had helped cut the deal with Roosevelt to build the canal. Not only did Boyd have no political base, he was estranged from his old friends and even some of his family because of his association with Noriega. Still, he was a more colorful character than the other two (a political asset in Panama). He had publicly urinated on the U.S. flag during a 1959 anti-Yanqui demonstration and, at about the same time, had helped Noriega get a scholarship to a military academy in Peru, where his career started. Boyd was Panama's ambassador to the U.N. when Bush was the U.S. ambassador. He boasted of his close personal friendship with the Bush family.

Hoping to stymie observers and journalists, Noriega prepared a basic plan for election fraud: He hoped to make it difficult for his opponents to vote by destroying voter registration lists and substituting his own truncated lists of eligible voters. Noriega was careful not to overdo it. He put more effort into making sure that his supporters—government employees, PRD members, and especially the PDF—had the correct paperwork to vote "early and often." Many PDF members even had special, legal passes that allowed them to go to the head of the line—useful if one planned to visit ten or fifteen polling places.

An assortment of U.S. and Latin American polling services rolled through Panama during the spring. Their published findings revealed public sentiments that Noriega's own pollsters either missed or chose to ignore. In terms of "name recognition," Noriega was at the top of the list in Panama. But he appeared dead last in terms of popularity of public figures. The opposition slate, the polls said, was beating his three friends two to one. Noriega did not like bad news, so he ignored the polls that should have made him consider canceling the election.

Instead, Noriega, who controlled all the media, filled radio, television, and newspapers with pictures of his slate and emphasized their commitment to Panamanian sovereignty and resistance to the United States. Noriega himself was barely visible; he had maintained a very low profile since the indictments. He had become very security conscious and traveled in as many as seven identical limousines. He used elaborate disguises and appeared only at heavily guarded events, which received saturation media coverage.

The opposition slate was, on the other hand, extremely visible. For a while, Noriega permitted them exactly ten minutes of TV airtime per day; eventually, that "privilege" was revoked. When the powerful Eleta family, which owned Channel 4, sold Endara airtime, Noriega slapped the family with a cooked-up bill for back taxes totaling $4 million.

So the opposition candidates went to city squares and open fields, and as time passed, they began to draw large, enthusiastic crowds. The campaign seemed to transform the candidates who appeared to enjoy each other's company. The grim and pedantic Arias Calderon gradually relaxed in front of crowds that reacted enthusiastically. Their applause provoked emotional oratory from Arias Calderon about the shame Noriega had brought to his country.

Ford was also a crowd-pleaser. His mocking denunciations of Noriega, even more raspy and catchy when broadcast over loudspeakers, were popular. Endara also worked hard, though he had dreaded the prospect of campaigning. He spoke adequately and seemed confident. He smiled more and more, suggesting that the campaign was sound in the karma department.

The first embarrassment and Noriega's first opening came on April 5 when the PDF arrested an American named Kurt Frederick Muse. Muse, a thirty-nine-year-old businessman, had grown up in Panama. He was arrested with several Panamanians by the PDF in raids netting about $350,000 worth of communications equipment from eight apartments around Panama City. Muse was accused by the PDF of being the principal American agent in a clandestine radio network that was attempting to promote the opposition candidates and undermine the government. Rumors had circulated in Panama City that the CIA was operating such a clandestine radio station but few, if anyone, had ever heard any broadcasts. The PDF charge against the conspirators—threatening state security—was flattering.

Later in the month, Bush's $10 million plan (the second "finding") was reported in Panama, in connection with the stories about the alleged radio station. Carla Anne Robbins, Miami bureau chief of *U.S. News & World Report*, broke the story and some suspected that her sources had to have had a motive for making the disclosure. Whatever the case, there were no denials from Washington following the stories on the finding or the alleged secret radio station.

The story infuriated many Panamanian opposition members who regarded it as a deliberate leak by Noriega allies inside the administration. They believed Nestor Sanchez was the culprit.

Noriega, however, failed to follow through, simply repeating the usual banalities about interference and aggression. "They Sold Their Country for $10 Million," blared posters, headlines, and televisions up until election day. Noriega, supremely confident, went on with his business, making sure the PDF and his people on the payroll were happy. On election day, Sunday, May 7, everything would be legal, orderly, calm—and observer-proof. Noriega believed he could fool anybody, especially Jimmy Carter, whom Noriega described as a "patsy."

On Saturday, May 6, twenty-one U.S. officials, legislators, and legislative aides flew from Washington to Panama to serve as President Bush's personal election observers. All opposed Noriega and many had made his wickedness part of their oratorical repertoire.

Ambassador Davis and General Woerner stood arguing on the broiling tarmac at Howard Air Force Base as the aircraft carrying the delegates taxied to a stop. The problem between them was a question of visas. The delegates did not have visas to enter Panama. In fact, according to the government press, they were not observers but "invaders" who had not been invited (like the Latin American team that Carter supervised) and who had no right to enter Panama. Woerner spoke urgently to Davis. There was reliable information that Noriega would use the visa issue to create a very dangerous situation. If the delegates were refused visas at the U.S. air base and then left the base, Noriega might have them arrested. Noriega could then enact a patriotic tableau on television: The Americans could assert their rights to enter Panama and Noriega, playing the patriot, could refuse.

Woerner was concerned. Noriega was unpredictable and Woerner wanted to brief the delegates about the situation. The fact was that they had not been invited and might soon be arrested as illegal aliens.

Davis scoffed: No invitation was necessary. "The government doesn't exist," Davis said. "There is no government of Panama." When Woerner pointed out that Noriega was running things, Davis said, "Fine, but we don't recognize them. We don't have anything to do with them." He and Woerner planned to have an aide hand over the passports to the PDF officer at the immigration desk at the base. Davis was bone certain that the man would stamp them. How could he not? If the PDF refused to stamp the passports, Davis planned to ignore the decision. "There's no way Noriega is going to keep senators and congressmen and other high dignitaries from the United States from going out and observing these elections," he told Woerner.

The animosity between the two men was apparent when they boarded the plane. Davis spoke first. "Look, we've got all your documentation," he said. "We're going to have to see if they accept it, but if they don't we have cars and vans to take you around. . . . Fred Woerner has different views. Fred, I want you to tell them what it is."

Davis's tone made it clear that he disagreed with what Woerner was about to say, but Woerner was blunt. He made it clear that they would risk injury by resisting arrest. He said that U.S. troops would increase the risk of bloodshed. He said that if any of the delegates were arrested he would follow procedures and see to their release. Most of the delegates, still in their seats, resented Woerner's warning. Like Davis, they thought it inconceivable that a pip-squeak Panamanian would bother official Americans.

According to Davis, U.S. policy was to confront the PDF and let the bodies fall where they may. "[Woerner] was afraid of military confrontation. His whole attitude was wrong all the way through." Davis believed his attitude reflected Bush's policy.

As the delegates, the ambassador, the general, and assorted escort officers and flunkies were boarding the buses for their downtown hotels, an embassy aide appeared with the passports, all properly stamped. A member of Woerner's staff, as it happened, had managed to smooth out the matter. Now the delegates had legal authorization from a regime whose existence most of them denied. Davis felt vindicated, confident that no Panamanian, including Noriega, could tell U.S. officials what they could not do.

Jimmy and Rosalynn Carter visited Noriega that same day for forty-five frosty minutes. Noriega, proclaiming that Carter had "an eternal visa" to Panama, was happy to be photographed with the ex-president and his wife. But Noriega hardly bothered to conceal his scorn for Carter during the conversation that followed. He did not concede the possibility of leaving power, under any circumstances.

On election day, the Carters and the other observers traveled around the city from the 7:00 A.M. poll opening to the 5:00 P.M. closing, looking in at polling places. The turnout was enormous, the largest anyone could remember. There were relatively few skirmishes or loud disputes at the polling places. As far as the observers and most visiting journalists could tell, all was in order and both sides began to claim victory in the early afternoon. Collection and counting were to begin almost immediately after closing at the Atlapa convention center, and the official returns were to be announced the next day, Monday, May 8. By the end of the day it appeared that Noriega had prevailed. "So far it's OK," Carter told reporters just as the polls were closing. "It's the counting that's the problem." Noriega looked forward to letting the gringos count the votes.

By early Sunday evening, the count was clear: Noriega had suffered one of the greatest humiliations of his life. The voters had cast their ballots for the opposition (or against him) by as much as three to one. The numbers meant that many of his most trusted supporters had voted early and often—and had voted against him.

They were all screwing with him, laughing at him. Stunned and enraged, he dispatched paramilitary teams to burn ballots and in some cases trash polling places.

By Monday morning it was clear that Carter had played Noriega for a patsy. Carter was the hero of the pro-government press that morning for his "OK" remark of the previous day. But now Carter wanted to ask Noriega some questions, and as the morning wore on he repeated his requests more urgently. Noriega's office refused to make an appointment. Around noon, Carter specifically mentioned his suspicions of fraud and destruction of ballots, and Noriega's office stopped returning his calls.

While Carter gathered more information, thousands of Panamanians surrounded Endara, Ford, Arias Calderon, and the others and marched toward Atlapa. But the PDF drove them away. "You can feel it, you can feel it, Endara is the president," the crowds chanted.

In the late afternoon, Carter decided to see what was going on at Atlapa for himself. He got as far as the door when a guard told him to get lost. Carter went almost immediately to the Marriott, just a short walk away, to hold a press conference.

"The government is taking the election by fraud," Carter said. "It's robbing the people of Panama of their legitimate rights. . . . I hope there will be a worldwide outcry of condemnation against a dictator who stole this election from his own people." Carter said the people had rejected the military by three to one.

The candidates stayed in the streets, still campaigning, confident that somehow, someone would prevent Noriega from stealing the election. What were observers for?

On Tuesday, May 9, the congressional delegation reported to Bush. The facts were plain enough for everyone. The delegation painted a very grim picture and wanted some sort of action. Senator John McCain of Arizona, for example, stated that the United States might have to use force in Panama, a thought that had occurred to everyone.

Carter gave Bush moderate and wise advice when he briefed him the same day. He did not try to goad Bush into action, telling the president to "take a little time" and see what Noriega did. "Any sort of military involvement there would immediately alienate the Panamanian people, who respect their nation's sovereignty as do we," Carter said. "And obviously unilateral action is much weaker than action in concert with other democratic countries." Carter suggested that Bush invite Latin American nations to help persuade Noriega to leave.

Bush jumped at Carter's suggestion because it helped him escape the political hazards of a genuine showdown with Noriega. U.S. diplomats sought out their contacts, who were eager to talk and participate. "The Panamanian people have spoken," Bush said. "And I call on General Noriega to respect the voice of the people. And I call on all foreign leaders to urge General Noriega to honor the clear results of the election."

On Wednesday, May 10, the candidates invited the public to join them in a march across the city. In a macabre way, May 10 was probably the day of greatest strength for Noriega's relentless opponents.

Up and down Via Espana, crowds waited for the candidates. The PDF assaulted them with clubs, birdshot, and liquefied tear gas. An old woman walking out of a bank was beaten bloody. Demonstrators hiding in the same bank lobby panicked when PDF soldiers pumped gas into the lobby and beat people who tried to escape.

When the candidates reached the banking district on Via Espana, they stood shoulder to shoulder in the center of a huge crowd. "Murderers, murderers, murderers," chanted the crowd at the PDF soldiers who blocked the street. The soldiers pointed guns at the candidates' stomachs. After a long and tense standoff, the crowds and the candidates melted away into side streets, planning to converge again at a designated intersection farther along Via Espana. Then they passed the Continental Hotel and El Carmen cathedral and headed in the direction of the Comandancia.

The PDF attacked the crowd near the cathedral just after the candidates passed. For the next ten or fifteen minutes, as the PDF surged in one direction and then another, the crowd ebbed and flowed. Louis Martinz and others stayed on the streets until a spray of gas came toward them, and they retreated into an office building lobby. They dashed in and out again and again. Once, Martinz lingered and, as he ran toward safety, noticed that a car had blocked the entrance to the building. Four armed men in civilian clothes grabbed him and tried to shove him into the backseat. Martinz used a sturdy six-foot flagpole as a brace and managed to stay out of the car—and yell to his friends for help. After at least a minute of tussling, one of the four pried Martinz's fingers from the flagpole, threw it to the ground, and shoved Martinz into the back of the car, which then sped away, its rear right door swinging open as Martinz kicked and struggled. A few blocks away the car stopped and the paramilitaries, assisted by a Doberman, subdued Martinz. The paramilitaries took him to a PDF building near the Comandancia, where nearly one hundred prisoners with similar stories were also locked up.

About half an hour later, Endara, Arias Calderon, and Ford reached the Santa Ana neighborhood, just a few minutes' walk from the Comandancia. The PDF policemen who had harassed them along the route faded away to lurk in doorways or just look the other way. Suddenly, men in civilian clothes, some with T-shirts inscribed "Dignity Battalion," materialized, running toward the three politicians, swinging long steel pipes, tire irons, and planks with jutting nails.

Arias Calderon's bodyguard managed to push him down a side street but only after he had been struck several times. One of the paramilitaries, however, lunged past Endara's bodyguards and punched him in the face, knocking the rightful president of Panama's glasses to the ground. As Endara bent to retrieve them, the man ground the glass into the pavement with his shoe. Then, as Endara began to raise his hand, another paramilitary swung a lead pipe hard, directly at Endara's skull. Blood streamed from Endara's head as he sprawled unconscious. His bodyguards circled him and managed to carry the inert, 250-pound president–elect down one alley and then another. Paramilitaries chased them until they reached a car and sped away.

Ford's bodyguards had shoved him quickly to his car, but the paramilitaries pursued and swarmed around the vehicle. Guns were drawn. Ford's chief bodyguard, twenty-two-year-old Manuel Alexis Guerra, embraced him, trying to shield his body from the arms and hands reaching into the car. Gunfire rang out. Guerra's head was next to Ford's right shoulder. "They killed me," Guerra said to Ford, very quietly. "No, no, they didn't," Ford said. Then blood erupted from Guerra's mouth all over Ford's right arm and side. It shone bright red and slick on his gleaming white *guayabera* shirt. Ford slid out of the car and was suddenly all alone.

When a paramilitary hit him in the face, opening a gash under his eye, Ford stayed on his feet, trying to confront his attackers, only to be clubbed again and again. The attackers hit hard, but they also withdrew immediately to stay out of his striking range, as if they were afraid of him. Finally, he was shoved into a PDF van and driven away.

Still bleeding and semi-conscious, Endara was taken to opposition headquarters at the Ejecutivo Hotel. There was no news of Arias Calderon or of Ford; reports about the others, especially Martinz, were grim. A paramilitary arrest made murder much easier. Indeed, the PDF would not admit Martinz was even in custody. "Martinz was forty-nine," a friend told a journalist on the phone, already using the past tense.

Hospitals were filling up with injured demonstrators. Two of Gabriel Lewis's sons, Eduardo and Samuel, both suffered bloody head wounds. Endara finally went to the hospital himself, and Arias Calderon, who had hidden out in a small factory, got home long after dark. His shirt was wet with blood. He was limping and deeply bruised on his thigh, back, and ribs. His wife, Teresita, had been gassed and chased. Their son Martin was bloodied, but sixteen-year-old Ignacio, who had also been in the streets, had escaped serious injury. By that evening the film of Ford's ordeal was on the news. Panamanian politics appeared in a stark, primary color—the color of blood.

Ford was locked up in the same building where Martinz had been taken. Many of the prisoners were isolated or alternately ignored and yelled at. Hours went by and Ford, his lacerations still untended and his shirt still bloody, was shoved down a corridor and into a dingy room.

"Louisito!" Ford exclaimed.

"Billy," Martinz, whose own cuts and bruises were also untended, replied, embracing his friend. "Tell me what happened."

Shortly afterward a *civilista* named Olimpo Saens, who had not been beaten, joined them and then all were packed off to La Modelo prison. Ford was taken to the infirmary where his face was stitched and then returned to the same room with Martinz and Saens. Shortly afterward Saens was taken away. When he returned to the room his face was bloody and his arms bruised. He brought news. Citing outside interference, Noriega had nullified the election.

Ford, Martinz, and Saens tried to sleep in the stifling heat. "Jesus, this table is so hard," Ford exclaimed. "Billy, the floor is harder," Martinz replied. Saens was silent.

Toward dawn a guard came in, threw some clean clothes at Ford and told him he was to be released. Ford replaced his blood-caked clothes with PDF prison issues—his first ever jungle-patterned Hawaiian shirt and shorts, complemented by black street shoes and no socks. Martinz examined the design closely. "No problem, Billy," he said. "All coconuts. No pineapples."

Saens was soon taken away again. This time the beating was more severe and one of his tormentors scrawled the stars and stripes and the words "he sold his country for $10 million" on his chest with a felt pen.

Martinz was pushed into another small room in another part of the jail. A guard told him the room next door was the "AIDS cell," where he would soon be taken to contract the disease. For two more months, with occasional beatings and frequent interrogations, Martinz and eighty-five other political prisoners remained in custody in the same cell. They were never put in the "AIDS cell," but it was a daily threat until they were released from prison in July.

The events of May 10 anointed the election landslide in blood. The opposition were clearly in the majority and belonged in power. Now it seemed inconceivable that Noriega could remain; his removal seemed a political necessity for Bush. "One way or another, it seems to us, [President Bush] has to restore the Panamanian election," said an editorial in the *Wall Street Journal*. The editorial reflected the political pressure on the president.

Bush listened carefully to Carter and sought international help. But his first action was to dispatch 2,000 troops to Panama to resume military posturing. Just two days after the bloody street violence, C-141 transports began to land in Panama every half hour. "Invasion fever" was in the air. Military dependents headed for the shelter of the bases.

In the past, SOUTHCOM had coordinated its convoys with the PDF to let them know when they could expect heavy truck traffic on Panamanian highways. It was a gesture of cooperation and promoted safety. After May 10, there was still coordination. But now armed escorts accompanied the convoys. It was a new dimension in muscle flexing.

"I'm worried about the lives of American citizens and I will do what is necessary to protect the lives of American citizens," Bush said on May 11. "We will not be intimidated by the bullying tactics, brutal though they may be, of the dictator Noriega. The United States will not recognize . . . a regime that holds power through force and violence at the expense of the Panamanian people's right to be free."

Bush also appealed to the PDF for a coup. "I would love to see them get him out," he said on May 13 as he flew to Starkville, Mississippi, to give a commencement address at Mississippi State University. In the give-and-take aboard Air Force One, a reporter asked what Panamanians should do. "They ought to just do everything they can to get Mr. Noriega out of there," Bush said.

There have been few if any occasions when an American president has been more explicit in asking a foreign military force for a coup. And there was probably no country in the world where the United States was better prepared to help foster a coup. U.S. help was crucial; it was obvious that any coup attempt would involve fighting within the PDF. The United States could play a decisive role. The Americans, for example, could intercept communications to the benefit of the coup-makers. In the event of troop movements on the ground or in the air, the United States could intervene, to block roads or seize aircraft and airports. However, Bush stressed that the responsibility lay with the Panamanians. "If the PDF asks for support to get rid of Noriega, they wouldn't need support from the United States to get rid of Noriega. He's one man and they have a well-trained force," he said. To most Panamanians, those were pro-forma remarks.

On May 16, Bush finally telephoned Endara to congratulate him. Nine days after his victory at the polls, Endara had become something of an afterthought in the U.S. calculations. Bush told him that the sanctions would remain and assured him they were targeted at Noriega and not the people of Panama. Endara did not debate him. Bush also said that the United States did not oppose the PDF as an institution. Again, Endara, still bandaged, did not argue, though the call offered little comfort.

The candidates tried to return to the streets and called a general strike on May 17. But it fizzled quickly. Ford made it clear that there was nothing more the Panamanian people could prove by sacrificing themselves to the PDF. He told interviewers that the people alone could not overthrow the heavily armed PDF. "We're not going to ask our people to confront these monsters," Ford said. "We're not going to take them to the butcher shop."

It was a sad moment for the opposition, and fittingly enough, Ambassador Davis was recalled to Washington as a gesture of U.S. anger at Noriega. That meant that the opposition's best American friend, a man who had risked his own safety repeatedly to show solidarity, was gone. At his departure press conference, Davis was outspoken. He flatly accused Noriega of attempting to murder the candidates.

11

Find the Scapegoat

ON May 12, 1989, Noriega received another blow. Carlos Andres Perez, the president of Venezuela, suggested that the Organization of American States (OAS) tell the general to disappear. To blunt the impact, he offered Noriega asylum in Caracas.

Perez, an ally of Jimmy Carter during the Panama Canal treaty controversy, had offered the United States his diplomatic assistance in the Noriega affair many times. But he had always been rebuffed and insulted by the Reagan administration. Now the Americans seemed more open: Bush endorsed the Venezuelan's idea and began to assemble a reasonable facsimile of a new Panama "policy." He knew that the cooperation of the OAS would help internationalize the Noriega issue and take the heat off himself—if only for a minute.

It was clear that the administration had run out of ideas on how to shelve Noriega. If Bush had other tricks up his sleeve, he would never have accepted assistance from the OAS, which in the past had been an active critic of U.S. intervention in Central and South America. When an emergency meeting of the OAS was scheduled for May 17, the consensus was that it represented nothing more than diplomatic posturing. Despite Perez's stand against Noriega, no one believed that the May 17 meeting would produce significant results. The OAS couldn't oust Noriega. Nothing was happening. Bush was using the OAS to attempt to conceal his own policy vacuum.

At the time the OAS got involved in the Panama situation, it was having its own troubles. Noriega had weathered his fiscal crisis, but the OAS was plunging deeper and deeper into its own. Administrators were even considering a second mortgage on the organization's Washington headquarters, a handsome building at Constitution and 17th Street. Earlier in the year, three hundred employees had been sacked and there were rumors that after May there would be no money for secretaries' salaries.

How had such a prestigious organization fallen into such a hole? One factor was that Reagan and Bush never paid any attention to it. Another problem was that most of its members were far behind in their dues. Founded in 1948, the OAS was chartered to be a regional United Nations. Dues payments were based on the U.N. model and the United States was obliged to pay over 60 percent of the annual budget. By May 1989, the United States owed the OAS over $50 million in unpaid annual dues. The general impression within the OAS was that these dues would be paid *if* the organization "helped" Bush with Panama.

In the days leading up to the May 17 meeting, U.S. diplomats lobbied OAS representatives vigorously: The United States wanted all OAS member nations to follow its lead and recall their ambassadors from Panama. The United States also wanted the OAS to demand Noriega's resignation. Furthermore, the Americans wanted pledges from every OAS member to do everything possible to remove Noriega.

There was, not surprisingly, resistance. Many OAS members recoiled from the suggestion that each should take action against Noriega. To some Latin Americans, the agreement amounted to tacit permission for a U.S. invasion.

Once the May 17 meeting actually started, it quickly became obvious that the U.S. lobbying effort had failed miserably. Many OAS representatives were so eager to denounce U.S. intervention that they argued against any resolution that mentioned Noriega's name, let alone his resignation. Some representatives believed that any resolution directly calling for Noriega's departure constituted, in itself, an act of intervention. One popular draft resolution omitted Noriega's name, spoke of Panama in general, specifically denounced intervention, and warned the United States that it had to honor the canal treaties.

In the early morning of May 18, the delegates produced a resolution condemning "abuses" by Noriega; this time he was named. The resolution called for a "transfer of power, in the shortest time possible, and with full respect to the sovereign will of the Panamanian people." The language was so tame that even Jorge Ritter, Noriega's foreign minister, called it fair. At the White House, Marlin Fitzwater praised the OAS and spoke of the resolution as a diplomatic triumph. "We're gratified that the OAS countries shared the United States's position," he said.

The OAS had also voted to dispatch diplomats to Panama to begin the "transfer of power." One was Ecuador's Diego Cordovez, famous for his work on negotiating the Russians out of Afghanistan. (The others were OAS general secretary Gen. Joao Baena Soares of Brazil, Trinidad's Bhoendradath Tewarie, and Guatemala's foreign minister Mario Palencia.) Between May 23 and late August, the team made five different reporting trips to Panama. After each visit, the team extended the deadline for its report and spoke of progress.

In late August, the negotiators said they were on the verge of success. They said they had worked out a plan by which Noriega would step down on September 1, when the terms of both Delvalle and Solis Palma ended. (The constitution required Noriega to either call a new election at that time or recognize the May 10 election.)

The OAS plan called for an interim government that would hold new elections. The plan thus accepted Noriega's nullification of the May elections and allowed him to remain in Panama.

The United States continued to encourage the OAS negotiations. "Our position," said a State Department official, "is that Noriega should leave office. We want a democratic transition. The United States is not insisting that Noriega leave Panama. Our position is he should leave power. Everything after that is up to the Panamanians; it ceases to be our business."

The negotiations continued, growing more heated against a background of intensified military posturing. In Panama, U.S. troops (bristling with assault weapons) traveled in fast-moving convoys, escorted by armored vehicles. They certainly looked as if they planned to attack someone, even if White House orders still limited confrontation.

Noriega denounced the military activity and snubbed OAS negotiators. He called them idiots in public and laughed at their plans. He refused to step down and even forgot to pay lip service

to the constitution. He named a new president, Francisco Rodriguez, a high school classmate who had been Panama's comptroller for seven years. The OAS episode came to an end with the
Latin American diplomats accusing the United States of subvert-
ing their success with its military bluster.

Still, despite the failure and recriminations, the OAS interlude
had been worthwhile. The OAS had served Bush's domestic political needs; it gave him an answer to the question "Now what?"
The negotiations also reinvigorated the OAS as an institution;
diplomats from many Latin American countries used the May 17
meeting as a forum to express opposition to U.S. military intervention in Panama. The negotiations also helped Noriega, at least
for a while. They gave him the opportunity to triumph again.

As time went by, Gen. Fred Woerner became more certain that
Bush might one day decide that the removal of Noriega was urgent enough for him to call for a large-scale U.S. military operation. Woerner instructed his staff to prepare for that contingency.
When Admiral Crowe, assessing the mood in Washington that
spring, told him to get ready to use force, Woerner told him he
was well along in his preparations.

Woerner's plans were dramatically foward-looking and politically astute. His fundamental assumption was that the PDF was
rotten throughout and that it had to be dismantled. Noriega would
not so much be removed from power as the power of the PDF
would be removed from him—and from Panama. Woerner's plans
amounted to a death warrant (figuratively speaking, since Woerner
assumed that the PDF would snap under the mere threat of U.S.
firepower) for the organization that had run Panama for twenty-
one years—and that the United States had nurtured with extensive
training and millions of dollars. His plans called for a new uniformed force whose single mission was public security and whose
members would all be freshly recruited. In Washington, meanwhile, Bush regularly reiterated his support for the PDF as an
institution, as is, minus the single person of Noriega.

Woerner's plans not only contradicted stated policy on the
PDF but also meant comprehensive change in Panama—a social
revolution in which the United States would play a major role.
The plans called for a U.S. military presence, the equivalent of
U.S. occupation, until the new Panamanian security force could
be recruited and trained. Indeed, U.S. troops would have to de-

ploy immediately throughout the capital to prevent the looting that was likely to occur once the PDF had collapsed, taking public authority with it. Woerner's plan included measures to prevent such disorder. Woerner also wanted to plan for a quick and effective assumption of power by Endara, Ford, and Arias Calderon.

Woerner addressed the obvious and troubling human, economic, and political questions raised by the prospect of large-scale action. He was blunt in saying that he opposed the use of force in Panama. He was convinced that the objective—to remove Noriega from power—was not worth the cost. If the United States attacked Panama, the first and most obvious target was Noriega's Comandancia, the PDF's equivalent of the Pentagon. Wooden tenements, built at the turn of the century to house canal construction workers, surrounded the concrete building. If U.S. forces attacked the Comandancia with heavy firepower, it was inevitable that these tindery structures would catch fire. Then perhaps all of El Chorrillo, as the thickly populated neighborhood was known, would burn to the ground. El Chorrillo was important in Panama's history and helped give the capital city its raffish élan. It was the birthplace of the boxer Roberto Duran, who was, its residents often told outsiders, not really that tough by the standards of the neighborhood. Its mostly poor and black population had voted against Noriega in the May election in great numbers.

The planning remained at the quiet, obscure level. Woerner was forbidden to discuss his scenario with the State Department for a number of reasons, including the possibility of leaks. No one wanted to explain why the United States was planning to "disassemble," as Woerner put it, the PDF when Bush regularly expressed his support for it.

Meanwhile, on the ground, things were getting dangerous in Panama.

Early in the summer of 1989, Woerner sent a cable to his superiors at the Pentagon in which he predicted that an American would be killed. He now says that he was "trying to shock them into realizing that the military posturing was bound to provoke the kind of situation we were trying to avoid. We wouldn't commit to military intervention, but the posturing would make it a necessity." He pointed out that there would be a casket with a flag on it.

"Are we going to eat that?" he asked. "Tolerate it? Or are we going to leverage it? What do we want to do?" Woerner got an answer several weeks later. It was a bureaucratic form letter, a brush-off, saying, basically, "Thank you for your interest in national security." Not long afterward he got another answer.

In late July, an aid to Gen. Carl Vuono, the army chief of staff, called Woerner. The aide said that Vuono was about to depart for Panama and wanted to see Woerner as soon as he arrived. Vuono would not stay the night. He would talk to Woerner and return to Washington immediately. Woerner called his wife. "I'm going to be sacked," he told her.

"Is there somewhere we can talk?" Vuono asked as soon as Woerner greeted him on the tarmac. The two old friends went into a small meeting room just off the runways. "Fred, I've got some very bad news. The president has decided to make a change," Vuono said.

"Why, Carl?" Woerner asked. ("Even though I was expecting it, it was like a sledgehammer," Woerner said later.)

"I don't know," Vuono said. "I was told by the secretary of the army that the president had made the decision, that it's irrevocable, and that I could not enter into it. I told the secretary that I had to tell you in person. You're a friend. I know the job you've done down here. I insisted that I had to come down and tell you in person, so here I am."

The two men discussed timing and some logistical arrangements and then Vuono flew back to Washington. Woerner told only his wife and managed to keep his own counsel at headquarters. Shortly afterward, Admiral Crowe urged Woerner to see him in Washington on his next trip, which took place in mid-August.

"I can't tell you anything because the decision was made while I was in the Soviet Union without any consultation," Crowe said. In other words, Woerner's fate had been sealed by White House civilians, probably by Bush himself, without consultation with the army chief of staff or the chairman of the Joint Chiefs.

Woerner still wanted answers. So he and Crowe went to Richard Cheney, the secretary of defense.

"Fred," Cheney said, "the president has decided to make a change."

"Mr. Secretary, you can call it what you want, but I'm being relieved from command for the first time in almost thirty-five years of service. I have served this country faithfully and I believe that I am entitled to more of an explanation than that," Woerner said. According to Woerner, Cheney said, "There is none. It was purely a political decision. It had nothing to do with your performance."

It was clear to Woerner that the administration wanted him to go quietly. Still trying to follow orders, he did what he thought was expected of him. "I'm a soldier," Woerner said. "I was not going to make any political issue of it myself, although I would not be dishonest if asked." Woerner rejected the suggestion that he explain his departure by saying that his wife had been pressuring him to retire. He also refused to sign a statement suggesting that he had requested voluntary retirement. Like Barletta, Woerner insisted on his own words. He stated flatly that he was retiring. Anonymous civilian officials, however, told reporters that the problem in Panama had been Woerner. He was not aggressive enough. That was why Noriega was still there, they explained.

"You could say that I was hurt," Woerner said. "I had been a soldier for thirty-five years. I was hurt by the loss of my command and the retirement. I was also disappointed by the integrity of the system . . . that a military man would be used as a scapegoat for a failed political policy, particularly with the irony that it was a policy that [the military man] had tried to change. . . ."

U.S. military posturing had been going on all summer in Panama. In one episode, more than 1,000 U.S. military personnel conducted an exercise that appeared to be a rehearsal of a kidnap raid. Helicopters and jet aircraft flew low over Noriega's house near Fort Amador as U.S. raiders splashed ashore nearby. In Panama City, U.S. Marines descended from helicopters by rope to practice emergency evacuation of the embassy. During several of the skirmishes, the United States and the PDF seized each other's personnel. In one case, U.S. troopers took Maj. Manuel Sieiro, Felicidad Noriega's brother, into custody.

U.S. troops were always heavily armed, and during one standoff, a U.S. assault weapon was accidentally fired, shredding a mango tree and nearly starting a firefight.

By the time Woerner left for Washington to demand explanations for his dismissal, U.S. military maneuvering in Panama had escalated to a new level. On August 11, Panama's foreign minister described the situation as "a state of imminent war."

———

By September 1989, there was still no operative U.S. policy toward Panama. There had been many so-called policy options (economic sanctions, threats, negotiations, the elections, the OAS episode), and all had been described as major anti-Noriega efforts. But each had been only a diversion or postponement. Each had served only to distract attention from the stark fact that if the administration really wanted to get rid of Noriega, it would have to "play hardball."

Bush maintained his tough-guy act. On September 1, he declared that "Panama is . . . as of this date without any legitimate government. The United States will not recognize any government installed by General Noriega. Our ambassador will not return, and we will not have any diplomatic contact with the Noriega regime. . . . We will continue to stand by the people of Panama until their fight for self-determination is respected and democratic government is restored."

State Department spokesperson Margaret Tutwiler called Noriega's government "an outlaw regime."

George Bush's appointment of Gen. Max Thurman to succeed Woerner was a surprise. For one thing, Thurman was due to retire in a matter of weeks after thirty-five years in uniform.

Some suspected that Thurman was a clue to a secret U.S. plan that had already been put into motion, a plan in which he would play a vital role. Those who knew Thurman believed that his appointment meant that something serious was afoot. There was always action where Thurman was. He was restless (he slept no more than a few hours a night), very smart, and had reached one of the two top four-star billets in the United States outside the Pentagon. He had risen in the ranks despite having proposed unorthodox solutions and bucked conventional wisdom. Thurman was his own troubleshooter. He was also cagey and liked and respected in Congress.

Thurman threw himself into marathon briefings to prepare for his new job. Those who noticed such things quickly realized that although there were twenty different Central and South American countries in SOUTHCOM's bailiwick, Thurman concentrated his energies on Panama.

Thurman needed the briefings. Unlike most of his predecessors, he was almost completely ignorant of Latin America, which he had rarely visited. He didn't even speak Spanish. If Bush had a plan for Panama, it apparently did not require a savvy, experienced Latin American hand. "MacArthur didn't have to speak Korean to plan the Inchon invasion," said one former intelligence officer.

Just as Thurman began his briefings, Admiral Crowe told him (in strictest secrecy) that there was a very high probability that Bush would call for large-scale military action in Panama in the near future. "We're going to go [but] I can't tell you when," Crowe told Thurman. "Your job is to put that place on alert, get the population down, get things we don't need out of there, and be prepared to go." Crowe told Thurman to examine existing plans from "top to bottom, and start getting us ready." Crowe had always opposed military action in Panama, and he hadn't changed his mind. But he was experienced enough to realize that the accumulated failures of the Reagan and Bush administrations virtually guaranteed military conflict.

Thurman's appointment was, in many ways, the catalyst in the process of deciding to invade Panama. Thurman, who had never been part of the Panama debate and so had brought no preconceived opinion about using force in the situation, began to settle the issue simply by following orders. Following Crowe's instructions, he began to prepare for military action. He set about updating existing plans ranging from a commando snatch of Noriega to a massive, armed assault against Panama. They were only contingency plans, but they were the only plans being made in Washington or Panama by Americans, and because of the policy void, they began to look pretty good.

Thurman had not commanded troops for fourteen years. He was a good example of the corporate administrator–type of military officer, as opposed to the battlefield commander. He looked like a hardworking clerk—slightly built, almost frail. His eyeglasses were more noticeable than his unremarkable medals. His nicknames—"Mad Max" and "Maxatollah"—were tributes to his demanding, driving performance in bureaucratic positions. Thurman was a tough, hardheaded office organizer, "a McNamara in a green suit," as one officer who worked with him put it.

On Saturday morning, September 30, 1989, Max Thurman formally took command. "The United States will not recognize nor accommodate with a regime that holds power through force and violence at the expense of the Panamanian people's right to be free," he said. He promised to challenge "tyranny in all its insidious forms."

On Sunday, October 1, two years and a few months after Sandra Noriega's wedding, Tony and Felicidad Noriega hosted a party in their Golf Heights home to celebrate the baptism of their grand-daughter. For the PDF, whose members constituted a large percentage of the guest list, the party was a gathering of the survivors and the loyal elect. The ranks of Noriega loyalists had dwindled since Sandra's wedding day, a fact that was all too apparent on that October Sunday as the crowd sipped Scotch (Noriega's drink) and champagne served "Remon-style" in tall tumblers. It was a special party. The officers invited that day knew they were Noriega's elite. As much as he trusted anyone, he trusted them. They had passed all his tests.

All feared that death would be the price for disloyalty. Noriega had delivered the message repeatedly, most recently in a television speech with a veiled threat. At one point in the speech, Noriega said that the wives of the PDF officers who had led the March 1988 coup attempt would be allowed to visit the men who would be in jail for a long time, perhaps forever. Anyone else who tried a coup, he continued, could forget about visits. Their wives would be widows.

Noriega was very drunk, and he screamed obscenities and made a spectacle of himself at the party. His heavy drinking was no secret to the men of his security team. He felt no compunctions about misbehaving around them. He felt confident that no one would betray him.

The newest member of the security team was Maj. Moises Giroldi, commander of the two-hundred-strong Urraca Company. The Urraca unit was headquartered inside the Comandancia compound and served as the palace guard. It controlled sufficient firepower to annihilate any raiders of the compound. Any attempt to take over the Comandancia meant first taking out Giroldi and his troops.

Giroldi was an aggressive soldier whom Noriega had always held in check, especially when he wanted to confront U.S. troops.

During the 1988 coup attempt, Giroldi risked his life to save Noriega, who rewarded his bravery with an instant promotion from captain to major and the new command. He also became part of Noriega's personal entourage. The coup experience had bonded the men—Noriega became godfather to Giroldi's third child.

No one in the PDF officer corps was a straight-arrow, but Giroldi came close. He didn't take advantage of the various ways the officers made extra money. He still lived with his ailing father and his wife and children in a small house. His wife worked in a bank.

Giroldi was a true believer in military rule and distrusted all civilian politicians. It was possible that he had never knowingly met a *civilista*. He often spoke of Torrijos, who had drawn him to the uniform and whose memory he venerated.

Second in command of the security team was Capt. Ivan Castillo, Noriega's personal bodyguard, a friend of long standing. He was ready to put his body between Noriega and bullets. He also procured women for Noriega and escorted them home afterward.

Capt. Ramon Dias, another team member, was a Noriega pal who had supervised construction of the Causeway house and now managed its maintenance and supplies. Dias had been trained in antiterrorist techniques. His mission was to keep his eyes and ears open.

Lt. Adolph Murillo's official position was chief of the PDF's Immigration Office at Howard Air Force Base, where he and his staff also ran an observation/listening post—a vital part of Noriega's security screen. Murillo and his men collected all kinds of information, paying special attention to unusual flight activity and the arrival of new units. Noriega had to be warned if the United States decided to make a full military lunge.

Noriega trusted Murillo because they were almost family. Noriega's "Aunt Louisa," who had taken him in as an infant, was in fact Murillo's aunt. Louisa Sanchez still lived in the old neighborhood. Murillo visited sometimes, but Noriega had stopped calling ten years earlier.

Noriega had guided Murillo's career since he had entered the PDF. When Murillo was crippled during training for a special assignment in Israel, Noriega bent the rules to allow him to stay in uniform. He made him a member of his personal staff and eventually gave him the intelligence job.

Murillo felt a sense of protectiveness toward Noriega. He believed the general had been an alcoholic for many years— probably even in high school—and the baptismal party had confirmed his opinion. Murillo thought Noriega was listening to the wrong people—and listening to them when he was drunk.

Capt. Asuncion Gaitan ranked near the top of Murillo's list of dangerous influences. Murillo noticed that Gaitan often waited until Noriega was drunk to discuss business matters. Gaitan commanded Noriega's personal escort, the men who rode in the jeeps when the Mercedeses rolled out and guarded the Golf Heights house.

Gaitan also served as Panamanian liaison with the various Cuban military and intelligence programs, an important part of the scenery in Panama. Cuban military advisers had trained the 7th Company, the Machos del Monte, or Mountain Men, a well-armed special operations force trained for only one purpose: to protect and, if necessary, rescue Noriega.

——————

At the baptismal party, Noriega gave Giroldi an astounding order in front of many of the guests. Giroldi and his men were, from now on, to shoot down all U.S. aircraft in the sky, anywhere. This included helicopters, planes, anything that belonged to the U.S. military. U.S. aircraft were a common sight in the skies around Panama City in October 1989. The order was tantamount to telling Giroldi to declare war on the United States. And Noriega made it clear that he wanted it obeyed.

One man decided it was time to act.

12

Bloody Fiasco

MOISES Giroldi had often discussed Noriega with his wife, Adela, a spirited young woman who, like many PDF wives and members, had risen from the lower classes. In the middle of September, the Giroldis had taken a tentative step. Adela had told a friend who worked for a senior officer at SOUTHCOM that her husband might want to talk to someone at SOUTHCOM about the problems in the PDF. Adela was very discreet, but it was clear that she was talking about a coup. The friend reported the news to her boss at SOUTHCOM. The response: The United States was ready whenever the Giroldis were willing. It was decided that Adela's friend would serve as the intermediary for communication in the future.

Noriega's actions at the baptismal party convinced Adela Giroldi that the moment for action had come. Her convictions had grown slowly and reluctantly. At the bank where she worked, she heard horrible stories about the state of affairs in Panama. No one respected the PDF as an institution anymore. Her husband's uniform meant nothing now, and his disillusionment was growing. Noriega was sober for only about an hour a day, and he tried to offset the alcohol with amphetamines. He and his friends talked about money most of the time, and Giroldi had heard enough to convince him that Noriega was a narco-trafficker, just as the *civilistas* said.

The order to attack U.S. planes was the final turning point for Major Giroldi. If obeyed, the order would surely provoke the United States to kill him and all his men. The PDF would be destroyed. But what, Giroldi worried, would Noriega do if he ignored or disobeyed the order? There was no telling; the general was crazy and Giroldi knew that many of the younger PDF officers realized this.

Giroldi was scared, scared for himself and his family, scared for Panama, but also scared for Noriega, for whom, despite all, he felt an almost filial respect.

He knew, however, that he had to act. After the Giroldis arrived home from the party, Mrs. Giroldi called her friend. A short time later, both were sitting in the friend's living room, telling two CIA agents what they had in mind.

Giroldi planned a tender coup. He would persuade Noriega that it was time for him to retire—with wealth and dignity. There would be no violence. He would quietly seize Noriega the very next morning, around the time he arrived at work. Once Giroldi had Noriega and his staff in custody, the rebels would announce the news in a radio communiqué. Noriega, Giroldi believed, would see the wisdom of this solution. He would ultimately see how much Giroldi respected him. What Giroldi planned was less a coup than an abrupt change of command ceremony.

The agents listened as Giroldi made several requests. First, he wanted protection for his family in the event his effort failed. To ensure this, his father, wife, and three children would enter Fort Clayton even before he went into action. Giroldi also wanted visible U.S. support of a practical kind. Giroldi was concerned about Noriega loyalists, particularly the 5th Rifle Company stationed at Fort Amador, just a few minutes by armored vehicle from the Comandancia. Their commander, Capt. Moises Cortizo, was a close friend of Noriega.

Giroldi was worried that the 5th Rifle Company might draw on the support of an Israeli-trained bodyguard unit at Fort Amador or the Mountain Men stationed at Rio Hato, fifty-five miles down the highway. Giroldi asked that U.S. troops seal off Fort Amador and establish a roadblock on the road from Rio Hato.

The CIA agents reminded Giroldi that U.S. law forbade their participation in the murder of a political figure. Giroldi firmly assured them that he had no intention of killing Noriega. Beyond that warning, the agents had nothing to say. There was no contingency plan. The agents provided no advice and made no demands about the eventual political outcome. They gave Giroldi a telephone number but didn't ask for his. If things went right, he would be available at Noriega's desk at the Comandancia. If things went wrong, he would probably be unreachable by phone.

Later, Giroldi met with PDF captain Javier Licona, a close friend who commanded a ceremonial cavalry unit based at the Comandancia. Licona agreed to join Giroldi and was pleased by Giroldi's assurance that he had the complete backing of the United States. Licona and Giroldi were confident they had enough men based at or near the Comandancia to seize Noriega, the building, and the nearby streets without trouble.

The CIA agents filed their report. They felt that Giroldi was, as CIA director Webster paraphrased, "sincere and that he had a less-than-even chance of succeeding because his plan wasn't very well thought out." The report also noted that Giroldi had saved Noriega's life, and that he was, in PDF terms, an honest man.

Less than thirty-six hours after his own change of command ceremony, General Thurman heard about Giroldi's plans. The news did not surprise him, but his almost instantaneous analysis would surely have terrified Giroldi if he had known about it. Thurman did not believe Giroldi. The major's approach, Thurman believed, was part of a plot masterminded by Noriega to set him up and provoke the use of military force. Thurman had been warned that Noriega would challenge him early and here it was. To be sure, suspicion was in order, but Thurman was more than suspicious. He was certain that Noriega's personal challenge had started. A fake coup fit the scenario perfectly. Thurman reported the news and his analysis to Washington. When Thurman was certain about something he sounded that way.

The real certainty that Sunday evening was that Thurman, Giroldi, and Noriega all failed to understand what was happening.

———

At 2:30 A.M. Monday, Joint Chiefs chairman Gen. Colin Powell, himself in his new job only since Saturday, passed the word of the Giroldi coup to Defense Secretary Cheney. After approving sanctuary for the Giroldis, Cheney phoned national security adviser Brent Scowcroft, who decided to wait until Bush's regular 9:00 A.M. Monday meeting with his top aides to tell the president.

"Get the lawyers" was Secretary of State James Baker's first reaction at that Monday morning meeting. Baker was concerned about the political fallout if the administration even appeared to violate the laws governing covert operations. While the news was what they had been asking for, now that a coup was about to happen, Bush and his men were extremely wary.

Thurman's skepticism influenced the attitude at the White House as the president and his men waited for news. Bush gave his permission for roadblocks if and when Giroldi did make a move, but he stressed caution. He wanted to be absolutely sure that the canal treaties permitted such action, and he wanted to avoid confrontation between U.S. forces and the PDF. Bush also began to prepare for possible military action. Later in the day, an American unit, A Company, First Battalion, 508th Infantry, moved close to Fort Amador.

Giroldi's requests for U.S. help were not extravagant, and despite Thurman's skepticism, some Americans thought the United States had hit the jackpot with Giroldi's plan. They thought it likely that it would be possible to bring Noriega to trial if Giroldi succeeded. Giroldi had said he wanted to protect Noriega, but the situation was fluid. Perhaps there would be an opportunity to intervene, even if Giroldi wanted Noriega to retire in Panama. It was understood that no PDF officer would announce that he was arresting Noriega for the North Americans. "Any PDF guy who handed over the commander to the gringos would have to hang up his jockstrap. No one would ever forgive him," said one American officer.

Thurman made no contingency plans to exploit the circumstances a coup effort might create, because Giroldi, he firmly believed, was a fake. He continued to believe this even after Giroldi sent word to SOUTHCOM that the coup was on for Tuesday morning. He had not moved on Monday, as he had planned, because Noriega had not shown up at the Comandancia.

That night, Captain Licona brought Giroldi some distressing news. He was convinced that Battalion 2000 would defend Noriega, regardless of what its commander may have led Giroldi to believe. Giroldi waved away Licona's worries. Whatever the PDF did, they both felt confident that they could count on the United States.

———

On Tuesday, at 6:30 A.M., Adela Giroldi, her three children, and her father-in-law showed up at the main gate of Fort Clayton for protection—as planned. They told the guards who they were and were ordered to wait. For close to half an hour, they waited and waited. Dozens of Panamanians and Americans noticed them as they arrived for work. Finally, the Giroldis were taken to a room on the base and locked in. There was no phone, no way for Mrs. Giroldi to inform her husband that someone might have seen her family waiting and informed Noriega.

The Giroldis' arrival did not shake Thurman in his certainty that Giroldi was plotting against him. Awaiting Noriega's next move, Thurman went to a crisis command center in "the tunnel" deep inside Quarry Heights, part of the hill that overlooks Panama City. At the center were map boards, secure communications equipment, and an open line to Washington. As Thurman waited, his officers maintained constant visual surveillance of the Comandancia and the compound.

Giroldi expected Noriega to arrive just minutes before his 8:30 staff meeting. His plan was to stop the general as he walked from his limousine to the building entrance. It was possible that Noriega might even decide to visit Giroldi before going to his own office. Surrounded by the overwhelming firepower of the Urraca rebel troops, Giroldi would tell Noriega, respectfully, that it was time to go. Giroldi planned to put his troops in position sometime after 8:15. Meanwhile, the men moved in and out of the compound anxiously.

At 7:50 A.M., two Mercedeses and two jeeps came through the compound gate. Noriega sat between Gaitan and Castillo in the back of one of the Mercedeses. Despite his famous network of sources, Noriega had no idea what Giroldi had in mind. So it was a moment of mutual surprise.

Noriega's early arrival threw his would-be captors into confusion. They began firing into the air and some fired at one of the Mercedeses, to no effect. Noriega's driver zigged and zagged and screeched to a halt near the doorway to Noriega's private staircase. Castillo and Gaitan shielded their boss as they all hurried into the building and into Noriega's office on the second floor. One slammed the door shut as the racket of gunfire continued in the compound and then in the corridor outside the office.

Noriega went to his telephone, called his girlfriend, Vicky Amado, told her what he knew and whom she should call. He then made more calls. Either Vicky or Noriega himself contacted friends at the Mountain Men headquarters as well as other officers who pledged their assistance.

Gaitan and Castillo opened the door a crack and fired bursts of automatic-weapon fire into the corridor while they tried to figure out what was happening. Giroldi and other rebels positioned themselves around a corner down the hall and yelled at them to give up. Giroldi told them that the rebels controlled the building. Indeed, the Centurions and the Dobermans, the riot control units, had rallied to Giroldi's side. They had been able to arrest Noriega's staff and others and lock them in a room on the top floor.

Gaitan and Castillo cursed the rebels and managed to keep them at bay until 8:30, when they ran out of ammunition, a full forty minutes after Noriega had arrived at his desk, forty minutes in which he had had uninhibited use of the telephone. Finally, all three threw out their weapons and surrendered to Giroldi in the corridor.

Noriega was defenseless. There was no guarantee that the rescuers whom he had called would be able to reach him, even if they were willing to try. If the United States blocked access to the Comandancia, for example, it was unlikely that many PDF units would try to get through. Who could blame Panamanian troops who refused to fight U.S. units equipped with heavy armor and air power?

Noriega flatly refused to resign as Giroldi set up shop at his desk and began a PDF version of a town meeting. The question was what to do with Noriega if Giroldi failed to persuade him to resign. Between 8:30 and 9:00, Noriega remained in the office, in captivity, as the debate raged. Some rebels wanted to shoot him on the spot. All watched as Noriega burst into tears and begged for his life. Some of his captors jeered, yelling that a narco-trafficker deserved to die.

Others, including Giroldi's ally Licona, recommended that he be taken to the SOUTHCOM gate, less than five minutes away, and left there. This faction even succeeded in moving Noriega downstairs and toward a truck. But Giroldi prevailed, flatly refusing to kill Noriega or deliver him to SOUTHCOM. Giroldi continued to try to persuade Noriega to resign. He insisted that Noriega be treated humanely and with respect. Around 9:00 A.M., Giroldi saw to it that Noriega was made comfortable in a bedroom down the hall, a very comfortable bedroom with a telephone, which Noriega promptly put to use. He called Vicky again to find out what she knew.

His earlier calls had already produced action. By the time

Noriega had surrendered, hundreds of Mountain Men had poured into the Rio Hato airport and set about seizing planes—a 727 and two smaller aircraft—to fly them to Omar Torrijos Airport on the outskirts of the capital. Giroldi had been right to fear that unit but wrong to assume they would travel by road. Their decision was based on speed. The American roadblocks were useless. In fact, they weren't even in place. Thurman had not blocked either road. There was no sign of any U.S. action.

At this point, Giroldi made an enormous concession. He accepted the argument that it was in everyone's best interest for Noriega to end the day in U.S. custody. It was the beginning of a triumph for Bush—if he had known about it.

The decision to hand Noriega over was easier to make than to accomplish. It was imperative that U.S. authorities conspicuously "seize" Noriega from the rebels, who hoped to maintain some national dignity. The rebels would not resist the seizure of Noriega; in fact, they would make it easy. One U.S. official put it this way: "We would have had to stage something to make the U.S. look like the aggressor."

The rebels attempted to work out an arrangement with Maj. Gen. Marc Cisneros, Thurman's second in command. His office was at Fort Clayton. Some of the rebels knew Cisneros, a seasoned, Spanish-speaking officer. They believed he would quickly understand the subtleties required.

Licona and three other rebels passed through the rebel roadblocks at intersections near the Comandancia and set off for Fort Clayton, twenty to twenty-five minutes away. A face-to-face meeting with the U.S. officer was, they all felt, the best way to accomplish the transfer. Noriega, meanwhile, ordered his friend Colonel Madrinan to round up the wives of the rebels and hold them until further notice.

In Washington, Deborah DeMoss, still dedicated to justice for Hugo Spadafora, heard about the gunfire at the Comandancia just moments after it started. In the ensuing moments, more and more information reached her and her colleagues of the minority staff of the Senate Foreign Relations Committee. (She had left Jesse Helms's personal staff but remained close to him.) The sources were varied. Some were Americans at SOUTHCOM and the U.S. embassy. Some were Panamanian opposition members who had telephoned the rebels inside the Comandancia. Some were the actual rebels who told DeMoss's colleagues they had Noriega under control. They said that the United States could get him if the details could be worked out. They warned that it was imperative for the United States to block all the roads to the Comandancia and show support in any way possible. They also wanted to be sure the proper authorities in Washington knew what was going on.

DeMoss promptly called Helms, who immediately placed calls to Baker and Thurman. He told their aides that he had important information from Panama. For the next two hours, DeMoss and her colleagues were on the phones almost constantly. They spread a map of Panama City on a table in a conference room and began writing in what was happening. Among the events was the arrival of the Mountain Men in Panama City. They passed the U.S. embassy at 10:35 A.M. The information that came to the office was exact, accurate, virtually up to the minute. It included the precise location of the bedroom where Noriega was detained in the Comandancia and which doorway was most convenient to reach it.

DeMoss called the State Department crisis center with each new piece of information. But the government officials ignored her and Helms. Helms finally reached Baker in the late morning, but Thurman did not return the senator's call until even later. The official at the State Department crisis center listened to DeMoss's reports with weary condescension and assured DeMoss that the State Department and SOUTHCOM had more information and that what they had was more accurate. DeMoss was unfazed and continued to call and pass on her running account of what was happening in Panama and inside the Comandancia.

The Licona delegation reached the Fort Clayton gate at 9:30 and told the guards the electrifying news: They represented rebel PDF officers who had control of Noriega. They wanted to turn him over to the United States. Could they please see Cisneros? Half an hour passed before the Panamanians got to Cisneros and several other U.S. officers.

The atmosphere was chilly. It was quickly obvious that Cisneros was not happy to see them. He was wary, aloof, and noncommittal. He told Licona that he had no authority to help, left the room, and remained absent for more than half an hour, conferring with Thurman by telephone. When he returned, Cisneros limited the discussion to one question: Would the rebels deliver Noriega to a U.S. base?

Licona telephoned Giroldi at the Comandancia, where there was growing consternation. It was obvious that the United States wanted Noriega, but they wouldn't bargain over conditions. Without assurances about Noriega's future and the procedure for transferring him, Giroldi refused to agree to deliver the general.

At about 10:45 A.M., a rebel communiqué was broadcast over the radio. A misunderstanding among the rebels had delayed the broadcast until then. In the communiqué, Giroldi announced that he controlled the Comandancia and that Noriega would soon retire. "This is strictly a military movement. There is no politics involved," the communiqué said. The rebels recognized Noriega's man Francisco Rodriguez as president and Giroldi called for a "return to Torrijosism." Around the city and in government offices, workers celebrated, trampled on Noriega's framed photos, and sent out for beer.

The celebrations were distinctly premature: Noriega's rescuers, the Mountain Men and Battalion 2000, had already passed the U.S. embassy and were approaching the rebel roadblocks at the intersections near the Comandancia. At the roadblocks, Giroldi's intermediaries came forward. They tried to negotiate, but the rescuers demanded Noriega's release.

Near the Comandancia, the rescuers' heavily armed scouts easily reached windows and balconies from which they could look into the compound. They outnumbered those within and had more arms.

There was growing consternation inside the Comandancia. The wives and even the mothers of rebels had telephoned. They told the men that they were in Madrinan's custody and begged them to surrender to Noriega—or else they would be killed. Noriega always played hardball.

In the late morning, the calls from the Comandancia to DeMoss's office stopped. Her last, brief call convinced her that confusion reigned in the building. A little while later, Licona, still at Fort Clayton, called the Comandancia. A Noriega loyalist told him that Giroldi could not come to the phone. Licona could return when he wanted, the voice said.

Noriega, whom Giroldi had invited out of the bedroom to try to negotiate a conclusion, was now contemptuous. "You guys are dead meat," he yelled. "My troops are on the way." He challenged Giroldi to kill him and then sneered that Giroldi would be better off if he killed himself. "To be a commander you have to have balls," Noriega said. "You don't have balls."

At about 12:30, the Noriega loyalists who had been locked up on the top floor were released. They dashed down the stairs, out a side door, and into the streets. Moments later, the Mountain Men and Battalion 2000 troops began firing antitank weapons, rocket-propelled grenades, .51-caliber machine guns, and M-16s at the Comandancia and at rebel positions in the compound. They riddled the roof of the Comandancia and blasted out the windows of Noriega's own office. For twenty minutes, glass and concrete splintered and flew; there was almost no return fire. Then the firing ceased—abruptly and entirely. Rebel emissaries met the rescuers and spoke to them on the phone. At 1:30, the rebels began dropping their weapons and forming ranks, their hands on their heads. Giroldi capitulated by handing his M-16 to Noriega, the man who remained commander in chief.

PDF officers streamed into headquarters from all parts of the city as Noriega, flanked again by Castillo and Gaitan, reasserted his control. The general appeared to ignore Giroldi, who stood, with his hands on his head, weeping openly. While Giroldi watched, Noriega declared, "I'm tired of these bastards," took out his pistol, and shot a rebel directly in the face. An officer who had shoved Noriega earlier in the day had his hands cut off before he was shot.

In the midst of the turmoil, Noriega spotted his pal Dias, who managed the Causeway house. He handed him a pistol and ordered him to shoot Giroldi. Dias refused and handed the pistol back to Noriega. Noriega strode away and guards hustled Giroldi off in the other direction.

Noriega appeared in public shortly afterward, beaming, shaking his fists in the air, and talking to the cameras. "The gringo piranhas want to do away with me," he laughed. Very quickly he issued a statement to reporters. "The incident this morning corresponds to the permanent aggression and penetration by the forces of the United States against the tranquility of our country," he said.

The coup attempt was all but over when Thurman finally realized that it had actually occurred. His information came from analysis of telephone intercepts and lagged behind events.

Colin Powell, also ill informed, told Thurman to prepare a plan to send troops to the Comandancia to get Noriega, but he also said to hold off until Bush gave the order. However, Powell did give Thurman the authority to send a covert team to seize Noriega if there was no chance the rebels would deliver him to a U.S. base. The president insisted, Powell told Thurman, that there be no evidence of U.S. military intervention. He also wanted to avoid any confrontation between the United States and the PDF. If Thurman could meet those requirements, he was free to try to capture Noriega. Very shortly afterward, Noriega appeared in public, triumphant.

Thurman's actions throughout the episode were puzzling. At 9:00 A.M., for example, he had ordered U.S. troops to seal off Fort Amador. There was no sign of any PDF activity at the base, and the action accomplished nothing beyond revealing that the United States was indeed a participant in the events. As it happened, the tanks moved into place just as the rebels announced that the United States could seize Noriega.

"It's not a coup until it's broadcast on the radio," Thurman had said as the morning wore on. After the rebels broadcast their communiqué shortly before eleven, Thurman ordered marines to block the road from Rio Hato, even though the Mountain Men from Rio Hato were already at the Comandancia.

Thurman was the last of the major participants in Panama to learn that Noriega was (or had been, by the time Thurman caught up) a prisoner. The unfolding of events suggests that Thurman's disbelief was a contributing factor in the rebels' downfall. Had he believed Giroldi, he might well have learned of Noriega's whereabouts sooner. Apparently, he chose not to return Helms's call quickly despite the urgency of the message. And, although he could have seen the Comandancia with his own eyes, he stayed underground. "Max never saw daylight," said an American officer who followed all the developments. "But the real problem was that Max let his ego get in the way."

White House officials were fully aware of Giroldi's plans and what they might achieve. White House staffers had alerted the Justice Department and the Drug Enforcement Administration that somehow or other the U.S. forces in Panama might well have Noriega in custody before the day was out.

Throughout the morning, Bush and a few advisers (Baker, Cheney, Powell, Scowcroft, Scowcroft's deputy Robert M. Gates, and John H. Sununu, the chief of staff) contacted Thurman several times. Thurman told them each time that he did not know for sure where Noriega was. He also told them that he believed Giroldi was working for Noriega. For the most part, the men watched

CNN, which carried the news that something was happening in Panama.

By early afternoon, journalists in Washington began to ask questions about a report that the State Department and the CIA had received from Panama City. It was the report, moot by the time it was sent, that the rebels wanted to turn Noriega over to the United States. Reporters began to ask more questions. Marlin Fitzwater flatly denied that the administration had been informed in advance of any coup plans. "If we were, the president doesn't know about it, the secretary of state doesn't know about it, and the secretary of defense doesn't know about it," he stated. In fact, all three had known since Monday morning.

When it was visibly obvious that Noriega had triumphed, Bush attempted to put even more distance between himself and the events. "There were rumors around that this was some sort of an American operation," Bush said. "I can tell you that is not true."

After Noriega appeared in public, Thurman emerged from the "tunnel" and went back to work in his office. As much as anyone, he had helped Noriega survive. His judgment was dead wrong. Giroldi had also been wrong, wrong to believe that he could persuade Noriega, wrong to believe that the Bush administration would back its rhetoric with even minimal action.

While Thurman went back to work, Giroldi was tortured— for information and for revenge. His interrogators shot him in the elbows and kneecaps and fractured a rib, one leg, and his skull before they shot him to death Tuesday evening, some forty-eight hours after he had made his first contact with U.S. intelligence agents.

13

Corpses and Cover-ups

ON October 5, two days after the coup attempt, Noriega traveled to Santiago de Veraguas, 157 miles from Panama City. In a nationally televised speech delivered to an enthusiastic crowd of government workers, the general gave his first public account of the coup that almost toppled him. Wearing a straw hat with a band that resembled the Panamanian flag, occasionally grabbing at a foot-high statue of Christ on the lectern, and pumping his fists in victory, Noriega was triumphant.

He told the crowd that the United States had helped the rebels but "left its agents in the lurch." He compared the American betrayal to the U.S. performance in the Bay of Pigs invasion of Cuba in 1961, but vowed that he had never been afraid. When the rebels told him to resign, he replied, "You've got to kill me first." Or so he said.

In his speech, Noriega declared that there would be new "wartime laws." "We can no longer play democracy when they have us surrounded and besieged," he said. "There can be no place here for laws applying to traditional times."

Noriega asked his audience to turn in fellow workers who had celebrated his apparent downfall. "Those officials who won't fire the traitors, will be traitors as well," he declared. "We have to make a list." Some women in the crowd chanted "Traitors out" and "Let's make the list."

Noriega also vowed to crack down on "foreign priests who are seditious," an apparent reference to Father Villaneuva and Monsignor Sebastian Laboa, the papal nuncio. And he proclaimed a catchy new slogan for Panama: "Al indeciso, palo; al enemigo, plomo; al amigo, plata" ("To the undecided, a club; to the enemy, a bullet; to the friend, money").

Noriega told the crowd that the PDF officers who had died fell in combat during his rescue. "I'm a man of peace," he said. "I fire on my enemies, not against my brothers."

In fact, Noriega was a man of rage. As soon as the coup collapsed, he ordered a far-reaching roundup. He learned that many of his most trusted officers—his "brothers"—had known about Giroldi's plans, though not all had taken an active role. One old Noriega crony, an intelligence officer, decided to stay home the day of the coup. He pleaded sickness and hoped to remain uninvolved. When the rebellion began to collapse he summoned a doctor to his house like a truant student trying to get a medical excuse for absence. But he did not fool Noriega, who had him arrested and beaten.

Even Murillo, "Aunt Louisa's" real nephew, Noriega's spy at Howard Air Force Base, got in trouble. After the guns had been put away, he submitted a political analysis of the coup and urged Noriega to consider popular feelings. Gaitan read the analysis, accused Murillo of sounding like Giroldi, and had him arrested. Noriega did not intercede. (Another officer saw to it that Murillo survived and was later released.)

In the days following the coup, morticians around the city toiled over the broken bodies of the PDF rebels, including Giroldi's, all of whom officially died in the fighting. However, the wounds on the bodies made it clear that the victims had been tortured and executed. Noriega had ordered the killings. As he had threatened, he murdered the members of his own extended family.

In public, Noriega tried to shore up his benign, paternal image. Shortly after his speech in Santiago de Veraguas he appeared at a reception with twelve-year-old Sarah York, a schoolgirl from Negaunee, Michigan, with big glasses and gaps between her teeth. The child seemed, mysteriously, to have developed a crush on Noriega. She had written him fan letters and the general had invited her to Panama to help him tell his side of the story to the

American people. The two appeared hand in hand in public. Sarah wore a rosary around her neck and said Noriega was a man of peace.

———

Some of the rebels escaped Noriega's wrath. Captain Licona and a colleague elected to stay at Fort Clayton. Others who were involved, or who were close to Giroldi, hurried with their families from their various offices and homes to Fort Clayton, or other U.S. bases. (The other two PDF officers who went with Licona to see Cisneros at Fort Clayton decided to return to the Comandancia; one had left thousands of dollars in cash in his desk. They were both shot.)

Mrs. Giroldi, who had learned of her husband's fate late Tuesday (October 3), remained at the base, in complete isolation, with her family. On Friday, October 6, family members picked up Giroldi's corpse at a mortuary, and she was finally given a more complete explanation of the events surrounding her husband's death. The next day, a U.S. government plane carried her and the forty or so Panamanians who had found shelter on U.S. bases to exile in Miami. Major Giroldi was buried in Panama a few days later.

Mrs. Giroldi put her sorrow and anger on paper. "My husband didn't have anything to be ashamed of. He didn't steal or traffic in drugs. I know that he was free of guilt and poor till the end. . . . I accuse you, General Manuel Antonio Noriega, of assassinating my husband, Major Moises Giroldi Vera, who was a bigger man and loved his men and country more than you. . . . I ask the next officer who tries [to make a coup] that you not allow [Noriega] to live, that you kill him instantly as only the mafiosos and the narcotics traffickers know how. [My husband] gave you [Noriega] the opportunity to live. But you couldn't do the same for him. Damn you a thousand and one times . . . damn you. You will not even find peace in hell."

U.S. officials cautioned all the exiles to be careful. They were to say nothing to embarrass the U.S. government. Government officials were very apprehensive about any utterance from the exiles. They found Mrs. Giroldi's statement, for example, told her not to show it to anyone, and formally classified it "Secret." (A *Washington Post* reporter obtained a copy.)

During the first few days after their arrival in the United States, Mrs. Giroldi and the others spoke guardedly to reporters.

Deborah DeMoss visited and learned, among many other details, that two of the rebels who had telephoned her office to ask for help had been killed. DeMoss bought candy bars for the Giroldi children and tried to console their mother.

The widow said that Noriega himself had killed her husband "even though my husband was his trusted friend. My husband could have killed Noriega, but he would not do that. He thought the commander's fate should be decided by the people." In her view, the United States had bungled badly. "Really, all they [the United States] had to have done was to cry wolf. No Panamanian soldier would give up his life for Noriega. They would have just run."

———

Bush and his men were on the defensive from the moment the coup collapsed. On the night of Noriega's triumph, Helms gave a speech accusing the administration—"Keystone Kops" in his estimate—of squandering an extraordinary opportunity. On "Nightline," Senator David Boren of Oklahoma accused the administration of talking tough but acting less than courageously. On the same program, Mario Rognini, Panama's minister of commerce and Noriega's frequent spokesman, cited troop movements during the day as proof of U.S. involvement. Administration spokesmen, however, continued to insist that the coup was a surprise, and that the United States played no role and took no action.

Over time, officials used a number of tactics to attempt to conceal the fact that they had sacrificed an extraordinary opportunity. Very early on, officials told reporters that the rebels, Giroldi in particular, were terrible people, not worthy of U.S. help. "Giroldi's a bastard," one Pentagon official told a reporter, "a sort of mini-Noriega." Another official called Giroldi a "bad apple," and said he "just wanted to be a new Noriega and that's not exactly what we wanted."

Defense Secretary Cheney also disparaged the dead rebels. "It was not a pro-democracy group that had taken over the PDF. It was more of a power struggle within the PDF itself between two contending factions," he said. His statement on "Nightline" was, at best, a misleading assessment.

On the same day, press secretary Marlin Fitzwater stated unequivocally that the United States knew nothing whatsoever about Giroldi or the others. "We didn't know what was going on; we had no direct communication with the coup leaders; we had no sense of their plans or intentions or possibilities at all," he said.

During the first week of October, the administration's denials of involvement collapsed when Rognoni promised on "Nightline" to deliver film of U.S. troop movements and eyewitness testimony of some of the hundreds, perhaps thousands of Americans and Panamanians who had seen the troops on the roads and outside Fort Amador.

Efforts to control the damage quickly caused more problems for the administration. Some U.S. officials who were familiar with Panama found the administration's defamations of Giroldi repugnant, and spoke to reporters. "Giroldi was a professional military guy. He was not tainted. I can show you lots of [stuff] on these guys. He's not among them," one official said. "We've been encouraging them to do a coup for a while . . . here they do something and we have the secretary of defense saying they're anti-democratic forces. That's very dangerous. They won't do anything for a long time," said another.

According to aides, Bush seethed with anger as he tried to find out what happened from bureaucrats trying to avoid blame. Guillermo "Billy" Ford, one of Panama's vice presidents–elect (he had been beaten after the May 1989 election) was visiting Washington and met with Bush. "Just because we didn't help out this time, doesn't mean we can't help next time," the president told Ford. "We cannot fight a monster like Noriega with rocks," Ford said.

Some wondered what administration officials were covering up. Jesse Helms provided one answer on Thursday, October 5, with an accurate, moment-by-moment description of the events of Giroldi's coup. Helms's version of events and nonevents, based on what DeMoss had learned, directly contradicted the administration version and vividly revealed the lost opportunity.

Helms provided a clear chronology and precise detail (Noriega's rescuers, for example, traveled in nineteen trucks and four armored vehicles and passed in front of the U.S. embassy on their way to the Comandancia). He mentioned that one of Noriega's allies was a suspect in the Spadafora murder. Helms thrust Noriega, and not the dead rebels, into the spotlight. U.S. authorities could have arrested him easily, Helms said, but Noriega had escaped because the administration bungled the job.

Now, on the same day that they admitted that they had deliberately lied about U.S. involvement, administration officials set about branding Helms as a liar. Cheney called Helms's account "hogwash." Later, he called the speech "a bunch of hogwash," and on another occasion said "any charge that we were somehow offered Noriega and didn't take him is hogwash."

A person identified as a "senior White House official" denied all aspects of Helms's account and attacked DeMoss's competence. "My personal feeling is that the Senator was badly misserved by his staff," the official told a *New York Times* reporter. The Helms speech was "so factually inaccurate that I suspect the Senator will feel uncomfortable when it is analyzed." An impartial analysis of the entire situation reveals something quite different: DeMoss and her colleagues had assembled more information on the Panama situation faster than the entire U.S. intelligence community. The information had then been ignored.

The president's office summoned Deborah DeMoss and one of her colleagues on the committee staff to the White House. DeMoss was under the impression that White House aides wanted information, and she was eager to cooperate. But Brent Scowcroft and John Sununu, who greeted the visitors, were furious, not curious. Indeed, there was only one request for information. The two men demanded the names of all of DeMoss's American and Panamanian sources. DeMoss refused to provide the names.

Both men angrily and harshly insisted that the Helms speech was wrong. It was simply not possible to telephone the Comandancia, they said. They insisted that SOUTHCOM had all the available information, and that the DeMoss story was a lie.

"You say it's a lie, we say it's true," DeMoss said. "We have good sources. You don't." The meeting lasted half an hour. When it was over, DeMoss concluded that the administration was, as she put it, "in deep kimche."

Back at the office, DeMoss decided to ask Noriega what happened. She dialed his number at the Comandancia, reached an aide, identified herself, asked to speak to Noriega, and then waited for several minutes. The aide, who had apparently been speaking to Noriega, returned to say that he had to be sure he was speaking to the real Deborah DeMoss. How could he tell he was not speaking to an imposter?

They discussed the problem and quickly agreed that Noriega could verify her identity by calling the U.S. Senate and asking for her. DeMoss and some of her colleagues waited at her desk. About half an hour passed and then a man who said he was an intelligence adviser to Noriega called her. Noriega, who was unavailable, had deputized him, he said, to answer any questions she had. The two spoke for an hour and a half. He confirmed the rumors that Giroldi was dead and said he had died "in combat." He provided his own account of what happened and answered all her questions, though he asked very few of his own. DeMoss regarded him with some skepticism and did not believe his story about Giroldi. But most of his statements corroborated what DeMoss had already learned, especially that Noriega had been under rebel control and that the rebels had asked the United States to take him off their hands.

The administration's denials of Helms's account were risky. But the officials made Helms himself the issue. The question became whether Jesse Helms could be taken seriously.

Helms, it turned out, did not have enough allies in the Senate, and certainly not in the press, to sustain interest in his account. And very quickly a new allegation shifted the spotlight away from an inquiry into the details of the episode.

Cheney made the allegation. On Friday, October 6, he suggested that the real culprits in the Panama fiasco were Senators David Boren, William Cohen, and their colleagues on the Senate Intelligence Armed Services Committee. The committee's strict rules on covert operations, Cheney said, hampered the administration's efforts to get rid of Noriega. It was a reminder of the July 1988 episode when the administration falsely accused members and staffers of the intelligence committee of leaking news about a Reagan "finding" that commissioned a covert operation.

Cheney's attempt to make Boren and Cohen the scapegoats was unfounded and ironic. The senators had not been consulted on the day of the coup attempt, and they certainly had not impeded administration action.

Cheney's low blow, delivered in an appearance before the committee and later with reporters, angered both senators—and, once they tried to defend themselves, produced new headlines. Stories about the fight between the administration and the committee replaced stories about Helms's version of the coup. Administration officials attempted to paint a picture of themselves as aggressive go-getters whose hands were tied by a cautious Congress. The tactic worked well. Scowcroft attacked Boren again on the same issue on a Sunday (October 8) television talk show, creating even more headlines during the next week.

When Cheney appeared before the intelligence committee he forcefully advanced the claim that the administration had not bungled an opportunity but had behaved in an emphatically correct fashion. There had been no dithering, as critics claimed. There had been a sagacious decision. "We made a good policy decision, and if I had to do it all over again, I'd make exactly the same decision," Cheney said. The decision was not to commit U.S. troops. Cheney went on the attack by the end of the week. "We are not in the business of willy-nilly running around the hemisphere toppling governments we don't like," he said. "How many dead Americans is General Noriega worth?" he asked.

Bush himself told reporters that his critics were reckless. "I didn't use military force because it wasn't warranted under the existing circumstances. . . . I'm not just being stubborn, but as I look at all the information, I wouldn't today have made a different decision then," he said. "Any commander in chief must have the lives of American citizens and of American soldiers foremost in mind when he makes a decision."

In fact, Bush and Powell had actually authorized Thurman to use U.S. troops, though the operations had to be covert. It was the appearance of Noriega in triumph that prevented U.S. military action, and not a decision made in Washington.

The *Washington Post* reported the Powell-Thurman telephone call authorizing military action in its Sunday, October 8, edition, shedding new light on the extent of U.S. involvement. Meanwhile, administration spokesmen intensified their attack on the dead rebels. They hoped to blunt the bitterness of the survivors who had arrived in Miami. "This was the gang that couldn't shoot straight," a U.S. embassy officer chuckled.

Bush presented his first full account of the events at a White House press conference on October 13. (His opening statement concerned legislation to protect the flag from desecration but the first question concerned the attempted coup.)

"Here is my position," Bush said. "I have not seen any fact in all the reports that have come out that would make me have done something different in terms of use of force. And I reiterate that. . . . And there's been endless interviews and discussions and stories, many of which are false, that come out as to what we were asked to do or not to do. But I've seen no fact that would make me change my view."

In the statement, Bush seemed to suggest that there were some coups he would support and some he would not. Until then, Bush, in his frequent and fervent appeals for a coup, had proclaimed only one U.S. demand—the removal of Noriega. He had not specified one type of coup as favorable over another. He did not define his new criteria, yet whatever his new standards were, they seemed operative retroactively: The Giroldi coup, Bush implied, had not measured up.

In the question period, reporters tried to clarify Bush's position and his extensive remarks were studied closely in Panama and the United States. "I would simply reiterate that we have no problem with the PDF itself," he said. Then, once again, without being specific, he seemed to say there were good coups and bad coups. "I think this rather sophisticated argument that if you say you'd like to see Noriega out, that implies a blanket, open carte blanche on the use of American military force . . . I don't want to mislead somebody, and to me that's a—you know—a stupid argument that some very erudite people make," the president said.

A reporter asked about future options. "I wouldn't mind using force, and if it could be done in a prudent manner. So, in other words, I am not ruling out the use of force for all time. I'm reiterating the fact that it was not proper to use force under the existing circumstances. And I feel more confident in that than I ever have—more confident, not less confident, from anything I've seen."

"Is it responsible or consistent to, on the one hand, call publicly for Noriega's ouster but then to do nothing?" a reporter asked. Bush answered, "Yes. Absolutely. Totally consistent. I want to see him out of there, and I want to see him brought to justice. And that should not imply that that automatically means, no matter what the plan is or no matter what the coup attempt is or what the effort is, diplomatically and anything else, that we give carte blanche support to that."

The reporter pursued the issue and said: "Some people would say you don't have to give carte blanche support to all situations like that, but you have to lend a hand. . . ." Bush replied: "What they're saying is—and it's only a handful of critics—'You said you wanted Noriega out. You say you have no argument with the PDF. An element tries to get him out. And you didn't support him.' And I'm saying, yes, I want him out. And yes, we have no argument with the PDF. But I am not going to give carte blanche support to an operation, particularly when they don't ask for the support. And I have to reserve that right. I have at stake the lives of American kids. And I am not going to easily thrust them into a battle unless I feel comfortable with it, unless those general officers in whom I have total confidence have . . . feel comfortable."

His answer was misleading. In saying that the rebels had not asked for support and in implying that U.S. troops remained immobile all day, Bush reverted to the lies that had collapsed on October 5 when his men finally admitted the U.S. troops had moved at the rebels' request.

Bush insisted that each and every official and officer who had been involved "did a good job—a good job," and that he had never been angry at anyone. A question about his emotions produced a lengthy and revealing reflection from Bush. He said he was "relaxed, even in the face of criticism. . . . I mean, normally I might be a little more tense. I wouldn't blow up, I don't think. And that's why I had ulcers twenty years ago, because I didn't—I kept it all inside. . . .

"The American people are strongly supporting the position I took. They're not dumb, they're not dumb."

Reporters shouted several more questions. One was "Will you talk to Mrs. Giroldi?" Bush did not answer.

14

No Way Out

"THE key lies in dropping the focus on Noriega's personal fate," Spanish prime minister Felipe Gonzalez said on October 11. Gonzalez and many others feared the possibly violent consequences of another flare-up between Bush and Noriega, so Gonzalez volunteered his diplomatic services once more. He proposed that Noriega step down but remain in Panama. He suggested new elections. Once again, diplomacy was futile.

By the autumn of 1989 several things were clarified. One was the degree of embarrassment that Noriega caused Bush: It was high and rising. The next crisis was guaranteed to be a domestic political ordeal for Bush, who appeared completely unable to handle Noriega. As time passed, the political costs of U.S. inaction would become greater and greater. The Noriega situation revived discussions of the "wimp" factor. It was a reminder of the reservations many Americans held about Bush and the questions still unanswered about what he and Noriega knew about each other.

Most Panamanians believed that if the United States wanted to get rid of Noriega, it could. The questions were how much they wanted him to leave and whether large-scale military action was necessary to bring about his departure. Among the illusions exposed by the miserable U.S. performance during the coup attempt was the idea that limited military action, such as a commando raid, could take Noriega out. At this point, such action—if Thurman chose to pursue it—would require precise, definite knowledge of Noriega's whereabouts. U.S. intelligence could not reliably and consistently provide this information. Noriega was too clever to stay in one place very long.

Even with military backup, capturing Noriega fell into the covert operation category and his death, from whatever circumstance, had to be considered a possibility. If Noriega was killed during a commando raid, it would look like a U.S.-engineered murder and a violation of U.S. law.

To guarantee Noriega's removal, Fred Woerner's plan to overwhelm the PDF with massive U.S. military force began to look like the only recourse. If Noriega was killed in a military operation, no U.S. law was broken. To be sure, the chances of his surviving such an attack, especially with specific efforts directed at him, were very slim. But "no one even joked about that," said an officer who was involved.

Logically, an invasion was inevitable. Politically, it was unthinkable in the early autumn. An invasion was a momentous event and Panama was not a momentous strategic issue, especially compared with the political upheaval in Eastern Europe, where the cold war was ending. In strategic terms, Panama was not a crisis. The military bases continued to function and canal operations were not threatened. The continued safety of the canal was never more than a rhetorical issue: The entire world had an interest in its continued physical security.

Defense Secretary Cheney suggested that Noriega was not worth "dead Americans." And Bush himself complained that his critics wanted him to "unleash the full military and go in and 'get Noriega.' I suppose you could have gone to general quarters," the president said. "But that's not prudent and that's not the way I plan to conduct the military or foreign affairs of this country." Bush stuck to his refusal to drop the indictments. But U.S. officials talked to a Noriega lawyer about a deal: Noriega would agree to leave office and the United States would agree not to press for extradition. The effort got nowhere.

As time went on, White House planning edged closer and closer to "hardball." In late October, for example, the administration launched another covert operation to knock Noriega from power. It was called Panama 5 and resembled, in broad outline at least, the four failures that preceded it. The CIA was in charge; they had a budget of $3 million and once again their aim was to foment a coup. Panama 5 represented a new consensus between the administration and the congressional intelligence committees. The operation's permissible tactics included violence. There was a very good chance Noriega would be killed. But since his death was not the stated aim of the operation, it would not be a violation of U.S. law.

When the outlines of the plan appeared in the press (in mid-November 1989), it was clear just how much the ground rules had been relaxed. There were, for example, "no restrictions," one source said, except the ban on murder. "It is an unimpeded effort to try to topple Noriega," another person familiar with the plan said. "We're going into it with the understanding that there may be loss of life, though the effort will be not to kill anyone." One person quoted put it this way: "What it boils down to is that we want him alive in the United States or dead."

The administration also moved to make "hardball" legal. At the Justice Department, assistant attorney general William P. Barr asserted that U.S. law enforcement officers could make an arrest in a foreign country even if the foreign government did not grant permission. Barr and other officials explained that such powers were necessary to combat narco-traffickers and terrorists. "There are still lawless countries in the world that sponsor terrorism directed at the United States," Barr said.

To some legislators, Barr's claim represented a dramatic and dangerous change in policy and was nothing less than a license to kidnap. When newspapers reported that the army's lawyers were also issuing unusual legal pronouncements the belief grew that the administration was paving the way for a raid. The Office of the Army Judge Advocate General prepared a "memorandum of law" that declared that U.S. troops could take part in a covert operation against a foreign political figure.

Representative Don Edwards, a Democrat from California, was one of the legislators who viewed these developments with alarm. "I can think of no law passed by the Congress or any provision of the Constitution that licenses the United States to be an international outlaw," he said. But Oliver B. Revell, associate deputy director for investigations of the Federal Bureau of Investigation (FBI), waved away "concern that we were going to mount up like the Lone Ranger." His agents, he said, had no plans to use the expanded licenses.

Perhaps the FBI didn't, but Max Thurman did. On November 3, a month after the coup attempt, Thurman went to the Pentagon to explain his plan to remove Noriega from power. It was a modification of the plan Woerner had left behind—a plan Woerner had forthrightly declared he hoped would never be used. But Thurman, a master at the briefing-as-sales-pitch, advocated military action against Noriega just as vigorously as Woerner had opposed it.

Thurman had declared war on Noriega even before he briefed Colin Powell and the Joint Chiefs of Staff in early November. After the coup fiasco, Thurman made it plain that life at SOUTH-COM was going to be different. In conversations and at staff meetings he told his listeners that they were literally at war—at war with Noriega, at war with America's enemies in Central America, and at war against drugs. He wanted SOUTHCOM on a combat footing—and fast. He made no secret of his belief that Woerner and many of the Spanish-speaking officers on his staff had suffered from "clientitis," or too much knowledge, and therefore sympathy, with the place and its personalities. Thurman seemed to regard his predecessor's expertise as a contributing factor to the crisis.

Thurman ordered all officers to wear battle fatigues instead of the more formal uniforms that had been the norm for office work. Thurman himself seemed to revel in the new uniform. "Max got very macho around that time after the coup," a SOUTHCOM officer recalled. He chose to wear the combat uniform when he traveled to Colombia for a meeting with President Virgilio Barco. In symbolic terms, his choice of apparel was insulting and reinforced the stereotype of Americans as military interventionists. An aide persuaded him to change to a different outfit before going to see Barco. Thurman's attitude soon made the papers and the press exposure may have had something to do with his dropping his plan to compel officers to carry gas masks at all times.

Thurman's plan was strategically the same as Woerner's, but there were a number of tactical differences. Thurman's plan was almost entirely military in nature, unlike Woerner's. Woerner's scenario called for extraordinary controls on U.S. firepower, especially in the densely packed wooden tenement neighborhood called El Chorrillo that surrounded the Comandancia. Woerner was concerned about civilian casualties, and he devoted as much if not more effort to planning the aftermath as he did to planning the attack. He foresaw, for example, the potential for looting once the

PDF, the only authority in Panama, had collapsed and included in his plan measures to prevent such disorder. Woerner also wanted to implement a quick and effective assumption of power by Endara, Ford, and Arias Calderon. In short, Woerner designed his attack plan to bring about the political aims of the administration, as he saw them.

Thurman's plan diminished most if not all of the "civic action" and politically oriented elements of Woerner's plan. There was little or no discussion at the November Pentagon meeting of nonmilitary concerns, nor was there any hesitation over Thurman's intention to put heavy U.S. firepower into the El Chorrillo neighborhood. Thurman received a "warning order," or green light. He was instructed to be ready to execute the plan as quickly as possible.

Word spread throughout the Pentagon that a large-scale operation with virtually no chance of failure was being planned. The roll call of units involved grew even bigger than Thurman's original proposed force. The planners even found a role for the F-117, the Stealth bomber. Eventually, the units involved totaled 25,000 men and women.

Though planners routinely used the word *invasion* to describe the operation, only part of the attacking force would actually come from elsewhere to attack targets in Panama. The rest of the troops and most of the support facilities, such as helicopter refueling points, were already in Panama on the bases. It was, as one military historian put it, as if the U.S. forces stationed at Fort Benning had been ordered to assault Columbus, Georgia, the adjoining town.

When Thurman returned to Panama he accelerated his preparations. It was clear from the signals that he was planning military action: The U.S. civilian population in Panama City and environs was shrinking rapidly. (At Thurman's insistence, more personnel and dependents were moved to the bases. Thurman even recommended evacuating all U.S. dependents, a clear public signal that he wanted to get Americans out of the way.)

Thurman also continued to rehearse combat tactics. The rehearsals, now more urgent, took place under the cover of the "treaty enforcement" military maneuvers. By that autumn, U.S. troop movements were part of the landscape in and around Panama City. SOUTHCOM continued to alert the PDF a day in advance, so there would be no unpleasant surprises. Thus, U.S. armored units would from time to time take up positions at Fort

Amador, a base the United States and the PDF shared. Officially, they were there to practice defending U.S. personnel who lived at the base. The positions they took were also the positions from which they would attack the PDF's 5th Rifle Company, if the attack ever happened.

The unique setting also meant that personnel who lived on the bases often went to restaurants or stores that were very close to targets Thurman proposed to attack—including the Comandancia. Indeed, off-duty GIs in civilian clothes regularly moved about in Panama City near those targets. Thurman exploited this circumstance by ordering company commanders and other officers to carry out visual reconnaissance of the targets they were assigned to attack, including the Comandancia. The vast majority of U.S. military personnel did not know about these operations, but it was not long before Noriega learned about them. He assumed the civilian clothes reconnaissance was part of the plan to kidnap him.

———

Noriega was absolutely certain there would never be a large-scale U.S. attack in Panama. Neither he nor anyone in the PDF believed the United States would go beyond limited military action to back up a raid or raids aimed at abducting him. The exposure, in mid-November, of Panama 5 seemed to vindicate his position. Noriega used the occasion to announce, in a government paper, that the government could not guarantee the safety of Endara, Ford, Arias Calderon, and other opposition figures if any harm befell him. Noriega warned that if he was attacked, the United States could spend the $3 million allocated to Panama 5 to buy flowers for the graves of his opponents.

Meanwhile, he all but ignored his many political, diplomatic, and economic, to say nothing of his military, problems. As Christmas drew near, Noriega remained very much his same old self even though he was running out of money and the country smelled of collapse. He drank more and more but otherwise intelligence and counterintelligence remained his obsessions. His simple goal was to survive in power. His telephone tappers, for example, were among his most important advisers. The tappers had been paying close attention to the telephone conversations of U.S. embassy staffers, about 80 percent of whom mentioned plans to go home for Christmas. This was a sign to Noriega's analysts that there would be a lull in the tension and some members of the counterintelligence staff made plans themselves to get away to Cuba for the holidays.

On December 12, Noriega dispatched an old friend on a diplomatic mission. Noriega wanted Prime Minister Gonzalez of Spain to approach the United States on his behalf with a view to opening new talks about his possible resignation. Noriega had less intention of resigning than ever, but he had learned that an ongoing negotiating process was one of the best ways to ward off sharp conflict with the United States. The time seemed right for another flutter. Noriega had not learned that even the deepest wells of diplomatic patience could run dry, especially when he had publicly scorned diplomats and the diplomatic process.

Sending an envoy to Madrid was just one of several steps Noriega took in December to shore up his defenses against a kidnap attempt. Just as U.S. prosecutors had indicted him, Noriega backed up a Panamanian court that had issued arrest warrants for Thurman and Cisneros. The charge was "constant harassment" of Panamanian citizens with the relentless motion and noise of trucks, planes, and helicopters. SOUTHCOM said any attempt to arrest the two generals would be regarded as "terrorism."

On Friday, December 15, Noriega used the National Assembly to bolster his personal defenses on the legal and diplomatic fronts. "The Republic of Panama is declared to be in a state of war while the aggression lasts," a resolution adopted by the National Assembly declared. "To confront this aggression, the job of chief of government of Panama is hereby created, and Manuel Antonio Noriega is designated to carry out these responsibilities as maximum leader for national liberation." Could one country (such as the United States) conceivably abduct a person who had the standing of "chief of government"?

"You have invited me to occupy a trench, and I will not fail you," Noriega told the legislators. He repeated his claim that the United States wanted to keep the canal, and he set the stage for a new crisis between himself and Bush. By December 31, according to the treaties, the administrator of the canal was to be a Panamanian. The treaties, assuming amity between the countries, made the selection of the administrator the shared responsibility of the Panamanian government, the president of the United States, and the U.S. Senate. Noriega had nominated Carlos Duque, his presidential candidate, for the job. The United States, denying the existence of the Noriega regime, named Fernando Manfredo, the veteran deputy administrator. That same day, the National Assembly voted to strip Manfredo of his citizenship. If Noriega chose to, he could accuse Bush of breaking the treaties and create a diplomatic incident. Or he could let the issue die. "We will sit by the canal and watch the bodies of our enemies float by," Noriega said, "but we will never destroy the canal." Bush administration officials, in public statements, attached no importance to the legislative action that made Noriega "chief of government," nor to any of his remarks.

On Saturday, December 16, Noriega visited Chiriqui and spent part of his weekend reading Ernest Hemingway's *A Moveable Feast*. Before the day was out, he received some bad news from Madrid. The Spanish prime minister was not encouraging about the proposed negotiations. Gonzalez doubted the United States would, as he put it, "fall for it." Gonzalez had a message for Panama: "Tell your general time is not on his side . . . there is very little time left. . . . Very, very little."

In Panama City it was another Saturday night. As usual, U.S. military personnel went out for dinner all over town. PDF soldiers at a roadblock in the vicinity of the Comandancia detained a U.S. Navy lieutenant and his wife shortly before 9:00 P.M. They were told to wait in their car while the PDF verified their identification papers. The PDF shook down motorists in general and gringos were particularly affluent targets. But near the Comandancia tensions were higher than in other parts of the city because the PDF were on the alert for U.S. spies—spies who would probably look like off-duty personnel out for a good dinner.

While the navy officer and his wife waited, a car with four young U.S. officers, all male, came down the narrow street. The driver said he had taken a wrong turn and gotten lost, which was easy enough to do in the narrow side streets of the neighborhood. The PDF refused to allow the four men to continue on their way. A crowd of civilians gathered, words were exchanged, and, according to the Americans, PDF soldiers tried to drag them from the car. The driver hit the accelerator and, as the car pulled away, the PDF opened fire, hitting two of the Americans. The driver raced to Gorgas Hospital, where one officer was treated for a grazed ankle. Lt. Robert Paz, U.S. Marine Corps, died fifteen minutes later from gunshot wounds. Not long afterward, Brent Scowcroft told Bush about the incident.

The ordeal of the navy lieutenant and his wife, who had witnessed the scene from their car, was just beginning. They were taken to a nearby PDF office where they were blindfolded with masking tape and then put in a pickup truck and driven to another building, possibly the Comandancia. PDF soldiers who appeared to be drunk beat up both of them, saying their indentification was fake and demanding that the lieutenant tell his real unit and mission. They kicked the lieutenant in the head and the groin repeatedly and threatened to kill him. They also threatened to rape his wife and threw her against a wall with such force that she cut her head. Then they made her stand with her arms over her head for at least thirty minutes, until she collapsed. After four hours of terror and torture, the PDF took the two Americans to Fourth of July Avenue, just a few blocks away, and released them. They got back to Rodman Naval Station after 2:00 A.M. and told their story.

15

Pulling the Trigger
DECEMBER 17, 1989–JANUARY 4, 1990

AT 4:00 A.M. on Sunday, December 17, 1989, the PDF issued a statement that accused four Americans of running a roadblock and firing at Panamanians. Three Panamanians, including a one-year-old girl, were wounded, according to the report. SOUTHCOM denied that Robert Paz, or any of the Americans, was armed. Both accounts made news. Most people in Panama suspected there was some truth to each nation's version.

At the U.S. embassy on Sunday morning, a young Marine Corps guard telephoned his mother in the United States and talked about the killing. The conversation caught the attention of Noriega's wire tappers, who quickly sent a transcript of the chat to G-2—and probably to Noriega himself. The marine told his mother he had been at the embassy since 10:00 the night before "waiting for the war to start." He was joking, as the rest of his conversation made clear. No one, it seemed, around the embassy believed that the shooting would cause a crisis.

"There's really nothing going on," he said. "Whatever happens, the United States has taken the position that the four military gringos that were involved were out of bounds, owing to the fact that they had no reason to be there. The whole world knows that they shouldn't have gone there. They messed up. If the United

States set up a barricade anywhere and someone acted in the same way we would also start firing."

Informal word around the embassy seemed to indicate that the shooting was an "isolated incident." The marine said that "it wasn't the Panamanians' fault. They're doing their job. It's nothing to do with Noriega's war declaration, nothing like that. It was only that four gringos went to a place that they shouldn't at the wrong time and then they got it."

Meanwhile, a PDF officer sent a "back channel" (which was the only channel) message to U.S. officials. According to one of the officials, the message "tried to reassure us that that Saturday night shooting was an accident, an isolated incident that was unintended."

In public, Noriega's press repeated the original PDF account. SOUTHCOM issued the false claims, the government press said, to prepare "U.S. and international public opinion for intervention in Panama." At a press conference, Foreign Minister Leonardo Kam said that the incident was "a grave escalation in the permanently hostile policy of provocation and intimidation that the U.S. Army has been systematically pursuing against the Panamanian people." On Monday, December 18, Noriega himself spoke to an interviewer from WBAI in New York City and took the same line.

In private, Noriega did not believe any of his own words. Nor did he believe that the United States would mount a major military operation against Panama. Like the marine at the embassy, Noriega expected business as usual. He returned from Chiriqui and made plans to go to Colon on Tuesday, December 19. Noriega completely miscalculated the significance of the Saturday night shootings.

———

On Sunday morning, December 17, Bush went to church at a military base in Arlington, Virginia. He ignored reporters' questions about how, if at all, he would respond to the shootings. After church, Bush went to brunch in the White House. One of the guests was Vice President Dan Quayle. Bush told Quayle that he had decided to take military action to remove Noriega. It was as simple as that.

After the brunch, Bush stayed in the residence and met for an hour and a half with Quayle, Jim Baker, Dick Cheney, Colin Powell, John Sununu, Brent Scowcroft, Scowcroft's deputy Robert Gates, and Lt. Gen. Thomas W. Kelly, director of operations for the Joint Chiefs of Staff. Marlin Fitzwater was also present. The death in Panama was the reason for the Sunday afternoon gathering. Bush set the agenda.

"Look, here are my objectives," the president said. "I want to get Noriega. I want to be able to have Endara and Calderon and Ford establish themselves as leaders of a democratically established government. I want to . . . ensure the safety of Americans. How can I do that?" Bush, according to one of the participants, sat beneath a painting called *The Peacemakers;* it depicted Lincoln and several of his generals discussing plans beneath a rainbow in the sky.

Powell was ready with maps and easels. He described what a military historian later called a "mini–Normandy invasion" involving some 25,000 men and women who would walk, swim, ride, fly, and jump. The plan also involved rubber boats, tanks, helicopters, and airplanes. All the services had roles to play.

When it was over, the PDF would cease to exist as an organization. Indeed, the centerpiece of the attack was a coordinated ground and air assault on the Comandancia. Other U.S. troops would engage PDF units elsewhere in Panama City and in Rio Hato, Colon, and other locations and seize the major installations. With all command and control mechanisms severed, the PDF would disintegrate.

Cecil B. deMille and Willy Loman would have approved of the operation more than Dwight Eisenhower. It was a showcase spectacle, a demonstration of Pentagon prowess. Some parts of the plan had only a tenuous connection to the actual demands of the situation. The Stealth fighter-bomber, for example, was known for its ability to evade enemy air defenses, especially radar. But this capability was superfluous; the PDF had no air defenses. Nevertheless, two Stealths were assigned missions. Each would drop a 2,000-pound bomb. The targets were two PDF barracks buildings at Rio Hato, one of which housed the Mountain Men battalion.

The navy's SEALS were ordered to incapacitate Noriega's Lear Jet, thus preventing his escape from Paitilla Airport in the city near the bay. A gunship crew or a mortar crew could have cratered the runway (and helicopter pads) and accomplished the same objective, but the SEALS got the job.

Bush asked about the possibility of a much smaller operation, a commando raid, for example, that would scoop out Noriega without such massive U.S. troop deployments. Powell explained that catching Noriega was the hard part because of his extraordinary skill at hiding. Massive force would overwhelm the PDF: It wouldn't matter if Noriega was caught right away because he would have no institution to command. There was no mention of the possibility that American firepower would kill Noriega.

Bush inquired about possible casualties among Americans and Panamanian civilians and he discussed Noriega. "This guy is not going to lay off," Bush said. "It will only get worse." After a while the room, with his advisers sitting in a circle, was silent. "Let's do it," Bush said. The strike was under way. U.S. forces would go into action about 1:00 A.M. on Wednesday, December 20.

In public that Sunday, the administration made appropriately cagey sounds. "We are extremely concerned that a climate of aggression has been developing that puts American lives at risk," said State Department spokesperson Margaret Tutwiler. "We don't discuss contingency plans or options. We never rule anything in or out."

On Monday, December 18, the administration began political preparation for the attack. Marlin Fitzwater said that Noriega had already declared war on the United States—in a speech Noriega gave the previous Friday. Americans in Panama, he said, were in danger.

What Noriega had really said was that the United States, through its constant military menace, had created "a state of war." Noriega himself did not declare war. Fitzwater and other officials had ridiculed Noriega's Friday statement, and said it was not important. But on Monday, Fitzwater said, "We are very concerned that the declaration of war . . . may have been a license for harassment and threats and in this case even murder of a United States citizen. When you put all of these together you begin to discern a certain climate of aggression that is very disturbing."

The signals continued all day Monday. At Fort Bragg, the XVIII Airborne Corps, of which the 82nd Airborne Division was a component, went on alert. The exercises were ostensibly part of a previously scheduled training program. A Pentagon statement said that they were "not related to the incident in Panama."

Bush himself was reflective, not bellicose. "One of the frustrations that I've had during this year is the whole Panama situation, an enormous frustration," he said. "It's an enormous frustration to me that the democratic system that was voted on in Panama was totally put down by force."

While administration officials set about making the case that Americans in Panama were in grave danger, another event took place. Several hours after Bush spoke to reporters on Monday, an off-duty U.S. Army lieutenant shot a PDF policeman twice on a Panama City street. The policeman escaped with wounds in the arm and leg. He said the attack was unprovoked; the gringo just looked at him and shot him. The lieutenant, who had emerged from a laundromat just moments before, said he opened fire because he thought he was in danger. SOUTHCOM admitted the American was carrying the gun illegally and tried to forget that the incident had happened. There was talk of an investigation.

Throughout Tuesday, December 19, Bush maintained a deliberately tranquil public countenance. Part of the president's agenda that day, according to the official schedule, was to discuss a greater role for the military in the war on drugs—an almost coy hint of what was afoot. At 3:00 P.M., he met in the Oval Office with the advisers who attended the Sunday meeting. CIA director Webster and Attorney General Richard Thornburgh joined them to review the plans.

At 6:00 P.M., Bush went to the residence and began to telephone congressional leaders to notify them that a military operation was afoot. By 6:30, he was at a White House Christmas reception, singing carols and shaking hands. By 9:00 P.M., he was back in his office, on the telephone again.

Officials told reporters in Washington that they should follow events in Panama closely, and stay tuned throughout the evening. Meanwhile, Americans in Panama were depicted as if they were on the brink of a slaughter. "Noriega's irresponsible declaration of a state of war last week, followed only hours later by indiscriminate and unprovoked violence against Americans, clearly increases tension in Panama," an official said. "We find the unwarranted use of violence against Americans by the Noriega regime unacceptable."

Life in Panama, despite the rhetoric, was much the same—except for the noticeable and dramatic increase in activity on the U.S. bases. C-141 Starlifters were landing in Panama every ten minutes. The bases were sealed, officially to keep secrets in, a plausible step if the bases were not in the country about to be attacked. The security precautions fueled the rumors that there would be action.

By Tuesday evening, the invasion was the talk of Panama City, especially among the girlfriends of U.S. military personnel. One young woman called Colonel Madrinan's office at DENI about eight o'clock to report that her gringo boyfriend had called to tell her to stay home. He had said that the attack was just hours away. Shortly afterward, a young woman who lived in El Chorrillo telephoned a G-2 office. Her U.S. soldier boyfriend had told her to move out—fast; El Chorrillo was a target. A government official called the Comandancia to say that the wife of an American soldier had told her the attack was imminent. A man who worked at a U.S. base and lived in El Chorrillo was telling his neighbors that the attack was just hours away. The stories proliferated.

While Panama City was ringing with advance word of the invasion, U.S. forces detained three journalists who had driven to Fort Clayton, just outside the city, to look around. The troops confiscated their notes and film and forced them to kneel with their hands on their heads. Rarely had any military operation had less of the element of surprise. Nevertheless, military authorities were determined that no independent reporters were going to see it.

———

Mike Harari, the "former" Israeli intelligence agent, knew it was time to go. He went to Noriega's Golf Heights house late Tuesday afternoon and stayed into the evening, talking to Felicidad and waiting to speak to Noriega. The two men had grown distant in recent months, as Gaitan, the head of Noriega's escort and his liaison to Cuba, had become more and more influential. Gaitan despised Harari and told Noriega he was disloyal and avaricious. Gaitan had envied Harari's power and made no secret of his own anti-Semitism.

After a while, Harari could no longer see Noriega with ease and often waited with Felicidad in the evenings for Noriega to come home. As often as not, Noriega stalked right past them, straight to the bedroom. The story went around the PDF that Noriega had vetoed a Harari plan to sell radios to the PDF, the sort of transaction that once had cemented their relationship. Noriega told his bodyguard that if Harari wanted to see him it meant Harari wanted something.

Harari had decided to pull up stakes in Panama. If Noriega no longer wanted his advice, so be it; he was not that useful to Harari anymore. But on Tuesday evening he lingered into the darkness as long as he could, hoping to see Noriega. Finally, he departed with a driver and bodyguard. He reappeared not long afterward in Israel. In interviews he said that he had never known Noriega as well as people said.

———

Guillermo Endara, Ricardo Arias Calderon, and Guillermo Ford heard the rumors, but they, as much as anyone, knew about U.S. bluster and inaction. Each man received an invitation to dinner at Howard Air Force Base that night—a common occurrence in previous months. The officers' club was a convenient and safe place for them to meet U.S. officials or visiting legislators. About 8:30, with no sign of dinner, a U.S. embassy official told the three Panamanians he wanted to tell them something very important, but he needed promises that they would not leave the base or make any telephone calls. The three men agreed and the embassy officer told them about Operation Just Cause, as the attack was dubbed, in broad outline.

Then he asked them to think about taking over the government of Panama. He told them that if they did, the United States would support them.

Endara was stunned. "I felt like a big sledgehammer hit my head," he said. He realized, as he recalled later, that, if he assented, he would assume the presidency "under occupation by American forces." He realized that history could condemn him as a "puppet." He knew that Latin American leaders would sneer, but he also knew that circumstances in Panama were unique. He saw no alternative. Shortly afterward, the three men were sworn in as the new government. They remained under U.S. protection that night—and for some time to come.

———

Noriega returned to Panama City around 8:00 P.M., accompanied by Marcela Tason, Gaitan, Castillo, and a few more guards and assistants. They went to a small house on 50th Street that was one of several offices Noriega kept around the city. Intelligence reports poured into the office and all of them pointed to massive U.S. military action.

Noriega telephoned Norma Trevia, Vicky Amado's mother.

She was worried. She told him that there were American reporters in Panama, whom she mistakenly identified as the Pentagon press pool. She also believed, again mistakenly, that the role of the Pentagon press pool was to arrive before the troops. (In fact, the Pentagon press pool was still in the United States, under tight military control, and did not reach the scene until most of the operation was over.)

Noriega called Mario Rognoni, who was also worried. Gaitan was worried. Everybody seemed worried except Noriega. To Castillo, it was as if Noriega knew something no one else did. He would not share his information but dismissed reports of an invasion as disinformation, perhaps designed to scare him into fleeing. He got drunker and drunker.

PDF units shifted around in a disorganized way. Action seemed to depend on how seriously individual units took the rumors. At Paitilla airport, for example, the PDF presence remained relatively light. Some troops took up defensive positions and patrolled the area with armored personel carriers equipped with .50-caliber machine guns. Noriega's plane remained in one of the darkened hangars.

At 11:00 P.M., Tason, whom Noriega trusted as much as anyone, considered all the evidence and made a decision. She headed off for Las Malvinas, a dark and smoky nightclub in a nearby mall where the customers were mostly PDF officers or civilian cronies and friends. "There were always a lot of BMWs outside and fat guys in guayaberas inside," a young woman who knew the place said. Tason's husband, Ulysses Rodriguez, a nightclub singer given to gold chains and bawdy talk, was performing that night.

Noriega also decided that entertainment was what he needed. A sergeant on his staff was ordered to pick up one of Noriega's occasional girlfriends and bring her to La Siesta, a hotel near the airport that had been converted into a PDF officers' club. It was another of Noriega's haunts. Noriega climbed into the back of a four-door Hyundai for the trip to the club. A Mercedes and a Toyota Land Cruiser filled out the caravan.

There was a scattering of PDF officers in the bar and restaurant at La Siesta. Noriega greeted the young woman in his suite and there were more drinks. Noriega was almost as drunk as he had been at the christening party. Nevertheless, he kept his wits about him. He told Castillo there were too many armed guards just outside his suite, and armed guards attract the attention of commandos. Send some away, he said. That order represented the only military decision Noriega made that night.

The guards left Noriega and the young woman alone.

At approximately 12:30 A.M., ahead of schedule, on Wednesday, December 20, explosions rocked La Siesta. Castillo ran outside and saw "a sky full of paratroopers." Operation Just Cause had begun and troopers of the 82nd Airborne Division and Army Rangers were jumping from planes right over his head. Castillo rushed back in to find Noriega at the door of his suite, still dressed in his military uniform. Castillo told him to put on civilian clothes; there was no time to waste. Noriega obeyed instantly. He, the young woman, and Castillo hurried to the Hyundai, where a lieutenant named Pinto was at the wheel. Castillo told Pinto to stay near populated areas, his theory being that the United States would not assault them. Tracers and fires began to light the sky in the neighborhood of the Comandancia and elsewhere in the city.

"What are we going to do, what are we going to do?" Noriega asked over and over again.

The young woman wanted to go home. Pinto pulled over to the curb and let her out.

Noriega issued an order: Return to the club, he said. He had forgotten a talisman of some sort that he liked. Castillo told him they should stay as far away from the club as possible. They headed for Pinto's house, which was not far away and had a telephone.

Noriega called the Comandancia, but no one answered. He reached Maj. Edgardo Lopez, the PDF information officer. Lopez was weeping. U.S. troops were everywhere. He said that he might seek asylum in a foreign embassy.

Noriega called Vicky and urged her to move in with her mother in Paitilla. He learned from servants that his daughter Sandra and her family had left their apartment to seek asylum in an embassy, presumably taking Felicidad and the other girls along with them.

Castillo assembled another carload of bodyguards and they set out for San Miguelito and the house of Noriega's close friend Balbina de Perinan, the director of immigration. It was an alarming, disheartening ride. At the intersection of Via Tocumen and Via Espana, Noriega watched as an officer he knew played his own small part in the disintegration of the PDF that was taking place all over. The officer stopped his vehicle at the roadside, removed his holster and web gear harness, placed them on the ground, and strolled away.

Noriega spent two hours at de Perinan's house, listening to the radio and making phone calls. The news was overwhelming and Noriega became silent and withdrawn. The operation was bigger than anything he had imagined. But neither he nor his friends had any plan, and Noriega still had no aim except to avoid capture. He decided to call Tason.

Tason, who had fled Las Malvinas and gone home with her singer husband when the invasion began, proposed they all rendezvous at the home of Eliana Krupnick, a friend, not far from the Marriott. As Noriega and his bodyguards were about to leave, he saw three U.S. Blackhawk helicopters descend toward a nearby field. He and the guards began to run to their cars, but Castillo warned them to slow down and not attract attention. There was another U.S. helicopter, a gunship, hovering nearby.

Eliana, a businesswoman, was, according to PDF gossip, one of Noriega's closest friends. Noriega established himself in a ground-floor room with a bed, a bar, a telephone, and a television. Jorge Krupnick, a businessman, went to his bedroom as soon as Noriega arrived.

Tason and Krupnick tried to pull the situation together and make a plan for Noriega and for themselves. The women made phone calls, and each brought more confirmation of the enormity of the American operation. Noriega was at loose ends. He telephoned a good friend of many years who told him not even to think about coming to his house. Noriega's guards, meanwhile, decided that the Krupnicks' live-in gardener was a security risk, and they locked him in a closet.

From time to time, the house shook from nearby explosions. As the night wore on, no one, least of all Noriega, had an answer to his question: "What are we going to do?" Perhaps Noriega should seek asylum in an embassy, someone said. Tason opposed the idea vigorously. She said it was tantamount to surrender. She believed the PDF would resist if Noriega remained at large and if they got some help. She telephoned the Cuban ambassador and asked him for immediate Cuban military assistance. The ambassador said military help was out of the question, but Noriega was welcome at his house at any time. Tason reached Gaitan, who was on the run himself, and he too urged defiance. Gaitan persuaded Noriega to make a defiant speech into the phone, which he recorded at the other end.

"We're in trench warfare now," Noriega proclaimed from the Krupnick house, "and we will maintain the resistance. . . . We must resist and advance. . . . We ask the world for help, with men, dignity, and strength. . . . Our slogan is to win or die, not one step backward."

Noriega's steps were toward the car. With dawn about to break, he, Castillo, and the drunken Ulysses Rodriguez set off for Campo Lindbergh, a neighborhood on the fringes of the city where Rodriguez's sister had a small apartment. On the way they saw looters, whose wildness alarmed them as much as the U.S. troops. Rodriguez's nephew let the men in and then he vanished. There were just two rooms and one bathroom, sparse furniture, some food, a radio, and a telephone. Castillo quickly set the ground rules. Since there were no curtains on the windows, they had to low-crawl if they wanted to move about. The three men had to make the sounds of only one, lest a neighbor get suspicious and call the U.S. troops. Castillo insisted, for example, that they flush the toilet only when all three had been there, and that they all wash their hands at the same time.

Now Noriega could catch his breath and figure out what to do and where to go next. He had won his war, at least by his own standards. He had avoided capture. His problem was that the U.S. forces had picked a different war to fight—and they had won it handily. In and around Panama City, Colon, and environs, the PDF had ceased to exist. Noriega was a fugitive now with a vast U.S. posse looking for him and only his scattered and largely fugitive friends to support him.

———

There were few surprises as the operation unfolded. The Dignity Battalions, for example, put up more of a fight than the PDF, and some members hung on as tenacious snipers for several days. The SEALS, who were assigned to prevent Noriega's escape from Paitilla airport, ran into fatal surprises. As H-hour approached, top commanders ordered them to launch their operation one hour earlier than they had planned. The navy commandos quickly found themselves under fire. They managed to complete their mission, but four SEALS were killed and sixteen wounded.

The Stealths provided more surprises. As they bore down on Rio Hato at H-hour, the pilots were troubled. Until just two hours before takeoff the mission had been to obliterate the two barracks buildings with two 2,000-pound bombs. But then the mission changed (or so the later official version claimed). The pilots were ordered to miss the barracks, *not* hit them. The objective was to stun and confuse the defenders. In other words, the Stealths were there to say a loud "Boo!" with 4,000 pounds of high explosive. The new targets were spots in open fields, spots about a hundred yards from each building, but the equipment was acting up. The pilots found that the clouds and high humidity over Panama played tricks with the plane's targeting system, tricks they had never been trained to handle.

The first Stealth dropped a bomb that exploded in an open field 260 yards away from the Mountain Men barracks and, as it happened, only eighteen yards from the other barracks building. The bomb was clearly off target. Nevertheless, the pilot spoke the code word that signified he had hit the target on the nose. This information confused the second pilot, who also missed his target and dug a huge hole near a basketball court.

It was the understanding of the U.S. Army Ranger commander that the bombs would kill the defenders of the barracks and not just scare them. But the enormous roars mainly served to wake everyone up. Some fled, but others stayed and opened fire on the U.S. Army Ranger paratroopers, 850 in all, who descended toward them.

One paratrooper was shot through the head as he stood in the doorway of the airplane. When the Ranger commander realized that his men were easy targets he ordered the transport planes down from 500 to 375 feet for the drop. That meant a trip from door to ground of mere moments, during which each man had to unhook his hundred-pound pack and let it fall ahead of him. Many failed to do so and came down very fast. Four paratroopers were killed and 253 were wounded. Eighty-six were part of "an orthopedic nightmare," as one doctor described the broken ankles and legs, sprains and tears that the paratroopers suffered because of the hard impact on the ground. Altogether, twenty-three Americans died in the fighting.

Freezing weather at Pope Air Force Base in North Carolina and at Fort Polk in Louisiana delayed some elements of the 82nd Airborne Division who were supposed to jump at 12:30. They did not arrive over Panama until 5:00 A.M. Their comrades had long since seized the runways. It would have been safer and faster for the planes to land with the tardy troops, but the order to jump was not changed. Many of the paratroopers and much of their equipment came down in the wrong place, but casualties were light.

The assault with the fewest surprises (apart from Dignity Battalion resistance) was the centerpiece of Just Cause, the attack on the Comandancia itself. Shortly before 1:00 A.M., mechanized units rolled down the hill from U.S. bases toward El Chorrillo, and U.S. helicopters and AC-130 Spectre gunships attacked the building from the air with bullets, rockets, and even 105mm artillery.

In the first few minutes, local civilians saw PDF soldiers running pell-mell from the building and thought another coup was under way. Then, from inside the Comandancia and from balconies of nearby buildings, PDF soldiers and Dignity Battalion paramilitaries fired AK-47s and M-79 grenades up at the U.S. aircraft and at the armored vehicles and foot soldiers making their slow way toward Noriega's headquarters. Some U.S. armored vehicles bumped into a pair of garbage trucks that formed a roadblock at an intersection several blocks from the Comandancia. There were more collisions, disorder, confusion, and shooting.

Exploding shells and tracer bullets set fires that were clearly visible from the other side of the city within just a few minutes. U.S. loudspeakers told residents to stay in their houses, but U.S. gunships fired directly into one building after another as crews tried to kill the snipers scattered throughout the neighborhood. Wooden structures blazed and collapsed, and when people ran into the streets many fell under the torrent of firepower from the sky. The assault continued until approximately 6:00 A.M., when U.S. troops moved up to the pockmarked, scorched, but still standing Comandancia. It was 10:00 A.M. before they entered the structure and counted the bodies, many of which were clad only in underwear.

In densely packed El Chorrillo, fires razed nearly 2,000 dwellings, making some 15,000 residents homeless. Many of them crowded into an open field in front of Balboa High School. Hospitals, such as Santo Tomas, filled up. The counting of the civilian dead began, and it continued for a long time.

———

Bush had stayed up until 4:00 A.M. Not long after 7:00 A.M., he addressed the television cameras. "My fellow citizens, last night I ordered U.S. military forces to Panama. . . . I took this action only after reaching the conclusion that every other avenue was closed and the lives of American citizens were in grave danger," he said.

After Bush spoke, Cheney, Powell, and Lt. Gen. Thomas W.

Kelly of Powell's staff provided a confident televised briefing. The official assessments started strong and stayed that way for many months. Cheney, for example, said the Stealths had achieved "pinpoint accuracy." And despite what had happened at Rio Hato, military spokesmen denied there had been any opposition on the ground. They also denied any orthopedic casualties, and stuck to both stories until contradictory evidence appeared in the media.

On Wednesday, December 20, there was a vacuum of power in Panama, at least among Panamanians. U.S. troops seized the government television station in the middle of the night and promptly placed the logo of the U.S. Defense Department on the screen. However, they neglected to seize the main government radio station. Noriega's voice was heard all over the city for much of December 20. As far as the public knew, he was on the loose and on the radio. Gaitan had succeeded in getting the tape to the government radio station. "Not one step backward," he said, over and over.

The safety of American civilians was one of the reasons for the invasion, but many remained unprotected throughout the action. At one time or another, nearly a dozen were taken prisoner and three were killed.

The U.S. Defense Department may have been in charge, but as December 20 wore on, U.S. troops made no effort to prevent looters from ransacking the city. These looters did more damage to the economy than all the economic sanctions. They emptied department stores, supermarkets, pharmacies, boutiques, fast-food shops, and whatever could be entered easily. The looting, which U.S. troops often watched, cost $1 billion, according to the Panama City Chamber of Commerce.

The hunt for Noriega intensified, and military briefers continued to suggest that his capture was imminent. But in fact, U.S. authorities had no clue as to where he was. They feared that he had made his way out of the city to Chiriqui, where, under the command of his friend Luis Del Cid, the PDF structure was still intact. The prospect of a long and bloody search loomed up. In the late afternoon of December 20, the White House announced a $1 million bounty for information leading to Noriega's capture.

On Thursday, December 21, Bush held a press conference during which he said, "This operation is not over, but it's pretty well wrapped up." Noriega obviously was still at large, and "I won't be satisfied until we see him come to justice," Bush said. He cited "the declaration of war of Noriega" as a reason for the invasion. "Every human life is precious," Bush said, "and yet I have to answer, yes, it has been worth it."

"The Ma Bell approach" was the most important tactic in disarming the 2,000 or so PDF soldiers west of the capital, where there had been no U.S. military action aside from reconnaissance. In town after town, U.S. troops surrounded the PDF garrison while Spectre gunships circled overhead. Then a U.S. officer telephoned the garrison and demanded instant surrender in return for safety. It worked every time. One PDF soldier was slightly injured. There were no U.S. casualties.

The United States, meanwhile, went about its postinvasion follow-up. There were many tasks, apart from providing rudimentary food and shelter for the thousands of Panamanians displaced by the invasion. U.S. troops provided all police functions and U.S. officers supervised the birth of the Public Force, a Panamanian public security organization whose members were recruited for the most part from the ranks of the old PDF. To be sure, most of Noriega's closest aides were in custody or on the run, but there were some familiar faces. Col. Roberto Armijo, for example, a senior officer, was captured and promptly appointed the new commander. His deputy, who flew in from Miami on U.S. military aircraft on December 20, was Col. Eduardo Herrera-Hassan.

And then there were the files that U.S. troops gathered from Noriega's offices and other sites around the city. U.S. forces bundled up Noriega's legendary archives, all the film, video, paper, and disks that made up the hidden history of Panama and the people from all over the world who did business there.

———

Noriega managed to establish intermittent communication with Vicky, her mother, Rognoni, and a few others. His goal was to escape Panama to some other country. First, however, he might try to make it to Chiriqui, where, with the threat of maintaining a small guerrilla presence, he could try to bargain his way out. In the meantime, however, Noriega remained in the apartment. U.S. troops were ubiquitous; they had staked out the embassies of Cuba, Nicaragua, and a few others where Noriega might expect to find shelter.

The only good news Noriega and his friends had was the conspicuous return, on Friday, December 22, of Monsignor Sebastian Laboa, the papal nuncio, who had been in Spain on vacation when the invasion began. Laboa had flown from Madrid to Miami and then telephoned U.S. authorities. An air force plane flew him into Panama, and U.S. ambassador Arthur Davis, who had returned immediately after the invasion, escorted Laboa to the nunciature. The return was good news for Noriega because Laboa was neutral—and U.S. troops had not posted guards outside the papal compound.

In Rome, a Vatican spokesman, referring to Panama, lamented the "illusion of the recourse to force as a means for resolving problems."

On December 23, Del Cid announced that he would surrender in Chiriqui. The news eliminated any hope Noriega had that he could make some sort of deal from the hills. Castillo said the news depressed Noriega very much. He lay on his cot, stared at the ceiling, and began to talk to Castillo about turning himself in. And sometimes he talked about suicide. Noriega dreaded an ignominious end. "He didn't want to end his life being shot by some GI Joe from Missouri," Rognoni said, "some guy from Biloxi."

To Castillo, Noriega looked defeated, depressed, and more and more edgy as the radio brought more bad news. He told Castillo that he had to be a realist. He had no desire to emulate Japanese soldiers who remained on the run for decades, especially if he had to stay on the run with Ulysses Rodriguez.

Rodriguez passed the time in the hideout drinking and telling Castillo and Noriega about his plans to challenge the U.S. Army. Noriega quietly told Castillo to get the keys to the Hyundai and the Land Cruiser away from Rodriguez.

Then Rodriguez told them he had an idea that would solve their problems. Noriega and Castillo had no choice but to listen as he spelled out his plan. Somehow, he would bring a homosexual friend they all knew to the apartment and the man would help Noriega dress up like a woman, so he could make an escape to somewhere else. How did they like it?

Noriega and Castillo were enraged. In the old days Noriega was famous for his pitiless and very loud dressing down of people who annoyed him. Now he had to be content with furious whispers. He berated Rodriguez. It was a ridiculous idea. It was undignified. It was stupid and, anyway, Noriega said furiously, the man would just turn them all in.

By midday on December 24, Noriega was ready to move. He directed an intermediary to call Laboa and tell him he wanted asylum. He wanted Laboa to come pick him up at a place another messenger would later identify. Laboa said Noriega was welcome but refused to personally pick him up. He would send his car and a representative, Father Xavier Villanueva, the pastor of Christo Rey. Villanueva, who made a point of praying for the soul of Hugo Spadafora at every mass, was a close friend of Laboa's and one of Noriega's most outspoken foes.

Noriega's intermediaries said the general would come to the parking lot of a Dairy Queen. Another Noriega friend, who had arrived at the nunciature, knew the place and would do the driving. Villanueva got in the front seat of Laboa's four-door, smoked-window Toyota and another priest got in the back. The car slipped into traffic. But just a few minutes out of the nunciature's gate a red light on the dashboard began to flash. They were about to run out of gas.

The first gas station they found had no gas and neither did the second. Villanueva remembered there was a church nearby. He rattled the locked gate and shouted "Father, father" until an upstairs window in the rectory opened. "Do you have any gas?" he shouted. The priest said no. "Give me all that you have in your car," Villanueva shouted. The priest, who recognized Villanueva, quickly assented and asked no questions as Villanueva siphoned the fuel.

There was no sign of life when they finally reached the Dairy Queen parking lot. Villanueva assumed that Noriega, or one of his people, was watching the lot from somewhere. He jumped out of the car to make himself conspicuous. He opened the trunk and closed it. Several minutes passed. Villanueva surmised that Noriega was shocked to see him and feared a trap, so Villanueva decided to call Laboa.

Inside the Dairy Queen, Villanueva learned that looters had visited the place not twenty minutes before and had taken all the money and all the equipment they could carry, including the telephone. Villanueva was the first person to enter the place after the pillaging and the woman owner was wavering between shock and hysteria. Villanueva hurried away. He had to find a telephone—and Noriega.

Villanueva found a phone but to his own amazement realized he was so tense he could not remember the telephone number at the nunciature. He walked slowly and conspicuously back into the parking lot. When he returned, he saw a van that had been parked down the street begin to move. It pulled up in the parking space

immediately to the left of the Toyota; the door slid open. Villanueva saw Noriega inside. He was wearing a T-shirt, blue Bermuda shorts, and a baseball cap. He looked exhausted and
terrified. Villanueva thought Noriega's legs were scrawny. The
other priest opened the rear left door of the Toyota and Villanueva
addressed Noriega.

"Get in," he said.

The driver of the van walked between the two vehicles and
held up a blanket as if to conceal the scene. Noriega hopped into
the rear left seat of the Toyota. The van driver said he was going
to follow, but both Villanueva and Noriega quickly said no. "Get
lost," Noriega said, just as the man slid the blanket, which in fact
concealed an Uzi and a hand grenade, under Noriega's seat. The
door slammed shut. Neither Villanueva nor the other priest had
seen him put the weaponry in the car.

Villanueva got back in the front seat and slammed his door
shut. He whirled around and stared Noriega in the face.

"Do you know me?" Villanueva asked.

"Yes," Noriega replied.

At the nunciature, Noriega walked toward the building without attempting to retrieve the Uzi and the grenade, which the
priests promptly discovered and confiscated. Villanueva watched
Noriega enter the building and then he saw a man appear atop the
compound wall, drop into the garden, and run toward the building. Then he recognized the man: It was Madrinan. Villanueva
thought of the diamond ring that he might be able to retrieve for
the Mitrottis. But Madrinan wore no jewelry as he sought asylum.

When Noriega entered, he thanked Laboa for agreeing to
accept him and immediately announced his intentions. "I would
like to ask Spain for political asylum," Noriega said. "Good, let's
ask for it," Laboa replied.

Noriega was shown to a room on the second floor, the same
room with the faulty, flickering television and no air-conditioning
where so many of his enemies had sought shelter. Laboa made
only one change for Noriega. He disconnected the telephone.

Laboa telephoned the Spanish ambassador and the two men
agreed that with an extradition treaty between Spain and the
United States, there was little point in Noriega's going to Spain.
"What about Mexico?" Noriega asked when Laboa told him of the
conversation with the Spanish ambassador. Laboa called the Mexican ambassador, who said he would call back.

Laboa informed Thurman about his guest, and in the late

afternoon Thurman held a press conference to announce the news. He also surrounded the nunciature with troops and set up barbed-wire barricades on all the streets in the neighborhood. Reporters set up shop up the hill in the Holiday Inn and kept their cameras focused on the scene.

Noriega had created a whole new situation. Even though he was just a flip of a grenade away from U.S. forces, he was, at least for the moment, as good as inside Vatican City—and untouchable. His presence in the nunciature frustrated the principal objective of the American invasion. He might stay with Laboa for years, a tropical Mindszenty. (Jozsef Cardinal Mindszenty, a fugitive from the Hungarian government, stayed in the U.S. embassy in Budapest from 1956 to 1971.) His room was austere but far more comfortable than he imagined a U.S. prison cell would be. And he was among friends. On the night before Christmas 1989, Noriega was just one of twenty-three individuals under the Vatican's protection in Panama City. Most were PDF officers—Madrinan and Gaitan among them.

Laboa told Noriega he would never throw him out, and he meant it. The nuncio, who shaped Vatican policy toward Panama from the beginning, defined his own objective early and very clearly: that Noriega willingly give himself up to U.S. authorities. His task, as he saw it, was to create the climate for Noriega to make that decision. Laboa knew Noriega well. "He is a man," Laboa said, "who, without his pistol, is manageable by anyone."

A little after 9:00 P.M., Rome time, Thomas P. Melady, the U.S. ambassador to the Vatican, received the news about Noriega from the State Department. He was preparing for midnight mass at St. Peter's basilica. About twenty minutes into the mass, one of Melady's staffers, who had received an urgent message, beckoned to the ambassador. The State Department wanted him back at the embassy to receive instructions, which were to tell Cardinal Agostino Casaroli, the Vatican's top diplomat, to call James Baker—and fast. Melady returned to St. Peter's in time for communion. After mass, he passed the message on to one of Casaroli's aides, along with two phone numbers where Baker, on vacation in Texas, could be reached and the hours when each number should be called. Melady watched as the aide delivered the note to Casaroli, who read it and continued on his way out of the basilica.

On Christmas Day in Panama, Thurman showed up outside the gate of the nunciature and spoke to Laboa for about forty minutes. Laboa continued to meet and talk on the phone with other U.S. officers and officials as time went on.

On Christmas Day in Washington, the administration tried to take a tough line with the Holy See. Reporters learned that Baker, who had not heard from Casaroli, had left a very strong message with the Vatican that they should turn Noriega over to Thurman. Other officials were just as blunt and not very diplomatic.

Vatican spokesman Joaquin Navarro-Valls seemed not to notice the tough talk in Washington. Instead he celebrated the fact that the bloodshed in Panama all but stopped. By Christmas Day, in military terms, Panama was calm. "I can announce with satisfaction that the conflict in Panama seems to be nearing a solution without further shedding of blood. And this is good news for Christmas Day," Navarro-Valls said. He added that the Vatican would not turn Noriega over, that Noriega's legal status was being examined, and that it was too early to say what would happen. "Concerning the situation of General Noriega in particular, I can confirm that at this moment he is in the Apostolic Nunciature in Panama City, after having expressed the will to end the conflict," he said. The pope himself remained aloof, except to lament deaths caused by "absurd imprudence."

Over the next several days, U.S. and Vatican diplomats met in Rome several times. They tried to clarify issues and to reach agreement on the definition of the word *asylum*. The U.S. position remained unchanged, but the Vatican diplomats ignored the pressure. They simply requested copies of the Florida indictments to study them.

In Panama, Thurman tried to scare Noriega and disturbed everyone in the nunciature with a campaign of psychological harassment. Armored vehicles gunned their engines and almost nudged the gate of Laboa's residence. Troops burned and bulldozed a nearby field in the middle of the night to make a helicopter landing area. And, beginning on December 27, the 4th Psychological Operations Group of the U.S. Special Operations Command went to work. For two days and nights they blared rock music from huge speakers directly at the nunciature at deafening levels.

Sometimes they played tapes and sometimes they broadcast SOUTHCOM's radio, whose early morning announcer intoned, "Goooood morning, Panama!" The psychological warriors selected songs with Noriega in mind: "Voodoo Child," "You're No Good," and "I Fought the Law." In the places where such initiatives are graded, the music was a hit. "It was a very imaginative use of psychological operation," said Lt. Col. Ted Sahlin of the army's John F. Kennedy Special Warfare Center and School at Fort Bragg. "I am the music man," Thurman said when questions arose about who had authorized the stunt.

Inside the nunciature, the din kept Laboa and others awake. Noriega claimed he could not hear it.

Thurman produced more spectacles. On December 26, he issued a two-and-a-half-page document that asserted Noriega was a "truly evil man." It was a truly remarkable document. Sometimes it was prissy: "according to our sources he never attempted to call his wife." Sometimes it was silly: It announced that Noriega wore red underwear "to ward off the evil eye." The demonization campaign, a hit in the American press, also included the announcement that U.S. soldiers had seized over a hundred pounds of cocaine belonging to Noriega. It was in fact tamale flour, as the army admitted when the *Washington Post* learned the truth.

Laboa was unimpressed by the campaign. In conversations with friends, he left no doubt that he believed Noriega was evil—and that over the years he had had plenty of American companions in his evil.

While the rock music blared, U.S. troops embarked on a vast search of the city and the country, turning up over 75,000 weapons, mostly of Cuban origin, in warehouses and other sites. On December 29, eighty U.S. troops ransacked the residence of the Nicaraguan ambassador. Afterward, Bush offered a halfhearted apology, saying the raid was a "screw-up," but added, "I would like to know what the man's doing with rocket launchers and grenades and Uzis and automatic weapons up to his eyeballs in his house." Bush's description was an exaggeration. In any case, the Nicaraguan, like most diplomats in Panama City, kept weapons for self-defense.

That same day (December 29), Vatican spokesman Navarro-Valls finally spoke sharply. He referred to the United States as an "occupying power" and let it be known that neither noise, nor propaganda, nor implied violence would intimidate Laboa. "An occupying power cannot interfere with the work of a diplomatic mission nor demand that a person seeking asylum there be handed over to it," he said. In Panama that day Laboa insisted that the music stop—and it did.

Laboa continued his efforts to establish a propitious climate for making Noriega realize he had to surrender. In the meantime, he all but ignored his guest. "I spoke very little with him," said Laboa. "I had one precise objective and that was to create the necessary and correct atmosphere for the plan I had. So from the first day to the day before he left I would just say, 'Hello, general,' 'Good morning, general,' 'Did you sleep well?,' or 'Do you need anything?' I didn't want to create too much of a familiar environment."

Once Noriega heard some upsetting news and asked to see Laboa. Was it true that Laboa had given U.S. forces permission to break in if Noriega took Laboa hostage? Yes, of course, Laboa said, just as he gave the fire department permission to enter if the place was on fire. But, Laboa said, he did not expect Noriega to take him hostage, so what was the problem? Laboa did not encourage conversation. With that quick explanation, the meeting ended.

Laboa went about his business, quietly lobbying for Noriega's voluntary surrender. Endara frankly admitted that he hoped Noriega would go to the United States for trial. The new president of Panama had to build a new government apparatus—including the judicial system—from scratch. Laboa also felt pressure from Panama's bishops, who wanted him to turn Noriega over to the United States. Laboa used that pressure to his own advantage. He encouraged the bishops to go over his head and write to the pope himself. Then Laboa assisted the bishops in writing their letter, which, as one of them said, "repeated our long-standing accusations against Noriega for his violation of human rights."

Noriega had plenty of time to think. He remained in his room much of the day and often ate there alone, or with Gaitan and others. He wore only an undershirt and green shorts, with sneakers and dark socks. When one of Laboa's assistants asked to take his photo he turned up in a pair of trousers and a long-sleeved shirt.

The U.S. troops who cleared the helicopter landing zone nearby terrified Noriega. He ran into the corridor in the middle of the night, concealing himself with a sheet he held up to his chin. "Are you listening? The gringos will climb over the wall. They're burning up the lot next door," he said to two young Panamanian lawyers who had moved into the nunciature to help Laboa; they had rushed from their beds when they heard Noriega shouting.

The next day one of the lawyers found Noriega watching skaters at Rockefeller Center on his still-flickering television.

When the young man asked how he passed the time, Noriega gestured at a Bible, a book by Isabel Allende, and the television. He told the young man it used to be different. "You know, my life has always been . . ." The sentence trailed off as Noriega fluttered his hands to show how hectic it had been. "I've learned that nothing is so important that you can't do without it. . . . Life goes on. We are just molecules." He joked about the austerity of the nunciature. "Many people have benefited from sanctuary here, and they don't even give anything in return. They never even offered a Betamax," he said.

By Saturday, December 30, the situation began to change. Thurman's harassment of Laboa had ceased, as had the would-be bullying talk from Washington. The Vatican, in close coordination with Laboa, announced it had determined that Noriega "was not considered to be in diplomatic or political asylum but a person in refuge against whom there were criminal charges." The Vatican statement was not clear about how long "refuge" would last.

On New Year's Eve, Laboa invited all his guests to sit down together for dinner "to create an air of serenity and peace on the last day of the year." Before dinner, Villanueva spoke to Laboa; he told him with some passion that he refused to sit down to eat with Noriega. Laboa said he understood. "You are very calm," Laboa said. "Please stay that way."

The dinner was tense. When he finished his meal, Noriega withdrew to a corner by himself and seemed very gloomy. He watched Laboa leave the room to speak on the telephone, and he snuffed out a candle with his empty, overturned coffee mug. Noriega went to bed before midnight.

By January 2, 1990, more and more Panamanians gathered at the barbed wire barriers that had been erected about two hundred yards away from the nunciature. They shouted "Assassin" and "Kill him. Kill him." There was no tension between the Panamanians and the U.S. troops. Indeed, U.S. troops continued to receive near adulation from many Panamanians. Public opinion was overwhelmingly in favor of the invasion. Many of its victims, especially the homeless and the bereaved of El Chorrillo, were embittered. But they, like everyone else, believed that just as the United States had saved them from Noriega, now the United States would pick up the pieces and restore what it had destroyed. Some Panamanians found the outpouring of support for foreign intervention embarrassing, but they also viewed it as a unique aspect of Panama's unique history as a U.S. creation and ward.

Deputy Secretary of State Lawrence Eagleburger arrived in Panama on January 2, as did Monsignor Giacinto Berloco, a Vatican diplomatic heavyweight. That same day, Laboa invited Noriega to sit with him in the ground-floor reception room. It was a formal, forbidding place with a marble floor, light blue walls, two chandeliers, a small velvet-covered couch, a coffee table, and four chairs. Laboa took the couch and gestured Noriega to a chair.

Now Laboa was ready to apply pressure. He urged Noriega to see that the best course was for him to surrender to U.S. justice and defend himself in a courtroom. Laboa also told him, "You can stay here. We will never throw you out." The meeting lasted fifteen minutes.

On January 3, Laboa again invited Noriega to talk. This time, while still assuring Noriega he could stay, Laboa suggested that Noriega should think about the crowds outside who wanted to kill him. They might invade the nunciature.

"But we have the U.S. Army out there," Noriega told Laboa.

"They will not fire on the Panamanian people," Laboa said. The priest told Noriega that he could very well, and very soon, end up like Mussolini, killed by his enemies and strung up for the world to see. Laboa's mention of Mussolini shocked Noriega. He thought for a few moments and then pointed out that the United States might even stage an attack and then step in and seize him. "I did not contradict him on that point," Laboa said. They talked for about half an hour and then Laboa left Noriega to listen to the distant chanting of the crowd and the hourly chimes.

It was a tense afternoon. One of the priests discovered a weapon under Noriega's mattress. When did it get there? How many more were there in the building? Laboa did not know. Later in the afternoon, however, Noriega told Laboa: "Your solution is the best. I am going." Noriega wanted the United States to agree to several conditions. He wanted to wear his uniform; he wanted total secrecy, neither journalists nor bright lights when he turned himself over; and he wanted to be able to call his family and write letters that he would entrust to Laboa to deliver.

Laboa relayed the news to SOUTHCOM. The U.S. authorities agreed to the conditions and haggled a bit about the timing, demanding an earlier surrender than Noriega had proposed. It was finally set for 8:30 that evening.

At 7:00 P.M., Noriega turned up for mass in the small, ground-floor chapel of the nunciature. It was the third day in a row he had attended mass. He sat in the back pew—there were only five—on the left. His nearest companions were nuns who lived and worked in the nunciature. Noriega had not sought spiritual advice during his stay. He had not asked any of the priests to hear his confession, and he certainly had not received communion, which, in Villanueva's view, would be a "sacrilege."

Noriega's mere presence in the chapel distressed Villanueva. "Does God love this man?" he asked Laboa, tears welling in his eyes, as they prepared for mass in the sacristy.

"Obviously," Laboa replied.

In his homily, Laboa spoke about the transience of earthly accomplishment and earthly loyalty. When they collapse, he said, God remains steadfast. "If we trust our lives to God, we can change our lives," Laboa said. He spoke of the thief on the cross next to Jesus. "He spent his life stealing and in just one moment he asked God to change his life. And Jesus told the thief, 'Indeed, I promise you. Tonight you will be with me in paradise.' "

Tears sprang to Noriega's eyes as Laboa said those words. His face contorted. He appeared on the verge of a sobbing outburst but regained control. At communion time, Noriega approached Laboa with the others.

One of the first rules any Catholic learns is that if one has committed serious ("mortal") sins one must confess the sin or sins to a priest, express contrition, and perform some penance before one can receive communion. Laboa suspected Noriega had done none of these things and he knew the man had sinned. Noriega's approach made Laboa's mind, and heart, race. "I thought at that moment I could have asked, 'Are you prepared for this?' " Laboa said.

He betrayed no sign of his inner turmoil. "I thought in that particular moment that charity is more important than the requirement of confession. . . . It was possible that at that moment he felt repentant for everything—and I don't have the right to deny him." When Noriega stood in front of him Laboa thought, "Lord, you know better than I do. I leave it in the hands of God." He gave Noriega the communion wafer.

After mass, Noriega went to his room and wrote two letters—one to the pope, the other to his wife. He thanked the pope, told him that Laboa had been fair, and that he himself was entirely innocent of any crime. He said he had helped the Panamanian people. He asked for the pope's prayers. "I go now on an adventure," he told his wife.

Just before 8:30, his friends stood near the front door as if they were in a receiving line. Noriega, wearing his tan uniform with four stars on each shoulder board, came down the stairs shortly afterward. He embraced each of his friends and kissed both the women. Madrinan withdrew slightly as Noriega stepped toward him, clicked his heels, and saluted Noriega. Then the two men embraced.

Noriega walked out into the dark and utterly silent night with Laboa, Villanueva, and another priest. The walk from the front door of the building to the gate was about fifty paces. Just before they reached the gate, Villanueva spoke to Noriega, for the first time since he confronted him in the Dairy Queen parking lot.

"I will pray for you every day," Villanueva said.

"Thanks," Noriega replied.

Laboa opened the gate and Noriega stepped off the nunciature's property. A U.S. soldier, who was, in Villanueva's recollection, "gigantic, enormous," lunged forward and grabbed Noriega around his arms. Then American hands were all over Noriega. Several soldiers patted him down thoroughly and audibly in the hot, dark quiet. Villanueva heard the slapping sounds and thought to himself: "They want to know if he has three balls."

U.S. troops surrounded Noriega to escort him to the field, where two helicopters waited with their motors running. No one spoke. Noriega tried to walk with his chin up, almost march, like a military man. But in the darkness he stumbled repeatedly; the soldiers held his elbows to guide him along without falling as they made their way almost at a trot.

When they reached the helicopters another U.S. soldier grabbed Noriega roughly, pulled his wrists behind his back, and fastened them together with heavy industrial tape. Noriega spun around and looked with terror at the priests. The blades of the helicopter began to turn faster and the motors began to whine. "It's for your own security," one of the priests said.

A parade of images of Noriega flashed through Villanueva's mind: Noriega waving a machete, Noriega waving his fists, Noriega as an assassin. Now he was standing with his wrists bound with tape. U.S. soldiers hoisted him aboard the helicopter. As it lifted off, Villanueva reflected that the Americans treated Noriega "as if he were a package."

The helicopter flew across the bay to Howard Air Force Base, just a few minutes away. DEA agents were waiting and they formally arrested Noriega. He gave up his uniform for a flight suit. Shortly afterward DEA agents escorted him aboard a plane for the flight to an airbase in Florida. On the way, Noriega signed autographs for some of the crew and the agents.

Before dawn on January 4, 1990, Noriega was in a cell near Miami beginning his "adventure." Now the goal of the invasion and of U.S. policy had been achieved. Noriega's debacle was a triumph for Bush. It was, said Lee Atwater, "a political jackpot."

Epilogue

IN the weeks that followed Just Cause, there was more adulation in Panama for the U.S. troops and tremendous popular support for the invasion. The operation had given Panamanians a new page in their history, and December 20 promised to be a day that would be celebrated for years to come. Most Panamanians were grateful to their "bigger brother" (as officials in the new Panamanian government described the United States). Bush had not only carted away Noriega, he had pledged $1 billion to "repair the wounds, repair the damage." For most Panamanians, that pledge was the most important part of the entire Just Cause episode. After the ruinous U.S. economic sanctions (which Bush lifted) and the invasion's destruction, most Panamanians thought the Americans owed them the money.

One year later, Noriega still occupies what is popularly known as the "Dictator's Suite" at the Metropolitan Correctional Center near Miami. The suite is actually a one-story building with a bedroom/cell, conference room, and office. Noriega has a color television, an exercise bicycle, and a private shower. The office has a desk with six chairs and, for the benefit of his legal team, two safes, two computers, a copier, and a shredder. Noriega's upkeep, protection, and transportation to and from court appearances cost the government approximately $360,000 for the year.

These days, Noriega, charged with drug trafficking and racketeering, follows the rules. His bed is made every morning by 8:00. Then, as he says, there is: "tennis at eleven, tea at three." He reads, he writes many letters, and he makes telephone calls. Guards stroll along the prison's paths with him, bring him his meals and library books, and play basketball with him.

Noriega keeps in touch with his wife and daughters, his girl-friend Vicky Amado, Amado's family, and a number of other people. They speak often and cryptically. His enemies claim that he has given instructions over the phone as to how to protect his money, and that he has advised his friends on how to manipulate events in Panama. His phone conversations attract considerable attention.

Noriega enjoys virtually unlimited access to a telephone, with ground rules that were established very soon after he arrived in Miami. The phone itself remains out of his reach on a guard's desk. Whenever he wants to make a call, he tells the guard the party and the number. The guard puts the call through, enters it in a log, and then hands the speaker/receiver to Noriega. Many of his calls go to the Miami switchboard of Frank Rubino, his principal attorney, where the operator patches him through to Panama and other foreign countries. Prison authorities can monitor and tape all of Noriega's conversations—except those between him and his legal team.

Noriega was successful in an early legal initiative and was granted the status of a prisoner of war. He is allowed to wear his PDF uniform in court appearances and signs his letters MAN POW 0001. A U.S. Army colonel visited Noriega in jail and gave him a copy of the Geneva Convention in Spanish. Red Cross officials have visited him and ascertained that he is not being mistreated. As a POW, Noriega receives 75 Swiss francs, or $59, a month, payable by the United States.

On November 16, Noriega made a strong case that it was not possible for him to get a fair trial, telling U.S. district judge William M. Hoeveler that he was a victim of a "totally unfair and unjust system." Noriega was careful to say that "the one shining light through this legal nightmare has been your honor."

Noriega currently stands at the center of a very complicated legal and political battle, just the kind of snarl he has always enjoyed. "I feel a little like we're in *Alice in Wonderland* at this point," Judge Hoeveler said as the first anniversary of Just Cause drew near. Noriega's phone calls are part of the problem. Many of his conversations have, in fact, been taped, but no one knows how many copies of these tapes were made or who received them. Jose Blandon, Noriega's spurned adviser and one of the government's star witnesses, has said he has heard some of them. According to Blandon, the prosecutor asked him to listen to them and try to explain what Noriega and his friends are talking about.

In November 1990, CNN reporters, who somehow obtained copies of the tapes, revealed that some of the recorded calls were indeed between Noriega and his defense team. This news touched off two separate legal proceedings, both of which pleased Noriega. One was Rubino's motion for dismissal of U.S. charges against Noriega on the grounds that U.S. authorities had breached client-lawyer confidentiality. The other was a First Amendment test that intensified when CNN elected to ignore Hoeveler's order not to broadcast the tapes until he had reviewed them. After CNN broadcast a few incomprehensible remarks, Hoeveler began a criminal investigation of CNN while he considered Rubino's request for a dismissal of charges.

On December 6, the FBI swooped down on Blandon's house, trying to find out how CNN got the tapes. Blandon denied giving anybody anything. He said government prosecutors had come to him with the tapes. But the investigation threatened to weaken if not finish him as a government witness against Noriega, a blow to the prosecution but good news in other quarters, since Blandon would surely have explained how Noriega had helped Americans like Oliver North at the same time he was working for the cocaine cartels.

Noriega's long record of service to the United States lay at the heart of the other bizarre legal tangle that has delayed his trial. On the surface, however, the issue was Noriega's money—and how he got it.

As Operation Just Cause began, the U.S. Justice Department successfully asked a number of foreign countries to freeze Noriega's bank accounts on the grounds that the money was the fruit of narco-trafficking. (The amount of the overall sum was in dispute. The Panamanian government claimed Noriega had hundreds of millions.)

By mid-1990, the Justice Department action no longer seemed

as smart as it had in January. Noriega said it was a tactic to deny him a fair trial. He said he could not pay his lawyers because the United States had stolen all his money. Rubino announced that an enormous portion of the funds in question came from the United States. He said he could prove that at least $11 million of the frozen funds had been paid to Noriega by the United States over the years.

Rather than contend with Rubino's plan to show that Noriega had been an employee of the U.S. government, Justice Department officials went to Switzerland to beg Swiss officials to thaw at least $6 million. A U.S. official told Hoeveler that getting the money that had been frozen at U.S. insistence in the first place was "rather like trying to un-ring a bell."

As he awaited the outcome of those legal proceedings Noriega maintained a wide-ranging correspondence. He continued to exchange letters with young Sarah York, who announced plans to write a book about the "kindler, gentler" Noriega she knew. He also wrote to the eighth-grade students at the Suzanne Middle School of Walnut, California. Another correspondent was Carlos Lehder Rivas, the Colombian cocaine trafficker who was sent to a maximum security prison at Marion, Illinois. Lehder counseled Noriega to plead guilty. "Your lawyers will concoct fairy tales to get your gold," the Colombian said.

As the first anniversary of Just Cause approached, there was serious question in Panama about how the government should observe the occasion. Some whose fortunes had declined after December 20, 1989, wanted to declare a national day of mourning.

Opinion polls put several obvious facts into numbers. President Endara's approval rating slipped (from 90 percent) into the teens—a number that was perhaps half the unemployment rate, which was estimated at somewhere between 20 and 30 percent. Endara had added to the problem by firing thousands from the government payroll. At least 40 percent of the population lived in poverty; 75 percent believed that the new Public Force (PF), the uniformed police force of perhaps 11,000 that succeeded the PDF, could not guarantee public safety.

Other statistics corroborated this belief. Violent crime had tripled. In one five-month reporting period there were 7,532 thefts and burglaries, 1,357 armed robberies, and 77 rapes. There were episodic strikes and schools shut down from time to time when the government failed to pay the teachers. The medical system, a legacy of Torrijos that Noriega had looted, had no funds to make it work.

One poll found that only 37 percent thought the invasion brought more benefits than problems.

Endara was an amateur at politics. Arias Calderon and Ford, the two vice presidents, were each more powerful, and each man quickly began his 1994 presidential campaign. They squandered their early popularity with public, and sometimes very unpleasant, bickering. Arias Calderon, for example, who supervised the PF, criticized Ford for his economic policies. Ford, the man who had become famous for his bloody shirt, publicly called the PF "faggots."

The government survived because it was a U.S. domestic political imperative that it survive. If it failed, what was Just Cause all about? The new civilian government had no protector other than the United States.

A U.S. official, describing United States policy, provided a strong clue about why things had gone wrong. "One objective is to reduce Panamanian dependency on the United States. The other objective is not to let the democratically elected Panamanian government go down the drain," he said. The trouble was that both objectives—though contradictory—succeeded, slightly.

Bush's pledge of $1 billion to Panama faded. The $1 billion of January became, by April, a request to Congress for half that amount, or $500 million. Eventually, Congress approved $420 million, but as the anniversary approached, only $120 million had reached Panama. The sum shrank as Panama receded from the headlines.

Meanwhile, it turned out that portions of the U.S. money had strings attached, strings that offended Panamanians. In fact, what the United States demanded from Panama (with $84 million held back until Panama said yes) in a Mutual Legal Assistance Agreement produced a rancorous debate between the two governments. Top Panamanian government officials spoke passionately of national interest and of breaking away from the United States once and for all.

To hear Panamanians tell it, the United States wanted to push Panama around, for the convenience of U.S. law enforcement agencies and for the continuing political justification of Just Cause, no matter how much it cost Panama. At issue was the strict secrecy and therefore the survival of the entire Panamanian banking industry, which had rebounded in 1990 and which, with 113 banks, accounted for a full 25 percent of the economy.

Over the years, depositors, ranging from the Vatican to the cocaine cartels, had quietly put their money in Panama's banks. Panamanian officials, like officials in Switzerland, agreed that U.S. investigators could breach the secrecy if there was evidence that a depositor was a narco-trafficker.

But according to Panamanian officials, the United States demanded so many breaches that the banking system was threatened. The United States, for example, wanted to open the secret accounts to investigate matters that were not crimes in Panama. The integrity of the secret banking system aroused far more talk from government officials about offended sovereignty than the invasion.

Over time, one of Noriega's predictions came true. He had said that if he was thrown out the mostly white middle and upper classes—the *rabiblancos* and *rabiblancas*—would reassert their power and once again exclude the poor and dark-skinned population from national life. The Endara government showed no sign of building a bridge between the mostly white elite, who did reassert their power, and the rest of the country.

———

The dismal performance of the PF was understandable. Nearly all its members came from the defunct PDF, a military organization whose principal mission was crime. Old habits—and training—died hard. One former PDF officer enthusiastically outlined a comprehensive intelligence-gathering plan to a U.S. officer. The gringo dryly praised the thoroughness of the scheme but noted that most of the proposed actions were prohibited in a democracy. "But sir, if you can't control them," the Panamanian said, referring to proposed targets in the press, the church, student organizations, and opposition political parties, "you don't control anything."

The first commander lasted twelve days, until government investigators found his bank records. His successor was Col. Eduardo Herrera-Hassan. Once again, he, Panamanian civilian leaders, and the U.S. government set off on a collaborative enterprise. Once again, all of them lost out.

Herrera-Hassan made all the proper vows about democracy. But he sometimes referred to "authentic democracy," which described, as far as one can tell, exactly the opposite of what the

United States and Endara wanted in Panama. After all, he was the embodiment of what the United States and Endara said would be expunged—military power. He was, in fact, the embodiment of the most romantic memories of the Panamanian military at their strongest, during the heady days of Torrijos.

It very quickly became obvious that the PF was not succeeding on anybody's terms. U.S. troops became the force of law and order in Panama. Meanwhile, all Herrera-Hassan's suspicions about civilians and the United States were confirmed. The PF, in his view, did not get the money it deserved while the government in general turned its back on the poor and the dark-skinned. He grew angry at government decisions about pay and vacation time and the refusal to pay death benefits to PDF widows.

In the late spring, an incident took place that raised serious questions about just what Just Cause had accomplished.

Several Panamanians who had endured torture in Noriega's prisons were having dinner in a Panama City restaurant. When they saw a PDF officer who had tortured them enter the restaurant, the men pointed, banged silverware on their glasses, and shouted that there was a criminal sadist in their midst.

The ruckus attracted a joint U.S.-Panamanian police patrol who arrested the torture victims and detained them for several hours.

By August, rancor between the civilians and Herrera-Hassan reached new levels. Endara sacked his police chief while the disgruntled military man was on a trip to Miami. October brought a series of harmless and never fully explained bomb explosions in Chiriqui. Government officials, by then facing periodic strikes and protest marches, said they had uncovered a plot to overthrow the government. The mastermind, the officials said, was Herrera-Hassan, who was in Miami again.

Herrera-Hassan returned to Panama one week later to deny the charges. He was quickly arrested and sent to Naos Island, a small rock·very close to the capital at the mouth of the canal. His prison had once been the barracks for one of Noriega's palace guard units.

───

By early December there was still no consensus about how to mark the invasion anniversary. Protests against the government were getting bigger. Union leaders who represented government workers and angry students picked Wednesday, December 5, for a strike and a large-scale street demonstration.

Shortly before 5:00 P.M. on the day before, three former PDF officers who had not been integrated into the new PF hijacked a tourist helicopter from Paitilla airport at gunpoint and flew straight to Naos Island. According to Herrera-Hassan, he was just as surprised as his guards were to see the helicopter set down. He left his grim prison dinner, walked past the docile guards, and flew away with his old friends to Panama City, where they sprinted from the helicopter to a waiting car.

Herrera-Hassan spent several hours in hiding at the San Miguelito police station, making telephone calls to PF commanders in the city and elsewhere. Then he and his friends decided to seize the PF headquarters. By 8:00 P.M., he had succeeded in doing so with no opposition from the PF officers (or several U.S. officers) who were in the building at the time. Journalists flocked to the place. Herrera-Hassan said he respected the civilian government, but he wanted the government to address the concerns of the PF.

Some journalists thought Herrera-Hassan was trying to figure out what to do. He had about a hundred men with him, many from PF units whose members fondly recalled the old days. His phone calls had not roused others to flock to the headquarters, and in the darkness, U.S. troops threw a ring around the building.

"It seemed to be a military coup attempt," said Louis Martinz, who had become a presidential aide and Endara spokesman after Just Cause. "What's the whole point of escaping from prison," Martinz asked, "and trying to rally the troops behind you if it's not to topple the government?"

But the government was unwilling to risk trying to arrest Herrera-Hassan. Endara had no confidence that the PF would obey orders to make the arrest. No one wanted bloodshed.

At 9:45 A.M., Herrera-Hassan abruptly broke the stalemate and surprised everyone by leading his armed supporters out of the headquarters. He told reporters that he was headed for the National Assembly, where he and his men would present a list of grievances. No, he was not planning to overthrow the civilian government. He supported the civilian government, he said.

The crowd flowed through an American roadblock and reached the Curundu neighborhood where small children and dogs began to scamper after them. There was no sign of any PF personnel.

Suddenly, over five hundred U.S. troops in combat gear arrived on the scene, firing in the air and ordering the Panamanians to drop their weapons and lie face down. Most obeyed instantly, and journalists photographed U.S. troops binding the wrists of Panamanians in uniform. One Panamanian policeman was killed and five were wounded in the encounter.

Very quickly the Americans had most of the Panamanians in custody. But where was Herrera-Hassan? He had refused to lie down and had simply kept on walking. Finally, the U.S. troops spotted him and twenty of his followers in an apartment building. Col. James Steele, commander of the U.S. Military Support Group, who had talked to Herrera-Hassan through the night, went to escort him to PF authorities who arrested him. SOUTHCOM announced that he had been "taken into custody by Panamanian authorities with U.S. assistance." Herrera-Hassan was taken to a maximum security prison out of the city. U.S. troops stood guard outside.

———

Endara finally decided that December 20, 1990, should be a day for "reflection." To be on the safe side, he closed all government offices but deliberately refrained from making any public comment or observation on the anniversary.

"Of Bush's objectives," said Jose Alberto Alvarez, president of the Panama Bar Association, "only one was really achieved—getting rid of Manuel Noriega. They didn't need to send in a Stealth bomber if they wanted to get Noriega. They could've captured him without an invasion, without destroying the country."

Thousands of Panamanians, mostly victims of the invasion and the political decisions that followed, turned up late in the evening of December 19, 1990, in a bulldozed field in El Chorrillo between Fourth of July Avenue and the former site of the Comandancia, which had been demolished.

Shortly before 1:00 A.M. on December 20, the demonstrators set off firecrackers, not to celebrate but to simulate and recall the violence of a year before. There were prayers for the dead and speeches about the sad plight of people made homeless by Just Cause. Some of the demonstrators kept a vigil until dawn near a cross made of two tree branches.

About 4:00 P.M. on December 20, several thousand people, all dressed in black, turned up at El Carmen cathedral. Speakers attacked the government and the United States for the failure to pick up the pieces after the invasion. The speakers also mourned the dead and some members of the crowd burned a U.S. flag.

As 1991 began, the question of how many Panamanian civilians had been killed during Just Cause was an explosive issue. Hospitals in Panama City and Colon had reported heavy casualties. U.S. and Panamanian authorities had carried out several mass burials. Individual officials and officers made their own counts, but neither U.S. authorities nor the Panamanian government made any effort to provide an accurate total. Estimates of the civilian death toll ranged from 202 to 4,000. The only consensus was that most of the dead were civilian and poor and dark-skinned.

Two U.S. Army officers who were ideally placed to make a count put the number of civilian dead at about 1,000. In a memo, Maj. Joseph A. Goetzke, the chief of the Special Claims Branch, said that "estimate of 1,000 civilian casualties is about right. Some were killed in Chorrillo section of Panama City, where about 10 blocks of high-density housing [slums] were destroyed as the result of our ops [operations]. Other civilian casualties are from shop owners shooting looters, Dignity Battalions shooting Noriega opponents, neighborhood protection/vigilante groups shooting Dignity Battalion members and stray rounds from US-PDF firefights."

There were other U.S. estimates. In June 1990, Thurman told an interviewer that the death toll was "on the order of 504 Panamanian deaths—all classifications, both military and civilian." That estimate conflicted with the official numbers that SOUTHCOM had issued. On January 11, 1990, SOUTHCOM said that 314 PDF soldiers had been killed and 202 civilians. On March 26, SOUTHCOM revised the numbers. Instead of 314, the PDF dead were only 50 while SOUTHCOM stood by 202 as the total number of civilian dead. The Panamanian government, when asked, cited the U.S. figures.

Whatever number was accurate, Operation Just Cause was the single bloodiest episode in Panamanian history. Official indifference to finding the truth became a burning political issue. "There may have been many more civilians that were killed," said Dr. Gregory Bloche of Physicians for Human Rights, whose team came up with the number 302, one hundred more than the SOUTHCOM figure. "We don't know the exact numbers, because it is in no one's perceived interest, certainly not in the United States's or in the Panamanian government's interest, to find out exactly how many civilians were really killed in the invasion."

Archbishop Marcos McGrath appealed for a government investigation to settle the issue. "I feel that neither the U.S. government nor the Panamanian government are interested in finding out the truth," McGrath said. "The issue has become political. Those who favored the invasion want a low number. Those who were against it want a high number."

The injured and the bereaved had few advocates in early 1991. Two of them were the Kiyonaga brothers, John, thirty-seven, and David, forty-one, partners in an Alexandria, Virginia, law firm. They pursued a class-action suit in the U.S. District Court in Washington on behalf of all noncombatant casualties of Operation Just Cause. The suit asked the court to direct the U.S. Defense Department to establish a procedure in Panama by which Panamanians who were injured or bereaved by U.S. firepower could file claims for financial compensation. The military used such procedures in the Dominican Republic, Vietnam, and Grenada.

The lawsuit began in January 1990 when the brothers went to Panama at the request of invasion victims. They looked around, listened, and got angry. It was plain to them that terrible injustices had taken place. In July they had over two hundred clients, and one of them was the family of Otilia Lopez de Perea, who was twenty-one when she was killed on December 23, 1989. The young woman had gone into labor, and she, her twenty-five-year-old husband Ismael, his mother, and a neighbor at the wheel set off for the hospital. But first they fastened a white flag on their Volkswagen. When they reached a U.S. Army roadblock on the Transisthmian Highway they asked for an escort to the hospital. U.S. soldiers told them the white flag was enough—and waved them through. They drove approximately five hundred yards, where U.S. troops at the next roadblock saw them and opened fire. They shot directly at the car for almost ten seconds. The couple, and the baby, were killed and the neighbor wounded. SOUTHCOM, in a later review, confirmed those facts and said, "although tragic in nature, [evidence] indicate[s] that the US personnel acted within the parameters of the rules of engagement in effect at that time."

In the course of the year, the Kiyonagas uncovered a memo that put such incidents in a broader context and suggested why the U.S. and the Panamanian government were so reluctant to count the dead who paid for the new page in Panama's history.

The army memo stated that "Payment of individual combat-related claims under a program similar to the USAID program in Grenada would not be in the best interest of the Department of Defense of the US because of the potentially huge number of such claims."

Chronology

OCTOBER 1968: Omar Torrijos overthrows Arnulfo Arias and establishes military rule in Panama.

AUGUST 1970: Manuel Antonio Noriega is made head of G-2 (Panamanian intelligence).

DECEMBER 1976: Noriega and Bush (at the time director of the CIA) have luncheon meeting as heads of respective intelligence agencies.

JULY 1981: Omar Torrijos killed in a plane crash.

DECEMBER 1983: Second meeting between Bush and Noriega; topic of discussion is support of the Contras. Two months earlier, according to Noriega, Bush had asked him to act as intermediary between the United States and Cuba at time of invasion of Grenada.

JUNE 1985: Lt. Col. Oliver North meets with Noriega in Panama.

SEPTEMBER 1985: Hugo Spadafora is murdered in Panama. President Nicolas Ardito Barletta is deposed and replaced by Vice President Eric Arturo Delvalle.

JUNE 1986: Seymour Hersh breaks story about Noriega's shady, complicated past in the *New York Times*.

OCTOBER 1986: Eugene Hasenfus is shot down over Nicaragua. Iran-Contra scandal begins to unfold.

JUNE 1987: Gen. Fred Woerner takes command at SOUTHCOM. Roberto Diaz Herrera breaks ranks and makes explosive public statements about Noriega and corruption within the PDF.

JULY 10, 1987: "Black Friday"—massive Panama City street demonstration in opposition to Noriega. Demonstration is violently suppressed by the PDF.

JULY 27, 1987: Diaz Herrera is arrested.

OCTOBER 1987: Joel McCleary, Jose Blandon, and Gabriel Lewis confer on the Blandon Plan that proposes Noriega's retirement in April 1988. Lewis submits outline to the State Department.

NOVEMBER 1987: Adm. Daniel Murphy, Ret., meets with Noriega in Panama and discusses a proposed retirement date for the general of April 1989.

DECEMBER 21, 1987: The Blandon Plan collapses; Jose Blandon is fired by Noriega and begins exile in the United States.

DECEMBER 30, 1987: Pentagon official Richard Armitage meets with Noriega in Panama City.

FEBRUARY 1988: Noriega is indicted in Florida on thirteen counts of narco-trafficking and racketeering.

MARCH 1988: Attempted coup within the PDF is suppressed by Noriega.

NOVEMBER 1988: George Bush is elected President of the United States.

FEBRUARY 1989: Bush allocates $10 million to help the opposition ticket in the May election.

APRIL 1989: The PDF arrests Kurt Frederik Muse in Panama City. He was running a clandestine opposition radio station funded by the United States. Later in the month, the $10 million allocated to the opposition is exposed. Opposition members claim they never received the money.

MAY 7, 1989: Panamanian elections are held. Former president Jimmy Carter leads a delegation of international observers and declares that even though the electoral process has been tampered with, the opposition ticket has won overwhelmingly. Noriega annuls election results.

MAY 10, 1989: Opposition candidates lead a march in Panama City and are severely beaten.

MAY 11, 1989: Bush sends 2,000 troops to Panama in response to election and beatings.

OCTOBER 1989: Moises Giroldi is killed in coup attempt within PDF.

DECEMBER 20, 1989: The United States invades Panama.

DECEMBER 24, 1989: Noriega turns himself in to the papal nuncio in Panama City.

JANUARY 3, 1990: Noriega turns himself in to the U.S. Army and is flown to jail in Florida to await trial.

Notes

I BEGAN GATHERING information for this book in 1984 when Louis Martinz, a friend from Panama, visited New York and told me about how someone named Noriega was making life difficult for him and for many other Panamanians who opposed the military's growing power. Martinz's accounts, and, over time, those of Panamanians whom I encountered through him, convinced me that Panama was a seedy, stirring, seething, and intriguing place. I kept in touch.

I assembled the research in a variety of places and a variety of ways. I made three trips to Panama—in late summer 1987, in spring 1988, and in January 1990, after the invasion called "Operation Just Cause." I also visited Washington often, and conducted many interviews in the course of three visits to Miami. Eventually (with many phone calls to all those places and others), I interviewed hundreds of participants and witnesses whose stories have helped me to make sense of the bewildering and violent events that have made up this episode of recent history.

Some of the sources—such as Manuel Antonio Noriega, his former close associate Jose Blandon, Ambassador Arthur Davis, Gen. Fred Woerner, and Elliott Abrams—played important public roles. I talked to them, to other public figures, and also to many less-well-known individuals who knew what was happening. For reasons ranging from discretion to abject fear, some sources have requested and received anonymity.

If by some terrible mistake my source list became a guest list, and they all showed up in the same place, it would be a raucous and probably violent gathering. Deep animosities and differences in perspective and philosophical outlook run through the list. I

listened to conflicting accounts of many events, as I had anticipated. In investigating Panama, I very often spoke to people who
had strong motives for what they did. After all, many of the
sources had their survival riding on the outcome of events inside
Panama. Sometimes people tried to shape future policy by promoting their own versions of events. Others told stories to ridicule a policy, or to protect or smear a reputation. There were the
usual obvious partisan slants.

I have every confidence that some of my interpretations will
be disputed. In that regard, I recall talking to a very well-informed
and highly decorated former U.S. official about the events I portray in Chapter 1. I had learned from many sources that he and
Noriega were close friends—or at least Noriega thought so. But
the U.S. official (who requested anonymity) asserted, without
being asked by me, that he hardly knew Noriega and had not
exchanged a word with him in many years. He provided an account of President Nicolas Ardito Barletta's career that omitted
any mention of the murder of Hugo Spadafora, a murder in which
Noriega was a suspect and which, in the almost universal consensus of Panamanians, was also an important factor in Barletta's
ouster. The former official thus provided a distortion by omission
that was comparable to explaining how the United States entered
World War II without mentioning the Japanese attack on Pearl
Harbor. I didn't bother to challenge him because the episode was
very instructive. I knew the man was powerful, and now I knew
that he was a liar—and not a very good one.

More people told the truth than not—often under very intimidating circumstances. After 1968, an independent media all
but vanished in Panama until it was restored as part of the 1978
treaties. But very shortly afterward, the military began harassing
the media, and for much of the time in which I closely followed
events, Noriega kept the independent Panamanian press silent. He
himself used newspapers, radio, and television to manipulate information as he saw fit.

Noriega wrote almost lovingly once about the power of rumor, and he created a situation in which the real media in Panama
City was rumor—rumor that he tried to manipulate but over
which he himself finally lost control. After all, when aides told
him there were signs on December 19, 1989, that the United States
was about to invade, he dismissed the reports as rumors. Most
rumors vanished quickly, but they had such power (as noted in the
narrative) that they deserve this comment.

Panama's sad press circumstances made me all the more grateful for the U.S. and international press, many parts of which I followed closely. Specific citations appear in the chapter notes below.

A number of reporters wrote frequently about Panama and were consistently excellent, especially when there were different accounts of events in the air in Panama City, Miami, Washington, and New York. I want to salute a few: Andres Oppenheimer of the *Miami Herald*; Jose de Cordoba of the *Wall Street Journal*; Alexander Cockburn, David Corn, and Christopher Hitchens of *The Nation*; P. J. O'Rourke of *Rolling Stone*; Stephen Kinzer, Elaine Sciolino, Larry Rohter, David E. Pitt, James LeMoyne, Richard Halloran, Stephen Engelberg, Jeff Gerth, Lindsey Gruson, and Mark A. Uhlig of the *New York Times*; Julia Preston, John M. Goshko, William Branigin, Jim McGee, David Hoffman, Joe Pichirallo, Bob Woodward, Ann Devroy, and Lee Hockstader of the *Washington Post*; Peter Eisner, Roy Gutman, Jim Mulvaney, and Patrick J. Sloyan of *Newsday*; Mike Billington of the *Fort Lauderdale Sun-Sentinel*; Lars-Erik Nelson of the *New York Daily News*; Charles Lane and Spencer Reiss of *Newsweek*; Linda Robinson of *U.S. News & World Report*; Elaine Shannon of *Time*. Also T. D. Allman, Connie Bruck, Frances FitzGerald, and Lally Weymouth. Peter Jennings and Ted Koppel consistently broadcast original reporting and Peter Collins of the ABC Miami bureau and Chris Isham of the ABC New York staff were particularly well informed.

The bibliography lists the books and documents that were part of the research.

Below, chapter by chapter, are general accounts of where the information in each chapter came from, followed by more detailed explanations and amplifications in instances in which I, as reader, thought I, as writer, should add a word to satisfy curiosity or bolster my interpretation of events.

CHAPTER 1: FRIDAY THE THIRTEENTH

I base my descriptions of Noriega's office and the towns of Pasa Canoa and Chitre on my own observation in the course of my visits to Panama. My descriptions of Noriega and Barletta come from my interviews with them (four separate meetings with Barletta) as well as scores of interviews about them with Panamanians, Americans, and others.

Many people who knew Dr. Hugo Spadafora well were eager to talk about him. I interviewed his brother Winston extensively, as well as his sisters and his close friend Jose "Pepe" Pretto. Another friend, journalist Guillermo Sanchez

Borbon, provided extensive and invaluable reporting and was generous to me with his time when he was an exile in Miami and later at *La Prensa* offices in Panama City.

Laura Bocalandro, an attorney who represented the Spadafora family on a pro bono basis, provided extensive background and documentation on the murder, as did Stephen J. Schnably, another lawyer who volunteered his services.

18, since 1981, CIA director William Casey. : Author's interview and testimony of Francis McNeil, Jose Blandon, and confidential sources.

18, proposed his assassination: *New York Times,* June 12, 1986.

19, Noriega also liked to . . . : Author's interview with Jose Blandon; Lally Weymouth, *Washington Post,* October 14, 1987; Col. Roberto Diaz Herrera, *Panama: mucho mas que Noriega.*

19, In 1983, Noriega had . . . : Author's interview with Ricardo de la Espriella.

19, busting drug traffickers: From *Sixteen Years of Struggle Against Drugs,* a compilation of Drug Enforcement Agency letters to the PDF.

19, "We have the rabid dog": Based on an NSA intercept and confirmed by congressional and intelligence sources.

19, becoming the first president . . . : Author's interview with Nicolas Barletta.

21, White House–level reports . . . : Statements by Norman O. Bailey and confidential sources.

26, "I am tired of Noriega . . .": Episode happened during a radio interview between Hugo Spadafora and Mayin Correa transmitted by Radio Continente, January 18, 1982.

31, Moments later there was a call . . . : Author's interview with Francisco Ginesta, Queenie Altimirano, and Nicolas Barletta.

33, He telephoned Noriega: The entire episode of Barletta at the Comandancia is based on author's interview with Nicolas Barletta, corroborated by Diaz Herrera in *La Prensa* interviews in June 1987 and on author's interview with staff photographer at *La Prensa.*

34, "Listen, we're supporting you . . .": Author's interview with Elliott Abrams and Nicolas Barletta.

34, But nothing else happened . . . : Nestor Sanchez testimony, July 11, 1988.

34, "Yes, Nestor . . .": The phone call from Nestor Sanchez to Noriega has been corroborated by both Barletta and Sanchez. Sanchez said he made the call on orders from Elliott Abrams. According to Sanchez, he and Abrams discussed the situation in Panama in the late morning. Sanchez said he put forth the position that Washington had to be tough on Noriega and tell him he should not get rid of Barletta. Sanchez said he told Abrams that someone should somehow get the message to Noriega that the United States opposed a coup. He and Abrams agreed, according to Sanchez, that Abrams would call Barletta and that Abrams would find someone to deliver a strong message to Noriega. Late in the afternoon, according to Sanchez, Abrams called him, told him to telephone Noriega, and gave him very precise instructions. According to Sanchez, Abrams said that Sanchez could tell Noriega that officials would view negatively any break in constitutionality in Panama. Abrams, according to Sanchez, stressed that Sanchez should say no more and no less. Sanchez made the call, which lasted no more than a minute.

Abrams said that he had never heard of a phone call from Sanchez to Noriega on the day in question until I mentioned it to him in March 1989.

(Sanchez had alluded briefly to the call in public testimony in July 1988.) Abrams said: "A telephone communication between Sanchez . . . and Noriega . . . would not be improper if it were coordinated. That is, Nestor had a responsibility then to reveal all of this to an interagency group, and if memory serves me right he never did so and I was unaware of such a call. I don't think I would have forgotten it either. I would have been outraged. . . . Now, what Nestor would have done at that point was to call me so that I could have gotten him instructed. We would have thought probably for a while. Somebody like Rich Armitage [would call Noriega] and say, 'You may not do this. You must not do this' rather than to say, 'Make it constitutional.' "

CHAPTER 2: CASEY, NORTH, AND NORIEGA

I base the information in this chapter on interviews with many sources, including people in the narrative, most notably Jose Blandon, Louis Martinz, Joel McCleary, Winston Spadafora, Deborah DeMoss, Guillermo Sanchez Borbon, and Roberto Eisenmann. I also drew upon testimony gathered by the Senate select subcommittees cited in the Bibliography.

37, Spadafora was a problem and he should solve it: U.S. surveillance of the meeting, reported in a *National Intelligence Daily,* a top-secret intelligence digest.

38, The general was not amused: Author's interview with confidential source.

39, Then he bought a house . . . : The entire episode of Cesar Rodriguez and Floyd Carlton is based upon the Kerry report, the testimony of Jose Blandon and Floyd Carlton, as well as author's interviews with Deborah DeMoss and confidential sources.

44, In fact, those meetings . . . : Author's interviews with President de la Espriella, Jose Blandon, and confidential sources.

44, North told them he would see if he could help: The account of this meeting and the October 1985 encounter is based on author's interviews with confidential sources and interviews with Jose Blandon; also see *In These Times,* February 24, 1988.

44, Langley headquarters on November 1: See Frank McNeil's *War and Peace in Central America;* author's interview with Jose Blandon, *Wall Street Journal,* May 6, 1988; *Washington Post,* May 8, 1988; and Connie Bruck, *American Lawyer,* August 1988.

45, Two weeks later . . . : See Frank McNeil's *War and Peace in Central America.*

45, A month later . . . : Whole episode is based on author's interview with Elliott Abrams, Gen. John Galvin, and Jose Blandon.

45, Spadafora's murder confirmed it: See page 276 of *Inside the National Security Council,* by Constantine Menges: "With Poindexter as NSC advisor, I told Nancy, there seemed to be little or no chance that any of my international political ideas would get a hearing. In September of 1985, when the Panamanian military strongman, General Noriega, had illegally coerced the elected president of Panama into resigning, it was the first step back from democracy in Latin America. The sub-cabinet officials on Latin America seemed to do nothing. Then, I wrote a plan for the United States to use peaceful political and economic means to help Panamanians restore their constitutional system. I told Poindexter that this was important in demonstrating President Reagan's commitment to democracy, and I warned that a Noriega-led military regime in Panama would make it far more vulnerable to destabilization and ultimate takeover by radical pro-Cuban/Soviet elements. I tried unsuccessfully for months to get this issue before President Reagan."

46, (Six days later . . .): *New York Times,* May 11, 1988, and author's interview with confidential sources.

47, "I'm going to do . . .": Author's interviews with Deborah DeMoss and Winston Spadafora.

48, Sanchez Borbon's friends . . . : Author's interview with Guillermo Sanchez Borbon.

48, At his hearing . . . : Author's interview with Arthur Davis; also *Wall Street Journal,* April 29, 1986.

49, The document. . . . : McCleary episode is based on author's interviews with Joel McCleary and Jose Blandon, the document itself, and confidential sources.

50, Much of the testimony . . . : Helms Subcommittee hearings, April 1986.

52, On April 17, 1986, the Pentagon announced . . . : *Wall Street Journal,* April 29, 1986.

52, His task was made . . . : Jose Blandon interview and testimony; the CIA denied Blandon's story.

53, In May 1986, two people . . . : Entire episode based on author's interviews with Seymour Hersh, Howard Simons, and Roberto Eisenmann, and *New York Times* starting June 12 and 13. Hersh left the employ of the *New York Times* three months later.

CHAPTER 3: MYSTICAL GUERRILLA WARFARE

I interviewed Guillermo Sanchez Borbon on a number of occasions for the basic facts of his ordeal and did the same with Berta Mitrotti and her son Jaime for the story of the Mitrotti murder. I used Col. Roberto Diaz Herrera's autobiography for some of the account of his activities. I also interviewed Jose de Jesus "Chuchu" Martinez and many others. Andres Oppenheimer, Latin American correspondent for the *Miami Herald,* who consistently provided some of the most thoughtful reporting on Panama, interviewed Diaz Herrera in Caracas and his report became the definitive document on the episode—definitive, that is, until Diaz Herrera told a different story in his book.

57, Noriega decided, on no evidence . . . : Author's interview with Jose Blandon.

57, The first, in Costa Rica . . . : The entire Santa Elena episode is based on Frank McNeil's *War and Peace in Central America,* the Kerry report, and interviews with confidential sources.

58, The *Pia Vesta,* another North scheme . . . : For entire *Pia Vesta* episode, see *Wall Street Journal* article, March 9, 1988; *In These Times,* February 28, 1987; and Jose Blandon's testimony. Noriega's aim, I concluded, was to leave a trail of conflicting evidence. He succeeded.

59, The story of Barry Seal . . . : For the Barry Seal episode, see Guy Gugliotta and Jeff Leen in *Kings of Cocaine;* the Kerry report (summary); and "Uncle Sam Wants You: Murder of a Witness," WBRZ-TV, Baton Rouge, Louisiana.

60, A representative of Noriega . . . . : The Oliver North section is based on the "Stipulation" accepted by both sides in his trial; on Jose Blandon's testimony; on *New York Times,* April 7, 1989; and on interviews with confidential sources.

61, On October 5 . . . : See Frank McNeil, *War and Peace in Central America.*

63, " . . . This country has become a nightmare": *Miami Herald,* July 11, 1986.

64, " . . . oppose the system politically in an open fashion": *Wall Street Journal,* July 10, 1987.

76, That June there were duties . . . : Author's interviews with confidential sources and Andres Oppenheimer's "Odd Man Out," published in *Tropic,* the Sunday magazine of the *Miami Herald,* August 13, 1989.

CHAPTER 4: THE LONG WHITE SUMMER

I interviewed many people (noted in the narrative) while also witnessing the demonstrations on the streets of Panama City.

79, On Saturday, June 6 . . . : Author's interviews with Arthur Davis, Gen. Fred Woerner, Mayin Correa, Col. Al Cornell, and many others.

83, "the moment when everything's up . . .": Diaz Herrera quoted in his deposition by Ken Anderson, a human rights lawyer who visited the Diaz Herrera house.

85, "I have no doubt . . .": *U.S. News & World Report,* June 22, 1987.

85, "I have confessed . . .": *New York Times,* June 12, 1987.

85, Strange things . . . : Entire Gabriel Lewis episode is based on author's interviews with Gabriel Lewis, Arthur Davis, Susan Davis, and Gen. Fred Woerner.

90, "As far as Congress . . .": Senator Dodd, quoted in *New York Times,* June 16, 1987.

91, "Panama's corrupt military dictator . . .": Robert Greenberger, *Wall Street Journal,* July 20, 1987.

95, "Knowing that you could be . . .": Louis Martinz, *New York Times,* July 16, 1987.

96, "Eduardo Villarino . . .": *Newsweek,* August 24, 1987.

99, When Noriega had been . . . : Blandon incident based on author's interview with Jose Blandon.

CHAPTER 5: ADMIRAL MURPHY PAYS A CALL

For my account of the Blandon Plan I used my interviews with Jose Blandon, a copy of the original document composed by Joel McCleary, and extensive interviews with individuals mentioned in the narrative and others. McCleary, it should be noted, had always been closer to Gabriel Lewis than to Noriega, a fact that made McCleary a more enthusiastic and more capable opponent of Noriega. Even when he was on the general's payroll McCleary made his opposition to Noriega's increasingly authoritarian actions very clear within the inner circle.

The Senate aides who visited Panama produced an excellent report cited in the Bibliography. Deborah DeMoss and Greg Craig helped me with their accounts of their visit.

My account of Adm. Daniel J. Murphy's visit to Noriega is based on his testimony to the Senate on July 11, 1988, testimony to the same panel by Sarkis Soghenalian, and extensive interviews with confidential sources.

103, From the beginning of the talks, there was one fundamental issue: See Frank McNeil, *War and Peace in Central America.*

103, Noriega spent several hours . . . : Lally Weymouth quotes are from her article in the *Washington Post,* October 14, 1987.

107, Blandon understood why: The testimony of Sarkis Soghenalian and other Senate testimony.

108, On November 17, Deborah DeMoss . . . : This episode is based on author's interviews with Deborah DeMoss and other sources.

110, "Japanese empire in World War II . . .": *Washington Post,* January 19, 1988.

112, It was time for another . . . : Entire episode taken from author's interview with Arthur Davis, and confidential sources.

CHAPTER 6: INDICTED

I base my portrait of Eric Delvalle on scores of interviews with his family, friends, and others.

114, "Don't come back": *Washington Post,* January 10, 1988, and author's interviews with many Panamanian sources.

116, Just a few days before . . . : *New York Times,* January 26, 1988.

118, "We got involved with indicting . . .": "The Cocaine General" Thames TV, September 22, 1988.

119, Two nights later . . . : "60 Minutes," CBS, February 7, 1988.

120, "He signed the orders . . .": *Fort Lauderdale Sun-Sentinel,* March 6, 1988.

122, "State Dept. Aide . . .": *New York Times,* February 19, 1988.

124, "I'm staying as long . . .": Quotes are from *Fort Lauderdale Sun-Sentinel,* February 26, 1988.

CHAPTER 7: NORIEGA STRIKES BACK

Most of this chapter is based on my interviews with the following: Ricardo de la Espriella, Jose Blandon, Gabriel Lewis, Ambassador Arthur Davis, Gen. Fred Woerner, Elliott Abrams, William Rogers, and many anonymous Panamanian and American sources. The General Accounting Office (GAO) report cited in the Bibliography was very helpful as was a confidential and highly authoritative paper prepared by Kenneth I. Juster, a colleague of William Rogers, about these events. Mr. Juster made the paper available to me. In addition to the specific newspaper, magazine, or television reports cited, I also found very strong corroboration and new insight in the reporting of Lally Weymouth in the *Washington Post* (April 10, 1988) and of Frances FitzGerald in the *New Yorker* (October 16, 1989).

Many Panamanians and Americans attested to Noriega's lifelong avidity for information ranging from trivial romantic gossip to strategic intelligence. He respected technology and, according to Panamanians and Americans who worked closely with him, usually consulted with Mike Harari so that he was sure to have the most advanced equipment with which to observe and record. For Noriega, information was ammunition. U.S. forces seized as many of Noriega's files as they could find and Noriega's defenders believe they have since expunged material that could embarrass, humiliate, or incriminate Americans and others. His archives will probably be controversial as long as Noriega is. After all, according to Panama City café gossip Noriega kept duplicate copies of his most useful material in bank vaults in different parts of the world.

127, "All imaginable pressures": *Time,* March 14, 1988.

129, "If the government of President Delvalle . . .": *Washington Post*, March 3, 1988.

129, "Panama's new president Solis Palma . . .": Author's interview with Elliott Abrams.

129, "What do you mean . . .": Ibid.

129, "You just had endless pulling and hauling . . .": Ibid.

130, "There was no communiqué . . .": Author's interview with Gen. Fred Woerner.

131, "They were kisses": *New York Times*, March 16, 1988.

131, "specialization courses in different military installations . . .": Ibid.

131, In another he bit it off and spit it out, smiling: *Washington Post*, March 26, 1988. William Branigin correctly reported this incident and several others as *bolas* or rumors, but some *bolas* turned out to be true.

133, "Everything in life is being born and then you disappear . . .": *Washington Post*, April 10, 1988.

133, "hanging on by his fingernails": *New York Times*, May 30, 1988.

133, "not far enough": *New York Times*, March 26, 1988.

133, Gridiron dinner incident: *New York Times*, March 28, 1988.

134, Three American companies with large operations in Panama . . . : GAO report, p. 26; *Washington Post*, June 7, 1988.

136, "We have ruined a healthy capitalist economy . . .": *New York Times*, May 8, 1988.

136, "What good is it to be the legitimate president of Panama . . .": *Fort Lauderdale Sun-Sentinel*, April 1, 1988.

136, Delvalle himself told an interviewer . . . : *Washington Post*, April 30, 1988.

137, Sosa's personal preference was a commando raid: *New York Times*, March 30, 1988.

137, ". . . I hope you can indicate to me that you, in fact, did not mean [the charges] as stated": AP, *Newsday*, April 6, 1988.

137, ". . . There is no doubt, however . . .": Ibid.

138, He had checked: Author's interview with Elliott Abrams.

138, "They just set impossible preconditions": Ibid.

138, ". . . They can shoot at you, they can attack the bases physically": Ibid.

138, "They've got some ideas that would make your hair stand on end": *Wall Street Journal*, April 1, 1988.

138, "harebrained": *New York Times*, April 14, 1988.

138, "cockamamy": *Miami Herald*, April 2, 1988.

139, "Under what international law . . .": *New York Times*, April 14, 1988.

139, "engaging in dangerously irresponsible behavior": *New York Times*, April 2, 1988.

139, ". . . I believed that the posturing was not productive": Author's interview with Gen. Fred Woerner.

140, "It shows they are even afraid of palm trees": *Miami Herald*, April 14, 1988.

140, "At this point in time, we don't categorically rule anything out": *New York Times*, April 14, 1988.

140, ". . . They didn't, oddly enough, run Panama anymore": Author's interview with Elliott Abrams.

141, "Blackmail? No. Leverage? Yes": Author's interview with confidential American source.

142, "The only way this crisis is going to end is when Noriega leaves": *New York Times,* March 20, 1988.

142, ". . . I want Noriega to have some sleepless nights": *Fort Lauderdale Sun-Sentinel,* March 28, 1988.

142, "This proposal is like getting the fox out of the hen house . . .": *New York Times,* March 23, 1988.

142, "Our policy is that General Noriega must go . . .": *New York Times,* April 29, 1988.

143, "They panicked in the United States": *New York Times,* May 15, 1988.

143, "The president, being the president . . .": *Time,* May 16, 1988.

144, "Everything fell apart, everything fell apart": *New York Times,* May 14, 1988.

145, "I am not like Reagan, with his astrologers": *New York Post,* May 31, 1988.

CHAPTER 8: BUSH, NORIEGA, AND FRIENDS

I based the various accounts on my interviews with Dr. Arnulfo Arias, Col. Eduardo Herrera-Hassan, Ricardo de la Espriella, Gen. Fred Woerner, and many confidential Panamanian, American, and, in government jargon, "third-country" sources. In addition to the citations below, the GAO report was very useful, once again, as was the reporting of Frances FitzGerald in the *New Yorker,* October 16, 1989.

146, "Given all the evidence . . .": Author's interviews with confidential source in the United States. When this anecdote gained currency later, several confidential sources, upon hearing it, claimed authorship.

147, ". . . up to his eyeballs . . .": *New York Times,* March 1, 1988.

148, despite a law requiring the CIA director to share his knowledge of any crimes with the attorney general: *New York Times,* May 8, 1988; also author's interview with confidential sources.

148, ". . . for the narcotics traffic": *Washington Post,* May 8, 1988.

148, "I wasn't aware of them": *New York Times,* May 21, 1988.

148, "They were extremely strong": *New York Times,* May 8, 1988.

148, "Briggs said there were a lot of allegations . . .": *New York Times,* May 14, 1988.

148, Watson memo: *New York Times,* May 14, 1988.

149, "Available to me as an officer of the NSC . . .": *Washington Post,* May 8, 1988.

149, "clear and incontrovertible evidence . . .": Ibid.

149, "The second meeting": *Washington Post,* May 8, 1988.

151, "resupply of the Contras": *Newsweek,* May 23, 1988.

152, his first phone call was to Gregg's office where he spoke to Colonel Watson: Ibid.

152, "gone bad": *Washington Post,* May 15, 1988.

152, "There are a lot of people around the world . . .": *New York Times,* May 8, 1988.

152, "when it became demonstrably clear . . .": *Miami Herald,* May 3, 1988.

152, "brought Noriega to justice": *Washington Post,* May 14, 1988.

153, "Not that I was ever aware of": AP, *Christian Science Monitor,* May 9, 1988.

153, "tell the truth": *New York Times,* May 21, 1988.

153, ". . . that I did brief him on such matters at that time simply is not true": *New York Times,* May 14, 1988.

153, It seemed a likely possibility: *Washington Post,* May 15, 1988.

154, "I could make that assumption . . .": AP, *New York Times,* May 20, 1988.

154, "I can tell you [Briggs] did not go into the fact . . .": *Washington Post,* May 15, 1988.

155, "You do what you were assigned to do": "ABC World News Tonight" transcript, May 16, 1988.

155, "Wasn't he on trial?": Ibid.

155, "George Bush can't make a speech these days . . .": *New York Times,* May 20, 1988.

155, "Drug dealers are domestic terrorists . . .": Ibid.

156, "I can see why the vice president said what he said": Ibid.

156, "political dynamite": Connie Bruck, *American Lawyer,* August 1988; see also *New York Daily News,* May 3, 1988.

CHAPTER 9: OPEN SEASON ON AMERICANS

I based the accounts on interviews with Ambassador Arthur Davis, Gen. Fred Woerner, Guillermo Endara, Guillermo "Billy" Ford, Ricardo Arias Calderon and his wife, Teresita de Arias, Louis Martinz, Col. Eduardo Herrera-Hassan, and many confidential American and Panamanian sources.

158, "He looked and acted like a soldier": Author's interview with Gen. Fred Woerner.

158, "He hardly touched the benefits that were available to him": Author's interview with confidential Panamanian source.

158, "had enough guts to make an effort . . .": Author's interview with confidential source.

159, "no longer viable": Author's interview with confidential Panamanian source in Miami.

159, "There was never any plan . . .": Author's interview with confidential U.S. military source.

159, The next day, March 29 . . . : The account of this meeting is based on a confidential American source and corroborated by secondary sources informed by eyewitnesses; see also *New York Times,* October 27, 1989.

160, The Panamanians, especially Villalaz, were disappointed: Author's interview with Maj. Augusto Villalaz in Panama.

160, Harari was happy to act as Noriega's hatchet man: *Miami Herald,* April 25, 1988.

161, "Our greatest dreams . . .": Author's interview with confidential American source.

161, The PDF simply ignored American inquiries . . . : *Army Times,* March 27, 1989; *Army Times,* March 20, 1989; see also U.S. SOUTHCOM *Information Booklet.*

161, . . . open season on U.S. civilians . . . : Ibid.

162, "Look at them": Author's interview with a confidential source and later corroborated by intelligence sources.

162, He knew how to read the signals: Above and what follows is based, except where noted, upon author's interview with Gen. Fred Woerner.

163, He and his handpicked band of exiles . . . : *Washington Post,* April 23, 1989.

163, Elliott Abrams was named as custodian . . . : Ibid and GAO report, pp. 10–11.

164, "play hardball": Author's interview with confidential source; see also *Washington Post,* April 23, 1989.

164, The phone call worked. Delvalle would remain quiet: *New York Daily News,* July 28, 1988.

165, "I'm usually angry at Congress, yes": *New York Times,* July 28, 1988.

165, "I think the matter was handled in such a way . . .": *Washington Post,* July 29, 1988.

165, "Someone, somewhere . . .": Ibid.

165, In response, the White House took the extraordinary step . . . : *New York Times,* August 18, 1988.

166, "Due to circumstances beyond Elliott Abrams's control . . .": *New York Times,* July 22, 1988.

167, "Welcome to the territory of Panama . . .": AP, *New York Times,* August 14, 1988.

167, "You're half saint, half witch": Author's interview with Louis Martinz.

167, "They make me feel like I'm a real president": Author's interview with confidential Panamanian source.

168, "There must be no misunderstanding about our policy . . .": William Scott Malone, *Washington Post,* April 23, 1989.

168, when Panama assumed sole control of the canal: *New York Times,* January 19, 1989.

CHAPTER 10: THE ELECTION

I base the various accounts on interviews with Ambassador Arthur Davis, Gen. Fred Woerner, Senator John McCain of Arizona, Guillermo Endara, Guillermo "Billy" Ford, Ricardo Arias Calderon and his wife, Teresita de Arias, Louis Martinz, and many confidential American and Panamanian sources.

170, Davis and Maisto had been forced to defend the policy: Author's interview with Panamanian businessmen who were present.

170, "I believe," he said, "that we should be seriously debating and deciding now . . .": *Army Times,* March 27, 1989; author's interview with Gen. Fred Woerner.

170, "We are frankly ill prepared . . .": *Army Times,* March 27, 1989.

172, After hours of wrangling . . . : *Army Times,* March 30, 1989.

173, "I remember": Author's interview with Guillermo Endara.

173, "Such a man is very dangerous": Author's interview with Teresita de Arias, wife of Ricardo Arias Calderon.

173, "If we talk about amnesty . . .": Author's interview with Louis Martinz.

175, Many PDF members even had special, legal passes . . . : *New York Times,* April 28, 1989.

175, "name recognition": *New York Times,* February 19, 1989.

176, Muse was accused by the PDF of being the principal American agent . . .": *Washington Post,* April 29, 1989.

176, Later in the month: Carla Anne Robbins, *U.S. News & World Report,* April 25, 1988. Robbins, a highly respected reporter, did not merit the criticism expressed by some Panamanians, who leaked stories frequently themselves, often with less accuracy. Nestor Sanchez denied leaking anything.

176, "patsy": Author's interviews with confidential American and Panamanian sources.

177, Ambassador Davis and General Woerner . . . : All of the subsequent episode, unless otherwise noted, is from author's interviews with Gen. Fred Woerner and Ambassador Arthur Davis.

178, "So far it's OK": *New York Times,* May 8, 1989.

179, "You can feel it . . .": *New York Newsday,* May 9, 1989.

179, "The government is taking the election by fraud": *New York Times,* May 9, 1989.

179, "take a little time" and see what Noriega did. "Any sort . . .": *New York Times,* May 10, 1989; *Washington Post,* May 10, 1989.

180, Up and down Via Espana, crowds waited for the candidates . . . : Unless otherwise noted, the following sources described the events of May 10: Guillermo Endara, Guillermo "Billy" Ford, Ricardo Arias Calderon, Teresita de Arias, Louis Martinz, and many other participants and eyewitnesses. There was also extensive media coverage.

183, "One way or another . . .": *Wall Street Journal* editorial, May 12, 1989.

183, "I'm worried about the lives of American citizens . . .": *New York Times,* May 12, 1989.

184, "They ought to just do everything . . .": *New York Newsday,* May 14, 1989.

184, "If the PDF asks for support to get rid of Noriega . . .": *Washington Post,* May 14, 1989.

184, Again, Endara, still bandaged . . . : Author's interview with Panamanian source.

184, He flatly accused Noriega of attempting to murder the candidates: Tribune Wire Report, *Tampa Tribune,* May 16, 1989; see also *New York Times,* May 16, 1989.

CHAPTER 11: FIND THE SCAPEGOAT

Unless otherwise noted, my accounts of the events in this chapter are based on interviews with Gen. Max Thurman, Gen. Fred Woerner, and Deborah DeMoss, as well as a number of confidential American and Panamanian sources. A report prepared by the Joint Debriefing Center of the U.S. Army, portions of which I learned about, was also helpful in its wealth of personal detail concerning the PDF.

186, there would be no money for secretaries' salaries: Author's interview with an OAS official and the *Washington Post,* May 17, 1989.

186, "helped" Bush with Panama: Author's interview with an OAS official and *Newsday,* May 19, 1989.

187, ". . . the sovereign will of the Panamanian people": *Newsday,* May 18, 1989.

187, "We're gratified that the OAS countries shared the United States's position": *Newsday,* May 19, 1989.

187, ". . . it ceases to be our business": *New York Times,* August 16, 1989.

189, ". . . the posturing would make it a necessity": This quotation and the following account are taken from the author's interview with Gen. Fred Woerner and also from the *Washington Post National Weekly Edition,* January 22–28, 1990.

191, "a state of imminent war": *New York Times,* August 12, 1989.

192, ". . . diplomatic contact with the Noriega regime": *New York Times,* September 2, 1989.

192, ". . . democratic government is restored": *Newsday,* September 2, 1989.

192, "an outlaw regime . . .": *New York Times,* September 2, 1989.

192, liked and respected in Congress: Portrait of Thurman is based on author's meeting with him and extensive interviews with confidential American military sources. Also, *New York Times,* December 28, 1989.

193, ". . . and start getting us ready": *Washington Post National Weekly Edition,* January 22–28, 1990.

193, "a McNamara in a green suit": Author's interview with Col. Harry Summers, Ret., and his column in the *Army Times,* August 14, 1989; *New York Times,* December 28, 1989; *Washington Post National Weekly Edition,* January 22–28, 1990.

193, "tyranny in all its insidious forms": *New York Times,* December 28, 1989.

194, Portrait of Giroldi based upon author's interview with confidential American military sources.

195, He also procured women for Noriega and escorted them home afterward: Portraits of the PDF are based upon the report prepared by the Joint Debriefing Center of the U.S. Army and corroborated by author's interviews with confidential American and Panamanian military and civilian sources.

CHAPTER **12:** BLOODY FIASCO

Unless otherwise noted, my account of the events in this chapter is based upon interviews with Deborah DeMoss and a number of confidential American and Panamanian military and diplomatic sources. The report prepared by the Joint Debriefing Center of the U.S. Army was once again helpful.

197, Adela's friend would serve as the intermediary for communication in the future. The portrait of the Giroldis is based upon author's interviews with confidential American military sources and others.

199, ". . . his plan wasn't very well thought out": *Washington Post,* November 14, 1989.

199, When Thurman was certain about something he sounded that way: Account is based upon confidential American military sources close to the action in Panama and Washington, D.C.; also in author's meeting with Thurman he expressed concern about an early challenge from Noriega.

199, his top aides to tell the president: *New York Times,* October 8, 1989.

199, "Get the lawyers": *Washington Post National Weekly Edition,* October 23–29, 1989.

200, he stressed caution: *New York Times,* October 8, 1989.

200, Later in the day, an American unit: Ibid.

200, ". . . No one would ever forgive him": Author's interview with confidential U.S. intelligence source.

203, "We would have had to stage something . . .": Ibid.

205, ". . . There is no politics involved": *New York Times,* October 4, 1989.

205, "My troops are on the way": *New York Times,* October 11, 1989.

205, "You don't have balls": *Time,* October 16, 1989.

206, "I'm tired of these bastards": *Washington Post,* October 14, 1989.

206, had his hands cut off before he was shot: *Fort Lauderdale Sun-Sentinel,* January 1, 1990.

206, "The gringo piranhas want to do away with me": *Miami Herald,* October 5, 1989.

206, ". . . against the tranquility of our country": *New York Times,* October 4, 1989.

207, If Thurman could meet those requirements: *Washington Post,* October 8, 1989.

207, "It's not a coup until it's broadcast on the radio": Author's confidential interview with U.S. Army officer who was close to the action.

207, ". . . Max let his ego get in the way": Ibid.

207, before the day was out: *New York Times,* October 4, 1989.

208, something was happening in Panama: *Miami Herald,* October 4, 1989.

208, ". . . and the secretary of defense doesn't know about it": *Newsweek,* October 16, 1989.

208, "I can tell you that is not true": "Nightline," ABC News transcript, October 3, 1989.

208, after he had made his first contact with U.S. intelligence agents: *Fort Lauderdale Sun-Sentinel,* January 1, 1990.

CHAPTER 13: CORPSES AND COVER-UPS

My accounts of the events in this chapter are based upon interviews with many Panamanian and American sources, including Deborah DeMoss, and the transcript of the Jesse Helms speech in the *Congressional Record* of October 5, 1989. Also, the report prepared by the Joint Debriefing Center of the U.S. Army was once again helpful.

209, "left its agents in the lurch": *New York Times,* October 9, 1989.

209, "There can be no place here . . .": *Miami Herald,* October 8, 1989.

210, "Let's make the list": Ibid.

210, ". . . to the friend, money": Ibid.

210, "I fire on my enemies, not against my brothers": *New York Newsday,* October 6, 1989.

211, ". . . You will not even find peace in hell": *Washington Post,* October 14, 1989.

211, told her not to show it to anyone, and formally classified it "Secret": Ibid.

212, ". . . He thought the commander's fate should be decided by the people": *New York Times,* October 12, 1989.

212, ". . . They would have just run": *Washington Post National Weekly Edition,* October 16–22, 1989.

212, "Keystone Kops": *New York Times,* October 6, 1989.

212, "a sort of mini-Noriega": *Time,* October 16, 1989.

212, "just wanted to be a new Noriega . . .": *Washington Times,* October 6, 1989.

212, "It was not a pro-democracy group . . .": "Nightline," ABC News transcript, October 4, 1989.

212, ". . . we had no sense of their plans or intentions or possibilities at all": *Newsday,* October 5, 1989.

213, "Giroldi was a professional military guy. . . ": *Washington Times,* October 6, 1989.

213, ". . . They won't do anything for a long time": Ibid.

213, "Just because we didn't help out this time . . .": *Washington Times,* October 6, 1989.

213, "We cannot fight a monster like Noriega with rocks": Ibid.

214, "a bunch of hogwash": *New York Times,* October 6, 1989.

214, "any charge that we were somehow offered Noriega . . .": *Miami Herald,* October 6, 1989.

214, "My personal feeling is that . . .": *New York Times,* October 16, 1989.

214, "so factually inaccurate that I suspect . . .": Ibid.

215, The committee's strict rules on covert operations, Cheney said, hampered the administration's efforts to get rid of Noriega: *New York Times,* October 9, 1989.

215, a Reagan "finding" that commissioned a covert operation: "Nightline," ABC News transcript, October 3, 1989.

215, creating even more headlines during the next week: *New York Times,* October 9, 1989.

216, "We made a good policy decision . . .": *Miami Herald,* October 7, 1989.

216, "We are not in the business of willy-nilly running around . . .": *Miami Herald,* October 7, 1989.

216, "How many dead Americans . . .": *New York Daily News,* October 9, 1989.

216, "I didn't use military force . . .": *New York Times,* October 7, 1989.

216, "This was the gang that couldn't shoot straight": Author's interview with a confidential U.S. embassy source.

216, ". . . But I've seen no fact that would make me change my view": President Bush's press conference is quoted from a transcript printed in *New York Times,* October 14, 1989.

CHAPTER **14**: NO WAY OUT

My accounts of the events in this chapter are based upon interviews with Deborah DeMoss and many confidential sources. Also, the report prepared by the Joint Debriefing Center of the U.S. Army was once again helpful.

219, "The key lies in dropping the focus on Noriega's personal fate": *Washington Post,* October 12, 1989.

220, "no one even joked about that": Author's interview with a confidential U.S. military source.

220, ". . . not the way I plan to conduct the military or foreign affairs of this country": *Washington Post National Weekly Edition,* December 25–31, 1989.

220, Noriega would agree to leave office and the United States would agree not to press for extradition: Ibid.

220, launched another covert operation to knock Noriega from power: *Washington Post,* December 24, 1989.

221, "no restrictions": *Los Angeles Times,* November 16, 1989.

221, "We're going into it with the understanding . . .": Ibid.

221, "What it boils down to is that we want him alive in the United States or dead": Ibid.

221, William P. Barr's legal position: *Washington Post National Weekly Edition,* January 1–7, 1990; also *New York Newsday,* December 21, 1989.

221, "There are still lawless countries . . .": *Los Angeles Times,* November 9, 1989.

221, "memorandum of law": *Los Angeles Times,* November 16, 1989.

221, "I can think of no law . . .": *Los Angeles Times,* November 9, 1989.

221, "concern that we were going to mount up like the Lone Ranger": Ibid.

222, Thurman went to the Pentagon to explain his plan to remove Noriega from power: *Washington Post National Weekly Edition,* January 1–7, 1990.

222, "Max got very macho around that time after the coup": Author's confidential interview with a SOUTHCOM officer.

223, "warning order": *Washington Post National Weekly Edition,* January 1–7, 1990.

223, as one military historian put it: Author's interview with Col. David H. Hackworth, Ret.

224, He assumed the civilian clothes reconnaissance was part of the plan to kidnap him: Author's interview with confidential U.S. military and intelligence sources.

224, buy flowers for the graves of his opponents: Author's interview with Louis Martinz.

224, the counterintelligence staff made plans themselves to get away to Cuba for the holidays: Report by the U.S. Army Joint Debriefing Center.

225, new talks about his possible resignation: Interview with a confidential Panamanian source.

226, "We will sit by the canal . . .": *Washington Post National Weekly Edition,* December 25–31, 1989.

226, nor to any of his remarks: Theodore Draper, *New York Review of Books,* March 29, 1990.

226, *A Moveable Feast:* Interview with close friend of Noriega.

226, ". . . there is very little time left . . .": Ibid.

227, They got back to Rodman Naval Station after 2:00 A.M. and told their story: *New York Times,* December 18, 1989.

CHAPTER 15: PULLING THE TRIGGER

For some of the information about the PDF and Noriega, the report prepared by the U.S. Army's Joint Debriefing Center was helpful once again. Panamanian and American sources corroborated certain material. I went to Panama early in 1990 and talked to many Panamanians and Americans. I saw the places where Operation Just Cause's most notable events took place, such as El Chorrillo and Noriega's office at the Comandancia, and was able to compare what I saw in 1990 with what I remembered from my previous visits. I also traveled outside the city to a number of places, including Rio Hato. I interviewed Guillermo Endara, Ricardo Arias Calderon, Guillermo Ford, Monsignor Sebastian Laboa, the Reverend Xavier Villanueva, and many other Panamanians and Americans about what they saw and heard before, during, and after the invasion. My account of military actions is also based, in addition to specific citations below, on extensive interviews with U.S. military personnel who took part in Operation Just Cause in one way or another and who saw it with their own eyes, or from a distance. Dozens of participants directly contributed in one way or another to my account and even greater numbers contributed to the research of attorneys and other individuals who investigated the invasion and its aftermath and who shared their findings with me.

228, At the U.S. embassy: The transcript of the marine's conversation was included in the report of the Joint Debriefing Center.

229, "tried to reassure us . . .": *New York Times,* December 19, 1989.

229, "U.S. and international public . . .": *Washington Post,* December 24, 1989.

229, "a grave escalation in the . . .": *New York Times,* December 19, 1989.

229, I base my account of Bush's Sunday actions on this and subsequent pages on several sources including accounts in the *Washington Post National Weekly Edition,* December 25–31, 1989; the *Washington Post,* December 24, 1989; and the *New York Times,* December 23, 1989.

230, "mini–Normandy invasion": Author's interview with Col. David H. Hackworth, Ret., and extensive interviews with military personnel involved with Operation Just Cause.

231, "We are extremely . . .": *New York Times,* December 18, 1989.

231, "We are very concerned . . .": *Newsday,* December 19, 1989. Theodore Draper provided a comprehensive account of this episode in the *New York Review of Books,* March 29, 1990.

231, "not related . . .": *New York Times,* December 19, 1989.

231, "One of the frustrations . . .": *Newsday,* December 19, 1989.

232, I base the account of the shooting on accounts in the *New York Daily News* on December 19, 1989, and December 20, 1989, and interviews with confidential American sources. The incident remains controversial. The *Los Angeles Times,* one year later, quoted sources who said that the U.S. personnel, with the tacit approval of senior U.S. officers, deliberately tried to provoke the PDF. The Pentagon denied it.

232, I base the account of Bush's actions on Tuesday on the same *Washington Post* and *New York Times* accounts cited in the second note for page 229 and the *New York Times,* December 20, 1989.

232, "Noriega's irresponsible declaration . . .": *New York Times,* December 20, 1989.

232, "We find the unwarranted . . .": *New York Times,* December 20, 1989.

233, The abundance of clues that the invasion was imminent was also reported in *Newsday,* December 19, 1989.

233, The telephone calls were mentioned in the Joint Debriefing Center report.

233, I base the Harari episode on the *New York Times* of January 3, 1990, and the *Wall Street Journal* of March 7, 1990, which describe Harari's mysterious departure in greater detail. Many Panamanians and Americans (including myself) believe that American intelligence friends helped Harari get out of Panama, but accounts are full of uncertainties. I also used my own interviews with confidential U.S. sources and the report of the Joint Debriefing Center.

234, I base my account of Endara, Arias Calderon, and Ford on my interviews with the three men.

234, I base my account of Noriega's actions Tuesday night, Wednesday morning, and afterward on interviews with confidential U.S., Panamanian, and Colombian sources as well as the report of the Joint Debriefing Center.

238, "We're in trench warfare . . .": *Newsday,* December 21, 1989.

238, I base my account of military operations on extensive interviews with participants and observers as well as extensive media coverage. Michael R. Gordon of the *New York Times* reported extensively on the Stealths in stories that appeared on February 27, 1990, April 11, 1990, and July 2, 1990. *Newsday,* January 9, 1990, the *New York Daily News,* April 13, 1990, and *Newsweek,* April 16, 1990, also provided accounts of the Stealths' performance.

239, "an orthopedic nightmare": *Los Angeles Times* Service report printed in *Miami Herald,* January 8, 1990.

239, Freezing weather at . . . : *Washington Post National Weekly Edition,* January 8–14, 1990, and interviews.

239, The assault with . . . : I base my account of the action on my own visits to the area and interviews with participants and witnesses. Also, the *New York Times,* December 26, 1989, provided a good account of the collisions and subsequent action near the Comandancia. Francisco Goldman provided an invaluable account of the assault in *Harper's,* September 1990, as did Martha Gellhorn in *Granta* 32, Spring 1990.

240, "My fellow citizens . . .": *Newsday,* December 21, 1989.

241, "pinpoint accuracy": *New York Daily News,* December 26, 1989. The Michael R. Gordon pieces in the *New York Times* also record this.

241, The looting estimates were reported on "Nightline," January 2, 1990, and in the *Wall Street Journal,* January 4, 1990.

241, "This operation is not over . . .": *Wall Street Journal,* December 22, 1989.

242, "The Ma Bell approach": *New York Times,* January 11, 1990.

242, I learned about Noriega's files from many confidential sources. Also, Doug Vaughan reported on the issue in *Details,* September 1990.

243, "He didn't want to end his life . . .": *New York Times,* January 20, 1990.

243, I base my account of Monsignor Laboa's and the Reverend Villanueva's actions here and for the remainder of the chapter on my interviews with them, except where otherwise noted.

246, "He is a man": *New York Times,* January 6, 1990.

246, Ambassador Melady provided his account of Christmas Eve and subsequent days in an interview conducted by Robert Moynihan in *30 Days,* February 1990.

246, On Christmas Day . . . : Typical of the comments was "We want them [the Vatican] to reject his [Noriega's] request for asylum, walk him to the door, take him outside, and let him go. We are not asking the Vatican to extradite him, we just want them to let him go. We will take care of the rest." That and others appeared in the *New York Times,* December 26, 1990.

247, "I can announce with satisfaction . . .": *New York Times,* December 26, 1990.

248, "I am the music man": *Newsweek,* July 16, 1990.

248, "truly evil man": *New York Times,* December 27, 1990.

248, "screw-up": *Fort Lauderdale Sun-Sentinel,* January 30, 1990.

248, "An occupying power . . .": *Catholic New York,* January 4, 1990.

249, "repeated our long-standing . . .": Archbishop McGrath, quoted in the *New York Times,* January 4, 1990.

249, The U.S. troops . . . : Enrique Jelenszky and Rolando Domingo were the Panamanian lawyers who stayed at the nunciature to assist the nuncio. Their accounts, prepared with the help of *Dallas Morning News* writer David Marcus, appeared in that newspaper, the *New York Daily News,* and the *Miami Herald* of January 7, 1990.

250, "was not considered . . .": *New York Times,* January 4, 1990.

254, "a political jackpot": *New York Times,* January 5, 1990.

EPILOGUE

During my visit to Panama early in 1990 I interviewed scores of Panamanians, Americans, and others who were participants in and observers of the post-Noriega era. I continued to monitor developments until the book went to press through the media and through frequent conversations in person and on the telephone with a variety of sources. Lawyers John Kiyonaga and David Kiyonaga provided extensive help on the human cost of the invasion as well as various U.S. Army documents regarding incidents in Panama and legal precedents based on events in Vietnam and Grenada. Both Kiyonagas had lived in Panama prior to the invasion and David, a founding member of the American Chamber of Commerce in Panama City, practiced law there for eight years and maintained an office and a home there. The Kiyonagas' father, Joe, was CIA station chief in Panama City, 1971–1975. Charles C. Thompson II, a producer with CBS's "60 Minutes," investigated the question of civilian casualties extensively before CBS aired its program on September 30, 1990. In the face of criticism, Thompson reviewed and extended his reporting and produced a "White Paper" that silenced his critics. Thompson made the paper available to me, and it is available for the asking from CBS.

255, "repair the wounds, repair the damage": *Washington Post,* December 16, 1990.

255, I learned bits and pieces of information about Noriega's living conditions and his activities while in jail from a variety of sources, but the most comprehensive account appeared in the *Miami Herald,* October 21, 1990.

256, Noriega's legal battles were covered throughout the year; some of the best accounts were in the *Miami Herald,* November 25, 1990, and the *Washington Post,* December 30, 1990, and T. D. Allman's in *Vanity Fair,* February 1991.

256, "totally unfair and unjust system": *Washington Post,* December 30, 1990.

256, "the one shining light . . .": Ibid.

257, "I feel a little like . . .": Ibid.

258, "rather like trying to un-ring a bell": Ibid.

258, *La Prensa* published various polls during 1990. *Newsday* provided reliable statistics on December 20, 1990. The crime statistics appear in an overview of developments during 1990 by Steve C. Ropp of the University of Wyoming that appeared in *Current History,* March 1991. Another valuable overview, by John Otis, appeared in *In These Times,* December 5–11, 1990.

259, "One objective is to reduce . . .": *Washington Post,* December 16, 1990.

259, I base my account of the Mutual Legal Assistance Agreement dispute on interviews with Panamanian and American officials and extensive media coverage.

260, "But sir, if you can't control them . . .": Report of the U.S. Army's Joint Debriefing Center.

261, Friends in Panama told me about the incident of the torturer in the restaurant and an extensive account appeared in the *New York Times,* July 22, 1990.

262, I based the account of Herrera- Hassan's escape, protest, and recapture on interviews with witnesses and friends of his as well as the *Washington Post,* December 6, 1990, the *Miami Herald,* December 6, 1990, *U.S. News & World Report,* December 17, 1990, and the *New York Times,* January 20, 1991.

262, "It seemed to be a military . . .": *Miami Herald,* December 6, 1990.

263, "Of Bush's objectives . . .": *Fort Lauderdale Sun-Sentinel,* December 16, 1990.

263, Eyewitnesses told me about the demonstrations in Panama on December 19 and 20, 1990.

264, As noted above, I relied extensively on the investigation done by the Kiyonaga brothers and the extensive reporting of Charles C. Thompson II of

CBS, which more than corroborated what I had learned through my own interviews and simple observations.

264, "estimate of 1,000 civilian casualties . . .": A memo brought to light through a Freedom of Information Act request by the Kiyonagas.

264, "on the order of 504 . . .": Television interview footage obtained by CBS.

264, "There may have been . . .": CBS "White Paper."

265, "I feel that neither . . .": Ibid.

265, I interviewed John Kiyonaga several times. The story of Otilia Lopez de Perea also appeared in an unpublished dispatch filed to the *Washington Post* in October 1990.

265, "although tragic in nature . . .": This was contained in a reply from SOUTHCOM to questions submitted by a *Washington Post* reporter about the incident. SOUTHCOM confirmed the facts of the story.

266, "Payment of individual . . .": From a memo by Maj. Joseph A. Goetzke, Chief, Special Claims Branch, obtained by the Kiyonagas through a Freedom of Information Act request.

Bibliography

BOOKS

Cockburn, Leslie. *Out of Control: The Story of the Reagan Administration's Secret War in Nicaragua, the Illegal Arms Pipeline, and the Contra Drug Connection.* New York: The Atlantic Monthly Press, 1987.

Conte-Porras, Jorge. *Diccionario Biografico Illustrado de Panama.* 1986.

Diaz Herrera, Col. Roberto. *Panama: mucho mas que Noriega.* Caracas, Venezuela, 1988.

Emerson, Steven. *Secret Warriors: Inside the Covert Military Operations of the Reagan Era.* New York: G. P. Putnam's Sons, 1988.

Greene, Graham. *Getting to Know the General: The Story of an Involvement.* New York: Simon & Schuster, 1984.

Gugliotta, Guy, and Jeff Leen. *Kings of Cocaine: Inside the Medellín Cartel—An Astonishing True Story of Murder, Money, and International Corruption.* New York: Simon & Schuster, 1989.

Gutman, Roy. *Banana Diplomacy: The Making of American Policy in Nicaragua, 1981–1987.* New York: Simon & Schuster, 1988.

Instituto Panameno de Estudios Comunitarios. *El Movimento Civilista (Junio 1987–Junio 1988).* Panama: Partido Democrata Cristiano, 1988.

Jorden, William J. *Panama Odyssey.* Austin: University of Texas Press, 1984.

Kwitny, Jonathan. *The Crimes of Patriots: A True Tale of Dope, Dirty Money, and the CIA.* New York: W. W. Norton & Company, 1987.

Mack, Gerstle. *The Land Divided: A History of the Panama Canal and Other Isthmanian Canal Projects.* New York: Alfred A. Knopf, 1944.

Martinez, Jose de Jesus. *Mi General Torrijos.* Panama City: Centro de estudios torrijista, 1987.

McCullough, David. *The Path Between the Seas: The Creation of the Panama Canal, 1870–1914.* New York: Touchstone (Simon & Schuster), 1977.

McNeil, Frank. *War and Peace in Central America: Reality and Illusion.* New York: Charles Scribner's Sons, 1988.

Menges, Constantine C. *Inside the National Security Council: The True Story of the Making and Unmaking of Reagan's Foreign Policy.* New York: Simon & Schuster, 1988.

PDF Compilation. *Panama: 16 Years of Struggle Against Drug Traffic.* Panama: Panamanian Defense Force, 1986.

Raviv, Dan, and Yossi Melman. *Every Spy a Prince: The Complete History of Israel's Intelligence Community*. Boston: Houghton Mifflin Company, 1990.

U.S. SOUTHCOM. *Information Booklet*. Public Affairs Office. Effective January 1989.

Woodward, Bob. *Veil: The Secret Wars of the CIA, 1981–1987*. New York: Simon & Schuster, 1987.

BIBLIOGRAPHY ON TRANSCRIPTS

Juster, Kenneth I. *U.S. Policy Toward Panama: The Premature Demise of Economic Sanctions*. Confidential draft.

Panama Canal, Permanent Neutrality and Operation: Treaty Between the United States of America and Panama, signed at Washington, September 7, 1977, with Attached Protocol and Protocol of Exchange of Instruments of Ratification signed at Panama, June 16, 1978.

U.S. General Accounting Office. *Testimony*. GAO Review of Economic Sanctions Imposed Against Panama. Statement of Frank C. Conahan, Assistant Comptroller General for National Security and International Affairs before the Subcommittee on International Economic Policy and Trade, and Western Hemisphere Affairs, Committee on Foreign Affairs, House of Representatives.

U.S. House of Representatives. *U.S. Narcotics Control Programs Overseas: An Assessment*. Report of a staff study mission to Southeast Asia, South America, Central America, and the Caribbean, August 1984 to January 1985, to the Committee on Foreign Affairs. February 22, 1985. Washington, D.C.: Government Printing Office, 1985.

U.S. Senate. *Drugs, Law Enforcement and Foreign Policy: A Report of the Subcommittee on Narcotics, Terrorism and International Operations*. April 13, 1989. Volume I, The Report.

U.S. Senate. *Drugs, Law Enforcement and Foreign Policy: A Report of the Subcommittee on Narcotics, Terrorism and International Operations*. April 13, 1989. Volume II, Exhibits.

U.S. Senate. *Drugs, Law Enforcement and Foreign Policy: A Report Prepared by the Subcommittee on Terrorism, Narcotics and International Operations of the Committee on Foreign Relations*. December 1988.

U.S. Senate. *Drugs, Law Enforcement and Foreign Policy: Hearings before the Subcommittees on Terrorism, Narcotics and International Communications and International Economic Policy, Trade, Oceans, and Environment of the Committee on Foreign Relations*. 100th Congress, 1st Session; May 27, July 15, and October 30, 1987. Part 1.

U.S. Senate. *Drugs, Law Enforcement and Foreign Policy: Panama. Hearings before the Subcommittee on Terrorism, Narcotics and International Communications of the Committee on Foreign Relations*. 100th Congress, 2nd Session; February 8, 9, 10, and 11, 1988, Part 2.

U.S. Senate. *Drugs, Law Enforcement and Foreign Policy: The Cartel, Haiti and Central America: Hearings before the Subcommittee on Terrorism, Narcotics and International Communications of the Committee on Foreign Relations*. 100th Congress, 2nd Session; April 4, 5, 6, and 7, 1988. Part 3.

U.S. Senate. *Drugs, Law Enforcement and Foreign Policy: The Cartel, Haiti and Central America: Hearings before the Subcommittee on Terrorism, Narcotics and*

International Operations of the Committee on Foreign Relations, 100th Congress, 2nd Session; July 11, 12, and 14, 1988. Part 4.

U.S. Senate. *Situation in Panama: Hearings before the Subcommittee on Western Hemisphere Affairs of the Committee on Foreign Relations.* 99th Congress, 2nd Session; March 10 and April 21, 1986.

U.S. Senate. Staff Delegation. *Report on Panama,* December 8, 1987.

Index

CRIME
SCHOOL

CAROL O'CONNELL

G. P. PUTNAM'S SONS   NEW YORK

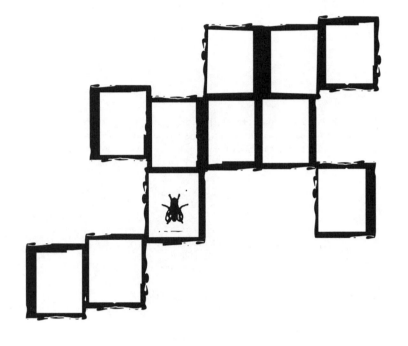

cRiME

ScHOOL

This is a work of fiction. Names, characters, places, and incidents either
are the product of the author's imagination or are used fictitiously, and
any resemblance to actual persons, living or dead, business
establishments, events, or locales is entirely coincidental.

G. P. Putnam's Sons
Publishers Since 1838
a member of
Penguin Putnam Inc.
375 Hudson Street
New York, NY 10014

Library of Congress Cataloging-in-Publication Data

O'Connell, Carol, date.
Crime School / Carol O'Connell.
p.   cm.
ISBN 0-399-14928-7
1. Mallory, Kathleen (Fictitious character)—Fiction.
2. Police—New York (State)—New York—Fiction.
3. New York (N.Y.)—Fiction.   4. Policewomen—Fiction.   I. Title.
PS3565.C497C75   2002   2002022860
813'.54—dc21

Printed in the United States of America
1   3   5   7   9   10   8   6   4   2

This book is printed on acid-free paper. ∞

BOOK DESIGN BY MEIGHAN CAVANAUGH

FOR THE TEACHERS

Thelma Rantilla once said, "Every child, at the age of ten, should be dropped on its head in the center of New York City and forced to find its own way home." Thus, this schoolteacher put a dull knife into the heart of every parent—and twisted it—*slowly*. For this and additional outrages, she became my personal hero. However, because she went everywhere in a rarified air of distraction, I believed she had no idea that I was on the planet.

The last time I saw her, she was carrying a carton with the year's end debris of papers and books. Her hair was a dangerous nest of sharp pencils, and her head was tucked in to avoid eye contact with anyone who might slow her quick trot to the door and flight into summer vacation.

As I pursued her down the hall, hurrying to keep up, I had no idea of what I might say beyond good-bye.

Miss Rantilla suddenly halted, then turned on me and said, "You know, every once in a while, you show a flash of talent—*just* a flash."

I was stunned, stopped cold and speechless. This bought her the time she needed to make her escape.

cRiME ScHOOL

PROLOGUE

HIGH IN THE SKY, APARTMENT WINDOWS WERE SMUDGES of grimy yellow, and this passed for starlight in New York City. Loud Latin rhythms from a car radio drifted down First Avenue. The sedan turned sharply, brakes screaming, narrowly missing a small blond girl with fugitive eyes. The child stood on tiptoe, poised for flight, arms rising like thin white wings.

A book was knocked from the hands of a woman on the sidewalk as the little girl sped past her in a breeze of flying hair and churning legs, small feet slapping pavement in time to the music of a passing boom box—a rock 'n' roll getaway. The eyes of the running child were not green, not Kathy's eyes, yet the startled woman saw her as a familiar wraith rocketing through space and years of time.

Fifteen years, you fool. And Kathy Mallory was not so small anymore, nor was she dead—not the makings of a ghost.

Sweat rolled down Sparrow's face. If not for the stolen book, would her mind have made that stumble? Again, the woman looked back the way she had come, but there was no sign of the man who had followed her from the bookshop. She had circled round and round, taking the long way home to lose him, and he had not hurried his steps to keep up with her. He had moved with inexorable resolve to the measured beat of a march. His body had no language, no life.

If a dead man could walk.

Sparrow's hands were clammy, a sign of anxiety, but she blamed it on the weather, so hot and muggy in this gray hour after sundown. And she blamed her costume for the stares from other pedestrians. The mutton-sleeve blouse and long skirt were too bizarre for a twenty-first-century heat wave. A match flared close beside her as a man, a harmless type, lit a cigarette, then passed her by. Her heart beat faster, and she rationalized away the second warning, taking it for guilt.

If not for the book—

She looked down at her empty hands and panicked—then sighed. The precious paperback lay on the sidewalk at her feet, and she bent low to snatch it back. On the rise, another figure, quiet as smoke, moved along-side her in the half-dozen mirrors of a drugstore window. She could still be surprised by these chance encounters with herself, for the surgically altered face needed no makeup to cover a history of broken bones and ravaged skin. The blue eyes of her reflection looked back across a gap of seventeen years, fresh off a Greyhound bus from the Southland.

Sparrow nodded. "I remember you, girl."

What an unholy haunted night.

She hid the book behind her back, as if a tattered novel might be worth stealing. In fact, she planned to burn it. But the book was not what the stalking man wanted. Sparrow looked uptown and down. He would be so easy to spot in this crowd of normal humans. Apparently, she had lost him at some turn of a corner. Yet every inch of her prickled, as though a thousand tiny insects crept about beneath her skin.

She hurried homeward, not looking back anymore, but only paying attention to a voice inside her head. Fear was a good old friend of hers, who broke into her thoughts to say, *Hello,* and then, *Ain't it gettin' dark?* And now, *Run, girl!*

ONE

GREENWICH VILLAGE HAD LOST ITS EDGE LONG AGO, becoming a stately old lady among New York neighborhoods. One of the grande dame's children stood beneath the great stone arch in Washington Square Park. The boy wore trendy camouflage pants, all dressed up for a revolution—should one come along the way buses do.

A guitar case lay at his feet, open to donations from passersby, though no one slowed down to drop him a dime. People marched past, sweating and cursing the heat of August, hurrying home to cold beers and canned music. It would take spectacle on a grander scale to get their attention tonight.

An unmarked police car crawled by in air-conditioned silence. Detective Sergeant Riker rolled down the passenger window and listened to a ripple of melancholy notes on soft nylon strings.

Not what he had expected.

Evidently, the teenage musician had missed the point of being young.

Thirty-five years ago, Riker had been the boy beneath the arch, but his own guitar had been strung with steel, electrified and amplified, ripping out music to make people manic, *forcing* them to dance down the sidewalk.

What a rush.

And the entire universe had revolved around *him*.

He had sold that electric guitar to buy a ring for a girl he had loved more than rock 'n' roll. The marriage had ended, and the music had also deserted him.

The window closed. The car rolled on.

Kathy Mallory took the wheel for every tour of duty, but not by choice. Torn between drinking and driving, her partner had allowed his license to expire. The detectives were nearing the end of their shift, and Riker guessed that Mallory had plans for the evening. She was wearing her formal running shoes, black ones to match the silk T-shirt and jeans. The sleeves of her white linen blazer were rolled back, and this was her only concession to the heat. If asked to describe the youngest detective on the squad, he would bypass the obvious things, the creamy skin of a natural blonde and the very unnatural eyes; he would say, "Mallory doesn't sweat."

And she had other deviations.

Riker's cell phone beeped. He pulled it out to exchange a few words with another man across town, then folded it into his pocket. "No dinner tonight. A homicide cop on First Avenue and Ninth wants a consult."

The jam of civilian cars thinned out, and Mallory put on speed. Riker felt the car tilt when it turned the corner, rushing into the faster stream of northbound traffic. She sent the vehicle hurtling toward the rear end of a yellow cab that quickly slid out of the lane—*her* lane now. Other drivers edged off, dropping back and away, not sporting enough to risk sudden impact. She never used the portable turret light or the siren, for cops got no respect in this town—but sheer terror worked every time.

Riker leaned toward her, keeping his cool as he said, "I don't wanna die tonight."

Mallory turned her face to his. The long slants of her green eyes glittered, thieving eerie light from the dashboard, and her smile suggested that he could jump if he liked. And so a nervous game began, for she was watching traffic only in peripheral vision. He put up his hands in a show of surrender, and she turned her eyes back to the road.

Riker held a silent conversation with the late Louis Markowitz, a ghost he carried around in his heart as balm for anxious moments like this one. It was almost a prayer, and it always began with *Lou, you bastard.*

Fifteen years had passed since Kathy Mallory had roamed the streets as a child. Being homeless was damned hard work, and running the tired little girl to ground had been the job of Riker's old friend, Louis Markowitz, but only as a hobby. Lost children had never been the province of Special Crimes Unit, not while they lived. And they would have to die under unusual circumstances to merit a professional interest. So Kathy had become the little blond fox of an after-hours hunt. The game had begun with these words, spoken so casually: "Oh, Riker? If she draws on you, don't kill her. Her gun is plastic, it fires pellets—and she's only nine or ten years old."

After her capture, the child had rolled back her thin shoulders, drawn herself up to her full height of *nothing*, and insisted that she was *twelve* years old. What a liar—and what great dignity; Lou Markowitz could have crushed her with a laugh. Instead, with endless patience, he had negotiated her down to eleven years of age, and the foster-care paperwork had begun with this more believable lie.

Now Kathy Mallory's other name was Markowitz's Daughter.

The old man had been killed in the line of duty, and Riker missed him every day. Lou's foster child was taller now, five ten; she had upgraded her plastic gun to a .357 revolver; and her partner was not allowed to call her Kathy anymore.

The homicide detectives were speeding toward a crime scene that belonged to another man. The East Side lieutenant had sweetened his invitation with a bet, giving odds of "Ten'll get you twenty" that they had never seen a murder quite like this one.

Revolving red and yellow lights marked the corner where police units and a fire engine blocked the flow of traffic along the borderland between the East Village and Alphabet City. All the action was on a side street, but the fire escapes were crowded with people hanging off metal rails, as if they could see around corners of brick and mortar. Cars honked their horns against the law, and hollered obscenities flew through the air.

Mallory's tan sedan glided into the only clear space, a bus stop. She killed the engine and stepped out onto the pavement as her partner slammed the passenger door. Riker's suit was creased and soiled in all the usual places, and now he loosened his tie to complete the basic slob ensemble. He could afford dry cleaning, but he was simply unaware of the practice; that was Mallory's theory.

The sidewalks were jumping, buzzing, people screaming, "C'mon, c'mon!" Crime made do for theater in this livelier part of town. Young and old, they ran in packs, off to see a free show, a double bill—murder *and* fire. And these were the stragglers.

The detectives walked in tandem toward the spinning lights. The uniforms behind the police barricades were doing a poor job of crowd control. The street and sidewalks were clogged with civilians chomping pizza and slugging back cans of soda and beer.

"What a party," said Riker.

Mallory nodded. It was a big production for a dead prostitute. The East Side lieutenant who owned this case had not provided any more details.

They had waded ten heads into the fray before the harried policemen recognized them and formed a human plow, elbows and shoulders jamming taxpayers. The uniforms yelled, "Coming through! Make way!" One officer pulled back the yellow crime-scene tape that cordoned the sidewalk in front of a red brick apartment building. Riker moved ahead of his partner. He descended a short flight of steps to a cement enclosure below the level of the street, then disappeared through the basement door.

Mallory waved off her entourage of cops and remained on the sidewalk. Soon enough, she would be barraged with information, some of it wrong, most of it useless. She leaned over a wrought-iron fence to look down at the sunken square of concrete. Garbage bags and cans were piled near the basement window, but the bright lightbulb over the door would not give an attacker any cover of shadows. The arch of broken glass had no burglar gate—a clear invitation to a break-in.

In the room beyond the shattered window pane, local detectives were getting in the way of crime-scene technicians as they slogged through water in borrowed firemen's boots. Riker, less careful about his own shoes, splashed toward the dead body on the gurney, and dozens of floating red candles swirled in his wake.

The corpse wore a high-collared blouse with French cuffs, and her long skirt was tangled around cheap vinyl boots—strange clothing for a prostitute in the heat of August.

Mallory recognized the chief medical examiner's assistant. In the role of God Almighty, the young pathologist lit a cigarette despite the waving arms of an angry crime-scene technician. And now he ambled across the room to finally have a look at the body. After pressing a stethoscope to the victim's heart for a few moments, completing the belated formality of declaring death, the doctor showed no curiosity about the short tufts of blond hair, evidence of a crude attempt at scalping. He seemed equally unconcerned about the clot of hair stuffed in the woman's gaping mouth.

Mallory wondered why the firemen had not removed it to attempt resuscitation; it was their nature to destroy crime-scene evidence.

A police photographer made a rolling motion with his hand, and the pathologist obliged him by turning the corpse on its side, exposing the silver duct tape that bound the hands behind the dead woman's back. The noose was removed for the next shot. The other end of the severed rope still dangled from a low-hanging chandelier of electric candles. The East Side lieutenant had not exaggerated. Beyond the era of lynch mobs, hanging was a rare form of murder. And Mallory knew this had not been a quick death. It would have taken a longer drop to break the woman's neck.

Torture?

She turned around to face the crowd and saw a man who had once been a uniformed cop in her own precinct. Six minutes away from losing his job, he had decided to quit NYPD, and now he was a fireman. "Zappata? Who broke the window, you guys or the perp?"

"We did." The rookie fireman sauntered toward her. His smile was cocky, and Mallory thought she might fix that if she had time. He would not look up at her face, for this would wreck his delusion that he was the taller one. He spoke to her breasts. "I need you to do something for me."

Not likely, you prick.

Aloud, she said, "Only one engine turned out?"

"Yeah, not much of a fire. Mostly smoke." He pointed to a young man with electric-yellow hair and a dark suit. "See that idiot dick *trainee*?

Go tell him he doesn't need statements from everybody on my damned truck."

"He's not with me. Talk to his lieutenant." And, of course, Lieutenant Loman would rip off the fireman's head—less work for her. She turned back to the window on the crime scene. "So your men cut the body down?"

"Nope, the cops did that." Zappata was too pleased with himself. "She was stone dead when we got here. So I preserved the evidence."

"You mean—you left her *hanging*."

"Yeah, a little water damage, some broken glass, but the rest of the scene was cherry when the cops pulled up."

This was Zappata's old fantasy, running a crime scene, as if he had the right. Mallory searched the faces of the other firemen, a skeleton crew gathered near the truck. There were no ranking officers in sight. If Zappata had not been an ex-cop, the rest of these men would never have followed his lead. An ambulance would be here instead of the meat wagon parked at the curb. And now she understood why three departments had converged on the scene at one time. "You made all the calls tonight?"

"Yeah, I got lucky. The meat wagon and the CSU van were only a few blocks away. They showed up before the detectives." Zappata grinned, awaiting praise for assuming powers that were not his—*police* powers.

She decided to leave the fireman's destruction to the reporters hailing him from the other side of the crime-scene tape. Cameras closed in on Zappata's face as he strolled up to a cluster of microphones and a rapt audience of vultures from the press corps. Now he shared with them every rule and procedure he had personally violated to run the show tonight—and run it wrong.

Mallory walked down the steps to the cement enclosure and stood before the basement window. From this better angle, she could see one end of the rope anchored to a closet doorknob. The floor beneath the chandelier was clear of any object that might have been used for a makeshift gallows.

She could picture the killer placing a noose around the woman's neck and pulling the other end of the rope to raise her body from the ground. The victim's legs were not bound. She would have struggled and tried to run across the floor, then kept on running, feet pedaling the air until she died.

The murderer was male—an easy call. This hanging had required upper-body strength. And Mallory knew there had been no passion between the victim and her killer. When a man truly loved a woman, he beat her to death with his fists or stabbed her a hundred times.

She was looking at her partner's back as Riker bent down to grab something from the water. When the man turned around, his hands were empty, and he was closing the button on his suit jacket. If she had not seen this, she would never have believed it. Riker was a dead-honest cop.

What did you steal?

And why would he risk it?

Riker joined the others, and they moved away from the body. None of them noticed when a young man entered the basement room. Zappata's nemesis, the rookie detective with bright yellow hair, approached the gurney and leaned over the victim. Mallory saw a wet wad of blond hair come away in his hand as he removed the packing from the corpse's mouth.

That chore belonged to a crime-scene technician.

You idiot.

What else could go wrong tonight?

The young cop blocked Mallory's view as he leaned over the dead white face, as though to kiss it.

What are you doing?

In the next moment, he was straddling the body.

What the—

The fool was pumping the victim's chest, performing emergency first aid on a dead woman. Now he grinned and shouted, "She's alive!"

No! No! No!

Three detectives whirled around. The horrified pathologist moved toward the gurney. Riker was quicker. Hunkering down beside the victim, he held one finger to her nostrils. "Oh *shit!* She's breathing!" In a rare show of anger, Riker's hands balled into fists, and he yelled at the younger man, "Do you know what you've done?" Unspoken were the words, *You moron.*

Too much time had elapsed since the woman's death. An inexperienced cop had just turned a perfectly good corpse into a useless vegetable.

The chief medical examiner broke the silence of the hospital room with a dry pronouncement that "human vivisection is illegal in all fifty states." Dr. Edward Slope had the physical authority of a tall gray general. This impression persisted despite the tuxedo, a physician's Gladstone bag and heavy sarcasm in the presence of a dying woman. The pale patient swaddled in bedsheets took no offense. The involuntary movement of her eyes was mere illusion of awareness. "I say the autopsy can wait until she's dead."

"That's just a technicality," said Riker. "She used to be dead." And all the detective needed was a superficial exam by this man, whose word was never questioned in court.

"She'll die again soon enough." The medical examiner held up a clipboard and read the patient's chart. "Her attending physician has a note here, 'Do not resuscitate.' She's brain dead. Give her another ten hours without life support. That'll kill her." He turned to the bald man beside Riker. "Loman, bring the body to my dissection room in the morning. But first—check for a pulse."

Lieutenant Loman seemed close to death himself. A virus epidemic in the East Village precinct had short-staffed his squad, and the longer duty hours were showing in his bloodshot eyes and pasty flesh. "Not my case, Doc." Loman clapped one hand on Sergeant Riker's shoulder. "It's his body now."

"No way!" said Mallory. And now, for Loman's benefit, she glared at the patient, clearly estimating the value of a comatose hooker as being right up there with a dead cat.

"It's *your* case, kid." The lieutenant's voice was still in that cautionary zone of rumbling thunder. "A deal is a deal. Sparrow was Riker's snitch. He *wants* the body."

Mallory gave Riker the squad's camera, as if she might need two free hands to finish this fight. She turned to face Loman. "So a john strings up his hooker. That's not a case for Special Crimes, and you *know* it." As an afterthought, she remembered to say *"Sir,"* then promptly abandoned the protocol for speaking with command officers. "Palm it off on the cops in Arson."

"The guy's a freaking *psycho!*" Lieutenant Loman moved away from the bed and advanced on Mallory, yelling, "*Jesus Christ!* Look at what he did to her!"

What remained of the victim's hair was a fright wig of wild spikes, and saliva dribbled from her lips. Adding to this portrait of dementia, her eyes rolled back and forth like shooting marbles.

Riker drew the curtains around the bed, closeting himself with the patient and the medical examiner. "Just a quick look, okay?"

"No," said Dr. Slope. "Tie a note to one of her toes so I'll know who won the body. I'm late for a dinner party."

Beyond the flimsy curtain, a fast, light rapping on the door escalated to two-fisted banging, then stopped abruptly. Riker could hear muffled words of argument from the guard he had posted in the hall. When the banging resumed, Mallory raised her voice to be heard above the racket. She was telling Lieutenant Loman, thanks anyway, but he could keep the dying whore. To his credit, the man never pulled rank on her when he went ballistic, shouting that he was understaffed, that his men were stacking up corpses in a heat wave while tempers were exploding and homicide rates soared.

August was a busy season for cops and killers.

Dr. Slope had formed a shrewd guess about the incessant banging on the door. His wry smile said, *Gotcha.* "The attending physician wouldn't allow his patient to be stripped for an audience of cops. Am I right?" He stared at the camera in Riker's hand, as if he suspected the detective of being a closet pornographer.

"The doctor's a kid, an intern," said Riker. "Even if he did the exam— what good is his testimony in court?"

The door banging was louder now, accompanied by shouts of "Let me in, you *bastards!*"

Dr. Slope dropped his smile. "And that would be our earnest young doctor trying to get to his patient. Any idea how many laws you're breaking tonight?"

"Well, yeah—I'm a cop."

Riker heard the door open. Mallory was speaking to the young doctor in the hallway, saying, "This is a *hospital.* Keep the noise down." The door slammed, and her bargaining with Lieutenant Loman resumed. "I've got my own problems with manpower," she said. "I'd need at least three of your men to make it worth my while."

"You're nuts! *Nuts!*" The lieutenant's voice was cracking. If Mallory had not been Markowitz's daughter, he would have slammed her into the wall by now.

Behind the thin protection of the curtain, Riker lowered his voice to plead with the chief medical examiner. "Just five minutes? A fast exam, a few samples for—"

"Not a chance." Slope turned in the direction of the banging. "You have to let that doctor in."

"Why? What can he do for her now? He'll stop the—"

"If this woman has family, you're leaving the city open for a lawsuit. So we'll go by the book."

As Slope reached for the curtain, Mallory ripped it aside. Behind her, the door was closing on the East Side lieutenant. As a parting gift, Loman must have released his pent-up aggression on the doctor in the hall, for the banging had ceased.

"I made Loman give us two detectives for grunt work." Mallory turned to face Dr. Slope. "Dead or alive, we need the exam. *Now.*"

The chief medical examiner was a man who *gave* orders, and he was not about to take this from her. All of that was in his voice when he said, "The victim will be dead by morning. This can *wait.*"

Riker braced for a new round of hostilities, but Mallory surprised him. "Maybe you're right," she said. "A cover-up is better." And now she had the pathologist's complete attention.

Dr. Slope folded his arms, saying, "What do you—"

"A lot of mistakes were made tonight," said Mallory. "No one called an ambulance. A rookie fireman decided the victim was dead. Maybe because she didn't blink—who knows? He used to be a cop, so he preserved the crime scene." She pointed to the hospital bed. "And he left that woman hanging."

Her foster father had been Edward Slope's oldest friend and the founder of his weekly floating poker game. The doctor had known Mallory in her puppy days, loved her unconditionally, and knew better than to trust her. He turned to her partner for confirmation of this highly un-likely scenario.

"It happened," said Riker. "It's the East Village virus. No senior men were riding on that fire truck tonight."

Mallory all but yawned to show how little this case mattered to her. "So Loman's detectives go along with a call of homicide—by a *fireman*. And then *your* man, a *doctor*—the only one authorized to operate a damn stethoscope—he confirmed the death."

"If he confirmed it—"

"I hear things," she said. "I know all about the corpse that woke up in your morgue last month—another victim who wasn't quite dead. Was your assistant on that case too?"

"I'm sure this woman was dead at the time—"

"You'll never be sure." She stepped back to appraise his tuxedo, then reached out to run one red fingernail down a satin lapel. "But what the hell. It's a party night." This was one of Mallory's more subtle insults: The fireman, the police and Slope's own assistant had all done their part to turn a woman's brain into coma soup—but why should that spoil the doctor's fun? "No great loss." Mallory glanced back at the door, then lowered her voice to the range of conspiracy. "She's just a whore. We'll let the nurses wash the body and destroy the evidence. No one will ever know what happened tonight."

She turned her back on an outraged Edward Slope, and this was Riker's cue to step forward and soften the damage, saying, "I *need* this exam. It's gotta be now." And last, the finishing touch, he saved the doctor's face with a bribe. "You'll get a police escort to the party. Traffic's murder tonight."

"You've won my heart." Dr. Slope set his medical bag on the bed, then turned to Mallory. "*Kathy*, take notes." This was the doctor's idea of get-ting even, for she always insisted on the distancing formality of her sur-name. He smiled, so pleased by her irritation, as he pulled on latex gloves.

"No makeup." Riker leaned over the bed to take the first photograph. "Looks like Sparrow was in for the night. So the perp wasn't some john she picked up on the street. Any sign of drugs?"

Dr. Slope examined the woman's eyes, then the fingernails. "Nothing obvious." There was no bruising on her arms nor any fresh puncture wounds. He clicked on a penlight and examined the nasal passages, then pulled an empty syringe from his bag. "She's not snorting it, but I'll get a blood workup."

When the sheets had been pulled away and the hospital gown untied, an old stab wound was exposed on Sparrow's left side. "Looks like a knife was twisted to widen the cut—sheer cruelty." Dr. Slope was impressed. "I gather this isn't the first time someone tried to kill her."

Through the camera's viewfinder, Riker watched the other man's gloved fingers explore the scar. "It happened a long time ago."

"A street fight?"

"That's my guess." Riker knew Mallory could give exact details of that fight, but she was continuing the long silence of Kathy the child. "Sparrow was real good with a knife."

"In that case, I'd hate to see the damage to her opponent." The pathologist looked up. "Or perhaps I did—on the autopsy table?"

Riker merely shrugged, for he disliked the idea of lying to this man. "It wasn't my case." And that was the truth. He turned the camera on Sparrow's face. Even after seeing proof of her identity, it had taken him a while to recognize those naked blue eyes undisguised by mascara and purple shadow. Two years ago, the prostitute's hair had been bleached to straw. Tonight, what was left of it was a more natural shade of blond. And there had been other changes since he had last seen this woman.

Awe, Sparrow, what did you do to that wonderful shnoze?

Once, her broken nose had been a dangerous looking piece of damage in the middle of her pretty face, hanging there like a dare. Now the nose was remade, and all that remained of her character was a slightly prominent chin that stuck out to say, *Oh, yeah?*, the bad-attitude line of a true New Yorker.

At their last meeting, Sparrow had been in her early thirties. The street life of drugs and whoring had aged her by another twenty years, but now she seemed brand-new again—so young. "She had a facelift, right?"

"Rhinoplasty too," said Slope, "and dermabrasion. Her last surgery was a brow lift. There's still some post-op swelling. Nice work—expensive. I gather she was a pricy call girl."

"No, nothin' that grand." Sparrow had never been more than a cheap hustler with an accidental gift for making him laugh. When she was a skinny teenager, Riker had turned her into an informant.

You were soaking wet that night, too stoned to come in from the rain.

She had strutted up and down the sidewalk, shaking her fists at skyscrapers and hollering, praying, "God! Give me a lousy break!" All of Sparrow's deities lived in penthouses, and she had truly believed that manna would fall from heaven on the high floors—if she could only get the gods' attention.

But you never did.

Over the years, she had peddled her body to pay for heroin, always vowing to kick the habit tomorrow—and tomorrow. *Lies.* Yet Riker remained her most ardent sucker. He gently touched a short strand of her butchered hair. "What did the perp use on her? Scissors or a razor?"

The pathologist shrugged. "Haircuts are not my area."

"It was a razor," said Mallory, who paid hundreds of dollars for her own salon expertise.

Riker imagined the weapon slashing Sparrow's hair, her eyes getting wider, awaiting worse mutilation as the razor moved close to her face— her *brand-new* face—stringing out the tension until she lost her mind.

Mallory moved closer to the bed. "What about that mark on her arm? That looks like a razor, too."

"It *might* be," Slope corrected her. "So be careful with your notes, young lady. I *will* read every word before I sign them." He bent low for a better look at the long thin scab on Sparrow's arm. "This is days old—not a defensive wound." He consulted the patient chart. "Her doctor did a rape kit. No semen present. No sign of trauma to the genital area." He glanced at Mallory. "I can't rule out sex with a condom and a compliant hooker. So don't get creative." After rolling the nude woman onto her stomach, he examined the back of each knee, then checked her soles and the skin between her toes. There were no fresh punctures.

Sparrow had beaten her addiction. She was clean again.

And young again—starting over.

Where were you going with your new face?

After reviewing the notes, Edward Slope signed them, thus completing his own hostage negotiation, and Mallory opened the door to set him free. He backed up quickly, making way for a man in the short white coat of a hospital intern. The young doctor crashed into the room with a jangling, rolling cart full of metal and glass equipment and a running nurse at his heels.

Dr. Slope stayed to watch the intern and nurse as they outfitted their patient with tubes and wires. "What's the point of this if she—"

"She's got brain activity." The intern tracked Sparrow's rolling blue eyes with the beam of his penlight. "I never should've listened to the damn cops. They told me this woman was revived twenty minutes after death. That can't be true." He turned on a startled Riker. "And you had no right to keep me out of here. Suppose she'd gone sour before I got her on life support?"

"That's enough." Edward Slope looked down at the *smaller* doctor, then held up a wallet with his formidable credentials. Satisfied that the younger man's testicles had been neatly severed, he continued. "Your patient was never in any danger while I was here." He reached down to pick up the clipboard that dangled from a chain on the bed rail, then pointed to the bottom of the page. "I see a clear order not to resuscitate." He glanced at the intern's name tag. "I assume this is *your* signature?"

"Yes, sir, but that was before I saw the EKG results."

"Screwed up, didn't you." This was not a question, but Slope's opinion of inexcusable error.

The intern had the look and the whine of a petulant boy. "I *told* the cop my patient needed life support."

"Nobody told me anything," said Riker. "I didn't know."

"*She* knew!" The young doctor whirled around to point an accusing finger, but Mallory was gone, and the door was slowly closing.

Riker settled into a chair beside the bed. He was fifty-five years old but feeling older, shaken and suddenly cold. Yet he managed to convince himself that no cop would leave herself so exposed to a charge of manslaughter by depraved indifference to human life—and that Mallory had *not* just tried to kill Sparrow.

Two

THE HIGH-PITCHED LAUGHTER OF CRIME-SCENE TOURISTS drifted in from the street, unhampered by a bedsheet draped over the broken window. The basement floor was no longer covered by water, but the air was hot and dank. Mallory removed her blazer and folded it over one arm as she moved about the room, taking in each detail.

Beads of moisture trickled down the cheap metal cabinets of the kitchenette to make wet tracks through black fingerprint dust. A fold-out sofa made do for a bed, and wrought-iron lawn furniture passed for a dining room set. The wooden crucifix was the only wall decoration. Crime Scene Unit's airtight metal canisters and plastic bags were stacked by the door, awaiting the van's return.

Though the work of collecting evidence was done, Riker kept his hands in his pockets to pacify Heller, a great bear of a man with slow brown eyes and rolled-up shirtsleeves. The forensic expert ran a blow-dryer over a small paper box and muttered, "Freaking clowns." This was his least colorful name for the firemen who had broken the window and hosed down his crime scene. "My crew didn't find a camera to go with this film box. Maybe your perp took a snapshot for a souvenir."

A soggy cockroach was also drying out, perched on the edge of the sink and basking in the warmth of Heller's floodlights, a bug's idea of the Riviera. New York City roaches were not afraid of bright light. Nor did they fear fire, flood or cops with guns, and it would take more than all of that to kill them.

"Well, this is all wrong." Riker stood beside the table, examining a plastic bag filled with dead insects. "Hey, Mallory. Ever see so many flies turn out for a body that wasn't dead yet? There must be a thousand bugs here."

"At least." Heller switched off the blow-dryer, then turned his head with the slow swivel of a cannon. "And the perp brought the flies with him. He carried them in that jar."

"What?" Riker leaned down for a closer look at the evidence bag that held a large glass jar coated with black dust. "You didn't find any prints."

"That's how I know it belonged to the perp. He wore gloves." Heller sorted through a stack of elimination cards marked with the fingerprints of firemen and police. "All I got here is the victim's prints and that idiot Zappata's." He nodded toward the plastic bags. "The jar's got a crack in it. Either the perp dropped it, or the fire hose knocked it off the table. I skimmed those flies off the water, but I know they were all dead before they hit the floor. I can even tell you how they died."

Riker raised one eyebrow to say, *Oh, yeah?* "Did they drown? Or did you find smoke in their little lungs?"

Heller's glare of quiet disdain was an unmistakable message: *Don't fool with the master.* "The inside of the jar smells like insecticide. So do the flies." He pulled four specimen bottles from his pockets and lined them up on the table. Four dead flies floated in clear liquid. "They're in different stages of decomposition. I'd say he's been collecting them for a week. And I got twenty bucks that says an entomologist will back me up."

"Naw." Riker waved him off, for he knew this was a sucker bet. In or out of court, the man from Forensics was rarely challenged.

"So he's been planning this for a while." Mallory turned to the makeshift curtain. Was the freak just passing by when he looked down, saw Sparrow for the first time—and decided to murder her? Was that the day he started collecting his flies and hoarding them? Or maybe the whore had bumped into him on the street, a New York kind of accident, a chance collision with violent insanity.

Heller crouched beside his toolbox and began the work of putting away unused razor blades and cotton swabs, brushes and bottles of dust. "Lieutenant Coffey called. He's on his way over."

Mallory wore her I-told-you-so smile. Riker ignored her and hovered over Heller, prompting him. "So? Was Coffey pissed off?"

"You bet. The lieutenant heard a scary rumor that you guys accepted this case for Special Crimes. How do you plan to sell him on this one? Given it any thought?"

"Yeah." Riker glanced at his partner. "She's gonna handle it."

Heller nodded. "Excellent choice."

Mallory studied the scorch marks at the base of the brick wall, then turned to the evidence bag of ashes and paper fragments. "Did the perp use anything fancy to start his fire?"

"Just a match," said Heller. "I'll test for accelerants, but I don't think I'll find any."

A rocking chair and a small magazine rack blocked the bathroom door. The scorched wall was the only logical place for them. "And you're positive none of the firemen moved any furniture?"

He nodded absently as he placed each aerosol can in its proper compartment in the tool box. "One of Loman's detectives got statements from everybody on the fire truck."

She pointed to a couch cushion leaning against another wall. A large square of material had been cut away. "What's that about?"

"I cut out a scorch mark and bagged it. That was the perp's first try at arson. It should've gone up like a torch. The couch must've come from out of state. New York law doesn't require fire-retardant upholstery. Lucky for you it didn't burn. Inside of four minutes, the whole place would've gone up in flames."

"And destroyed all the evidence," said Riker. "You're sure that's not what he wanted?"

"Yeah, I'm *damn* sure. This guy was looking for a fast, controlled burn. Lots of smoke, but no major damage. He was real careful to clear the area around his bonfire."

Mallory agreed. The hangman had wanted to call attention to his work, not destroy it. A wet mound of bright cloth and sequins lay at her feet. "Some of these clothes have scorch marks."

"Another experiment," said Heller. "He picked them because the material's so flimsy. More bad luck. The law *does* call for fire-retardant costumes. Eventually, they'll burn—everything does. But the guy's in a hurry. So next, he collects all the paper—junk mail, magazines. He even burned the window shade."

"So our boy's an amateur at arson." Riker leaned down to examine the pile of wet cloth deemed unworthy of evidence bags. "I spent four years in Vice. Never heard of a streetwalker with a costume collection like this." He drew out a scanty garment with sequins and sewn-on wings. "I've seen this one before. June, I think. Yeah, Shakespeare in the Park. The play was *Midsummer Night's Dream*. I *loved* the fairies."

With a rare show of surprise, Heller turned to stare at the man voted least likely to have an up-close encounter with culture.

Riker shook his head, saying, "Naw, must've been October—the Halloween Parade."

The forensic expert sighed, then returned to the task of putting his tool box in order.

Mallory looked down at the carefully labeled insect collection on the table. Heller was deluded if he thought Lieutenant Coffey would pay for an entomologist. It would be a fight just to keep this case in Special Crimes Unit. Among the evidence containers stashed near the door was a bag of votive candles. There were at least two dozen in various stages of meltdown. All were covered with fingerprint dust. "The candles belonged to the killer?"

"Yeah. Part of his little ritual." Heller pointed to the area beneath the ceiling fixture. "Check out the wax." Melted droppings had survived the fire hose, and they formed a circle on the cement. "There were spots of red wax on the victim's skirt. So I know she was lying on the floor while the candles were burning. I used the wicks for a time frame. The last one was lit fifteen minutes before the place was hosed down. That's how much time he had to hang the woman and start his bonfire."

"That can't be right," said Mallory, risking heresy. "We have to add on another ten or twelve minutes before Sparrow was cut down and revived. But she isn't even brain dead."

"She was starved for oxygen, but her air supply wasn't completely cut off." Heller reached into the evidence pile and selected a canister. After breaking the seal, he pulled out a section of rope. "With a hangman's noose, he could've killed her in a few minutes. But this is a fixed double knot. The noose didn't tighten with the weight of the body. Satisfied?"

Yes, she was. Mallory could see it now—Sparrow hanging quietly, sipping air and playing dead, waiting for the freak to leave. Cagey whore. She must have had great hopes. The window had been bare and all the lights left on. Help would surely come any moment. Then her lungs had filled with smoke, and Sparrow had blacked out. Or perhaps she had been dimly aware of her rescuers, the conversation of firemen all around her, and not one hand lifted to help a lady down from the ceiling.

"The jar of dead flies doesn't fit," she said.

"You're right." Heller interrupted his work to stare at the perfect circle of wax droppings. "A very tidy job, *meticulous*. Even the scalping. You can't trim a moustache without making a mess, but there wasn't one stray hair on that woman's clothes. And the candles—each one an equal distance from the next. Your perp is compulsively neat. I can't see this guy catching bugs."

Mallory could. She pictured a man ripping garbage bags open, then waiting patiently with his can of insecticide. He would have worn gloves to harvest the dead and dying flies, and still it would have made him queasy to touch them.

The basement door opened, then slammed with a bang. The commander of Special Crimes Unit had arrived. Before his last promotion, Jack Coffey had been a middling man with a forgettable face, hair and eyes of lukewarm brown. Now, at age thirty-seven, the stress of a command position had widened the bald spot at the back of his head and added a premature decade of worry lines and character. Riker noticed the lieutenant's hands were balled into fists, and he counted down the seconds, waiting for the man to explode.

Coffey's gaze passed over the two men and settled on his only female detective. His tone was too calm, too reasonable when he spoke to her. "Imagine my surprise when Lieutenant Loman dropped off the paperwork for a hooker." His voice jumped ten decibel levels when he shouted, "And she's not even a *dead* hooker!"

Mallory never flinched. She had the slow blink of a drowsing cat, and her serenity would cost the lieutenant one game point.

"We're tossing this case back to the East Side squad," said Coffey. "*Tonight!* What the *hell* were you guys thinking? This is assault, not murder. Loman says it's a damn sex game gone wrong."

"Autoerotic asphyxiation?" Heller kept his eyes on his tool box as he shook his head. "I've seen a few teenage boys strung up, and even some old guys, but no women. Her hands were tied with—"

"She was a damn *hooker*," said Coffey. "She did whatever she was paid to do. And bondage is part of the trade."

"Sparrow was never into freaks and their games." Riker said this so casually, an offhand line dropped into the conversation.

The lieutenant's reaction was predictable. "We're not tying up a squad so you can keep faith with one of your snitches."

Riker shrugged, then lit a cigarette as he leaned against the wall, leaving the fight to his partner. Coffey could make no personal connection between her and Sparrow. Mallory had been ten years old the last time she had spoken to the whore.

"The perp is a serial killer," she said. "Loman's squad would've botched it."

Riker sucked in his breath. *Awe, Mallory, what are you doing?* Was she *trying* to lose this case? No cop on the force had ever heard of a serial hangman. It would have been better to run with Heller's portrait of a tidy psycho with a penchant for dead flies.

"A serial killer?" Coffey wet his lips, tasting the words. "So, tell me." His cursory glance swept the entire room. "Where are the rest of the bodies?"

"In a Cold Case file," she said. "It's the same MO. The rope, the hair—everything."

And now the fun begins. Or this was Riker's impression of Jack Coffey's smile. Hands on his hips, the lieutenant squared off with Mallory. "And where *is* that file?"

"They haven't located it yet."

Riker relaxed a little, for his partner was on safer ground now. The Cold Case files dated back to 1906, and the squad had recently moved this staggering inventory to new headquarters. What were the odds that they would rush to unpack a hundred cartons just to appease Special Crimes Unit?

Jack Coffey's tight smile never wavered. "Then you pulled this information from the computer. Where's the printout?"

"The case isn't in the system," she said. "Most of the older files aren't. Just basic inventory—names and numbers."

With budget problems and lack of manpower, it would take Cold Case Squad years to make complete computer entries for every unsolved murder of the last century. Mallory might get away with this.

Not so, said the look in Coffey's eyes. "If you've never seen this file—"

"Markowitz told me about it," she said.

The lieutenant's mouth dipped on one side. "Well, how *neat.* Your corroboration is a dead man. How damn *convenient.*"

Riker was also skeptical. He knew she had the talent to tell a better lie than that one.

Heller slammed the lid of his tool box. And now that he had everyone's attention, he rose to his feet, saying, "I was there when she heard about the other hanging."

Jack Coffey's smile evaporated as he faced the man from Forensics, and so he missed the stunned surprise in Riker's eyes.

"I don't know all the details," said Heller. "But neither did Markowitz. It wasn't his crime scene. He only got a quick look at the room and the body, but he couldn't get it out of his mind. Damn strange way to kill somebody."

Heller would never back anyone in a lie. No one on the force had stronger credibility. And so Lieutenant Coffey's eyes rolled up, as if his concession speech might be written on the ceiling. "Mallory, I wanna see that Cold Case file. Until I do, your hooker isn't draining resources from Special Crimes. You got that?" He was walking toward the door as he said, "You can use that man Lieutenant Loman gave you, but that's all—"

"*Two* men," said Mallory. "Loman promised two."

Jack Coffey was close to joy when he turned on her. "Oh, did he?

Well, I guess the bastard scammed you. He only came across with one detective—*half* a detective. The guy's a whiteshield, no experience. And here's the best part, Mallory—it's the same idiot who resuscitated the corpse. So Loman's squad gets rid of a half-dead hooker and a screwup cop. What a deal, huh?"

Score one for the boss.

Riker was almost happy for the man. Jack Coffey needed these small victories to keep him going. Over time, the lieutenant had learned the value of a hit-and-run game. And now that he had scored, he slammed the door on his way out.

Heller knelt on the floor to close the snaps of his tool box, then glanced up at Riker. "Markowitz never told you about that hanging, did he? Naw, he'd never give up details from another cop's crime scene. That's a religion in my job, too. I was the *only* one he could talk to." Heller aimed his thumb at Mallory. "And Markowitz never told *her* a damn thing. She was only thirteen years old. The way I remember it, we caught her listening at the door."

Riker stubbed out his cigarette. "What else can you tell me?"

"The woman's hands were bound. Rope or tape—I'm not sure." Heller stood up and mopped his brow with a handkerchief. "So that knocked out murder dressed up as suicide. And Markowitz said the perp must've planned it. He brought his own rope to the party—just like your guy. But why plan a hanging?" The criminalist grabbed his suit jacket from the back of a chair, and only now did he notice that, despite the sweltering heat of the basement, Riker was the only one not stripped to shirtsleeves.

Before Riker could check the movement, his hand touched the button that kept his jacket closed. "What about money? Lou always loved money motives."

"No," said Heller. "On his own time, he looked into that and came up dry. He didn't see any sex angles either."

"And the victim didn't step off a piece of furniture," said Mallory. "The noose was around her neck when the perp raised her from the floor—just like Sparrow."

"But there was no fire," said Heller. "*No* candles, *no* jar of flies." He made this sound like an accusation against her. "And there wasn't any hair in the victim's mouth. Your old man never mentioned any of that."

Riker jammed his hands in his pockets. "Mallory, why did you have to elaborate so much? You told Coffey the hair was—"

"It's not a problem," she said. "Without a name or a case number, no one can find the file. We don't even have a date."

"She's right," said Heller. "That case was years old when Markowitz told me about it. It bothered him for a long time. Too many things didn't fit." He shrugged. "That's all I remember."

The door opened, and a technician from Crime Scene Unit entered the room to pick up an armload of canisters. Heller grabbed two evidence bags and followed his man outside to the waiting van.

Riker took one last look at the departing bag of ashes and unburned fragments. He could see the charred spines of magazines, yet some miracle had preserved the brittle tinder of an old paperback novel. It had not even been scorched when he had retrieved it from the water. He could feel the wetness on his skin under the pressure of his holster's strap.

Mallory was attracted to the damp spot spreading across the breast of his suit. Her gaze dropped lower. "I bet you never used that button before."

True, he never bothered to close his jacket, but on any other night, there would be nothing to conceal.

You spooky kid. Always picking up on the oddest things.

Mallory met his eyes, and her gaze was steady. She was clearly waiting for him to say more.

To confess?

Damn her, she knew he had robbed the crime scene. But she could not pose a direct question. A cop could never ask a partner, Did you break the law?

Riker went out in search of a cold beer, and Mallory stayed behind to double-check Heller's work. On the subject of forced entry, she deferred to no one. There were no recent scratches on the outside of the lock. Even after dismantling the mechanism, she could find no sign of a metal pick.

Sparrow, why did you let the hangman in?

The prostitute had been good at reading men and sorting out the mental cases. It was unlikely that the collector of dead flies had been her customer; he would never have gotten past her radar—unless she had been dope sick and desperate. Then she would have opened the door to any drug dealer, however squirrelly. But Dr. Slope had found no signs of recent addiction, and there were no syringes listed on the evidence log.

The junkie hooker had always been careful to keep a supply of clean ones. In what had passed for a childhood, Kathy Mallory had stolen boxes of needles from a local clinic—presents for Sparrow, a little girl's idea of payments for shelter from the streets.

One hand drifted down to a tear in the couch cushion and touched a hard lump. Heller's crew had missed something. Her fingers dug into the upholstery and pulled out an ivory comb with delicate prongs. Sparrow had always worn it in her hair. The oriental carving was elaborate, unforgettable. This was the only thing of value that the whore had not sold for drug money. The antique comb had been stolen long ago to buy the first story hour. The whore had laid her present down with a sigh, saying, "Baby, you don't have to *pay* for stories. They're *free*."

No. Young Kathy had shaken her head to tell the woman that she was wrong. And the child's logic had been indisputable: All hookers would be beggars if this were true; their lies would be worthless—*if* this were true. But then, Sparrow had never understood precisely what the little girl was buying.

How long had they kept company—and why?

Mallory's early history on the streets was not linear, but called up in shattering events remembered out of order. And now her memories were so distant, they could be twisted any way she liked. She decided that, at best, Sparrow had been merely a bad copy of a dead mother.

A whore and nothing more.

She had not recognized the prostitute's new face at the crime scene. On the way to the hospital, Riker had broken the news, and he had done it so gently, as if the victim were a family member—and not the dangerous debris of the past. But soon enough, Sparrow would be dead, and only Riker would know the story, but he could never tell it.

Mallory's hand closed over the comb. It had not been dropped through the tear in the couch cushion, but buried there. So Sparrow had had some time to hide it, but when? While the hangman was knocking at the door? Perhaps he was already inside when she pushed her precious comb deep into the upholstery so it could not be stolen. Had there been time for con-versation? Had Sparrow tried to talk him out of killing her?

She stared at the bedsheet covering the broken glass. Why had the man risked burning the window shade before he made his escape?

You wanted a big audience for your work—not just the cops—civilians too. Fame? That's what you want? Yes, he had even left an autograph, a signature of dead flies.

The door opened. Mallory rose to a stand, then whirled around to face Gary Zappata. The rookie fireman stood on the threshold. His sleeveless T-shirt and chinos were a size too small, the better to show off his gym-sculpted torso. His dark hair was slicked back, still wet from a shower, and he stank of cologne.

"This is a crime scene, Zappata. Did you forget the rules?" She nodded toward the door in lieu of saying, *Get the hell out.*

"Hey, I'm here to help." He shut the door, then sauntered into the room. There was arrogance in his smile and his every move. "So, Detective . . ." One hand waved about, feigning frustration, as if her name might be dif-ficult to remember. "How's it going?"

"I'm working here. What do you want?"

He hooked both thumbs in his belt loops and strolled over to the couch. "Just tying up loose ends."

"Zappata, don't waste my time. If you've got something—let's hear it."

That made him petulant, but he forced a smile. She was forgiven. "I can help you, babe. I know things about that fire. For instance, the candles had nothing to do with it."

"Great tip. Thanks for stopping by." Mallory turned her back on him to study the blackened wall of the burn area. After a moment, she glanced over one shoulder with a look that asked, *Still here?*

The fireman ignored this blatant dismissal and flopped down on the couch. "The guy's not a pro." He draped one leg over the upholstered arm—just to let her know that he planned to stay awhile. "A real arson-ist would've made a fuse to the door. You know, when a blaze gets hot enough, the *air* can ignite."

"Did you learn that in fire school?"

He disliked this reminder that he was new at his trade. Even when he had been a cop, his police career had not lasted long enough to lose the rookie status. "Listen, Mallory." This was an order. "The guy's an amateur at homicide too. These freaks always stick with what worked in the past. So this is definitely our perp's first try at murder. 'Cause of the botched fire."

Our perp?

Mallory looked up to the window, attracted by the silhouette of a man pacing across the makeshift curtain. His hat had the crown of a uniformed officer. Riker must have requested a guard for the crime scene. Bad move. This unapproved use of manpower would not sit well with Lieutenant Coffey.

Zappata left the couch to hover over the wet pile of flashy silks and rayon. He picked up the sparkling costume that Riker had so admired. "I wonder what the hooker looked like in this."

"Drop it!" Mallory strode across the room, aiming herself at the man, planning to walk over him or through him. He backstepped to the door, clutching the costume to his breast in a lame attempt to hide behind a swatch of sequins and fairy wings.

"Don't *touch* her *things!*" She ripped the garment away from him and shouted, "Get *out!*"

His hand was on the knob when he noticed the guard's shadow rushing across the bedsheet curtain. And now there were footfalls on the cement steps leading down to the basement door.

The fireman was as nervous as a schoolgirl afraid of losing her reputation. He puffed out his chest and summoned up a bit of bravado.

The cop outside was coming closer.

Zappata opened the door, yelling, "I'm done here, you *bitch!*" He stomped out of the apartment, as if this were his own idea.

Mallory wondered if the fire department knew that their rookie was a physical coward. But he was forgotten when she looked down at the ivory comb in her hand.

Sparrow, how did the hangman get in? Did he bring you presents, too?

Sergeant Riker could smell the apartment-house odors of meals cooked and eaten hours ago. His stomach rumbled as he stepped off the elevator.

The landlord's floor was divided in two. On one side was Charles Butler's apartment, and across the hall was a consulting firm of elite head-hunters. And here Kathy Mallory broke the law in her off-duty hours, investigating the deluded, the grifters and other poseurs to weed them from a clientele of wildly gifted and generally unstable job candidates for think tanks. Riker called them Martians.

Lieutenant Coffey had given her a direct order to dissolve this business partnership, and tonight, Riker had his first glimpse of Mallory's response, an elegant solution. She had nailed a new brass plaque on the old familiar door. Once, this had been the entrance to Butler and Mallory, Ltd. Now it was called Butler and Company. She had become a *silent* partner.

Attracted by the aroma of a recent meal, the detective strolled across the hall to the private residence. His nose for fast food told him it was Chinese take-out. Before he could knock, the door opened, and he was looking up—and up—at Charles Butler.

The man was at least a head taller than most of the world, and his nose was also above average, a wonderful hook that could perch a pigeon. His heavy-lidded eyes bulged, and the small blue irises were surrounded by vast areas of white, giving Charles a startled look that he shared with frogs and frightened horses. From the neck down, Mother Nature had gotten it right—better than that in Riker's estimation, for the body was well made, aiming for the angels in form and power.

"Riker, *hello!*" When Charles Butler smiled, he took on the aspect of a lunatic, but such a charming loon. Over the past forty years of his life, he had learned to be self-conscious about this idiosyncrasy. The line of his mouth waffled with embarrassment, apologizing for every happy expression.

"Hey, how are ya?" Riker noted his friend's rare departure from Savile Row suits. The denim shirt screamed of money; nothing off the rack could fit so well. And apparently Mallory had introduced Charles to a tailor shop that customized her own blue jeans. The two of them were still struggling with the concept of casual dress.

"I hear you're on summer vacation."

"Yes, Mallory's idea." Charles pushed a curling strand of light brown hair away from his eyes. He was always forgetting appointments with his barber. "No more clients until the fall." And now the man looked worried. "She's all right, isn't she? You didn't come by to—"

"Oh, no. She's fine. I should've called. Sorry." And Riker's regret was genuine, for Charles must have thought that he was here to break the news of Mallory's premature death. "It's late. I should leave."

"Nonsense, I'm glad you stopped by." Charles stood back and ushered his guest inside. "I was only worried because we had dinner reservations, but she wasn't home when I—"

"She never called to cancel? I'll rag her about it." And that neatly explained the reek of Chinese take-out in the home of a gourmet cook. Riker passed through the foyer, then paused a few steps into the front room. "She rewired your stereo, didn't she?"

"How did you—"

"I'm a detective." Perfection was Mallory's signature, and it was writ in what could not be seen. She had made the machinery, its wires and speakers invisible. And the sound was remarkably well balanced, creating the illusion of an orchestra at the center of Riker's brain. The concerto was bright and hopeful, a portrait of Charles Butler in strings and flutes.

There were never any CDs lying about in Mallory's personal car, and he sometimes wondered if she ever listened to music, perhaps something metallic with New Age clicks and whirs.

"Can I get you a drink?"

"I wouldn't say no to a beer." Riker sprawled on the sofa while Charles crossed the formal dining room, heading for the kitchen.

Though the detective had been in this apartment many times, he scrutinized the room of paneled walls and antiques. Books and journals were piled on all the tables and chairs, the sign of a man with too much free time. Riker found what he had been looking for—food, a bowl of cashews partially hidden under a newspaper, and he had devoured all of them before Charles returned with two beers foaming in frosted glass. Any man who kept his beer steins in the freezer was Riker's friend for life.

"I have to tell, you—" As the detective accepted his beer, he spied a fortune cookie on a small table next to the sofa. "This isn't exactly a social call." He grabbed the cookie, then remembered his manners and asked, "You mind?"

"It's yours." Charles settled into an armchair. "What can I do for you?"

Riker unbuttoned his suit jacket and pulled out the stolen waterlogged paperback. "Can you fix this?"

Charles stared at the soggy cover illustration of cowboys and blazing six-guns—so far removed from his own taste in literature. His face expressed some polite equivalent of *Oh, shit*, as he attempted a lame smile. "I think so. It might take me awhile."

"I got time." Riker cracked his cookie open. His printed fortune fell out. He watched this sliver of paper drop to the floor and let it lie there, for he was that rare individual who ate the cookies for their own sake. And now he looked around for another.

Charles excused himself for a few minutes, then came back with a sandwich wrapped in a napkin, and Riker happily traded his wet book for the roast beef on rye. A moment later, his happiness was destroyed. The paperback lay open in the other man's hands, and the detective could see a piece of paper stuck to the back cover. If he had not been so tired and hungry, he would have thought to leaf through the book before handing it over. "What's that?"

"A receipt." Charles gently peeled up the paper. "From Warwick's Used Books. Odd. I thought I knew every bookshop in Manhattan." He closed the old novel and stared at the lurid cover. "So this is rather important to you." He was too well bred to ask why in God's name this might be true.

"Yeah, you can't get 'em anymore. That western went out of print forty years ago. It's the last novel Jake Swain ever wrote." Riker wolfed down his sandwich, then drained the beer stein, stalling for time, for the right words. *Sheriff Peety rides again.* What was the other character's name? He had blocked it out of his mind long ago and hoped it would remain forgotten.

"I'll have to get started before this dries out." Charles rose to his feet, and Riker followed him into the next room. The library walls were fifteen-feet high and covered with a mosaic of leather bindings. A narrow door set into one bookcase opened onto a small boxy room. Glue pots and rolls of tape, brushes, tweezers and spools of thread lay on a long work table where the bibliophile repaired the spines and pages of his collection. Charles swept aside volumes with gold-leaf decoration to make room for a paperback that had cost fifty cents in the year it was published.

"You can't tell Mallory about this," said Riker. "Promise? I don't want her to know I wrecked it."

Stole it, robbed it from a crime scene.

But his partner would never know about that if Charles believed—

"It's *hers?*" Charles should never be allowed near a poker game; his face expressed every feeling, every thought. And just now, he was thinking that Riker had lied to him. The office across the hall contained all the books that Mallory owned. Most dealt with computers; none were fiction. And, before leaving college to join NYPD, she had received two years of an elite education at Barnard. No way could he believe that this book was her property. Yet he nodded and said, "Understood." Charles reached up to a shelf above the work space and pulled down a bundle of blotting papers. "You were never here. We never had this conversation."

"Great. Thanks." Riker imagined that he could hear the man's beautiful brain kicking into high gear and making connections at light's speed.

Charles teased the block of pages away from its paper spine, then noticed his guest's anxiety and mistook paranoia for concern. "Don't worry. I can put it back together." After setting the cover to one side, he peeled away a top sheet of advertising and stared at the underlying page. "Oh." His face conveyed that everything had suddenly been made clear. "Well, I can't blot this one. I'd lose most of the ink. I can save the inscription, but Louis's signature is gone."

Calmly, the detective asked, "What?" And inside his head, he screamed, *What?*

"This *is* Louis Markowitz's handwriting, isn't it? I imagine there'll be trouble when Mallory sees the damage."

Startled, Riker looked down at the inscribed page. An old friend's quirky penmanship trailed off in a wash of blue ink. "No, it's okay. She hasn't seen it yet. I was gonna give it to her later—a present."

Charles read the inscription. "So it's a gift from Louis to Mallory. Almost poetry. I gather he wanted her to have it after his demise. A posthumous good-bye?"

"Yeah, something like that." Untrue. On the only day when that note could have been written, Louis Markowitz had not been anticipating his own death; he still had many years ahead of him, time enough to raise Kathy Mallory. The old man must have forgotten that the book existed, and so had Riker—until it floated past him in Sparrow's apartment.

"Louis's funeral was some time ago." Charles used clamps and cotton batting to fix the page to a board, then picked up a palm-size heater and switched it on. "You're delivering this a bit late, aren't you?"

"Yeah." Riker was slowly coming to terms with shock. A dead man had corroborated his lie—fifteen years before it was told.

An hour later, every surface in the room was covered with a book leaf pressed between blotting papers. Only the inscription page was exposed. The detective stared at the scrawl of blue ink, the words of a man who had loved a homeless child. The lines suggested that the book had been inscribed after the old man had seen convincing proof that the ten-year-old was dead and gone. Yet that grieving cop had obviously clung to the insane idea that Kathy *might* come back.

Riker bowed his head over the page to read the passage again.

Once there was a little girl. No, scratch that, kid. You were always more than that, bigger than life. I could have set you to music—the damn Star-Spangled Banner—because you prevailed through all the long scary nights. You were my hero.

After Charles had bid Riker good night at the elevator, he saw a crack of light under the door to Butler and Company. Mallory? He had not seen her face since early June. And now he forced himself to walk, not run, as he entered the office and passed through the lighted reception area, then moved quickly down a narrow hall, pulled along by the dim glow from Mallory's room—where the machines lived.

He paused at the open doorway, staring at the back of his business partner. She sat before a computer workstation, one of three. Most of her personal office was lost in shadow, a sharp contrast to the halo, a silhouette of burnished gold made by lamplight threading through her hair.

What could he say to her? He doubted that she would regret or even recall their missed dinner date, for she was in holy communion with her machines and oblivious to human disappointment.

Years ago, he had written a rather poetic monograph on her gifted applications of computer science. Over the course of his career, he had evaluated many wizards who could force electronics to do remarkable things. But she was a creature apart, employing an artist's sensibility similar to a composer of music. She merged with the technology, fashioning effect by thought, blending the psyches of musician and mathematician to write original notes for electronic bells and whistles.

During his study of her, Charles had indulged in a fanciful, albeit unpublishable, notion that Nature had planned ahead for this new century, that some long-sleeping gene had awakened when she was made. Later, after learning more about her childhood, his vision had altered and darkened, for Mallory had been hammered into what she was—the perfect receptacle for something cold and alien. And her intimacy with machinery chilled him.

Once, he had been ambivalent about computers. Now he saw them as perverted soldiers that blurred the demarcation line between her fingertips and the keyboards. He had sought to dilute their influence with offerings of fine art and the soft edges of antiquarian objects. Mallory had fought back, encroaching on the office kitchen with ugly technology that he could not abide. Then she had invaded his personal residence, staging a surprise attack to reconfigure his stereo system. Stunned, he had been assaulted from all sides by musical perfection via enemy components that removed the necessity of human hands for turning the knobs and fine-tuning the song. The sheer beauty of it had seduced him for a time. But now, seeing her like this, he was back in combat mode, dreaming new schemes to disconnect her computers, to unplug them all—and Mallory too.

It was a good fight.

She never looked up as Charles approached. He stood beside her chair and stared at the monitor. Her only task tonight was the harmless typing of text. All that angst for nothing. Bracketed question marks pocked the glowing screen. A battered notebook lay on the metal surface of her workstation. It was open to a page of faded coffee stains and lines of blue ink from an old-fashioned fountain pen. Charles could even describe that pen; Louis Markowitz had willed it to him. For the second time in one night, he was staring at a sample of an old friend's handwriting. Mallory was deciphering her foster father's shorthand scribbles between the clearly written words, *duct tape* and *rope*.

She raised her face to his, and they exchanged grins of hello. Their technology wars had caused no hard feelings between them. They still smiled and waved at each other across the great divide.

THREE

RIKER WATCHED THE SIDEWALKS ROLL BY THE PASSENGER
window of Mallory's tan sedan. The landscape kept changing on
him. Early memories of beatniks in funereal black gave way to colorful
flower children, hippies with love beads, and bless the girls with diaphragm
earrings who had bedded every boy with a guitar.

Rock 'n' roll. Salad days.

Nose rings were the next new thing in another parade of fearless children with hair every color of the chemical-neon rainbow. Girded in tat-
toos and vintage corsets with cruel metal spikes for nipples, they had flung
themselves into the badlands of the East Village.

This morning, he saw a girl in a white polo shirt and jeans still creased
from the store hanger. Another yuppie strolled by in a similar uniform.
One day, while Riker's back was turned, the kids had all gone shopping at
The Gap.

He turned to his partner behind the wheel. "Maybe I should do the interview with Tall Sally." He might as well have added the words "just to be safe." It was not the size of the ex-convict that worried him, but Sal's history with Sparrow when Kathy Mallory was a child. "It's not that you can't handle it—"

The car stopped before the light turned red. No warning! Not fair! She hit the brakes hard and slammed him toward the dashboard. His teeth were saved by a seatbelt, but it was a near thing. "So that's a definite no," said Riker.

After the silent wait for a green light, the car moved on, and Mallory lowered her dark glasses. "You think I should do the old woman instead?"

Enough said. According to a police report, the elderly witness was very fragile in mind and body. Mallory might want to take her out for a drive.

The detectives pulled up to the curb in front of the crime scene. Riker stepped out of the car and watched it drive off, passing only one other moving vehicle. Sparrow's street had a tranquil character in the early morning light. There were flower boxes on some of the window ledges, a sign of gentrification, law and order, though last night's mob had made off with all the blooms, and now the headless stalks were turning brown.

The detective on loan from Lieutenant Loman was hovering near the front steps of the apartment building. All dressed up in a suit and shiny new shoes, the youngster shifted his weight from foot to foot, suspecting that he was in trouble—and he was.

Riker's gaze traveled over the smoke-stained bricks, then down to the yellow crime-scene tape lying on the sidewalk. It had been pulled aside so a man in coveralls could board up the broken window. A familiar uniformed officer stood guard over Sparrow's basement apartment. Riker smiled. "Hey, Waller. Go grab some food. I'm gonna be here awhile." He nodded toward the workman and the young detective. "I'll make sure they don't run off with anything."

After the patrolman had crossed the street and passed out of earshot, Riker turned to face the worried young cop in the dark suit. The new man was in that whiteshield limbo between a uniform's silver badge and a detective's gold. And he was too young to have been promoted without a father-in-law at Number One Police Plaza. His sole distinguishing feature was bleached hair that went beyond blond; it was yellow, the color of a baby duck.

And Riker christened him accordingly.

Department politics dictated that he handle Duck Boy with great care, and so he held up the young detective's report and crumpled it into a tight ball, saying, "This sucks." Riker was not usually that fancy with his critiques. The wadded-up paper should have made words unnecessary, but he was feeling expansive this morning. He looked toward the window of a first-floor apartment directly across the street, then squinted to make out a woman's head piled high with white hair.

How he loved old ladies, the watchers of the world.

He opened the crumpled ball of paper, Duck Boy's idea of an interview, and read the closing words aloud, "'Religious fanatic. Ramblings of senility.' That's *it?* What the hell kind of a witness statement is this? When I send you back to Lieutenant Loman, he's gonna think I didn't raise you right."

Officer Waller had returned with his breakfast in a brown deli bag, and now Riker crossed the street with Duck Boy following close behind, and they climbed a short flight of stairs leading up to the front door of a narrow building.

"This is a school day." The senior detective pushed the buzzer. "Keep your mouth shut and *listen.*"

The door was opened by a bespectacled elderly woman in a long and flowery summer dress. Her lenses were thick, and one eye was clouded with cataracts, yet she recognized Duck Boy immediately, and it was obviously not a pleasant memory. "Oh, you've come back."

Riker detected a trace of the Southland in her accent. "Emelda Winston? I'm Detective Riker. May I call you *Miss* Emelda?"

"Why, of course you may." Her eyes lit up, and even her red-painted toes were thrilled, curling and uncurling in her sandals. She belonged to him now, charmed by this old custom of address never observed in northern climes.

"Now you boys come right in." She stepped back to open the door a little wider. "I've got a nice breeze goin' in my parlor."

When the two men had been seated awhile on a gigantic horsehair sofa, Miss Emelda returned to the front room, rolling a tea cart laid with white linen, glassware and a plate of chocolate chip cookies.

"So you're here about Sparrow." She lifted the pitcher of lemonade and poured each of them a glass. "You know, *I* was the one who called in the fire."

"So that was you?" Riker glanced at the younger man. "No one told me." He bit into a cookie that was definitely homemade, for it lacked the preservatives to keep it from turning to stone. "So, Miss Emelda, how well did you know Sparrow?"

"Not well at all, I'm afraid. That poor girl. She just moved in a few weeks ago."

"Then you don't know what she did for a living?"

"Oh, yes. She was an actress. But I don't see how she made a living at it. I went to her dress rehearsal yesterday. The play was in the basement of the elementary school, and they were only planning to charge a few dollars a ticket. I suppose they'll cancel it now."

Riker nodded. "I wondered why Sparrow was wearing those clothes. Long-sleeved blouse, long skirt—boots. So that was her costume for the play?"

"Yes, they were doing a period piece, something by Chekhov, I think." The old woman smiled. "Sparrow was surprisingly good. A very moving performance."

After consuming two more rock-hard cookies and nearing the dregs of the lemonade, they were old friends, Riker and Miss Emelda.

"Ma'am," said Duck Boy, violating orders of silence, "why don't you tell him about the angel."

"Oh, yes—last night. Well, the crowd parted, just for an instant, mind you, and there was the angel floating in front of Sparrow's window." Miss Emelda clapped her hands. "Just *glorious*. But there was nothing about the angel in the morning papers."

Riker continued to smile, as if she had just said something perfectly rational. "Can you describe the angel?"

"I think it was a cherub." She fished in the pocket of her dress and pulled out a small Christmas tree ornament. "I showed this to the young man." She nodded toward Duck Boy, then spoke to Riker in a stage whisper. "But he didn't seem to understand. He thinks I'm pixilated."

Riker shook his head in sympathy. "Kids today, huh?" He stared at the ornament in her hand, a pair of white wings attached to the disembodied head of a child with gold curls. The detective turned to the window behind the sofa and its view of Sparrow's apartment across the street. And now he knew that the old woman's angel was a cop. Last night, Mallory's black jeans had disappeared in the dark; Miss Emelda had only discerned the blond hair and white blazer, a winged thing on the fly.

"It was a miracle," she said, hands clasped in prayer.

Riker was satisfied that, thick lenses or no, the old woman could see well enough. He drained his glass, then leaned forward, speaking as one gossip to another, "Just between you and me, who do you think did it? Who hung Sparrow?"

"The reporters. Naturally."

Duck Boy rolled his eyes, then winced when his supervisor kicked him. This act was hidden behind the safe cover of the tea cart's linen. It was a clear shot to the shinbone, and Riker hoped it hurt like hell. He turned back to his star witness and smiled. "I never trusted reporters myself."

She nodded. "They're everywhere. Even in the trees—watching us all the time. I saw one of them out there with his camera. And that was *before* I smelled smoke. Very suspicious, don't you think?"

"Yeah," said Riker. "So this reporter—did you get a good look at him?"

"I'm sorry, no, not his face. His back was turned. I remember his camera. Oh—and he wore a white T-shirt and blue jeans. He might've had a baseball cap. Yes, he did. I'm sure of it now." She made a delicate moue of distaste. "I remember when reporters wore suits and ties."

Riker glanced back at the window, attempting to judge the zone of Miss Emelda's vision. She could not have seen anything across the street in great detail, or she would never have made Mallory into an angel. "How close was this guy?"

"He was in a tree. Didn't I tell you that? Oh, yes, right in front of my building. Then that van showed up with the other news people from the TV station. The name of the news show was painted on the side of the van, but I can't remember which one it was—I'm so sorry. Well, as you can imagine, it was quite a time. The fire engines came a minute or two after that. Of course the fire didn't amount to much—thank the Lord."

"Amen," said Riker. "So the guy with the camera climbed a tree *before* the news van showed up?"

"Yes, and before I smelled smoke." Miss Emelda walked behind the sofa to stand before the window. She pointed at a nearby oak on the sidewalk. It was large, one of those rare specimens that thrived in cement. "That's the tree."

"Ma'am?" Duck Boy took out his pencil and notebook. "Did the suspect's videocam have a network logo?"

A confused Miss Emelda turned to the senior detective, silently asking what language the youngster was speaking.

"I know," said Riker. "All cameras look alike to me."

"I can show you mine." The woman bustled out of the room, then returned with an old Instamatic. "Now his was a bit smaller than this one, and maybe the brand was different. His could've been a Polaroid. But the pictures popped out the front, same as mine. They develop themselves right before your eyes. I'll show you."

Duck Boy was blinded by the flash and caught in the act of snapping his pencil in two.

The carpenter was gone when Riker emerged from Miss Emelda's apartment and crossed the street with Duck Boy. He had one more piece of information from his witness, and—serendipity—the man he most wanted to hurt was within reach. Ex-cop Gary Zappata was starting down the steps to Sparrow's basement apartment when Officer Waller grabbed him by the arm and roughly pulled him back to the sidewalk.

"Back off! I got business here!" The shorter man puffed out his chest the better to display a fire department logo emblazoned on his T-shirt, as if this passed for credentials.

Riker guessed that Zappata had been asked to turn in his fireman's shield and identification. Soon there would be a hearing on charges of gross misconduct, the prelude to being fired from his new job.

Officer Waller blocked the entrance to the basement room.

"Get out of my way," said Zappata. "I won't tell you twice."

Unimpressed, the policeman responded by tipping back a can of orange soda and draining it dry. The pissing contest was officially under way, and Waller was already winning. A true son of New York City, he bit into a bagel and looked up at the sky, ignoring the ex-cop, soon to be an ex-firefighter.

Zappata turned to see the two detectives step onto the sidewalk. He pointed to the senior man and yelled, "Hey, you!"

Riker so rarely answered to that form of address, and he liked the commanding tone even less. He waved the man off, saying, "It can wait."

You weasel.

After opening the door to Waller's patrol car, Riker motioned Duck Boy to follow him into the front seat. When the windows had been rolled up, he said, "Did you get all that?"

"All *what?*"

"Sparrow's acting gig. We just expanded her social circle. I want names for everyone at that dress rehearsal. And the reporters were on the scene *before* the fire engines turned out. Even if the old lady was slow to call in the fire—they shouldn't have beaten the engines. You're gonna find out why that news van was in this neighborhood. And I don't care who you have to sleep with. But you wear a condom when you bang a reporter. You don't know where those bastards have been." Riker reached across the other man's chest and opened the car door. "Move!"

The young detective was quick to scramble out, and then he was off and running down the street. The duckling was launched.

Detective Riker took his own time stepping out onto the sidewalk. Now he was looking down at the short fireman.

Gary Zappata rolled back his muscular shoulders, gearing up for a fast round of King of the Hill.

Of all the stupid kid games.

The detective made a point of looking at his watch to convey that his own time was worth a lot more. He glanced at the fireman, as if he had just noticed him standing there. "Yeah, what?"

Zappata nodded in Waller's direction. "He won't let me in."

"I got orders." Officer Waller leaned down to attach the crime-scene tape to a gatepost. "Only Special Crimes detectives get in. Punk firemen don't."

Riker shot a warning glance at the man in uniform. Waller had never served with Zappata, the former loose cannon of the SoHo precinct. A nutcase ex-cop was too dangerous to have for a friend or an enemy.

"Where's your damn partner?" Zappata demanded.

Right about now, Mallory should be walking into Macy's department store in search of New York's tallest whore. "She's busy. So am I." The detective was more blasé about making his own enemies. And now he flirted with the idea of putting this man on the short list for Sparrow's hanging. Was that ludicrous? Would Zappata have the balls to beat up a Girl Scout in a fair fight? In this idle moment of indecision, Riker put a cigarette in his mouth, then slowly fished through his pockets for matches—just to make the man a little crazier than he already was. "You got one minute of my time." Did that make the fireman angry? Oh, yes, and so tense his facial muscles were twitching. Some days, Riker really loved the job.

"Your partner got me suspended from the fire department," said Zappata. "I guess I stepped on her toes last night."

"Yeah, I heard about you playing detective on the crime scene."

"That bitch is the one—"

"Nobody heard it from her. She never rats on anybody."

"Then how—"

"*You* figure it out. And now maybe you can explain the damn lightbulb over the front door."

"What?"

"Zappata, I got a witness who says that light was out when the firemen got here. Now, I don't figure you guys carry spare bulbs on the truck, so I'm guessing some *jerk* figured the bulb might be loose. So this freaking *idiot* reached up, twisted it. And sure enough, it wasn't burnt out—just loose in the fixture."

Riker knew he was onto something. There was too much white in the fireman's eyes—fear. "But this criminally stupid fireman never thought to mention it to the cops. I guess he figured we wouldn't care if the perp was some stranger hiding behind the garbage cans, waiting to surprise that poor woman in the dark. Naw, better we should think Sparrow opened the door for somebody she knew. Then we could waste a few days spinning our wheels."

There was no one Riker hated more than Zappata. If Sparrow had come down from the rope in time, her coma-blind eyes would not roll aimless in their sockets, and she would not drool.

He had one last salvo to take this man down. "I'm guessing this moron fireman took his gloves off before he touched the bulb." Riker turned to the uniformed police officer. "Waller! Get a CSU tech over here." He pointed to the light fixture over the door. "Have him take that lightbulb and dust it for prints."

Riker turned his back on the subdued Zappata and walked down the street toward his next appointment on Avenue A, where he planned to kill off a ten-year-old girl for the second time.

The doors opened and the carnage began. Two inexperienced women were roughly pushed aside, and a man fell down on one knee. Shopping in the city was no game for tourists, otherwise known as the halt and the lame. Behind the display counters, men and women, flushed with adrenaline, waited on the enemy. Onward marched the hordes of customers— and one tall blonde in Armani sunglasses.

Everything Detective Mallory wore flaunted the idea that she was a cop on the take. The silk-blend T-shirt allowed her skin to breathe in style, and the dark linen blazer was tailor made. Even her designer jeans bore the detailed handwork of a custom fitting. And with dark glasses to cover her green eyes, she bore no resemblance to a hungry child who had once robbed this store on a regular basis, ripping off items from the shopping list of a drag queen hooker.

Tall Sally had always been fanatically devoted to Macy's and prized their goods above items stolen from any other store. Over time, the salespeople had become too familiar with Sal's apprentice shoplifter, ten-year-old Kathy Mallory. Sometimes the clerks had departed from the armor of New York attitude to lean over their counters and wave. This had confused the little thief, for she had only targeted Macy's once a week, and she had never been caught in the act of stealing.

How had they recognized her?

As a little girl, she had not seen the obvious answer in her own intense green eyes and a face that was painfully beautiful—unforgettable. The homeless child had passed by a hundred mirrors in this department store but failed to notice her own reflection in any of them. It had been a shock to discover that salesclerks could see her.

One day, the child had attempted to solve this old puzzle, deciding that unwashed clothing had made her stand out from the crowd. She had taken more care with her wardrobe, donning freshly stolen jeans before setting out for Herald Square. Her dirty hair had been swept up under a baseball cap, the better to blend with cleaner shoppers. And the little girl had added one more touch to her disguise, a pair of wildly expensive designer sunglasses with real gold frames—which no one in that middle-class throng could possibly afford.

And *then* she had felt truly invisible.

Fifteen years later, Detective Mallory had upgraded to even more expensive sunglasses, and the salespeople had also changed. She scanned the unfamiliar faces as she passed the counters, hunting a clerk who was seven-feet tall with long platinum-blond hair. Apparently, staid old Macy's had relaxed the hiring policy. Or perhaps Tall Sally had convinced them that a job in their store was the fulfillment of a lifelong dream—and this was true. She found the transvestite working behind a cosmetics counter. Of course. Now Sal could steal all the makeup in the world, and without the assistance of small children. Voice jacked up to a high falsetto, the salesclerk said, "May I help you, miss?"

Don't you know me, Sal?

No, there was no sign of recognition in the heavily painted gray eyes. Mallory held up her gold shield and ID. "This is about Sparrow."

"Put that away." Tall Sally's voice dropped into a deeper, more masculine register. "Why're you guys hassling me? I see my parole officer every damn week."

Mallory lowered her badge. "Does Macy's know about your rap-sheet? . . . No?" What a surprise. Sal had lied on the job application, failing to mention convictions for grand theft and corrupting the morals of minor children. Mallory laid her leather folder on the counter, keeping the badge in plain sight. Sal's eyes were riveted to the detective's gold shield, regarding it as a bomb. "Sparrow used to work with you. Does that help?"

"It's a big store, honey. What department did she work in? Can't say I recall the name."

What about me, Sal? Remember running out on me?

Aloud, Mallory said, "You and Sparrow were booked for prostitution in the same raids. You both gave the same street corner as your employment address. Don't even *try* to jerk me around."

"Well, back in the day, I knew a lot of whores. You can't expect me to remember every—"

"Does Macy's personnel director know that you're a man?"

"I'm the real deal, Detective." Sal thrust out a chest of formidable breasts. "In *all* my parts, if you know what I mean."

"Sex change?"

Tall Sally nodded.

The parole officer had not mentioned this, and Mallory knew the thief had been incarcerated in an all-male facility. The surgery must have been recent. "Expensive operation. You didn't get that kind of money working in a prison laundry. Doing your own stealing these days? Or do you still use little kids?"

"I had some money saved."

In other words, Sal had stolen a *lot* of money. Mallory had a vivid memory of Sal holding a set of lock picks just beyond the reach of a child and making threats, saying, "Kid, if you get caught, forget my name, or I'll mess you up real bad." Ten-year-old Kathy Mallory had snatched Sal's picks, then walked up to a delivery truck and opened the rear doors in record time. The student had surpassed the master.

Remember leaving me behind?

As always, the drag queen had been standing a safe distance away while Kathy had done the robbery alone, a little girl with puny arms struggling to unload VCRs into a grocery cart. At the first sight of a police car, Tall Sally had climbed into a station wagon, obeying all the laws and traffic lights while driving away and abandoning the child.

Two uniformed officers had seen Kathy standing just inside the open doors of the delivery truck—nowhere to hide, no way to run. The small thief had walked to the edge of the truckbed, raised one thin white hand and waved at the policemen. *Big* smile. Grinning, they had waved back, and their car had rolled on by.

All these years later, Tall Sally did not recognize the child all grown up and still holding a grudge.

"So it's just a coincidence," said Mallory. "You get a vagina installed about the same time Sparrow gets a new nose."

"That junkie whore got her nose fixed?" Tall Sally's voice had shifted back to fluttery high notes, for this was *girl* talk. "So tell me, how's it look?"

And now Mallory could believe that the two prostitutes had no recent history. Tall Sally had always been an inept liar, embroidering details to death and advertising every falsehood—but not this time. There was no exaggerated protest. Sal had never seen Sparrow's new face.

Along Avenue A, half-naked men with jackhammers ripped up the street, choking the air with particles and shaking the pavement in front of the bookshop. Riker had the taste of dust in his mouth as he stood before the display window and perused the titles of worn paperbacks. This morning, he planned to be the first customer.

John Warwick was walking toward him now, thin and wasted, moving slowly, doing his old man's shuffle. He bowed his white head, unwilling to meet the eyes of passing pedestrians. And now he paused at the door to his shop.

"Hey, John. Remember me?"

The bookseller turned his face to the window and spoke to the detective's reflection in the glass. "Riker. What's it been, fourteen, fifteen years?"

"Sounds right. I came about that old western you tracked down for Lou Markowitz."

The bookseller drew back, as if he feared that Riker would strike him. "It's not for sale. You can't have it. It belongs to the girl."

"She's dead," Riker lied. "And you *know* that. Markowitz *told* you—"

"No." Warwick shook his head. After fifteen years, he still believed that a ten-year-old Kathy had merely been lost. How close to the truth he had come. And he had sussed out his truth aided only by his paranoid distrust of police.

"So you still have the western?" This was impossible, for Riker had found that book in Sparrow's apartment, but evidently Warwick had lost track of the shop's inventory.

"Of *course* I have it. You think I'd give it to anyone but her?"

"It's over, John. The kid's never coming back." And now he posed a question disguised as frustration. "When was the last time you heard anyone ask for that book?"

"Every day for the past two weeks." Warwick winced. "This woman—a tall devil with blond hair."

Close, but Riker knew that the man was not describing Mallory.

"Sparrow," said Warwick. "That was her name. She wrote it down on a piece of paper—her phone number too. I threw it away."

"But before this woman came along? Nothing, right? Not a whisper in fifteen years. Doesn't that tell you—"

"The child is alive," said Warwick. "You couldn't catch her. No one could." His thin arms were rising as if to defend himself from a blow. "And you *can't* have her book."

Riker wondered how he would phrase questions about Sparrow. He needed a time line for the last days of her life, but he could not interrogate this man in the name of the law. Given Warwick's psychiatric history, that would mean knocking at the door of a very scary closet. "John? Can we sit down and talk about this? Just for a few minutes. Then I'll go away."

Warwick pulled out a gray linen handkerchief. He removed his glasses and made a show of cleaning them while casting about for something to say. "Markowitz put me through a lot of trouble tracking down that novel. He told me to—"

"She's dead. She can't come back for the book."

"You can't have it!" Warwick shouted, then shrank into himself, hunching his shoulders and furtively looking from side to side, as if he believed those loud words had come from someone else. He continued in a hoarse whisper. "Because she *might* come back."

John Warwick was a member of Lou Markowitz's choir. He would never give up his vigil, but the threat this posed to Kathy Mallory was very small. Riker was satisfied that this man had never known her name. In the worst possible case, the bookseller might meet her on the street one day and recognize the remarkable green eyes. Or was he still waiting for a ten-year-old child?

Riker stepped back to reappraise this fragile little person, who had always teetered on the edge of sanity. The threat of any authority figure terrified John Warwick. Yet, he was making a stand against the police, though he trembled to do it. And this was bravery in any man's philosophy.

Please. Don't make me do this the hard way.

The detective sat down on an iron bench in front of the store. Now that he no longer loomed over Warwick, the smaller man relaxed. "I can't make you talk to me," said Riker. "And I can't go away until you do." He would not risk another cop canvassing this street and stumbling onto a connection between Sparrow and a green-eyed child who loved westerns. He looked down at the sidewalk and whispered, "Please."

Shaking his head, Warwick unlocked the door to his shop and shuffled inside. Two minutes later, he was out on the street again, eyes wild and close to tears. "She *stole* it! Yesterday, that book was on the shelf behind my register, and now it's gone. That woman stole it when my back was turned."

Playing the public servant, Riker pulled out his notebook to take down a citizen's statement on a theft. "You said her name was Sparrow? So she was in your store yesterday."

"And every day for two weeks. Yesterday she was the last customer. It was just a few minutes before I closed the store. So I *know* she's the one who stole it. You write that down."

Riker glanced at the hours posted in the shop window. Poor Sparrow. She had wanted the book so badly, but there had been no time to read it before she was mutilated and hung.

FØUR

THE SUNLIT ROOM WAS RACKED WITH GLEAMING COPPER–
bottom pots, more spices than the stores carried and every cooking utensil known to God and Cordon Bleu—and even here, antiques
prevailed. Charles Butler lit a flame under an old-fashioned percolator. He
was dressed in yesterday's shirt and jeans, and his eyes were sore from
working through the night on Mallory's account, though he would never
get credit for mending her present, a waterlogged paperback western.
Riker had never understood this man's one-sided infatuation with her.
Charles was hardly a virgin in the area of abnormal psychology, and he
must know what she was.

The detective sat at the kitchen table and opened the restored book to
the page with the inscription. Apart from Lou Markowitz's lost signature,
there was no sign of damage, and he toyed with the idea of actually giving it to Mallory. "Good as new. It's magic."

"The paper was very brittle." Charles set the table with coffee cups and forks. "I had to treat it with a matte polymer so the pages wouldn't crumble. Of course, that would've destroyed the value of a rare book. So I did some research first."

Apparently, this was not a joke. Riker glanced at the stack of volumes on the kitchen table, all reference materials of an avid book collector. Among the titles he found *The Role of the Western in American Literature.* "The book is worthless, right?"

"Yes, sorry." Charles laid the old receipt from Warwick's Used Books on the table alongside the paperback. "I can't imagine why Louis paid so much money for it."

"I told you they were hard to find. It took a while to track this one down."

"Ah, he hired a book tracer. I use one from time to time. Well, that explains it." Charles leaned down and pointed to the faded date on the receipt. "Wasn't that the year Louis took Mallory into foster care?"

Riker felt queer and cold, the sensation of a misstep on a ladder. There were no regrets over stealing the book; he would risk his badge to do it again. No, his great mistake was made in that sentimental moment when he had decided not to destroy it. The second error was bringing the book to the man who loved Mallory. "Hey, I really appreciate all the time you—"

"It's not like I had something better to do." Charles set two plates of pie on the table, then turned down the flame on the stovetop. "I don't think I care for summer vacations. Oh, I almost forgot. I found a list of Jake Swain's work. Did you know he wrote eleven other books?"

"Yeah, I knew that." Riker wondered how much of the truth he could tell before the whole mess came unraveling.

His host poured coffee into the cups, then sat down on the other side of the table. "Interesting that Louis would go to so much trouble." His tone was merely conversational and curious, not suspicious—not yet. "If he hired a tracer, he must've wanted it very badly."

Of course, this would be confusing. Charles and the late Louis Markowitz had shared a reading list of more respectable authors. Perhaps he was hoping that this bad novel was some inside joke between Mallory and her foster father.

"No tracer," said Riker. "The bookshop owner found it for him." He sipped his coffee and tasted bile rising in his throat.

"So—how did you know about Swain's other books? They're very obscure. Did Louis mention them?"

"Yeah, Lou read 'em all." Riker knew he would not be believed, though he was telling the truth.

Charles was incredulous. "Why would he read books—like—*that?*" His gigantic vocabulary had failed him. He could find no better euphemism for *god-awful crap*.

Riker jabbed at the pie with his fork. "Because it's great literature?"

"No, I don't think that's *quite* it. May I?" Charles reached for the western, then opened it to a page near the end. "In the last chapter, there's a rather strange gunfight."

There was no need of the book to refresh his memory. Charles could read as fast as most people turned pages, and he retained everything in eidetic memory. Yet he kept the small conventions of normalcy—always trying to pass for a less gifted man, less of a freak. Riker wondered if this was partly his own fault. Perhaps he should stop referring to the brilliant clients of Butler and Company as Martians. He sometimes forgot that this man hailed from that same far planet.

"Here it is." Charles looked up from the page. "First, a gun shoots a red flame like a blowtorch. Then the crowd lets out a cheer. Oh, and the mayor has a few words to say. And *then*, at the other end of Main Street, an aging dancehall girl faints when she actually *hears* the sound of the bullet entering the opponent's body." He looked up at his guest. "Now, given all the action and conversation between firing the shot and hitting the target, I estimate that the bullet took six minutes to travel down the street." He closed the book, pronouncing it, "Wildly implausible."

Riker gave him a slow grin. "You only say that 'cause you never saw Lou on the firing range. A man could wait around all day for one of his bullets to hit a target." He sipped his coffee, stalling for time, hunting for words that would not sound like lies. "There were usually two gunfights in every book." And now he remembered the name of the gunslinger. "Now I never read this particular book, but I'm guessing that last shootout was between Sheriff Peety and the Wichita Kid." He shook his head slowly in mock sadness. "So that's how it ends."

"*You* read them, too?"

"Yeah, maybe half of 'em." And he had read the books under duress.

Lou Markowitz had wanted a second opinion, for he had never understood why a ten-year-old girl could be so attached to the trashy westerns.

Charles was still skeptical, crediting the detective with better taste in reading material if not suits and ties. And though it would not occur to him to call a friend on a lie, he clearly required more proof.

"In the first book," said Riker, "Sheriff Peety watches this little boy grow up in a sleepy burg called Franktown, Kansas. The kid and his mother rode in one day on the Wichita stagecoach." More of the story was coming back to him now, and his appetite had returned. "Well, the kid follows the sheriff around like a little shadow. In fact, Peety was the one who started calling him the Wichita Kid. It made the boy sound like a gunslinger. Just a joke, see? But the boy *loved* that name. It really made him strut."

By the time the Wichita Kid had obtained his first six-shooter, "a rusty old gun he bought for a dollar," Riker was done with his pie. "It was the kid's birthday. He'd just turned fifteen. And that morning, the sheriff wakes up to gunfire. So he comes runnin' out to the street." The detective looked down at the floor and made Charles see a body there. The stranger in Franktown was an unarmed cowboy lying on his back in the blood and the dust.

"His unblinking eyes stared into the sun." Riker surprised himself with this hokey line quoted verbatim. "And guess who's standing over the body?" His hand formed an imaginary gun, and he blew smoke from one finger. "Looks real bad for the Wichita Kid."

The situation worsened when the boy stole a horse and rode out of town. In the next chapter, the lawman was saddling a black stallion. "He's riding out after the Kid." And Riker had finished his coffee. "Sheriff Peety can hardly see. He's got tears in his eyes. He *loves* the boy. But Wichita killed a man, and he's gotta hang for that. At the end of the story, the sheriff runs the kid off a canyon wall. It's a long drop, hundreds of feet to the bottom of that canyon. But Peety's still tracking the boy in the book after that one."

"So it's episodic. A series with the same characters."

"Yeah, and every story has an ending like that one. I guess that's what gets you hooked."

Charles nodded, then slid the paperback across the table. The matter was closed.

The detective picked up the novel and quickly hid it in his pocket, as if it were a dirty book instead of a dangerous one.

The Ice Queen cometh.

Whiteshield Ronald Deluthe watched the pretty woman crossing the squad room. He recognized money when it walked in the door, shod in a brand of running shoes that no civil servant could afford. No one had to tell him what Mallory spent at her tailor's or the hair salons. And he wondered if she was on the take.

What green eyes you have. How cold they are.

She was blind to him, looking right through him, and yet he resented her less than the others. As a merely average man with an amateur dye job of bright yellow hair, Deluthe knew he was beneath her notice and contempt. It had nothing to do with his rank.

He turned back to his work, typing a meticulously detailed explanation for the news van beating the fire engines to last night's crime scene. Detective Riker would have nothing to criticize this time.

Mallory paused to read the paper sign taped to the side of his computer monitor. Originally, it had been taped to his back. The joke had gone unnoticed until he had removed his jacket and discovered the sheet of paper stuck to the material—and his new job title, *Resurrector of Dead Whores*. He had gamely put the sign on open display and earned a few smiles from passing detectives.

Mallory was not amused.

She ripped the sheet off the monitor, wadded it into a tight ball, then dropped it on his keyboard. He stared at the small white marble of compacted paper; her crumpling style was more serious than Riker's. He looked up as she moved away from him, calling after her, "Ma'am?"

Did that sound too needy?

She ignored him, but all the detectives did that. He abandoned his report and followed her down a hallway that opened onto a large room with no distraction of windows. Every wall was lined with cork and cluttered with bloody photographs and the paperwork of current cases. Earlier in the day, a detective had given him a brief tour of the Special Crimes facilities, also known as the mens room and the lunch room, but not this place. Of course not. Why bother? Folding chairs were set up in audience formation for briefings he would never be invited to attend.

Near the door, a table held a large-screen television set. Mallory stood beside it, speaking to an older man, Janos.

A *real* detective.

Deluthe knew better than to interrupt. But rather than hover like a schoolboy awaiting permission to take a piss, he wandered the perimeter of cork walls, perusing pinned-up pictures and paperwork. None of it pertained to the hanging hooker. Obviously it was not an important case, and his report was only one more piece of busywork for the son-in-law of the deputy commissioner, a little something to keep him out of the way.

Mallory fed a videotape into the mouth of a VCR. Deluthe was drawn to the screen and its images of fire engines and the crowd that had turned out for last night's hanging. Now he understood why the news director had refused to copy film and outtakes from the fire. The videotapes had already been collected by Mallory.

Detective Janos flicked the remote control and froze the picture. "That one?" He pointed to a figure standing well back in the gathering, a man dressed in a T-shirt and jeans. "Yeah, he might be the old lady's man in the tree."

Deluthe winced at this reminder of Miss Emelda and all that he had missed in his first interview with her. But he had learned a lot from Sergeant Riker, the only detective who had bothered to teach him anything. Perhaps the useless trek to the television station had been a training exercise and not a total waste of time. He cleared his throat before speaking to Mallory. He would rather die than let her hear his voice crack. "I thought *I* was supposed to talk to the newspeople. Sergeant Riker told me—"

"I got there first." Mallory said this with no inflection, yet he drew the inference that he had been somehow remiss.

She undoubtedly knew everything that he knew and then some. Comparing his notes with hers would only be asking for more humiliation. "I'm almost finished with my report." His *useless* report. "What do I do now?"

"I know what you can do." Mallory smiled.

A sucker grin? Yes, and Deluthe braced himself, wondering if she would tell him to get lost or worse.

She pulled out her notebook. "Never mind if this takes a few days. You just stay on it." The detective wrote down the address of a warehouse and the item she wanted, then ripped off the page and handed it to him. As an afterthought, she said, "That murder could be fifteen or twenty years old."

And this vague time frame was supposed to help him locate an evidence carton for a homicide with no name or case number? He could search for years and never find a box with a hangman's rope. In effect, Mallory had just told him to get lost. And now she glared at him, perhaps wondering why he was still here.

He marched down the hallway, then crossed the squad room, saying a silent good-bye to the walls and wondering if he would ever see this place again. A few minutes later, the young man slid behind the wheel of his car and discovered that he was out of gas.

My name is Fool.

Deluthe was surrounded by cops with motorcycles and cars. Any of these men could siphon out a pint of fuel, enough for him to reach a gas station. But rather than admit to one more stupid mistake, he abandoned his vehicle and walked toward the subway, hoping it would drop him close to the warehouse. And there he might spend the rest of his temporary assignment, wandering long corridors of dusty shelves stacked with ancient evidence cartons.

Count on it, Fool.

When he reached the subway track, the last car was running away into the tunnel. He sat down on a wooden bench assigned to screwup cops who missed their trains. The public-address system came alive with an electronic squeal that hurt his ears. An inhuman voice was telling Ronald Deluthe that, wherever he was going, he could not get there, not from here, not today. There was a fire on the tracks, and no more trains were coming his way.

New York was not a town of second chances.

On the other side of the grimy storefront window, an old man sat hunched over a desk as high as a pulpit, the better to catch shoplifters among the aisles of used books, though he had no customers this afternoon. The plaque on the edge of the desk said, "John Warwick, proprietor."

Charles Butler entered the shop, announced by a buzzer. Near the door, a table and two chairs were cooled by the steady breeze of a fan. This told him that Mr. Warwick was more than a merchant. Only a man who loved his trade would sacrifice valuable floor space to carve out this niche for weary readers.

The bookseller looked up from his work, peering through thick lenses that enlarged his pale gray eyes. And now Charles could see that the man was not elderly, but closer to his own age of forty. He had been duped by Warwick's premature white hair and slumping shoulders that mimicked a hump. The old-fashioned spectacles had also added to the illusion of extreme age. And, although the room was warm, the sleeves of his frayed white shirt were long and buttoned at the cuffs.

"Mr. Warwick?"

This was said in a civil voice, but the bookseller seemed confused. Then he took it as a command to come down from his perch, and he was quick enough to rise from his chair but slow to descend the short flight of steps to the floor. Moving in the cautious manner of one with brittle bones, he shuffled across the room to stand before Charles, then lowered his head and stared at his shoes.

Awaiting orders?

"Uh, could we sit?" Charles gestured toward the readers' table.

Obediently, Warwick eased into a chair, as if he did not trust it to hold his leaf-light body. And now he waited for further instructions. His head was still bowed in resignation, accepting another man's authority over him.

Charles recognized the behavioral cues of a patient or a prisoner, someone who had remained too long in an institution. He quickly ruled out prison. Given Warwick's eccentric masquerade as a senior citizen, the most likely scenario was long-term care in an asylum. The symptoms of institutionalization were so pronounced, the damage of prolonged confinement had likely begun when this man was quite young, perhaps in childhood. He wondered if the cuffs of the shirt hid scars of a razor across the frail wrists. How to proceed with such a delicate soul? Well, gently and with references, of course. "I got your name from a friend of mine. Perhaps you know him. Sergeant Riker?"

Warwick looked up for a moment, then lowered his face to stare at the tabletop, keeping custody of the eyes. Charles pulled out his business card and slid it across the table. The bookseller picked it up with grave suspicion in his myopic eyes. "This doesn't say what you do."

A valid point. A long string of academic degrees followed several PhDs behind Charles Butler's name, but the card did not mention his profession, and this had been Mallory's idea to prod him into word-of-mouth advertising by way of explanation. "I'm in human resources. I evaluate people with unusual gifts, and then I place them with projects in the private sector or gov—"

"You're a *psychiatrist*." Warwick spat out this last word as if it had a bad taste.

"No, I'm not." Charles looked down at the card. "A few of those degrees *are* in psychology, but I've never been a practicing—"

"And now you're going to tell me that Riker didn't lie to me. Am I right—*Doctor?*" Warwick spoke to the tabletop when he whispered. "I'm crazy not to believe him. Right again?"

"I've never known Riker to lie." Charles softened his voice, not wanting the man to acquiesce because of some imagined threat. "I'm sure he wouldn't—"

"More tricks." Warwick conquered his ingrained posture of compliance and sat up straight. His eyes darted from one bookshelf to another, then locked with those of his inquisitor. As the little man drew a deep breath, he seemed to be inhaling energy. His voice was stronger now. "You go back and tell Riker—" One tremulous finger rose from a closed fist, and he pointed it like a weapon. "You tell him—she's *alive!*"

"Who do you—"

"I'm not senile, if that's what you're thinking. First Markowitz, then—"

"*Louis* Markowitz?"

"You think I'd forget that name? There's nothing wrong with my memory. You tell that to Riker."

"I didn't come here to examine you." When Charles smiled, as he did now, he knew it made him look like an escaped fool who had dodged his keeper. Such a silly face. Even the most paranoid of lunatics could not perceive him as a threat.

Warwick relaxed by slow degrees. "It's been a long time, but I remember everything. She was a rare one. Most runaways are teenagers. The little ones like her, they usually go where they're kicked—juvenile facilities, foster homes. You know how she survived the hunt? She was smarter than them. *So* smart."

"Them? The police?"

"Markowitz and Riker. They staked out my store. What fools." Warwick pushed the thick spectacles up the bridge of his nose. "As if they could ever catch her."

"Who? What was her—"

"The little girl who loved westerns," he snapped, as if his interrogator should know this.

Charles called up an old photograph from an archive of eidetic memory. It was the picture that Louis Markowitz had carried in his wallet. Perfect recall included a tear in the protective plastic sleeve. "This child's hair—was it long and wavy? Was it blond?"

"And matted and dirty." Warwick nodded. "Her face was dirty, too." Eyes focused on some middle ground, he was also looking at a memory. "Her jeans were always rolled up in fat cuffs. Clothes never fit her— except for the running shoes. They were always spanking white. I think she stole a new pair every week. Markowitz said she was robbing New York City blind. But she never stole from me. She'd take a book off the shelf and put back the last one she borrowed." He smiled now, but not with happiness—more like defiance. "You see? I don't forget anything."

"How long did this stakeout last?"

"Off and on? Two months—and they couldn't catch her."

Charles recalled a different series of events: Louis had been en route to his wife's birthday party when he had just *happened* upon a strange child robbing a car. Rather than spend the night filling out paperwork, he had taken Kathy home to the party, and his wife had mistaken the baby felon for a present. What a lovely story—told so many times. Riker was not even mentioned in that version. And nothing had ever been said about stalking, *hunting down* a little girl over a period of months.

"And what was your part in this, Mr. Warwick? You just loaned her the books?"

"No, no." The man was exasperated, perhaps still believing that this was a psychiatric interview, a test of trick questions. "The girl *took* the books, like she had a right to them. She'd take one, then bring it back. That's how Markowitz figured out that she came from a small town."

"Pardon?"

"Markowitz said, in her part of the world, my little store was probably the size of a public library. He said to me, 'The kid brings the books back because her mother raised her right.' Then that bastard confiscated her westerns, all but the last one."

"The book you traced for him?"

Warwick nodded. "I had to track down all the buyers at the estate sale where I got the others. He paid me, then put the book on the shelf—so she would find it. But she never did. I never saw her again. The last time Markowitz came in, he told me the little girl was dead. He scribbled a few words in the book, then left it behind."

"So you know what he wrote on the—"

"It was a love letter to a dead child. The words weren't meant for you." Warwick sighed, then looked down at his hands. "He wanted me to believe she was dead, but it was just a trick. He was crying that day. I— almost believed him."

"Interesting pattern," said Charles. "The little girl and her books. She must have come in here quite a few times before you reported her to the police."

"I never did that. I *never* betrayed her." The bookseller said this with great pride, as if he had defeated yet another trap of the inquisition.

No, that was wrong.

Charles decided that the man's pride stemmed from honoring some unspoken pact with a child, for he was certain there had been no conversation between the bookseller and young Kathy Mallory. "I bet you couldn't get within three feet of her." He was working with Louis Markowitz's description of the feral child raised as his own. "Edgy as a cat, wasn't she?"

Every detail dropped into its proper slot as Charles arrived at an uncomfortable conclusion: Warwick had not wanted the little girl to be caught and locked away in some institution—like the one that had imprisoned him and probably drugged him every day so he would not pose problems for the staff. Warwick had not seen the comforts of adoption or foster care in Kathy Mallory's future. No, this ex–mental patient had seen a kindred malady in a small child, something abnormal and dark. One sick mind had reached out to a—

Charles shook his head in a futile attempt to empty out this idea. Seeking some better reason that he could believe in, he leaned toward the bookseller. "Her clothes, her hair—you had to know she was homeless. But you never reported her. Why *not?*"

He saw the question in Warwick's eyes, *Would you buy a lie?* And it was all Charles could do to keep from shouting, *Hell, yes!*

John Warwick reacted as if mere thoughts were screams. He ducked his head under some imagined blow. His bony shoulders were rising, and his chin disappeared into his shirt collar, a frightened turtle in retreat.

With deep apology in his voice, Charles leaned forward to lure the man back out with an easier question. "What sort of books did she like?"

The man's neck slowly attenuated, eyes still wary, searching the room for hidden enemies. "Only westerns." Warwick almost smiled. "And only one writer." The agitation had abated, and he seemed merely tired as he leaned back in his chair. "All of Jake Swain's work went out of print long ago—and for good reason. It was terrible writing. But she read those westerns over and over, the same eleven novels."

"Any idea why?"

"Who knows?" The bookseller shook his head. "The child was so small and skinny, so vulnerable—always alone. I suppose she read them for comfort. She always knew what would happen in her books." Warwick turned his face to the window on the street. "She never knew what might happen out there."

FiVE

SERGEANT RIKER CROSSED THE SQUAD ROOM OF SPECIAL
Crimes Unit, a haphazard arrangement of fifteen desks littered
with deli bags, pizza boxes and men with guns. On the far side of the
room, a wide glass panel gave him a look inside Lieutenant Coffey's private office, where Mallory stood before the desk, her eyes cast down in
the manner of a penitent schoolgirl.

What's wrong with this picture?

The senior detective strolled into the meeting and assumed his usual
position, slumped down in the nearest chair with a cigarette dangling at
one side of his mouth. After a heavy lunch, Riker was not inclined to
waste energy on actual words, and so his eyes merely opened a little wider
to say, *Okay, I'm here. What?*

"I understand you sent that kid—" Lieutenant Coffey paused to glare
at his sergeant's cigarette, as if that ever worked. "The guy from Loman's
squad—what's his name?"

"Duck Boy."

"You sent him down to the warehouse to go through eight million boxes of old evidence. I'm guessing you hoped he'd get lost down there."

Riker shrugged. That had been the general idea, but not *his* idea, and Mallory was not stepping up to claim the credit. She was busy with her upside-down reading of all the lieutenant's paperwork.

"Well, the kid got lucky." Jack Coffey lifted an evidence carton from the floor and settled it on the edge of his desk. "It only took him five minutes to find your hangman's rope."

Mallory seemed not to care. Behind the cover of the carton, she teased a red folder from the mess on the lieutenant's blotter and opened it. Riker caught the glimpse of a full-color autopsy photograph, then turned back to his commanding officer, feigning interest in the adventures of Duck Boy. "So how did he do it?"

"Last month, the warehouse roof sprung a leak and damaged a few cartons." Coffey opened the box flaps and pulled out a bulky object in brown wrapping. "A clerk remembered repackaging the evidence. The paperwork was wrecked, except for a few of the case numbers. So Duck Boy— let's find another name for him, okay? So the kid used the numbers to pull a file from the ME's archive."

The lieutenant unwrapped a coil of rope, then knocked the carton to the floor and reached out to grab the red folder from Mallory's hands. "And this is a twenty-year-old autopsy report. It washes out any connection to Sparrow. So we're kicking the hooker back to the East Side precinct. Now she's Lieutenant Loman's headache." He dropped the rope and the folder on his desk. "I guess we're done here."

With an attitude of *not so fast*, Mallory swept the rope off the desk and into Riker's lap, then opened the ME's folder and spread the contents across the blotter. She tapped a photograph in the center of her array. "Take a look at this one."

Riker and Coffey leaned over for a closer inspection of a corpse bloated with gas and thriving maggots.

"This was another scalping." With one long red fingernail, Mallory called their attention to the blond hair matted and plastered to the woman's skull. "It was hacked off with a razor."

The lieutenant's smile said, *Nice try, but no sale.* "I'm looking at a woman with a short haircut, and I don't see any hair packed in her mouth."

"She was a blonde," said Riker. "Like Sparrow."

"Not good enough." Coffey rooted through the companion paperwork, then handed a sheaf of stapled pages to Riker. "Here, read the report. The woman was found hanging, but that wasn't the cause of death. Dr. Norris was chief medical examiner in those days. He said she was strangled first."

"Wouldn't be the first time that hack got something wrong." Mallory sifted through the other photographs. "Markowitz said he was drunk half the time."

"No." Riker slapped the desk. "I remember that old bastard. He was drunk *all* the time."

Coffey clasped his hands behind his head and leaned back in his chair. "So, you guys think a pathologist, drunk or sober, could overlook a wad of hair packed in a victim's mouth?"

"Last night, a *pathologist* pronounced Sparrow dead," said Mallory.

The lieutenant's smile widened. "That's pretty lame."

The boss was entirely too cheerful, and this made Riker uneasy. Though he had no faith in premonitions, he did have a clear vision of Jack Coffey digging a deep pit for Mallory, then concealing it with twigs and branches.

And there was no way to warn her.

She picked up the old autopsy report and leaned over the desk to dangle it in front of the lieutenant's face. "Did you *read* this?" Her unmistakable implication was that fault had somehow shifted onto Coffey. "No one assisted on this autopsy. And that's odd, because Markowitz said it took two assistants to cover the old drunk's mistakes. Norris *never* worked alone."

Jack Coffey was unimpressed. "Your point?"

"He wouldn't want any witnesses if he was suppressing evidence. So he omitted a few things from the—"

"No, I don't think so." Coffey ripped the report from her hand.

Fun's over.

The lieutenant was not smiling anymore. "All right, Mallory. Let's talk about another fairy tale. The old file in Cold Cases? Nobody on that squad remembers a search request from you. I ordered you to requisition that file. I can guess why you didn't waste the time." He looked down at the report to refresh his memory. "Natalie Homer. Her murder was never one of their cases."

"They're lying," said Mallory. "They lost the file."

Even Coffey had to admire gall on such a grandiose scale. "You're telling me they were too embarrassed to admit they lost a file? So they *lied?*"

"That's right," said Detective Janos. Three heads turned to the open doorway and a man built like a refrigerator with salt-and-pepper hair. "Natalie Homer *is* a Cold Case file." Janos's soft voice was at odds with a face that resembled mug-book shots of the most violent offenders. "They assigned it to an independent."

"So they lost the paperwork *and* Mallory's request?" Coffey was not yet convinced. "And they *lied* about it?" His tone of voice implied that a lying cop might be a new concept in this room.

"Take the charitable view." Janos smiled. "Cold Cases moved to a new office. They're a little disorganized. If the boys didn't make a copy before they released the folder, they'd never find it again. The copy holds the transfer sheet. Very minimalist filing system. So, today, a hanged hooker is big news—front pages. And they get a request for a connected file—a *lost* file. Yeah, I think they'd lie to you, boss."

"But *you* found the file?"

"Better than that," said Janos. "The name of the catching detective was in the ME's report. So I took a ride over to his last known address. This old guy answers the door—he's got the damn file in his hand. He says to me, 'What took you so long?' And here we are." Janos nodded toward the stairwell door on the other side of the squad room. "That's Lars Geldorf."

Riker swiveled his chair around to face the window on the squad room and a lean, white-haired man. "He's gotta be seventy-five years old."

Lars Geldorf had grown tired of waiting for a summons, and now he walked toward the lieutenant's office, not hobbling but making good time. No one had told this retired detective that he had grown old. He wore a silk suit in the best tradition of all the young Turks of his day. The swagger agreed with an arrogant smile, and anyone could read his mind: Geldorf was thinking, *I'm going to save your damn hides.*

"He's gonna be trouble," said Coffey.

Riker agreed. He was reminded of his own father, another cop who had not had the grace to take up knitting after being pensioned off. Geldorf had the same way of walking, as if he owned all the real estate under his feet. The old man strolled into the private office and shook Coffey's hand in silence, trusting that his name and his fame had preceded him. Then he opened his suit jacket, so as not to wrinkle the silk when he sat down.

Just like Dad.

Riker noticed more trouble when the suit jacket opened. Geldorf wore a revolver holstered at the hip. The old man was definitely back in the game.

Lieutenant Coffey dropped his polite smile. "I understand you've got something for me."

"It's all in here." The retired detective held up a zippered pouch with the smell of new leather. "The Natalie Homer case. I got the details on your perp's MO from the morning paper." His eyes narrowed with a foxy smile. "Too bad you couldn't keep the press away from the crime scene." This was an unmistakable criticism, for he had done an excellent job of keeping his own case details under wraps. Until today, no one had ever heard of the twenty-year-old hanging of Natalie Homer.

Jack Coffey held up the old autopsy folder. "But your case didn't have the same MO."

"Oh, yeah," said Geldorf. "It *did*. Every detail matches."

"Natalie Homer's autopsy didn't mention any hair in her mouth." And the newspapers had made much of that. Coffey opened the red folder and glanced at the first page of the old report. "The chief medical examiner was—"

"Dr. Peter Norris," said Geldorf. "A drunk and a third-rate hack. I'm glad he's dead. And you're wrong, son. *I* pulled the hair out of her mouth before the meat wagon showed up." He leaned back and smiled in self-congratulation. "In those days, all the worst press leaks came from the medical examiner's office."

Lieutenant Coffey read aloud from the old autopsy report, "'Manual strangulation.' According to the ME, your victim was strangled *before* she was strung up."

"Oh, yeah. What a psycho." Geldorf smiled. "Or maybe he only wanted it to look that way." He glanced up at Mallory. "What's your theory?"

"I like the psycho," she said.

The old man turned to Riker. "And what about you? I'll give you a hint. You wouldn't expect the victim to have a coil of rope lying around the house."

Riker only drummed his fingers on the arm of the chair. He recognized all the signs of this ritual—Learning from the Master of Old Farts. Previously, he had believed that this was his father's invention, a game devised to drive his son insane. He reached over to take the leather pouch from the retired detective. It was a tense moment, for this file was Geldorf's ticket to ride with Special Crimes Unit, and he would not loosen his grip. Mallory caught the old man's eyes and silently conveyed a threat, *Hey, this is going to happen, old man.* And Geldorf's hand slowly opened. Riker grabbed the pouch and unzipped it, then riffled the contents. "So what happened to the hair you took from her mouth?"

"It's with the rest of the evidence. After the case went cold, I packed it myself."

Lieutenant Coffey shook his head. "No hair."

"So they lost it," said Geldorf with a casual lift of one shoulder. "Happens all the time."

Riker handed the lieutenant a photograph from the pouch. Natalie Homer's mouth was stuffed with a gag of wadded blond hair.

Detective Janos stood behind Geldorf's chair and leaned down to the old man's ear to say, "Tell them about the candles."

What the hell?

Twenty-four candles and a jar of dead flies were the only details not mentioned in the morning papers. Why would Janos confide in the old man? Riker glanced through the rest of the crime-scene photos but found no pictures of votive candles.

"That summer, the East Village had rolling blackouts," said Geldorf. "The electricity was off for three hours after sundown, and Natalie had three candles in her apartment."

Mallory pulled a bag of melted red wax from the carton. The long tapers were fused together.

"Now you see?" said Geldorf. "This is how they treat evidence. Those candles were brand-new. Check out the wicks. Never been lit. So I figure the perp showed up while it was still light. Early evening works with Norris's call for time of death."

The candles were the right color, red, but the wrong shape. Riker counted only three candles—not the dozens found in Sparrow's apartment.

Geldorf was awaiting a compliment on his astute reading of three unlit wicks.

"Nice work." There was no sarcasm in the lieutenant's voice, though the old man had botched the chain of evidence. Jack Coffey was always respectful to the visiting ghosts. "I need a few minutes alone with my people. Detective Janos will look after you."

When the office door had closed on Geldorf and his keeper, Coffey shook his head. "There's still no case connection." He held up the photograph Riker had given him. "This perp has to be in his forties by now, and stringing up blondes is a young man's game." He tossed the picture back to Riker. "You guys don't have a serial killer. And Sparrow's still alive. You don't even have a corpse yet."

Riker turned to his partner. Mallory had been raised by the best poker player in the universe. She was the source of all his hopes for keeping Sparrow's case in Special Crimes Unit.

"I say he's picking out another victim right now." Mallory took the pouch from Riker's hand and held it up as her hole card. "I can link these two cases."

"You think so?" Coffey bent down to the carton at his feet and pulled out a plastic bag with a smaller segment of the rope. It was not a good container for water-damaged evidence. Riker could smell mildew when the lieutenant opened the bag. And now he was staring at a classic hangman's noose with a neat row of coils below the loop.

Sparrow's case was lost.

"Try explaining this away." Coffey reached into a stack of paperwork and pulled out a photograph of the more recent hanging. "The nooses aren't the same, not even close. Sparrow's has a simple knot." He held up the rope used on Natalie Homer. "This one is guaranteed to kill. If your perp knew how to tie a hangman's noose, why didn't he use it on the hooker?"

Mallory kept her silence. She only stared at the noose, the last piece of evidence Coffey had been withholding, waiting for her to show him everything she had. It looked like a clear victory for the boss, yet Riker sensed that the man's graceful-winner smile was premature, that Mallory was not quite played out.

Jack Coffey continued. "You know why this case bothered your old man? Markowitz didn't know the hanging was just for show. The autopsy report was sealed. He never knew the woman was strangled before she was hung."

"He *knew!*"

"*Prove* it!"

Mallory pulled a battered notebook from her back pocket and handed it to the lieutenant. "You're wrong about the hanging."

Even without the reading glasses that Riker never wore, he recognized Lou Markowitz's handwriting as Jack Coffey flipped through illegible pages of shorthand punctuated by single words.

Coffey looked up at Mallory. "I can't even read most of the—"

"I can," she said. "The tape on Natalie's wrists was so tight it dug into her skin. But no sign of cut-off circulation. And you won't find that in the autopsy report—*another* screwup. Markowitz could read a corpse better than that drunk Norris. He knew the perp bound a dead woman's hands. He *knew* she was dead before she was hanged, and that rope *still* bothered him."

Lieutenant Coffey closed the notebook. "You just made my case. It was a garden-variety murder dressed up like a psycho hanging."

"No! The killer always planned to hang Natalie Homer, but something went wrong."

"That's reaching, Mallory."

"If the perp didn't plan on a hanging, why would he bring a rope?" She snatched the old notebook from the lieutenant's hand, then stalked out of the office. An outsider would have read her exit as cold anger. Coffey did. In reality, Mallory simply had a flawless sense of timing.

And the time was now.

"Makes sense," said Riker.

"The hell it does. Natalie Homer's dead body was in that apartment from Friday till Sunday night. Lots of time for the perp to come back with his rope. She's forcing these cases to link."

"Everything she said panned out." And Riker would have regarded this as a miracle, but what were the odds that God was on Mallory's side? "And you gotta wonder what else she found in Lou's notes." He silently complimented his partner on her early departure with the notebook. "Give us a week. How's it gonna look if another body turns up *after* you bounce Sparrow's case back to Loman's squad?"

"That's crap, Riker. There's no connection here, and you *know* it. All you've got is two women with bad haircuts and lots of rope." Coffey covered his face with one hand, for it would never do to let the troops see his frustration. "So here's the deal. You keep Geldorf and his file out of my shop. And he *never* gets a look at Sparrow's evidence."

"Deal." The detective tapped out his cigarette on the sole of his shoe, then rose from the chair. He was uncomfortable with this win. It was going too smoothly.

The lieutenant gathered loose papers and photographs into the red folder. "And keep Geldorf away from the reporters. I don't wanna read any headlines about a trumped-up case connection." He tossed the ME's file to Riker, then dropped the rope into the cardboard box at his feet. "And get this crap out of my office."

Riker leaned down and picked up the evidence carton. "I've got a place to stash everything—the old man too." The boss would not want to hear the name Butler and Company, no hint that Mallory's ties to that firm were still binding.

"Good," said Coffey. "If you can't make a case in forty-eight hours, you lose the hooker to Loman." He lowered his head, pretending interest in the papers on his desk blotter. "I called the hospital. It doesn't look good for the hooker. She's going sour." He looked up. "Sorry about that. You and Sparrow go back a long ways, don't you?"

Riker nodded. He understood everything now. His partner had entrusted him with the endgame, the humiliating part, for Jack Coffey had just made it very clear that this was only charity for an aging detective and a dying whore.

Lars Geldorf opened the door, and Mallory followed him into an apartment that stank of stale ashtrays and yesterday's meals. The frayed furnishings and a small-screen television set were character references for an honest cop living within the means of his pension. A large mirror over the mantelpiece reflected light from windows overlooking Hell's Kitchen along Eighth Avenue. There were no signs that a woman had ever lived here. The dust was thick, the window glass was yellowed with the nicotine of a million cigarettes, and the walls were all about Geldorf.

Framed newspaper clippings were grouped with photographs of his younger self posed with politicians and cops who had died before Mallory was born. One citation hung by itself in the most impressive frame. It was hardly evidence of a stellar career, but he obviously took great pride in it.

The retired detective paused to rock on his heels and smile, to allow time for his guest to admire these mementos. Then he led her into the next room, where another large mirror had pride of place. It almost covered a line of cracked plaster, but its real purpose was less functional. The old man stood before the looking glass, a peacock in a silk suit that was decades out of style. His gold pinky ring gleamed as he straightened his tie and smiled, *loving* what he saw. And now he pointed to another cluster of photographs. "That one in the middle was taken the night we cut Natalie down. I shot it myself."

Mallory stared at the framed crime-scene photo. The hair had been removed from the victim's mouth. The prone corpse lay on the floor, displayed in an open body bag, and two grinning detectives stood over the dead woman, posed as hunters with a trophy kill. But the real trophy was the third man, only a visitor on this scene, a celebrated cop who stood between the case detectives and a head above them. The two grinning men appeared to be restraining Louis Markowitz, an unwilling subject for a macabre souvenir. His face was slightly blurred by the sad shake of his head.

Below this photograph was a desk buried under papers and flanked by file cabinets. The most modern piece of office equipment was an early-generation fax machine. Cartons were piled on cheap metal storage shelves, and two large bulletin boards were littered with personal notes. The absence of a computer was no surprise to Mallory. This old man still lived in the century of the typewriter.

"I don't see why we can't work out of my place." Geldorf pulled a large box from a shelf. "I'm all set up here."

"Coffey wants tight security," she lied. "And a downtown location is better."

"Tight security." Geldorf nodded. "Good idea."

The box bearing Natalie Homer's name had been half full when he began to load in more papers. Cartons this size did not travel with Cold Case files. A thick folder should have been sufficient for reports and statements. "You've been working this murder for a while?"

"Oh yeah, I never let go of a case I couldn't close on the job," said Geldorf. "After I retired, I just kept collecting stuff, scraps and pieces. When I was ready to do more interviews, I'd check out the Cold Case file and make it official."

"So you only work your own cases?"

"That's right. You should've seen this room twelve years ago. So many cartons, you couldn't move. You had to go out in the hall to change your mind." He waited for her to smile at his little joke—and he waited. Then, slowly, he turned around to face the shelves that were bare. "So, one by one, I'd close another Cold Case file, get rid of another box, another ghost. Now I've only got a few left." He lowered his head and focused on the task of packing his box. "When I was on the job, I only got days to work a murder. Now I got years." His smile was sheepish when he said, "I shouldn't have told you. Now you know what a lousy detective I was. But I'm gonna make it right. I'll close 'em—every one." He dropped more papers into his carton, then folded the cardboard flaps. "I'm all yours now—full time."

"And I appreciate that." She had already laid plans to keep him out of her way. The baby-sitting detail would be split between Charles Butler and Lieutenant Loman's whiteshield, also known as Duck Boy.

She donned her sunglasses, then turned around for a sidelong look at the mirror and Geldorf's reflection. She had been wrong about the peacock trait. All the posturing arrogance fell away when he believed that he was unobserved. It must have been a great strain to keep up that facade. The old man in the looking-glass room shrank and sagged, and his eyes were full of worry. He must see every young cop as a potential threat to his dignity.

Good.

Keeping him in line would be no problem.

Geldorf sealed the box flaps with tape. "So now you'll wanna talk to everybody who saw my crime scene." He glanced in her direction.

"You're wondering how your perp found out about the hair in Natalie's mouth."

Mallory turned around to smile at him. *Crafty old man.* "You knew it wasn't a serial killing."

"Couldn't be." His sly grin explained everything: He had simply wanted to come back to the job—to come in from the cold of his old age. "My prime suspect died nineteen years ago."

She almost liked him. With only an exchange of nods and knowing glances, mutual admissions of lies were made and vows of silence taken. They were allies now, and neither of them would give the other away.

"At best, what you got is a copycat." He lifted the heavy box in his arms, and she showed him respect by not offering to help with the load. Geldorf walked behind her, saying, "When I find out where your perp got his information, maybe I can close out Natalie's case. Oh, yeah, I think we can help each other."

You can dream, old man.

She had no intention of working Natalie Homer's homicide. The trail was twenty years old and a cold one. She opened the door for Geldorf, then took his proffered keys and locked it.

"The link is in the details." He struggled with the bulky carton as they walked toward the elevator. "I had complete control over my crime scene. No leaks to the media. You know how I pulled that off? I told a uniform to take bribes from the reporters. Well, this kid gets twenty bucks apiece from those bastards, then tells 'em he found the woman swingin' from a rope."

"So they figured it was a suicide." Mallory approved. It was always wise to tell the truth when you lied. "And Natalie Homer got lost on page ten."

"And just one newspaper, a couple of lousy paragraphs." He set down the box and pushed a button to call for the elevator. "So now you'll wanna rule out the possible leaks. Lucky I saved my old case notes."

Yeah, right.

"You can handle those interviews," said Mallory. "I got you an assistant to go along as your badge." Then she would be rid of Geldorf *and* Duck Boy.

"What about the big guy? Butler? Was that his name?" Geldorf pulled out a card given to him an hour ago at the offices of Butler and Company.

"*Doctor* Butler," said Mallory, though Charles had never used that title. "He's a consulting psychologist with NYPD." Fortunately, there was no useful information on the business card to contradict that lie. "He'll be working closely with you."

Charles Butler wore a suit and tie, for this was a workday. Many thanks to Riker's intervention, the tedium of a summer hiatus was finally at an end. He passed through the reception area of Queen Anne furniture and Watteau watercolors, then strolled down a short hall, leaving behind centuries of antique decor that separated the other rooms from Mallory's domain of electronics, of plastic and metal and wire. Her private office at the rear of Butler and Company had some charming features. However, the tall arched windows were hidden behind cold steel blinds, and a plain gray rug strove to disguise the hardwood floor as concrete.

Her three computers sat atop workstations perfectly aligned at the center of the room, and all the monitors were lit. Square blue cyclops eyes focused upon the intruder, and Charles recalled his old dream of kicking in the glass and blinding the little bastards.

The free space of three walls was devoted to gray metal shelving units stocked with manuals lined up precisely one inch from the edge and software components keeping company with hardware. Mallory had refused his offer of paintings, preferring not to clutter the giant bulletin board that covered her fourth wall from baseboard to ceiling molding.

Sergeant Riker was still at work pinning photographs and papers to the cork surface. The detective had given Charles a new project, a present, actually *two* gifts: a twenty-year-old murder and a seventy-five-year-old man.

"When will they be back?"

"Half an hour, give or take." Riker sifted through the contents of a leather pouch and selected more papers. Handwritten notes and typed statements had been arranged on the wall in no particular order.

"All this to pacify Mr. Geldorf?"

"Yeah," said Riker. "Think it might keep you busy for a while?"

"Absolutely, and thank you." Charles was wondering how to broach another subject without seeming ungrateful. He decided that oblique angles were best. "After Louis died, did Mallory keep any of those old westerns?"

"No!" Riker dropped the pouch on the floor, then bent down to retrieve it.

"What a pity." Charles faced the wall and studied a diagram of the murder victim's apartment. "I wanted to read the books, maybe figure out what Louis saw in them. I suppose I can track down other copies, but that—"

"No, you can't." Riker turned his back on Charles to pin up the full-color photograph of a gutted woman on a dissection table. "You can't get 'em anymore. Just cheap paperbacks. Nothing you'd find on a library shelf."

"That's what John Warwick said—almost the same words."

Riker spread one hand flat on the cork and slowly leaned into the wall. He bowed his head, perhaps bracing for the accusations, a litany of deceits, years of lies, his own and Louis's.

If that were true, he would wait forever.

Charles sat down at the edge of Mallory's steel desk. He waited patiently until Riker turned round to face him, and then he smiled for the man. His inadvertently foolish expression had the same relaxing effect on the detective as it had had on John Warwick. "Perhaps you could just tell me what happened in the next book?"

"Yeah, give me a second." Riker settled into a metal folding chair and remembered to exhale. He was obviously relieved, perhaps assuming that nothing more had transpired between John Warwick and a disappointed customer. "It's been a while. You remember the plot of the first book?"

Charles nodded. "A fifteen-year-old boy shot a man in the street."

"An *unarmed* man. In the next book, you find out that cowboy had a gun after all, and it was a fair fight." Riker turned his head for one furtive glance at the office door. Assured that they were alone, he continued. "The Kid took the other guy's six-shooter 'cause it was better than his old rusty one. But the sheriff never saw that second gun. The Kid had it stashed in his belt *before* Peety got to the crime scene."

Subsequently, Charles learned that the lawman had remained unaware of this exculpatory evidence—while the boy was growing into premature manhood as a fugitive.

"Now they're a year older," said Riker, "Sheriff Peety and the Kid." And it was miles too late for the boy to clear his name. "Wichita won another gunfight and killed another man."

Riker glanced at the door again, knowing that he would never hear Mallory coming up behind him. She was that quiet. He turned back to Charles and his story. "The Kid's name is no joke anymore. He's a bona fide gunslinger, a real outlaw. At the end of the first book, the sheriff runs him right off the rim of a canyon, a three-hundred-foot drop. The Kid was still in the saddle at the time. Down he goes, horse and all."

"But he survived."

"Yeah, the horse too. When the next book opens, the Kid lands in the river, and the fall knocks him out. He gets washed ashore beside his half-dead horse. An Indian girl finds him and drags him back to her village. She's his age, just sixteen. On the last page, the sheriff's chasin' Wichita again, and the girl buys the Kid some time. She throws herself under the sheriff's galloping horse." He splayed his hands to say, *You see how it works?* He tossed the leather pouch to Charles. "You and Geldorf can finish setting up the wall, okay? Play detective. Knock yourself out."

Charles's smile was brief, merely polite this time. The detective had made an interesting point, but the aspect of cliffhanger suspense did not explain why anyone would bother to read the novels twice. And young Kathy Mallory had read them again and again. Why?

The bookseller's theory of a child needing comfort from a fictional world would not hold up. Charles glanced at the surrounding shelves of dry technical journals and reference books. Mallory never read fiction. Louis Markowitz had once told him what a fight it had been to instill a sense of make-believe in his foster daughter, and ultimately he had lost that battle. To Louis's sorrow, she had remained a hardened realist throughout her childhood.

And though she had displayed an early penchant for cowboy movies, he had surmised long ago that it was largely for the companionship of Louis that the little girl had indulged the man in Saturday mornings of gunfights and cavalry charges. From what Charles knew of the early warfare between foster father and daughter, young Kathy would rather have died than admit to this need for his company. For all the years that man and child had known one another and loved one another, she had kept

Louis at a distance, never addressing him in any form but Hey Cop and Markowitz.

Charles wondered if Kathy Mallory regretted that now. He thought she might.

Lieutenant Coffey and Detective Janos looked up when Duck Boy appeared in the doorway and hovered there in respectful silence, waiting to be noticed.

Coffey motioned him into the room. "Yeah, kid, what is it?"

"Sir, I finished all my paperwork." He held a thick sheaf of papers in his hand.

"If that's the report on the warehouse—"

"No, sir. It's something Sergeant Riker requested, but I can't find him. Do you want it? Does *anybody* want it?"

The lieutenant accepted the report, briefly noted Duck Boy's other name on the first page, then dumped it into his out-basket at the edge of the desk. "Deluthe, you did good work today. But the paperwork goes to Riker and Mallory from now on." He turned to Janos. "Did they give you an address?" What his tone implied was clear: *I don't want to know where they are.*

And now his detective was writing in his notebook, saying to Deluthe, "This is where you can find them."

The younger man nodded and stared at the basket with his discarded report. "So you'd rather have *them* not read it?"

Jack Coffey leaned back in his chair and smiled. There was a brain at work here. At least, the boy had the makings of a smart mouth. And the rookie detective had earned a fair hearing. "Okay, sit down."

Ronald Deluthe settled into a chair next to Janos.

"You can report to me," said Coffey. "But I only want the gist of it, okay?"

"Yes, sir. I spoke to the mobile news crew. The other night, they were in the area following up on a lead. That's why they got to the crime scene ahead of the fire engines. They were just cruising up and down—"

Damn, a speechmaker. "What was their lead?"

"Well, this guy phoned in a tip an hour before the prostitute was hung.

The news show has a public line called *Cashtip*. But that wasn't the first call they taped. The—"

Janos leaned forward. "The station *taped* these calls? The news director only gave Mallory video. *Bastards.* So they were holding out on us." He slapped the trainee on the back. "That was real nice work, kid."

"Thank you, sir." Deluthe continued his dry recital of facts. "They had another tip for a homicide a few blocks from the crime scene, but that one was last week, and it didn't pan out."

"So let's get past that," said Coffey.

"Yes, sir. So the same guy calls back to tip them on Sparrow's murder. This time, he didn't give a name or address. He just told them to look for the smoke. Well, they didn't plan to send out their mobile unit. This guy burned them once before. But then, it turned out to be a slow news day, and they decided—" And now Deluthe must have sensed that interest was waning. His voice trailed off as he said, "Well, I guess that's the gist."

Janos put one meaty hand on Deluthe's arm. "Back up, kid. What about the first tip—the murder that *didn't* pan out?"

"That was five or six days ago. The tipster gave them a name and specific location. But when the news van got to Ms. Harper's building, the neighbors told them she was in Bermuda. Then the reporters went to the local police station, and a desk sergeant told them the same thing. He said Ms. Harper had gone to—"

"Hold it." Coffey retrieved the report from his basket. "How did a cop know where she was? Did this woman ever file a complaint?"

"I don't know, sir. I only spoke to the television people."

Detective Janos was shaking his head. "You never mentioned this to Mallory or Riker?"

"It was in my report, but I—"

"Yeah, yeah." Janos moved around behind the desk and scanned the pages, reading over the lieutenant's shoulder. "The address is there. I'll get a warrant on Harper's apartment. It's worth a look. Maybe Mallory was right about the perp going serial."

Jack Coffey pretended not to hear that. He smiled at Deluthe. "Good work. *Damn* good work. So you got the perp's voice on tape?"

"No, sir. I asked the news director for a copy, but he said that would compromise the integrity of his—"

"Janos!"

"Yeah, boss."

"Go get that tape!"

Charles stared at the old photographs taken after the body was cut down. Among Natalie Homer's few shabby possessions, all that was hopeful were the potholders, each one decked with a red bud, the promise of a rose. He had come to think of this woman, twenty years dead, in a possessive way, for Riker and Mallory showed so little interest in her. And he had developed a bond with Lars Geldorf, the lady's only champion.

"I'm not sure I follow you." The retired detective paced the length of the cork wall with the attitude of an inspector general.

"It's an homage to an old friend," said Charles Butler. "Did you know the first commander of Special Crimes Unit?"

"Lou Markowitz?" said Geldorf. "Oh, yeah, I met him once. He was on my crime scene—just stopped by to talk to my partner. Great cop. It was a goddamn pleasure to shake his hand." He turned back to the mess on the wall. "Sorry, you were saying?"

"Well, Louis's office used to have a cork wall like this one. It took me awhile to figure out his logic. You see, it emerged as he shuffled things around every day." Charles pointed to one cluster of papers held by a single tack. "The top layers have pertinent information that overrides what's underneath. You can see the progression of the case at a glance. No time wasted on bad leads and insignificant data. And there's relevance in the juxtaposition. Oh, and prioritizing. The least relevant items are on the outer edges."

"Not bad, Dr. Butler. Not bad at all."

"Call me Charles." He was entitled to a doctor's credential, in fact several of them, but his background in abnormal psychology only served as an adjunct to client evaluations. Perhaps a practicing psychologist would have predicted Mallory's reaction.

He heard no footsteps behind him and only turned around because of Riker's comment from the doorway, a soft *Jesus Christ*. The words were outside of Geldorf's hearing range. The old man kept his eyes on the cork, and Charles kept watch over Mallory. How long had she been standing there in the center of the room? She took no notice of him, and the moment was almost like stealing, for he was free to stare at her, unafraid that his tell-all face would say foolish things.

He had been working close to the wall for hours, and now he stepped back to see it from Mallory's vantage point. A frozen whirlwind of papers and pictures spiraled out from the center pastiche of crime-scene images. It was the jumble of a brain turned inside out, exposing a unique thinking process, trains of thought splashed over the wall in a starburst pattern as Louis Markowitz's mind of paper debris reached out, stretching— awakening.

Without a word, and unnoticed by Geldorf, she left the room. Riker put up one hand in the manner of a traffic cop, warning Charles not to follow her, then disappeared down the hall. A few moments later, the door in the reception area slammed shut.

Lars Geldorf called his attention to the square crime-scene photographs. "These are the originals. The blow-ups might be easier to read."

"I thought the size was unusual." The Polaroids were much smaller than the eight-by-ten pictures once pinned to the cork wall of Louis's office. Charles pointed to a photograph of the corpse hanging from a light fixture. "What's this dark area on her apron?"

"Grease. And those spots are cockroaches." Geldorf leaned down to the cardboard carton at his feet and picked up an envelope. "I had enlargements made." He pulled out a group of pictures. "Now these are grainy, but you can see the bugs better."

"Indeed." They were gigantic.

"Oh, you like bugs? I got shots of flies and maggots too." Geldorf opened another envelope, and this one contained twice as many insects, all in very sharp focus. "A medical examiner took these shots. That old bastard *loved* bugs. A drunk *and* a freak."

Charles leafed through the images. "I gather he was an amateur entomologist." None of the medical examiner's photographs included cockroaches. "It seems he preferred flies and larvae."

The fax machine rang, bringing Riker back to Mallory's office in an uncharacteristic hurry. The detective watched a sheet scroll out of the machine, then ripped it off and left the room.

"I'll be right back." Charles walked down the hall, following the sound of a one-way conversation. He found the detective in the reception area, slumped in a chair behind the antique desk and speaking into a telephone that was circa 1900.

"Oh, the warrant was easy," said Riker to the caller. "But the super didn't have keys to Harper's apartment." One leg was on the rise, then settled back to the floor; Mallory had trained him not to put his feet up on office furniture. "I'll make the calls for Heller and Slope. . . . Yeah, the locksmith just opened the place. . . . Right. Mallory's already on the way."

Riker set the ornate receiver back on its cradle, then looked past Charles to the young man who had just emerged from the office kitchen with a sandwich in hand. "Kid? You're driving. Go get your car and pull it up front. I'll be down in a minute."

The recent fax wafted from Riker's hand to the desk. Charles read the words *Guys, come home. All is forgiven. Love, Special Crimes Unit.* "Did Jack Coffey send that?"

"Naw, too affectionate for the boss. And he's still pretending Mallory doesn't work here anymore." Riker looked down at the fax. "No, I'd say this is Janos's style."

"There's been another hanging?"

The detective shrugged into the sleeves of his suit jacket. "Good guess, and keep it to yourself. Yeah, Mallory was right. We got a serial killer." He paused with one hand on the doorknob. Without turning round, he said, "Tell me something, Charles. Would you want to live in a world where all of Mallory's lies came true?"

SiX

THEY WERE EXILES NOW, LOCKED OUT OF THE ROOM. This was Heller's punishment for breaking a commandment of Forensics: Thou shalt not disturb my freaking crime scene.

The detectives' walk-through had turned into a run-through, battling fat black insects on the wing and biting back vomit all the way to a rear window that had not been dusted for prints. Now Mallory sat outside on the steps of the fire escape, keeping her partner company. The air was sweeter here, but muggy and almost too thick to breathe. The sun was hot, the day was dead calm, and cigarette smoke hung about Riker in a stale cloud.

On the other side of the locked window, most of the insects were still trapped in the apartment. Their buzzing penetrated the glass, loud and incessant. A ripe corpse had emptied its bowels postmortem, attracting every blowfly in the neighborhood and adding to the odor of putrid flesh.

Mallory looked down through the metal grate. More civilians had joined the gathering below. There was nothing to see, but New York was a theater town, and the yellow crime-scene tape was the cue to form a sidewalk gallery. Last week, the killer had probably stood on that same patch of pavement. After calling the reporters to his crime scene, he would have stayed to watch them enter this building, then leave, unimpressed with his work. "I wonder how long the perp waited for the cops to show. Hours? Days?"

"Must've driven him nuts." Riker took a drag on his cigarette. "I've got uniforms canvassing the block. We might get lucky."

No, Mallory doubted that they would turn up any witnesses who recalled a man loitering on the sidewalk. Too much time had passed between the death and the discovery of the corpse.

Riker flicked his cigarette over the rail of the fire escape. "I wonder if we'll find any more bodies, maybe a few in worse shape."

"Not likely. Janos said there were only two calls on the *Cashtip* line." And, despite the killer's telephoned confession and a reporter's visit to the local police station, Kennedy Harper's body had been left to rot for six days in the heat of August. "He must've figured the cops just weren't paying attention."

"Well, he got that part right," said Riker. "And now we know why he burned Sparrow's window shade. Hard to miss a woman hanging in full view of the street. He wanted a guaranteed audience for his second show."

Heller stood on the other side of the glass, raising the sash. "Okay, all the windows are open, and the worst of the stink is gone. You two delicate little pansies can come back inside."

Without being asked, the tenants kept their distance from the stench of the crime scene. They were gathered at the other end of a long hallway, where Ronald Deluthe questioned a man with greasy coveralls. A large cluster of keys dangled from his utility belt.

"You're the building handyman, the super?"

"Good guess, kid."

Deluthe could translate that to mean, *Who else would I be, you moron?* Not a promising beginning for his first interview of the day, but he pressed on. "So a body is rotting away for maybe a week, but you never smelled *anything?*" He paused a moment to flick a fly off his face. "No-body complained?" An army of insects walked up the walls, and some were strolling across the ceiling.

The high-pitched whine of a woman chimed in behind the detective's back. "Oh, we complained all right! You think this lazy slob would take six minutes to check it out?"

The far door opened, and Mallory stepped into the hall in time to catch the handyman demonstrating a New York gesture for love and friendship, his middle finger extended from a closed fist.

"Harper got new locks!" The man edged closer to the whining tenant so he could yell in her face, "And I got no keys for 'em! You want I should break down her damn door?"

At the other end of the hall, Mallory called out to Deluthe, "Chase down the locksmith. Find out when he was here."

"Oh, I can tell you that." The handyman's keys jangled as he turned to flash a lewd grin at the pretty detective. "It was two weeks ago. I watched him do the work." His eyes undressed Mallory layer by layer, removing her blazer, her T-shirt, her bra.

And now *he* was the focus of *her* attention. "Was Kennedy Harper home that day?"

"Yeah." His eyes traveled all over her body. "So?"

The detective's long legs were encased in blue jeans, but, in the handy-man's eyes, they were naked. He looked up, suddenly startled. She was moving toward him with long strides and swinging a camera from its strap like a weapon.

Ronald Deluthe wondered if she was only pissed off, or had he missed something—again.

Mallory stood toe-to-toe with the man in coveralls. "You had keys to the other locks." This was an accusation.

"Sure. I got keys for the whole building."

That was so obvious. The buckle on the man's utility belt sagged from the weight of his keys, each one tagged with an apartment number. And now Deluthe waited for some caustic comment from the witness, but the handyman kept a respectful silence, for Mallory stood with one hand on her hip, exposing the shoulder holster and a very large gun. Her eyes were even more intimidating. Did she ever blink? She took two quick steps toward the handyman, who had nowhere to go but flat up against the wall.

"Why don't you have the new keys? You were here with the locksmith. Harper was home that day."

"I *asked* for 'em. She wouldn't give 'em to me."

Mallory looked down at the cluster of tags and metal hanging in front of the man's crotch. He squirmed when she reached for it.

"You've still got the old ones." Mallory stared at the key tag for apartment 4B. "You had access *before* she changed the locks."

"And she had no problem with that." He was a model citizen now, eager to help and talking fast. "Five years and no complaints. Then one day, out of the blue, I'm a suspicious character. She can't trust me with her damn keys. Go figure." He turned to Deluthe. "Don't write that down, kid."

Deluthe folded his notebook into a pocket, then took out his Miranda card to read the prime suspect his rights. "You have the right to remain—"

"What are you doing?" Mallory took his card away, then handed him the camera. "We're done with this man. Go outside and take pictures."

Deluthe nodded. He was growing accustomed to humiliation and busywork. The killer had no way to know that the body had been discovered, not this time. He would not be among the onlookers. This was Mallory's way of telling him, once again, to get lost.

Riker stood near the kitchenette, where the odor was strongest. He stared at the jar of dead flies on the floor, then counted exactly two dozen saucers, each one containing the melted remnants of a red candle. They formed a perfect circle, and at the center lay Kennedy Harper's remains. She had a noose around her neck, and the double knot was the same as Sparrow's, but this woman had not been found hanging. The light fixture had come loose, and the body had crashed to the floor long before the police arrived. A broken bulb and a shattered white globe lay close to a nest of wires pulled down from the hole in the ceiling. The corpse at his feet was bloated with gas, and the face was partially concealed by shards of broken plaster. Only one eye, clotted with white dust, was visible. It had retracted into its socket.

Or the maggots had eaten it.

Riker turned away, wondering if this woman had been as pretty as Sparrow. He hunkered down on the floor in front of the kitchenette sink and picked up her wallet with his gloved hand. Opening it, he stared at the photograph on her driver's license. Yes, she had been very pretty, but Kennedy Harper had borne no resemblance to Sparrow beyond the hacked-off hair of another scalping. He set the wallet on the floor, positioned as he had found it among the spilled contents of a purse. He moved to one side to allow a crime-scene technician room to dust the jar of dead, dry flies. Even before the man shook his head, Riker knew there would be no fingerprints.

The detective looked up to see Heller standing by the door with a uniformed officer and signing a receipt for an armload of garments in clear plastic bags. After ripping the plastic away from one hanger, the criminalist held up a pale green blouse and motioned to Riker. "You might wanna look at this." Heller turned the blouse around to display a large faded *X* on the back. Affixed to this stain was the dry cleaner's We're-so-sorry sticker.

"I've seen this mark before," said Heller, "on a shirt I found wadded up under Sparrow's sink. She used hers for a cleaning rag."

"So it's not a random killing." Mallory joined them over the body. "We've got a stalker."

"Yeah," said Riker. The *X* on the blouse worked nicely with her theory on the new locks installed a week before the murder. "He sees the women on the street. Then he marks their shirts to make it easier to follow them home in a crowd—like tagging animals in the wild." Unlike Kennedy Harper, Sparrow had not complained about the stalking, the terror. Prostitutes were not given the same service as human beings.

Sparrow, why didn't you come to me?

The East Side lieutenant had put in a personal appearance instead of sending one of his minions to the crime scene, and Mallory saw this as an admission of guilt for the mistakes made on his watch.

"I brought her package." Lieutenant Loman spoke only to Riker, pretending that Mallory was not in the room. "The complaints started a few weeks ago. Some pervert was following the girl."

After accepting the envelope, Riker pulled out four papers encased in plastic, each bearing the same brief message. Loman was tense, almost standing at attention, and Mallory wondered if this was a habit from the days when Riker had held the rank of captain.

"Kennedy found those notes in her pockets." Loman mopped his bald head and brow with a handkerchief. "Pretty harmless stuff."

Riker responded with a noncommittal nod, then scanned the paperwork attached to the evidence bags.

The lieutenant stared at the stained green blouse draped over the detective's arm. "She brought that into the station house. She said the perp did it on the subway. You should find a T-shirt marked up the same way. And the notes—every time she found one in her pocket, she'd been in a crowd of people—the subway, a store. That's why Kennedy never got a good look at the guy."

Mallory noted the use of the victim's first name. It was common for homicide detectives to speak of the dead with this familiarity; but Loman's squad had only known Kennedy Harper as a living woman, one civilian complainant out of thousands. She stared at the man in silent accusation.

You turned that woman into a pet, didn't you?

The lieutenant avoided Mallory's eyes while he waited for Riker to say *something*—anything. "She never saw the perp's face. What could we do?"

"Did you put an extra patrol on this street?"

And now the lieutenant was forced to acknowledge Mallory, for Riker looked up from his reading, and he was also showing interest in her question.

"No," said Loman. "It was that damn virus. The uniforms were spread too thin for extra patrols."

Mallory only shook her head. It would be gross insubordination to call him a liar out loud. Kennedy Harper was dead before the virus had grown to an epidemic in this part of town. And Loman's men had found lots of time to visit with pretty Kennedy Harper. She had even come to the attention of the squad's commander.

Riker selected one piece of paper with dried blood on it and held it up to the lieutenant's eyes.

It was a moment before Loman spoke. "That was the last note. The perp used a hatpin to nail it into the back of her neck. Kennedy walked into the station house—dripping blood—and the note was still staked to her skin."

Mallory knew there was only one reason for a victim to go to that extreme. It was the woman's plea for them to take her seriously—because they never had before.

Riker read the bloodied note aloud, "'I can touch you any time I want.'"

"That was the day she snapped," said Loman. "Told us she was leaving town. Well, we thought that was a real good idea. One of my men got her some coffee and a first-aid kit. I made her plane reservation for Bermuda."

How kind of you, how helpful.

"Did you do anything else for her?"

"Yes!" Loman turned to Mallory, and he was on the offensive now. "The girl was in shock. I got a police escort to take her to the hospital. And then they drove her back home. After that, all she had to do was take a cab to the airport."

You left her alone.

Mallory edged toward the lieutenant. "There was no follow-up?"

"No! What the hell for? As far as we knew, she was on the way to Bermuda."

Chief Medical Examiner Edward Slope had arrived to give this case his personal attention. He knelt on the floor and rolled the corpse to expose a ruined face for the police photographer.

"Well, this is different," said Heller, and everyone in the room turned to look at the dead woman. Flies crawled among the strands of long blond hair that trailed from her mouth. The rope's double knot had snagged on her teeth and pried her mouth open, spreading the lips in a death's head grin. "Looks like she almost got away."

Only Mallory was watching Lieutenant Loman's reaction. His face was pale, and his mouth was slack. This veteran of a thousand crime scenes was about to be sick. He was most vulnerable now, and she stepped closer, her shoulder touching his. "So then, the reporters stopped by with their murder tip . . . and still no follow-up? *Sir?*"

"My men didn't know about that." Again, he spoke only to Riker. "The desk sergeant never mentioned any reporters. As far as he was concerned, the lady was in Bermuda. He was going off duty, and it wasn't worth his time to walk up a damn flight of stairs and talk to us. I promise you, his head's gonna roll."

Ah, too late.

Mallory perused the folder. "We need more men to work this case."

"Well, now you guys got two more. Just tell me—"

"Three," said Riker. "Make it three. You came up one short the last time you promised her some help."

"You got it," said the lieutenant. "We're finished?"

Riker nodded, giving a man who outranked him permission to leave. Loman turned on his heel and started across the room. Mallory wondered if he would make it to the street before he vomited.

Dr. Slope supervised the removal of the body, then remained behind to study a drawing of the apartment floor plan. Heller squatted next to the victim's fallen purse and began to draw another diagram on his sketch pad, noting all the scattered items and their positions.

Mallory knelt beside him and studied the objects around the purse. "Looks like a struggle."

"No." Heller drew black crayon circles around the fallen items. "It's a nice tight pattern. These things just fell out when she dropped her purse. The way I see it, she was standing here when something made her jump."

Riker stared at the front door. "I count three locks and a chain, but no sign of a break-in. This woman was nervous as hell. I don't see her opening the door for a stranger."

"Maybe we're looking for a cop," said Mallory.

"I wouldn't rule it out." Heller pulled on a new pair of gloves. "But I don't think the door was locked when the perp arrived. This woman was planning a long trip, so she ran some errands after the cops brought her home." He picked up a packet of fallen traveler's checks. "A trip to the bank, right?" Next, he pulled a bottle of pills from a small pharmacy bag. "And she refilled this prescription. But she forgot the receipt for the dry cleaner. So she came back to get it."

Riker pulled out his cigarettes. "Is this a guess or—"

"It's a fact," said Heller. "The dry cleaner said she dumped out her purse to look for the receipt. But she'd left it at home. I found it on the counter next to the sink. Now remember, she's got a plane to catch. She plans to grab that receipt and run right out again. So she doesn't lock the door this time." Heller rose to his feet. "She's standing here, reaching for it, when the perp startles her, and she drops her purse. I say he walked in right behind her."

Click.

Ronald Deluthe snapped pictures of civilians on the sidewalk. He had quickly divided the crowd into categories. The out-of-towners were the people disguised as the Statue of Liberty. Their spiked crowns of green foam rubber were purchases from a street vendor working the crowd with a carton of souvenirs. The visitors smiled as they posed for the camera, then took their own pictures of the young detective with exotic bright yellow hair. He had become a tourist attraction.

All the blasé faces belonged to the natives who were almost bored by murder. And lots of them fit Miss Emelda's loose description of the hangman. T-shirts and jeans were the uniform of this neighborhood, and five of the men wore baseball caps.

Click, click.

The freelance reporters were easy to spot. They were the ones hustling every cop in uniform. The pros with real media jobs were disgorged from vans with network logos. Their technicians were setting up pole lights and carrying cameras. A brunette with a microphone was headed his way. She ignored the officers standing behind the blue sawhorses. The woman only had eyes for Deluthe as she worked her way around the semicircle of barricades—so she could be close to him.

She was pretty. He took her picture.

Click.

The reporter smiled for him.

Click, click, click, click.

She called out to him—a siren song, "It's a murder, right?"

"No comment," he said. This time, the crime scene was under tight control. Even the uniformed officers could not give any helpful information to reporters, however pretty they might be.

Deluthe was out of film and praying that Mallory and Riker would not show up before Officer Waller got back from the store.

He was saved. The uniformed policeman was fast approaching, elbowing his way through the crowd. Perfect timing. There *was* a God. Waller handed over the backup film, and Deluthe opened the camera to remove the used roll.

A face in the crowd distracted him. The spectator was staring up at a high window while everyone else watched the front door. The young detective looked up at Kennedy Harper's fourth-floor apartment. All he could see was blue sky reflected on glass. He reloaded the camera, but before he could snap a picture, his subject slung a gray canvas bag over one shoulder and backed up into the crowd. The bag looked like one in the trunk of Deluthe's car, where he kept a change of clothes for a baseball game in Central Park.

And now he remembered to shoot the man.

Click.

Shit.

He had only caught the back of the civilian's head turning away from the camera. Deluthe wondered if he should chase the man down. But what pretext could he use? *Excuse me, sir. You looked up instead of down.* That scene might not play half as well as his attempted arrest of the building handyman.

The odd spectator was forgotten when Deluthe spied a familiar face behind the barricades. It was the fireman who had left the prostitute hanging at the last crime scene. Gary Zappata's eyes were fixed on the door to Kennedy Harper's building.

Waiting for what?

Click.

Detective Mallory stepped out on the sidewalk, followed by her partner. Zappata's angry eyes locked onto Sergeant Riker.

Click.

The detectives would not give his opinion any credence, but they had to believe a picture. Zappata clearly wanted Riker dead.

Mallory walked up to Deluthe, giving him no time to explain his theory on the fireman. She was saying, *ordering*, "Get out your notebook."

Deluthe complied, and now his pencil hovered over a clean page.

"Get your film developed," she said. "And don't take any grief. You tell the techs you want it *now*. Go back to Special Crimes and clear a section of wall in the incident room. Pin up this paperwork." She handed him a large manila folder. "You'll find some still shots of news film on my desk. Compare the faces to the ones you shot in this crowd. Meet Riker back here when you're done. He'll give you another list. *Run.*"

No baseball game tonight.

Detective Janos was a human tank, physically and psychologically. Nothing stopped him. However, if Lieutenant Coffey had sent him out in search of the Holy Grail, he would have been back with it long before now. The more difficult errand had been securing a voice recording for the tip line of a local news program.

He was exhausted.

The television people had called him *Babe*, then misused the word *synergy* twice in five minutes, saying nothing intelligible for another twenty minutes of wasted time. Everyone on the news staff had labored under the whacked impression that the Constitution of the United States allowed them, even encouraged them, to conceal evidence of murder.

Yet Janos had not killed any of these people. That was not his way. He had merely loomed over the news director, one hand outstretched, saying, "Give me the tape."

Another member of the staff, the anchorwoman, had expounded on freedom of the press, making it clear that she had never read the pertinent passage of First Amendment rights.

And Janos had replied, "Give me the tape."

Half an hour had passed by before the network attorney arrived to yell at his clients, "Give him the tape, you fucking *idiots!*"

More time had been spent convincing an overworked support technician at One Police Plaza that he could not simply leave the tape and go; he needed a copy for his lieutenant. Mere looming had done the trick with the small man in the lab coat.

And now, finally, Janos carried his hard-won trophy down the hall to the incident room. He opened the door and paused on the threshold, taking a moment to admire a crude flat scarecrow nailed to the rear wall. The boys had been busy while he was away.

He looked down at a gray canvas bag near the baseboard. A pair of wadded gym socks had been dropped on the floor, apparently rejected as feet for the image on the wall. Janos agreed with this aesthetic decision—less was more. In the space below a tacked-up baseball cap was a photograph showing the back of a man's head; this was in keeping with Miss Emelda's sighting of a suspicious character in her tree, a man without a face. Beneath this picture, a T-shirt had been spread out and pinned to the cork. Sturdy nails supported a pair of blue jeans to fill out the lower half of the body. Crime-scene gloves were positioned where the effigy's hands would be, and a nail had been driven into one latex palm to hold the strap of a cheap instant camera, yet another detail from Miss Emelda's description.

Interesting.

However, the truly original touch was a halo of fat black flies impaled around the scarecrow's cap. One was a large horsefly speared on a long pin, but still alive, twitching, buzzing—

At the sound of footsteps, Janos turned around to see the yellow-haired youngster from Lieutenant Loman's squad. Judging by the slim build, Janos assumed that the scarecrow's clothing belonged to this detective. And there was more damning evidence: Ronald Deluthe's face was flushed red with sudden guilt—perhaps because he carried a living, squirming fly impaled on a hatpin.

"Deluthe, you're very young to be this jaded." Janos smiled at the blushing whiteshield, who now realized that this was a compliment and resumed breathing.

This meeting place had been chosen to increase the prostitute's anxiety, but Daisy was too stoned to appreciate the decor of framed photographs and citations that screamed, *This is a cop bar!* Detective Mallory kept fifteen feet of mahogany and five drinking men between herself and the aging whore with electric-red hair.

The skeletal woman perched on the edge of her stool, one eye cocked on the door. Riker was ten minutes late, and the woman would not wait for him much longer. Mallory put on her sunglasses when the hooker glanced in her direction, though it was doubtful she would be recognized; they had both changed so much. Kathy the child had grown into a woman, and Daisy the whore had become a superannuated corpse.

In the old days, this redhead had been a long-haired blonde who had shared heroin with Sparrow. They had done everything together. Mallory had a childhood memory of the two prostitutes vomiting in the same toilet bowl.

Daisy's bright red mouth formed a suggestive smile for a male customer. The man turned to catch the attention of the bartender, another recent redhead, though, unlike Daisy's color, Peg Baily's was a shade found in nature. Also, Baily was softly rounded, glowing with good health, and in her younger days, she had been a decorated police officer.

The customer arched one eyebrow to ask why a sickly hooker had been allowed to stay so long. Tradition demanded that Daisy be kicked into the street, literally, with the press of a boot on her backside. Peg Baily held up two fingers to let him know that the whore was on the way out in just a few minutes.

Trouble.

This was a new location for the bar. Perhaps it was a coincidence that Baily had moved her business to Riker's neighborhood, but Mallory thought otherwise.

The bartender looked up at the clock on the wall, then turned to the detective. "Your partner's not gonna show, kid. I'm tossing that hooker out of here right now."

A whore wasting from AIDS was bad for trade.

Mallory turned to the window—and inspiration. The former Angie Riker was opening the door to a barber shop across the street. Riker's ex-wife was leading a parade of four teenage boys, the brood of her second husband. Mallory wondered if it was pure accident that her partner had set this time for the interview. Or was he still keeping close tabs on Angie?

The bartender rapped the mahogany to get Mallory's attention, saying, "Time's up, kid."

"Quick question, Baily? You knew Riker when he was married, didn't you?"

"You *know* I did." Peg Baily's eyes were suddenly unfriendly, silently asking, *What are you up to?* "I was his partner. You know that too. What's this—"

"How come you never told him his wife was playing around behind his back?" As a child, Mallory had learned many things by listening in on her foster parents' late-night conversations. "You knew Angie was a slut. But even after the divorce, you never told Riker. He still doesn't know you held out on—"

"You wouldn't be threatening me, would you?" Baily leaned on the bar. "I wouldn't like that, kid. And if you say one word to him, I'll mess your face up so bad."

Mallory smiled, for she was younger, faster, and had no healthy sense of fear. Oh, and she was the one with the gun.

Riker had arrived. He stepped out of the car at the curb and watched Deluthe drive off in search of a parking space.

The two women fell into an uneasy silence. The bar's lighting was lowkey. Mallory and Baily had no worry of being caught in an act of voyeurism, for Riker was standing in bright sunlight, and the plate glass would act as a mirror. He was slowly turning round, responding to Angie, who hailed him with waving arms. His ex-wife left her children on the curb and crossed the street, dodging traffic and mouthing a happy *Hello!* As the former Mrs. Riker drew closer, Mallory realized that Peg Baily's new hair color was the exact same shade of carrot red.

Riker faced the window again, pretending interest in the posted hours of his favorite bar as his ex-wife came up behind him. Angie was still a pretty woman, but he would not look at her. She stood beside him, cheerful and chattering, probably asking how he had been—as if they did not see each other all the time. His own apartment was only a block away from hers. However, it was enough that Riker could be near this woman, that he could see her face every single day; he never spoke to Angie anymore—he never would again. It was just too hard on him.

The woman put one hand on her ex-husband's sleeve.

Peg Baily's hands curled into fists.

Riker lost his slouch and stood up straight, rigid and stone silent. He stared at the window, seeing nothing, hearing nothing. Angie's shrug said, *No hard feelings.* Then, giving up on him, she crossed back to the other side of the street.

Not wanting to witness any more of this, Peg Baily walked off to fetch a glass of club soda for her ex-partner, who never drank on duty. Mallory continued to watch the man lingering on the sidewalk, staring at his shoes and collecting his sorry wits. She was now convinced that there had been no affair between Riker and Sparrow. He was still in love with his ex. And why would he take up with a whore when Peg Baily was still waiting for her own turn?

He entered the bar and waved to Baily. She started to slide his soda down the bar when he put up one hand to stop her, then ordered cheap bourbon.

More trouble.

He loosened his tie as he sat down beside Daisy, and the hooker promptly ordered a champagne cocktail.

Riker was working on his second shot of bourbon as he listened to the prostitute's slow drawl, so like Sparrow's. Years ago, the hookers had been the best of friends, two small-town southern girls against the city. So far, the interview had turned up nothing useful, and now he stirred up a memory of old times. "Remember that little blond girl who used to run with Sparrow?"

"Wasn't just Sparrow. That kid used to work a battalion of whores." Daisy signaled Baily for another champagne cocktail.

"What was her name?"

"Oh, darlin', she had a lotta names. One hooker called her the Flyin' Flea, and Sparrow called her Baby."

"And you?"

"Hey Kid—that's what I called her. First time I ever saw her was in a crackhouse." The hooker paused to inhale her drink. "She came in lookin' for Sparrow. What a dirty little face. And those eyes—tiny green fires, but so *cold*. Nothin' warm and cuddly 'bout *that* little girl. And *mean?* Oh, darlin', you got no idea. Ah, but her face—I saw it when it was clean. God don't make angels that pretty. But I don't mean to say that God made her. I don't blaspheme. My mama raised me better."

This was going to take awhile. Riker had no idea how Daisy made a living on the city streets where time was money. She hailed from a more temperate climate, where customers and cops could wait around all day for a whore to finish a thought.

"So, like I was saying, I'm in this crackhouse, and I hear a noise in the dark. At first, all I see is her eyes—cold, empty. *Scary* eyes. That little girl had no soul. She comes up to me and hands me a cigarette case—*real* silver. And she gives me this ratty old book with cowboys on the cover. Not *my* taste. Well, she swipes away the needles and trash so she can sit down beside me. Then she kicks out one little foot to make the rats run. And she says, 'Read me a story.' She don't say please, nothin' like that. Just says, 'Read me a story,' like that's my job in life."

"So the kid couldn't read?"

"Oh, yeah, she could," said Daisy. "Better'n me. She helped me with the hard words. But that night—that first time—she lays her head down in my lap and waits for her story to begin. So I read till she fell asleep. Then I sat up all night long to keep the rats away from her. I had to, don't you see?"

Riker nodded. "You were her mother that night."

"Other nights it was other whores—when she couldn't find Sparrow."

Riker looked up from his drink. Mallory sat at the other end of the bar. If she lowered the dark glasses, would Daisy recognize her? Not likely, but the long green slants of her eyes had never changed. They might spook a whore who believed in ghosts.

"So you looked after the kid," said Riker.

"Sometimes," said Daisy. "Well, she could never count on Sparrow. That junkie whore was always gettin' stoned and wakin' up in strange places. Lucky the kid knew how to fend for herself."

Yeah, what a lucky little girl.

Sometimes Kathy had lived out of garbage cans, finding a cold supper there. "You remember the day Sparrow got stabbed?"

"Oh, darlin', I'll never forget. I went to the hospital to visit. The kid was there, too. Poor baby, she fell asleep sittin' bolt upright on the edge of Sparrow's bed. Too tired to lie down or even fall down. That's the last time I saw the kid alive."

"Remember anything else? Did Sparrow say who stabbed her?"

The hooker was wary now.

"Hey," said Riker, "I don't need a witness. That stabbing is old history. This is a personal thing, okay?" A twenty-dollar bill slid across the bar. "Do you know who stabbed her?"

"I'd be guessin'." The prostitute's hand closed over the money. "Only *guessin'*—hear me? Sparrow might've mentioned Frankie D. You remember that twisted little bastard?"

Riker nodded. Frankie Delight had been that rare drug dealer who was not strictly cash and carry. "So Sparrow was trading skin for drugs?"

"No, she'd never do that freak for a fix. I don't care how bad she was hurtin'. No, darlin', she was tradin' brand-new VCRs. Still in the cartons. One of Tall Sally's jobs went wrong and—"

"I know that story," said Riker. And ten-year-old Kathy Mallory would have been on the stealing end of that arrangement.

The great VCR heist.

He remembered the report from Robbery Division. A patrolman's log had mentioned sighting suspicious persons in the vicinity of the crime, among them a little blond girl with green eyes. Lou Markowitz had read him the details, then said, in a tone between awe and pride, "The kid robbed a damn *truck.*"

Daisy nudged Riker's arm to call him back to the world, asking, "Whatever happened to Frankie?"

Riker had never been certain until now. "I heard he left town." One could say that the dead were way out of town. "So, Daisy, what's Sparrow been up to? You guys keep in touch?" He doubted that this whore read the papers, and her television set would have been pawned long ago to buy drugs.

"No, we don't talk no more." She stared at the bottom of her glass. "Not for a long time. But I did hear a rumor today. Some bitch told me that Sparrow was the hooker who got herself strung up last night. Well, I knew that wasn't true. My Sparrow got clean—kicked them drugs. And she stopped liftin' her skirt for a livin'. That was years ago, darlin'. *Years* ago."

He gave her another ten dollars. She snatched it from his hand, then climbed down from her barstool and backed up all the way to the door, eyes trained on Peg Baily. Daisy whirled around and fled rather than risk an injury by staying a second too long.

Riker ambled toward the end of the bar, where his partner waited, attracting stares from every man in the room. He sat down beside her. "Well, that was a waste of time. We're not gonna find a stalker with hookers. Sparrow got out of the life years ago."

Mallory the unbeliever shook her head. She would not seriously consider any good thing said about Sparrow.

Once a whore, always a whore?

"How did it go with the theater group?"

"That was a dead end," said Mallory. "Sparrow was a last-minute sub-stitute in the play. None of those people met her before the rehearsal. And that was the day she was hung."

"Well, somebody got her that job. We might find a tie between Spar-row and Kennedy Harper."

"No, Riker. This wasn't a Broadway production. She answered an ad posted on a supermarket bulletin board. The director gave her the part be-cause she showed up in costume and knew all the lines."

Riker tried to imagine Sparrow memorizing Chekhov. He drained his shot glass and laid his money on the bar. "So what's next? Morgue time?"

"No. Slope's working on a fresher corpse right now."

"Okay," said Riker. "A local cop, Waller, looked over your videotape. He gave Janos a name and address for the man in the T-shirt and jeans. You know that big church on Avenue B?"

"A priest?"

"You got it." Riker stared at his empty glass, turning it over in his hands. "If you want off this case, I can work it alone."

"No." She gathered up her car keys, then left an obscene tip on the bar. "I'll see it through."

The East Village park was full of music, rock and rap, Hispanic and soul. It poured out of radios and CD players. Some youngsters sported earphones, and Riker had to guess their songs by the cadence of their struts, their bounces and glides.

At the heart of Tompkins Square was a stellar memory of the night his father had thrown him out of the house—an elegant solution to the prob-lem of a teenager's dissident music. Young Riker had waged a showdown in the old band shell, the spot claimed by another boy, whose music had been a self-portrait, cool and dark, a jazz riff played on a clarinet. Riker had shot back a volley of rock 'n' roll, louder and longer. And they had dueled awhile before laying down their instruments.

After a bloody fight, each boy had won his cuts and bruises. And after too many beers, they had ended the night blind drunk, arms wrapped round each other for support, one musically discordant creature in a four-legged stagger walk.

How he had loved those days.

Startled pigeons flew up in the wake of a passing boom box. Riker put out his cigarette and returned to the church, where he discovered that Mallory's plan to torture a priest had somehow gone awry.

The church was no cathedral, but it held all the trappings of stained-glass windows, a giant crucifix and rows of votive candles blazing at the feet of plaster saints.

Mallory had laid out twenty dollars for a disposable camera just to rattle the priest, and the man's laughter was a disappointment. He *liked* the idea of taking part in a photo lineup of murder suspects. "No, don't smile, Father," she said. "So Sparrow belonged to your parish?"

"Now how did you manage to make that sound like a guilty thing?"

Father Rose was having entirely too much fun sparring with her in this novel departure from a priest's workday. She doubted that he would make her shortlist for a double hanging. She glanced at Riker, who sprawled in the front pew, waiting to play his role of the easygoing policeman, everybody's friend.

Mallory lowered the camera so the priest could see her slow grin. She had a repertoire of smiles, and this one made people nervous. "A witness can place you at the crime scene last night."

"Yes, there was quite a crowd—even before the fire engine showed up." The priest turned to the side. "Want a profile?" He froze in position, waiting for the flash. "Your witness is an old woman. Am I right? *Very* thick glasses? She was sitting in the window across the street, watching the whole show and—"

"A *show?* Is that how you saw it, Father?" She shot him again. "Why were you at the crime scene? Forget something?"

"So I *am* a suspect." He seemed almost flattered.

"You were out of uniform last night."

"I leave the collar home when I work at the neighborhood clinic. I donate my time three nights a week. Mostly bandaging cuts, dispensing aspirins—that kind of thing."

She looked up from the camera so he would have no trouble reading distrust in her eyes. "I want names. Who can vouch for your time—say an hour before the fire?"

"The nurse who runs the clinic. We were leaving together when we heard the fire engines. Is this—"

"When did you talk to Sparrow last?"

"Sunday, but I didn't—"

"Did she mention any enemies? Somebody out to get her?"

The priest shook his head.

"No? You don't know or you won't say? Want to lawyer up, Father? You have the right to an attorney during—"

"That's *enough*, Mallory." Riker rose from the pew, acting the part of an annoyed superior. "Go check out his story."

She walked down the altar steps, passing her partner as he climbed upward in dead silence. Riker was already departing from the script. There was nothing amiable in his face as he squared off in front of the priest. Mallory stayed to watch.

"I know you tried to get access to that crime scene," said Riker. "My witness is no old lady. He's a big hairy fireman."

"Yes, he must be the one who told me Sparrow was dead. Well, she's Catholic. She was entitled to last rites."

"The fireman said you knew her name before the cops identified her. You *knew* that was her apartment. So you've got what—two hundred people in your parish?"

Father Rose wore a slightly pained expression. He understood that this was a test. "I recognized her face when—"

"So you had a good view of the *show*, right? Front row—close to the window. Notice anything unusual?"

"The hair jammed in her mouth?" The priest was rallying, almost smug. "No, too obvious. That made headlines, didn't it?" He folded his arms. "You must mean the candles. I don't recall any mention of them in the newspaper." Father Rose waved to a nearby alcove that housed a plaster saint and a few small flames burning among tiers of candles. "Like those. Yes, I saw them in the water." His smile was wider now. "But Sparrow's were red. *Mine* are white."

So Father Rose had failed to notice a thousand dead flies spread on the water. At least one crime-scene detail was secure.

The priest was smiling, triumphant.

"Having fun, Father?" Riker moved closer, forcing the other man to backstep. "Sparrow is a friend of mine, and I'm not enjoying this much. So do me a favor and stop *grinning* at me."

Father Rose's head snapped back, as if the detective had sucker-punched him—and he had. Riker backed off a few paces to reward the priest's more somber attitude. "Maybe we have a religious connection. How would you explain all those candles?"

"Well, they weren't for ambiance." And lest Riker take this for humor, the priest hurried the rest of his words. "All the lights were on in Sparrow's apartment before the firemen broke the—"

"Why do *you* light candles?"

"Ritual." The man was not so sure of himself anymore. "Burnt offerings. A light in the darkness. Hope?" This last word waned to a whisper as he watched the detective descend the stairs.

Riker's back was turned to the priest when he asked, "Did you know Sparrow was a prostitute?"

Mallory watched the priest's stunned reaction. He opened and closed his mouth like an air-drowned fish. And she knew he could tell them nothing more, not even if he violated every secret of the confessional. Sparrow had never confided in him. The two detectives walked down the wide center aisle, then paused at the sound of running footsteps.

The priest called out, "Wait!" He hurried from statue to statue, lighting all the wicks. "Just another minute. *Please.*" He lit every candle on the altar as well. "I'm sorry." The priest walked toward Riker. "*So* sorry. Sparrow is a special person to me." His face showed deep contrition. "She has a good heart—better than most. She's better than she knows."

Riker nodded and cracked a smile, raising his opinion of this man who could admire a whore.

"And I was wrong about the ambiance," said the priest. "Maybe that *is* your angle. Candles make for great theater—even when all the electricity is turned on. Look around you."

Candles flickered beneath the crucifix. The man on the cross writhed in an illusion of lights. And all along the wall, flames beneath the other figures created animation, action—actors.

"Thank you, Father." And Mallory meant that. His idea was worth consideration, but from a different angle. What if religious candles had the same significance as a jar of dead flies?

SEVEN

AUTOPSY—*AUTOPSIA*—SEEING WITH ONE'S EYES.

When Mallory was a child, she had learned her essential Latin from Chief Medical Examiner Edward Slope.

A refrigerator and sinks gave the doctor's dissection room the character of a large kitchen. Long tables were laid with tools for slicing and dicing meat. A small metal platform the size of a butcher block held intestines in a shallow tray, and another body part lay in the bed of a hanging scale. Dr. Slope called out the weight, then switched off his recorder. "Hello, Kathy."

"Mallory," she said, correcting him as she always did. She approached the steel table and looked down at the gutted remains of a woman her own age. A wide red cavity ran from the breast bone to a mound of blond pubic hair, and the smell of chlorine mingled with the reek of meat gone bad.

Hoc es corpus. This is the body.

Today she had missed these words that began every autopsy, but now she watched the process in reverse. A few organs had been set aside. The parts that would be buried with Kennedy Harper were being returned to her hollowed-out corpse. Mallory leaned down for a closer examination of small holes in the cadaver's flesh. "What's this? It looks like a shotgun splatter."

"That's from the maggots exiting the dried-out skin." He picked up his magnifying glass and held it on the area above the collar bone. "You see? The rims of the holes are turned out." One bloody, gloved hand pointed to ravaged skin at the cadaver's throat. "Now this is more interesting. The rope did lots of damage here, but the killer wasn't responsible for it." He watched her face and waited for the student to ask the master, *Why not?*

If she encouraged him in this old game, it would take forever to glean a few simple facts. The doctor was determined to continue her education, and he was too fond of long lessons. So she waited him out, arms folded, blinking only once before he gave in.

"The damage was self-inflicted." He turned his eyes down to the work of coiling the large intestine. "This woman was very cool under pressure."

That sounded like another contradiction, but she recognized an old logic trap. *No, I'm not going to ask.*

As Dr. Slope finished stitching skin to close the gaping wound, he shifted his tactics, offering Mallory a bizarre piece of candy. "You'll *never* attend another autopsy like this one." And with this hook, he led her over to the steel counter by the refrigerator, where he wadded his bloody surgeon's gown and tossed it into a barrel with his gloves.

"I've seen a lot of hanging victims, mostly suicides, but nothing like this." He sorted through a group of photographs. "Normally, I find a ligature mark at the back of the neck where the knot is." He selected a picture of the victim's face, taken when the rope was still caught between her teeth. "But this woman was facing the knot. Now I never expect a classic hangman's noose. It's usually a slip knot."

"I *know.*" She kept her sarcasm to one syllable, a subtle reminder that she had been present when the noose was removed. "This one was a double knot. Heller already—"

"And it didn't close off the carotid artery. So Miss Harper didn't black out or succumb to euphoria."

"Transient cerebral hypoxia," said Mallory.

"You *do* pay attention." Dr. Slope graced her with a half smile as he unfolded a diagram of the crime scene. "Heller assisted on this part. We choreographed the last minutes of her life like a ballet." The doctor pointed to the roughly sketched countertop by the kitchen sink. "This is where Heller's forensic team found footprints and partials. Note the distance to the ceiling light." His finger moved across the paper to a drawn circle. "That's where she was left hanging, playing dead." He looked up at Mallory. "Miss Harper was still alive when the killer left the scene. First, she kicked off her sandals. We found them under the body. When she raised her leg, she could just barely reach the counter with one toe. So she pushed off to make her body swing away and back again."

The doctor laid out photographs of the Formica surface covered with Heller's black dust. One close-up showed a partial footprint layered over the mark of a toe. "Here you've got more of the foot," said Slope. "Her body swings in a wider arc each time she pushes off. Finally, she lands both feet on the countertop. Now her weight is supported at two points—feet on the counter, neck in the noose. See here?" He pointed to a shot of two full footprints on the Formica beside the sink. "Both soles are flat. Now she has the leverage to rotate her body until she's facing the knot. That gives her an inch of air between her throat and the noose. She worked her chin under the rope. That's when it snagged on the upper teeth. I can't tell you how long she hung there."

Patiently waiting for the cavalry to come and rescue her—just like Sparrow.

"She couldn't dislodge the rope or the hair in her mouth," said Slope. "She could've screamed—but no intelligible sounds."

The neighbors didn't come. The cops didn't come.

Dr. Slope pushed the photographs aside. "I can tell you she died six days ago, but the cause of death wasn't asphyxiation. It was heart failure." He picked up a pharmacy bottle bagged and tagged as crime-scene evidence. "I called the prescribing cardiologist. Miss Harper had a congenital heart defect—inoperable. All her life, she's been living with a time bomb in her chest."

"Good practice for a hanging," said Mallory.

"It does explain a lot, doesn't it? Twisting on the end of a rope, but no panic. And she nearly escaped."

Mallory thought of the day this woman had walked into a police station with a bloody note staked to her neck. The hanging scenario worked well with that kind of poise. But now she had two victims who were accomplished at playing dead while their hearts were beating a million times a minute. What were the odds against *that?* She turned to the medical examiner and smiled.

You wouldn't hold out on me, would you?

The doctor would never volunteer what he could not swear to in court and back up with evidence, but if he thought this was the end of the autopsy, he was dead wrong. She glanced back at the dissected woman on the other side of the room. There was cutting and there was cutting. "So I've got a perp who can't tell the living from the dead. That's *it?* That's *all* you can tell me? The hangman's just another screwup who can't find a pulse?"

Dr. Slope hesitated for a moment. He had always fancied himself a great poker player, born with a face of stone that gave up nothing in his hand. Yet Louis Markowitz had beaten him in every bluff, and everything that cop knew about poker and Slope he had passed along to his foster child. Even if she could not read the doctor's face, she knew what he was thinking: She was an ungrateful brat, and he was going to put her in her place.

The man's voice was testy, but still in the lecture mode. "You assume he believed his victim was dead. Well, *I don't.* After he strung her up, she was getting oxygen, but not enough to keep her conscious for long. So I know the killer left the scene immediately. Otherwise, there wouldn't have been time enough or strength enough for Kennedy's aerial ballet. He didn't stay to *watch* her die."

Just like Sparrow—a pattern.

A few minutes with this medical examiner was worth ten hours with any psychiatrist, for most witch doctors were light years removed from the carnage of murder. She turned her back on Slope and crossed the room to the steel table and the body of Kennedy Harper all sewn up with crude stitches—a Frankenstein scar. Mallory was striving for the sound of boredom when she asked, "What else can you tell me? Anything *useful?*"

The doctor's poker discipline was shot to hell. His face was now an easy read, waffling between surprise and indignation. He marched up to the table and confronted her across the body, firing off another contradiction. "I'd say your man's not the violent type. That may seem a bit odd—"

"Odd?"

"All right, *Kathy*—it's *insane*. But he didn't go off on either of the women. He didn't beat them or—"

"He cut off their damn hair."

"But no cuts to the flesh, no fractures from a fist. And the other one, Sparrow—she didn't have a single defensive bruise. I've seen every unspeakable act a man can commit on a woman's body." The doctor looked down at the corpse laid out on the table, the woman he so admired. "But I don't see that kind of violence here—no loss of control, no rage."

This did not square with a note staked to the neck of a living woman, and she was about to tell him that when he held up one hand to forestall any more arguments.

"I'm out of my depth," he said. "This man didn't *care* if the women lived or died. He's a walking paradox—a serial killer who's not all that interested in killing."

The murder of Kennedy Harper had taken over an entire wall of the Special Crimes incident room. Mallory posted the autopsy pictures next to Heller's crime-scene diagrams. Sparrow also had a wall to herself. The throwaway whore had become a priority case.

Rows of metal folding chairs were filling up with detectives. Four men gathered around the audio equipment and listened to the *Cashtip* recording of the killer's voice playing again and again, unwilling to believe that it did not offer more. The volume was turned up each time they heard the ambient sound.

Pssst.

One man timed it by the second hand on his watch. Mallory used a natural clock, a quirk of the brain that told her this sound occurred every twenty seconds. It reminded her of Helen Markowitz's spray starch on ironing day.

She walked to the hangman's wall and stared at a photograph of the back of a man's head. The image, crowned with a baseball cap and encircled with dead flies, was as worthless as the lame description of T-shirt and jeans played out in the clothing pinned to the cork.

Pssst.

Janos stood beside her. "So what do you think of our scarecrow?"

"Is that what we're calling him now?"

"Yeah." He turned to look around the room. "Hey, what happened to your partner?"

"He'll be back." She had kept track of all the passing minutes since Riker had slipped out of the room. After the ambush in front of Peg Baily's bar, he would not miss an opportunity for a drink today. Each up-close encounter with his ex-wife was a prelude to a binge. Her internal timepiece had moved well past his three-minute walk to a nearby watering hole.

Pssst.

Riker would down his bourbon in no time. Mallory allowed extra minutes for his return trip. He would not walk back here with the same urgent speed. She factored in another minute so he could trade insults with the desk sergeant before climbing the stairs and ambling down the hall to the incident room.

Mallory turned her face to the door, and her partner appeared.

Pssst.

She saw nothing amiss. Riker prided himself on never stumbling in the daylight hours. There were no new spills on his suit, nothing more recent than his interview with Daisy, and that splash of bourbon had dried long ago. He sat on the chair next to hers and peeled the wrapper from a roll of mints. "Did I miss anything?"

"No. We're still waiting to hear from Tech Support."

Pssst.

The detectives around the tape player walked away from the machine, allowing the recording to play out at full volume, and still the suspect's voice was subdued.

"—*a woman has been murdered in the East Village*—"

It was an empty monotone, lacking the bravado of a man on a quest for fame, and one more motive died.

"—*name is Kennedy Harper*—"

The mechanical tone almost qualified as a speech impediment, or that was the excuse offered by technicians at One Police Plaza. They had not yet fixed the suspect's home state.

"—you can find the body at—"

This man, so adept at theatrical staging, was so bland in his recital of bare facts—a death, a name, an address.

Pssst.

Mallory was fleshing out the portrait of a killer whose emotions were dead, not the type for a thrill kill. He was a tidy man, well organized. A man with a plan? She stared at the scarecrow on the back wall. *What the hell do you want?*

"We got it!" Janos hovered in front of a computer monitor and read the pertinent details as he scrolled down the screen. "The scarecrow is from the Midwest. They're still trying to nail down the state. The techs say he wasn't calling from a cell phone or a pay phone. And the ambient sound might be from an early model humidifier or an automatic plant mister."

Jack Coffey entered the room and shut off the tape player. "Listen up!" All conversation stopped, and every pair of eyes turned his way. "Riker's witness, Miss Emelda, is worth her weight in gold. Our perp was the old lady's man in the tree—the guy with a Polaroid camera."

He held up two plastic bags, each containing a small box with a Polaroid logo. "These film cartons were left at both crime scenes, and they weren't left by accident." He held one higher than the other. "And the box we found today has a twenty-year-old expiration date." He tossed the bags on the table. "Kennedy Harper died six days ago—that's official. Six days and twenty years ago, another hanging victim was found."

The lieutenant turned to face Mallory. "It was an anniversary kill. And *now* we have a solid connection to the Cold Case file." He pointed to Janos. "You're the primary on Kennedy's case. And, Desoto, you got Sparrow."

Mallory watched Riker's face go gray. His eyes were all the way open now, and his head was shaking from side to side, silently saying, *This can't be.* How could he lose Sparrow's case to another detective? He was rising from his chair when she caught his sleeve and pulled him down.

"If we can't get Sparrow back, we'll work her case on the side."

Was he hearing her? Yes, he was nodding.

Jack Coffey had finished handing out assignments to the others, and now he stood before Mallory and Riker. "You guys are working the Cold Case file. We got a copycat, and I wanna know where he got his information."

The lieutenant paused, correctly reading Mallory's expression of ennui. "You're not baby-sitting Geldorf. *Use* that old man. Just keep him the hell out of Special Crimes."

Lars Geldorf was hoarse from explaining and explaining, then shouting in exasperation. His opponent was a small wiry woman with dark Spanish eyes, a deeply suspicious nature and a mission to clean Manhattan. She pulled a mop from her rolling cart of cleaning supplies and said, once more, "I'm gonna do Mallory's office now." Nothing would stop the intrepid Mrs. Ortega, certainly not this old man—gun or no gun.

The retired detective informed her that this room could *not* be cleaned until his case was wrapped. He distrusted all civilians, and she should understand that it was nothing personal. Charles intervened, suggesting that, since it was so late in the day, Mrs. Ortega could skip this room. The cleaning woman countered with, "Mallory's orders, not yours." And eventually, the matter was settled.

Mrs. Ortega ruled.

But Geldorf was adamant that Charles remain in the room until "that— that *woman*" was done. Then, with great dignity, he left the office with his relief watcher, a young detective with unnatural bright yellow hair.

After the door slammed behind them, Mrs. Ortega plugged in her vacuum, then shook her head, saying, "Damn, that baby cop's got one bad bleach job."

Charles nodded. "It's interesting, though. Perhaps he's making some kind of statement."

"Yeah, like—look at me, my head glows in the dark."

"Exactly what I was thinking." Charles turned his attention to the cork wall. Where should the giant cockroaches go? Well, the only place for them was underneath the maggots. Where else?

The carpet was spotless when Riker strolled in. He nodded his hello to Charles, then flashed a big smile for the cleaning woman. "Hey, how've you been?" He was genuinely happy to see her, though she used him for verbal sniper practice each time they met.

She glared at a spot on Riker's suit, singling it out from all the other stains, then stopped her work to clean him with a bottle of solvent and a cloth, as if he were any other object in her path. "Next time you drink crummy bourbon for lunch, mop it up."

Charles's nose was larger, but Mrs. Ortega's was truly gifted. However, she was not an olfactory savant. She had not identified the alcohol by scent nor discerned that it was stale, not fresh, and neither had she found the bouquet a bit wanting—a lesser brand. This was only a parlor trick. Cheap bourbon was Riker's habitual choice, and the spill might reek, but it was dry, suggesting a drink earlier in the day. After erasing the evidence of his on-duty imbibing, she went back to dusting the shelves and muttered, "My tax dollars at work."

"Mallory's on the way," Riker said to her back. "You got fifteen minutes." The detective also knew *her* soft spots, and now Mrs. Ortega's duster doubled its speed. She would not want Mallory to walk in while there was still a dust mote at large.

"You never finished the story," said Charles. "What happened to that Indian girl after she—"

The man shook his head to say, *Not now,* then quickly glanced at the cleaning woman. When Mrs. Ortega had packed up her cart and gone home, Riker was still uneasy as he continued the unfinished tale. "The Wichita Kid got away. When the next book opens, you find out the Indian girl is dead." He sagged back against the wall, and his face turned toward the open door.

Keeping an eye out for Mallory?

Yes, and he was also telegraphing the terrible importance of the books, which had nothing to do with plots and everything to do with a recent murder and a child who loved westerns.

"Sheriff Peety's horse crushed the girl's skull," said Riker. "So he broke off the chase and carried the body back to her village. Wichita never found out that the girl died to save him. He just went on loving her for the rest of the book." The detective was about to say more when something caught his eye, a folded newspaper on the desk. His left shoe began to tap in a steady rhythm, though he was not given to nervous mannerisms.

The newspaper belonged to Charles. He had finished the detailed account of a hanged prostitute and noted the similarities to Natalie Homer's murder. However, the most startling lines described the crime-scene floor awash in water from a fire hose. Given the time of night and the degree of dampness in a paperback western called *Homecoming*, he now knew how the book had gotten wet. It was possible that the detective had innocently dropped it in the water, but the man's uncharacteristic anxiety suggested that the truth was even more out of character than Riker telling lies and drinking on duty. Though Charles suspected the book had been stolen, all he would say to his friend was, "Tell me how the story ends."

Riker's eyes were on the door, and there was some strain in his voice when he said, "Sheriff Peety hears about another gunfight with the Wichita Kid—another man killed. He picks up the trail outside of El Paso, Texas. At the end of the book, the sheriff's riding into an ambush—forty-to-one odds. He knows what's comin'. He *knows* he can't win. But he keeps on riding."

The apartment had a formal dining room, but Charles preferred the casual warmth of the kitchen, where a Bach concerto played at the low volume of background music. He turned down the gas flame under a bubbling pan of red sauce for Sergeant Riker's favorite meal. His dinner guests had not waited on ceremony. Riker and Mallory sat at the table demolishing salads of olives and purple onions, red lettuce and fettuccine, as if they had not eaten in days and days.

Charles poured out a sample of cabernet sauvignon, then set the bottle on the table. "You're going to love this." It was an old vintage, deep red and fine. He swirled the glass, and the bouquet summoned up the warm sun of France, country air and the scent of rich earth among the ripe grapes. He tasted it. Potent magic, a rare wine to stimulate the intellect and turn a stammering fool into a poet. He owned first editions of Blake that had cost him less, but this was truly a work of art that one could swallow.

And Riker did. He slopped it into a glass and slugged it back in one long thirsty gulp, neatly bypassing every taste bud.

After a time, Charles closed his mouth and opened his eyes again. "Anyway," he said, turning back to the stove, "it was the best I could get on short notice."

"It's wonderful," said Riker. Food had greatly improved the man's mood, perhaps with a little help from the wine.

"I'm glad you're taking an interest in Lars Geldorf's case." Charles opened the oven and released the aroma of warm garlic bread. "He thought you were only humoring him." After setting the bread basket on the table, he watched them empty it by half before he could ladle spaghetti and meatballs into their bowls, and it was a race to pour the sauce before they picked up their forks. Now he worked between the movements of silverware to add the grated cheese. "Riker, what do you call that detective, the one with the yellow hair? He was here and gone so fast."

"The son-in-law of the deputy commissioner. That's the kid's full name."

"Ronald Deluthe," said Mallory.

"Alias Duck Boy." Riker inhaled his spaghetti, then smiled at his host. "So Charles, how was *your* day? Did the old guy give you any trouble?"

"Not at all." He sat down at the table and salvaged what he could of the bread and the wine. "I like his stories." He turned to Mallory. "Did you know that your father visited Natalie Homer's crime scene?"

"I know." Mallory opened a small notebook to a page of Louis Markowitz's handwriting, then pushed it toward him. "Take a look."

Charles recognized a few of the lines she had transcribed last night on her computer. He found it easy to break the simple shorthand code. "So Louis was in the room for only a few minutes."

Riker nodded. "That was after Geldorf removed the hair from the woman's mouth. Lou didn't know about that."

Charles read on for a few more lines. "He thought Natalie Homer was gagged with tape—not hair—but he doesn't say why." And now he turned the pages faster, easily deciphering chains of sentence fragments. Apparently it was typical of Louis Markowitz to write down only the last words in a long passage of thoughts. "Lipstick." He turned to Mallory. "Maybe he saw a piece of tape with her lipstick on it? Of course that word is miles from the part about the gag."

"Cryptic bastard." Riker reached for a slice of garlic bread and dipped it into his spaghetti sauce. "He wrote in code so the lawyers couldn't subpoena his personal notes. What about Geldorf's stuff? Have you seen all the photos—the reports?"

"Not yet. Lars is bringing in another carton tomorrow."

Mallory's fork hung in midair. "He was holding out on us?"

"I wouldn't put it that way," said Charles. "He has a few things that didn't qualify as evidence. Said he didn't want to confuse the larger picture with minutia." Or, in Geldorf's words, *the small shit*. "He has a few more photographs and notes."

"A *carton* of 'em," said Riker.

Charles looked from one detective to the other, then realized that the short answer should have been, yes, Geldorf had been holding out on them. "Well, he probably didn't think you'd care. But when he found out you were planning to work on the case—"

"Never mind." Mallory pushed her bowl aside. "What've you got so far? Anything unusual?"

"A few discrepancies—one major problem."

Riker helped himself to a second bowl of spaghetti. "Did you point that out to Geldorf?"

"No, I thought it might be rude."

"Good," said Riker. "Whatever you come up with, bring it to us, not him. Geldorf's not a cop anymore. He's just visiting."

Mallory rested one hand on Charles's arm, and it had the effect of a warm current of electricity. She so rarely touched anyone. "What's the problem?" she asked.

Well, there was a flock of butterflies crashing about inside his chest cavity. That was a problem. And he was wondering how long this contact with her would last if he sat very, very still, if he never moved the arm beneath her hand, not by so much as a hair.

Mallory leaned toward him—so close. "Charles, are you breathing?"

"What?"

She lifted her hand from his arm, realizing that he was not choking on his supper, and the man with total recall forgot the threads to their conversation. Heat was rising in his face, the prelude to a blush. Riker gave him the kindest of smiles, the one that said, *You poor bastard*.

"The problem?" said Mallory, impatient with him now.

Oh, the lock on Natalie Homer's door. "Sorry." Damned sorry. "According to the landlady's statement, the odor in the hall was overwhelming, and she was desperate to get into Natalie's apartment. The old woman had the key, but it wouldn't open the door. You see, the lock had been changed or another one added—that part's not clear."

The detectives exchanged long glances.

"Natalie had security issues." Charles paused again as both of them turned to stare at him. "She was being stalked. Perhaps this is something you already know? I don't want to—"

"Go on," said Riker. "You're not boring us."

"Well, the landlady made one more try at opening the door—right before she called the police. Now the first officer on the scene made a very detailed report—but no mention of kicking down a door or breaking a lock. He just entered the apartment. So, obviously, some third party opened that door before—"

"And Geldorf didn't catch this?" Riker refilled his wine glass. "Naw, I don't see him missing a thing like that. There should be paperwork for repairs on a busted lock. It travels with the Cold Case file."

"No," said Charles. "I read every word of that file. Between the landlady's call and the police response, there was a four-hour interval. I gather a bad smell wasn't a high priority. So, during those four hours, somebody opened the door with a key."

"The perp must've had Natalie's key," said Riker. "He'd be the one who locked up after the murder. So he forgot something and went back to—"

"No," said Mallory. "He wouldn't risk it—not that day."

"I agree," said Charles. "Between the heat and the insects, that body was badly decomposed. The stench was incredible—that's in the officer's report. The killer would've realized the police were on the way. Also, this was a Sunday evening. Most of the tenants would've been at home. More risk of—"

"Okay," said Riker. "Let's say the intruder wasn't the killer."

"But someone with his own key," said Charles. "Maybe a lover. If he saw the crime scene—it was horrific—that might've left him unhinged. Now he's not the man who murdered Natalie Homer—"

"So he's the one who did the copycat hangings." Mallory turned to Riker. "It fits with the anniversary kill, a woman with Natalie's long blond hair. Then Sparrow—"

"Poor Sparrow." Riker poured the last drops of wine into his glass. "Nothing personal, the freak just needed another blonde."

On toward midnight, Mallory circled the block once more, then cut the car's engine and turned off her headlights as she coasted silently to the curb. Her eyes were fixed on a third-floor window dimly lit by the screen of Riker's television set. She knew what he was doing up there. He was chain-smoking cigarettes and sipping bourbon—medicine for missing his ex-wife. Every glass in the apartment might be dirty, yet she knew he would not be drinking from the mouth of a bottle.

Riker's rules—only winos did that.

Mallory covertly kept him company for a while, sitting in the dark of her car, keeping watch on his window. It was the kind of thing one partner did for another—as if she could fly that high when his gun went off.

A year had passed since the last time his ex-wife had inspired a day-long binge. Mallory had helped him stagger up all those stairs, then rolled him onto an unmade bed, where he had slept in his clothes, but not his shoes. And she had also removed his gun that night and taken the bullets away.

He was a sorry alcoholic; that would never change. And Mallory was also constant.

The light in the window went out.

'Night, Riker.

She started up her car and headed home.

He would not kill himself in the dark; it would be too difficult for a blind and trembling drunk to thread his finger into the trigger. And she could not foresee him dying in the bathroom by the glow of his plastic Jesus night-light.

EiGHT

THE REAR OFFICE WAS FLOODED WITH MORNING LIGHT. Charles thought the room temperature had chilled by a few degrees since he had last looked in, but little else had changed. Mallory was still averting her eyes from the paper storm on her cork wall, an anathema to someone who straightened paintings in other people's houses. She sat at a metal workstation but no longer communed with her network of computers. The three machines hummed among themselves while she leafed through Louis Markowitz's old notebook. The only human sound was the tap of Lars Geldorf's pacing shoes.

Impatient to begin the day, the retired detective removed his suit jacket and loosened his tie, but this clue was lost on her. Occasionally, she looked up from her reading to watch his travels about the room—*her* room—as he inspected metal shelves stocked with electronics. Geldorf wore a brave pretender's smile and nodded in a knowing way, though he had no idea what her machines could do. They were new, and he was old.

She rose from her chair and approached the cork wall to stand before a haphazard arrangement of crime-scene photographs. Charles observed tension in her face, a small war going on at the core of her as she struggled with the urge to place every bit of paper at perfect right angles to the next.

Lars Geldorf hurried across the room to join her. And now Charles understood what the last fifteen minutes of silence had been about. Mallory was teaching the old man to follow her lead. There should never be any doubt about the hierarchy in this room, and Geldorf should not call her *honey* one more time. Charles decided that she must like the old man, for this was the mildest and most drawn-out show of contempt in her repertoire.

She lifted the edge of a grainy photograph to expose a small square one pinned beneath it. Then she looked under the other eight-by-ten formats in this group, each one covering a picture from an instant camera. "All you've got are Polaroids and blowups."

"Yeah," said Geldorf. "So?"

"Where are the originals?"

"That's all of 'em, kid."

"Mallory," she corrected him.

"Suppose I call you Kathy?"

"Don't." And that was a threat. "So there was no police photographer on the scene?"

"Yeah, we had one, a civilian. But he didn't last three minutes." Geldorf waved one hand to include all the images of a hanged woman, two days dead in the heat of August, an incubator of maggots. "The photographer got sick and dropped his camera. We couldn't get it to work after that. So we borrowed one from a neighbor."

Mallory stared at a shot of the hanging rope draped over a light fixture. "What's that brown smear on the ceiling?"

"Bugs on their way to a meal," said Geldorf. "Cockroaches *love* their grease. And here." One bony finger pointed to another photograph depicting a large brown glob on the kitchen floor. "Roaches swarming over a frying pan." He squinted. "You see those little logs on the floor? Those are sausages and more bugs. The ceiling light was coming loose and cracking the plaster. Must've been a nest of 'em up there. I had more blowups made."

Geldorf edged a few steps down the wall, where the medical examiner's materials were grouped together. He perused the pictures of flies hanging with their spawn. "Charles? What did you do with my best cockroaches?"

"They're pinned up under the maggot pictures. Seemed like the only logical place for them."

"What?" Mallory stared at him, clearly wondering where logic entered into this.

Geldorf answered for him. "Flies are the only useful bugs at a crime scene. Roaches can't tell you nothin'."

"Right," said Charles. "So I pinned them up under the more useful—" There was not much point in finishing his thought, for Mallory had tuned him out. She was staring at her nails. Perhaps she had found a flaw in her manicure that would take precedence over an insect monologue.

She looked up. "Done? Good. Let's get the roaches up front."

When Charles had removed the covering pictures of flies and their larvae, Mallory appraised the giant cockroaches pouring out of the ceiling and making their way down the rope to the corpse. The photo that caught her attention was a shot of the victim's apron and a rectangular stain spotted with brown insects.

Geldorf stepped close to the wall. "Looks like she dropped her frying pan in the scuffle and splattered the grease. There was a utility blackout at dusk, so—"

"No." Mallory looked down at the baseboard where the actual skillet leaned against the wall. She tapped the picture of the apron stain. "That's *not* a grease spatter."

Charles knew she was paraphrasing a line in Louis Markowitz's old notebook, the words, *No splash—a smear.* Louis had found that observation worthy of an underscore, but it was never explained until now. The two long edges of the rectangle were fairly well defined. This was not a splatter pattern.

Mallory turned to the retired detective. "Natalie was cooking a meal, maybe expecting company. You interviewed her friends?"

"She didn't have any," said Geldorf. "When she was married, her husband wouldn't let her get a job. Never gave her any money. She hardly ever left the apartment. After the divorce, I guess she forgot how to make new friends." He stared at the close-up of the sausages on the floor. "It was probably a meal for one."

Charles noted Mallory's skepticism, then counted up the sausages. During a summer of utility blackouts that made refrigeration unreliable, Natalie Homer would not have purchased more food than she could eat at one sitting, and such a slender woman could not eat so many sausages— not by herself. Who was the dinner guest? He inclined his head toward the smaller man. "Natalie was also alienated from her family, right?"

"Yeah," said Geldorf. "A year after she got married, her sister stopped talking to her. But that wasn't in the statements. How'd you know?"

"It fits a pattern of spousal abuse. Forced dependence, isolation." Charles turned to Mallory. "Her husband may have knocked her around a bit during the marriage."

"Right again," said Geldorf. "That's what Natalie told me."

Mallory's voice was all suspicion now. "You *talked* to her?"

"Yeah, of course I did. Twice, sometimes three times a week."

"I think I mentioned the stalking last night." Charles walked toward the center of the wall and a cluster of papers. "These are samples of her complaints." He unpinned the paperwork and handed her five stalker reports.

"The trouble started right after her divorce." Geldorf leaned down to pick up an envelope propped against the baseboard. "This is the rest of 'em."

"And after she died?" Mallory stared at the thick envelope. "All those complaints—no leads on the stalker?"

"She never saw the guy's face," said Geldorf. "The first time she came in, we thought she was just paranoid. I mean, sure men were gonna follow her around."

"Because she was pretty," said Mallory, though not one image on the wall could have told her that. In death, Natalie was grotesque.

"She was beautiful." Geldorf bent down to the carton he had brought in that morning. He pulled out a brown paper bag and removed a packet of photographs. "I didn't think these belonged with the evidence." He held up one smiling portrait of a young woman with blond hair falling past her shoulders. Natalie's eyes were large and blue.

Mallory folded the envelope of complaints under one arm, then carried the pictures to a clear section of wall and pinned them up with machinelike precision, each border exactly the same distance from the next. "A pro took these shots."

Charles agreed. The lighting was perfect, and the subject's pose was not candid but artful.

"The photographer was another dead end," said Geldorf. "That woman was older than I am now."

Mallory had yet to open the envelope of complaints. She merely hefted its weight in one hand. "Natalie spent a lot of time in your station house. A *lot* of time. When you figured out that she wasn't paranoid—what then?"

"We went after the ex-husband and told him to stay away from her. He was a cool one. Never owned up to nothin'."

"And after the murder?"

"We hauled him in for questioning. But he had an alibi for the time of death. He was in Atlantic City all weekend. That's where he was gettin' married to the next Mrs. Homer. Jane was her name. They never left the hotel room all weekend. That's what the staff said. But how much would it cost to buy an alibi from a maid and a bellboy? And the statement from the second wife, Jane—that was worthless. Two days married, and that bastard had her cowed."

Mallory was not listening anymore. She had discovered one of the stalker's notes in a clear plastic evidence bag. She took it down from the wall and stared at a brief message penciled on thin airmail paper. The letters were painstakingly drawn in varying sizes and scripts.

"All seven of 'em say the same thing," said Geldorf. "We figured they were traced from magazines. No newsprint smudges on the paper. Natalie found 'em under her door at night when she got home from work. Be careful," said Geldorf, as she pulled them out of the bag. "That paper's really fragile, and you don't wanna smudge the pencil."

Charles expected Mallory to be annoyed with this lecture on the handling of evidence, but she only stared at the paper, transfixed by the words, *I touched you today.*

Geldorf never noticed her reaction. Hands in his pockets, rocking on his heels, he stared at the photographs of the murder scene. "That kid photographer who dropped his camera—he wasn't the only one who got sick that night. There was this young cop—the uniform who found the body—I can't remember if it was Parris or Loman."

Mallory looked up from her reading. He had her undivided attention now.

Geldorf continued. "We couldn't get him back inside the apartment again. An hour later, he's at the station house, still batting off flies and stomping his feet to shake roaches out of his pant legs. Well, there weren't any bugs on him—not one—not then, but he could still *feel* them. Oh, and the stink. You can't take a picture of that. But you know what I remember best? I could hear it outside in the hall when I was walkin' toward that apartment. When I opened the door—it was *so* loud—so many of 'em. Scared the hell out of me." He closed his eyes. "I can hear it now. The roar of flies—*thousands* of flies."

Sergeant Riker entered the office, arms laden with the bags of a delicatessen breakfast. "Did I miss anything?"

Riker lured Geldorf down the hall to the office kitchen with promises of coffee and food. After settling the deli bags on the table, he fumbled with the wrappings, hunting for a bacon-and-egg on white toast dripping with heart-attack grease. He spread the packages on a red-checked tablecloth, the only bit of charm to survive the ruthless takeover of Mallory's machine decor.

After writing down the delicatessen's phone number, he handed it to Geldorf. "Lose this and you'll starve." While he and Mallory covertly worked on Sparrow's case, Geldorf would have to fend for himself. Charles would be no help in foraging for food around the office; on principle, the man ignored all kitchen appliances with control panels more complex than the dashboard of his Mercedes.

"Deluthe should've made the deli run. What good is a slave if he doesn't do errands?"

Geldorf grinned. "Mallory's got him chasing down personnel files for all the cops from my crime scene."

"Well, that should keep him occupied." A whiteshield in training pants would have to stand in line all day long at One Police Plaza. But Duck Boy's report would reinforce the fiction that they were working on Natalie Homer's murder. He handed a paper coffee cup to the retired detective. "I hear you've been working cold cases for six years. You missed the job, huh?"

"Yeah, I like to keep—" Geldorf was facing the kitchen door when he stiffened slightly, then sat up very straight. This was Riker's clue that Mallory was standing behind his own chair. Obviously, she had been training the help again. Every time she entered a room, Duck Boy had this same conditioned response.

She laid a stack of paperwork beside his coffee cup. Riker leafed through the familiar forms of citizen complaints. Natalie Homer had been a frequent visitor to her local police station. This was a replay of Lieutenant Loman's squad making a station house pet of Kennedy Harper.

"There's a big gap in the dates for these complaints," she said.

Geldorf nodded. "The pervert gave her a breather. Two weeks later, he was stalking her again, and he was escalating. That's when he started leaving those notes under her door. And phone calls—no conversation, and no heavy breathing either. I think he only wanted to hear her voice."

Riker fished through his pockets for matches and cigarettes. "Was the ex-husband in town during those two weeks?"

"Oh, yeah. The guy never missed a day of work at the post office. But I knew he was guilty."

After emptying the cigarettes from his crumpled pack, Riker hunted for one that was not broken. "So you never developed other suspects."

"What for? Erik Homer did it," said Geldorf. "If only the bastard hadn't up and died on me. He had a heart attack a year after the murder."

Mallory laid down another sheet of paper. "This is the ex-husband's statement. There's just one line about Natalie's son. How old was the boy when his mother died?"

"Oh, six or seven. The kid's father had sole custody. After the divorce, she never saw her son again."

Mallory's eyes locked with Riker's. He nodded, holding the same thought: Natalie's son would be twenty-six years old today, a prime age group for serial killers. He lit a cigarette, then exhaled and watched the smoke spiral up to the ceiling. "You know where that kid is now?"

Geldorf shook his head. "After his father died, the stepmother told me she gave the boy to Natalie's sister—a cop hater. Zero cooperation."

"So she's holding a grudge." Riker looked back at the kitchen counter, seeking something to pass for an ashtray. "All this time and no leads on her sister's murder. I can't blame her."

"Me neither," said Geldorf. "But Natalie's sister didn't have the boy. That's all she'd say. I figure she fobbed him off on another relative. A few months after I checked out the Cold Case file, I asked her to tell the kid that I never gave up on his mom. Then I left her alone."

Riker stole a glance at Mallory. Was she also wondering if Lars Geldorf had triggered a murder spree?

The old man grinned at each of them in turn. "I know what you guys are thinking. You figure the boy's grown up and gone psycho, right? You think he's your perp for that hooker hanging?" He shook his head. "How would he get the details? Only the killer could've told that little boy about the hair packed in his mother's mouth. I don't see his dad sharing that with him."

Mallory pulled up a chair at the table. "So you never talked to the boy."

"No. There was no point in it." Geldorf rose from his chair. "I'll be back in a minute."

When the bathroom door had closed at the other end of the hall, Mallory handed Riker a twenty-year-old statement signed by a rookie patrolman. "Is that Lieutenant Loman's first name? Harvey?"

Before Riker could respond, *Jesus Christ, yes it is,* Charles Butler entered the kitchen, saying, "I can tell you why Natalie had those photographs taken. It was an actress portfolio." He handed Riker a photocopy of a newspaper column. "I found that on microfiche at the library. It's the only mention on the death of Natalie Homer."

And the press had not wasted much type on the lying headline, SUICIDE. Riker skipped over the first dry lines and read the short story of Natalie Homer's life and death. "'She served cocktails at a local bar from six o'clock till closing time.'" And every Wednesday afternoon she sat in the cheap seats of off-Broadway theaters, watching matinees in the dark and learning another trade. She was too poor to pay for acting lessons, so said her landlady. The rest of Natalie's days were spent dogging miles of pavement, making the rounds of theatrical agencies that never found her any work. Every day she reminded them that she was still alive and still determined to make it in New York City. "'That girl worked so hard,' said the landlady. 'She was tired *all* the time. You *say* that when you write about her. You say something *nice.*' According to police sources, the young actress was found at the end of the day '—at the end of a rope.'"

Mallory waited for Detective Janos at the address he had given her along with his promise that she would find it interesting, but he had said nothing about the actress connection, not within earshot of Lieutenant Coffey.

The lot next to the narrow building was a dusty construction site. The only structure was a portable restroom the size of an upended coffin, and a troupe of children formed a wriggling column at the door. The day-camp supervisor, a very tired woman, called out her thanks to the men in hard hats. Her young campers were making a toilet stop while roaming the neighborhood on a nature walk, though the flora of this East Village street was limited to scrawny city trees dying of heat and urine showers. And the wildlife only amounted to one dead squirrel in the gutter and a pigeon strolling down the sidewalk. The bird was followed closely by a homicide detective carrying a rolled newspaper. The children were impressed by the man's large size and his brutal face. They laughed, pointing fingers like guns, and then used one another for human shields.

"Hey, Mallory." Detective Janos joined her at the door of the narrow shop that now served as a makeshift theater for art films. "You were right. Everybody wants to be in show business. Kennedy Harper worked second shift. That left her days free for auditions."

"So she had an agent?"

"No, she didn't need one. There's open auditions all over town." He handed her a page torn from an old copy of *Backstage*. "Heller found a sheet like this in her trash—ripped to shreds. I'm guessing the auditions didn't go well." He handed her his rolled newspaper. "This is a recent edition."

The pages were turned back to columns of dates and locations for open casting calls. "There's at least five auditions a day."

"Not if you scratch the out-of-town locations and the song-and-dance gigs. More like one or two. I just came from an audition. Must've been a hundred actors standing in line on Spring Street. I figure that's how he found Sparrow and Kennedy. He just walked down the line and picked out the blonde he liked best."

"So now we're three for three," said Mallory. Natalie Homer, Kennedy Harper and Sparrow had all been aspiring actresses.

"Yeah, and I think you're right about consolidating the cases, but Coffey's never gonna buy that. The boss figures our chances are better if we work the fresh hangings. And he'd go nuts if he knew I was here." Janos's implication was clear: There would be no more covert meetings. He turned to the grimy window of the Hole in the Wall Theater. "An actor in Sparrow's play tipped us off to this place. They're running a videotape of her dress rehearsal."

A handmade poster taped to the window had retitled Chekhov's play *The Three Sisters* as *The Hanging Hooker*. Alongside the poster was the attendant publicity. Front-page stories of New York tabloids had also given star billing to the comatose prostitute.

You're famous, Sparrow. You made it.

And now, if only the whore would finish this dragged-out affair of her dying.

After Janos had walked back to his car, she paid the three-dollar admission at the door, then passed through a curtain to enter a dark room that stank of smoke and sweat. There were chairs for twenty, but only two other patrons watched the television monitor. One of the men rose from his chair, muttering, "Rip off." He was obviously disappointed that *The Hanging Hooker* was actually a classical play—no nudity and nothing lewd. The second man followed him out of the room, equally offended, leaving the detective to watch the video alone.

Only the keenest observer would have noticed the change in Mallory as her young face took on the conviction of a stubborn child. She sat very still, eyes fixed on the screen, a window she watched with great expectation—waiting for Sparrow. She had been waiting for years.

An elderly crone appeared on stage in company with a young actress, a beautiful girl so far removed from the drooling, eye-rolling dementia of the coma patient. The voice that filtered through Mallory's shock was familiar and not.

"*—Nothing ever happens the way we want it to—*"

Sparrow was dressed in the clothes she had worn to her hanging. The southern accent had been erased, and a gifted surgeon had made her too young for the part of Olga. Years had passed since Mallory had last checked up on Sparrow, and now she saw another change in this woman, something surgery could not provide. The whore was lit from within—fresh fire. Even Sparrow's eyes had made a comeback, clear and bright, seeing the world for the first time—all over again, an encore of youth. This was what she had looked like on the night they first met.

And how old was I, Sparrow? Eight? Nine?

It was winter then, a sudden storm, and a feverish young Kathy Mallory had crawled into the last remaining telephone booth in New York City, the only one with a door that she could close against the stinging snow. She had fed money into the coin slots, a daily habit and the only constant of a childhood on the streets.

More than a thousand miles away and years away, a dying woman had written a telephone number on the little girl's palm. All but the last four digits had been smudged off her hand before that terrible day had ended. Kathy continued to obey long after her mother had died. Though she had forgotten the reason for these telephone calls, she continued making up numbers to replace the three that were missing. Whenever she heard a feminine voice on the line, the child would become inexplicably hopeful and say the ritual words, *It's Kathy. I'm lost.*

None of the startled women on the receiving end of these calls had known who she was, thus giving themselves away as impostors. That night, one of them had cried into the telephone, "Won't you tell me who you are? How can I—"

Click. And another connection was severed, another woman left in tears, and hope died. The child had become an addict of hope, and the best part of this game was that she could get it back again every day, any time she wanted it.

The fever had given way to violent chills. Her small hands were shaking as she tried her last coins, her last call, saying, "It's Kathy. I'm lost."

Out of a thousand women, only Sparrow had responded, "Where are you, baby? I'll come get you." This had been said with the lilt of the Southland—so like a dead mother's voice.

Anticipation had kept Kathy from giving into sleep and death while she waited for the Southerner to come and find her. The little girl's eyes had begun to close when she saw a shadow on the other side of the fogged glass. It was coming for her, moving quickly, flying through the storm.

The door opened, and a woman's arms reached into the telephone booth to gather up the shivering child, warming Kathy with fake fur and perfumed body heat.

While the delirium lasted, the little girl believed that her dead mother had come to carry her home, and all that was lost had been restored. The night of the snowstorm, pressed up against the warm breast of a whore, was the happiest time that Kathy Mallory had ever known.

"—*our life is not over yet,*" said the actress on the screen.

The summer heat was stifling in the small theater, yet the young detective remained in her seat after the play was done. Head bowed, she sat in absolute darkness, awaiting the video's next run—so she could continue to nurse her deep hatred of Sparrow.

Riker had already made a case for combining the investigations, and he had lost. Mallory should have handled this, but she had failed to show, and this worried him. Coming late to any appointment was outside the pathology of a punctuality freak.

She was still wearing dark glasses when she entered Jack Coffey's private office and pulled up a chair without waiting for an invitation to sit down. Riker smiled in the belief that she had picked up this bad habit from him.

Lieutenant Coffey leaned back in his chair, only glancing at his wristwatch to remind Mallory that she was late. "Riker tells me the scarecrow has a type—stage-struck blondes."

"Hmm. His victims were stand-ins for Natalie Homer." Mallory seemed almost bored as she leaned toward the stack of newspapers at the edge of the desk. "Her case is the key to the scarecrow's hangings."

The lieutenant was not rising to this bait, but it was early in the game, only round one by Riker's reckoning. The boss kept his silence, expecting Mallory to elaborate. She picked up a newspaper, cast it aside after a minute, and opened another. After folding back a page, she glanced at Coffey, her eyebrows arching to ask him why he kept her waiting.

"The scarecrow is a copycat, and a bad one," said the lieutenant. "He was nowhere near Natalie Homer's crime scene."

Did that sound defensive? Riker thought so.

"And I say he was there." Mallory lowered her sunglasses to scan a column of newsprint that interested her more.

"Too many things don't fit," said Coffey, "all those candles, the wrong noose. I know this perp never saw that crime scene."

"I would've thought just the opposite," said a friendly voice, and Coffey spun his chair around to stare at the tall man whose head barely cleared the top of the door frame. Misunderstanding the look of surprise, Charles Butler glanced at his watch, saying, "Oh, sorry. I'm too early?"

The lieutenant would be wondering why a civilian had been invited to the briefing. Riker gave up on the idea of damage control and braced himself for a shouting match. It was predictable that Coffey would do all the yelling. Mallory would sit back and let the man knock himself out. And perhaps then she would drop the bomb of Lieutenant Loman's presence on Natalie Homer's crime scene.

There were no free chairs, and Charles Butler was always self-conscious about inadvertently dwarfing people and their furniture. He leaned against the glass wall, believing this would make him smaller and more polite. "The inconsistencies make sense to me."

The lieutenant was forcing a smile. "So you're siding with Mallory?" *What a damn surprise.*

"Yes," said Charles. "The scarecrow is working from a twenty-year-old memory—bound to be errors. At least he has a fair idea of how many flies were at the original crime scene. I understand he brings them in a jar."

Coffey turned an accusing eye on Mallory, but before he could nail her to the wall for this breach of case details, she said, "He's our consulting psychologist. I know how much you hate the department shrink."

The lieutenant nodded, for this was true. The consultant on call for Special Crimes was an incompetent hack and an irritant to the entire squad. A year ago, he had offered the job to Charles Butler only to discover that the city of New York could not afford a man with more than one PhD. "It's just too bad we don't have the budget for him."

Riker had the distinct impression that the lieutenant was overacting.

"Not a problem." Mallory was still working through the stack of newspapers. "He can't earn any more money this quarter."

"Right," said Charles. "It's a tax thing. I'm at your disposal, free of charge."

The lieutenant was rightly distrustful of something for nothing, but he had not yet worked out the potential for treachery.

Mallory folded the last newspaper from the pile on the desk. "There's nothing in here on Kennedy Harper. And the reporters botched the story on Sparrow's hanging. They're still calling it a hooker's sex game. Sounds almost accidental. Charles thinks this will send the scarecrow into a homicidal rage. The next kill could be any day now."

Riker could see that this opinion was a big surprise to her new consulting psychologist.

"If you believe the papers," she said, "the only women at risk are hookers. It's time to go public."

"All right," said Coffey, "we'll give the actresses a sporting chance to stay alive." He turned to face his generous gift from Mallory—Charles Butler. "Let's say you're right about the scarecrow being pissed off. Why doesn't he call the media and set them straight?"

"It's just my impression, but I think he wants the police to work it out."

"And he's stalking the next victim right now," said Mallory. "We need the public tip lines up and running."

Coffey shook his head. "We don't have to panic every blonde in the city—only women who fit the profile. And we're not gonna mention the Cold Case file to the press." He turned to Charles Butler. "Any more ideas about the scarecrow?"

"I assume his tie to Natalie Homer is very strong. He's restaged her murder twice."

"Well, that's one theory." Coffey turned to his detectives. "I put Gary Zappata on the short list."

Mallory abandoned her role as the Laid-back Kid. Her fist came down on the arm of her chair. "What *possible*—"

"Hold it." The lieutenant put up one hand to silence her. "Did you know his father was a detective? Yeah, Zappata wanted to be one, too." Coffey turned to Charles. "When this guy was a cop, he was real close to getting fired. That's when our desk sergeant sold him on the idea of applying to the fire department. Sergeant Bell told the kid it was easy to make the fire marshal's squad. Then he could carry a gun and play detective."

Riker nodded. This friendly gesture fitted so well with Bell's philosophy: Always stay on good terms with a psycho cop.

"The other night," said Coffey, "our boy turns up on the scene of a murder and runs the damn show."

Mallory's red fingernails drummed the arm of her chair. "So Zappata is hanging women—as a *career* move."

"Hear me out." This was not a request. Coffey was ordering her to keep her mouth shut. "I can place him on two crime scenes. His face is in the crowd shots outside of Kennedy Harper's place."

"So he's got a police scanner in his car," said Riker. "You know three people who don't?"

The lieutenant ignored this remark and spoke to his new consultant. "This man was voted most likely to come back here with a shotgun and blow away his ex-coworkers. Does that help you?" Coffey shuffled the papers on his desk until he found the report he wanted. "Zappata started his shift the minute Sparrow's 911 call came in. The firehouse was two blocks from the scene. I'm surprised their Dalmatian didn't suss out the smoke a lot faster."

"You figure he hung her, then ran two blocks to the firehouse to set up an alibi?"

"Yeah, Mallory." Coffey paused a beat, perhaps to remind her that sarcasm was insubordination. "The sloppy noose and a slow death bought him some time. But he *did* want her to die." He turned back to Charles. "According to a report filed by Zappata's own crew, he physically restrained another fireman when the guy tried to cut Sparrow down."

Riker faced his partner. "It's got some merit." And this, of course, was code for, *Play nice, or he won't consolidate the cases.* And when was she planning to bring up Lieutenant Loman's connection? That would get the boss's attention *real* fast. He caught her eye and mouthed the name.

Mallory shook her head, then turned to Coffey. "How would Zappata get details of a twenty-year-old murder?"

"I think his old man told him," said Coffey. "Look at all the details that don't match up. He knew there were candles, but not how many. He knew there was a noose, but not what kind. This fits with third-hand information. Twenty years ago, Zappata's father might've had connections to one of the crime-scene cops. We're checking that now."

"There wasn't any fire at Kennedy Harper's apartment. If Zappata was—"

"Maybe he was practicing, Mallory. Or maybe he knew that woman. Suppose he killed Sparrow to draw us off the—"

"No," said Mallory. "You *want* it to be Zappata. I don't like that creep either, but there's a problem with your theory. Sparrow could've taken him down with a dull kitchen knife." She spoke with something close to pride in an old enemy. "Even without a weapon, that whore would've done a lot of damage. She was that good."

Riker could attest to that. Sparrow would have been damned hard to intimidate. Once, the hooker had survived a stabbing that should have been fatal. Fifteen years later, she was still proving impossible to kill. Against the best medical advice of her doctor, she had lived through another night.

Jack Coffey was smiling at Mallory—always a bad sign. "So why didn't Sparrow bone the perp like a fish? No answer? I'll tell you why. He rushed her in the dark. The lightbulb over her door was unscrewed."

Riker stared at his shoes. He knew what was coming. He had forgotten to tell her—

"One more thing," said Coffey. "And you can thank your partner for this. He called CSU back to the scene to dust that bulb, and they found Zappata's prints."

Riker glanced at Mallory. To the extent that she was capable of pity, that would best describe her smile and the slow shake of her head. "That's good," she said. "You found a fireman's prints—at the scene of a fire."

Damn fine shot. Elegant, simple. All that remained was to have her name engraved on the winner's cup. But Riker could see that Jack Coffey was not about to concede. The boss was smiling when he said, "All right, here's my best deal. We keep the motive open—the suspect list too. But you and Riker stay on the Cold Case file." He splayed his hands to say, *See? I'm a fair man.*

The actress hangings, old and new, would remain with their assigned primaries and their separate lines of investigation. Riker knew that was not going to change. But Mallory had poisoned the lieutenant. All day long, it would worry Jack Coffey that she might be right, that the next kill would happen on his watch.

While Mommy drank paper-cup tea with another mother, the child had been drawn away from her and toward the sound of flies round the other side of a garbage drum. He was quite impressed by the sight of them, a living, swarming blanket over something small yet wonderfully stinky at the center of a piece of wax paper. The grass of Tompkins Square tickled his bare knees as he knelt before the frenzy of insects and wondered what they were attacking. Might their prey still be alive and twitching? Hopeful, he prodded the fetid meat, using a common stick of the sort that is issued to all boys at their birth. He found the underlying flesh to be squishy but definitely dead, impervious to pokes. Somewhat disappointed, he continued to watch the writhing mass of legs and wings and fat black bodies. The loud buzzing was really evil, quite delightful.

The boy's interest waned, and he wandered to a nearby bench and a man clad in jeans and a baseball cap. This figure was as rigid as any beast in a long parade of dead hamsters, songbirds and goldfish. He was as lifeless as the flesh beneath the flies, though not one winged thing dared approach him. The child solved this mystery as he drew closer to the bench and caught a whiff of insecticide on the man's clothes. An open gray bag on the ground held a canister of the stuff Mommy used when she chased down lone bugs flying through the rooms of their apartment. The bag also contained a large glass jar half filled with dead, dry flies and a few that were still alive.

A collector.

Well, now the world made sense again as the boy connected the man to the foul-smelling meat and the swarm. An excellent solution—no need to chase the flies down.

The man took no notice of the little boy, and this was odd behavior to a child who knew himself to be the center of the universe. The man never blinked, never moved. The boy's eyes rounded as he watched intently for some sign of life. At the end of his attention span, perhaps half a minute, he pronounced his subject dead as a dead hamster. But just to be sure, and only in the spirit of scientific enquiry, he poked the dead man's leg with his stick.

The corpse turned its head, and the child screamed.

Fast mother steps came up behind him, fleshy arms wound round his small body, lifted him and bore him away. As the boy bounced with his mother's running gait, he looked over her soft shoulder to see the dead man don a pair of yellow rubber gloves. Now the man approached the mass of buzzing flies with his insecticide can and rained down clouds of aerosol poison on the swarm.

The young actress had won a seat on the subway by beating another straphanger to a crack between two passengers on the plastic bench. She carved a wider niche with her squirming backside and settled in for the long ride home to the East Village.

After inspecting her suit jacket for battle scars, she removed one long blond hair from the lapel. The pale blue linen matched her eyes, and it was the most expensive outfit she had ever owned. Perversely, she regarded the suit as her lucky charm, though it had failed her in one audition after another.

In dire need of distraction from the sweaty press of flesh, she balanced a new packet of postcards on her knee and penned her weekly lies to the Abandoned Stellas. She borrowed a phrase from the rack of advertisements posted above the car's windows. *New York is a summer festival.*

A canvas bag hit her in the side of the head.

"Hey!" she yelled, just like a real New Yorker. "Watch it!" She looked up to see the crotch of a man's faded blue jeans a few inches from her face. He reeked of insecticide. She lowered her eyes to the postcard and wrote the words, *I love this town.*

She wanted to go back home to Ohio.

Last year, as the family's first college graduate, she had qualified for the traditional entry-level job of all theater majors—serving fast food to the public. And this had come as a bitter surprise to the Abandoned Stellas, two generations of tired truck-stop waitresses, impregnated and deserted before the age of seventeen.

Grandma, the original Stella, had cashed a savings bond to send the aspiring actress to New York City, a place with *no* roadside diners, and more money had followed every month. The second Stella, also known as Mom, still waited on tables and sent all the tips to her daughter, the only Stella ever to leave Ohio.

The train's air conditioner was not working, and Stella Small resented everyone around her for using up precious oxygen. She singled out the woman seated next to her for The Glare, a practiced stare that said, *Die.* The other woman, beyond intimidation, happily chomped a meaty sandwich that was still alive and moving of its own accord. Rings of onion and dollops of mayonnaise slithered from the greasy slices of bread and added a new odor to the stink of sweat and bug spray. Stella slipped the finished postcard into her purse and began to spin a new lie, this one for her agent. How would she explain losing a role to an idiot with no acting experience?

The train was one stop away from Astor Place and home. The smelly sandwich eater got up, leaving a residue of tomato slices on the plastic seat. This prevented other passengers from sitting down, but Stella could not stand up against the press of new passengers, nor could she edge away from the scratching man seated next to her. Had she already contracted body lice? The flesh of her upper arm felt crawly, itchy. Her hand moved to her sleeve to scratch it, then touched something alive and twitching.

Oh, shit!

A fat black fly. And now a rain of flies fell down on her head in the numbers of a biblical plague. Incredibly, most of them were dead. Others still twitched, only sick and sluggish, crawling slowly across her lap—down her legs.

Up her skirt! *No!*

She jumped up from the bench, wildly slapping her hair and her clothes. Insects dropped to the floor around her shoes and crawled in all directions. Stella screamed and set off a chain reaction of squeals from other riders. People were trampling one another to get to the other end of the car. Dry fly carcasses crunched underfoot as she jumped up and down, trying to shake loose the bugs that were still alive and crawling up her pantyhose. Other riders joined the hysteria dance, feet stomping, hands waving, fingers flicking. One passenger accidentally dislodged a note taped to Stella's back; it drifted to the floor as the train lurched to a stop, and all the doors opened. The small piece of paper and its message ran away, stuck to the bottom of another woman's shoe.

NiNE

CHARLES BUTLER STOOD AT THE CENTER OF THE SPECIAL
Crimes incident room, only glancing at the flanking walls, each
one devoted to a hanged woman. Now the rear wall—that was fascinating. The halo of dead flies around the scarecrow's baseball cap was definite
proof of creativity. He turned to the detective beside him. "Seriously?
Ronald Deluthe did this?"

"Yeah." Riker diddled the controls of a small cassette player. "I may
wind up liking that kid."

Pssst.

"Then why not stop treating him like a half-bright child?"

"Okay, I'll buy him a beer. That's the highest honor I'm allowed to
confer on a lame trainee." Riker raised the volume of the cassette to play
a few words spoken in an empty monotone. This was the voice of the
scarecrow alone in a gray landscape, a monotonous plain with no rise of

emotion, no depth of despair. The only relief in this flatline existence was the ambient sound.

Pssst.

Charles stared at the other walls papered with handwritten notes and typed reports, fax sheets and photographs. He could perceive no order in this work of many hands and minds. "Can we take the paperwork back to—"

"No," said Riker. "We can't remove anything from this room. Can't copy it, either. Coffey's orders. So just read *everything*."

And now that Charles understood his role as a human Xerox machine, he walked along the south wall, committing the paperwork of Kennedy Harper's murder to eidetic memory. Obviously all the autopsy information had been pinned up by Mallory. It was a small oasis of perfect alignment on an otherwise sloppy wall where neighboring papers hung straight only by accident.

The detective walked alongside him, working the volume of the cassette player as they crossed over to the opposite wall. "Listen to this one more time."

Pssst.

"Regular intervals," said Riker. "We know it's automated. Our techs think it might be a plant mister in a florist shop or a commercial greenhouse."

"I'd rule out a workplace," said Charles. "If the scarecrow was worried about being interrupted, you'd hear that in his voice. But it's level, isn't it? Utterly flat." He listened to another sentence fragment, then—*Pssst.* "There—a breath pause. The rhythm of his speech works around the ambient sound. It's like punctuation. I'd say he's been living with that noise for a very long time. It might come from a machine related to health issues." While Charles was speaking to Riker, in another compartment of his mind, he was absorbing the text of Edward Slope's autopsy report on a living woman. "Doesn't this coma patient have a last name?"

"Sparrow," said Riker. "That's it."

Mallory was in the room, but Charles could not say just when she had arrived. Cats made more racket with soft padding paws. He sometimes wondered if this was her idea of fun, watching startled people jump—as

Riker did when he noticed her strolling along the wall behind them. She showed little interest in the photo array of Sparrow's nude body. Only one picture at the edge of the group attracted her, a close-up of a vicious wound on the victim's side. The scar was an old one, a gross knot of flesh grown over a hole. Mallory closed her eyes, a small but telling gesture, and he read much into it. She had more in common with Sparrow than a paperback western retrieved from a crime scene.

Mallory looked up to catch Charles staring at her. "What?"

Pssst.

"There's something I'm curious about." He stepped back to the group of photographs taken at the hospital. Edward Slope's signature appeared on the last page of notes in Mallory's rigid handwriting. He pointed to the picture of Sparrow's scar framed by the gloved hands of the medical examiner. "Evidently, Edward spent some time exploring this wound, but you didn't mention it in any of your notes."

"It's old history," she said. "Nothing to do with this case."

"So you know how it happened."

Pssst.

Riker was suddenly leaving them with uncommon speed, moving to the other side of the room, and that was the only warning that Charles had trodden on some personal land mine.

"It's an old knife wound. *Very* old. A waste of time." She ripped the photograph from the wall. "It shouldn't even be here."

"But you told Coffey this woman was good with a knife."

"None better." She crumpled the photograph in one hand, and Charles could see the bright work going on behind her intelligent eyes.

Because he was handicapped with a face that could not run a bluff in a poker game, most people wrongly assumed that he could not tell when he was being lied to. Mallory never made that mistake. He guessed that she was simply wondering what half-truth might be most misleading.

"It wasn't a fight," she said. "Sparrow never saw the knife coming."

"So she had a blind side?"

"No!" She wadded the photograph into a ball, then rolled it between her palms, making it smaller and smaller. "Yes." And now her voice was smaller too. "You could say she was blindsided by a joke." The little ball of paper disappeared into her closed fist. "Sparrow was laughing when he did it to her." And while Charles was watching this little magic show, her other hand flashed toward him, and he was lightly stabbed in the chest by one red fingernail.

"And now you can *forget* the scar," she said to him, *ordered* him. "We're clear on that?"

Oh, yes, the threat was very clear. Mallory crossed the room with long strides. She could not leave him fast enough. Charles wished she had slammed the door on her way out; that would have told him that she was merely angry, that he had simply annoyed her. But that was not the case; he had damaged her somehow. There would be no more mention of Sparrow's scar, not ever, for he sensed that it was also Mallory's scar. However, the photograph was locked in his memory. He could not let go of it, and now it began to grow, attracting other bits of paper, a fifteen-year-old receipt from Warwick's Used Books, an inscription to a child on the title page of a western. When had Mallory witnessed that piece of violence?

If one truly wanted to maim a human being for life, it was best to start when the victim was very young—ten years old?

Now that the field was clear of explosives, Riker was strolling back to him, folding a cell phone and saying, "Okay, Charles, you got your wish. I gave Duck Boy a real job. He's taking the old man on a field trip—an interview with the cop who found Natalie Homer's body. Are you happy now?"

Hardly.

At the top of the page, Ronald Deluthe had identified the interview subject as the first police officer to enter Natalie Homer's crime scene. During a testy silence, he wrote down a careful description of Alan Parris's apartment, noting worn upholstery, cracked plaster and all the dust and grime of a man who had hit bottom before the age of forty-two.

Parris's personnel file had listed only the dry statistics of a short career with NYPD, but the garbage pail overflowing with beer cans indicated a serious drinking problem. The sink in the galley kitchen was piled high with dirty dishes and one cracked teacup with a delicate design, perhaps something the man's ex-wife had left behind when the marriage ended twenty years ago—only a few months before Natalie Homer's death.

Alan Parris's T-shirt was stained; his boxer shorts were torn; and dirty toenails showed through the holes in his black socks. The man was so underwhelmed by the interview style of Lars Geldorf that he appeared to be nodding off.

No, Alan Parris was drunk.

"You're *lying!*" Geldorf paced the floor and raised his voice to rouse the man from lethargy. "I *know* one of you bastards leaked the details. It was you or your partner. Now give it up!" The old man leaned down, bringing his face within inches of Parris's. "Don't piss me off, son. You won't like me when I get mad."

All the incredulity that Parris could muster was a small puff of air escaping from pursed lips, a lame guffaw. He kept his silence, showing remarkable patience with the retired detective and his ludicrous threats.

Lars Geldorf's promised anger was unleashed, and Deluthe took faithful shorthand, recording every obscenity. The old man finally succeeded in triggering Parris's temper. And now the four-letter words were flying both ways as Deluthe's pencil sped across the page of his notebook, not resting until Geldorf stomped out of the apartment.

This was Deluthe's cue to pull out his list of prepared questions. The script Geldorf had outlined for him was reminiscent of days in uniform and visits to elementary schools in the role of Officer Friendly. "Just a few more questions, sir." He gave Parris a lame smile, and the man rolled his eyes just as the schoolchildren had done. Another tough audience.

Screw Geldorf.

Deluthe dropped his smile, then folded the paper and slipped it back into his pocket. "What about neighbors? Do you remember anyone in the hall near the crime scene? Maybe there was a—"

"It was a long time ago, kid." Parris leaned down and moved a newspaper to one side, exposing a beer can crushed and discarded after some previous binge. He upended it over his open mouth to catch the last drops of flat, warm liquid.

Though the ex-cop showed no sign of anxiety, soon he would be eager to get to a liquor store and replenish his supply of booze.

"Take your time," said Deluthe. "I've got all damn day for this." *Now* he had the man's attention. "I saw the photographs of the crime scene. If it was me, I couldn't have forgotten anything about that night."

"You got that right, kid. But I never talked about the murder. The leak didn't come from me." Parris stared at the front door left ajar, then raised his voice, correctly sensing that Geldorf hovered on the other side. "And you can tell that old bastard—it wasn't me he posted outside in the hall. It was my *partner!* Maybe somebody got by *him.*" His voice dropped to a mumble. "But I couldn't say for sure. Harvey never talked about that night, either—not even with me. We worked together for years, and we *never* talked about it."

"If your partner was posted at the door, then you were inside the apartment the whole time."

"No—only a few seconds. I'm the one who found the body. God, the smell. It was enough to knock a man down. When I went home that night, it was still in my clothes, my hair. I can smell it now. I can still feel the cockroaches crawling up my legs. And the flies—a million of 'em. *Jesus.*"

"So you closed the door and waited for the detectives and Crime Scene Unit?"

"Naw. The way that woman was hanging, I couldn't see the tape on her wrists. Me and Harvey figured it for a suicide. Like I said, I was only in there a few seconds. Suicides don't rate a visit from CSU. The dispatcher only sent detectives."

Deluthe flipped back to notes of yesterday. "Wasn't there someone else on that scene?"

"The photographer? Yeah, he came with the dicks—just a kid. Younger than me, and I was only twenty-two. He got sick and dropped his camera—broke the damn thing. So I borrowed another one from a neighbor. Then the dicks sent me out to buy more film. I think I made two runs to the store that night."

"Did your partner mention any civilians around the crime scene while you were gone? Harvey—" Deluthe checked his notes, as if his own lieutenant's name might be easy to forget. On Riker's orders, no one would be apprised of the case connection to a command officer. He put his finger to a blank page. "Loman, right? Harvey Loman? Was he outside the door the whole time?"

"Yeah. Well, no. When I got back from the store, he was down the hall settling a beef with some old lady." Parris paused for a moment, then covered his eyes with one hand. "Awe, what the hell."

Deluthe's pencil hovered over his notebook. "What?"

"There were two kids right outside the door—real young, a boy and a girl. Harvey—he never saw them. Well, the door was open 'cause of the smell, and those kids got an eyeful before I chased them away. That always bothered me. Probably gave them nightmares. I felt bad about it, sure, but I had no—"

"So your partner lost control of the crime scene. He screwed up. And you didn't want him to get in trouble, right?"

Parris's head lolled on his chest, as if he could no longer support the weight. "Geldorf, bad as he is now—he was worse in those days. He would've nailed Harvey's hide to the wall for letting those kids get past him. That old prick still thinks he's God. I hate detectives. No offense, kid."

"Did the kids see the hair in the victim's mouth?"

"Yeah, they saw everything. The body hadn't been cut down yet. The dicks were still shooting pictures."

Neither of them had heard the door open, but now Lars Geldorf was standing on the threshold. The old man was smiling, and Deluthe could guess why. The retired detective was relieved that another cop had lost control of the crime-scene details. And now no one could ever say that this major screwup was *his* fault.

Pssst.

Charles Butler studied the stalker's notes to Kennedy Harper. By comparison, the old ones left for Natalie Homer were almost poetry. He turned to Riker. "Did you tell Deluthe to ask if Natalie's door was locked when the police arrived?"

"No, Deluthe can't ask about that, and I'm hoping Alan Parris won't volunteer anything." Riker turned off his cassette player. "We have the old statement from Natalie's landlady, and she says that door was locked."

"I'm sure it was when she called the police. But when they arrived—"

The detective put one hand on Charles's shoulder. "If the door wasn't locked when the first cop showed up, then eight million New Yorkers had access to the crime scene. That makes it hard to narrow it down to a boyfriend with his own key. The district attorney won't like that if the case goes to trial. You see the problem?"

Charles nodded absently. He was still preoccupied by the difference in the notes. "The man who killed Natalie Homer loved her obsessively. He crushed her windpipe with his bare hands—an act of passion. I rather doubt that he made a habit of it. Emotionally, the scarecrow is his polar opposite." He tapped the autopsy report on Kennedy Harper. "And the date—an anniversary murder suggests long-term planning. The man who did this was only obsessed with the act itself. A hanged woman, a few dozen candles, a jar of flies—all props. The scarecrow decorates his stage and goes away. It's that cold. Oh, and he's quite insane."

"Suppose we bypass a jury trial?"

"Wise decision."

"What are the odds of getting the scarecrow to confess?"

"Nothing easier. All you have to do is catch him. He'll tell you everything he knows. In fact, he's doing that right now, but no one is listening." Charles unpinned the plastic bag containing a bloodstained note. It was disconcerting to see that the scarecrow's rigid printing so closely resembled Mallory's.

"You analyze handwriting?" asked Riker.

"No, sorry, I don't do voodoo." Charles turned the bag over and showed Riker the deep grooves on the back of the paper. "If his pen had pressed down any harder, he would've torn the paper. I suppose you could read frustration or anger into that."

"He staked that note to a woman's neck with a hatpin—a live woman. Yeah, I'd say he was angry."

"Oh, the rage is limited to his penmanship. It wasn't directed at Kennedy Harper. I don't think he expected her to feel any pain from the hatpin. She was an object—a bulletin board. But I think he definitely has issues with *your* people. He had to know she'd head for the nearest police station. This note was meant for *you*." Charles crossed over to Sparrow's wall and stood before the photographs of the coma victim. "A recent razor slash on Sparrow's arm—I'm guessing that's an escalation because the police clearly were *not* getting his message. Incidentally, why didn't she report that assault?"

"Because she had a whore's rap sheet. Sparrow didn't think the cops would care. And she was right about that."

Riker handed a cup of coffee to Charles, who must be uncomfortable at the small table built for people of normal size. But the man had wanted privacy, and there was not a more secure room than the one that housed the lockup cage. "We can finish this up at your place if you like."

"No, I'm fine, really." The man sipped from his cup and pretended to find the brew passable. "Just one more question."

"Shoot." The detective turned a chair around and straddled it, bracing his arms on the wooden back. "Anything you want."

"I gather Louis took an interest in Kathy some time before the night he brought her home. When exactly was that?"

Riker's blood pressure soared, but he had to smile. Brilliant Charles. A police station was the perfect location for stressful questions. But this time the truth was harmless. "This is just between us?"

"Of course."

"Late one night, a social worker turns up in the squad room. Now Lou owes the woman a favor, so she begs him to find this kid—a very special kid. I guess Kathy was nine, almost ten. She used subway tunnels to get around town, but she didn't always ride the trains. Earlier this same night, the kid played a game of chicken with an engineer in the tunnel. She stood on the track till the train was almost on top of her. At the last possible second, she jumped out of the way." Riker's own private theory was that the child had wanted to die that night.

"She almost gave this poor bastard a heart attack. So now the engineer's afraid she'll electrocute herself on the third rail. He calls out the Transit cops, and they block off the tunnel. Six of those clowns couldn't catch one little girl. She *laughed* at them. So now the social worker arrives. This woman walks into the tunnel and rounds up the kid in two minutes flat. You know how she did that? Kathy walked right up to her, this tall blonde—"

"Like your friend Sparrow."

"Yeah, and the kid was real happy to go anywhere with this woman. Kathy even held the social worker's hand while they were filling out paperwork at Juvie Hall. So the kid's in custody. She's been cleaned up and fed, all settled in for the night. But now the social worker goes home and leaves her alone in that place. Well, no tall blonde—no Kathy. The kid left five minutes later, and the guards never figured out how she got away. She was their only escapee—ever."

"Sounds like she picked up bad habits from the Wichita Kid."

Riker froze. How long had the door been open? How *long?*

Jack Coffey stood on the threshold, saying to him, "You've got a visitor."

And then, as if Charles Butler knew how dangerous the westerns were, he said, "I'm so sorry."

When Riker returned to his desk in the squad room, an old friend was waiting for him. There was nothing in Heller's expression to say that he had good news or bad, for he was the king of deadpan. He held up a business card. "You know this guy, right?"

Riker took the card and read the name aloud, "Warwick's Used Books." His stomach knotted as he eased into the chair behind the desk, and his mouth was suddenly dry. "Yeah, I interviewed him."

Heller slowly swiveled his chair, turning away to look out the window. "John Warwick came in while I was here, and Janos palmed him off on me. So this little guy's all excited. He waves a newspaper in my face. Then he goes into a ramble about some paperback book. He doesn't *ask*—he *tells* me I found it in Sparrow's apartment. Says he *knows* I found it—and he wants it back. Seems the hooker stole it from his store an *hour* before she was hung." He turned back to face the desk and the sorry-looking detective. "Warwick says you'll vouch for that 'cause you took his statement."

"Yeah, I did." Riker tapped the side of his head, a gesture to say that the bookseller was not quite sane. "The paperback probably went into the fire, but I didn't tell that to Warwick."

"*I* told him," said Heller. "And you're right—he *is* nuts. The little guy broke down and cried. I guess that book was pretty important to him—and Sparrow."

"I guess." Riker was recalling his suit jacket all buttoned up—very fancy for a sweltering crime scene. And Heller, a man who could do a post-mortem on a dead fly, would have noticed the damp spot on the breast of that jacket—and every other detail of that night in Sparrow's apartment.

Heller looked down at an open notebook in his hand. "Warwick says the title is *Homecoming*, by Jake Swain." He looked up. "But I figure you already knew that."

This man had run cops off the force for stealing trinkets from crime scenes. If Heller developed a case for tampering with evidence, he would prosecute in a New York heartbeat, no exceptions for friendships that spanned twenty years. They stared at each other, and the silence went on for too long.

"After Warwick left," said Heller, "I went back to the lab and sifted through ashes and fragments. Some of the magazines were intact, but no sign of a paperback. Now that's strange—even with the age of the book, the brittle paper. You'd think the core would've survived, a good chunk of pressed pages. There are tests I could run. You want me to keep on looking?"

Riker slowly shook his head, and this must have passed for a confession.

Heller nodded, then ripped the sheet from his notebook and dropped it into a wastebasket. "Well, I guess that's the end of it." With no good-bye, he rose from his chair and crossed the squad room to the stairwell door.

Riker knew he would keep his badge for lack of physical evidence to hang him—but this man was no longer his friend. And *that* was what Heller had dropped by to tell him.

Cafe Regio on MacDougal Street was filled with the metropolitan babble of foreign languages. Charles Butler looked around the large single dining area crammed with people, paintings and eclectic furnishings. He spied an acquaintance at a corner table.

Anthony Herman was a child's idea of a pixie, not quite five feet tall with a small bulbous nose and pancake ears sticking out at right angles. His light brown hair was swept back to display a pronounced widow's peak, a sure sign of witchcraft, though his true profession would seem rather boring to most. The little man nervously adjusted a red bow tie while doing his best to hide behind a menu, though it was long past the dinner hour.

When Charles sat down at the table, the antiquarian book dealer handed him a package wrapped in brown paper and said, "That's the whole set. Don't open it here."

A very generous check crossed the table and found its way into Herman's pocket. The little man looked around, as if the other late-night diners might be watching this exchange and making notes or taking blackmail photographs. His toes just barely reached the floor to tap it, and his fingers rapped the table. "If you ever tell anyone I was tracing those—"

"I know," said Charles. "You'll hunt me down and kill me. Your reputation is safe." He set the package of books on the table. "How did you find them so fast?"

"There's a collector," said Herman. "Well hardly that—not at all discriminating, but the man's a repository of every western ever written. I had to go to Colorado. That's why the bill is so high. The books didn't cost a dime. I won them shooting pool with a rancher who thinks that crap is high art."

While Charles was grappling with the odd idea of Anthony Herman as a pool hustler, the man added, "The rancher also has first editions from the penny-dreadful era. If you want them, *you* go shoot pool with the old bastard."

"I don't suppose you read any of these novels?" Charles watched Herman's eyes grow a tad fearful. "You *did* read them, didn't you?"

"I might've *glanced* at one on the plane." The little man's mouth dipped down at the corners, silently intoning, *What a question*, making it clear that he was hardly the type to read this sort of trash, and his client should know better.

Charles opened the package, despite the book detective's sudden violent shaking of the head, begging that he not do this in public. After leafing through a chapter of the first volume, he smiled at Herman, another great speed-reader, for this was a talent that went along with the trade of manuscript comparisons. "Light stuff, isn't it? Lots of white space. How long was the plane trip? Three or four hours?"

"All *right*." Herman bowed his head. "I read them. All twelve."

"I'm sure you had other reading material with—"

"It's your fault, Charles. I just had to know why you wanted them so badly. Then I got caught up in the whole thing."

"They're not very good, are they?"

"No. The writing is awful, the plots are thin. Very bad—*very*—all of them."

"But you read the entire series."

"Don't do this to me."

"So what did you think of the resolution to the ambush?"

"Oh, that was the best." Herman's sarcasm was surprisingly light, and his face had gone suddenly sly. "No, wait. The best one starts in *The Cabin at the Edge of the World*. In the previous book, the Wichita Kid was bitten by a mad wolf. The animal was frothing at the mouth, the whole nine yards."

"But there was no rabies vaccine in Wichita's century."

"I know that," said Herman, no dilettante in the field of history. "Rabies was a death sentence in that period."

"So he's cured with a folk remedy," said Charles. "Something like that?"

The little man's smile was coy. "No, that's not it."

"Well, I know he's alive in the last book, so he can't possibly die of—" Charles leaned back in his chair and smiled, for he had just exposed himself as another victim of Jake Swain. "Touché."

And now—a turnabout.

He spread the books over the table for all to see, then studied the lurid covers of smoke and guns and rearing horses, much to the discomfort of Anthony Herman. "I know someone who thought the world of these novels. She read them over and over. Now that you've had a chance to evaluate the lot of them—any helpful insight?"

"Well, no." Herman seemed honestly mystified. "The only reason for reading any of them is to find out what happens next. I assure you there's no reason to read them more than once."

"There has to be more to it than that." Charles gathered the westerns into a stack, then looked up at the book detective. "So what's it all about?"

"Ultimately," said Herman, "it's about the redemption of the Wichita Kid."

Riker had finished his first drink by the time he came to the end of the written interview. The detail was fanatical, right down to Alan Parris's dirty toenails. "And all this conversation—this is word for word?"

"I take shorthand." Deluthe sipped his beer, then tried to make his voice sound casual when he asked, "So what're my chances for getting a permanent assignment to Special Crimes Unit?"

"Today? Slim and none. You got no experience, kid." Only a handful of detectives were ever promoted to first-grade, and ten of them were in Special Crimes Unit. "We don't take whiteshields. And you're what— twenty-five, twenty-six? Most of the guys are in their thirties and forties. We only got one cop your age."

"And *coincidentally* Mallory is the daughter of the former commander of—"

"You're out of line, Deluthe. She grew up in Special Crimes Unit. When she was still in grammar school, she logged more time on the job than you've got."

"He's right." Their bartender had been introduced to Deluthe as Riker's former partner from younger days. Peg Baily leaned into the conversation to replace Riker's empty glass with a fresh bourbon and water. "That kid was our only technical support. In those days, we had crappy secondhand computers. Didn't work half the time. The kid got the whole system up and running when she was thirteen years old." Peg set down a beer for Deluthe. "But you're wondering how Mallory got the rank of detective, first-grade. She chased down the perp who murdered her old man. Highest-priority case in New York City. That's getting ahead the hard way."

Peg Baily wandered down the bar to fill another glass, and Riker completed the trainee's education, giving equal weight to every word. "Nobody ever questioned Mallory's right to a place in Special Crimes." As he leaned toward the younger man, his face relaxed into a smile. "Now, as the son-in-law of a deputy commissioner, you've got a lot more to overcome."

"Suppose I divorce my wife?"

"It's a start." Riker pulled a wad of papers from the pocket of his suit jacket and slapped it on the bar. "This is your background check on the cops at Natalie's crime scene. We already had this information. Mallory pulled it off the computer. Took her two minutes."

"So that assignment was just busywork."

Riker ignored this statement of fact and spread the sheets flat on the bar. "This is only worthless because you took a computer spit-out, some-

thing a clerk gave you over the counter. Now a look at the original files—
that might've turned up some dirt. But you can still learn a lot from the
official fairy tale. I'll teach you how to read the disappearing ink." He put
the first sheet aside, saying, "There were five cops on the scene, three
dicks, two uniforms. Four of them left the precinct in a group. That's a
standout fact."

"I *saw* that," said Deluthe, defensive now. "But it had nothing to do
with the murder. That was six years later."

"But all in the same four-week period. That tells you Internal Affairs
was all over that copshop."

"There are no charges on their records, nothing to say—"

"Deluthe, I *told* you this was a fairy tale. Now do you want your bed-
time story, or do we call it a night?"

"Sorry."

"Just drink—quietly." Riker's finger moved across the lines of text. "So,
one of the uniforms, Alan Parris, was fired for insubordination. Now that's
bogus. You'd have to shoot a sergeant to get fired on a charge like that."
Riker turned to the next page and the next man. "The week before
that, his partner, *your* boss Harvey Loman—he gets reassigned to another
precinct. That tells you Loman rolled over on his partner to cut a deal with
Internal Affairs."

He moved on to another sheet. "Here we got one detective who resigned to take a job in the private sector. The real story? They forced him
out. Not enough proof to hang him. This guy's next job was cleaning out
toilets. He drank himself to death years ago."

Now the final sheet. "And here we have one more dead detective, a
suicide. So, dead or alive, four out of five men leave the department at the
same time. The man who shot himself was probably looking at jail time.
That means he was the last one to give it up, but there was nobody left
to rat on. If he hadn't died, he would've been the sacrifice, the cop who
went to prison."

Of course, Riker was cheating. The nest of shakedown artists in that
station house had been the worst kept secret in NYPD. "Your interview
with Alan Parris only looks good on paper. The two witnesses—the little
kids in the hall? Parris gave you a lot of convincing details, but nothing to

help you find them. That story could be smoke. So Parris goes on the shortlist."

"But the FBI profiles for serial killers—"

"And that's another fairy tale," said Riker.

The remainder of Stella Small's night was a self-imposed blur. She was using rum concoctions to drown the image of a subway full of dead and dying flies and stampeding passengers. Another hour had ended in yet another crowd. On the next bar stool was a tourist in a T-shirt emblazoned with the city motto, "I love New York."

New York sucks.

The young actress's sinuses were clogged with cigarette smoke, and she fancied that she could still smell the insecticide from the subway fiasco. Her head was swimming in rum, and the world swirled around her. Perhaps it had been a mistake to order drinks decorated with paper parasols. But she was not up for the humiliation of tears in a room full of out-of-towners, and the booze, so much tastier than Valium, kept her eyes dry.

One of the customers slammed into her back as he moved toward the men's room. Stella turned to yell at him, but he was lost among a gathering of drinkers.

Damn tourist.

Another patron took advantage of her distraction to cop a feel of one breast. Stunned for a moment, she spun her stool around too late. The man who had sat beside her was gone, lost in the crowd. Stella laid her head down on the bar and knocked it twice against the wood.

I will not cry, I will not cry.

And she did not. She gathered up her house keys and left the bar. Half a block down the street, she noticed a man who was definitely on a mission, marching in the perfect parade-time of a soldier. No—more like a toy soldier, so mechanical, all springs and levers. Mimicry was her art, and she employed it now, stiffening her limbs to follow the marching man.

When he arrived at the broad avenue, he turned left, then stopped, and so did Stella. By the better light of a street lamp, she could see the gray gym bag in his hand. This was the bastard who had cupped her breast in the bar.

The mechanical man turned sharply on his heel, suddenly changing his direction. Stella saw the spinning red light before she reached the avenue where two police officers were patting down a teenager pressed to the hood of their car. She turned to look for the windup man and found him escaping, marching off in double time, afraid that she would report him as a deviant. Well, that was a small victory, but one to savor.

A few minutes later, she was fitting her key into the door lock, though she had no memory of having climbed the stairs to her apartment. Her blue linen blazer was neatly folded over one arm. Miraculously, the material was unmarked despite the subway panic, the rain of flies and the assault of the mechanical pervert. It had come through the day-long odyssey stain-free and hardly wrinkled—certain proof that the suit was magical.

Stella opened her front door and walked into a muggy wall of heat at least ten degrees higher than the outside air. Her one-room apartment had the decor of student housing with mismatched furniture dragged off the street one step ahead of the garbage truck. And all the houseplants had succumbed to neglect, even the artificial varieties. Never once dusted, her plastic ivy had taken on the gray color of authentic death.

She stepped out of her skirt, then clipped it on to a hanger with her blazer. When her lucky suit was in the closet and out of danger, she switched on the air conditioner and stood in the cool breeze as she stripped off her blouse. Before she could toss it on the couch, which was also her bed, she noticed the black ink stain on the white material, a large X made with a thick marking pen.

Weary beyond belief, the actress whispered somewhat insincerely, "I *love* this town." What was she doing here? She stared at the family photograph on the wall, and the Abandoned Stellas smiled back at her. Gram and Mom were so hopeful for her prospects far from the roadside diner and the randy, fertile truck drivers, the fathers of them all.

Stella held up the blouse, shaking her head in deep denial, as if this might make the big black X fade away. She sank down on the couch, then cradled her head in both hands and cried, finally releasing the day in tears.

Had a fellow thespian done this to her during the morning cattle call? The blouse had been fully exposed when the actors were herded into the waiting area. She had put on the blazer just before walking onstage to deliver her lines to a casting director.

No, most likely the vandal had been in that crowded subway car. Was he the same freak who had unleashed the downpour of dead and near-dead insects? Maybe he had been one of the local barflies in the last crowd. Yes, the tourist who had slammed into her back to distract her while he mutilated her only good white blouse.

"Creep." Her other suspect was the pervert who had cupped her breast. "Creep number two."

She wadded up the shirt and dumped it in a wastebasket lined with a plastic bag. And now, since it was trash night, she picked up all the stray bits of debris around her one-room apartment. She held her nose before braving the door of the refrigerator, knowing the smell of rancid milk would make her vomit. And there were other horrors growing on the wire shelves, unidentified critters with coats of furry fungus, abandoned bits of fruit which had crawled off to die in the back of the box. But she never attempted the door to the freezer, for there an arctic winter had settled in to seal half a package of peas in a block of ice, preserving it for future generations.

All the rest was swept into the trash bag, a major job and an important step in making a fresh start. There was another audition tomorrow, and her lucky blue suit had come through the day unscathed.

A good omen.

The *X* on the discarded blouse was now covered with rotted garbage, solidified milk, bottle caps, candy wrappers and deli containers. Stella never saw the folded note in the garment's small breast pocket; it was lost in the clutter of her life. And so she never read the words, *I can touch you any time I want.*

TEN

THE EARLY MORNING TEMPERATURE WAS EIGHTY-TWO degrees, and the East Villagers were already showing some wear as they moved down First Avenue in the rush-hour traffic of wheels and feet.

The tour guide stood at the front of the bus beside the driver. Microphone in hand, she pointed out the more colorful examples of New Yorkers in the wild. However, most of the Finnish tourists were fixated upon one specimen; though this man was clad in the common uniform of T-shirt and jeans, he stood out from all the rest. His torso and head appeared to be made of one rigid piece of wood, and his hands swung by his sides to the beat of a metronome—*tick, tick, tick.* He carried a gray canvas bag, but its weight never hampered the synchronous movement of both arms, and every step was of equal length and speed, never slowing to avoid other people on the sidewalk, never deviating from a straight line.

For the past hour of gridlock, the bus passengers had been bored out of their minds. Their translator had taken sick this morning, and the American tour guide had not yet grasped that they neither spoke nor understood English, except for the word *tourist* and a few helpful obscenities. Now they crowded together on one side of the vehicle, their sense of expectation heightened as they watched the strange man moving down the sidewalk.

Something was about to happen.

The traffic was beginning to move again, and the bus kept pace with the wooden man, following him as he turned a corner and marched down a side street. Most of the other pedestrians moved out of his way, but two smaller people collided with him. Their bodies yielded to the impact—his did not. Crossing Avenue B in advance of the bus, the man kicked a dog, but not in anger. The spaniel was simply in the way of his foot. The animal's owner yelled at him, and he passed this woman by, blind to her raised fist and every living thing in his path.

He pivoted neatly to march in front of the bus, and the driver slammed on the brakes. The riders smiled in unison. Finally—something of interest—a near-death experience.

The Finns moved to the windows on the other side of the bus, and every pair of eyes followed the man's progress to the opposite sidewalk, where he took a baseball cap from his gray bag and pulled it low to shield his face. Then he reached into his pocket for the giant I LOVE NEW YORK button and pinned it to his T-shirt. He moved through a crowd of people, pushing them out of his way without raising a hand, walking into their bodies, never seeing or hearing them, and they fell off to the side with angry shouts and obscene gestures.

The Finnish tourists heard a loud bang, and some of them ducked, for they had seen entirely too many movies about New York and its heavily armed residents.

The man stopped, and so did the bus. It knelt down on one blown-out tire as the driver muttered a word for defecation and frustration. The tour guide cautioned her disembarking passengers not to wander off before the replacement bus arrived. Even if the Finns had understood what she was saying, her warning would have been unnecessary, for they had no intention of going anywhere.

They formed an audience on the sidewalk, and, behind the safety of their sunglasses, they watched the wooden man. He stood near the door of an apartment house. A fence of bars protected a tiny courtyard and a bed of daisies gamely growing in the heat. The man moved closer to the iron gate. He opened his canvas bag and pulled out a camera, then stared at his wristwatch.

The Finns understood that he was also waiting for something to happen. They waited with him, watching him between the bodies of pedestrians marching toward the subway. Except for the large souvenir button on his T-shirt, many of the commuters were dressed in the same casual clothes, but the wooden man could not quite blend in with real life.

He glanced at his watch again, and the tourists nodded to one another. It would not be long now.

The man turned his entire body to face the door in the courtyard fence, and twenty pairs of Finnish eyes were looking over his shoulder.

Beyond the iron bars, a red door flew open. A slender blonde crossed the small courtyard with a fast click of white high heels. Her blouse was also white, and the pale blue skirt matched the garment slung over her arm. The young woman opened the iron gate and hurried to the curb, one hand raking through her long hair, combing it on the run. She lifted a waving arm to fish a cab from the stream of traffic.

The Finns stared at this attractive woman, wondering if they should recognize her from television or the cinema. They wanted her to be an actress, for they had not seen one celebrity in the past two days.

After donning sunglasses, the man moved toward the pretty blonde as a tight group of pedestrians passed between them. The sun glinted off a piece of metal when the man lurched forward through the press of bodies and collided with the young woman.

She yelled, "Damn tourist!" And the twenty Finns were startled, but took no offense.

The man pointed his camera at her. Some reflex made the woman toss her hair and pose for him with a smile. A cab stopped, the blonde stepped in and rode off, never noticing what the wooden man had done to her.

The show was over. The man moved on. And the Finnish tourists looked the other way. In the best tradition of New York City, they had elected not to get involved.

The cab was trapped in midtown traffic, and Stella Small's anxiety was climbing with every dime on the meter. She banged on the bulletproof glass that separated her from the driver. Of course, he would not turn around. What was the point? He spoke no English, and Stella knew that when she yelled, "There won't be any ransom! I'm dead broke!"

The turbaned cabby nodded to assure her that they would be moving soon. He was very polite, more proof that he was not a native New Yorker.

She looked down at her watch for the third time in as many minutes, and she was still late.

"Okay, you win!" She waved money so the man could see it in his rearview mirror. After paying him, she stepped out of the cab two blocks from the hotel. Her pale blue blazer was carefully folded over one arm to protect it from soot and the droppings of low-flying pigeons.

She was swept up in the crowd of pedestrians and moving along the sidewalk at a fast clip. Two women walking toward her were actually slowing down, completely misunderstanding the concept of rush hour. And now they were breaking the prime law of survival in New York City, going beyond dangerous eye contact to overt staring. Stella wondered if they had recognized her from a recent walk-on part in a television soap opera.

Dream on, babe.

An old man stopped to gawk at her, and Stella smiled for him.

Yes, it's me, the famous actress with no speaking roles.

She was attracting hard looks from everyone she passed. A middle-aged couple stopped to point at her, their mouths working in silence, obviously starstruck. The daytime soaps must be more popular than she had supposed.

Don't you people have regular jobs?

The actress pushed through the hotel door and walked into an icy wall of machine-made air. Near the entrance, a bored young man never even glanced her way. He plucked a sheet of paper from his stack and waved it in her general direction. A woman near the closed doors to the ballroom was calling out the names that began with *R*. Stella Small sighed—saved by her rank in the alphabet.

She donned her suit jacket and joined the other actresses in an area roped off for the cattle call. None of these women paid any attention to her. Each pair of heavily made-up eyes was glued to a line of script on the handout sheet. Stella looked down at her own sheet. One line, *six* words. How much study did that require?

She stood near the wall behind a potted fern, away from the press of other bodies, determined that no one would wrinkle her lucky suit or stain it. When her name was called, she entered the ballroom beyond the great doors and stood before a long dais decked with bottles and glassware, paperwork and food trays. On the other side of the linen table cloth, the casting director and producer were seated in the company of assistants. Before Stella could even say her line, these men and women were all agog, eyes popping. She flashed them with her best smile. They were dazzled, riveted, stunned—though still awaiting her first word.

The actress felt a slick of something wet on her hand and looked down at a long thick line of blood seeping through the sleeve of her blazer. Inside the casing of linen, more blood was rolling down the skin of her arm and dripping off the tips of her fingers.

"I hate it when this happens." Line delivered, though it was the wrong line, Stella Small closed her eyes in a dead faint, and the back of her head met the hardwood floor.

Green curtains formed three walls of the emergency-room cubicle, a thin layer of privacy for the young couple. Stella Small's legs swung from the edge of the metal examination table, and the physician's smile was shy as he treated her wounded arm.

The doctor's head snapped to one side, suddenly distracted by a shadow looming close to the flimsy curtain. Though the silhouette was all wrong, Stella instantly recognized this scene from the movie *Psycho*. One shadow hand was on the rise, reaching higher, higher, and then—the green curtain was violently ripped to one side. And now the startled young doctor was staring at a stout woman with a pyramid of dark hair and a long black dress that flowed like a nun's habit.

Stella had always suspected that her agent could smell fresh blood from great distances. Martha Sutton was a formidable woman, a drama queen extraordinaire and scarier than *real* nuns.

"Nice entrance."

"Oh, Stella, *Stella*." The woman's gleaming eyes appraised the lacerated arm and the bright red stains on her client's clothing. "You look *marvelous!*" In agentspeak, this meant *publicity worthy*.

The young doctor turned back to his chore of irrigating a long thin wound. "I think we can get away without stitches." He applied a few small bandages shaped like butterflies. "It's a clean cut—very shallow. But I don't see how a camera could've done this. Even if a piece of broken metal was—"

"I'm telling you," said Stella, "this tourist bumped into me with his damn camera. I was standing outside my building, hailing a cab—"

"All right, have it your way." The doctor walked away from the examination table, saying, "But it looks like you've been slashed with a razor."

Martha Sutton's eyes turned gleeful and sly. She whispered to her client, "Great line. We'll keep it in the act."

"But it was a *camera*." Stella was more insistent now.

The agent pointed toward the far wall, where a man was standing behind a glass door. "See that guy? He's a reporter. Now how bad do you want a career, baby doll?"

"Oh." And by this, Stella meant, *I've got religion—I've seen the light.* Aloud, she said, "I've been slashed with a razor."

"That's my girl," said Sutton. "And play up the idiot who carried you across that hotel lobby. He's one of my clients. Lucky he didn't have the brains to stop your bleeding. That trail of blood on the carpet was priceless. Now remember to spell your name for the reporter. He's another idiot." The agent turned to leave, then stopped with an afterthought. "I made you an appointment for another audition. Something different—a police station. I just got off the phone with a cop in SoHo. He only wants blond actresses with dry-cleaning problems. Do you by any chance have a blouse with a big *X* drawn on the back?"

Stella nodded. "Some bastard got me with a black pen."

"Wonderful. The cops are looking for a serial vandal. Pray for a slow news day. Maybe we'll get your face on TV. And take that blouse with you. It'll make a great prop."

"But I don't have it anymore," said Stella. "I threw it away."

"No, honey, don't tell me that. Look me in the eye and tell me you *saved* that blouse."

Well, how hard could it be to mark up another one?

"Okay, I saved it."

"That's my girl."

Two hours later and home again, fresh from the shower and clean of blood, Stella Small opened a can of beer in hopes that it might dull the throb in her wounded arm. She spotted a pair of sneakers only partially hidden by her cast-off clothes. No, bad idea. Her agent had given her too much Valium, and tying shoelaces might be too hard. She reached under a chair for a pair of sandals.

Stella flopped down on the couch in a cloud of dust and consulted a copy of *Backstage*, the only newspaper she ever read. The turned-back page with the schedule of auditions listed nothing for today. Yet she could not lose the nagging idea that she was supposed to be somewhere this afternoon.

She picked up her TV remote and flicked through the channels until she found a children's program.

Good. Cartoons were easy.

The television screen went black, and no button on the remote control could bring it back to life. This was a bad omen, but Stella was not completely shattered—not yet. She had a fascination for how long a disaster streak could go on and how awful it could become before playing itself out. The young actress was also determined that no life experience would ever go to waste if she could only stay alive in this town.

A bug was moving up her leg. Mid-scream, she stopped and smiled. It was only a spider. She flicked it off her skin and watched it crawl across the floor. It was a big one, but the Abandoned Stellas had always said that a spider in the house was good luck. However it *was* a big one. She rolled up her newspaper and smashed the creature flat.

The Abandoned Stellas had said a lot of things.

She reached down to the floor and picked up the bloodstained suit jacket. While going through the pockets, preparing to throw it away, she found a note in her agent's handwriting.

Oh, right—the cattle call. She read the address of the SoHo police station and the time when she was expected—along with a few hundred other actresses. The station house was within easy walking distance, and there was at least an hour to kill.

The telephone rang, and Stella cringed. She let her answering machine take the call. The young woman from Ohio was much too fragile to deal with New Yorkers right now.

She paid more attention to the machine when the words, *police department*, filtered through her Valium fog. Stella grabbed up the phone. "Hi! Is this about the actress interviews in SoHo? . . . No? Midtown? I thought . . . Oh, right. Sorry. I didn't know . . . Yes, I'll be there."

And now she recalled her agent dragging her out of an emergency room, though she had been told to wait there until a police officer arrived. She had left the hospital in the company of a tabloid reporter who had taken precedence over the law.

How much trouble was she was in?

The timing would be close. With a little luck and a functional subway, she could make the appointments at both police stations, but only if the SoHo interviews went by alphabetical order. Martha Sutton's note reminded her that she needed a vandalized blouse for a prop.

After rummaging through the closet and the drawers, every article of clothing was strewn about the small apartment, and all the effort of last night's cleaning binge had been undone. This was so disheartening. Just looking at the mess made her weary. She turned to the smiling portrait of the Abandoned Stellas, but they had no homilies to cover a life spinning out of control.

In the pile of clothes at her feet, she found an old thrift-shop garment that would do nicely. Then she went off to make another mess of the kitchenette, emptying the catch-all drawers in search of a pen to make a large *X* on the back of the blouse.

The ground floor of the SoHo police station was packed with actresses, all sizes and every color of hair, though Special Crimes Unit had specifically requested blondes. Jack Coffey stood near the street door and stared at the double-parked news vans. Reporters were roaming the sidewalk in gangs.

He turned to Detective Wang. "Exactly what did you say to the talent agencies?"

"Just what you told me. I said we were investigating vandalism on the subway."

Detective Desoto folded his cell phone and turned to the lieutenant. "One of the agents tipped the reporters. She told them we were hunting a sex maniac with a thing for blondes." He looked toward the open door and its view of reporters milling on the street. "But none of those bastards made a connection to Special Crimes Unit."

Lieutenant Coffey silently thanked the city accountants for being too cheap to paint the name of his unit on the door at the top of the stairs. "Okay, take the actresses up to the squad room, ten at a time. And pass the word—nobody mentions Special Crimes. I don't want anybody handing out cards to these women—I don't care how pretty they are. Now weed out the brunettes."

Coffey watched the actresses being herded toward the staircase, where Desoto pulled out the women with dark hair. The first group of blondes climbed the stairs behind Detective Wang. They were all so young, so unprepared for what was going to happen to them.

A few minutes later, when Lieutenant Coffey entered the squad room, the actresses were lined up in a tight row, all but standing at attention. Detective Janos played the part of their drill sergeant, pacing back and forth in front of them, inspecting his troops. "If you're jerking us around to get your names in the paper, you'll be charged with obstruction of justice. That means time in lockup."

Though the man had a gentle voice, he also had a thug's face and the gravitational mass of a small planet. The blond heads turned in unison, following his movements back and forth.

"Our lockup isn't very clean. Fleas, lots of fleas."

Two dishwater blondes were edging toward the stairwell door while the other women were still debating flight.

"Oh, and lice are a problem, too." Janos sighed. "So you'll be stripped and deloused in a gang shower."

After the mass exodus of actresses, all that remained was one intrepid blonde in the fairest range, and the large detective engaged her in a staring contest. She burst into tears, then ran toward the door, where another ten women were waiting in line. And Janos hollered, "Next!"

ELEVEN

 CHARLES STOOD APART FROM THE OTHERS AS THEY ARGUED in Mallory's private office at Butler and Company.

Chief Medical Examiner Edward Slope said, "No, Riker, I'm not going back to that hospital, not for at least ten years." And now that the subject of the dying coma patient was closed, he turned back to his study of Natalie Homer's *new and improved* autopsy photographs blown up to many times the original size.

Mallory's magic had created sharp definition from grainy enlargements, using her computer to refine light and shadow, replacing ambiguity with certainty and exposing details never seen in the originals. Although it appeared to be the camera's eye of truth, Charles suspected that she had cheated the pieces, the pixels that made the pictures, and the result was only the best guess of artificial intelligence.

"Okay," said Riker, somewhat testy. "Can you give me a second opinion on this?" He handed the pathologist an X-ray of Natalie's head, some-thing Mallory had not retouched.

The doctor held up the film to the light of the windows. "You're right. It looks like my predecessor missed everything but the cause of death. It's a skull fracture. I can't tell if it rendered her unconscious, but it certainly stunned her. The fracture agrees with a blunt object. I could swear to that much."

Next, Riker handed him an enlarged photograph of Natalie's right hand. "This is the burn shot."

Dr. Slope shook his head. "Can't help you on this one. No way to tell if the flesh was burned before the insects got at it."

Riker consulted a transcription of Louis Markowitz's notes and pointed to a line of type. "Right *here*. Lou says the hand was burned." And another argument had begun.

"That's because of the roaches," said Charles, stepping into the conver-sation in the role of a peacemaker. "Louis saw them clustered on her hand. That would indicate the presence of grease. If it was hot from the frying pan—"

"Speculation," said Edward Slope. "I only testify to facts." He glanced at his watch. "Unless there's something else—"

"About Sparrow," said Riker. "Maybe you could just talk to her doctor on the—"

"Not a shot in hell," said Dr. Slope. "Now Charles could take on that lightweight intern. He knows all the jargon."

"Sparrow's dying," said Riker. "I need a *medical* opinion."

"If it's coma related, then Charles is your man." Edward Slope walked toward the door, saying, "I promise you, nobody on that hospital staff knows more about the human brain."

The door closed, and a defeated Riker slumped into a chair behind the desk. "Sparrow's doctor hates cops. He won't even talk to me. Can you help?"

"Well, Edward exaggerates," said Charles. "I only published one paper on the comatose brain. However, I could probably negotiate a conversa-tion with her doctor."

"Sounds good. Thanks. But Mallory doesn't need to know, okay?"

Riker closed his eyes and put his feet up on her desk, a sign that she was not expected back for the duration of a catnap. And Charles was left to wonder why Riker would keep the hospital visit a secret. Surely his own partner had an equal interest in this crime victim. It was an interesting problem, and the solution lay in the certain knowledge that Mallory would not forgive any act of concern for an enemy.

Both men jumped at the sound of a crash in the next room.

"Kids." Riker's feet hit the floor. "You can't turn your back on 'em for a second."

When they entered the office kitchen, they found Ronald Deluthe dressed in a replica of Natalie Homer's apron, ruffles and all. He was holding an unplugged electric skillet. There were spills on every surface and puddles of water on the floor. Wet enlargements of crime-scene photos were spread across the tabletop.

"This is my fault," said Riker. "I told him to work out a fly-on-the-wall scenario."

Charles looked down at a splash of water near the stove. "So that's supposed to be grease from Natalie's sausages?"

"Yes, sir. Watch." Deluthe filled the frying pan with more water, then treated them to a demonstration of backswings and overhand strikes. Most of the liquid spilled behind him, and the remainder sloshed forward toward an imagined assailant, splattering an innocent refrigerator. His right hand was wet, and the rest of him remained dry. "It never spills on the apron. So she wasn't using the frying pan for a defensive weapon. I figure the killer was holding it."

"That makes sense," said Riker. "Slope confirmed the skull fracture. Maybe the perp used the pan on her head. Good job, kid."

"Now clean up the mess." Mallory had materialized in the doorway. Her eyes roved over the wet floor and the rivulets streaming down every wall. She turned to Deluthe in stone silence. He scrambled to grab a sponge from the sink, then knelt on the tiles and began to wipe the puddles.

"You're wrong about the frying pan," said Charles. "Natalie *did* use it as a weapon. But the mistake is understandable." He pointed to the electric skillet with its built-in computer panel for timing meals. "That's aluminum, and the handle never gets hot."

"What?" Deluthe slowly rose from his crouch on the floor.

Charles excused himself for a few moments, then returned to the kitchen, holding the frying pan found at the crime scene. "This is

Natalie's—solid iron. The handle would've been very hot. She'd need a potholder." He pointed one of the pictures on the table. "See the hooks on this wall? Here by her stove—one hook for each potholder, and they're all in place. But the sausages weren't done yet. See? The front burner is still glowing. She was interrupted."

"Right," said Deluthe. "She died."

"But first—something less dramatic," said Charles, "like a knock on the door. Natalie had time to hang her potholder on a hook before she opened that door to her murderer. She wouldn't leave sausages unattended for long, so you know the fight began immediately." He took the sponge from Deluthe and wiped spots off a crime-scene photo. "Judging by the number of sausages, I'd say you used too much water for your experiment." He glanced at a photo of Natalie's apron. In Mallory's enhancement, the longest borders of the grease stain were more sharply defined. Louis Markowitz's notebook entry had been correct. This was not a splash or a splatter. It was a smear.

After separating one photo from the rest, Charles pointed to a mass of roaches on Natalie's right hand. "Let's assume she burned her hand. She also had a bad fall, and it knocked her out or stunned her. Natalie never got to swing the skillet. But she *intended* to use it as a weapon. Oh, and the killer never touched it at all."

Deluthe folded his arms. "How could you know if—"

"Because your apron is dry, and the rest of the kitchen isn't." Charles ran the frying pan under the tap, then returned it to the stove's front burner. "Natalie's facing her killer. No time to pull down a potholder—she grabs the skillet—" He grasped the handle and raised the pan quickly, spilling a bit of the water on his hand and arm. More liquid hit the floor behind him on the backswing. "The hot iron and grease burn her hand. Natalie lets go of the handle before she can swing the skillet forward."

Charles released the pan, and it clattered to the floor beside him. "The killer advances. She backs off." He edged away from an invisible man. "She has grease on her shoes and loses traction. Her legs fly out from under her, and she falls facedown."

Deluthe was in denial. "How do you know she fell? Or how she landed?"

"Logic," said Charles. "If all the facts only fit one scenario, that's the way it happened. May I?" He held out one hand to take the proffered apron, then spread it on the floor. "Natalie's down. She's not moving. Probably hit her head on the corner of the stove. I know her skull fracture wasn't made by an iron skillet. That would've caved in her skull." He straightened up and turned to Deluthe. "You'll notice that my grease puddle is smaller than yours. It's covered by the breast of the apron." He tapped the photo of the garment. "The edges of the grease stain wouldn't be this straight if she struggled. So she was stunned or unconscious when he dragged her across the floor." Charles reached down and pulled the apron toward him. When he picked it up, the wet spot was the size and shape of the stain on Natalie Homer's apron.

"And that's what the fly on the wall saw." Charles's tone was almost apologetic when he said to Deluthe, "I'm sure you could've worked this out. But you've never cooked anything, have you?"

The floor had been recently mopped, and it bore the same chlorine odor as the city morgue. Riker could hear Charles Butler speaking to the young intern in the hallway outside the hospital room.

The rolling of Sparrow's eyes was involuntary; Riker knew that, but this guise of dementia might be a window on her mind—what was left of it. He resisted the temptation to close her eyelids, a service performed for the dead.

The detective sat beside the bed, making confetti out of the hospital's request to give the patient a more complete identity. He knew her full name, but he would never surrender it. Sparrow would not have wanted that. She had told him so one rainy night when he had given her coffee and shelter in his car. The prostitute had been sickly and bone thin all that winter. He had believed that she was only days away from dying, and that was before she had mentioned the plans for her gravestone.

He remembered laughing when their macabre conversation had turned to braggadocio. *Sparrow*—that was all she had wanted on her monument— no dates, no message, only the one name engraved in bold letters like a Las Vegas marquee, a token of fame. It fit her character so well, this gross presumption that cemetery visitors would know who she was . . . who she had been.

Done with his hallway consultation, Charles Butler entered the room and closed the door softly, as if Sparrow were not beyond being disturbed. "Well, you were right about her doctor. He hates policemen, but he's giving her the best of care. One might say he's on a mission to keep her alive." He nodded toward the pole beside the bed. It supported a plastic bag of liquid that flowed into the patient's arm. "That's an antibiotic to fight infection. And a collapsed lung explains the tube down her throat. Apparently this woman had a very hard life. For one thing, her doctor suspects a history of chronic respiratory ailments."

Riker nodded. "She got sick every winter."

"And then there's the long-term damage of malnutrition and drugs. Given her history as a prostitute, the doctor thinks venereal disease might account for a dysfunctional kidney. So it isn't just the coma—it's a gang of complications." He rested one hand on the detective's shoulder. "I'm so sorry."

Riker stared at the woman on the hospital bed—his friend until she died. "Could she be in there? I mean—with a brain going on all cylinders?"

"It's possible." Charles stared at a machine by the bed, watching the dip and spike of lines running across its screen. "Her present condition is best described as a dream state. In all likelihood, she'll be dreaming when she dies. No pain, no fear. Does this help you?"

"Yeah, it does. Thanks." Riker listened to her mechanical breathing and stared at the tubes running in and out of her body.

"We should be leaving soon," said Charles. "I promised Mallory I'd get you to Brooklyn on time."

"Yeah—soon." The box of tissues on the nightstand was empty. Riker set the paperback novel on the bed, then searched all his pockets for a handkerchief.

"I might have something to cheer you up," said Charles. "A lead on William Heart, the photographer who dropped his camera at Natalie's crime scene. I called a gallery that—" He picked up the western and idly leafed through the pages. "Did you finish this yet?"

"Never started it." Riker wiped away Sparrow's drool.

"I don't blame you. The writing is terrible." Charles stared at the woman on the bed. "I imagine Mallory was a child when she met Sparrow— maybe ten? Younger than that?"

Riker froze in the act of dabbing Sparrow's lips. He wanted a drink so badly. He was damned if he lied or told the truth, and even his continuing silence said too much.

Charles looked down at the book in his hand. "I managed to find a complete set of these westerns. I read them all last night."

The handkerchief dropped to the floor. Riker closed his eyes and hoped that his voice conveyed only weariness when he said, "Bet that took all of four minutes."

"Longer. I read them twice. And I still don't understand why Kathy read them so many times."

These days, it was rare to hear Mallory's first name said aloud. He knew Charles was speaking of Kathy the child he had never known. She had been all grown up when Lou Markowitz had introduced this man to his pretty daughter, the cop. On the day they met, Mallory had arrived at the SoHo cafe for a ritual breakfast with her foster father. Charles, normally a graceful man, had risen too quickly, knocking over his chair in a rush to play the gentleman. In another departure from grace, he had stared at her remarkable green eyes throughout the meal and smiled a foolish apology each time she looked his way. His every gesture, the food spilled in his lap and an overturned juice glass had said to her, *I love you madly.*

"No accounting for her taste in reading," said Charles. He was still turning the pages of the last western. "Even at the age of ten, she would've been brighter than most adults."

Only the bookseller could have revealed the little girl's obsession with westerns. Riker would never have believed that John Warwick, paranoia incarnate, would open up to a stranger. But how had Charles sussed out Kathy's childhood relationship to Sparrow?

"The paper seems to be holding up well." Charles fanned the pages of the book, testing his handiwork. "Have you made a decision yet? Do you plan to give this to Mallory? Or will you destroy it?"

The detective settled into a chair beside the bed. His smile was one of resignation, and he was only half joking when he said, "You're a dangerous man, Charles."

"Oh, I already burned my copies. Don't let that worry you. They went into the fireplace last night. I suppose Louis did something similar while Kathy was still very young. He wouldn't want evidence to tie his child to a little thief who loved westerns. I gather her early days were more—more *colorful* than I thought. So Louis destroyed all her books? All but the last one?"

Riker only nodded. The less said, the less this man would have to work with. "I can't tell you any more about the westerns."

"Especially the last one," said Charles. "Yes, I imagine you're giving me deniability of a crime. Something like that?"

Riker took a moment to digest these words. Was there anyone left who did *not* know that he had robbed a crime scene? That was the problem with spontaneous criminal acts, no planning, no time to cover tracks. And here he was still holding stolen goods. Any half-bright petty thief would have made a better job of it.

"I guess I'll never know what she saw in them." Charles looked down at the cover illustration of Sheriff Peety on a rearing stallion, two six-guns blazing fire, and the ricochet of sunlight from a golden badge. "Do you think she believed in heroes?"

Riker shrugged. Lou Markowitz had once held the darker idea that Kathy had identified with all the cattle rustlers and the stagecoach robbers.

A nurse entered the room to bathe the patient, and the two men took their leave. As they strolled down the corridor, Charles told the story of *The Cabin at the Edge of the World*, a book that Riker had never read. As they neared the parking lot, the Wichita Kid had been bitten by a mad wolf frothing at the mouth a century before the rabies vaccine was invented. When they reached the other end of the Brooklyn Bridge, the outlaw lay unconscious in a burning cabin surrounded by a mob of angry farmers with torches and pitchforks. A preacher was denouncing a witch, an old woman also trapped in the fire, and blaming her for the drought that was killing the crops.

"No, don't tell me," said Riker. "This con man, the preacher, he actually brings on the rain. That puts out the cabin fire and ends the drought. So now the farmers are real happy, and they decide not to kill the old lady. And then the preacher does another miracle and cures Wichita's rabies."

"Not even close," said Charles. "When the next book opens, the Wichita Kid is still surrounded by flames. There's no way out."

Riker knew a better escape yarn, a true one, but there was no one he could share it with now that Sparrow was dying. He had missed her company over these past two years, and now he was grieving for her, though she was not altogether gone.

The Mercedes was approaching the Brooklyn Bridge when Charles asked, "How did Louis trace Kathy to Warwick's Used Books?"

Riker stared at the window on the water. *Shoot me—shoot me now.* "We just got lucky one night."

He had a demoralizing old memory of running out of breath as he watched the child's shoes skimming along the sidewalk, outdistancing him with no effort at all. She had laughed as she dusted off Lou Markowitz, a man with fifty pounds of excess weight. Poor Lou had been wheezing when he caught up to Riker, who was hugging a lamppost, convinced that his heart had stopped.

"Then we spotted the kid in Warwick's window." He recalled the baby thief leaning one small hand on a bookshelf as she nonchalantly perused her westerns. Though she had just run two cops into the ground—nearly killed them—only Kathy's eyes seemed weary, just like any other child at the end of a busy day.

"So we go inside the store, and Lou tells the owner no more customers for a while. Then we go to collect the kid, but she's gone, and the back room was locked up from the inside. It drove us nuts. You've seen that place. There was no way she could've made it out the door without being seen." Then they had noticed the fear in the bookseller's eyes. Lou had gathered his hound-dog jowls into a dazzling smile to win over the merchant with personal charm—or so he had believed at the time.

The mystery of Kathy's escape had not been solved that night or the next. "Lou spent a week of off-duty hours staking out the store and reading all of Kathy's westerns." He had also developed a rapport with the fragile bookseller. "Finally, Warwick tells him how Kathy got away that night. For maybe three seconds, our backs were turned from the rear wall while we talked to the owner. That's when she climbed up the bookshelves—quick as a monkey, quiet as smoke—all the way to the top where there was just enough room to squeeze between the shelf and the ceiling."

"Then the bookseller must have watched her do it."

"Yeah, and he never gave her up, even though just the sight of a cop scared the shit out of him. The whole time Lou was talking to this frightened little man, Kathy was up there listening to him, laughing at him."

The detective shrugged. "So we were outmatched by a ten-year-old girl. Not our best night."

That was when Lou Markowitz had begun to realize who and what he was dealing with—no ordinary child, but a full-blown person. And he had amended the résumé of a street thief to include the grand title of Escape Artist. Kathy had earned Lou's respect. She had also cut out his heart, but that was another night, and the child had almost won that time, almost destroyed the man.

Though it would have been some comfort to him, Riker could never share the story of Kathy's best escape act. And now his mind reached back across the bridge, across the water to the sleeper in her coma dreams to tell her that she was not dying alone.

Sparrow, the secrets are poisoning me.

Mallory watched Charles's Mercedes drive off as her partner slid into the front seat of her tan sedan.

"It's that one." She nodded toward the building directly across the street. Natalie Homer's sister lived in an area of Brooklyn prized for views of Prospect Park. Apparently Susan Qualen was doing well in the world. "It's better if we catch her outside." Then the cop hater would have no door to slam in their faces. "The neighbors say she runs in the park— same time every day."

"Must be a health fanatic." Riker wiped the sweat from his brow. "She's gonna kill herself in this heat."

The front door opened, and a trim woman in shorts and a T-shirt appeared at the top of a short flight of stairs. Natalie's sister was tall and blond with a familial face. Before the woman could descend to the sidewalk, the two detectives were out of the car and moving toward her, each holding up a leather folder with identification and a gold shield.

"Miss Qualen? I'm Detective Mallory, and this is—"

The woman's face turned angry and hard. "Go away!"

Riker stood at the bottom of the stairs. "Ma'am? We'd rather do this at your convenience, but you—"

"I read about your last hanging in the papers," said Susan Qualen. "You bastards couldn't cover up that one. Not so easy this time, was it?"

"Ma'am," said Riker. "We don't work that way. Sometimes we have to withhold details so we can—"

"I've heard that one before. Twenty years ago, the cops told the reporters my sister was a suicide."

"The cops didn't tell you much, did they?" Mallory moved up the staircase, advancing on the woman slowly. "They told you it was murder, and you knew about the rope." But no cop would have revealed the details of the hacked-off hair jammed in Natalie Homer's mouth.

Mallory was one step away—touching distance. *Nervous, Susan?* "So how did you make the connection between your sister and a hanged hooker?"

"I read the story in the damn papers."

Mallory shook her head. "No, you're lying. The link had to be more than rope. All those details in the paper—why did you connect them with—"

"I'm done with you." Susan Qualen started down the staircase.

"Hold it." Mallory blocked her way. "Where did you get the—"

"My lawyer says I don't have to talk to you."

"No," said Mallory. "That's what people say when they *haven't* talked to a lawyer. Your sister's murder is still an open case, and you *will* talk to us."

Riker climbed a step closer to the woman. His voice was more reasonable and friendly. "We turned up some inconsistencies in Natalie's murder. We think her son might be able to straighten it out. So where's the kid now?"

"I don't know where he is," said Susan Qualen.

"I read a follow-up interview with the boy's stepmother," said Mallory. "She claims you took the boy after his father died."

And Riker added, "That would've been a year after Natalie's murder." His tone of voice said, *Hey, just trying to be helpful.*

"But we had a problem with that." The threat in Mallory's voice was impossible to miss.

"You see," said Riker, dialing back the tension, "the little boy never went to school after his mother died. When summer vacation was over—"

"So the family moved out of the school district."

"No, Miss Qualen," said Mallory. "The stepmother still lives at the same address." Mallory edged closer. "She told a cop named Geldorf that *you* had the boy. Why would she lie? And when that same cop called you, why didn't you set him straight?"

There was confusion in Qualen's eyes. Civilians were amateurs at deception, unable to remember the details of lies told in the distant past, and they were all so easily rattled. Riker smiled at the woman, as if they were old friends discussing weather and books they had read. "It would help if you could tell us what happened to Natalie's son."

"And where he is now." Mallory made the short step from accusation to attack. "Talk to me! What did you do with him?"

Susan Qualen lost her hard-case composure and made a mad sprint down the staircase, slamming into both detectives in her haste to get away. Mallory hit the sidewalk at a dead run, and Riker lunged to catch her arm, yelling, "Whoa! First, let's interview the stepmother. Then we can nail Qualen for obstruction. We'll toss her in the lockup cage for a while. It'll be scary but legal."

Mallory watched the woman's hands flailing as she ran down the sidewalk, escaping. Passersby must believe that they had drawn guns on her. Even now, the distance could be so easily closed, and when Mallory caught up to Susan Qualen, the woman would be vulnerable, breathless and frightened.

"Trust me," said Riker. "It'll be more fun my way."

Not likely.

William Heart cringed at the noise. The recluse was not good with human interaction and did what he could to avoid it. Worst was the knock at the door, the sound of a trap closing. He stood very still, hardly breathing, but his visitors would not go away, and now he heard the voice of the landlord saying, "I know he's in there. Takes him all damn day to open the door. Bang *harder*."

However, the stranger was more polite, only lightly rapping, as he said, "Thank you," to the dwindling footsteps of the landlord. And now the visitor spoke to the locked and bolted door. "Hello? Mr. Heart? Your gallery gave me your address."

The cultured voice was reassuring and carried the lure of a potential sale. William opened the door to see a fairy-tale bag of metaphors. This tall man had the body, the clothes and patrician air of a prince, but eyes like a frog and the beak of Captain Hook. The broad shoulders were threatening, magically enlarging in every passing second.

When William stepped back a pace, his visitor took this for an invitation. The man walked past him and paused by the couch, a threadbare affair of lumpy cushions and barely contained stuffing. It was the only piece of furniture that might accommodate his large frame. The chairs were made of flimsy wooden sticks.

"May I?"

William nodded, and the frog prince sat down.

"My name is Charles Butler." The man's grin was so foolish, William smiled against his will as Mr. Butler handed over a business card. "Your gallery dealer tells me you do crime-scene photography."

"No, that was a long time ago. I don't do it anymore."

Butler was staring at a radio on the coffee table, and William wondered if he recognized it as a police scanner. He cleared his throat. "I mean—I don't work for the police anymore. I do car wrecks, that kind of thing."

"Yes, I know. Your work is almost tabloid genre, wouldn't you say? High contrast, hard light, black shadow. And some cruelty in every image."

The photographer vacillated between flight and a faint. Charles Butler was obviously an art collector and well heeled, but several of the degrees on his business card related to psychology. William distrusted head shrinkers.

"I'd like to see your earlier work," said Butler. "The crime-scene photos. I'm particularly interested in Natalie Homer. Perhaps the name's not familiar. It was twenty years ago. The newspapers called it a suicide by hanging."

"I didn't keep—" William shook his head and began again. "I couldn't do the job. My camera was broken." Even as these words trailed off, he realized that he was not believed. Charles Butler's face expressed every thought and doubt. William could actually see himself being measured and evaluated in the other man's eyes. He even saw a hint of pity there.

"It's not a picture most people would want in their heads." This was a true thing. Only a specific type of ghoul sought that kind of image, and Butler did not seem to fit that category.

"So you did take at least one shot." The man was not posing a question but stating fact.

William clenched his sweating hands, then looked down at the leather checkbook which had suddenly appeared on the coffee table beside an old-fashioned fountain pen. And now he relaxed again, for this was merely a money transaction, a simple purchase.

"That's one photograph I'd be very interested in." Butler opened the checkbook. "*Very* interested." He glanced up at William and broadened his smile, killing all trace of alarm and increasing the comfort level in the room—then delivered his bomb. "You knew Natalie, didn't you?"

William could not have spoken had he wanted to.

Mr. Butler continued, "It's a reasonable assumption. Your landlord tells me you've lived here all your life. I understand you inherited the lease from your mother. And this building is only a block from where Natalie died. Must've been difficult to photograph the body of someone you knew."

"I didn't—know her." William wrapped himself in his own arms to quell the panic. He could see that, once again, he was not believed. In that tone of voice reserved for the confessional, he said, "She only lived in this neighborhood for a little while. I never spoke to her." Losing control of his nerves and his mouth, he continued in a chattering stammer, "But I used to see her on the street sometimes. She was so pretty. She didn't belong here. Anybody could see that. God, she was beautiful."

He had never lusted after her as the other watchers did, for her smile had reminded him of the painted madonnas and statuettes that had adorned this apartment while his mother was alive. Pretty Natalie in her long summer dresses.

William studied Charles Butler's tell-all face, checking for signs that he had given away too much. "It wasn't just me that watched her, you know. She turned heads everywhere she went. All those men, they just *had* to look."

"And after she died, you took her photograph," said the visiting mind reader. "Nausea doesn't come on in an instant. I'm guessing you had time to get off one shot before you vomited. You're such a fine photographer. It would've been a natural reflex action—taking that picture."

So he knew about the vomiting too.

"All right. I'll give it to you." William was actually relieved, though this certainly meant that Butler was a ghoul, the kind of customer who paid the rent, but a twisted type he had never wanted to confront outside of an art gallery. So this was really all the freak wanted, a grisly crime-scene souvenir.

Upon entering the bedroom, William locked and bolted the door behind him. When he emerged again, a print of the old photograph was in his hand.

After the man had departed with his purchase, William noticed that the amount entered on the check was more generous than the quoted price. He looked around at the evidence of his poverty, and he was frightened anew, for he suspected Charles Butler of being a compassionate man and not a freak after all.

William Heart returned to his bedroom. Again, he carefully locked the door and drew the bolt, though his landlord had no keys to this apartment. He lay down on the bed and stared at the opposite wall. Every night, before switching off the lamp, this was what he saw, a wall of a hundred pictures, all the same—the same face, the rope, the massing insects. This photograph was the best work he had ever done. The flies had been so thick and fast that the camera could only capture them as a black cloud surrounding the Madonna of the Maggots and Roaches.

TWELVE

ERIK HOMER'S SECOND WIFE, NOW HIS WIDOW, LIVED
in a large apartment on East Ninety-first Street. "It's rent control," she said. "Two-eighty a month. Can you beat that? This used to be
such a crummy area. But look at it now."

Detective Riker guessed that this woman's view of her neighborhood
was limited to what she could see from the nearby window. He nursed a
cup of strong coffee and longed for a cigarette, a little smoke to kill the
stench of a sickroom.

Jane Homer was a mountain of sallow flesh, and he could roughly guess
when she had become housebound, unable to fit her girth through a standard doorway. Her hair was a long tangle of mouse brown. Only the ends
had the brassy highlights of a bleach blonde. Vanity had died years ago.

On the bureau, there were dozens of photographs of her younger self
posed with her late husband. Jane had once been as slender as the first Mrs.
Homer. There were no portraits of her stepson.

A visiting nurse bustled about in the next room, chattering at Mallory while cleaning up the debris of a meal.

Mrs. Homer's handicap worked in Riker's favor. Like most shut-ins, she was eager to gossip, and now she was saying, "I saw the TV coverage the other night. Natalie's hanging was never on TV."

Riker smiled. "Yeah, the murders are a lot alike, aren't they?"

The woman nodded absently, and this gave him hope. He waited until he heard the door close behind the departing health-care worker. "Did your husband ever talk about the murder?"

"Oh, yes. Erik and Natalie's sister—what was her name? Susan something. No matter. They talked on the telephone for hours. Erik made the funeral arrangements—paid for it, too. He didn't have to do that, you know."

Riker thought otherwise. Taking possession of his ex-wife's body fit the pathology of a control freak. Even in death, Natalie never escaped Erik Homer. "What about the little boy? How did you get along with your stepson? I mean—after his mother died."

There was a touch of surprise in her eyes, or maybe guilt. "Junior was no trouble."

"No trouble? I'll bet." Mallory had quietly entered the room. She held a silver picture frame in her hands as she glared at the woman on the bed, saying, accusing, "You palmed him off on a relative after your husband died."

"Yeah," said Riker. "That was in your last statement to the police. You said you gave the boy away."

"Well, Erik's life insurance wasn't exactly a fortune." Jane Homer's eyes were fixed on the picture frame in Mallory's hand. It was something she prized or something she feared. "And I had all these medical problems that year. My thyroid gland and all. Junior loved his grandparents." The woman stared at Riker, then Mallory, perhaps realizing that she had made some mistake. She filled their silence with a rush of words. "I couldn't take care of him. You can see that, can't you?"

Mallory stepped closer to the bed. "You told a detective the boy went to Natalie's sister in Brooklyn."

"That's *right*," said Mrs. Homer, trying to appease Mallory with a feeble smile. "I remember now. My father-in-law had Alzheimer's. Well, his wife probably couldn't cope with that and a little boy too. So, after a while, Junior went to live with Natalie's sister. *That's* what I meant."

Mallory reached out across the body of Jane Homer to hand the silver frame to Riker. He turned it over to see a picture with the familiar backdrop of the Bronx Zoo. There were light creases through the image of a man and a woman, as if someone had crumpled it into a ball before it was framed. Had Jane Homer rescued this picture from a wastebasket? Yes, that was exactly what had happened. This one flattered her more than the others. The girl in the photograph was not yet wearing a wedding band, and she had been happy that day. A third person had been cut from the photograph. All that remained of the unwanted figure were the fingers of a small child caught up in the much larger hand of his smiling father.

"Was the boy having problems?" asked Riker.

Mallory leaned down very close to the other woman's face. "How did Junior adjust to his mother's death?"

"Natalie died in August," said Riker. "And we know your husband didn't send Junior to school in September."

"Tell me what you did with that little boy," said Mallory.

Jane Homer's eyes widened with the realization that she was caught in the middle of a police crossfire. "His grandparents—"

"No!" Riker scraped the legs of his chair across the floor, edging closer to the bed. "No, Jane, I don't think so."

Mallory leaned close to the woman's ear. "I know how Erik Homer treated his first wife. He never gave her any money—*never* let her out of the house. Is that—"

"Erik did the shopping. I didn't *need* to go out. I didn't—"

"Your first police interview was right after your marriage," said Riker. "The cops thought you were afraid of your husband."

"When did the beatings start?" Mallory raised her voice. "On your honeymoon? Was that the first time he knocked you around?"

"You have lots of photographs." Riker nodded toward the cluster of frames on her bureau. "I see you and your husband, but not the little boy. You never lived with Junior, did you?" He caught the sudden fear in the woman's eyes. "What did you do to Natalie's son? Is he *alive?*"

Jane Homer shook her head from side to side.

"Is that a no?" Mallory asked. "The boy's dead?"

The woman trembled, and her bosom heaved with sobs. Speech was impossible. Her mouth formed the words, *I don't know.*

Mallory moved closer. "How could you *not* know?"

Riker leaned toward her. "Did you think your husband went off on the kid, maybe killed his own son?"

The woman's head moved from side to side, splitting her halting words between the two detectives, anxious to please them both. "The night they found Natalie—Erik got back—very late. I asked him where the boy was. Erik—hit me—*hard.*" One hand drifted to her mouth. "He broke my tooth—then he—got rid of Junior's things—toys, clothes. And the pictures—he tore them to pieces."

Jane Homer stared at the photograph that Riker held, the image of her husband and her smiling self in better days. In a small act of defiance, she grabbed the silver frame from Riker and held it to her breast, covering it with both hands, protecting the happy times. Huge tears rolled down her face, and they could do no more with her—or to her.

Outside the SoHo police station, young actresses were ganging on the sidewalk, posing for the cameras of reporters and tourists. Uniformed officers grinned with their good luck—they had gone to cop heaven. They worked the crowd, tipping hats to brunettes and sending them on their way, then filling out forms for all the blondes, taking down names and telephone numbers, as women filed past them and through the front door to interviews with Special Crimes detectives.

Mallory's car pulled to the curb. She left the motor running after Riker opened the passenger door. He had one foot on the pavement. "You're not coming in?"

"No, I'm going over to Natalie's apartment building." Then she added, with no enthusiasm at all, "Come if you like."

"Naw, I did a drive-by. Too much renovation. The new owner probably rearranged half the walls." He kept her awhile longer with one foot on the floor mat of her car, acting as if a sidewalk choked with pretty women were an everyday thing with him. "I'm sicking a couple of uniforms on Susan Qualen. You're gonna miss all the fun when they drag her in." After a few seconds of dead silence, Riker realized that she was not even tempted. He stepped out onto the sidewalk, closed the door and waved her off, then disappeared into a blond sea of actresses.

Mallory drove across town and through the East Village, heading for the twenty-year-old crime scene and blaming Jack Coffey for another fatal mistake. He had pulled men off their independent lines of investigation to work on the actress interviews, as if they could find the next victim that way.

Another woman was going to die.

She turned the wheel on First Avenue and rolled along the side street toward Avenue A. Once, this area had provided cheap housing for the poorest of the poor. Now, none of the former residents could afford to live here.

Mallory parked her car in front of the building where Natalie Homer had lived and died. Only the architectural bones would match Lars Geldorf's old photograph. Peeling gray paint had been sandblasted to expose the red brick. The windows were modern, and the wrought-iron rails of Juliet balconies had been restored. According to Geldorf's personal notes, the previous owner had died, and all the old tenants had departed before the renovation.

Riker was right. This was a waste of precious time.

And a woman was going to die.

Yet she left her car and walked up the stairs to ring the bell for the landlord's apartment. The front door was opened by a softly rounded woman with a warm smile for a stranger. The new owner was obviously not a native New Yorker, but a transplant from some smaller, less paranoid town.

"Mrs. White?" The detective held up her badge and ID.

The woman's smile collapsed. "It's about Natalie, isn't it? I wondered when you'd come."

The civilian police aide for the midtown precinct was a short, thin woman with brown hair and a dim view of blondes. Eve Forelli held up her favorite tabloid with the headline: ACTRESS STABBED IN BROAD DAYLIGHT. She glared at the tall, pretty woman seated on the other side of her desk. "You look better in person."

And this, of course, was sarcasm, for the grainy newsprint photograph only showed the back of the actress's head; the face was pressed to the bosom of another actor, a man holding the unconscious, bleeding victim in his arms while he postured and smiled for the camera.

The blonde's blue eyes opened wide. "How could it be in the paper? It just happened this morning."

Forelli pointed to the line below the newspaper's banner. "It's the late edition." She could see that the younger woman was not following this. "It's a *second* edition." And it had been free, a promotional gimmick for a failing newspaper. "Now I need the correct spelling for your last name. The hospital only used one *L*. It doesn't look right." She handed the newspaper to the blonde. "And this story didn't even mention your name."

The startled actress tore her eyes away from the clock on the wall to scan the article. "Oh, damn, you're right."

"The *spelling*, Miss Small?"

"Just the way it sounds. Call me Stella." The woman flashed a smile. "Look—is this going to take much longer? I've been waiting for over an hour. I'm already late for another appointment in SoHo."

Eve Forelli only glared at the woman. This—*blonde* had left the hospital before giving a statement to the police. One of the little princes from Special Crimes Unit downtown had reamed out a desk sergeant and demanded the missing paperwork on the reported stabbing. Her supervisor, in turn, had crawled up Forelli's own scrawny tail. Further down the food chain, the frazzled police aide had screamed at the hospital staff. And, finally, the errant actress had been identified. And now Forelli prepared to marry an illegible attending physician's report to the crime victim's account. "So you were stabbed by—"

"Oh, Jesus, no!" said the actress. "I don't want any trouble with the cops. Look, I'm sorry, officer, but this—"

"I'm not a cop." Forelli pointed to the name tag pinned to her blouse, clearly identifying her as a civilian aide. "You see a badge here? No, you don't. I just do the damn paperwork."

"Sorry." Stella Small touched her bandaged arm. "A camera did this. No big deal."

Eve Forelli's face was deadpan. "A guy *stabbed* you—with his *camera*." Of course. And this added credence to her pet theory that the roots of blond hair attacked brain cells.

"No." The actress waved the newspaper. "The reporter got it wrong. I wasn't stabbed—I was *slashed.*"

"With a camera."

"But it was an accident." The blonde slumped down in the chair. Her blue eyes rolled back, and then she sighed—a clear sign of guilty defeat. "Okay, *this* is what happened. My agent thought getting slashed with a razor was better than a guy just bumping into me on a crowded sidewalk."

"Yeah, that would've been *my* choice."

"I didn't know the doctor was going to file a police report."

"Ah, doctors." Forelli sighed. "They fill out these reports for every shooting, stabbing and slashing. Who knows why? It's a mystery."

"You're not going to get me in trouble, are you?"

"Naw, what the hell." Forelli was overworked, very tired and feeling giddy. Inside the appropriate box of her form, she typed the words, *Professional bimbo collides with camera. Damn every tall blonde ever born.*

Her supervisor would not like this entry, assuming the lazy bastard ever bothered to read it—fat chance. All her best lines were lost on that illiterate fool. And now she would have to phone in the details to a detective from Special Crimes, another brain trust who had problems with the written word.

"But no more false police reports, okay? You can go to jail for that." Forelli was not certain that this was true, but it did have a frightening effect on the blonde.

After the actress had departed, the police aide opened a window and leaned outside to smoke a cigarette. She looked down to see Stella Small standing on the sidewalk below, looking left and right, lost in yet another blond conundrum—which way to go?

Forelli, for lack of any better spectacle, watched as the young woman removed a wadded-up blouse from her purse, then tossed it into a trash basket near the curb.

Before the clerk had finished her smoke, an older woman came along. This one, with ragged clothes and matted hair, fished the blouse out of the wire basket and briefly inspected it. Though the material was stained with a large *X* on the back, the homeless woman stripped off her shirt—right in front of a *police* station—*no* bra—and put the trash-can find on her back.

Mallory listened politely as Mrs. Alice White gave her a walking tour of the residence, rambling on about the problems of renovation. "The place was a rabbit warren, all broken up in small spaces. Now there's only a few apartments left at the top of the house." The rest of the floors had been restored to the former proportions and appointments of a family home.

"Where did the murder happen?"

"If I recall the old floor plan—" Alice White pulled open two massive wooden doors and stepped into a formal dining room. "It was probably in here."

Another doorway gave Mallory a view of the adjoining sit-down kitchen. *Always go to the kitchen.* This lesson was handed down from Louis Markowitz. Interview subjects were less guarded in that more casual room, for only friends and family gathered there.

Mrs. White's voice was jittery and halting. Police had that nervous effect on civilians, but Mallory suspected another reason.

Planning to hold out on me, Alice?

The woman paused by a large oak table surrounded by eight carved chairs. "Yes, I'm sure of it now. This was where Natalie's apartment used to be. And it was no bigger than this room."

Though the new owner had been a child when the victim had died, it was obvious that they had known each other. Whenever the conversation turned back to murder, the hanged woman was always Natalie to Mrs. White.

Mallory was done with the pleasantries, the getting-to-know-you courtship. She decided upon a style of bludgeoning that would leave only psychic bruises and fingerprints. She raised her face to stare at the chandelier above the table, perhaps the same spot where Natalie Homer had hung for two days in August. "You can almost see it, can't you?"

Gentle Alice White was *forced* to see it now; the woman's gaze was riveted to the ceiling fixture, and her mind's eye showed her a dead body twisting on a rope, rotting in the summer heat. And from now on, she would find Natalie hanging there each time she passed through her dining room.

The detective slowly turned on the freshly wounded civilian.

Can you hear the flies, Alice?

As if this thought had been spoken aloud, the startled woman's hand drifted up to cover her open mouth.

"Mrs. White? Could I trouble you for a cup of coffee?" Caffeine was the best truth drug.

"What? Oh, of course. I've got a fresh pot on the stove." Alice White could hardly wait to leave this room, this ghost, for the safety of the next room, and the detective followed her.

Mallory sat down at the kitchen table and unfolded a packet of papers, spreading them on a flower-print cloth. "I understand you bought this building five years ago."

"No, that's wrong." Mrs. White poured coffee into a carafe. "I didn't buy it." Next, she opened a cupboard of fine china cups and dishes, and this was a bad sign; she was putting out her Sunday best for company.

"I like coffee mugs, myself," said Mallory.

"Oh, so do I." The woman smiled as she pulled two ceramic mugs from hooks on the wall, then set them on the table.

"Maybe it's a clerical error." Mallory held up a photocopy of the ownership transfer. "This says you purchased the building from the estate of Anna Sorenson."

Alice White, carafe in hand, hovered over the paper and read the pertinent line. "No, that's definitely a mistake." She poured their coffee, then sat down across the table. "I didn't buy the house. Anna Sorenson was my grandmother. She willed it to me."

"And you visited your grandmother—when you were a little girl." Ten seconds crawled by, yet Mallory did nothing to prompt the woman. She sipped her coffee and waited out the silence.

"Yes." Alice White said this as a confession. "I was here that summer." Their eyes met.

"The summer Natalie died." Her hands wormed around a sugar bowl, and she pushed it toward Mallory. "The coffee's too strong, isn't it? Norwegians make it like soup." She reached for a carton of cream. "Would you like some—"

"No, it's fine."

And now it begins, Alice.

"So, the last time you saw Natalie Homer—"

"I was twelve." Mrs. White made a small production of pouring the cream carton into a pitcher, buying time to hunt for the right words. "She was so pretty—like a movie star. That's what my grandmother said. Natalie gave me her old lipsticks and a pair of high heels."

"So you spent some time with her. Did she talk about herself?"

"No—not much." Alice White was so rattled, she stirred her coffee, though she had added neither cream nor sugar. "I know her people were from the old country, but not Natalie. My grandmother said her Norwegian wasn't good." The woman forced a bright smile. "I don't speak a word myself. My parents only used it when they didn't want me to know what they were saying. So when Natalie spoke Norwegian to Gram, I knew I was missing all the good stuff."

Mallory shuffled her papers, then handed the woman another document. "This is a copy of Natalie's marriage certificate. Her maiden name was an odd one, Qualen. That's Norwegian?"

"Never heard of it." Alice White stared at the certificate. "Maybe it's a corruption. A lot of foreign names were changed at Ellis Island. I bet the original spelling was *Kv* instead of *Qu*. But that still wouldn't make it a common name."

"Good," said Mallory. "That'll make it easier to trace her family. It would help if I knew what state they live in. The only next-of-kin we have is a sister in Brooklyn. And she hates cops."

"So did my grandmother. She said they were all thieves. They were always ticketing the building for fake violations. Then Gram would give them some cash and—" She gave Mallory a weak sorry smile, suddenly remembering that her guest was also police. "But that was a long time ago. I've never had any problems like—"

"Can you remember anything that would tie Natalie to relatives out of state?"

"I think she came from Racine, Wisconsin. My parents live there, and Gram asked Natalie if she knew them."

Mallory reached for a folded newspaper at the edge of the table. It was days old. She opened it to the front-page picture of Sparrow being loaded into an ambulance. "Can we talk about this now?"

Alice White's eyes were begging, *Please don't.*

"You knew the police would come." Mallory pushed the newspaper across the table. "This hanging was a lot like Natalie's—the hair cut off and packed in her mouth. When you read the paper, you recognized the details. That's why you were expecting me. I know you saw Natalie's body. We have a statement from the police officer who saw you in the hall with another kid, a little boy. How old was he?"

"Six or seven." Alice White was mistaking Mallory's guesswork for absolute certainty. She showed no surprise, only the resignation of a true believer in police omniscience.

"The two of you saw everything," said Mallory, "before Officer Parris chased you away."

The woman nodded. "Officer Sticky Fingers. That's what Gram called him. Or maybe that was the other one." She looked up. "Sorry—the cops in uniforms—"

"They all look alike. I know. So you saw everything, the hair, and the—"

"I can still see it."

"Who was the little boy? Your brother?"

"No, I never knew his name. Gram found him wandering in the hall. She took him inside and went through all the stuff in his little suitcase. I remember she found a phone number, but there was nobody home when she called."

"Why didn't she turn him over to the cops?"

"She'd never—" Mrs. White shrugged. "Like I said, Gram hated the police. She'd never trust them with a child, not that one. You see, there was something wrong with the boy. He couldn't talk, or he wouldn't. Well, my grandmother figured somebody must be expecting him for a visit—because of the little suitcase. When she opened it up, everything was still neatly packed. He smelled bad—I think he'd messed in his pants. Gram gave him a bath and changed his clothes. Then she went from door to door, all over the building, the whole neighborhood."

"So you were alone with the boy when the cops showed up."

"Yes. My grandmother was the one who called the police, but it took them forever to get here. This awful smell was coming from next door. Gram was just frantic. She had a key to Natalie's place, but it didn't work. A few hours after Gram left, I heard the cops out in the hall. One of them yelled, 'Oh, God, no!' "

"And you were curious."

"You bet. More police showed up, men in suits. One of the men in uniform was guarding the apartment and shooing people away. I waited till he walked down the hall to talk to a neighbor. Then I went to Natalie's door. It was wide open."

"And the boy was with you."

"I was holding his hand. Gram told me not to leave him alone. Well, I saw the body hanging there—but it didn't look like Natalie. Her eyes and that beautiful long hair—it was just—" Alice White took a deep breath. "And the roaches—they were crawling down the rope to get at her. The men just left her hanging there while they took their pictures. Then another policeman chased us off."

"What happened to the little boy?"

"That night, a man came to take him away."

"Did you recognize him?"

"No, I was in bed. I only heard the voices in the other room. I think Gram knew him. Or maybe she tried that telephone number again, the one she found in the suitcase. Yes, she must've talked to him on the phone. He didn't have to say who he was when he came to the door."

"Did you tell your grandmother what you and the boy—"

"God, no. Gram would've been so angry. She told me to take care of that boy—not give him nightmares for the rest of his life."

Charles Butler was no stranger to Brooklyn. He frequently made the trek to this outer borough for a poker game with friends. However, like any good New Yorker, he only knew his habitual routes. Before Riker had allowed his driver's license to lapse, every other road had been a mystery, even this broad avenue along Prospect Park.

He waited in his car as the detective crossed the street and joined two uniformed policemen standing by a squad car. They were too far away for Charles to hear any conversation, and so he eavesdropped on their body language.

One of the officers shrugged to say, *Sorry*. Riker's hands rose in exasperation, and he must have uttered at least one obscenity, for now the officer's hands went to his hips to say, *Hey, it's not our fault*. Behind dark glasses, the slouching detective stared at one man and then the other, giving them no clue to his thoughts. Suddenly both officers were talking with upturned hands, offering new forms of *Sorry*, probably accompanied by a mollifying *Sir*. In an economy of motion, Riker waved one hand to say, *Awe, the hell with it*, then turned his back, dismissing them both. He was one very unhappy man when he slid into the front seat of the Mercedes.

"Not good news, I take it." Charles started the engine.

"Natalie's sister left town in a big hurry." Riker nodded toward the men in uniform. "And those two clowns just stood there and watched her drive away—with a *suitcase*." His head lolled back on the soft leather upholstery. "They keep changing the rules on me, Charles. Apparently, if you can say the word *lawyer* three times without interruption, the cops have to let you go. My fault. I used the word *detain* instead of *arrest*."

"Bad luck. Sorry." The Mercedes pulled away from the curb.

"Yeah. And I was really looking forward to scaring the shit out of that woman." Riker fell into a black silence until the great arches of the Brooklyn Bridge loomed up on the road before them.

Charles sensed there was more to the detective's dark mood than a lost witness. How else to account for this sadness? When the car stopped in traffic, he turned to the man beside him. "Is there anything I can do to help?"

"Yeah, there is." The detective stirred, then sat up a bit straighter. "I've been thinking about the Wichita Kid and that wolf bite."

This was highly unlikely, but now Charles understood that the real problem was none of his business. "You want to know how—"

"Naw, here's my best guess. I figure there's a one in a million chance the Wichita Kid could survive rabies without a vaccine."

"That's actually true, but I don't think Jake Swain was aware of it when he wrote the book." As they crossed the bridge, Charles launched into the story of Sheriff Peety's travels from town to town, hunting an outlaw infected with rabies. "So he's chatting up all the local doctors along the way when he meets one who's heard the story of the rabid wolf that bit—"

"Hold it," said Riker. "Don't tell me. The sheriff finds out that the wolf never had rabies in the first place. Am I right?"

"Right you are. He discovers that someone else was bitten by that same wolf and survived. The animal actually had distemper. Looks the same as rabies, lots of frothing at the mouth, but it's not transmissible to humans. However, the wound wasn't cleaned properly, so Wichita suffered a massive infection—fevers, hallucinations, but no symptoms of hydrophobia."

The detective politely raised one eyebrow, though he seemed to have lost interest. After a few moments of silence, Charles said, "You've had news from the hospital. Your friend—"

"Yeah." Riker turned his face to the passenger window and its view of the open sky over the water. "Her one good kidney is failing."

And even Jake Swain could not have written an escape for Sparrow. However, pressed by deep concern for a friend, Charles now came up with the next best thing—an emergency epiphany. "There was an eyewitness to Natalie Homer's murder. Does that cheer you up?" The car came to a standstill in heavy traffic halfway across the bridge. Riker turned around to face him with a look of surprise, successfully distracted from pain.

Charles changed gears as the traffic moved forward again. "My theory works nicely with the problem of the locked door."

The detective turned back to face the passenger window, his way of saying, *Oh, that again.*

"Bear with me. Previously, I assumed that someone used a key to open Natalie's door before the police arrived. But my witness wouldn't need a key—not if he opened the door from the *inside.*"

"And here's the flaw," said Riker. "That would mean your witness was in the apartment for two days—watching a woman's body rot."

"Yes. Now back up a bit. The night she died, Natalie was cooking a meal for two. She had no friends, and she was on bad terms with her sister. So the dinner guest was her son."

"Interesting," said Riker, which was his polite way of saying that it was not at all interesting. "So, before Erik Homer goes on his honeymoon, he leaves the kid with his ex-wife? No, Charles. This guy was a control freak. After the divorce, he *never* let Natalie see that kid, not *once.* This can't work."

"Why not? Erik Homer was getting married again. He had a new woman to control. And this babysitting arrangement would be for *his* convenience. *That's* what makes it work. And no one ever interviewed the boy. We don't know where Junior was for two days in August or any time after that." Charles could see that Riker was not buying any of this. "Only a small child would have stayed in that room with the body. The boy wouldn't want to leave his mother. Dead or alive, she was his whole world."

"Let's see if I understand this." Riker's voice was strained in an effort to quell the sound of condescension. "It was a studio apartment. No place to hide a kid, even a small one. But Junior managed to—"

"Riker, all over the world, mothers tell their children to wash up for dinner. It's a universal thing. The boy was in the bathroom the whole time that man was killing his mother."

"It was August," said the detective. "No air conditioner in Natalie's place. Rolling blackouts. The lights were off half the time. The stove burner was left on. *More* heat when—"

"Yes, and after two days, the little boy's survival instinct overcame trauma, and he left the apartment. This explains the unlocked door. Also, it very neatly explains your contrary reports of the boy's whereabouts. The father sent him away. Erik Homer didn't want the killer to find out that his son was a witness."

Charles and Riker were still at odds when they entered the back office of Butler and Company.

Mallory never acknowledged them. She was deep in conversation with her machines, speaking to them with keyboard commands. They responded with screens of data and papers pouring from the mouths of three printers. She sat with her back to the discordant men and the mess on her cork wall. Her vision was thus narrowed to a sterile field that hummed with perfect harmony.

Charles rounded the computer workstation and saw the cold machine lights reflected in her eyes. He looked down at the thick cable that fed her electronics through a dedicated line of electricity, and he played with the idea of *accidentally* kicking the plug from its socket and disconnecting her that way.

Riker rapped on the top of the monitor, and when this failed to get her attention, he said, "Charles thinks he's got an eyewitness to the murder of Natalie Homer."

"Hmm. Natalie's son." Mallory never lifted her eyes from the glowing screen. "He's the one who unlocked the door to the crime scene. But I don't know what name Junior's using these days, so we'll just stick with the scarecrow." She smiled at her computer, as if it had just said something to amuse her. "And now we've got a game."

THIRTEEN

CHARLES SAID A SILENT GOOD-BYE TO LOUIS MARKOWITZ. His old friend's personality was being erased from the cork wall by layers of lopsided pictures and papers.

Mallory walked along the cork wall, ripping down reports and sending tacks flying through the air. Photographs of fat black flies hit the floor where they mingled with enlarged cockroaches and smiling portraits from Natalie Homer's actress portfolio. Given that Mallory was a pathologically tidy creature, Charles thought this might qualify as a loss of control, a display of temper, though she never raised her voice when she said, "So Natalie's sister got away."

"Yeah," said Riker. "I put the dogs on her. We might get lucky before she ditches the car for a plane or a bus. Maybe Susan's more afraid of her nephew than us."

"She should be," said Charles. "If Natalie's son is the scarecrow—"

"He is." The soft plof of papers and pings of pushpins followed Mallory to the end of the wall, where she tacked up the print bought from William Heart. "It all fits." She pointed to the open bathroom door in the background of this photograph. "Charles is right. The boy was probably in there while his mother was being murdered. Two days later, he was found wandering in the hall with a suitcase and all the symptoms of shock. And that was *before* the first cop opened the crime scene."

"Okay," said Riker. "Say the scarecrow is Natalie's kid all grown up and not too shy about cold-blooded murder. If he knew who killed his mother, he'd just off the bastard."

"No," she said. "The boy was hiding, watching through a keyhole or a crack in the door. Maybe he never saw the killer's face."

"Or even the actual murder," said Charles. "The scarecrow doesn't imitate his mother's death by strangulation—only the postmortem hanging." And now he noticed the dead quiet in the offices of Butler and Company. "So where's Lars Geldorf?"

"I had Deluthe take him home. The old man is out of the loop. We're consolidating all the hangings. From now on, he doesn't get past the front door." She turned her eyes on Charles. "You've got a problem with that?"

"Well, he has so much invested in Natalie's murder." And now, judging by the hand gravitating to her hip, Charles realized that the correct response would have been, *Oh, hell no*. But he rather liked the old man, and so he persisted. "Lars could still contribute to the—"

"Wrong." She turned her back on him. "All Geldorf ever had was a stalker pattern and an ex-husband, every cop's favorite suspect. He spent all his time trying to break Erik Homer's alibi." A more linear personality was taking shape on the cork wall as Mallory finished pinning up a straight line of text and pictures. One red fingernail tapped the statement of Susan Qualen. "Natalie's sister hated her brother-in-law. Every other word on this paper is *bastard*. But later the same night, she was talking to Erik Homer for hours, and they weren't discussing funeral arrangements."

Charles nodded. "You think they conspired to hide the boy."

"Right," said Mallory. "They didn't want the killer to know there was an eyewitness. That's why no one could find Junior. He was shipped off to relatives out of state."

A computer beeped to call for Mallory's attention, and she sat down at a workstation to watch the text scrolling down her screen. "An hour ago,

I found rap sheets for Rolf and Lisa Qualen, a husband and wife in Wisconsin. They were arrested for kidnapping a little boy, but the age doesn't match Natalie's son." Mallory scrolled down the single-spaced text. "One hell of a lot of material." She watched bundles of paper pouring into all the printer beds. "I've got a time problem here."

Laden with Mallory's printouts, Charles had retreated to the comfort of his own private office, a soft leather chair and a wooden desk from a less technical age. When he had finished speed-reading the last of the court documents, a trial transcript and attendant reports from social workers and police, he looked up at his audience. The weary detectives were pressed deep into a plush sofa. They were raiding delicatessen bags and awaiting his synopsis on the arrest and trial of Rolf and Lisa Qualen.

"Mr. and Mrs. Qualen had a son named John, who drowned shortly before his eighth birthday, and that was a year before Natalie Homer's murder. Two days *after* Natalie's body was found, the Qualens abandoned their house in Racine, Wisconsin, and resettled in a small town a hundred miles away. That's where they enrolled their dead son, John, in grammar school."

"Freaking amateurs," said Riker.

"Hmm." Mallory finished her bagel. "Bad match for Natalie's son. The dead boy's birth certificate was off by two years."

"The school principal noticed that, too," said Charles. "He was told that the boy's scholastic records were lost in a fire. Eventually, he located those records in Racine—along with a death certificate for the real John Qualen."

"So that's when the cops were called in?" This was Riker's polite way of moving the story along, for it was not his habit to state the obvious. And now he glanced at his watch in yet another attempt at being subtle.

"Yes," said Charles. "The police suspected kidnapping, but the Qualens wouldn't cooperate with the investigation and neither would the little boy."

"Junior was scared," said Mallory.

"That was the case detective's opinion," said Charles. "The police had no idea where the boy came from. He didn't match any reports on missing children. So they put him in foster care, and the Qualens went to trial.

The kidnap charge was never proved, but they were found guilty of falsi-
fying records, and that got them a stiff fine. The foster-care records were
sealed, and the boy disappeared into the bureaucracy."

Riker pulled out his notebook and pen. "What've you got in the way
of case numbers?"

"For the boy? There's nothing attached to the court documents. Sorry."
He held up a sheaf of papers. "This is a brief filed by the Qualens' attorney. They tried to adopt the boy, but they weren't even successful in getting visitation rights."

"That's why I can't find him," said Mallory. "Social Services saw the
Qualens as a threat. So they changed Junior's name again and gave him a
new case number. We don't even know what age they settled on."

"With what we got so far," said Riker, "we'll never get a court order
to open sealed juvenile records. And he's probably out there right now
stringing up another woman."

"Then we'll know soon enough," said Mallory. "He escalated with
Sparrow. This time, he'll put on a bigger show."

Riker's kitchen was wrecked, drawers pulled out, cupboards rifled, and a
slice of pizza was glued upside down to the linoleum where he had dropped
it the previous night—or perhaps the night before. And he had not yet
found the playground tape. Years ago, he had put it away for fear of breaking it after running it so many times.

He glanced back at the living room. Charles Butler sat down on the
sofa, and a dusty cloud rose up around him. At the man's feet, cardboard
take-out containers and months of newspapers were loosely piled, as if set
apart for recycling, a practice Riker had only heard about, and all the ashtrays were overflowing with stale butts. However, Charles was so polite,
so well bred that no one would have guessed he was not accustomed to
squalor.

At last the detective found the videotape and fed it into the VCR in the
living room. He handed his guest the last clean glass (Riker's own version
of good breeding) filled with bourbon and a splash of water, then made
his own drink a bit stronger and settled into a leather armchair.

"A friend of mine confiscated the tape from a pedophile. The freak was cruising Central Park for victims." He turned to Charles and noted the sudden rigid set to the man's jaw. "Relax. He never got near the kid. He could only catch her on film." Riker hit the PLAY button on his remote control. "This is what really got Lou's attention. The film was a few years old when we saw it for the first time." In the absence of children of his own, the pedophile's video was Riker's substitute for home movies.

The screen brightened to a clear summer day, and the show began with the close-up shot of a small blond girl in a dirty T-shirt that fitted her like a tent. Riker pressed the PAUSE button. "Kathy's probably eight years old on this tape, but you can see she's been out on the street too long."

He pressed the PLAY button, but the little girl remained frozen on the grass at the edge of a playground. She tilted her head to one side, not yet committed to going or staying. The homeless child must have known that she belonged here with kids her own age. Perhaps she recognized a normalcy that had been ripped away from her. So here she was—looking to fill a need.

Doing the best you can.

Kathy came to play.

Charles Butler leaned toward the screen, spellbound by the beautiful little girl, a miniature Mallory. All around her the world swirled with action and sound, small feet running in packs and tiny screams of outrage and joy.

The solitary child hesitated another moment. Then, light stepping, cautious as a cat, she padded toward a row of swings, gray boards dangling from long metal chains. She took her seat among the rest, looking right and left with grave suspicion, and she began to swing in a small tentative arc. Now Kathy leaned far back to steepen the pitch and made a soft giggling sound at the wonder of flight. On the upswing, she soared above a line of cruel spikes atop an iron fence. An illusion of the camera made these spears seem close enough to impale her.

Fearing nothing from the hard ground below, she leaned farther back to make the swing fly higher. Reckless and grinning, she soared up and over the heads of wild-eyed women, mothers and nannies, their waving hands and their screams of *Come down!*

Riker turned to Charles. The man's mouth was working in a silent prayer, *Don't fall.*

Toes pointed toward the sun, she rushed up to the sky, laughing—laughing.

All the joy died when Kathy looked into the camera lens. Her eyes were suddenly adult and cold. Her hands let go of the chains, and she took flight; literally airborne, she flew out of the camera frame, and the screen went black.

Though Riker had watched this film a hundred times, his hand tensed around the bourbon glass. For him, the child was still flying and always would be—a tossed coin that could never land.

Charles slept soundly on his office couch, still wearing yesterday's clothes. Only Mallory was awake to watch the sun come up. She had returned to the offices of Butler and Company with a stack of morning newspapers, and now she sat in an armchair, sipping coffee and hunting for a police press release. It had not made any of the front pages. The scarecrow's crimes were old and stale, last week's news.

The dog days of August marked the close of tourist-hunting season in Central Park, the scene of another daylight stabbing, but today's headline victim was a man decapitated by a flying manhole cover described as the blown cork of a broken water main. The next runner-up was a woman killed by a stone gargoyle that had fallen from a crumbling building facade on Broadway. All the signs of a town out of control were here in black and white, decay and corruption from the sewers to the skyline.

And then there was Riker.

Yesterday, his sallow skin had been stippled with the small wounds of a shaving razor. His hands always trembled the morning after a binge. Booze poisoning was running its course and killing him slowly. With most cops on the decline, integrity was the first thing to go. Riker had clung to his long after everything else had been lost. He had always commanded great respect, even while crawling out of a bar on his hands and knees.

Why would he risk his job to rob Sparrow's crime scene?

It was a common form of larceny for cops and firemen, stealing cash and baubles from the dead. But she had believed that all the manhole covers would blow up and the town would fall down before Riker would steal *anything*. And she still believed that, for now she suspected him of a worse crime—holding out on his partner, secreting evidence and working it on the side.

Mallory turned another page in search of the official press release, a warning to every blond actress in New York City. She found the story at the bottom of page three. Lieutenant Coffey had come through on his promise to give the next victim a sporting chance, but the scarecrow had also warned his prey; he had all but pushed the women into the arms of the police. Why?

She blamed her lack of sleep for seeking logic in a madman's plan.

The young actress had grown up wearing the discards of the Abandoned Stellas, twice and thrice handed-down clothes bought from second-hand stores. Only the fabulous blue suit had never been worn by anyone else, and now it was ruined New York style—with blood—and she had lost her armor. Every passerby could see the genes of a third-generation bastard, the highway debris of traveling men.

This morning, Stella Small stood in front of an uptown cash machine and stared at her bank card. She never balanced her checkbook, for that sucked the last bit of charm out of life, and it also frightened her. She could roughly guess her account balance, enough for underwear, but she was hoping for more. A brochure was clutched in her other hand, and she paused to pray over it, *God bless junk mail*. Designer suits were featured on the second page of sale items. The fashion outlet store was only one block away, and she had an hour to spare before the next open audition. Stella had gambled a subway token on her belief in synchronicity, and now she fed her bank card into the magic slot.

Her eyes were scrunched shut. *Please, please, please.*

Stella's white blouse and skirt had been washed and ironed twice, yet she could detect the smell of a thrift shop in the material. It was the odor of failure. Her head was bowed and her shoulders slumped in a loser's posture. But that was about to change.

When she had finished her ritual prayer words over the cash machine, it disgorged all the manna she needed to replace the ruined audition suit. Her first thought was that this was her rent money, that the Abandoned Stellas had made an early deposit to her checking account. Her second thought was that there *was* a god of cash machines, and he loved theater folk.

She ran to the end of the block and joined a herd of shoppers gathered outside the department store, all awaiting the early-bird sale. Stella had her battle plan ready. The doors opened, and the chase was on. She sped past older women in support hose, descended the stairs to the basement level, then charged toward the back wall where the suits were hanging. If the clothes fit, if the producer liked what he saw—her entire life would change. Her future might be literally hanging on the rack before her eyes, and she was rushing toward it.

And then she stopped.

Damn—another New York moment.

A lumpy woman with brown hair and gray roots pulled the only blue suit from the group of size eights. Stella watched, dumbfounded, as the middle-aged shopper popped a button trying to close the blazer over her bulging stomach. Oh, and now the evil bitch had left a smudge of makeup on one sleeve.

Stella was distracted by the sight of her own face in a mirror on the nearby wall. Without intending to, she had slipped under the skin of the aging brunette, imitating the scowl, the narrowed mean little eyes and the absence of a soul.

The older woman gave up the attempt to shoehorn her body into the suit jacket, and she stormed away with heavy footfalls. Stella retrieved the fallen button and collected her prize from the floor where it had been dropped, but not, *Thank you, God,* trod upon. She checked the label. It belonged to a designer she had actually heard of. The price had been slashed in half, another divine act, or, as the Abandoned Stellas would say, *Jesus saves.*

She glanced at her watch. It was late, but she would make the audition *if* she hurried, *if* the line at the cashier was not too long, *if* the trains were not late. She was still chaining her conditions of success when she ran into the fitting room, where she stripped, tried on the suit and pronounced it a perfect fit.

Stella slung her old skirt over one arm as she walked toward the cashier's counter. Miraculously, there was no one on line. This afforded her the luxury of a few minutes of preening before a three-sided looking glass, admiring herself from every angle. The makeup stain was invisible as long as she kept her right hand by her side. And there was more than enough time to sew on a button during the subway ride. For a whole year, she had carried a small traveler's sewing kit in every purse she owned, just waiting for a day like today, when her life might hang upon a button.

She was knocked into the mirror by a hard slam to her back. Stella sucked in her breath, then braced both hands on the glass. In one of the three reflecting panels, she saw a man standing behind her, breaking the rules, for all New York collisions were hit-and-run affairs. Everyone else in the crowd was in motion, hustling from rack to rack, flinging clothes and hangers. Only this man was absolutely still, and he only had eyes for Stella.

FⓞuRTeeN

THE MAN IN THE DEPARTMENT STORE MIRROR WAS OB-
viously another fan of daytime soap operas. Stella smiled at his
reflection.

Yes, it's me.

He did not acknowledge her smile, nor did he make eye contact like
any normal person. The man stared at her as if she were an object all of
one piece and without eyes of her own to see him. She stiffened her
body, imitating his posture, then focused on her own reflection and watched
her eyes go cold and colder. Her mouth became a simple line, committed
to no expression. And now she had his likeness inside and out. There was
no one home inside of her anymore—just a little graveyard dust.

The man did not seem to appreciate or even notice her artful portrayal
of him. Beneath the brim of a baseball cap, his face was unchanged, frozen,
one inanimate object facing another—herself. Pushing the likeness just a
bit further, Stella's eyes had gone entirely dead, and she became—

The audition!

She was going to be late.

Stella broke off this eerie connection to glance at her watch. When she looked up again, she saw the reflection of his baseball cap just visible above the heads of female shoppers as he moved backward, blending into the crowd, a player doing his walk-on in reverse.

Mesmerized, Stella did not move until he was out of sight. Again, she looked at her watch. More time had passed than she would have believed possible. Other customers were moving toward the cash registers. She ran full out to beat a slow-moving elderly woman to the check-out counter. Hunched over, neck and neck with the stooped, white-haired shopper, Stella unconsciously mirrored the sudden alarm in her opponent's eyes. The old woman put on some speed toward the end, then gave up the footrace to youth; panting and wheezing, support hose bagging at the ankles, the loser stood in line behind the grinning actress.

When it was Stella's turn to be waited on, her mouth dipped down on one side, copying the face before her, and she also assumed the overly efficient air of the salesclerk. "I'm in a big hurry. Just cut the tags. I'll wear it." Stella pushed her old skirt across the counter. "And bag this, okay?"

"Suit yourself." The clerk's voice was the monotone of a telephone company recording. "No returns on sales."

Stella held out one pale blue sleeve so the other woman could snip off the price tags. "You be careful with those scissors, all right?"

The clerk's voice betrayed a sudden annoyance. "Like I said, lady—no returns." Not quite so efficient anymore, the woman allowed Stella's arm to hang in the air. Taking her own maddening time to put the blond actress in her place, the clerk picked up the old skirt twixt thumb and forefinger, then held it at the distance of a bad smell before dropping it into a bag. Finally, she reached for her scissors and *slowly* cut the tag strings from Stella's sleeve. The cashier glanced at the mirror behind the line of customers, saying, "You know this jacket is damaged, right? Stained?"

Oh, the makeup smudge.

"No problem. I can get that out."

"Yeah, *sure* you can." The clerk watched the blonde walk away with a black *X* scrawled on the back of the new suit. Then she turned a merciless eye on the next customer in line, an elderly woman slowly approaching the counter. "*Move* it, lady!"

Lieutenant Coffey watched the last actress leave the squad room in company with two detectives, the number of men it took to escort a pretty woman downstairs. The deputy commissioner's son-in-law passed them at the stairwell door, and now he walked toward the private office.

So Mallory and Riker had managed to lose Deluthe again.

While the lieutenant checked his list of blondes for the second day of interviews, the younger man stood at a respectful distance and waited to be acknowledged. Coffey liked the deference to rank, but he had his doubts that this youngster was going to make it as a detective.

"I thought you were watching Lars Geldorf."

"He's staying home today. I'm looking for Sergeant Riker."

"He'll be here in half an hour." Coffey held up a tabloid with the headline: ACTRESS STABBED IN BROAD DAYLIGHT. "Okay, kid, make yourself useful." He pointed to the handwritten notes and a telephone number scrawled across the top of the front page. "This midtown precinct never called back with a name on the actress. Find out who she is, then check the interview list. If we haven't talked to her, get her down here today."

"Yes, sir." Paper in hand, Deluthe swooped down on the nearest vacant desk and picked up the phone.

Jack Coffey had only a few minutes to settle in behind his desk before the rookie rapped on the frame of his open office door. The lieutenant waved him inside. "What've you got, kid?"

"The actress is Stella Small. I talked to a police aide, Eve Forelli. She says it was just a publicity stunt."

The lieutenant nodded toward the tabloid in the younger man's hand. "Did you *read* that article?"

"No, sir. I thought you wanted—"

"*Read* it. You'll find the first mention of blood in the opening paragraph. It's a puddle on a hotel carpet." He leaned over the desk and ripped the paper from Deluthe's hand, then pointed to the photograph of an unconscious woman. "Oh, and the dark stain on her sleeve? That's blood too." He slammed the newspaper down on his desk blotter, yet his voice remained calm. "In my experience, very few actresses ever mutilate themselves for a mention in the tabloids." And now he stopped, for it was not his job to train the rookie from Lieutenant Loman's squad. "At least you got her name. That's something." He consulted his list of blond interview subjects and found Stella Small among them. "Her agent set up an interview, but Small was a no-show. Apparently this woman doesn't watch the news or read the papers. *Find* her."

"The police aide already took her statement," said Deluthe. "The actress told her she had a street altercation with a tourist. You see, the guy hit this woman with his camera, and she needed a few stitches. That's it. So then her agent shows up at the hospital and gets the idea to make the wound a little more newsworthy. That's when it turned into a stabbing."

"A police aide did the interview? A *civilian?* Well, that's just great." He tossed the newspaper to the rookie. "Get a copy of that statement from Midtown, and get that actress down here."

"But it's just—"

"Busywork? Most of my damn day is busywork. I'm one goddamn busy man. Now can you handle this or not?" What he had really wanted to ask Deluthe was why the man dyed his hair. And of all the colors in the world, why choose glow-in-the-dark yellow?

Detective Janos stood at the front of the squad room and addressed the rest of the men. "We got a thirty-second spot on the morning news and a full minute on radio. We might get lucky with the tip lines." He held up the newspaper page that listed the dates and locations of open casting calls. "And there's two auditions today. We got twenty minutes to make the one on—"

"Hey!" Detective Desoto, who sorted the tip-line calls, yelled, "Listen up! A woman with an *X* on her back just passed the corner of Sixtieth and Lex. I got a guy calling from a pay phone. He says she was headed for the subway. She's got blond hair, and she's wearing a light-blue suit."

"A suit," said Riker. "I'll bet she's on her way to the midtown audition."

"It's on the West Side." Janos was heading for the door, issuing orders on the run. "Get a unit over there. She'll make the crossover over at Forty-second Street."

"Maybe not." Arthur Wang grabbed his gun from a desk drawer. "If she sees that X on her back, she might pack it in. I know my wife would—"

"Subway!" yelled Janos.

Every man but Deluthe was up and running. Sergeant Riker stopped to tap his shoulder, saying, "You're with us, kid."

And they were off. Lieutenant Coffey's busywork errand was forgotten as Deluthe fell in with the gang of running detectives heading downstairs for the cars. One by one, the unmarked vehicles raced their engines. Mobile turret lights were slapped onto the roofs as they sped down Houston, zooming toward the West Side Highway.

Heading uptown.

What a ride!

The police cars were strung out in a wedge, forcing cabs to dodge and weave, and terrifying the amateur drivers. Five sirens screamed, and bull horns shouted, *"Outta the way! Move it! Move it!"* Every cross-town light was magically green until the convoy pulled to the curb in front of the Forty-second Street station.

The men left their cars at a dead run, hustling down the subway stairs in close formation, flying through the long tunnel, leather slapping cement, adrenaline rushing, hearts on fire, finally emerging in the shuttle bay.

Full stop.

Something's wrong.

There were too many people milling around at this time of the morning.

Three detectives climbed up on a bank of concrete and scanned the heads of waiting straphangers, looking for the blonde with an X on her back. Six men circled around to the other side of the track to search the rest of the crowd, then returned, heads shaking.

The woman was not there.

The surrounding passengers had the makings of a mob, feet stamping, voices rising, tempers close to exploding in the hot muggy air around the shuttle bay. Most had wandered away from the track, but hopefuls still stood on the edge, eyes fixed on the dark tunnel with a New Yorker's certain knowledge that watchers, not switchmen, made the trains come.

The crowd was still growing, not conversing but growling, voices rumbling in one sentiment, *Death to all transit workers—kill them all.* Here and there, a passenger went off like a firecracker, screaming obscenities. It could only be a matter of minutes before the first punch was thrown. This vast space would become a bloodbath from wall to wall.

Near the police booth, a band of musicians were unpacking instruments and plugging in amplifiers. This was the city's emergency response to impending violence among disgruntled subway riders.

Janos folded his cell phone. "We got uniforms at the exits. No sign of her yet."

Detective Desoto had disappeared into the mob, and now he was running back to them. "The good news? A suicide. A jumper got himself smeared across the tracks. All these people are from the rush-hour crowd. That's how long they've been waiting."

"And now the bad news," said Riker.

"They just finished cleaning up all the blood and guts. The shuttles are on the way. We're gonna lose the whole crowd in five minutes flat."

Deluthe understood this worst-case scenario. What were the odds that any of these stressed-out citizens would miss a ride out of hell to talk to a cop? "Can't we just stop the trains?"

Desoto gave him a look that asked, *What hick town are you from?* "Maybe you didn't hear me, kid. The last guy who stopped the trains is *dead.*"

"We got five minutes," said Riker. "Deluthe, you work the passengers near the track. Hit on the women. Men are useless. They only see breasts, not backs. The rest of you guys are with me."

The detectives moved in tandem, walking toward the small band of musicians. Their body language changed as they drew closer to the light Latin tempo intended to soothe ugly tempers with the soft strings of a guitar and a bass—and a drummer with nothing to do.

While Deluthe was taking statements of "I didn't see nobody" and "I don't know *nothin'*," Riker was taking a guitar away from one of the teenage musicians.

Deluthe watched the action through breaks in the crowd near the track. The senior detective's hand flew up and down the neck of an electric guitar, playing riffs of rock 'n' roll, and he was good—*damn* good.

The younger passengers were drifting toward the music, fingers snapping, heads bobbing to the beat—reborn.

The musicians were playing backup as Riker was gliding and sliding, strings zinging, the crowd cheering. He ripped out notes in a one-handed frenzy as he rolled the other hand toward the band to jump up the tempo. The bassman's fingers moved faster and faster. The drummer went insane with his sticks, smashing cymbals and beating on skins.

Janos pulled a woman from the crowd, and now they were gyrating, twirling and writhing. Other detectives grabbed strange females, danced them ragged and discarded them quickly. All the people were in motion; the place was rocking, cooking, jumping. The beat vibrated across the concrete and came up through the soles of Ronald Deluthe's shoes.

The crowd formed a ring around Riker, hands clapping, whistling high and shrill. Janos swung a new partner around, then lifted her high off the floor and let her go—airborne. She squealed with delight when he caught her. Riker ripped out another riff, and the crowd went wild. A shower of coins chimed into an open guitar case, and the band went demonic, pushing the tempo, faster, harder, louder. The trains came; the people stayed—stoned on music. The detectives changed partners and fired questions, never losing the beat.

Two hands shot up with high signs.

Finale.

Riker made a cutthroat gesture to the band, and the music died suddenly, as if a door had closed upon it.

And the world stopped moving.

The musical detective wiped the sweat from his eyes and took a deep bow to thunderous hand clapping. He turned to Janos, hollering to be heard above the racket, "What've you got?"

"A woman spotted the *X*. Our blonde didn't cross over. She stayed on the downtown Lexington line, and she was crying."

"She's going home," yelled Desoto. "Yesterday another woman saw a blonde with an *X* on her shirt. Now here's where it gets a little weird. She was fighting off a gang of dead flies in the station at Astor Place, and that's where she got off the train."

Deluthe moved against the flow of boarding passengers and fought his way out of the mob in time to see the squad of detectives flying into the pedestrian tunnel. When he emerged from the subway at street level, the other men were piling into their vehicles. The caravan drove off, sirens squealing, red lights spinning. And the young policeman was left standing alone on the sidewalk, breathless, as if he had also danced to the music of Sergeant Riker's band.

FiF TeeN

THE BLINKING LIGHT ON THE ANSWERING MACHINE WAS pulsating to the beat of a human heart—Stella's. The message could only be from the police. They would want to know why she had blown off her appointment at the SoHo station, and she had also missed the morning tryout for a play. Her agent had given her one last chance to redeem herself, a late evening audition, and it was not the standard cattle call. This time, she would be one of four actresses up for the part.

And Stella had nothing to wear.

The contents of her closet and drawers were strewn about the apartment in piles of thrift-shop clothes and hand-me-downs. When she wore these garments, they changed her into something lesser, lower. And now, in her mind, she had already failed the last-chance audition. Before day's end, she would have no career, no agent and no point in living. Stella sat on the edge of the sofa bed, then fell back and stared at the ceiling, eyes wide, unblinking, playing dead—just getting used to the idea.

The brand-new suit jacket lay on the floor, marred with another *X*. She had discovered the stain on the subway after removing the jacket to sew on a button. And now her eyes were raw and red from crying. The rent money was gone, and she could not ask for more. The egos of the Abandoned Stellas had been worn away so long ago; they would never understand the fragility of hers and the great importance of a magic mantle of pale blue linen.

She could not go home to Mom and Gram, though she pined for them. Tomorrow, she would send another postcard, another lie: *Fame and fortune can only be hours away.* Then she would find a job as a waitress and never tell them that their worst fear had come true.

Another thought overshadowed failure and the loss of home—the stalker. She could not go to the police for help, not after spinning a lie to get her name in the papers. That woman, Forelli, would have informed them by now. She imagined the police department as a colony of telepathic spiders, all busy weaving traps to catch her. Adding to her crimes against them, she had missed the SoHo interview for vandalized blondes. And now that she had a suit jacket with a legitimate *X*, she was no better off. The cops would never believe it was the real thing.

Stella rose from her bed and straightened her spine. She was an *actress*. She would *make* them believe her. All it would take was attitude and the right persona, but which one? Turning to the mirror on the wall, she asked, "Who am I today?"

Nobody, said the mirror. *You're just a little girl from Ohio.*

Stella nodded, then picked up the ruined suit jacket and traced the nasty black *X* with one finger. Every nice thing was ruined in this town, Bitch City.

Heavy footsteps were coming down the hall. They stopped outside her apartment. The police? She held her breath and played the statue, eyes fixed on a white envelope sliding under her door. It must be a summons. Oh, she was in so much trouble. The footsteps trailed off toward the stairs. Overwhelmed by dread, her feet weighed a hundred pounds, each one, as she approached the envelope on the floor. It was another few minutes before she gave herself up for dead and opened it.

Impossible.

It was a gift certificate from a Fifth Avenue department store where she could not afford to breathe the air. So much money. This would replace her ruined suit with something from the designer section—and shoes, *new* shoes.

Fifth Avenue was singing to her, *Get your tail down to the store, babe.*

On her way out the door, she considered the source of this bounty, quickly ruling out her Sunday school God, Who would not have survived for six minutes in New York City. Her savior could only be an apologetic vandal, a disturbed soap-opera fan who had gone too far and wanted to make amends.

Blessed are the mental cases.

Halfway down the stairs she stopped. There was no air conditioning in the common areas of the building, yet she felt an icy sensation in her chest. In movie lore, scary cold spots marked the presence of haunts in abandoned houses. And women?

He knows where I live.

Sergeant Bell sat behind the front desk facing the door of the police station. He was waiting for Lieutenant Coffey's order to send up the suspect. In peripheral vision, he kept watch over the fireman. Gary Zappata was working the cops in uniform, slapping backs and politicking, though he had never had a single friend in this precinct.

The detectives walked in the front door—three of them, if Sergeant Bell counted the whiteshield from the East Side squad. Riker had a few words with Deluthe, who then raced up the staircase to Special Crimes Unit, his feet hitting every third step like a galloping puppy.

Riker and Mallory were in no hurry as they crossed the wide floor, walking in tandem. They ignored the rookie fireman swaggering toward them.

Zappata squared off, legs apart, hands on his hips, then yelled, "I know what you did to me, Riker! You cheap shit! You snitch!"

The desk sergeant silently begged, *Please, Riker, don't do anything stupid.* It was worth a lawsuit if the detective slugged this man. And perhaps that was what Zappata was hoping for, since he was out of a job with the fire department and could never come back to NYPD.

The fireman strutted toward the partners. "You ratted me out." He glared at Riker, then puffed out his chest. "You drunken asshole." Zappata turned his smug face to Mallory, saying, "Well, if it ain't the Ladies' Auxiliary. Stay out of my way, *bitch*." He glanced over his shoulder and smiled at the battery of men and women in uniform, as if expecting applause for this very big mistake.

Mallory never flinched, but Riker's hands balled into fists. Sergeant Bell thought of calling the lieutenant down to end this before it—

The desk sergeant looked up to see Jack Coffey standing at the top of the stairs, hands in his pockets, quietly watching.

The short fireman moved to block Riker's path.

Another big mistake.

"You couldn't face me like a man," said Zappata. "You back-stabbing piece of crap."

The two detectives closed their distance with the fireman.

Any second now.

The phones stopped ringing. The only noise came from a civilian clerk, fingers typing, lightly skimming the keys.

. . . *tap, tap, tap, tap* . . .

The fireman was playing to his audience of uniforms, and he was so cocky, rocking on his heels, smiling too wide for a man so off balance. The dead silence from the uniforms gave him no clue that Riker was about to pound him into the ground.

It was not a sucker punch, though Zappata never saw it coming, not from the Ladies' Auxiliary. One moment he was standing up—Mallory's fist shot out fast and sure as a hammer fall, and then he was lying on the floor, having a quiet nosebleed.

She stood over Zappata's prone body, braced like a prizefighter awaiting the payback that would surely follow when this man found his feet again. With one quick glance at Riker, she warned him away. Sergeant Bell smiled, and there were nods of approval all around the room. Markowitz's daughter would not look to her partner or anyone else to finish off Zappata. By Mallory's stance, he could even guess which knee she planned to smash into the fireman's testicles.

The man at her feet was conscious, but he would not or could not move. He lay on his back, staring at the ceiling with an idiot gape of wide eyes and slack mouth.

The clerk stopped typing. The uniforms were stealing glances at Mallory, the bomb at the center of the room. A telephone rang to jangle nerve endings, and then another phone went off. Papers shuffled, typing and conversation resumed. Officers walked to and fro, some stepping over Zappata's body on the way to the door—life went on.

Once the squad room door was closed and Jack Coffey was facing Mallory, she missed her opportunity to say, *I told you so*, but the sentiment was clear when she turned her back on him and walked down the hall toward the incident room.

Sergeant Bell opened the stairwell door and leaned in, asking, "Hey, Lieutenant? You still wanna question Zappata?"

"No, just roll him out on the sidewalk." Coffey planned to follow the lead of ten uniforms and the desk sergeant, to say that he had been looking elsewhere when the fireman *tripped*. A blue wall of cops was securely closed around Mallory. Not that Coffey worried about consequences. What were the odds that Zappata would file a police brutality suit against a *girl*? Mallory was going to get away with this. The lieutenant watched her disappear through the door at the end of the hall.

"Maybe you noticed." Riker slumped down in a chair. "Your favorite suspect has a glass jaw." He pulled out a cigarette. "Now Sparrow was a big girl, and real good in a street fight—better than Mallory. There's no way that twerp could've taken her down."

"Even with a razor in his hand?"

"You think he'd know what to do with it? I don't. We're looking for somebody a lot scarier than Zappata."

Riker stood before the back wall of the incident room and cleared a space for a photograph from Natalie Homer's actress portfolio. The hangings had finally been merged into one case. He pinned the woman's smiling face to the cork alongside the effigy made of clothes. Now they hung together, Natalie and the scarecrow, mother and child.

Detective Janos pinned a note near the newspaper account of a stabbed actress. "I talked to Stella Small's agent and the doctor who treated her razor cut. They both say the assault happened on a crowded street. Now that works with what you got from Lieutenant Loman. All the hassling went on in crowded places."

"That pattern won't hold up for Sparrow, not the week before the hanging." Riker walked over to the next wall and pulled a statement down, then handed it to Janos. "That's the interview with the director of the play. Sparrow told him she was between day jobs, and she spent four days learning the lines of the play before she auditioned. Well, that just impressed the shit out him. That's why he gave her the part. And there were no open auditions the week before she died, so she wasn't commuting on the subway at rush hour."

"Okay," said Janos, "but you know this whole town is one wall-to-wall crowd."

When the big man had left the room, Riker turned back to the wall and the job of merging the paperwork of all the cases. Janos was right. New York City was one big swarming—

"Crowds of hookers," said Mallory.

He jumped in his skin. She was standing right behind him.

"If you see one hooker," she said, "you see eight or nine."

Riker shook his head. "No, Daisy said Sparrow was out of the life. Maybe the scarecrow marked her while she was—"

"Sparrow was still working the streets."

"And how do you know that, Mallory? Were you stalking her again?" Only someone who knew her well would see the sign of damage in her face, her frozen stance. And now Riker added his words to the list of things he wished he had never said.

Years ago, Sparrow had told him about being covertly followed and catching the young cop in the act from time to time. Mallory had the bizarre idea that she could shadow people unnoticed, that she could walk down any street, enter any room, without attracting stares. At Riker's last meeting with Sparrow, the prostitute had turned to her own gaunt reflection in a store window, then covered her eyes with a bone-thin hand and said, "I know why Kathy's following me. The kid thinks I'm dying—and she wants to watch." Two years had passed since then, and he should have known that Mallory had not stalked Sparrow recently, for she had not recognized the crime-scene address or the surgically altered face. He had wounded her for no good reason.

Her voice was mechanical when she said, "I found the plastic surgeon. He does a lot of work on battered women. Sparrow's new face wasn't free, but he gave her an installment plan. That's where all her money went. She was still turning tricks to pay for the operations and chemical peels. So Daisy lied to you. What a surprise, huh?"

"But you don't *know*—"

"Yes, I *do*. Those payments weren't cheap, and hooking was the only trade Sparrow ever had. That and one pathetic acting gig. She never had a pimp, so she always hung with other whores, lots of them. Safety in numbers—in the *crowd*. Then you've got the summer conventions, the boat shows, car shows. Lots of men—hooker heaven—*crowds.*"

"All right," said Riker. "I'll find her hangout whores." Even in a coma, Sparrow still had the magic to string him along, and the price of being blindsided was very high. "I'll chase down Tall Sally and talk to Daisy again." If one of them could point him to a likely street corner, he would do a raid. He would wait until it was too late for arraignments and bail. Most prostitutes were junkies who would shop their own mothers before they would spend eighteen hours in lockup.

Deluthe pulled the new reports from the wall on Riker's instructions to copy updated material for Charles Butler. He was careful to keep his distance from Mallory, and she had almost forgotten he was in the incident room—until she found another mistake—his.

She stared at the front page of a newspaper pinned to the wall. The actress in the photo was a blond stabbing victim. Deluthe's initials appeared on a brief companion note in longhand, a few lines for the actress's name, her address and the words *publicity stunt*. But that would not square with the dripping blood reported in the article. "Where's the follow-up interview for Stella Small?"

Deluthe looked up from the Xerox machine. "I never got to talk to her. But I left a message on her answering machine."

Mallory searched the wall for other paperwork. "Where's the statement from the midtown precinct?"

"A police aide was supposed to fax it from the—"

"This article mentions an ambulance. Where's the attending physician's report?" She turned to look at him. It was obvious that he had no answers. Still, she would not follow her first inclination, which involved a bit of violence. Mallory *never* lost control of her temper. The incident with the fireman did not count, not in *her* scheme of denial. She had not struck Zappata in anger. That blow had been the simple expedient of getting Riker through the day without a suspension. Yes, *Riker* was the one with the bad temper, or so she decided, founded on absolutely no proof of this defect in his character. And *she*, of course, had reigned in her own temper, safely gauging her punch to harm no more than the fireman's ego. She had hardly tapped him. Though Mallory had created this version of events only moments ago, she found no flaws in it.

The whiteshield detective stood beside her, nonchalantly gazing at the photograph of a recently assaulted blonde actress, who lived in the East Village. Could this woman have more *precisely* fit the profile of the next murder victim?

Deluthe had his excuses ready now. "I was going to call the actress again. But I had to put it off. Sergeant Riker—"

"That was a mistake." Mallory's words all carried the same weight, and she kept her eyes on the board when she spoke to him. "Don't phone her. Go to her apartment. Get a statement."

Still he lingered, and then she said, "*Now*, Deluthe. *Before* she dies."

Mallory followed in the wake of the running rookie, though at a slower pace. Her feet were dragging, and she was feeling other effects of lost sleep. She pulled out a cell phone and placed a call to the police station with jurisdiction on the actress's assault.

Ten minutes after making contact with a midtown sergeant, she was sitting in the squad room. Her head rested on the back of her chair, and her eyes closed as she waited for the man to locate paperwork on Stella Small's stabbing. Finally, he returned to the phone, saying, "Sorry, Detective. I found the statement, but it won't help. Our police aide, Forelli—she's been doing creative writing on the job again."

One hand tightened around the phone, but Mallory's voice was calm when she said, "Read it to me."

"All right. 'Professional bimbo collides with camera. Damn every tall blonde ever born.' You see the problem?"

Mallory's face was devoid of expression as she studied her right hand. The pain had ebbed away since decking Zappata. She flexed her fingers, then curled them tight, and her fist crashed down on the desk, bringing on fresh hurt and restored focus. And then, so that clarity would last awhile longer, she smashed her fist into the wood a second time—crazy naked pain.

SiXTEEN

A FENCE OF IRON BARS PROTECTED A TINY COURTYARD
and the red door to Stella Small's apartment building. Mallory
stood outside the gate and pushed the intercom buttons. When none of
the residents responded, she pulled a small velvet wallet from the back
pocket of her jeans, then unfolded it and perused her collection of lock
picks. At the age of ten, she had stolen this set from her mentor, Tall Sally,
then lost it for a time—the rest of her childhood. The velvet wallet had
turned up in the safety deposit box of the late Louis Markowitz. Sentimental man, he had not been able to throw away baby's first toys.

Before she had made her selection of tools to work the fence lock,
Ronald Deluthe came through the red door and crossed the small courtyard to open the gate. "There was nobody home," he said, "so I left my
card under her door."

"How do you know she's not home?"

"I'm telling you," he said, "there's nobody in there. I checked."

Mallory pocketed the velvet wallet, though she did not believe that he would recognize burglar tools. "You *checked*. And how did you do that?"

"Well, I banged on the door. No answer. I couldn't hear anybody moving around inside. It didn't sound like—"

"What does a hanging woman sound like, Deluthe?"

"Right." He walked back to the red door and unlocked it.

"Where did you get that key?"

"The management company down the street." Deluthe held the door open for her, then slipped past her to lead the way up the stairs to the second floor. "They wouldn't give me a key to her apartment—not without a warrant." He stopped at the door to 2B. "This is it. You're sure it's legal to go in there?"

"*Yes*, if we believe she's *dying*." Mallory did not appreciate having to repeat a lesson that he should have learned at the police academy. Deluthe had obviously not excelled in academics. So far, in *every* way, the son-in-law of the deputy commissioner was a mediocre candidate for the NYPD Detective Bureau.

He motioned for her to move away from the door. "I'll take care of it." *Yeah, right.*

Mallory stood to one side, arms folded.

Apparently, Deluthe had learned nothing on the subject of locked doors either. Putting all his might behind his right foot, he kicked the door dead center, and, of course, the locks held. There was not even a dent on the heavy metal surface. Mallory decided that some lessons should be learned the hard way, and so she waited patiently as he made a second attempt to break his foot, then asked, "Are you done?"

It was gratifying to see him limp as he backed away from the door. She pulled out the velvet wallet, selected two pieces of metal and worked close to the door, blocking Deluthe's view. First she opened the top lock, the one reputed to be pick-proof.

He edged around to one side of her, trying to see. "What are you doing?"

"I'm using a bobby pin," said Mallory, who owned no hair pins. "I always carry one for emergencies." And now she was done.

Like most New Yorkers, Stella Small had not bothered with the other two locks. The knob turned easily, and the door opened onto a room of cheap furniture and cheaper clothes strewn about amid the general clutter of dirty dishes and an unmade bed. A couch cushion lay on the floor, half covering a copy of *Backstage*.

"Looks like she's been robbed," said Deluthe.

Mallory shook her head. She recognized Riker's modus operandi in this mess. "Stella was only looking for something to wear." In Riker's case, he would have been hunting for the wardrobe item with the fewest stains and cigarette burns.

"No corpse hanging from the ceiling." Deluthe looked up at the light fixture and smiled. "I *told* you she wasn't home." A pale blue garment lay in a heap on the floor—in plain sight, yet he did not find this at all interesting.

"That woman you guys were chasing," said Mallory. "What was she wearing?"

"A light blue suit," said Deluthe. And *now* he noticed the material on the floor. Sheepish, he picked up the blue blazer and unfolded it to display an *X* on the back.

"Stella Small is the next victim," she said, believing that this needed to be spelled out for him. Mallory took the suit jacket from his hands and checked the label of a very respectable designer. The lines were good and so was the material. She walked among the piles of clothing and hangers on the floor. With an eye for what was out of date, she could tell that most or all of the wardrobe was secondhand. Yet there was an innate sense of style in a few good pieces of vintage clothing. The ruined blue suit was the best of the lot. Though Mallory's blazers were all tailor-made, she pronounced this one excellent. A cash receipt in the pocket bore out her suspicion of a discount house, a liquidator of unsold designer stock.

A pile of unopened letters lay on a table near the door. The loose stack was labeled with a yellow Post-it that bore the words *hate mail*—all bills and none of them paid. Mallory opened the table drawer and hunted among the contents till she found the checkbook. All the actress had listed in the register were check recipients—no amounts, no running balance, and none of the checkbook entries were for credit-card companies. So the woman was flat broke and would not be doing any more shopping today.

Mallory turned to the window on the street. It cost money just to walk out the door in this town. The impoverished actress would probably be home soon. "Deluthe, stay here and wait for Stella. I don't care if it takes all day—all night. You got that?"

Given his choice of interview rooms, Riker had selected the lockup, the smallest space in Special Crimes Unit. The walls were brownish yellow, and it had taken years of cigarette smoke and the projectile vomit of junkies to produce this special patina. Half the room was taken up by a flimsy coop of chain-link steel and wood. The door of this cage stood open, as an invitation and a threat to the tallest platinum blonde in New York City.

The transsexual sat on a metal folding chair and knocked knees on the underside of the table. "Where have you been, man? I've got a date tonight."

Riker closed the door behind him—slowly—and glanced at his watch. "This shouldn't take long, Sal. Tell you what. If you're in a rush, we can do it tomorrow. Suppose I have a police car pick you up at the store on your lunch hour?"

"Oh, yeah. Now that's a favor and a half. No thanks." Tall Sally was staring at the clock on the wall and fidgeting with brassiere straps and flyaway strands of hair. "I already talked to that other cop. The blonde with the Armani sunglasses." And now, the ex-prostitute, ex-male, ex-thief forgot the ladylike facade. "*Armani.* Tell me that bitch ain't on the take."

"I know what you told that detective." Riker dropped an old folder on the table. "And I know you lied." He sat down and put his feet up on the table in the posture of a man who had all the time in the world. "Let's talk about Sparrow. Or, if you like, we can talk about old times." Riker turned the folder around so that Sal could read the name of the subject in capital letters, FRANKIE DELIGHT. "It's been fifteen years, but his murder is still an open case, and I can put you on the scene."

Score.

The transsexual was backing up while sitting in a chair, all four metal legs scraping the floor. "I had *nothing* to do with it! Frankie was seriously crazy. Must've been a hundred whores lined up to kill that little bastard."

"You're probably wondering how I know you were with him the night he died." Now that Tall Sally had decamped from the male gender and joined the ladies, Riker was the only man alive who knew that Frankie Delight was the corpse found in the ashes of a fire. "There's no statute of limitations, Sal. Murder never goes away."

"If Sparrow says I'm the one that knifed him, she's a liar."

Frankie Delight, known to the medical examiner as John Doe, had indeed been killed with a knife. Sal was reaffirming a long-held belief that criminals as a class were stupid to the bone.

"Now that's another problem," said Riker. "Sparrow got stabbed the same night Frankie died." He opened the folder and scanned the four sheets of paperwork necessary to requisition an electric pencil sharpener. "Here's a statement from the ambulance driver. He was heading for the scene when he saw a seven-foot-tall blonde hightailing it down the street." That was actually true. However, fifteen years ago, Riker had been the only one to hear that statement, and he had never written it down. "So, Sal, can you—"

"If it wasn't for me, that junkie whore would've bled to death." Sal's hand waved in the air in a girlie affectation. "Or the rats would've got her. I saved her damn life."

This did not work with what Riker knew about the ex-convict's character; Tall Sally did not have one.

"I know you used a ten-year-old girl to heist VCRs off a delivery truck." He opened the folder again, feigning interest in another piece of paper. This one was blank. "I got two cops who can place you on that scene. When their patrol car showed up, you left that poor kid behind."

"What makes you think that I—"

"You answer *my* questions, Sal. That's how it works. I know that little kid gave the VCRs to Sparrow. Then you caught Sparrow fencing them for heroin. You stabbed her and killed the drug dealer. I've got motive, opportunity—everything I need to close this case."

"Frankie was dead when I got there. You know my rap sheet. Any knives, *any* weapons? No!" Hysteria was rising in Tall Sally's voice. "*Frankie* stabbed Sparrow. And I carried that bleeding whore on my back for three blocks."

"You moved her body away from a crime scene—so you could go back and get your goods without wading through ten cops."

"No, that was the kid's idea. The brat drags me to this empty building on Avenue B. Used to be a crackhouse before the cops raided it. And there's the whore laid out on the sidewalk. So I'm carrying this half-dead whore, and the kid runs up ahead, looking for a phone that wasn't broke. She used *my* damn change to call 911! Then I laid Sparrow down—"

"And you went back to the crackhouse to get your VCRs. So that's when you saw Frankie's body? Is that your story, Sal?"

"Damn kid didn't mention that—a dead man lying next to my VCRs. So much blood. I swear, every drop in his body bled out. Still had the knife in his leg." Sal pointed one finger at Riker, saying, "And that was Sparrow's knife. Big ol' *S* on the hilt."

"Too bad we never recovered the murder weapon." That was a lie. Riker had personally disposed of that knife long ago. "Maybe the kid can back you up. Got a name for her?"

"No, just street names. I called her the Flying Flea. Damn that girl could run. Anyways, she's dead now. Sparrow said the kid got cooked in a fire."

Riker was finally convinced that this ex-con would never connect the name Kathy to a cop with the same green eyes. "The evidence makes you look bad, Sal. We can get you a lawyer, or we can make this old business go away. You run into Sparrow now and then, right? If you lie to me, I'll have your parole revoked."

They played a waiting game, and finally Tall Sally leaned forward, saying, "That other cop, the tall blonde? She said the whore got her nose fixed. Now if I did see Sparrow—it would've been before that."

"You can do better, Sal. I need to know how Sparrow was spending her time the week before she died."

"Man, I can't give you what I don't have. Three months ago, I was leaving town for the weekend, so I'm sittin' in traffic at the Lincoln Tunnel, and there's Sparrow, working the cars with all the other busted-up whores. Damn queen of the commuter blow job."

"You're lying. There haven't been any hookers around that tunnel for over a year."

"You don't drive much, do you, Riker?"

Why would Sal spin him a lie that was so easy to break? The detective heard voices on the other side of the door, and one of them was Ronald Deluthe's.

"Okay, you can go." He actually felt a breeze when Tall Sally sprinted from the room. Deluthe smashed himself against the door frame when the giant blonde sped by him. And Riker could not help but notice that Sal's hair color looked more natural than the cop's.

"Okay, kid, what've you got for me?"

"All the stuff you wanted me to copy for Mr. Butler." Deluthe set a pile of paperwork on the table, then took the chair that Sal had vacated. His back was turned to the door when Mallory appeared on the threshold.

Riker patted the paperback in his pocket. He had been hoping to find a private moment to give her the old western, but this was not the time. She was wearing dark glasses, her idea of hiding. Tall Sally would not be back, but there were more interviews to come, other whores who would remember Sparrow's golden shadow, a child with strange green eyes. Mallory must feel trapped.

No, there was something else on her mind. Her attention was focused on the young cop seated at the table. Soundlessly, she moved into the room and stood behind Deluthe's chair. She bent down to his ear and said softly, "I told you to stay at Stella Small's apartment—her *unlocked* apartment."

She might as well have shot him.

Deluthe's hand went to his chest as he lifted his head and stammered to the ceiling. "I got a uniform to stand guard in front of her door."

Mallory sat down at the table, the picture of calm, shaking her head slowly from side to side. "No, you don't get to issue orders to the uniforms. That's not your job, and you don't have the rank."

"And it pisses off their sergeants," Riker added.

Mallory lowered her glasses so Deluthe could see that she was three seconds away from doing some real damage. "That uniform was pulled off guard duty to settle a domestic dispute in another building. Nobody bothered to tell his sergeant that waiting for Stella Small was a matter of life and death."

Deluthe could not look away from her. He was waiting for the explosion of temper, but Mallory was only stringing out his imagination, his anticipation of what she *might* do.

"I'll go back." Deluthe was rising from his chair.

"No you won't."

He froze in an awkward stance, half sitting, half standing, awaiting permission to wet his pants.

She never raised her voice. "I patched things up with the cop's sergeant.

He gave me a guard for the door and another man to canvas the neighbors in her building. That was also your job."

"You didn't tell me that you wanted—"

"I shouldn't have to tell you every damn thing, Deluthe. Sit *down*."

He sank to the chair.

"The uniforms will do the job," she said. "You stay the hell out of it. Just sit on your hands."

Riker kept silent until she left the room, and then he turned to the problem of rebuilding the shattered whiteshield. "How long were you with Loman's squad? Four months?"

The younger man nodded.

"Did they teach you *anything?*"

"Yes, sir." There was a curious lack of sarcasm in Deluthe's voice when he said, "I know which guys take cream and sugar and who likes their coffee black. I know who wants mayo on their sandwiches and who wants butter. And I never get their deli orders wrong."

"Yeah," said Detective Janos. "The tunnel's crawling with whores."

Hookers had reinvaded old territories while the mayor was concentrating on a new psychosis, exterminating all winged insects that *might* be carrying the East Village virus. This summer, insecticides had killed two elderly people with severe emphysema, and the insects, who had killed no one, were being executed *en masse*. But the hookers had escaped the city-wide extermination of bugs and old people, or so said Janos as he lumbered down the sidewalk with Riker.

"You gotta see it for yourself." Janos's large hands were rising, thick fingers fluttering, delicately plucking words from the air. "All those whores at the mouth of the tunnel. Well, the whole tableau is just *gorgeously* phallic."

This from a man with the face and physique of a bone-crushing hitman. Riker turned around and waited for Deluthe to catch up. "Hey, kid. You wanna go down to the Lincoln Tunnel and roust some whores?"

"Yes, sir." Deluthe was grinning.

"You can't wear gloves. That's the giveaway that we're gonna chase 'em down. So think about it, kid. We're talkin' body lice and head lice, crabs and herpes—every disease in the world is down there."

Janos smiled. "It's God's little waiting room for dying whores."

"Should be fun," said Riker. "Still wanna go?"

"Yes, *sir.*"

Lieutenant Coffey watched the television set in the incident room. Stella Small was now the subject of a fifteen-minute news segment. The police were requesting public assistance in the hunt for a potential crime victim. "Prime-time news. This is too good to be true."

"Oh, they were happy to do it," said Detective Wang. "It's ratings week. This'll send advertising revenues through the roof. They *loved* the part about the serial hangman."

The reporter on screen interviewed a bartender in Stella Small's neighborhood. The tavern's customers leaned into the shot and waved to the audience. The camera panned to the window, then out the door and into the street, turning left and right. The reporter asked, "Where is she now? Have you seen her?" His voice had the tenor of a game-show host inviting the home viewers to play.

A banner ran across the bottom of the screen with telephone numbers for the police tip line as the picture changed to a group of small children in costumes. Coffey wondered how a local news station had obtained this video of a kindergarten play in Ohio. A child-size Stella Small wobbled onstage, precariously balanced atop a pair of grown-up's high heels. The little girl promptly fell off her shoes and landed on her little backside, endearing her to two homicide cops and eight million New Yorkers. Tiny snow-white socks waved in the air while the child cried, "Mommy!"

"Oh, no." Coffey knew where the film had come from. "It was that damn agent. She turned the reporters loose on Stella's family."

Ronald Deluthe parked the car some distance from the mouth of the tunnel where a battalion of women was working the lanes of congested traffic. Slow stepping in high heels, the whores flashed bosoms pearled with sweat. Cars crawled through the street market of skirts hiked up to buttocks, twin moons in every shade of skin, spangles and cheap wigs in copper and gold—red, *red* mouths.

Some of the women were diving into cars, heads down and disappearing from view, then emerging with cash.

"Hookers never file complaints," said Riker, turning to the young cop behind the wheel. "And they never identify suspects. You know why? When the perps get out on bail, they beat the crap out of the women—or they kill them. Dead witness? Case dismissed. That's our criminal justice system. So we need to convince the ladies they'll never make a court appearance. But leave that to me, kid. I've got more experience lying to women."

He loosened his tie and buttoned his suit jacket so the gun and holster would not show. "Give me fifteen minutes. I'll pick out some likely whores. Then we'll try to bag two or three."

Riker stepped out on the pavement and raised the hood of Deluthe's car, disguising it as a disabled vehicle. Then he wandered toward the women, weaving slightly and snapping his fingers, but not in time to the blaring music from a slow-moving car, for he was playing the role of a harmless drunk out of tempo with the rest of the world, so as not to trigger the hookers' cop radar.

Twenty minutes later, he had picked out three junkies, older prostitutes in Sparrow's age bracket. They would be climbing the walls inside of an hour in custody, and a dope-sick whore was a talkative whore. One looked familiar, but if he had ever arrested her, she did not remember him either. He had asked no questions about Sparrow, for these women were streetwise, but he had managed to pick out regulars who had worked this part of town when Sparrow was last seen whoring.

The detective looked at his watch. Where was Deluthe? More than the allotted time had passed, and one of his best whores was getting away.

A red sedan crawled by, and a pair of high-heeled sandals clacked alongside the moving vehicle as a woman leaned down to smile at the driver, singing to him, "Hey, sweet thing." The prostitute rolled onto the hood of the car and rode it into the mouth of the tunnel, shouting into the windshield, negotiating her price with the driver.

Riker turned around to see the rookie cop make a hasty exit from his car. Now Deluthe remembered to slow his steps as he approached the women. What was he carrying? Riker squinted, and then his hand went to his own jacket pocket.

Empty.

The paperback western must have fallen out in the car.

Deluthe was trying not to stare at all the undressed skin, and this attracted immediate attention. Alerted now, the women lifted their heads, all but sniffing the wind for the smell of a cop. Some edged away, and some stayed to watch from a distance, wary and tense, ready to fly. And Riker knew he would be lucky to catch a single whore.

Could it get any worse? Oh, yeah.

There was only one stiff breeze in the entire month of August, and it had to be tonight. Deluthe's suit jacket was blown open. Three of the hookers could see the gun in his brand-new shoulder holster. And now they were melting away in the heat.

The whore-store was closing.

All the brunettes edged away, but one blonde sang out to other blondes as she strolled toward Ronald Deluthe.

Go figure.

Riker had seen hookers gang together by race, but never by hair color. Two more blondes were drifting toward the young detective. And now the dark-haired whores had forgotten their fear and proceeded to steal all the trade, picking off commuters, climbing in and out of cars, raking in cash by tens and fives.

Deluthe was deep in peroxide heaven and mounds of pale skin escaping from halter tops. The women stroked his hair, his chest and thighs. They smiled at him with broken teeth and gold teeth, with a "Hey, baby" and a "Hi, sugarman." One whore tapped the book in his hand, saying, "So—you know how this story ends?"

Riker's jaw went slack as he watched Deluthe open the paperback western. The young cop then read aloud to a group of very attentive, nearly naked book fiends.

· SEVENTEEN

LIEUTENANT COFFEY CLOSED THE DOOR OF HIS OFFICE, wanting more privacy for this delicate telephone call to Ohio. He spoke gently to Stella Small the elder, while Stella Small the younger cried on an extension phone. The mother soon faded out of the conversation, but the grandmother remained on the line until weeping made talking impossible.

He set down the telephone and turned to the small television set in the corner of his office. The live coverage from Ohio had resumed as the two Stellas returned to the reporter in their living room. Beyond the couch where the women were seated, Coffey had a picture-window view of their trailer court. A circus of media was camped outside.

The reporter was asking the mother and grandmother about their telephone interview with Special Crimes Unit in New York. "Do the police believe they'll find Stella before she dies?"

No mercy.

The lieutenant looked up at the glass partition and counted up the whores passing by his office, ten of them. Leading this parade was Ronald Deluthe. Riker was the last one through the stairwell door. All the detectives in the squad room were smiling, heads swiveling to follow the women, and Jack Coffey had no trouble reading their minds:

More blondes. God is good.

The lieutenant opened his office door and called out to Riker. "Charles Butler is here. He said you sent for him."

Charles sat in a narrow, darkened room, rather like a theater audience. Rows of comfortable chairs were raised in tiers, and there was not a bad seat in the house. The stage was a large bright space on the other side of a one-way glass, where Ronald Deluthe was holding the door open for a group of blondes in various stages of undress. The women took chairs around a long table. He could see them all talking at once but heard nothing of their conversation.

Riker entered the room and flopped down in a front-row seat, his tired face illuminated by the light from the window.

"Hard day?"

"Surreal." The detective rolled his eyes. "I'm trolling for hookers with the baby cop, and the ladies are crawlin' all over him. Now you might think they want Deluthe's sweet young body."

"No," said Charles. "That would be too easy."

Riker sighed. "They wanna discuss *literature* with him." He held up the old western as he stared at the larger room beyond the glass. "What you're lookin' at out there—that's the Kathy Mallory Hooker Book Salon. Those women can name all the characters from Kathy's westerns. They used to read to her when she was a kid, but only for an hour at a time. Some of them knew the beginning of a story, and some knew the middle or the end."

"But none of them ever read an entire book."

"Right. So this is what they used to do between tricks—they'd marry up the plots of the whole series. Other hookers joined up from word of mouth. And then they started running ads in *The Village Voice*. It took them years to find each other. And tonight they see Deluthe come along with a book by their favorite author, and it's one they've never seen before."

"The last western," said Charles. "They wanted the story."

"Yeah. Well, Deluthe tells 'em he's only gotten a few pages into it. So he opens the book and starts reading to a gang of whores. Now the traffic *really* slows down. Nobody's ever seen anything like *that* in New York City. Then the kid stops reading, and he says, 'Hey, I know somebody who's read the whole book.' So now the hookers think it's a *great* idea to go to a police station. It gets better. They invite some more blondes with street-corner addresses. I had to send out squad cars to pick 'em all up."

"And how can I help you?"

"I've read maybe half those books, but that was fifteen years ago. You're the only one who's read 'em all. We're gonna trade plots for information. At least half of these women know Sparrow on sight. I need a time line for the week before the hanging."

"And you're hoping one of them got a look at the scarecrow." Charles turned to the glass and watched Deluthe set up room dividers to create two small cubicles and the illusion of privacy.

Following Riker's lead, he rose from his seat, and the detective put one hand on his arm, saying, "Just one more thing, Charles. Listen carefully. None of those whores knows Mallory's right name. Sparrow was the only one who ever called her Kathy. But you're gonna hear stories about a little girl with blond hair and green eyes. That kid is officially *dead*. If she doesn't stay dead, she's facing charges of murder and arson."

On that warning note, a startled Charles Butler was quickly ushered out of the room. Riker locked the door behind them, then opened his hand to display three keys. "That's all of 'em." For added security, he inserted a toothpick into the lock and broke it off at the lip of the metal. "We don't want any eavesdroppers."

The detective strolled into the interview room, saying, "Ladies, you came to the right place." He clapped one hand on Charles's shoulder. "We know how *all* the stories end."

And this earned them a round of applause.

If Riker had intended to shelter her from the hooker reunion of Sparrow's friends, he should have posted a guard. Locked doors had always intrigued her, though this one did not pose much of a challenge. Mallory teased the toothpick out with her fingernails, then made short work of picking the lock. Upon entering the darkened room, she removed her sunglasses and sat down in the front row of chairs facing the one-way glass. And now she waited for the performance to begin.

Something was wrong.

Mallory leaned closer to the glass. She recognized most of these prostitutes from the story hours of her childhood, even women who had been badly altered by scars and broken teeth. It was surprising how many had survived, though this was but a fraction of their original number. The common denominator for these women was not Sparrow, but herself.

What was Riker playing at?

Deluthe stood at the head of the table of whores, writing furiously in his notebook, probably taking orders for a deli run. Riker would not want him in the room when this interview started.

Mallory turned on the sound system. It was another shock to hear Charles Butler's voice. When he stood up, she could see his head above the gray partition of the far cubicle. Riker was introducing him to a prostitute. Would Charles have enough sense to wash up after shaking hands with Greta? His new friend, the whore, was missing half an ear, old damage from long ago.

Deluthe was on his way out the door to fetch the orders from the delicatessen, and now the interrogation would begin. Mallory raised the volume on the intercom. The sound system was intended to eavesdrop on one voice at a time, not six conversations. She closed her eyes to all distractions, then sifted through the babble, seeking out one man's voice and then the other's.

How did Charles know the plots of her westerns?

She listened a while longer, concentrating on a single voice. Charles had finished telling Greta how *Far Trails* had ended, and now he was asking her questions about Sparrow's movements.

Mallory shifted her attention to Riker's cubicle, where he was seated with another whore. A few minutes into this conversation, she knew he was trying to solve the wrong murder.

"Markowitz didn't know Sparrow was tight with the kid, he just wanted a pair of eyes on the street," said Belle. "You know, like if she saw the kid—"

"A little blond girl," said Riker, attempting to speed up the interview, for he already knew this part of the story. He had been the one who had approached Sparrow for information, but Lou Markowitz had put up the money.

"Uh-huh. The cops were really hot to find that girl. Offered Sparrow cash—not chump change either. And then, up front, she got a get-out-of-jail-for-free card, and it was signed by Markowitz himself."

Riker gave up the idea of moving this woman along any faster. Whatever drug she was doing, it was not laced with speed.

"So Sparrow started out the day as a hooker," said Belle. "Then she turned into a snitch that afternoon. And that same night, she was ware-housing stolen goods for a ten-year-old thief. So you can see how her ca-reer just wasn't going real well."

"Warehousing goods?" Riker feigned skepticism. He was hoping this was the shipment of VCRs. "It's not like the kid was ever more than a small-time thief."

"Hey, who's telling this story? Well, I'm walking down the street with Sparrow. She's already decided to blow off Markowitz. And along comes the kid wheeling a grocery cart full of VCRs. Brand-new, still in the car-tons. I ask her if she wants me to read her a story, and she says no. Well that was a first. The kid looks to Sparrow and says she needs a place to stash her stuff."

And now Riker listened to another version of the great truck robbery. In this one, Kathy took all the credit for the theft.

"So now the kid wants to change the goods into cash. Tall Sally's the only fence Sparrow knows, but the kid won't deal with Sal. Never would say why. So they got another buyer for the VCRs."

"Would that buyer be Frankie Delight?"

Belle shrugged off the question. "Who the hell knows? I sure don't. Now what happens at the end of *Shadowland*?"

Riker knew this book well. It was his personal favorite, and he did not even care about the glaring flaw of long-range shooting in the dark of a moonless night. "It ends with an ambush. Forty rustlers are up on the cliffs, guns aimed, waiting for Sheriff Peety to come through the canyon. And he's got a bad feeling about this trail, like he knows what's coming, but he's got no choice. He has to follow the Wichita Kid."

"'Cause that's his job." Belle recited words from the first page of almost every book. "His life is the law."

"Right. But all he's got is two six-shooters and no extra bullets. It's a cloudy night, no stars, not one, and that's the worst of it for him. He believes he's never gonna see their lights again. And he's lost without 'em—no markers in the sky to help him find his way. So he reins in his horse and sits awhile. He wonders what his life is all about. He's lost his faith, he's lost his way. Can't even see the badge on his chest—it's so damn dark. The book ends when the sheriff digs in his spurs. He rides into the canyon at a gallop, *knowing* it's a trap—a fight he can't win. The rustlers open fire. He looks up and sees the bright lights of guns firing from every ridge—like *stars*."

"That's beautiful," said Belle, rising from her chair.

Riker nodded to the next woman in line. "Your turn."

The second prostitute's name was Karina, and she had a few questions of her own. "Did I hear right? You talkin' about Frankie Delight? Whatever happened to him? Not that I care about that squirrelly little bastard. Just curious is all."

"Last time I saw him," said Riker, "he was toast—dead on a slab in the morgue."

Mallory's eyes snapped open. How could Riker know about the murder of Frankie Delight? The drug dealer's body had been destroyed in the fire. No one could have put a name on that charred corpse.

Crazy Frankie.

She closed her eyes again and called up the jittery image of a drug dealer in a deserted building on Avenue B, a skinny white boy in dreadlocks, ripped jeans and gold chains.

The jewelry? Was that how Riker had identified the body?

She could see the deserted building again, deep in shadow, half the interior walls knocked down and rats everywhere—only one way out. She could pinpoint the moment when Sparrow had realized that Frankie planned to rob her, to take the VCRs without paying. No knives had come out, not yet, but whore and dealer circled round and round.

Unconsciously, Detective Mallory's hand made the shape of a pistol as Kathy the child drew her pellet gun on the drug dealer. It was happening all over again. Frankie Delight was in her sights when he dropped to one knee, holding his sides because he was laughing so hard it hurt. Pointing to her plastic gun, he giggled out the words, "Oh, you're gonna make a big hole with that sucker." He turned to Sparrow, saying, "Hey, bitch. Your needles make bigger holes." Not done with humiliating a child, he turned back to Kathy as he rose to his feet, still in good humor. "You could really mess up a big-assed cockroach with that thing. You shoot that bug in the leg, and he'll never walk again."

And Sparrow was laughing, too—when he jammed his knife into her side, then twisted it to rip her up some more.

Oh, the look of surprise in the whore's eyes.

How Frankie had laughed at the comical sight of Sparrow sliding down the wall, leaving a smear of blood in her slow descent. His laughter had drowned out the screams of a child.

Riker lit Karina's cigarette. "So you're the one who set up the meeting."

"Yeah, Sparrow wanted to unload some VCRs. A little kid ripped 'em off. Can you beat that? Well, I knew this half-assed drug dealer, the only one who'd deal for goods. Everybody else was cash or nothin'."

"Sparrow wanted to swap the VCRs for drugs?"

"Yeah, but what she really needed was cash. Her rent was way past due. So she figured to get drugs for the VCRs, then change the drugs into money on the street—selling to the johns." Karina exhaled a cloud of smoke. With all the authority of a jailhouse lawyer, she said, "That's twice removed from the truck robbery."

Riker smiled. It was the first instance ever of laundering illegal proceeds with drug money—very creative.

May smiled at Charles, showing him all her broken teeth and one gold cap. "What happened after that ambush in *Shadowland*?"

"It's still going on when the next book opens," said Charles. "The gunslinger was clear of the canyon before the rustlers opened fire on the man who was chasing him."

"Sheriff Peety."

"Right. Well, it looks like there's no way out for the sheriff. He's almost out of bullets. But then, the Wichita Kid turns his horse around and comes riding back into the canyon to save him."

"I *knew* he would," said May. "But there were forty rustlers up on the ridge. How did Wichita shoot all of them?"

"Oh, he didn't shoot any of them. He shot the sheriff."

May's head tilted to one side to say, *What?* And now she leaned far forward, her expression clearly implying, *You're nuts.* And aloud she said, with great conviction, "Wichita would *never* do that."

"I swear that's what happened." Charles was perplexed by the sudden hostility. It was only a story. "He shot the sheriff. Mind you, it was only a shoulder wound, but it knocked Sheriff Peety right out of the saddle. Actually, it was quite a clever ruse. You see, when the rustlers thought the old man was dead, they stopped shooting at him." Not that there had been much danger of them hitting their target in darkness described as absolute. "The rustlers even cheered the Wichita Kid for making this really great shot from a galloping horse." In fact, it was an impossible shot, but logic was not the author's forte.

"I *love* that boy." The prostitute clapped her hands together.

"My turn," said Charles. "Now the last time you saw Sparrow was how long ago?"

"Four months, maybe longer."

Charles looked up at the woman behind May's chair. "Madam, you're next."

Mallory found it difficult to concentrate on conversations in the next room. A cascade of pictures was dropping into her mind, and she could not block them out. Through the eyes of a child, she watched Sparrow writhing on the floor, losing a river of blood from the knife wound in her side and crying, "Jesus! Jesus!"

Kathy knew Jesus, too. He was the King of Pain, crowned with thorns and stabbed with nails. And she had sometimes called on Him in this same way—with no expectation of help—just another ritual like the story hour.

Riker recognized the woman now, but not by her face, not even by her name. The prostitute's neck scarf dropped to give him a glimpse of a familiar scar, a souvenir from the man who had slit her throat rather than pay for her services. He would tread carefully with this one. She was the hooker who had tied Sparrow to the little girl who died in the fire, and all for three seconds of fame on the evening news.

The whore gave no sign of remembering the detective. All cops and customers must look alike to this aging parody of a dead actress. Marilyn's red mouth was drawn well outside the lines of her thin lips, but her voice was breathy and sexy, so close to the real thing.

"Sure I remember," said Marilyn. "It was maybe fourteen, fifteen years ago. I brought Sparrow's stuff to the hospital. That was the day after she got stabbed."

"Her *stuff*. You brought her *heroin?*"

"Oh, just a taste, a snort. Not enough to mess her up. I had a personal interest in Sparrow's health. She owed me money. God, she was strung out. What I gave her didn't help much."

Riker leaned over to light the woman's cigarette. "Did the little girl ever visit her?"

"Uh-huh. When I came in, she was sittin' on the edge of the bed. Sparrow was feeding her off the hospital tray. The kid was eating an apple one minute, and then she was dead asleep. Her eyes closed, and the apple just rolled out of her little hand. Ain't it funny—the things that stay with you for years?"

"What else happened that day?"

"Sparrow shook the kid till she woke up. Reminded her she had something to do—and fast. I never found out what that was about. So the kid climbs down from the bed. So tired. Poor baby. She was weavin' on her way out the door. And that was the last time I ever saw that child alive."

Mallory leaned forward, straining to catch the details of her hospital visit. That was the day Sparrow had sent her back to the deserted crackhouse—the day of the fire. This was a memory she did not want to relive, but images broke into her conscious mind against her will—the rats were eating the dead man, and she could hear the sucking sound that Sparrow's knife made when it was pulled from the body.

"No, babe," said Crystal. "Sparrow ain't worked the tunnel in a while. Last time I saw that whore, she was planning to get her nose fixed. Later, I heard she was working uptown hotels. I'm telling you, that must've been one hell of a nose job. I wouldn't last six seconds in one of those hotels before they threw my ass out the door. So what's the rest of the story?"

"First, tell me something," said Charles. "Why do you care about these books?"

Crystal gave this some careful thought, then smiled with her broken mouth. "It's like you're always waiting for the other shoe to fall. You know that saying? You do? Good. Well, babe, I've been waiting for fifteen years. Now give me the rest of my damn story."

"All right. Remember the first cowboy Wichita ever killed?"

Exasperated, she said, "Of course I do. All the girls know that story. That was the only one we got paid for."

"Pardon?"

"That first story—the kid paid for it. Well, she paid for the first hour. She'd give a whore something she stole, something real fine. I gotta say, the girl had good taste. Then, after that first time, all her stories were free. All she had to do was say, 'Read me a story,' and some whore would take her home."

"And you all read to her—because you had to know how the books ended?"

"Now you got it. But it was never the same book twice in a row. You'd wind up an hour into a completely different story—and no end. Or maybe you'd get the end, but you wouldn't know how it started."

"Well, in *Homecoming*, you discover that the first dead cowboy was a murderer. He was part of a gang that killed Wichita's father and stole his cattle."

"So that's how the Kid's mother wound up as a dancehall girl. I always wondered about that. She was the only churchgoing slut in Franktown."

"Right," said Charles. "It was either work in a saloon or starve, and she had a child to support. Well, in this book, Wichita's almost done. He's tracked down the last gang member, a man hiding out in Franktown. And he kills him in a gunfight."

"Does the sheriff arrest the Kid?"

"No."

"So the Kid just left town, right? He got away again?"

"Well, not in this one." Now Charles realized that this woman was unaware that *Homecoming* was the end of the series.

"You don't mean Wichita gave himself up?" She read a worse fate in Charles's giveaway face. "No," she said. "Don't tell me he *died!* Don't you *dare* tell me that!" She shouted, "How can the Kid be *dead?*"

All around the room, conversations stopped abruptly as ten hookers went into mourning for the Wichita Kid.

Mallory sat in darkness, eyes closed, slowly moving her head from side to side. She could not remember a book called *Homecoming*.

Riker waited out the silence. Finally, the whores rallied, for they had other unresolved issues.

"So tell me what happened to the horse," said Minnie. "Ol' Blaze rolled off a cliff at the end of one book. At least tell me the *horse* didn't die."

"Well," said Riker, "I know it looked like old Blaze was goin' sour, but the horse came back in the next book. Now this Indian girl—"

"Gray Bird? The one who loved the Wichita Kid? He talks about her in most of the stories."

"That's the one, yeah. She nursed the horse back to health with magic and herbs. The girl died, but the horse was good as new."

"Ain't that romantic?"

"Yeah."

Mallory left the building and walked past her car, heading for the next block and her office at Butler and Company. It was trash collection night, and the street was rimmed with garbage and a rancid stink. As she passed each metal can, something slithered away in the dark. Eyes shut tight, she pressed her hands over her ears, trying to kill the sound of rats' feet scrabbling across a rotted wood floor, racing one another to the fallen, bleeding Sparrow. She could not lose the smell of kerosene, smoke and burning skin.

Stopping by a pay phone, she fed coins into the slot. Mallory dialed three random numbers and then the four she knew by heart, though she had not performed this ritual since childhood. The phone was ringing, and she felt the same excited anticipation. But why? Was it comfort she expected at the other end of the line?

A woman answered, "Hello?" One more stranger out of a thousand calls from the street said, "Hello? Is anyone there?"

Mallory had not forgotten the ritual. She knew what came next, the words, *It's Kathy, I'm lost,* but she could not say them anymore.

"Hello?" The stranger's voice was climbing into the high notes of alarm.

Oh, lady, can you hear the rats on the telephone line?

Charles abandoned his previous theories. The child had neither believed in heroes nor had she relied on fictional people for friends. Far from it. She had once ruled a stable of prostitutes bound to her by stories. It was an ancient lure dating back to the cave, the need to know what happens next.

Brilliant child.

He pulled another chair into his cubicle for Gloria and Maxine. The women were not related but resembled each other and even dressed in twin red halter tops and shorts. They were younger than the rest. Their makeup was low key, and they were not battered where it showed. The two prostitutes had insisted on being interviewed together.

"We do everything together." Gloria's smile was very friendly. "*Everything*, hon."

On request, Charles was about to finish a story begun in *The Cabin at the Edge of the World*.

"And don't tell us that preacher made it rain," said Gloria.

"Oh, no, nothing like that. When Wichita comes out of the fever, the cabin is still in flames. Now if you recall the cliff-hanger in the previous book—"

"Like we'd forget that," said Gloria. "The farmers think the old woman's a witch and she caused the drought. They move burning bushes in front of all the windows and the doors. Every wall is on fire, and Wichita's dying. That's what the old woman thinks. So she gets down on her knees and screams to God for mercy."

"Right," said Charles, recalling the final sentence: " 'A scream that shivered the stars in the firmament.' Well, in the next book, Wichita wakes up and soaks the old woman with a bucket of water. He slings her over one shoulder, then leaves by the front door. Walks right through a wall of fire." And now he thrilled the prostitutes with another quotation from the page, " '—stripped to the waist, his long golden hair flying in the wind and burning with sparks, his skin steaming with the burnt sweat of his fever.' It's an imposing sight on the heels of a very loud prayer from the old woman. Now the fake preacher gets religion. He falls down on bended knee and declares the outlaw is an angel. Well, as you can imagine, that gives a few of the farmers pause. Then the Wichita Kid draws his six-gun, and the rest of them have second thoughts about this business of witch burning."

The prostitutes were enthralled. "The Kid walked through fire."

"Yes," said Charles. "But then, toward the end of the book, he guns down another man."

"Oh, he always does that," said Gloria. Apparently, this credential of a serial killer was a character flaw she could live with. "So the Wichita Kid walked through fire."

"Now," said Charles, "I believe you mentioned running into Sparrow recently."

"Last week," said Gloria. "Maxine and me, we were cruising for johns at the computer convention in Columbus Circle. Sparrow was there. Wasn't she, Maxine?"

"She was." Maxine resumed chewing her gum.

"She was workin' the crowd, same as us," said Gloria. "But nothin' obvious—no flash. She didn't look like a whore no more. She looked real nice, didn't she, Maxine?"

"Very nice."

"Excuse me," said Charles. "Did you ladies notice anything odd that day? Something out of the—"

"You mean Sparrow's new nose job? Or the guy who slashed her arm with a razor?"

Deluthe sat at a squad-room desk, very close to Maxine, as the woman concentrated on the computer monitor. They were attempting to create their own monster with photographic slices of other people's faces, eyes and noses, ears and mouths, assisted by FBI software.

A few desks away, a sketch artist was working with Gloria and using an old-fashioned pencil. "Can you describe him a little better?"

"Yeah, he was a cold one," said Gloria.

"Well, that doesn't—" The exasperated sketch artist saw Riker's hand signal to keep his mouth shut, and the man fell silent.

"The color of his hair," said Riker. "Was it light or dark?"

"Blond," said Gloria, raising her voice to be heard across the room. "His hair was blond, wasn't it Maxine?"

"No," her friend called back. "It was brown, average old brown."

"Maxine, you're nuts. He was blond, I tell ya. But real natural." The prostitute glanced at Ronald Deluthe's head. "Not a bleach job."

Hoping to strike a compromise, Riker said, "Maybe it was blond hair that went dark when he grew up."

"Yeah," said Maxine. "That's it. His hair looked like Gloria's roots." She turned to Deluthe. "Make it brown."

The sketch artist's version was in gray charcoal pencil. "No, this isn't working," said Gloria. "Start over. Make it a profile picture—like a mug shot, 'cause that's all I saw of him. Maxine saw his whole face." She called out to her friend. "Didn't you, Maxine?"

"I did."

Gloria went on with her story of the encounter for Riker's benefit. "Well, I was gonna say hi to her when this stiff-lookin' jerk comes up behind her. So I just stand there. Didn't wanna say nothin' to queer it for Sparrow. But the john, he don't say nothin', either. Sparrow hasn't even noticed him yet. Then this freak pulls a box cutter out of his gym bag."

Gloria looked up at Charles, who wore the expensive clothes of a man unfamiliar with box cutters. "It's a big metal grip with a razor." She turned back to Riker. "He cut her arm. I couldn't believe it. All them people around, and he cut her right there. Cold as you please. Then he walks away, real calm, like he does this kind of thing every day. He stuck the box cutter back in his bag before Sparrow even knew she'd been slashed. She didn't know till I told her. I said something like—Hey, you're bleedin'. Isn't that what I said, Maxine?"

"That's close." Maxine was no longer listening to her friend. She was staring at Deluthe's monitor. The computer-generated image was taking shape faster than Gloria's drawing. Deluthe had picked up on the other woman's cue of a cold stare. A pair of vacant eyes slipped into place on the screen.

"It's better," said Maxine. "But it still needs work."

Charles crossed the room with a photograph retrieved from the cork wall of Butler and Company. He handed Maxine a wedding portrait of Erik Homer, the scarecrow's father.

"The eyes aren't the same." She turned to Deluthe. "The mouth is, but don't make him smile like that."

Riker handed Gloria a roast beef on rye. "Do you remember anything about the bag he was carrying?"

"Nothin' special. Right, Maxine? His bag wasn't special."

Maxine shook her head. "It looks just like my gym bag. Got it on sale at Kmart. Paid almost nothin' for it."

Riker moved to Maxine's chair and handed her the container of soup she had ordered from the deli. "What did the bag look like?"

"It was gray with one stripe."

Deluthe stopped work. "A *red* stripe?"

"Yeah, just like mine."

The young cop stared at the image on his screen, then crossed the room to look at the sketch artist's pad. "I've seen this guy. He was in the crowd outside the last crime scene. I remember his bag. I've got one just like it. But his had a red stripe. That was the only difference."

"Kmart?" asked Maxine. "Nylon, right?"

"No, L.L. Bean." Deluthe turned to Riker. "My bag is canvas, and so was his."

Riker turned to Charles. "Keep the ladies company." He grabbed Deluthe by the arm and propelled him down the hall to the incident room. They walked to the wall where exterior crime-scene photos were pinned up alongside autopsy pictures of Kennedy Harper.

"Which one?" Riker pointed to the pictures of the crowd gathered outside Kennedy Harper's building. "Which face?"

The younger cop turned to point at the rear wall and the photograph between the scarecrow's T-shirt and the baseball cap. It was the picture of a man whose face was turned away from the camera. "He's that one. . . . Sorry."

A breeze swept papers and cigarette packs down the narrow SoHo street, and a car alarm went off with a high-pitched incessant squeal. An irate tenant on an upper floor leaned far out his window and hurled a dark missile to the pavement, but the bronze baby shoe fell short of the offending vehicle and narrowly missed the two walking men.

Riker glanced up at the civilian and yelled, "Lousy shot!" In a lower voice, he said to Charles Butler, "But it could've been worse. It's scary how many of these people have guns."

Another man emerged from a building just up ahead. He held a baseball bat. When he spotted Riker and Charles, he thought better of leaving the shadows of his doorway. As the two men came abreast of him, the bat disappeared behind the man's back.

"Now *that* guy means business," said Riker, when they were well past the car with the screaming alarm. "He'll get the job done."

They turned the corner at the sound of breaking glass and the bangs of wood on metal—followed by blessed silence.

They were heading toward Charles's building on the next block. Mallory would be at work in the back office at Butler and Company, and there might not be another opportunity to speak privately with Riker. "When you said the little girl was dead—well, obviously, you didn't mean Kathy had actually died. So presumably—"

"I've seen her death certificate. It was backed up by sworn statements from two fire marshals. And neither one of those guys owed any favors to me or Lou."

"You're not going to explain that, are you?" Charles's tone was fatalistic. "Not a hint, not a clue."

"Nope."

"And that business of murder and arson charges—"

"Not a chance."

EiGHTEEN

MALLORY STOOD IN THE OFFICE KITCHEN AND POURED another cup of coffee. Her eyes were closing. When had she slept last?

Old pictures were breaking into her thoughts again, wreaking havoc with her concentration. The rats were coming for the whore. Greedy vermin. Not content with the blood and meat of Frankie Delight, they wanted Sparrow too.

Mallory turned on the faucet, then leaned over the sink and splashed her face with cold water. She sat down at the kitchen table. Her coffee cooled in the cup. Her eyes closed, and down came the curtain between waking and sleeping dreams. Though she had never had the smoker's habit, one hand went up to her mouth as she lit a cigarette that was not there. She was ten years old again. Sparrow was bleeding, saying, "Don't cry, baby."

But Kathy could not stop crying. The frantic child shook Sparrow to keep her from drifting into sleep and death. "I'll get help!"

"Don't leave me," said Sparrow. "Not yet." The prostitute nodded toward the shadows where the rats were fighting over the corpse of Frankie Delight. "Keep 'em off me—till it's over."

"You *can't* die."

Sparrow gently touched the child's face. "Baby, I'm always telling you stories. *Read me a story*—that's all I hear from you. Suppose you tell me one. But mind you, don't make it a *long* story." Sparrow's eyes were closing as she smiled at her own little joke.

"You need a doctor!" Kathy shook Sparrow until the blue eyes opened. The child put her hands over the open wound, trying to keep the prostitute's blood from leaking out.

"Don't leave me for the rats," said Sparrow. "Tell me, how did that book end? *The Longest Road*, yeah, that one. The Wichita Kid decided he was goin' home. Did he ever say why?"

"It ends when he's on the trail." Kathy emptied Sparrow's purse on the floor, straining to see by the daylight streaming in from the street door. "Wichita stops his horse in front of the sign for Franktown." The room was growing darker; the day was ending; Sparrow was dying. The child found a handkerchief. "He just stares at that sign for a while." She used the square of white linen to cover the stab wound. The cloth was soaked with blood the moment she pressed it to Sparrow's side. "Then there's these lines near the end. But I don't—" Though the little girl knew all the books by heart, her panic was overwhelming her. Sparrow could not *die*.

"What lines, baby?"

Kathy bit her lip until it bled into her mouth. She needed this pain to concentrate, and now the passage came into her mind, clear as the spoken word, and she recited, " 'It was more than the call of home. He was riding toward his redemption.' "

"You know what that means, baby?"

"No." And she did not care. Kathy unclipped a long strap from Sparrow's purse and used it to hold the red handkerchief in place. "I'm going for help. I'll come right back."

"No, baby. *Stay* with me." Sparrow's next word was hardly more than a whisper, a sigh, "Redemption." Her voice was stronger when she said, "How can I put that so a little thief can understand?"

The rats were coming. The child stamped one foot and screamed at them, "You stay away! She's not dead! She's *not!*"

"That's right, baby. You tell 'em." Sparrow's voice was failing. "Redemption—that's when you buy back all your bad karma—so you can steal heaven."

What was karma?

The prostitute closed her eyes again, and this time Kathy could not wake her. The child's head snapped toward the shadows and the sound of a rat's feet. She waved her arms, but the creatures had no fear of her anymore. The lure of blood was strong. And now another rat appeared at the edge of the failing light from the street door.

"Stay away!" Kathy pulled out her pellet gun and fired on the rat, missing her mark. She was crying, vision blurring, yelling, "She's not *dead!* Not *yet!*"

The child reached down to the debris from the prostitute's purse and found something hard, a missile to throw. It was a silver lighter she had stolen for Sparrow. She held it tight, then picked up one of the cigarettes that had spilled on the floor alongside a can of hairspray. Kathy hunkered down beside the purse, smiling—inspired.

Once, Sparrow had nearly set her hair on fire, smoking a cigarette while waving the hairspray can.

Kathy lit the cigarette, puffing and coughing until it burned. She stared at the glowing ember and waited, fighting down the panic until the rat was close to her feet. She pointed the aerosol can at the animal, then pressed down on the nozzle, wetting the rat through and through. It squealed with the pain of hairspray in its eyes. The child dropped the cigarette on its fur and stood back as the animal burst into flames and screamed.

Another rat came out of the shadows, drawn by the smell of live cooking meat. Hunched over, Kathy crept forward to meet the creature. Holding the cigarette lighter low to the ground, she pressed the nozzle of the hairspray, aiming it at the tiny flame, and the chemical spray became a blow torch. The second rat was burning, running in circles, streaking fire round and round. It was crying in a human way and drawing cannibals from the corpse of Frankie Delight.

Kathy was numb, too stunned to care what the rats were doing to one another. Working by slow inches, the child struggled with her burden, dragging Sparrow out of the dark building and into the waning daylight where more rats awaited them, scrabbling out from between the garbage cans on the sidewalk.

In the kitchen of Butler and Company, Mallory lurched to one side. Chair and woman crashed to the floor. Her face was pressed to the tiles, and she lay there for a few seconds of absolute stillness, quietly seeking her true place in time and space. Then she rose to her feet and gripped the edge of the counter for support. Her hands were shaking when she splashed more water on her face. If she could not stay awake, Stella Small would die.

"It'll never work." Riker turned his back on Mallory's computers. "There's gotta be ten million people in Wisconsin."

"Closer to four and a half." Charles could quote the atlas statistic to the last individual, but that would be showboating. "And we're only looking at one small county where the boy went into foster care."

Riker shook his head. "We're running out of *time*. Stella Small could be hanging by her neck right now—still alive."

Mallory looked up from her monitor. "What do you want me to do, Riker? Go door to door with those worthless cartoons?" She nodded toward the cork wall where he had pinned up the hooker sketches.

Indeed, Charles thought the images were more of a guide to what the man did *not* look like. He was not thin or fat, not African or Asian descent, and his hair was neither long nor short.

Mallory turned back to her computer monitor. She was also showing signs of strain. "I'm checking every newspaper with a database. If anything jumps out—"

"It'll take forever," said Riker.

"And thank you for your support," said Mallory.

Charles watched the screen over her shoulder, scanning text as fast as she could scroll down the columns of newspaper archives, and, in another compartment of his brain, he addressed Riker's concerns. "You have two possibilities. Some recent event triggered these hangings, or the scarecrow started acting out antisocial behavior with early juvenile offenses."

"Then we're still screwed," said Riker. "The criminal records of juveniles are sealed."

"But not newspaper archives. The county is mostly small towns. Any sort of standout behavior would be worth a mention in a local newspaper." Charles could see that Riker was unconvinced. The man was looking at his watch, a reminder that Stella Small was running out of time, and now he left the room. A moment later, the door to the reception area slammed shut.

Mallory handed a cell phone to Charles. "I've got a Wisconsin detective on the line. She works in Juvenile. Can you give her a profile for the scarecrow?"

The small phone all but disappeared into Charles's larger hand as he described a tortured child to the caller, explaining that the boy had lost everything, his parents, his home. He was sent away to live with strangers, and they were also taken from him. Then police custody, foster care, more changes and strangers to deal with. "Too many traumas in quick succession. I'd look for a history of petty criminal acts and small-scale violence. Sociopathic behavior could've started as early as nine or ten years old. Or even—"

Charles watched Mallory's eyes close. Her fingers ceased to tap; her hands were suspended over the keyboard. And he wished he was dead. He had just created a general profile for her as well.

He quickly added one qualification never mentioned in Kathy Mallory's own childhood history and said to the caller, "You might find incidents of torturing and killing small animals."

Stella Small listened to the public-address system. A small fire had broken out on an upper floor, and all customers were urged to make an orderly evacuation of the store.

What fabulous timing. The new suit was paid for, and she was wearing it. However, she had not yet replaced her snagged pantyhose with the new ones, and a saleswoman was barring her way to the changing room. Stella shrugged. There was time enough to go home and change hosiery before the evening audition in Tribeca. She joined a stream of shoppers moving toward the escalator with great resolve despite the protests of store employees who tried in vain to turn the herd toward the fire doors and a stairwell.

There was one motionless standout among the onward marching shoppers and the arm-waving clerks. A man was waiting near the bottom of the escalator. Though he wore dark glasses, Stella recognized him from her last shopping expedition. This was the soap-opera fan who had stood behind her in the mirror of the discount store. Yes, it was the same baseball cap and stiff posture. She was sure of it now. He was the vandal, the stalker, the giver of gift certificates. And the gray bag—she had seen that before too, but where? She stared at him, wondering, *How crazy are you?*

He climbed up the steps of the down escalator, unhampered by all the people who blocked his way. He passed through the press of bodies, crushing them into the sides of the escalator as he closed the distance to Stella while the mechanical steps sought to take them both down. He came abreast of her and slapped a note on the lapel of her new suit jacket. The man never looked into her eyes. He might as well have taped his message to a kiosk instead of a living woman. She ripped the note off her jacket and read the words, *I can touch you any time I want.*

Charles sprawled on the leather couch, one of few office furnishings that was not an antique but was custom-made to fit his longer than average legs. He was nearly done with the last batch of fax transmissions. Occasionally, he interrupted his reading to glance at the portable television set. Mallory had given it to him so he could keep track of local news bulletins. And now he was startled to see a familiar face on the screen. "Mallory!" he yelled, to be heard in her office across the hall. "Riker's on TV!"

No response. Well, she was busy.

Charles turned back to the screen to watch Detective Sergeant Riker being introduced to the viewers. Poor man. He looked so pale beside the healthy orange glow of the anchorman's stage makeup. He held up a photograph of a fugitive witness, Natalie Homer's sister.

Stella fought against the tide of the crowd spilling off the escalator. She saw another exit sign and ran toward it, only glancing back once to see the baseball cap bobbing above the heads of the shoppers. Everyone was being turned away from the bank of elevators. Store employees barred the doors, shouting that the elevators had been disabled. Others directed people to the fire doors where a line of people filed through to a stairwell.

First Stella caught a whiff of insecticide, and then a hand grazed her face. She turned to see the stalking man walking away from her, moving toward the line for the stairwell. He turned around to look in Stella's general direction, never making eye contact, perhaps perceiving her as a store manikin. Was he waiting for her to join him in the line?

You think I'm crazy, too?

She turned around full circle, searching every wall for another red-lettered sign to show her a way out. The escalator was barred by three women with folded arms. Drunk with power, they turned shoppers back to the stairwell, shouting, "That's the fire exit!" And they were so unimpressed with Stella's note from a madman. "Lady, look around. You see any cops? No." And once again, she was directed to the stairwell, the only *approved* exit, where her personal stalker stepped out of line to wait for her by the fire door. This was so unfair. She had obeyed all the rules regarding New York wildlife. She had never tried to pet the lunatics grazing on the city sidewalks, never fed them or looked them in the eye.

Now Stella saw another sign and ran toward it. After closing the restroom door behind her, she depressed the lock button on the brass knob, for it was unlikely that a lunatic would be put off by the "Ladies Only" sign of sanctuary. All the stall doors were open, and there were no sounds but her own footsteps as she walked toward the line of sinks to lay her packages down on the long marble countertop. Stella never considered the possibility of burning alive in a blazing building. She had lived in this town too long to take any fire drill as seriously as the more immediate threat of a deranged stalker—or shopping—and she planned to wait it out until the store refilled with customers and clerks, a simple matter of killing time.

After stripping off her ruined pantyhose, she fumbled with the cellophane wrapper of the new pair. A clock on the wall gave her hours to make the late audition. She stared at the mirror, in love with the new suit. Her lipstick had been bitten off, but there was time for a complete overhaul of makeup, and she rifled her purse for cosmetics. Oh, wait. She should use the toilet before the fire drill ended. Stella gathered up her purse and packages from force of habit. No New Yorker would leave a possession unguarded.

She was sitting on the toilet when she heard the door open. Heavy steps, a man. He would have to be a store employee. Who else would have a key to the lock? The door closed again, and she sat very still, holding her breath and holding her water. After what seemed like forever, Stella knelt down on the floor and looked toward the stalls left and right.

No one there. And yet, after leaving the stall, she could not lose the feeling of being watched. And what was that sound? A fly? More than one?

"This woman is wanted by the police." The newscaster held up the photograph of Susan Qualen. Though the woman was in her forties, Charles thought the family likeness was striking. The picture of Natalie's sister was joined by a portrait of Stella Small.

"If you've seen either of these women today," said the voice behind the photographs, "call the number on your screen. And now a few words from Detective Sergeant Riker."

Riker leaned into the microphone. "Miss Qualen has information on the whereabouts of the missing actress. We have to find Stella tonight. She's in a lot of trouble, and she needs your help."

"As we speak," said the anchorman, "our broadcast is also being shown on our sister station in Wisconsin." He turned to his guest. "So you believe Susan Qualen is hiding in the vicinity of Racine?"

"Yeah, she could be en route right now," said Riker. "But I'm hoping she's still in the tristate area."

"If this woman has important information, why is she evading the police, Detective Riker?"

"Because she doesn't care if Stella Small lives or dies."

Very impressive, Riker.

No one could have put the case more eloquently.

He knew how to jack up the speed of the human heart from a startled flutter to *BAM, BAM, BAM!* And how to slow it down. Or paralyze it.

Though he neither liked his work nor disliked it.

Almost ready.

The man sat on the toilet seat, tailor fashion, so his feet would not show in the openings between the stall doors and the floor. He slowly unzipped the gray canvas bag on his lap and reached for the camera, ignoring the large glass jar beside it, for he had no interest in terror on a small scale.

The jar contained a black soup of flies. Some of the insects were still alive and moving slowly, drunk on insecticide. They animated the bodies of the dead, all in a panic, crushing and crawling over dry corpses, breaking wings and ripping off legs in a frightening struggle to reach the top of the jar, one inch of air—and life.

And then they struggled in the dark, for the man had closed the gym bag. With equal indifference, he aimed the camera lens at the opening between the stall door and its frame. He watched the blond actress through his viewfinder. The young woman stood by the sink, too wired to put her lipstick on straight. She picked up a tissue and made short nervous dabs at her mouth. Turning her head to one side, she sniffed the air now scented with the insect spray that clung to his clothing. She batted at an imagined fly, created by the power of suggestion and the low buzz from the jar in his bag.

The ready light on the camera had been amber and now it was green. As if the woman had heard the change of colors, she dropped her lipstick, then jumped at the sound of the metal tube hitting the tiles and rolling across the floor.

She gathered up her shoes, her purse and packages, then left the ladies' room, running barefoot.

Charles rose from the couch and stretched, then walked across the hall to the back office. Deluthe was nowhere in sight, and Mallory was facing a computer monitor, her hands resting on the keyboard and lightly tapping the keys.

"Mallory?" Charles bent down to retrieve another stack of paper from a printer bin. He had already scanned a thousand sheets of newspaper archives to no avail. "I haven't found anything yet." During the scarecrow's boyhood years, the children of Green County, Wisconsin, had been remarkably well behaved. "Perhaps this is a waste of time."

She only tapped the keys, giving no sign that she was even aware of him. He approached her with some caution, not wanting to break her concentration. If she ignored him to some purpose—

Oh, God, what's this?

Her eyes were closed in sleep, yet her fingers continued to type. Her repetitive movements produced only gibberish on the computer monitor, yet Charles could not rid himself of the illusion that the machines were now operating Mallory. He lifted her into his arms and held her tightly, regarding her sleeping face with enormous concern. He carried her back to his own office, where the machines could not get at her, and there he laid her down on the soft leather couch. Covering her hands with his own, he forced her fingers to stop typing across the air.

The store was empty and eerie. The customers and clerks should have returned by now, for there was no sign of a fire, no sirens and not a trace of smoke. Stella walked the vacant aisles alone—and not. Every manikin drew her startled eye. And now she was one of them, neither moving nor breathing. She could only stare at the gray canvas bag on the floor in front of the escalator.

Where was he now? Was he watching her? Her eyes searched the vast space with a thousand hiding places. She ran toward the bank of elevators and found a crude out-of-service sign posted above the dark call buttons. She tried the nearby stairwell door, but the knob would not turn. Another sign, this one merely an arrow, directed her away from the stairs and toward a freight elevator. It stood open, waiting for her. She stepped inside and pushed the button for the ground floor.

Stella was slipping her new shoes over naked feet when she looked up to see the man holding the doors to prevent them from closing. He appeared not to see her as he stepped inside and set his gray canvas bag on the floor. She could get around him if she acted right now—if she was fast. She willed her legs to carry her away.

The moment was missed, the elevator closed.

Stella watched the lighted numbers overhead. They were going down. The canvas bag on the floor was open, and she was staring at the razor tip of a box cutter. They descended in silence—except for the buzzing sound from his bag, low and ugly, insectile. The shrill high noise of her screaming was purely imagined.

When Mallory opened her eyes, her head was pillowed in Charles Butler's lap. What time was it? She had no idea. Her internal clock had failed her.

Unaware that she was awake, Charles absently stroked her hair, and she listened to the soft shuffle of paper, then watched the white pages sail by on their way to the pile on the rug below. She should rise now—time was precious.

The hand lightly moving over her hair was intoxicating. The human touch was rare since she had lost the Markowitzes, first Helen, then Louis. During the years that followed his wife's death, the old man had made a point of kissing his foster child twice at each encounter—a sorry effort to make up for her loss of a mother, and he had rarely missed an opportunity to capture her in a bear hug—hugging for two. And then he died.

She was always losing people.

Mallory closed her eyes and listened to footsteps in the hall. Now Riker's voice called out, "It's me. How's it going?"

"One possibility," said Charles, "though not what I had in mind. Here, take a look at this article."

"Foster Care Fraud," said Riker. "Catchy headline."

"That foster child ran away when he was twelve years old, but the police were never notified."

"And these people kept collecting his support checks?"

"Right," said Charles. "The boy was put in their care the same year Natalie's son was taken from the Qualens."

Another hand, Riker's, rested on Mallory's shoulder a moment, then gently brushed the hair from her face. "I've never seen her sleep," he said. "I always figured she just hung from the ceiling like a little bat. Damn, I hate to wake the kid up."

"Then don't," said Charles.

"But I got her a present—Susan Qualen. The woman turned herself in. Janos is walking her over here now—in handcuffs."

"Why here?" asked Charles.

"More privacy."

Stella pressed her back to the wall of the elevator and watched the man open a metal panel with one of a gang of keys hanging from his belt loop. A janitor? "So you work here?"

No answer. He was not aware of her on any level, and this was hopeful. It could all be one ghastly coincidence. This man worked here; he *belonged* here. Of course, he would give her a gift certificate from this store. He probably got an employee discount. And now he was merely rounding up a stray shopper and escorting her to safety. Stella acted the part of a woman who could believe all of this, but she could not sustain the role for long.

When he closed the metal panel, the light for the ground floor was no longer glowing. They were on their way to the basement level. Her heart beat faster, and adrenaline gorged every muscle for flight. When the doors opened, her legs ran away with her, flinging Stella headlong down a wide aisle of cardboard cartons. There were no hurried footsteps behind her. He had no worries that she would get away. Why should he? It would be so easy to follow her by the clack of high heels.

Idiot.

She slipped off her shoes and ran in barefoot silence down a corridor of boxes, running from the light, swallowed by the dark.

All the television stations ran hourly updates on the plight of Stella Small, showing photographs of her early years and reading excerpts from letters to her mother and grandmother, known to locals as the Abandoned Stellas. The written words of the youngest Stella were upbeat and hopeful, full of the dream: She was going to be somebody, and fame could only be minutes or hours away.

"What was that?" Riker turned off the volume, and now he could more clearly hear a knock on the door in the reception area. "That's gotta be her."

He answered the door and greeted Detective Janos with a smile. Natalie Homer's sister needed no introduction. His face was grim when he turned to the woman in handcuffs, only inclining his head a bare inch to say, "Miss Qualen."

Stella shrank into a small space behind a carton, playing the mouse, shaking and listening to the footsteps coming closer, stopping now. A nearby box was being moved. Eyes shut tight, her thoughts went out to the Abandoned Stellas. How sorry she was to let them down, yet she knew they would cope well with her dying, for that was their strength of purpose. They were younger than she was now when they had committed themselves to their own slow deaths at the roadside diner.

But wait. This was New York City—different rules: No cowards allowed.

An inspired Stella sat in the dark and prepared herself for something finer than slaughter by box cutter. Adjusting her chin to a determined angle, she created the role of a lifetime, imagining her own heart engorging and growing into the part, pounding harder, louder—*stronger*.

Can you hear it, you son of a bitch?

The box was moved aside. A hand reached out for her, and the greatest thing that ever came out of Ohio jumped to her feet. She raked his chest with five long fingernails that left red streaks on his T-shirt. He stopped, as if his batteries had suddenly run down, stunned that an *object* would fight back. And then she clawed his face.

Stella had drawn first blood, and now she ran for the light at the end of the box corridor, screaming, "I'm gonna *live*, you *bastard!*"

Janos leaned against the door to the back office, making it clear to the prisoner that she was not going anywhere. Mallory and Riker closed in on Susan Qualen. The woman backed into a computer station and slipped. Her handcuffs bound her wrists behind her, and she could not break the fall. She awkwardly managed a squat, then rose to a stand and revolved slowly, looking from face to face. "Why am I under arrest?" She jangled the chain of her manacles. "I haven't done *anything*."

"You got that part right," said Riker. "You wouldn't help us. You ran away."

The words were spoken in a monotone, but the woman behaved as if he had screamed at her. She bowed her head and stared at the floor. As a reward for this attitude of contrition, Janos removed the handcuffs, then stepped back.

Mallory kicked a chair toward the suspect. It fell over, and Riker commanded, "Pick it up!"

Susan Qualen did as she was told.

"Sit down!" said Janos.

"That day you came around—" Qualen's voice faltered and cracked. "I couldn't help you. I didn't—"

"You have to sign this." Riker held a small card that listed her rights under the constitution. "We'll get you a lawyer if you want one. Do you understand your rights?"

"I don't need a damn lawyer. I didn't do—"

"Then *sign* it!" Riker was not playacting. He was angry when he grabbed a clipboard from the desk, then attached the card and a pen. She accepted the board, fingers slowly closing around its edges, and quickly signed her name. Mallory tore the clipboard from the woman's hands and threw it across the room. Qualen jumped as it skittered across the floor for the last few feet before hitting the wall.

"And now," said Riker, "tell us that twisted freak didn't look up his Aunt Susan the minute he got to town."

"It's *your* fault!" Qualen faced each of them in turn. "You *lie* to people. You don't—"

"All those details in the papers," said Mallory. "You *knew* there was a link between the last hanging and—"

"And my sister? The police only told me Natalie was murdered. I read about her hanging in the newspapers—the fake suicide, a damn cover-up!" Susan Qualen's voice was in the high wavering pitch of hysteria. "Nobody wanted to solve Natalie's murder."

"Your nephew gave you all the details," said Mallory. "*That's* how you knew. When you saw the story in the papers, it was Natalie's murder all over again."

"*Stop it!* Junior didn't tell me *anything!*" She was in tears. "That little boy could barely speak. He was almost catatonic."

"So you sent him away. You conspired to hide the only witness who could've helped the police find your sister's killer."

"Oh, that's rich." Susan Qualen was not frightened anymore. She was angry. "Who do you call when a damn *cop* kills your sister—the *cops?*" She wore a grim smile and took some satisfaction in their stunned faces.

Running toward the light at the end of the corridor, Stella turned a corner of boxes and saw a small office walled in glass. The door was ajar, and she pushed it wide open. At the point of slamming it behind her, she regained her sanity, then closed the door quietly and turned a knob to lock it. The desk offered the only cover in a room made of glass, and she crouched behind it, taking the telephone with her. She dialed 911, but the call would not go through. And now she listened to an automated recording that instructed her to dial another digit for an outside line.

He was coming.

She could hear him walking at a mechanical clip. Stella held her breath as the man tried the knob, and then she heard metal on metal—a key in the lock.

Oh, you stupid fool. He's a damn janitor. He has all the keys.

Stella closed her eyes and covered her ears, blocking it out, wishing it away, this thing at the door. The lock came undone. The door opened, and that insect smell was in the room with her. She opened her eyes. Very slowly, deep in shock, she lifted her face. He was standing beside the desk, looking down at her, yet not really seeing her. And he said nothing; one did not converse with objects. She saw the sign behind him, the shield of the alarm company pasted to the glass wall encircled by metallic tape. If she could break the glass, that would trigger the burglar alarm and bring a watchman.

Susan Qualen was all but spitting the next words at them. "If I'd given him up, how long would that little boy have stayed alive? The only witness to a cop killing his mother. I lived in that neighborhood for years. Drug dealers bought the police for a song. And you guys always cover for your own." She put up one hand, sensing Riker's intention to interrupt. "Don't start with me. I did the right thing, and you *know* it!"

"He ran away from the foster parents," said Mallory, "a pair of chiseling—"

"And he went back to my cousins. They took him to Nebraska. When he grew up, he had a lot of questions about his mother. They told him everything they knew. Then he came back."

"Back home," said Mallory. "To you."

"He only spent a few hours with me. That was a long time ago."

"You didn't want to see him again." Riker folded his arms. "He scared you, didn't he?"

"No! He wasn't some whacked psycho. He was as normal as I am."

Janos pulled out his notebook. "Where's your nephew now?"

"I don't know."

"What does he call himself these days?"

"Junior, I guess. That's what he always called himself."

"I want a straight answer." Janos moved closer. "Did you hear the question? What name is he—"

"I don't know!"

"Right," said Mallory. "You don't know anything helpful. I keep forgetting that. So why did you run?"

Susan Qualen sank into the chair, trembling, not with fear but excess emotions, none of them good ones. Hate predominated overall.

"Okay," said Riker. "Here's an easier question. Why did you come back?"

Stella had no clue to the source of sudden strength in her arms. She picked up the heavy wooden desk chair and sent it hurtling through the glass wall, fracturing it into a hundred pieces. The man turned to a panel of buttons beside the door and cut off the alarm while it was merely a squeak and before the glass shower had ended. One long shard lingered in the frame, then toppled and shattered across the office floor. The broken pieces crunched under his shoes as he walked toward her, one hand rising, reaching out.

"No," she said. "No!" she yelled.

And now she realized that she was invisible to him. He walked past her and took a card from a rack on the wall, then fed it into the slot below the

time clock. Because this was such a normal act for any employee beginning his shift, it unhinged Stella's mind. The night watchman was never
coming to her rescue. *He* was the watchman.

"I came back to beg you not to kill Natalie's son." Susan Qualen doubled over, as if they had kicked her. "Killing is what you do best, isn't it?"
She was nearly spent. Anger was all that sustained her. "You gun-happy
bastards kill people all the time. *You* made Junior what he is. A goddamn
cop killed his mother. So I figure you owe him a life. You can't just put
him down like a sick animal."

Riker could see that Janos was losing the heart for this. The man's voice
was too soft when he said, "Tell us where your nephew lives. If we have
some control over the capture—"

"I don't *know!*" She shook her head. "That's the truth. I told you—I
only saw him for a few hours. That was three years ago, and *he* asked all
the questions."

Mallory gripped the woman's arm. "What did your relatives tell you?
What was he doing for a living when he—"

"He was a *cop!*" Susan Qualen's face was wet with tears. "Can you believe it?" Her words came out in a stutter of sobs. "A cop . . . like you . . .
so don't . . . don't kill him."

Stella backed up to the wall, cutting her bare feet on broken glass and
never feeling the pain. Her mouth was dry, and her eyes were on the box
cutter in his hand. Involuntary responses came first, cold chemicals flooding her veins. Her palms were clammy, and her heart banged in a full-
blown panic attack. There was nowhere to go but into the corner. She
pressed up against the plaster, eyes wide, staring at the razor. Her sweaty
hands spread out on the corner walls, and she climbed them, finding traction with the sticky flesh of palms and soles. Her feet were inches off the
floor, toes curling over the baseboard—a human fly.

"Please don't." She was stripped down to the naked personality of the
little girl from Ohio. "Please," she said. "Please," she whispered.

Jack Coffey looked up to see two visitors in his office. New Yorkers had come to know these women as the Abandoned Stellas of Ohio. They stood before his desk in sturdy serviceable shoes and their best dresses. They had brought him their frightened eyes and wavering smiles, brave then not, and all the baggage of hope. First, they destroyed him, they broke his heart, and then they said hello and "Did you find our Stella?"

Another bag of delicatessen food sat on the floor at Ronald Deluthe's feet. He was operating a laptop computer and scanning all the transcriptions of tip-line calls. The sightings of Stella Small spanned four states. Charles Butler sat beside him on the leather couch, rolling one hand to tell the younger man to scroll faster. "Stop. Highlight that one too."

Mallory stood over them, saying, "What? Let me see."

"Here," said Charles. "Multiple sightings in department stores. Look at this last one. Stella was shopping rather late this evening."

Deluthe shook his head. "This can't be right. The discount store I can see, but where would she get the money to shop on Fifth Avenue?"

"Hmm. Bergdorf's had a moonlight sale," said Mallory. "So did Lord and Taylor." She leaned over to look at another highlighted entry. "That designer outlet store checks out. That's where she bought a suit this morning, and the bastard ruined it."

"Well, she's not gonna find another one on Fifth Avenue," said Deluthe with absolute conviction. "You saw that place she lived in, all those unpaid bills. So the late sightings are bogus."

Mallory glared at him briefly, a small threat to tell him that he must defer to her in all matters of police work and shopping. "Stella has good taste."

Charles stared at the glowing screen. "This place was on the news tonight. There was a small fire on the top floor. The whole store was evacuated. Perhaps a—" He looked up to see the back of Mallory leaving the room. "Well, I guess it was worth checking out."

"Waste of time," said Deluthe. "The scarecrow always hangs them in their own apartments."

"*Twice* isn't quite the same as always." Charles picked up the deli bag and searched among the sandwiches for his own dinner. "Oh, and he's got the hang of setting fires now."

Suddenly, Deluthe was also leaving him, feet slapping the wood in the hallway, making a dead run for the front door.

It had never occurred to Mrs. Harmon Heath-Ellis that cabs might be scarce in the hours after all the bars had closed. She crossed the small park and passed the fountain, hoping to improve her chances of hailing a car on Fifth Avenue.

A group of six people had gathered in front of her favorite department store. Suppose someone recognized her? Her social stature was too secure to worry about being caught in town during the loser's month of August. However, she did fear being discovered near her brother-in-law's hotel.

The socialite waved frantically, though the only cab, indeed, the only vehicle on the avenue, was stopped at a traffic light a block away. She glanced back at the people in front of the store, *her* store. They were wearing what must pass for evening clothes in that third-world country, Middle America. The rubes were fixated on one window. Curiosity prevailed, and she walked toward the shabby little gathering. What was the harm? None of their social orbits could possibly intersect with hers.

The wealthy society matron looked over their shoulders and between their heads to see the lighted display. After all she had spent on haute couture, who was better qualified to critique the window dresser's art?

Well, this was different. And it was inevitable, she supposed. This must be the next big thing, the new wave beyond heroin chic—*dead*.

"That's no manikin," said the man directly in front of her.

Of course not. As any fool could see, this was a living woman playing the role of a department store dummy. It was an old idea with a new twist—literally. The model was slowly revolving at the end of a rope, allowing the public to view all sides of the blue suit and matching shoes.

"She *is* rather good," said Mrs. Harmon Heath-Ellis. "This one doesn't blink." Well, certainly the girl must blink, but not until the rope twisted her face away from the window. The model was quite pretty in a low-rent way. Her hair had not been styled by any reputable salon. The short spikes standing out on the scalp were so passé. Longer strands of blond hair trailed from the model's open mouth, and what sort of statement was that?

The window had been arranged with small kitchen appliances and utensils to create an interesting contrast with high fashion. Though somewhat nearsighted, the socialite recognized the designer by the cut of the light blue suit—quite respectable. Ah, but the rest—such tedious violence, no blood, no real drama.

An enormous woman in a muumuu—obviously an out-of-towner and an obvious Kmart shopper—was whimpering, saying, "Oh, God, she's dead!" A man joined in this opinion. "Hey, somebody call a cop!"

Mrs. Harmon Heath-Ellis smiled benignly in the spirit of giving first aid to the ignorant and unwashed, the *tourists*. But now a man pointed to the glass, his mouth working in astonished dumb show. The socialite stepped closer to the display window to see what she might have missed.

Her superior smile was frozen, and she was deaf to the oncoming screams of police sirens. Beneath the hanged model was a jar of dead flies encircled by flaming red candles. The woman looked up, and now she could not look away. What she had mistaken for a mole, a beauty mark, was a black fly crawling across the model's face and moving toward one wide blue eye.

The socialite was trembling, interior screams outshouting the sirens. She jumped at the screech of brakes and spinning red lights. Police cars disgorged men in uniforms and men in suits. There was one woman among them, but this tall blonde was hardly a civil servant. She wore a linen blazer of all too marvelous cut and line, a thing to die for. And now this young paragon of fashion pulled an enormous revolver from a shoulder holster and beat on the plate glass with the butt end of the gun.

Of course, the glass was holding up well. It was made to withstand such vandalism, and Mrs. Heath-Ellis was about to tell her as much, for she was privy to every detail of her favorite—

"Hey, Mallory!" Near the far corner of the block-long store, a policeman called out, "This door's open!"

Either young Mallory did not hear this man, or she did not care, so enraged was she, quite mad actually, beating, hammering the glass, electric green eyes full of rage. With one last mighty swing of the gun, the glass wall shattered, and the young blonde was climbing past the shards, tearing her fabulous threads to get at the twisting figure on the end of the rope.

The policewoman was slender, and yet she was able to lift the dead weight as if it were nothing. She cradled the other woman's limp body like a babe in arms, then lifted it high until the rope slackened. She was fiercely concentrated on the model's still white face. And every watcher knew she was willing the hanged woman to live.

There was a hinged panel at the rear of the display window, but rather than simply open this door, the entire back wall was ripped from its moorings by a large man. Oh, and that face—brutality incarnate.

"Good job, Janos," said another man, a less imposing figure with a bad suit, who climbed up to the raised floor, then quickly untied the thick knot of the noose. The rope fell away, and Mallory laid her burden down. The largest policeman, the brutal one called Janos, leaned over the prone body to remove the gag of human hair. With surprising delicacy, he pinched the model's nostrils closed and covered her mouth with his own. The young woman's body shuddered back to life in convulsions. Her hands rolled into fists that punched the air, batting at some phantom from an interrupted nightmare, and her mouth opened wide in a shrill scream. The large policeman gently gathered her into his arms and rocked her slowly. His voice was incongruously soft as he said, "Hush now, Stella, it's all over."

The small crowd of watchers went *wild*, screaming, cheering, whistling. The socialite was surprised by her own helpless laughter as she was engulfed in a hug from the heavyset woman in the muumuu. Her head fell upon this stranger's generous breast, and she began to cry.

NiNeTeeN

MALLORY LOOKED LESS LIKE A CRIME VICTIM AFTER removing the blazer torn by broken glass. The garment was neatly folded over one arm to hide her bandaged wound. And now her holstered revolver was on public display in a window on Fifth Avenue. She stood in full view of a sidewalk audience and watched the watchers. One of them picked up a small piece of glass from the litter on the pavement, and he slipped it into his pocket. Perhaps he prized this one above the other souvenir shards because of the small red stain. He was stealing a drop of her blood.

She turned to Ronald Deluthe. "Take another look. You're sure he's not out there?"

The rookie detective shook his head. "I don't see him."

She pointed to three uniformed officers standing off to one side. "What about them?"

This startled him. "You think the scarecrow is a cop?"

"When I say look at everyone, that means cops too."

"No, he's not there." And now, sensing that she had no further use for him, Deluthe climbed out of the display window, giving the forensic expert more room to work.

Heller pulled down the rope that dangled from an exposed pipe in the chopped-away ceiling. "Crude job for such a tidy killer."

"And he's taking more chances," said Mallory. "Heller, you said this woman fought back?"

"Better than that. Dr. Slope found blood and skin under her fingernails."

Good for you, Stella Small.

"What about store security?"

"They got everything," said Heller. "Cameras, alarms, even guard dogs. But none of it was working, and the animals were locked in a utility closet."

Mallory lowered her sunglasses. "This store doesn't have a night watchman?"

"Yeah, they got one." Riker climbed up on the raised floor of the display window. "The watchman's a retired cop, sixty-four years old. Maybe he slept through the whole thing."

Mallory turned back to the crowd of ghouls on the sidewalk. "And maybe the old man's dead."

"Well, that theory's *my* personal favorite." Riker knelt down beside Heller. "His basement office was wrecked. Broken glass everywhere, and there's blood on the floor. I didn't see any broken skin on Stella, so it might be the watchman's blood."

Without a word or even a nod to Riker, Heller closed his tool kit and climbed down from the display window. For the past hour, these two men had not traded one insult, and she wondered about this sudden rift in an old routine.

"Stella marked the perp with her fingernails," said Mallory.

"That's my girl." Riker stared at the bits of hair on the floor. "Not a very neat scalping this time, and you should see that basement office. The perp's not so fussy about cleaning up his messes anymore."

Mallory nodded. The scarecrow was coming undone.

A crime-scene tape cordoned off ten feet of space in front of the basement office. John Winetrob, the personnel director, was not permitted any closer to the broken glass wall. This aftermath of violence was beyond his comprehension. He froze when a policeman passed by carrying a bloody shard in a plastic bag.

Detective Arthur Wang gestured toward a cardboard carton the height of a chair. "Sir? Why don't you sit down?"

Before you fall down.

The man's shakes were easy for Wang to account for, but not only because of the crime-scene blood. The police were also making him nervous. The unshaven personnel director wore a suit but no tie, and his socks were mismatched. Dressing would have been difficult at this early hour while a uniformed police officer, six feet tall and armed with a gun, had waited at his front door.

For the past ten minutes, Mr. Winetrob had been talking nonstop, mostly inane chatter. Now he fell silent as the detective completed a cellphone call.

"No answer." Arthur Wang dropped the phone back into his pocket. "The watchman isn't home, but I didn't think he would be. And he hasn't turned up in any local hospitals."

"Thank you for trying," said Winetrob. "You don't really believe he could be dead, do you?"

Yes, that was exactly what Detective Wang believed. "We're still looking for him, sir. We've got twenty men doing a sweep, floor by floor. If he's here—if he's hurt—"

"What if he didn't come to work last night? Now there's a thought." The personnel director glanced at the broken glass wall of the night watchman's office, then looked away. "Maybe it's not his blood in there. You know, an old man like that, he could be at home right now, lying in his own bed, maybe—Oh, God. He could be having a heart attack. Can you send somebody over to his apartment? We must cover all the bases." He raked one hand through his sparse hair. "Yes—all the bases."

"Of course," said Wang. "I'll send a cop to check it out—real soon." Or maybe never. This errand would hit the bottom of police priorities this morning. The more important business was a look at the store's files. All the employees had been photographed, and this was the only helpful information Winetrob had given him so far—or so he believed.

Gently, Detective Wang helped the civilian to his feet and led him to an elevator that would carry them up to the personnel office. Later, Arthur Wang would wish that he had prioritized in a different fashion and paid closer attention to Winetrob's wacky ramblings, his hopes and fears.

When Deluthe had finished Janos's chore in the payroll department, he had been loaned out to Arthur Wang. Now he was posted at a secretary's desk outside the office of the personnel director. He had made short work of the first fifty photographs in the stack of employee files, and the man from Kennedy Harper's crime scene was not among them. More busywork. He glanced toward the open door. The senior detective was inside, drinking coffee and making notes on his conversation with Mr. Winetrob. Wang noticed him and called out, "Find anything?"

"Nothing yet, sir." Deluthe closed another folder.

Arthur Wang walked to the door and tossed a file on the secretary's desk. "That one goes in your stack. Put it back in alphabetical order, okay? When you're done, report to Riker."

Deluthe opened the file of the night watchman and stared at the photograph. His eyes drifted down to the name, that vital clue to the man's place in the file cabinet. The line below it was a familiar East Village address. And now, with utter disregard for the alphabet, the young detective jammed the folder into the center of the large stack and left his job unfinished.

He had more important things to do.

In the back office of Butler and Company, Mallory was on the phone, terrorizing a clerk at the Odeon, Nebraska, Police Department. "So what if your computer is down? What does that . . . Look, all I need is a photograph. . . . Yeah, *right*. . . . I told you that an hour ago. . . . So pull it out of the hardcopy . . . Then *fax* it! *Now!*"

Fortunately, there had been no computer problems at the Nebraska Department of Motor Vehicles. Charles was looking at a monitor and their only likeness of the scarecrow. The image was not very good, but most license photographs were less than professional quality.

After relocating in Nebraska, Susan Qualen's cousins had changed their family name, and the boy they had harbored was called John Ryan. No doubt the cousins had called the boy by his initials, J.R. for Junior, the only name he was accustomed to.

Mallory sat down at the workstation. "It'll probably take them an hour to figure out how a file drawer works."

"Bad luck," said Charles. "How do you suppose ordinary people like the Qualens became so adept at changing identities?"

"Nothing to it. Idiots get away with it all the time." She stared at her monitor screen. "The scarecrow must've picked up another alias when he came east. He's not in any local databases. You know what that means?"

"He's been planning this killing spree for three years?"

"No, I think he only planned *one* murder."

"The man who killed his mother?"

Mallory nodded. "In Nebraska, Junior was a small-town cop in uniform. Probably never got near a major investigation. So he comes to the big city. Figures he can find his mother's killer in a day—and without any help from us."

Charles agreed. And when the boy failed, his last resort was forcing NYPD to do the job for him.

"The scarecrow hates police," she said. "He's very clear about that. So tell me, why would he become a cop?"

"Perhaps he had control issues." Charles suspected that this was why Mallory had joined NYPD, but he could not complete this twinning image of her and the scarecrow. "It's an interesting choice, isn't it? His emotional problems must have been very tightly contained while he was a police officer. The deterioration probably started after he moved to New York."

He looked up to see Lars Geldorf standing just inside the door. Some tenant must have buzzed him into the building. Charles was unprepared for the change in him. The old man had aged another decade in a day.

Ignoring the unwelcome visitor, Mallory looked down at her keyboard. The retired detective walked a few steps into the room, then seemed at the point of falling down. Charles picked up a chair and rushed toward him, but the man waved him away and remained standing.

Lars Geldorf's eyes were fixed on Mallory. "I heard about that poor woman—Stella Small. You think the copycat hangings are my fault, don't you? If I'd done my job right twenty years ago—" His shoulders sagged, and he braced himself with one hand pressed flat on the cork wall, then turned his defeated eyes to Charles. "I think I *will* take that chair." He sat down and waited out Mallory's silence. It was clear that the old man would not leave without a word from her.

She continued her typing, occasionally looking his way, annoyed that he was still there. Her eyes trained on the keyboard, she said, "I can't discuss details of an active case. You *know* that."

"Yes," said Geldorf. "I know."

She could have killed the old man with only a few words, but she kept silent, and Charles saw this as the potential for kindness. Growing up in Special Crimes, she would have seen many of these old men coming and going, haunting police stations as confused ghosts, unable to come to terms with the end of things.

Mallory was done with Geldorf now, and he could make no mistake about that. The conversation was over, and yet he continued his vigil. After a time, his presence began to wear on her. She pushed her chair back from the workstation and swiveled round to face him. "So you want me to tell you what you got wrong? Is that it?"

Yes, that was what he had come for. He had to know.

She strolled to the cork wall and what remained of the old murder case, then ripped down a sheet of paper. "This is your report on the hanging rope and the duct tape. It's real short. 'Common items. Untraceable.' Wrong. The rope belonged to the building handyman. I got that information from the landlady's granddaughter."

"The handyman was out of town when—"

"On a family emergency. I *know*. That's why he left his tool box in the hall. The landlady promised to take care of it for him. But before she could drag it back to her apartment, the killer found it and stole the rope and the tape. If you'd talked to the handyman, you might've gotten a print from the tool box."

Geldorf had no comeback for this, but he would not look away from her.

She ripped two more sheets of paper from the wall. "And then there's the locked door. *Locked* when the landlady called the police. *Open* when the first cop showed up on the scene."

"I *caught* that," said Geldorf. The light was back in his eyes, and he rose to a stand as he defended himself. "That door was never locked. It was *stuck*. The landlady was old, pushing eighty. Tiny woman, no muscle. It was a hot night in August—and muggy. Wood swells in the damp and the heat. The door was stuck, not locked. And she admitted that when I—"

"Admitted what? That she was old? That you confused her? She never recanted her statement, and you didn't make any notes on that conversation. And what about Natalie's son? You never talked to him."

"What the hell for? What good would it do to torture a little boy? He'd just lost his mother. When you've been on the job a little longer—"

"Natalie came to you for help, and you just strung her along, you and your buddies. After she died, you built your case around the easiest target, an innocent man."

"I was *right* about the ex-husband!"

"No, you botched that too." She paused a moment, waiting for him to challenge her, but he said nothing. "And twenty years later, here we are, cleaning up the mess."

Geldorf shrank down to his chair. His gaze lowered to the floor at her feet. She had won. He was finished.

Mallory hunkered down beside his chair and looked up at his face. If she had been a cat, Charles might have seen this pose as a prelude to a lunge, but he hoped for something better from her. For a moment, he believed that she planned to soften her words with some comfort for a vulnerable old man.

How foolish was that?

"Listen to me." She gripped Geldorf's arm to shake him from his stupor of pity. He stared at her red nails, startled, as if she had just extended claws.

Mallory's half smile said, *I'm done playing with you.* "Here's the best part, old man. This killer might be a *cop*. So go home and lock yourself in. If the police come knocking, don't open that door. It might be one of your mistakes coming back on you. Scary, huh?"

Arthur Wang finished telling the Forensic expert about his conversation with Winetrob. He had intended it as a humorous story to break the tension in the night watchman's basement office.

"Sorry Arty. Winetrob was right." Heller pointed to the red smears on the cement floor. "That's not the watchman's blood. I called the hospital to check for broken skin on the victim. When they removed Stella's shoes, they found cuts on her soles and glass fragments in the wounds. I got a partial footprint off one of the shards—real small, a woman's print. This is *her* blood."

One of Heller's technicians nodded, saying, "And Winetrob was right about the watchman not showing up for work tonight. The security camera has a record of everybody who uses the employee entrance. He's not on the film."

"But the watchman isn't on vacation," said Wang. "I checked."

"Then maybe Winetrob's right about the heart attack, too."

Detective Wang produced a long piece of stiff paper sealed in an evidence bag. "So who's been using the old man's employee card? Somebody punched in on the time clock last night."

Heller turned to his assistant. "Maybe the watchman's still here. Call out the cadaver dogs. We'll do another sweep of the store."

Mallory ended her call with the Wisconsin detective, then turned to Charles. "The scarecrow *was* planning murder when he left Nebraska. There's nothing wrong with the police computers. The damn clerk didn't want to tell me she couldn't find the records. The file was deleted from the computer. The hardcopy is missing too—prints, photos, everything."

"Did the police talk to the relatives?"

Mallory nodded, then turned back to her computer monitor. "They had to wait for a warrant, then they tossed the cousins' house. The only New York address they found was Susan Qualen's. Her cousins haven't heard from Junior in three years. They had a falling out. They finally told him his mother's killer got away with murder. A bit late. When he came to New York, his Aunt Susan added her own poison." Mallory's fingers flew across the keys, entering new parameters to narrow her search. Her eyes were riveted to the screen. "Where are you hiding?"

"Maybe he doesn't live in New York," said Charles. "It's only a few minutes to New Jersey on the subway."

She shook her head. "He's living in the city. Deluthe saw him at Kennedy Harper's crime scene thirty minutes after we found the body. Either he works for NYPD, or he was picking up local radio calls on a police scanner. He's *here*."

"I suppose that makes sense," said Charles. "His aunt said he came home, and that would be the East Village."

"No," said Mallory. "Erik Homer had sole custody. Natalie never saw the boy after the divorce—not till the day she died. The scarecrow's home was always uptown with his father."

"But his father was a bully," said Charles. "And he's dead now. The boy never lived with his stepmother, so he wouldn't think of that place as home anymore. Natalie was the parent he adored, the one he still obsesses about."

Mallory abruptly stopped tapping keys.

Detective Janos listened to the theory on the missing night watchman, then nodded. "Yeah, we know. Another guy was filling in for him."

Heller's assistant glanced at the store's daytime security guard, then said, "Can we take this outside?"

Janos followed the man out the door of the manager's office. When he returned, Riker was still watching the same videotape for the tenth time. "This is crap." The image was too dark to make out details finer than the profiles of shadows punching in on the employee time clock. "No clear shots of anybody." Riker glanced at the store's daytime security guard. "I know, it's not your fault. You're sure this is the only tape of the new watchman?"

"Yes, sir. It rewinds every three days. So yesterday it—"

"Yeah, yeah," said Riker. And that would explain the grainy images. The camera had clicked once every three seconds. The shadowy figure had the jerky motion of an old silent film. "The time stamp on this video is too early for his shift. And why doesn't he punch in?"

"He's got his own time clock in the basement," said the guard. "No idea why he'd show up so early."

Riker waved one hand to tell the guard that he could leave. "Janos? What happening?"

"The regular watchman wasn't scheduled for a vacation. And his payroll checks are getting cashed."

Riker stared at the man on the videotape. "So maybe the regular watchman pays this guy out of pocket."

"That fits. Nobody's got a name for him." Janos read notes made from interviews with store employees. "We talked to a stock boy who does a lot of overtime. He says this new guy showed up one night, and nobody questioned it. He had the old man's keys on his belt and a security card to unlock the office door. That's the only place where you can turn off the alarms." He looked up from his notebook. "But the glass wall in the office was broken. So our perp wasn't the guy with the keys." He turned to the man on the screen. "Not that guy."

"Okay," said Riker. "What about the regular watchman?"

"I'm on that." Arthur Wang entered the room, a very worried man. "Couldn't reach him by phone, so I sent a uniform to knock on his door. The place doesn't stink like a ripe corpse. But that's all the cop could tell without going inside. He interviewed the landlord. The apartment's been sublet."

"Works with the vacation theory," said Janos. "Still it's worth a look inside. The old guy might've left something to give us a lead. Let's get a warrant and toss the place."

"It's in the works," said Arthur Wang. "So now we wait another forty minutes. The chicken-shit DA doesn't want to wake up a judge for a warrant."

"No judge is gonna sign that warrant," said Riker. "Not unless that uniform forgets he talked to the landlord. The sublet angle is a paperwork nightmare." He looked at Wang, and both men smiled in unison.

"But what if we *don't* know about the sublet tenant," said Wang. "Let's suppose the cop forgot to mention it when I talked to him."

"Yeah," said Riker. "Let's just suppose that."

"But it's still gonna take forty minutes to get a warrant."

"Fine. I don't see the scarecrow stringing up another blonde today. I'll be at Charles's place with Mallory." Riker looked down at his watch. "Where's my ride? Has anybody seen Deluthe?"

Pssst.

The old-model humidifier emitted a light spray of insecticide every twenty seconds, flooding the room with poisonous fumes. No cockroach would ever brave this atmosphere. Yet there were roach traps on the floor, strips of sticky tape along the baseboards and fly paper on every surface, all the added precautions of a man with a phobia.

Ronald Deluthe sifted though the Polaroid photographs of Stella Small madly beating flies from her hair in a subway car. In another shot, a blue garment was slung over one arm as she actually smiled for the camera— while bleeding. Then she was climbing into a cab, unaware of the line of blood on the sleeve of her blouse. In the next photograph, Kennedy Harper twisted on her rope, blurring the shot. Among the other Polaroids of the dead and dying, the prettiest subject was Sparrow, the vegetable woman in the hospital.

He glanced at the newspaper beside the telephone. *Backstage* was open to the columns for auditions. Two for tomorrow were circled in red ink. The mission was an ongoing thing.

Pssst.

TWENTY

LIEUTENANT LOMAN SET DOWN THE PHONE AND YELLED loud enough to be heard all over the squad room, "Hey, you bastards!"

Five heads turned his way.

"Has Deluthe been around this morning?"

"Blondie? No," said one detective. "I'd remember that."

The East Side lieutenant closed the door of his office and returned to his phone call. "No, Riker, he's not here. So, like I was sayin', the kid ain't the greatest cop material, but you got him all wrong. The brass didn't put him on any fast track. The deputy commissioner hates his guts."

"His father-in-law? Why?"

"Deluthe's marriage fell apart four months ago, and the wife's old man is out for blood. He ain't too subtle neither. Came right out and told me to crush his son-in-law. But I didn't want any part of it."

"And that's why you unloaded him on me?"

"The truth, Riker? I forgot Deluthe was alive. He was only takin' up desk space around here. Wasn't just me—*nobody* noticed him much. Then, the night that hooker got strung up, he comes walkin' in here with a bad bleach job."

"And *that* got your attention."

"Oh, yeah. So how's he doin', Riker?"

"Good. The kid's doin' good."

Pssst.

Ronald Deluthe listened to the police scanner as a dispatcher reeled off codes for domestic disputes and robberies. This address was not among the calls, and another few minutes would make no difference at all.

The insecticide permeated everything in the apartment including the closet and the clothes. There was no other discernible odor, though the body in the plastic bag was badly decomposed.

Pssst.

"Great!" Riker paced the length of the back office at Butler and Company. "Now I got two AWOL detectives." He leaned over the fax machine to read the last report from the Wisconsin State Police. "So Mallory's on the phone with these cops, and then what?"

"We talked about the scarecrow." Charles turned to the computer monitor. "She was working on this machine, and then she left. Just got up and left."

Riker glanced at his watch. "We'll give it a few minutes. Maybe she'll call in." He sat down at Mallory's desk and reached for the phone. While the detective waited on hold for Sparrow's doctor, Charles left the room to give him some privacy, saying, "I'll make some fresh coffee."

The office kitchen was only marginally more comfortable than Mallory's domain, though it housed fewer electronics. He loathed the coffee machine of chrome, plastic and computer components. The programmed brew was sterilized in his mind before it ever reached his taste buds. Unlike Geldorf, Charles was a Luddite by choice: he *could* work the machines, but he would not. Instead, he returned to his apartment, four steps from the door of Butler and Company, to light a flame under an old-fashioned coffeepot. The coffee was done by the time Riker had tracked him across the hall and into the kitchen.

The detective pulled up a chair at the table, and Charles set out an ashtray, inviting him to smoke if he liked. "So how is Sparrow?"

"'Bout the same. Still dying. They keep telling me that. She keeps hanging on. Then, an hour ago, the doctor thought she might be coming around. But he was wrong. A nurse confused a muscle spasm with a hand squeeze."

Charles filled two large mugs with coffee. "You check on her frequently, don't you?"

"Yeah."

"But not just because she's a crime victim and a witness. You really like this woman."

"We got a lot of history, me and Sparrow. She was one smart whore, and she made my job a little easier. All the dirt she ever gave me was gold. If she'd been on the payroll, she might've made lieutenant by now." As an afterthought, he said, "And she was good to Kathy."

Charles wondered how Riker could say that. According to the prostitutes, Kathy had been left to fend for herself most of the time—with a little help from the Hooker Book Salon. "Sparrow was an addict—hardly mother material. If she cared so much, why didn't she turn the child over to the authorities?"

"Because, more than clean sheets and three square meals, the kid needed somebody to love her. Sparrow loved Kathy like crazy. That was the best the whore could do—and it was a lot."

Charles set the coffee mugs on the table, then sat down. "But now Mallory hates this woman, doesn't she?"

Riker said nothing—and everything. The answer could only be yes. Charles held out a box of the detective's favorite pastries.

"Let me guess," said Riker. "A bribe?"

"Just one question. It's about the westerns and the prostitutes."

Riker smiled. "What a kid, huh? We only saw ten hookers last night. Figure most of them died or left town. That means Kathy was workin' whores all over the city."

"And you think that was her only use for the books—trading stories for a support network?"

"Who knows?" Riker shrugged. "Lou and I spent a lot of time trying to figure out the attraction. We didn't know about the Hooker Book Salon."

"You don't think she cared much about the stories?"

"Well, she always liked cowboys and Indians. Saturday mornings, she used to watch old westerns on TV with Lou. That was their only common ground for a while. She loved Helen at first sight, but it took Lou years to get that kid to trust him."

"You know," said Charles, "I always wondered why she never called him anything but Markowitz."

The detective looked at his watch. "I never did read that last western." He looked up and smiled. "So the Wichita Kid takes a bullet? Did I hear that right?"

"Yes."

"I guess I always knew it would end that way."

"If you only read the first six books, how did you—"

"I knew the sheriff would do his job."

"But the sheriff loved the Wichita Kid."

"That's why he had to kill him, Charles. That's what made Sheriff Peety a hero, bigger'n life. Now my job is a dirtier proposition. We give the bad guys a pass every day. They rat out their friends. We cut a deal, then watch 'em walk away."

"But not killers."

"No, that's the cutoff. Nobody walks away from that."

"Except Kathy Mallory. Last night, you said she was wanted for murder and arson."

"And the kid was posthumously charged," said Riker. "Case closed."

"But Kathy didn't actually die."

Riker drained his coffee mug. "And she didn't actually kill anybody. So?"

The detective never noticed the comical look on Charles's face as he was left hanging one more time. This would be maddening to most, but he was a patient man. "One more question? Are you disturbed by the parallels between Mallory and the scarecrow?"

Riker stared into his empty cup, considering his words carefully. "It's an old idea that cops and killers are twins. What separates us—that's what happens after the killing is over. You think this freak has any remorse about murder?"

Charles shook his head. "Not this man, no."

"But when a cop's involved in a fatal shooting, we take away his gun—so he won't die of remorse."

"So you don't see Mallory identifying with the scarecrow?"

"Never," said Riker. "I'm thinking now she knows what it was like to be Lou Markowitz."

"Hunting the lost child?"

"Natalie's son, one sick puppy. Some days you got nowhere to put your hate." Riker stared at his watch. "Why doesn't she call?" He pulled a crumpled fax from his pocket and glanced at the text. "So Odeon, Nebraska, was the last place the scarecrow called home."

"We were discussing a definition of home when Mallory got up and left."

Riker's fist banged the table hard enough to make the coffee mug dance to the edge. "She *found* him! Mallory knows where the scarecrow lives. Tell me everything you talked about." That was an order. "Every damn word."

Mallory stood on the steps of the East Village building, Natalie Homer's last address. She pressed the intercom button for the apartment on the parlor floor. There was no answer, and she heard no sounds within.

A man on the sidewalk was strolling toward her, regarding her with mild curiosity. He climbed the short staircase to join the detective at the front door. "I live here. Can I help you?"

It was Mallory's impression that he actually had some sincere desire to be helpful, and now she coupled him with another Midwest transplant. "Are you Mr. White? Alice White's husband?"

"Yes."

Mallory held up her badge, and no more words were necessary. Smiling, he unlocked his front door and opened it wide, never questioning her right to come inside. She wondered how these friendly Wisconsin folk survived in New York City. "Is your wife home?"

Mr. White consulted a note on the glove table in the hall. "This says she's gone to the store." He opened the large double doors to the front room and waved her toward a comfortable chair. "Please make yourself at home. I'm sure she'll be right back."

When they were both seated, he said, "I understand Alice gave you the guided tour. So what do you think of our renovations?"

"Nice job."

Mr. White leaned forward, eyebrows arched, expecting more from her. Then he gave up and sat back, perhaps realizing that this was her entire store of small talk. "Is there anything I can help you with?"

"I hope so." Mallory pulled out the two sketches of the scarecrow, the poster boy for the average man, and laid them on the coffee table. Beside these portraits she set down the computer printout of another likeness.

"Oh, he's from Nebraska," said Mr. White, after reading the address line of the driver's license. "I have a sister in Nebraska." His forehead puckered as he stared at the picture. "Terrible photography."

Pssst.

Deluthe was slowly becoming accustomed to the poison. He knew better than to touch anything, including the off switch for the machine that sprayed the insecticide into the air. He hunkered down before the body on the closet floor. The flesh was covered with green mold and black, and so was a good part of the bag's interior surface. The age of the corpse was evident by the white hair, and he sexed the body by one mannish square hand pressed up against the clear plastic.

Next to the closet, an umbrella stand held a baseball bat, the New Yorker's favored weapon for defending hearth and home. However, the white-haired man in the bag had no bloody wounds, no apparent cause of death.

The young detective stood up and turned round, though he could not have said why. He looked about the room. Everything was just as it should be.

Pssst.

"Well now," said Mr. White. "This could be most anybody." He looked up from the sketch, which had been no more helpful than the driver's license. "Sorry. I'm gone all day. It's my wife who knows all the neighbors on sight."

"Maybe you noticed a stranger hanging around your building at night. He wears a baseball cap and—" Mallory turned her head toward the sound of a small bell tinkling over the front door.

Alice White was home.

Deluthe walked toward the closed bathroom. He could not remember if he had left the door ajar. Between the automatic sprays of insecticide, the room was dead silent. He was almost certain that he was the only living thing in this apartment. *Almost* certain, he drew his gun as he reached for the doorknob. His skin prickled, and drops of sweat slid down his face as he conjured up a vision of Mallory standing over his dead body, making caustic remarks about his failure to call in for backup.

Yet he opened the door.

A hand shot out and smashed into his face. His nostrils gushed blood. His knees were weak and threatening to dump him on the floor. The man in the bathroom was raising his other hand. Was that a gun? Deluthe raised his own weapon.

No, it was an aerosol can.

Pssst.

Deluthe's eyes were on fire. He had taken a direct hit of insecticide, and now he was partially blind, only able to discern a blurry white shape, a floating face, as he hit the floor, landing on his knees. *More* pain.

Mrs. White entered the hallway, calling out to her husband, "John? Did you see my note?" She walked into the front room and set her grocery bag on the carpet, then noticed that her husband had company. "Oh, hello again. You know you're the third police officer I've seen today."

"What? Say again," said her husband.

"Early this morning, there was a young man in uniform. He came right after you left. I think he must have been a friend of George's. And then there was another one—" She stopped and turned to Mallory. "George is one of our tenants. He used to be a policeman years ago."

Mallory held up the sketches. "Does he look anything like this?"

"Oh, no," she laughed. "George is sixty-five if he's a day. A very heavy man, and not so much hair."

Deluthe moved back. Tears had washed his eyes, and now he could see the shadowy form of a man in front of him. When he aimed his gun, it was simply taken from his hand, for he had misjudged the distance of his assailant. Fists waving blind, he made contact with the other man's body. A savage kick to Deluthe's testicles doubled him over in pain, and a hard punch to his stomach took his breath away. He hit the floor and lay there, rolling on to his side, curling like a fetus and listening to the opening and closing of drawers, then the sound of something tearing. He tried to get his bearings in the room. Where was the umbrella stand, the baseball bat?

Next to the closet.

His vision was still blurred, but he could make out the dark rectangle of the open closet door. He crawled toward it and located the nearby umbrella stand by touch. As he reached up to grab the bat, he heard the running footsteps, gained his legs and swung at the thing rushing toward him.

He hit something. Yes, flesh and bone. The shadow man was down.

Mrs. White looked at the sketches and the photograph.

"Take your time," said Mallory. As if she had the time. "Have you ever seen him before?"

"Well, he looks like lots of people. He could even be that young policeman. I told him George wasn't here. But the man he sublet the apartment to—"

"He works nights," said John White. "Same as old George."

"So I thought he might be sleeping," said his wife. "And I told that to the officer."

"The first one?" asked John White. "Or do you—"

"Well, both of them," said his wife. "The second policeman was a detective. He asked if it was all right to leave a note under George's door."

Deluthe's legs were pulled out from under him. He cracked the back of his skull when he hit the floor. The baseball bat was still clenched in his right hand.

The other man's weight was on top of him, and together they rolled across the rug and knocked up against the wall. The assailant was beneath him now, and Deluthe smashed his fist into the face that he could barely see. His opponent did not seem to feel the blows, a hand was closing on Deluthe's testicles, and he screamed in agony.

When had he let go of the bat?

Mallory was deep in denial. "This man lives in your building, and you *never* got his name?"

"Well," said Mr. White, speaking for his wife, "it's not like he's a complete stranger. He's been visiting old George for years."

Once more, Mallory tapped the pictures on the coffee table. "Could this be your sublet?"

"It could be." Mrs. White picked up one of the sketches. "I'm not sure. It could also be one of those policemen. The detective—he's the one who wanted to leave a note. He came by just a little while ago, and I sent him upstairs. Well, I had to run to the store, so the young man said he'd let himself out."

Pssst.

Ronald Deluthe was lying on his side. He could taste the blood in his mouth as he ripped off the tape. His other hand was feeling around for the baseball bat. Blind fingers no sooner closed around the wood than it was twisted out of his grasp. His right arm was forced up behind his back, and he could feel muscle and bone ripping away from the socket. The pain was beyond anything he had ever imagined. Tiny points of shooting white lights were all that he could clearly see. His scream was muffled by another piece of tape covering his mouth.

"George's sublet is a very quiet young man," said Alice White. "We never hear a sound from that apartment."

"Well, we wouldn't, would we?" Her husband smiled. "It's on the top floor. So one day, I met him on the stairs. He had George's keys. He said the old man left town in the middle of night. Some family crisis." He smiled to reassure the skeptical detective. "Well, he *did* have George's keys, and he seemed presentable. There was no reason to—"

"And you were afraid of him." Mallory did not have to wait for a reply. It was in the man's face. And now she understood why no one had pressed the sublet for so much as a name to call him by. "Take another look." She held up one sketch. "Imagine him with a baseball cap and a gray canvas bag with a red stripe."

"Oh, that's the sublet, all right," said Mrs. White. "You never see him without that bag of his."

Mallory turned her eyes to the ceiling, as if she could see through all the floors of the building. "Is there a back exit?"

"We have a door to the backyard."

"That's it? No fire escape?"

"No."

"So if he wanted to get out, he'd have to—"

"You'd see him out there in the hall," said John White, who now finished sentences for the detective as well as his wife.

"Give me your keys." Mallory held out her hand. "Now!" Later, she would not remember screaming at this man to make him move faster. *"Keys!"*

When Deluthe regained consciousness, his hands were bound. He tried to lift his head. A rope was pulling tight around his neck, and his body bucked against the heavy weight of the man on top of him.

No breath. Eyes bulging, heart hammering.

Panic was magnified to monster-size primal fear. His legs kicked out, then thudded on the floor. His struggles ceased. His prone body was lighter now. Head swimmy, muscles relaxing, fear gave way to euphoria, and he closed his eyes. The heavy weight that had straddled him was suddenly lifted, and gravity ceased to hold his body down. He floated up into an ether of midnight black.

All sensation ceased.

The door closed. The room was dead quiet.

Riker yelled, "Yes, you *can* go faster! You're with a damn cop!"

Charles pushed the gas pedal to the floor and never flinched at the near miss of a cab and now a truck coming out of a side street.

The detour was a long one, twisting round the gridlock traffic of a broken water main on Houston. They were driving ten miles of bad traffic to travel one as the crow flies.

TWENTY-ONE

THE LANDLORD HAD DISOBEYED A DIRECT ORDER TO remain downstairs with his wife. He had silently followed Mallory to the top-floor apartment, and now it was too late to threaten the man—and unnecessary. John White quickly backed down to the lower landing when she drew her .357 Smith & Wesson, a cannon among revolvers. She favored it above all others for its drop-dead stopping power.

Pssst.

The door was ajar by the crack of a bare inch. She kicked it dead center, and it flew back with a bang and the sound of plaster crumbling where the knob had crashed into a wall. Fresh wet blood was splattered across the rug, and some of it had stained a baseball bat. Mallory only glanced at the body on the floor. Ronald Deluthe had a rope knotted around his neck. She entered the apartment, aiming her gun at every piece of furniture that might give cover to the scarecrow. The bathroom was empty. She kicked open another door—no one there.

Upon returning to the front room, she found John White crouching on the floor and holding the wrist of the fallen detective. Deluthe's left arm was twisted in an unnatural attitude. His nose was smashed to one side and still gushing blood, the only sure sign of a beating heart and life.

"I've got a pulse," said White, "but it's thready."

Mallory knelt beside the unconscious man, then put one finger between the rope and his neck. It was a tight fit. His oxygen had been completely cut off, but his lips were not yet blue. The scarecrow could only be a minute away.

John White was also working at the rope, but to a different purpose; he was trying to clear the man's air passage, saying, "I was a volunteer paramedic back in Wisconsin."

Mallory was not listening, nor did she watch as White performed mouth-to-mouth resuscitation. She stared at the open closet and its contents for a moment, then reached down and ripped back the lapel of Deluthe's suit jacket. His shoulder holster was empty.

The scarecrow has a gun.

She was rising, moving quickly toward the door and the inconvenient obstacle of Alice White. Mallory pushed the woman aside, shouting, "Call 911!"

"I did. You told me—"

"Call *again!* Tell them an officer's down!"

The last staircase at the end of the hall would lead her to the roof, and Mallory was running toward it. She had climbed to the door at the top of the stairs when she heard a scream from the apartment below. Apparently, Alice had noticed the moldy corpse on the floor of the closet.

Riker spoke into his cell phone. "Repeat that. An officer down?"

Charles was pulling over to allow an emergency vehicle to pass when the detective yelled, "Follow that ambulance!"

Mallory's revolver preceded her through the door of a small rooftop shed. Her eyes had not yet adjusted to brilliant sunlight when she took aim at the sound of footsteps. And now, in perfect focus, the profile of a young girl's head was lined up with the muzzle of the gun. The teen-ager had not yet seen the detective or the weapon, but she was shaking, and her face was a study in dumb surprise as she bolted for the rooftop door.

Mallory rounded the shed to see the back of a man's bloodstained shirt and jeans. He used Deluthe's gun to shade his eyes from the overhead sun. There were scratches on his face, the work of Stella Small. The scarecrow's right arm hung useless at his side, and she guessed that Deluthe had also done some damage before he was taken down.

Only steps away, a smaller man with carrot-red hair was huddled on the tar-paper ground amid a wash of white linen pulled down from a clothes-line, perhaps in the belief that wet sheets could protect him from bullets. On the other side of a low brick wall that separated one roof from the next, an elderly woman tended a coop of carrier pigeons. She was deaf to the whimpers of the little man in the sheets and blind to the one with the gun.

At the sound of a nervous giggle, Mallory glanced back over one shoulder to see the children standing behind her, three boys in staggered sizes, and these television babies showed no fear of either weapon.

The scarecrow was facing her now, dazed and weaving. Blood dripped into one eye from a gash in his brow.

A massive head injury—a bonus.

She could hear the children creeping forward to watch the show. None of them had the sense of sheep to get out of harm's way. Mallory left her back vulnerable when she whirled around and yelled, "Get inside!" Her gun produced no effect on the boys, but her eyes were promising some-thing nasty if they did not move and *right now*.

They shrank back behind the shelter of a door made of wood, not fire-code metal. Bullets would rip right through it. The smallest child had been left behind. He was walking between the guns.

Thou shalt not get the sheep killed.

That had been Louis Markowitz's prime rule and Mallory's hardest les-son, for it tied into a bizarre concept: When she pinned on the badge, she agreed, if need be, to *die* for the sheep. This had been a difficult pitch to a child of the streets, who possessed an ungodly instinct for survival.

But a deal was a deal.

The scarecrow's gun hand extended slowly. Mallory's finger touched lightly on the trigger. She could drop him any time she liked, but fast as she was, he might get off one round. His every movement told her he was not left-handed. The shot would go wild.

One dead sheep.

All the children were targets, the one in the open and the two behind the door. Or he might blow away the pigeon lady or the little man under the sheets. Mallory lowered her revolver to end the threat that would make him fire.

His gun slowly drifted toward the shed where the children were hidden but not protected. In sidelong vision, Mallory caught the motion of a wind-whipped flowery dress before she saw a terrified woman creeping toward the lone boy in the line of fire. Mother courage. The woman gathered the little boy into her arms, and the scarecrow paid no attention to her running backward with the child. His eyes were fixed on Mallory. His gun hand was on the rise.

She was faster. In a stunning flash, the muzzle of her revolver pointed at his eyes. "You really want this bullet, don't you?"

The threat was meaningless to him. This was not the cornered animal she had anticipated, but something even more dangerous. Perversely, she raised her revolver high to aim at the noonday sun, and then, pushing perversity to the nth degree, she taunted him, saying, "I know more about your mother's death than you do."

Magic words.

His gun was lowering, buying her time to reassess his injuries. The right arm was certainly broken. All his weight listed to the right leg, and she knew the left was about to fold. One eye was clotted with blood, and one eye was attentive as he awaited the rest of her story.

Just like the old days—just like a whore.

"And I even know what *you* did that night."

The scarecrow's one clear eye flickered with surprise. His left leg buckled, but he remained standing. He seemed unaware that he was aiming at the shivering pile of wet laundry. The little man in the sheets ceased to cry and laid his head down in a faint.

And the scarecrow was still waiting for his story.

"You found one of the stalker notes," said Mallory. "You found it on the floor the night she died." She had guessed right. He was nodding. "And you had a lot of time to read it—two days and two nights. Flies in your hair, roaches crawling in your clothes. The stove burner was on. The heat was suffocating."

His gun was getting heavier, and his aim was drifting again. The old woman was his accidental target. He was tired in every part of his body and tired of his very life. Yet Mallory held his attention. "You were in the bathroom when he came to kill your mother."

The pigeon lady was oblivious to the weapon, but her birds were restless, sensing tension in the air as a threatening storm. Their wings batted against the wire doors of the cage, and a shower of downy white feathers drifted from the coop in an eerie August snowfall.

Mallory walked toward him, slow-stepping. "You heard something." She circled around him, drawing his body and his gun away from the old woman. "You opened the bathroom door—just a crack. The man was bending over your mother." Now she was positive that he had *not* seen his mother strangled to death. The six-year-old child had believed that his mother was still alive while he watched a man mutilate her and hang her. If a fireman and a doctor could not tell the living from the dead, what chance did a little boy have?

The pigeon lady was on the move again. Mallory kept track of her in peripheral vision. The old woman crossed the roof, walking into the line of fire to pick up a heavy bag of birdseed.

Mallory backed off softly, slowly.

Easy now.

A hand tremor made his gun shake. He was sliding into profound shock and aiming from the hip.

"You watched him hang her—without a sound, no screams. She never—"

His head was shaking in denial.

Impossible. Mallory knew she could not be wrong about this part. Yes, she *was* right. She had simply not pushed this idea far enough. "*You* never made a sound. You—just—*watched*."

The man's head tilted to one side, as though some supporting string had been cut. His face contorted into a soundless scream, and the blood-clotted eye cried red tears. He was bleeding inside and out.

The birds were screaming, wings in a racket, beating the wire of the coop, frantic to get away.

"You *watched* that bastard kill your mother! You *let* him do it to her!" Of course he did—only six years old, traumatized and paralyzed, and now she played to the guilt of the innocent child. "You never called for help. You never even *tried* to stop him."

The doors of the pigeon coop flew open, and dozens of birds escaped before the wide eyes of their keeper. In tight formation, they flew across the roof in a roar of wings and cries, diving close to the scarecrow, then veering upward. His eyes were wild, following the flight of birds into the sun.

"You couldn't reach her up there on the rope." Mallory could see him as a small shivering boy, crying to his mother, no clue that she was dead. "How could you leave her—if she was still *alive?*"

He dropped his gun and never noticed its loss. On the next roof, the pigeon lady stared at the sky, arms fluttering in her own attempt at flight.

"After two days—the bugs and the heat—you couldn't take anymore. You left your mother all alone in the dark. You knew what the insects were doing to her when you closed that door and walked away."

His bad leg buckled, and he folded to the ground like a piece of collapsible lawn furniture. And there he made a stand of sorts, on his knees, as though his legs had been cut to stumps. Mallory stepped closer to kick his gun, sending it flying to the far side of the roof.

He was helpless. Both eyes were open now and looking in on some interior hell. She knelt down before him, facing him in the position of prayer. He raised his head a bare inch. Later, she would remember his eyes with an imagined film of dust, as though he had already been dead for some time—for years and years. It would have been a kindness to put a bullet in his skull—an act of mercy.

Resurrection time.

In the absence of kindness and mercy, she planned to rebuild him as her only witness to the murder of Natalie Homer. "I know it was a cop who killed your mother. And you're going to help me nail that bastard. It's revenge you want, and I can get that for you."

No, that was not what he wanted, *never* what he wanted. Mallory could see her error now, a very bad mistake.

Natalie's son was waiting for his bullet, staring at the revolver with a great hunger. He had foreseen this moment long ago as a little boy in the heat of August, waiting so patiently to be punished. And he had laid this out so clearly in the mad restaging of a crime that he believed was his alone. Three hangings, one endless shriek, *Catch me! Kill me!* He had even warned his victims and sent them into the arms of the police as his messengers, extensions of a scream.

Mallory could see all the way to the bottom of his madness, the rest of the damage done to a small child. "You thought your father sent you away—because he *blamed* you."

No response. The scarecrow was shutting down what remained of his mind. Mallory tried to touch him, and he shrank back, a reflex that she understood too well. Her hand froze, suspended in the forbidden act of reaching out. She was always clutching air—touching no one. Yet she tried again, gently grazing his battered face with the tips of her fingers.

A shadow blocked the sun. She heard the sick sound of the bat cracking his skull, breaking it open. There was time to catch him in her arms, and they fell together.

Ronald Deluthe stood over them, listing to one side. The baseball bat dangled from his right hand as he sank to the ground, where he sat bolt upright, legs splayed out, his eyes slowly closing.

The scarecrow's weight was on top of Mallory. His blood was on her face and in her hair. As she lay beneath the corpse, only her eyes were moving, slowly turning to Ronald Deluthe. She watched as his upper body pitched forward and his head hit the dusty tar paper between his spread legs.

Mallory had lost her weapon. Her gun hand absently stroked the scarecrow's hair, then came away with bits of red bone and flesh. But how could this be? She had yet to tell him how his mother had really died— that there was nothing he could have done to save her.

Charles Butler's Mercedes pulled up in front of the apartment building and double-parked alongside a row of police units and their spinning red lights. An ambulance was at the curb, where two men in hospital whites stood beside an empty gurney.

Riker was the first one out of the car, yelling, "What happened? Where's the wounded cop?"

"It's my fault!" An unnerved civilian rushed up to him, arms waving, as if this might help to gather his thoughts. "I'm sorry. I thought he was unconscious. I just took my eyes off the poor man for a minute. My wife was feeling a bit queasy, and I thought she was going to faint. You see, she saw the body in the closet. And when I looked back—well, the man was gone."

Riker barreled through the shed door, gun drawn, eyes going everywhere. He saw the little redheaded man rolling in wet sheets and moaning. On the neighboring roof, a confused old woman was staring up at the sky where her lost birds had gone.

He found Deluthe beside the shed, slumped over and holding a baseball bat in a one-handed death grip. Mallory lay a few feet away—underneath a corpse.

More sirens were coming, and she listened to them, as if from a great distance of miles and miles. The scarecrow's flesh was deceptively warm, and so was his blood. It dripped from the broken skull to soak her and stain her.

Riker rolled the heavy weight off her body and met with some resistance, for Mallory's hands were pressed to the dead man's face—still trying to make human contact.

TWENTY-TWO

CIVILIAN CONVERSATIONS BLENDED WITH THE STATIC of radio calls from police units, and yellow tape cordoned off the sidewalk in front of the apartment building. An ambulance and a meat wagon were parked at the curb, side by side, doors hanging open, awaiting the living and the dead. The man from the medical examiner's office zipped up the body bag on his gurney. A cigarette dangled from his mouth as he accepted a light from the homicide detective. "Dr. Slope's standing by to crack the old man open. So what's the story on the other corpse?"

"There's only *one* dead body," Riker corrected him. "This one." He looked down at the remains of George Neederland, the missing department-store watchman.

The ME's man looked up to the sky and a departing police helicopter. "Your guys just took another body off the roof. What's the—"

"Repeat after me, pal. There's only one dead body at this crime scene." Riker turned to see another reporter approaching the police barricade.

Nearby, a news van was unloading pole lights and camera equipment. He turned back to face down the meat-wagon man. "*One* body. If the press hears a different story, Dr. Slope's gonna fire your ass. I'll make *sure* he does."

In a less threatening mode, Riker turned to thank Alice White for the wet washcloth she pressed into his hand. He grabbed Mallory by the arm and forced her to stand still while he cleaned the red smears from her face. Then he stepped back to appraise the rest of her stains. "Damn, you look worse than Deluthe. You're sure none of that blood belongs to you?"

Mallory turned away from him and walked toward a crime-scene technician, calling out, "You! Stop!"

Riker strolled back to the ambulance crew. "You're right, guys. No wounds on Mallory." He turned to watch his partner issuing orders and signing the evidence bags for her crime scene, unaware that her bloody clothes and hair were making the civilian onlookers sick.

A paramedic hovering over Deluthe said, "He's coming around again."

There was no need to shield the youngster from the reporters and their cameras. His own mother would not recognize that swollen bandaged face. More bandages covered his scalp. He was being stabilized with injections and portable machines to keep him out of the danger zone of deep shock.

Riker waited until Deluthe's eyes flickered open, then continued the lecture where he had left off ten minutes ago. "When you found Natalie's address in the watchman's file, you should've come to me. *Never* go after a perp without backup. And that *door.* That was a major screwup, kid. When you saw the open door, you should've known the scarecrow was still in the building."

The young cop was coughing. It was a fight to get the words out. "Is this your way of telling me I'm fired?" The lame smile made his lip bleed again.

"Naw," said Riker. "I wouldn't waste time teaching you how to stay alive—not if you were on the way out."

The medic unhooked the monitor. "Okay, he's stable."

"Give us a minute," said Riker. When the two paramedics had walked around to the other side of the ambulance, he said, "One more thing, kid. We're promoting you to a stone killer—just for a little while." He pointed at the uniformed officers seated inside the ambulance, both men he trusted.

"Waller's got your ID and your badge. He'll field all the questions at the hospital. Just keep your mouth shut." He turned around to look at his partner in her bloodstains. "Oh, and Mallory's taking the credit for beating the crap out of you. But we'll clear that up tomorrow, okay?"

Before the ambulance doors had closed on the baffled Deluthe, Charles Butler joined Riker on the sidewalk. "Shouldn't Mallory see a doctor?"

"Right," said the detective. "*You* talk to her."

"There's something—not quite right with her."

"Oh, yeah?" Riker turned to watch her moving about the scene like an automaton. "How can you tell?"

Charles certainly caught the sarcasm, but he was selectively deaf to detrimental remarks about Mallory. "Under normal circumstances, she's compulsively neat. She'd never tolerate a smudge on one of her running shoes. Look at her now. She doesn't even see the blood on her clothes and her—"

"Yeah, she's not quite the little fanatic today." Riker smiled. "But that's a good thing, isn't it? Progress?"

Charles sighed. He pointed to the rectangular bulge in Riker's pocket. "Are you ever going to give her that book?"

"I will—when the time is right."

Mallory was walking toward them. Charles made himself scarce before she could order him behind the crime-scene tape again.

Riker grinned, so happy to see her alive and walking around in any condition. "You missed your chance to tell Deluthe how bad he screwed up today. I filled in for you."

"Did you tell him he killed an unarmed man—the *only* witness to Natalie Homer's murder?"

"No, kid, I saved that part for you. Wait'll he gets out of the hospital. He won't be expecting an ambush." This was a joke, but she seemed to be considering it. "So, Mallory, I hear you reamed out Geldorf."

"He had it coming," she said.

"Sure. That's why you told him the scarecrow was a cop. You'd need a pretty good reason to give up a detail like that. You figured the old man was on the perp's kill list, right? So you warned him. That was your twisted good deed for the day."

He could see that she was not about to admit any such human frailty.

Maybe it was all wishful thinking on his part, a fantasy of what he wanted her to be. He looked up at the clouds that threatened rain. "Not very satisfying this time, is it, Mallory?" No, he guessed not.

She raised her face to his, and he saw his Kathy, only ten, all played out at the end of a bad day, and he wanted to kill somebody to make her world right again. His hate was growing, going out to the man who murdered Natalie Homer. That worthless bastard had done so much damage. Twenty years later, the dead could not be officially tallied until Sparrow was taken off life support. And then there was Mallory, altered in ways that worried him.

Riker reached into his pocket and pulled out a brown paper bag containing a book. "Here, a consolation prize." He handed her the final installment of the saga of Sheriff Peety and the Wichita Kid. "You might like the inscription."

He had marked the page with a matchbook so she would find the brief message from her biggest fan, a love letter written before Louis Markowitz and Kathy had been properly introduced.

Riker walked away as she opened her present. He was heading for Mallory's car, planning to sabotage it so she could not drive home by herself. Also, she would not forgive him if he saw her cry, and he did not want that additional burden. He was still paying for all his old crimes against the child she used to be.

"Riker!" she called after him. "We're not done yet!"

So much for his grand idea that she could be moved to tears. Perhaps his fantasy life was getting out of hand.

The decor of the Manhattan condo was expensive and Spartan, though the living room had the smell of Brooklyn ghosts, Louis and Helen Markowitz. Their old house had reeked of the same canned-pine-tree air freshener. Riker supposed this was Mallory's idea of memento, for the room was bereft of family photographs or keepsakes. She must believe there was nothing here to give away any clue to her personality. Untrue. The white carpet had a low tolerance for dirt; chrome and glass gleamed from the toil of a cleaning fanatic; the dark leather chairs and the couch had severe right angles and hard straight lines. It was all black and white—no compromises—all Mallory.

And so it was easy to spot the small item that did not belong here. Evidently, he had not been the only one to rob a crime scene, and Mallory had been careless with her stolen goods. He knelt down on the rug and reached under the glass cocktail table to retrieve a delicate ivory comb. It was memorable for the elaborate carving and the look of money. Sparrow had worn it in her hair each time they met. And he had always been curious about this precious comb, this favorite possession of a junkie that should have been sold for a drug buy long ago. When Sparrow finally died, would the comb become Mallory's keepsake or her trophy?

He turned to see his partner enter the room, towel drying her hair as she walked toward him in a long white robe. Mallory was resilient, and she cleaned up well.

Riker folded a cell phone into his pocket. "Dr. Slope cracked the night watchman's chest. The old guy's been dead about two weeks. Natural causes. You figure the scarecrow planned his last murder that far in advance?"

"No. He made friends with the old man years ago. He wanted to spend time in the building where his mother died. That place was his idea of home." She accepted a glass of bourbon and soda from his hand.

Riker had been surprised to find the makings in her kitchen cabinet, and he wondered if she drank alone. Of course she did. She would never drink in public and risk losing control in front of witnesses. "So that's what triggered the hangings? The watchman's death?"

"We'll never know—thanks to Deluthe." Mallory stared at the pocket that hid his cell phone. "What did you hear from the hospital?"

"If you mean Deluthe, he'll live. Just busted up is all." Riker watched her finish the medicinal whiskey and soda. "He's got a broken nose, a hairline skull fracture and a dislocated shoulder. Oh, and he's gonna have a wicked scar on his face, lots of stitches. But the doctor says he doesn't seem to mind that. In fact, he seems real happy about it." He picked up the remote control for the television set. "But if you mean Sparrow—the doctor says she'll be gone before morning." He could not tell if this made any impression on Mallory. At least she did not smile.

"And now for the good news." Riker switched on the television and killed the sound of the broadcast, preferring to give his own narrative. "We got a very confused press corps with an inaccurate body count. They think the scarecrow's still alive, but badly wounded." He pointed to the image of a teenage witness being attacked by microphones. "That's all the girl could tell them."

Mallory nodded. "She was only on the roof for a few minutes."

And the young girl was still shaking on camera as Riker leaned closer to the set. "Here, watch this—her father's gonna deck a reporter." The punch was thrown. "Good job." And now the picture changed to three small boys all talking at once. "Oh, but these kids—they were great!"

"They didn't see *anything*," said Mallory. "Their mother took them off the roof before they could—"

"Yeah, but, in *their* version, you shot the poor bastard's legs off. Then you pistol-whipped him and shot him some more. But they knew he was still alive 'cause they saw him try to crawl away from you. Bless their lying little hearts."

"I need something to rattle a suspect." Mallory stood before the rear wall of the incident room, pinning another array of photographs to the cork surface. "We have to wrap Natalie's murder tonight."

Understandable. Come the morning, every fact of the scarecrow's death would be public knowledge. "All right," said Charles. "There were *two* stalkers. Only Natalie's killer would know that."

She said nothing aloud, but he knew that smirk so well. *Yeah, right.*

"It's a matter of style," he said, undaunted. "The first stalker was the ex-husband. I'm sure Lars was right about that. So perhaps he could be forgiven for—"

No. One look at Mallory and he knew that forgiveness was never coming from that quarter. Charles unpinned one of the stalker notes and held up the aged yellow paper. "Erik Homer was a wife beater, short on patience. I don't see him spending hours tracing individual letters of magazine script just to make this beautiful for Natalie. Rather artistic, isn't it?" He read the words to her. " 'I touched you today.' More like poetry than a threat. Not Erik Homer's style. When he met his second wife, the stalking ended, and Natalie had no more use for the police. That explains the two-week gap in her complaints. It was the second stalker who left her these notes, who loved her—and killed her."

"All right, I'll buy that." Mallory stepped back from the wall to give him a clear view of her rogues gallery, five men as they had appeared twenty years ago. Lars Geldorf's portrait came from a newspaper archive. Head shots of two other detectives and one patrolman were made from Mallory's computer enhancements of the crime-scene Polaroids. And another patrolman's picture was taken from a personnel file. "Next problem," she said. "We know the perp was a cop, but which one?"

"How can you be sure it was one of these men?"

"Because one of the uniforms called in the hanging as a suicide—and *three* detectives showed up."

Apparently Mallory was picking up cryptic bad habits from Riker.

"Just guessing," said Charles. "You don't usually send so many detectives out for a suicide call?" What was he missing here? He stared at the pictures of the men in suits. "So you've narrowed it down to these three because they all signed off on Natalie's stalker complaints? Is that it?"

"No."

Of course not. Miles too easy.

"You're right about one thing." Mallory pinned up a portrait of Natalie Homer smiling for her photographer. "He loved her. He was obsessed with her. She was the prettiest thing he ever set eyes on."

And you are beautiful. Had he ever told her that? No, never.

"But he was nothing special," said Mallory.

Far from special, far from beauty.

"Not in her class," said Mallory. "All he could do was watch her and follow her. He probably figured she'd laugh if she knew how often he thought about her—about the two of them—together. She was unapproachable, unattainable."

As far away as the moon. You would never—

"He was my best suspect." Mallory tapped Lars Geldorf's photograph. "The old man has an attachment to Natalie that just won't die. He was on the top of my list."

"Was," said Charles. "And now?"

"When Natalie's son looked through that bathroom door, if he'd seen a detective in street clothes, he wouldn't have known the hangman was a cop."

Though relieved that Lars was no longer in her sights, Charles's good logic held sway. "You're not forgetting that Junior saw that man a second time—two days later, outside the crime scene. The boy had to know that all the men in that room were police."

"Three detectives turned out for a suicide call," said Mallory. "And it wasn't the address that got their attention. One of the uniforms gave the victim's name. No patrol cop was ever dispatched to Natalie's apartment while she was alive. I checked. She always made her complaints at the station. You read Deluthe's interview with Alan Parris. The uniforms were in that room for two seconds before they shut the door and called in the report. They saw a scalped corpse on a rope. It was bloated with gas and maggots, face wrecked beyond recognition."

"But they knew it was Natalie," said Charles. "They knew that was her apartment."

"One of them did." She tapped the photographs of the uniformed officers. "Can you tell Loman from Parris?"

"That's easy," said Charles, though he knew neither man on sight. "Loman is the only one in the crime-scene photos. Parris wouldn't go back inside that room. Oh, I see. They *are* rather alike." Even Lars Geldorf had confused one for the other. Both in their early twenties, the patrolmen had the same regular features, dark hair and eyes beneath the brims of their caps. "When the boy was in the hall with Alice White, that second encounter should have reinforced his identification. But he saw *two* men in uniform."

"It's the uniform he remembered best," said Mallory. "If the boy couldn't tell them apart, how do we—"

"I suggest you flip a coin," said Charles, for logic could not take him everywhere.

Riker leaned toward the window by his desk in the squad room. News vans on the street below were double-parked at the curb. A few men with microphones assaulted the police entourage surrounding and concealing the wounded detective, whose head was covered by a white helmet of bandages. The rest of the reporters were looking up at the second-story windows, mouths open like dogs waiting to be fed. "Nothing like a good hungry mob to jack up the fear."

When Officer Waller and his partner came through the door, they were supporting Ronald Deluthe on both sides. Nursemaids could not have been more tender than these large men slowly walking him across the squad room and watching his face with grave concern. The dividing wall between detectives and uniforms came down when one of New York's Finest was wounded in the line of duty.

An angry rope burn circled Deluthe's neck, exposed stitches ran down one cheek like a dueling scar, and the dislocated shoulder was covered with a sling supporting his left arm. Riker saw the dead-white face as a sure sign that the boy had not taken any recent medication to block the pain.

Had that been Mallory's idea?

The wounded man's honor guard was dismissed. Riker did not want the uniforms to see what would happen next. When the stairwell door had closed behind the departing officers, Mallory unclipped a pair of handcuffs from her belt and manacled Deluthe's good hand to the one that dangled from the sling.

TWENTY-THREE

JACK COFFEY SAT AT THE TABLE BESIDE THE LOCKUP cage. He had used a pencil to jam the sash of the only window, and now the small room was hot and airless as he entertained the East Side lieutenant with a story about the three Stellas' reunion. "So this theatrical agent—real scary, like a nun gone psycho—she's got Stella Small an acting job on a soap opera. But the mother and grandmother plan to take the girl home to Ohio."

"Good idea." Harvey Loman's feet tapped the floor as his eyes strayed to a clock on the wall. He seemed mildly crazed by this tale that went on and on.

"Well, the poor kid's been through hell," said Coffey, pleased with the other man's agitation. "And she's knocked out with sedatives. So the agent leans over the hospital bed and smiles with real sharp little teeth. She says, 'Up to you, baby doll. It's a three-year contract with the hottest show on daytime TV.' Now the agent acts real concerned. She says, 'Oh, sorry, hon. Would you rather be buried alive in Iowa?' Then Stella's mother chimes in, 'We live in *Ohio*.' So the agent says, 'Yeah, yeah,' like there's a difference."

"Nice little story, Jack." Loman's political smile was flagging. He took out a handkerchief to mop his brow and bald head. "Now what the hell am I doing here?"

"We're closing out an old case of yours. Nobody told you? It's the Natalie Homer murder." Coffey could read surprise in the other man's face, but nothing more.

"That wasn't my case, Jack. I was only a uniform in those days."

"I know. I invited Parris too. He's on the way over."

Loman winced with real pain, then mopped his bald head and brow with a handkerchief. "Alan Parris?"

"Yeah," said Coffey. "Your old partner."

The man you sold out for a shot at the golden shield.

Lieutenant Coffey rocked his chair on two legs, enjoying the moment, for he had always disliked this man. "So, how come you never mentioned that old hanging? When you dropped off the paperwork—"

"I never made the connection to the hooker's case."

"Both women were hung by the neck and gagged with their own hair. How many connections did you need?"

"The crimes scenes were nothing alike." Loman stood up and jangled car keys in his pants pocket. "I'm not gonna stick around for this, Jack."

"I'm not giving you a choice, Harvey. You're on my list of material witnesses. So you stay till we wrap it." Jack Coffey was smiling as he rose from his chair, daring the man to push his luck in this precinct.

Still smiling, the commander of Special Crimes Unit stepped into the hall and locked the door the behind him.

The squad room was quiet and dim. All but one of the overhead fluorescents had been killed, and only a few independent lamps were left on, though all the desks were empty. The only bright light was focused on Mallory and the rookie detective. Ronald Deluthe wore a bloody T-shirt. His jeans and baseball cap, ripped from the wall of the incident room, were free of stains.

Riker stood by the window and watched the crowded sidewalk below. He saw Charles Butler's head above the crowd of normal-size human beings and that other species, the reporters.

Mallory was still instructing her star performer. "Keep your face down."

Well, that should be easy enough. Riker doubted that the boy would have the strength to lift his head. "We should send you back to the hospital, kid."

"He wants to do this," said Mallory, speaking for Deluthe. "So he *stays*."

Riker was about to make another comment but let it slide for Deluthe's sake. In the aftermath of killing the scarecrow, this was almost therapy, though that was not Mallory's motive. She only wanted an authentically battered doppelgänger.

"One problem," said Riker. "Even if they don't see his face, they'll recognize the hair. You can see that bleach job through solid walls."

"I know." Mallory resolved the problem with a mascara wand. After a few deft strokes, the fringe of hair beneath the bandages was turned to brown. "Deluthe, you've got everybody's attention now." She leaned down to his eye level. "So no more *bleaching*." And that was a direct order. "You're not invisible anymore."

Riker was startled. Empathy was not his partner's forte. She should have been the last one to work out the puzzle of Deluthe's bright yellow hair.

"I don't want to see any emotion at all," she said. "We're clear on that?"

"Yes," said Deluthe.

Mallory dabbed at his bleeding lip with a tissue, perhaps perceiving fresh blood as a sign of overacting. "When Janos brings you back to the squad room, I'll ask a few questions. Don't speak. Just nod."

"Yes, ma'am."

"A lot hangs on that nod." Jack Coffey crossed the squad room to join them. "We got nothin' else, kid. No physical evidence."

They could not even justify an arrest warrant. And since there was no need to mention that Deluthe had dispatched their only eyewitness with a baseball bat, the lieutenant led him down the hall in silence.

"So you got your perp." Geldorf's voice came from the stairwell door, where he stood with Charles Butler. "Nice work!"

"Hey, Lars." Riker returned the old man's broad smile. "You know all your lines?"

"Oh, yeah. Charles briefed me. Don't worry about—"

Mallory made a motion to silence Geldorf as the stairwell door opened again, and Alan Parris was escorted into the room by Detective Wang. Riker studied the suspect with the eye of a fellow alcoholic. The ex-cop showed no signs of a recent binge, but fear could sober a man. At least Parris did not reek of booze. His new suit was another sign of fear, disguising him as a respectable taxpayer instead of an unemployed drunk.

"Mr. Parris?" Mallory pointed to the door on the far side of the room. "Could you wait in there? Thanks."

Geldorf watched the man enter Coffey's office and take a chair near the glass partition. "He's gonna be way too comfortable in there. You need a closed room, no windows, no air." The old man was reborn, and all the annoying cockiness was back as he turned to lecture Mallory. "You want complete control over him. You decide when he takes a piss, when he eats—*if* he eats."

"It's not your call," she said, reminding the old man that he was visiting Special Crimes Unit on a provisional passport. "Parris thinks he's here for a friendly little chat."

"No, he doesn't," said Janos walking toward them. "When he saw Geldorf, he panicked. Now he wants a lawyer. So we gotta kill an hour till—"

"The hell we do." Riker strode across the room, entered the office and shouted, "What's all this crap about a lawyer!"

Parris's voice was surly. "You plan to crucify me for these hangings, right?"

"You don't watch TV? You don't listen to the radio? We nailed our perp this afternoon, okay? Now I read your statement, and I got some questions on Natalie Homer."

"I wasn't—" Parris turned to the door as two more people stepped into the office. Mallory sat down behind Coffey's desk, then glared at Lars Geldorf, warning him to keep silent and wait for his cue.

"Parris," said Riker. "You were saying?"

"I wasn't the one who took Natalie's complaints. I was a uniform, not a dick."

"But you *knew* her." Geldorf stood behind Parris's chair and placed one gnarly hand on the man's shoulder. "You saw her every day on patrol."

Parris shook off the man's hand. "She never even looked my way."

"That bothered you, didn't it?" Geldorf leaned down to Parris's ear. "She was so pretty. And here you got this gun, all this power, but she don't even know you're alive."

"Back off," said Mallory. Now everyone in the room, including Alan Parris, was united by a common enemy—Lars Geldorf.

The old man pretended to ignore her and reached into his breast pocket. He pulled out a Polaroid of Natalie Homer, a close-up of a dead woman with mutilated hair and flesh. "Not so pretty now, is she? Not so high and mighty anymore."

Mallory leaned over and snatched the photograph. "I said that's *enough*." Some of her anger was genuine. She disapproved of ad-lib remarks and unauthorized props.

"I want a lawyer," said Parris.

"I don't blame you," said Riker. "This is bull shit. But you haven't been charged with a crime." He turned on Geldorf. "Not one more word." This small gesture had endeared him to the smiling Alan Parris.

"Mr. Parris—*Alan*," said Mallory. "You were a cop. You know how hard this job can be. So what can you tell me about her? Anything that might—"

"Nothing. Every time she came into the station, there was a crowd of dicks around her. They talked to her for hours. For all the good that did her."

"You felt sorry for her." Riker nodded his understanding, his commiseration. They were brothers now.

"Damn straight. She deserved better."

"Tell me about the extra patrols in that neighborhood," said Mallory. "You checked in on her, right? Maybe you stopped by her place to—"

"Why *should* I? The detectives never asked me to." Parris turned to Geldorf. "You bastards liked her well enough, but you never *believed* her." He turned back to Mallory. "They only saw Natalie when she was really scared. I guess they figured that was just normal for her."

"But you knew better," said Riker. "You saw her every day. You knew what she was going through." She was always Natalie to Alan Parris, a first-name acquaintance and not a woman who had never given him the time of day.

Jack Coffey had left the door to the lockup room wide. And now Lieutenant Loman watched the back of a prisoner being marched down the
hall. Mallory was right. No one else could have been as convincing as this
young cop in bloodstains, chains on his wrists, chains on his ankles, falter-
ing steps and now a stumble. Janos's massive arms reached out to catch Deluthe before he could fall.

"The leg irons are overkill," said Harvey Loman.

Coffey stared at the sweat shining on the back of Deluthe's neck. The
mascara hair treatment was running in a brown streak that mingled with
the T-shirt's bloodstains. Then he realized that the game was not over
when Loman went on to say, "I can't see that pathetic bastard outrunning
Janos."

"Yeah, well, the DA's coming," said Coffey. "So we're going by the
book, leg irons and all. We're cutting a deal with the perp."

"Yeah? What's he offering?"

"A photo ID on the man who killed Natalie Homer." Lieutenant Coffey rose from the table and slammed the door. "So you remember that
crime scene pretty well."

"Like I could forget. That room was hell on earth. The stink and the
bugs. But it was a different kind of freak show for the hooker."

"Sparrow."

"Yeah, all those candles, a different noose. And she wasn't even dead. I
still don't see the connection, Jack."

"It's the scarecrow—Natalie's son. I think you met him once, Harvey."

Charles Butler entered the office and stood behind Mallory's chair.
Since he had been given no further instructions, all he could do was loom
over the proceedings, bringing his own discomfort to the party. And now
they were five—too many people and just the right number, each one
jumping up the energy level, the heat and the stress.

Mallory stared at the window on the squad room. "He's coming."

Five pairs of eyes watched Janos escort his prisoner to the desk beneath the only overhead light. From the distance of the lieutenant's office, only the chains, the bandages and the blood were visible. The battered face was shadowed by a baseball cap. Mallory glanced back at Charles, whose face could not hide a thought. He was merely curious. He had no idea that the injured man was Deluthe.

She leaned toward Alan Parris, talking cop to cop. "I've got one break on this case, a witness. You met him once."

"Yeah," said Riker. "You chased him away from Natalie's door. Remember? He was only six years old."

"One of those little kids in the hall?"

Riker turned to the glass wall and pointed at the wounded man being guarded by Janos. "He was Natalie's son."

"Oh, Christ!" Parris turned around for a better look at the man in handcuffs. "That's your perp?" From this angle, he could only see the curve of Deluthe's cheek. "So the kid went nuts."

Mallory nodded to say, *Yes, it's all very sad. Yeah, right.* "Natalie's sister hid the boy out of state. You can guess why."

Parris shook his head as he stared through the glass wall, eyes fixed on the young man in manacles. "Her son hanged those women. I can't believe it. *Bloody Christ.*"

Detective Wang entered the office and tossed a manila envelope on the desk. Riker picked it up and inspected the contents, pictures of three detectives and two uniformed officers as they had appeared twenty years ago. He laid them out on the desk blotter.

Predictably, Parris focused on the portrait of his own young self fresh from the police academy. He was about to say something when Mallory cut him off, saying, "This won't take long." She picked up the photographs and rose from her chair.

"Oh, yeah," said Lieutenant Loman. "I remember the little kids in the hall—one of them anyway." He was staring at the evidence bags that contained a twenty-year-old film carton and a set of notes written to Natalie Homer. "You know *why* I remember him, Jack? This tiny little boy—he reached inside the door of Natalie's apartment and picked up an empty film carton. He wanted a damn souvenir of that poor woman's murder. Cold, huh? I *wish* I could forget that kid."

Mallory stood before the injured detective, looking down on his swollen face. When she spoke to Deluthe, her voice was loud enough to carry across the squad room. "Take your time. This is what they looked like the year your mother died."

Deluthe kept his head down and stared at the photographs as she held them up, one by one, angling them away from the glass wall of Jack Coffey's office. And now she fed Deluthe his cue, the first question, "*This* one?"

The young cop nodded.

"Are you sure?"

Deluthe nodded again.

In a departure from the script, Mallory bent down to him and lowered her voice. "Don't talk, don't move. We've got some time to kill before I go back in there. I know you can't get that dead man out of your mind. You never will. He's part of you now—and what you did to him." She nodded toward the large man beside him. "Detective Janos volunteered to look after you for a while."

Deluthe stared at her with fresh damage in his eyes. "You think I'm a nutcase?"

Mallory nodded. "We *all* go crazy."

"Crazy is a place," said Janos. "You go, you come back."

"Happens so often, we even have a protocol for it—the suicide watch." She held up the photograph again. "Now tap this picture and we're done."

He stretched out his handcuff chain to do it.

Mallory counted to ten slowly. "Nod one more time."

He did as she asked, then lowered his head, eyes fixed on the floor, a genuine portrait of remorse.

"Good job." She prized realism.

Deluthe slumped over, fists clenched, eyes shut tight. The anesthetic benefit of shock was wearing off. She turned to Janos. "Get him back to the hospital."

Mallory made a show of looking at one photograph on the long walk back to Coffey's office. Arthur Wang blocked her way, handing her the evidence bags with the notes and the original film carton with the Polaroid logo. "The boss is done with these."

Detective Wang opened the door to the lockup room and handed Lieutenant Coffey a duplicate set of photographs. Mallory had only given him one line to say: "It's the one on top."

Jack Coffey stared at the picture for a moment, then laid it down on the table in front of Loman. "The scarecrow picked you."

"He picked you." Mallory pushed Lars Geldorf's photograph across the desk, then turned to Alan Parris, saying, "You can go now."

The ex-cop quickly left the office, and Geldorf sank down in the vacated chair. He clutched the portrait of himself at age fifty-five and shook his head. "This is crazy. *Crazy.*" There was a flicker of panic in his face when he looked past Mallory, raising his eyes to stare at the tall man standing behind her chair.

No need to turn around.

With only the eyes in the back of her head, she pictured Charles's wonderful tell-all face stricken with surprise—the real thing. No actor could portray shock and betrayal so well as an honest man with her knife in his back.

Welcome to my job.

She watched Lars Geldorf's face and saw the reflected sorrow of Charles Butler, who had finally understood his role tonight. He had been gulled into preparing this old man, his *friend*, for the close, the kill. And now he joined the list of the wounded as he walked toward the office door, eager to put some distance between himself and his assailant—Mallory.

Ah, but she was not quite done with him yet. "Charles?"

He stopped. She knew he would. There was a bruised and battered look about him when he turned to face her. Was he wondering how far ahead she had planned for this moment?

"I'm sorry. I wanted it to be Parris or Loman," said the queen of all

liars, and only Lars Geldorf believed her. The door closed on Charles Butler, and the old man's sole source of comfort was gone.

The room was colder now.

"I never set eyes on Natalie's son," said Geldorf.

"That's probably what kept him alive," said Mallory.

The old man turned to Riker. "Help me out here. I'm telling you, I
never—"

"Lars—don't," said Riker, deadpan. "It's over. Why would the kid lie?"

"My apologies." Mallory smiled. "I thought you botched this case because you were such a lousy detective. In fact, you were the one who fed
me that line." She picked up the small square Polaroids of the old crime
scene, then dealt them out across the desk like playing cards. "I know why
Parris isn't in these shots. He was only in that room for two seconds. And
you?" She stacked the photographs into a neat deck. "You're not in them
because you took all the pictures that night."

"I could've told you that!" said Geldorf.

She held up the empty film carton. "This always bothered me. The scarecrow left one at every hanging. It had nothing to do with Natalie's murder—only her crime scene. This one's twenty years old. The boy found it
in the hall while you were shooting pictures of his dead mother." She
dropped the film box on the desk. "A little something to remember you by."

"And now it makes sense," said Riker. "The kid's family always knew a
cop killed his mother. We wondered how a six-year-old would recognize
a cop in street clothes. We thought that narrowed it down to Parris or
Loman—the uniforms."

"The scarecrow set us straight," said Mallory, lying as easily as she drew
breath. "When he watched you shoot those pictures of his mother, he
knew you were police. And that was his *second* look at you."

Geldorf sat back in his chair and grinned. "You guys are good, but you
can't scam the master. I invented this little game you're playing. You got
nothin'." He stood up and buttoned his jacket. "Try this on some other
sucker."

"Not so fast, Lars." The man was stunned when Riker put both hands
on his shoulders and forced him back into the chair. "We haven't booked
you yet. The charge is murder."

And that charge hung on a pack of lies told by a fly on the wall.

"All those sausages," said Mallory. "Too many for one person, remember? Natalie was making dinner for her son. The boy was in the bathroom while you were killing his mother. We always figured the perp was someone she knew."

"Her ex-husband!" Geldorf shouted this in the tone of, *Are you blind?*

"No," said Riker. "He was Natalie's *first* stalker. Then he met his new wife, and the harassment stopped. You were the one who left the notes under her door. You scared her right back to the station house—back to you. What a joke. You and that beautiful girl. Even twenty years ago, you were twice her age."

"You didn't expect Natalie to be home that night," said Mallory. "She was always at work when you stopped by with your *love letters*. She caught you leaving that last one under her door. That's why the boy didn't hear any conversation before you killed his mother. How could you explain a thing like that?"

Riker was on his way through the door, saying, "I'll tell the boss it's a wrap."

And Mallory continued, "He said his mother reached for the frying pan and dropped it. Then she tripped and fell. That's when she hit her head on the stove. She was out cold, but you thought she was shamming. You pulled her through a puddle of grease, and then you rolled her on her back."

Were Geldorf's eyes a little wider? Yes.

"She was coming to," said Mallory. "Were you afraid she'd scream? Is that why you wrapped your hands around her throat and crushed the life out of her?"

Jack Coffey was standing in the doorway. "Is that when you panicked, old man?" He walked into the room and tossed a pad of paper to Mallory. "That's Loman's statement."

Geldorf craned his neck to read the upside-down lines of longhand on the top sheet. "Loman? The other—"

"Alan Parris's ex-partner." Riker strolled into the room, smiling. "He rolled over on you, Lars. He claims you tried to bury this case, concealing evidence and—"

"I was *protecting* my evidence!"

"Well, it's your word against his." Mallory looked up from her reading. "And he's a lieutenant." Though Loman's statement was worthless, only repeating Geldorf's own story of misleading reporters, she said, "And that's it. We're done."

Coffey cleared the evidence from the desk, sweeping it into the carton, packing up the debris of the day. The lieutenant paused to hand her a slip of paper. "I don't recognize this witness."

"That's the landlady's granddaughter, Alice White. She saw a man steal the rope and duct tape out of the handyman's tool chest." Another lie, another nail. "She's on the way in for a photo ID." Mallory picked up the photograph of Geldorf and casually dropped it into the box. "She'll testify that Natalie's son was in that apartment for two days. Just his dead mother for company—and the flies, the roaches. No wonder that little boy went psycho." In an echo of Susan Qualen, she said, "Who do you call when a cop kills your mother? The cops?" She turned to Geldorf. "He told us the buzz of the flies was deafening, but he was only six years old. I guess the noise got louder as he got older."

"You have the right to remain silent," said Riker, pulling out his Miranda card, preparing for the last formality that would allow their suspect to call for a lawyer.

They were cutting the timing very fine.

Mallory snatched the card away from her partner and handed it to Geldorf. "Look, it's been a long night. You know all the words. Just sign the damn thing, okay?" She held out the pen, and Geldorf accepted it like thousands of felons before him. So natural to take an object when it's offered. But now he only stared at the card.

Planning to lawyer up, old man?

In a preemptive strike, she slapped the desk. "Sign the card! Bring on the lawyers!"

They were coming to the closing shots—almost done, for Geldorf must realize that no deal was in the offering, and this was the sign of a case with abundant evidence. He began to shrink, shoulders slumping, hunching. His hands were rising, as if to beg. "I loved that woman. I *grieved* for her. Natalie was—" He had lost his train of thought, his reason; he had lost everything. The old man bowed his head, and Mallory strained to catch the mumbled words, "I was a good cop once. That's worth—something."

She stared at him, incredulous. "You were expecting a *deal?*"

"I don't care if he was a cop." Jack Coffey lifted the carton and feigned impatience. "We're not gonna offer him any—"

"It's *my* case." Mallory turned to Geldorf. "I know what you're thinking, old man. All that embarrassment to the department. And saving the city the cost of a trial—that should be worth something, too, right?"

Geldorf nodded.

Jack Coffey dumped the carton on the floor, saying, "Keep it simple, Mallory. I'm not giving him the moon."

She leaned forward, eyes trained on Geldorf. "This is the best deal—the *only* deal you get. The state won't request the death penalty. No cameras, no media circus, and the real story never leaves this room. If you waive a trial, we can probably get the DA to push your arraignment through night court—quietly." In fact, the arrangements had already been approved. Sentencing would follow in the morning. "All the standard perks for an ex-cop, and you'll do fifteen years in prison." A life sentence for a man of seventy-five.

She pushed a yellow pad across the desk. "Make up any version you like. Call it a crime of passion. Say you once loved a woman to death. You've got six seconds, old man. Take it or leave it."

"Time's up!" Jack Coffey's fist came down on the desk, and Geldorf jumped. "*Now* we book him. *Right now!*"

Lars Geldorf picked up the pad of paper, and his hand trembled as he began to write out his confession.

Mallory followed her partner across the squad room, not willing to let him out of her sight—not yet. He was one of few people who mattered to her, but that did not mean she trusted him. Riker sat down at his desk far from the pool of fluorescent light. The ember of his cigarette glowed in the dark as he dropped his match into a dish of paper clips.

"How's Sparrow?" This was a test. According to her paid informant, a nurse, Riker called for updates every hour.

"It's almost over," he said, "just a matter of hours."

Mallory bit back a comment that he would not like, and they sat in uneasy silence for a while, watching his smoke twist and curl. "You wanted

Sparrow's case so bad," she said. "Just keeping faith with a snitch? Or maybe you thought Frankie Delight's murder would come back to bite you." She wanted it to be one of these two things, something cold, less personal.

Riker shrugged. "There was more to it, but that's between me and Sparrow." He rose from the chair and stubbed out his cigarette. "I'm heading back to the hospital. I wanna be there when—"

"No you don't," said Mallory. "I *know* she's out of the coma. You weren't planning to tell me that, were you?" Mallory stared at him until he met her eyes. "It's *my* turn at Sparrow."

What a kick in the head, huh, Riker?

After all he had gone through on that whore's account, now he must stand back, virtually handing a helpless woman over to her worst enemy. And yet he could not raise a challenge. Her claim on the dying prostitute was so much stronger than his.

He nodded, and their deal was done.

Mallory watched from the window on the street until Riker emerged from the building. Reporters converged on him with cameras and microphones—star treatment. Sergeant Bell came running out the front door to rescue him with a press release of lies, waving the paper as bait. After the mob had deserted Riker for fresh meat, he stepped into the street and let two cabs go by unhailed, for he was a man with nowhere to go from here.

A lamp switched on at the back of the squad room. The chief of Forensics sat in a small patch of light, hands folded, waiting.

Spying, Heller?

The criminalist stared at her across the span of five desks. How much had he overheard? As Mallory strolled toward him, she could see that his eyes were red and sore from lost sleep.

"Warwick's Used Books." He simply put these words out in the air between them, then solemnly awaited her reaction. Mallory was stunned and feeling threatened. He misunderstood her expression. "So Warwick *was* a suspect. I *knew* it."

Mallory settled into a chair beside the desk. Dancing with this man was a tricky business, but she would not admit that she was mystified. "I can't give up any information on him." Always best to mix lies in equal parts with the truth. "The scarecrow wasn't Warwick. Does that help?"

Heller's face lifted and brightened, flesh deepening in the folds of a wide grin. "Well, I guess you won't need this." He handed her a sheet of paper. "Too bad. I called in a lot of favors to get it."

She scanned the brief synopsis of a psychiatric history: As a child, John Warwick had stood accused of murdering his twin sister. An eyewitness had cleared the boy, but not before the police had spent six hours wrenching a false confession from a terrified eight-year-old grieving for his twin and crying for his mother. Gangs of reporters had stalked the family, increasing the trauma of a guiltless child. And John Warwick had spent the rest of his childhood in a mental institution, clinging to the fictions of cops and newspaper headlines, irretrievably lost in deep pain and unable to believe in his own innocence.

She dropped the bio sheet on the desk, unenlightened and unimpressed. From what she remembered of the bookseller, he was not capable of killing even one of the thousand flies left at each crime scene. This connection of Heller's was so pathetic. Something had clearly gone awry in his good brain. And this foray into Warwick's past was outside the scope of Forensics.

Mallory smiled, for she was always happiest in the attack mode. "You shouldn't have messed in our business, Heller. If Warwick had been a solid suspect, you could've queered everything."

"I had to know," he said. "That bastard Riker couldn't trust me to keep the book quiet. It should've been recorded on my evidence log." There was no animosity in Heller's voice—far from it. He was one happy man.

The book.

Mallory was making linkages at the speed of a computer. Her machine logic flickered and faltered, for the paperback western had shown no trace of damage from the fire or the hose. Yet this book must be what Riker had snatched from the watery floor of Sparrow's apartment. And his other gift to her was the innocent deniability of a crime. He had risked everything to hide a dangerous connection between a whore and Markowitz's daughter.

"*Homecoming,*" she said, "by Jake Swain."

When Heller nodded, Mallory knew this man had solid proof against Riker, and no machine logic could have guided her to the next conclusion: Her partner was Sheriff Peety in a bad suit.

Riker commanded such deep respect that no one could believe him guilty of a corrupt act, not even when guilt was proven beyond doubt. And Heller, of all people, had been unable to believe his own evidence, for how could Riker steal *anything*? The criminalist had denied his own religion of all-holy fact. He had stepped a hundred miles out of character to doggedly hunt down proof of Riker's innocence where none existed. And Heller had actually found something that looked the same, that shined like truth—though it was only faith.

Without another word between them, they left the station house and parted company on the sidewalk. And there the young detective continued her silence as she endured a civilian's tight embrace and oft-repeated thanks. Mallory stepped back and stared at the smiling face of the next and final victim of the man who killed Natalie Homer. Susan Qualen had believed the press reports that her sister's only child was still alive.

And so the damage of a twenty-year-old murder would not end tonight. It would drag on well into the morning hours. Following Lars Geldorf's rushed arraignment and sentencing, Natalie's sister would be quietly told that the police had killed her nephew after all—with a baseball bat.

"So sorry, ma'am," Jack Coffey would say.

TWENTY-FOUR

WHEN CHARLES CLOSED HIS TIRED EYES, HE SAW A tiny thief who ran with whores and lived by guile, surviving on animal instinct to get through the night—an altogether admirable child. Louis Markowitz's hero.

"Charles?"

His heavy lids flickered open, and Kathy grew up before his eyes. She was so lovely, and he wanted to tell her that, for how else would she know? The tragedy of Kathy Mallory was some malady that had no name but was akin to an aspect of vampirism. This sad insight had come to him by simple observation. She did not look for herself in mirrors, nor in the reflections of shop windows, never expecting to find herself there. He turned to the antique looking glass above his mantelpiece. Literally a magic mirror once used in a stage act of the last century, it was full of wavy lines and smeared realities.

"Charles!"

"Yes," he said, without turning round.

"I want you to keep an eye on Riker tonight." Mallory walked back and forth across his front room, impatient with a cell-phone caller who had put her on hold. "You'll find him in that cop bar down the street." She was still in motion as she resumed her phone conversation. Red designs in the weave of the mirrored carpet seemed to track the floor behind her.

Charles stared at the ancient glass, his gigantic nose, her wonderful eyes. He was fascinated by her form elongating and twisting, her legs bending back to form the hocks of a padding cat. Beast and Beauty were trading places. The reversal went far beyond their positions in the backward space of the mirror room, where she continued to walk to and fro. Her human face was gone, distorted and stripped down to the bestial aspect of Mallory in the panther cage, badly wounded by her life, elegant paws bleeding as she paced. *She* bore the scars, *he* felt the pain. How insane—

"Charles?"

The SoHo saloon was crowded with cops and one civilian. Charles Butler had lost his jacket and tie somewhere between one death and another. His white shirt was wrinkled, sleeves rolled back, and his face was showing the wear of long days broken by catnaps.

Riker stared at his own tired image in the mirror behind the bar, then quickly looked away, saying, "Thanks anyway, but I'm taking a cab tonight. So pull up a glass. I hate to drink alone." Of course, this was a polite lie, for the detective did his best binge drinking all by himself.

Charles obliged him and ordered two rounds of Chivas Regal. "So Sparrow is dying. And you're not going to the hospital?"

"No." He prayed that Sparrow would be long dead before an old enemy turned up.

Awe, Mallory, what a gift you have for payback.

It made her the ultimate cop. She was the paladin everyone wanted, a perfect instrument of vengeance. In Riker's view, people should be more careful about what they wished for. Absent all humanity, its bias and fragility, the law was a sociopath.

Their drinks had appeared on the bar in front of them, and Charles had been left hanging again, awaiting some explanation for this failure to visit the deathbed of a whore. Riker cut the man off before he could ask one more time. "So tell me, how did Sheriff Peety outdraw the Wichita Kid?"

"The usual way. The other man drew his gun too late."

"Impossible," said Riker. "Drunk or sober—even with the damn sun in his eyes—that gunslinger was the best man."

"Yes, if you mean faster. And that day—" Charles's eyes were in soft focus now, and Riker knew he was projecting book pages on his cocktail napkin and quoting verbatim when he said, " 'That day, the gunslinger was a young god, walking out of the whirlwind of dust, growing larger, step by step. His birthright was dominion over all other men.' " He shuddered, then tipped back his shot glass, as if to kill a bad taste. "Terrible prose. You're right—Wichita was fast with a gun, but Sheriff Peety was bigger."

"What?" And now Riker was left to dangle while his bar-stool companion sipped his drink, taking his sweet time. Charles's expression worried him. It was almost a Mallory smile.

"A hero bigger than life. Your words, Riker. Well, he was Wichita's hero, too—always had been. The boy *loved* the man. So you might wonder—did Wichita deliberately draw too slow? Or did he lose that gunfight in his own mind before he drew his weapon? Perhaps, at the end, he still believed that Sheriff Peety was a great man, the better man. Maybe that's how the sheriff won. . . . Or maybe it was a suicide."

"Thanks, Charles. That might drive me nuts for another fifteen years."

"Happy to return the favor."

Riker recognized his own twisted signature in this exchange, and he smiled with the grace of a good loser. "Okay, you get one free question. Anything you want. Shoot."

"You said Kathy was posthumously charged with arson and murder."

"Right."

"Though she didn't *die*, and she didn't *kill* anybody. But I've still got a corpse and a fire. Does this have anything to do with why Mallory hates Sparrow?"

"Yeah."

Charles waited for the rest of the explanation. And he waited. Now the two men engaged in a contest to see who could outcreep whom with the most insipid smile.

Riker broke down first. "Okay, this is the deal. It took me a long time to piece this story together. You can't repeat it to anyone. And when I'm done, you'll wish I never started. Kathy Mallory's death is gonna drive you crazy till the day you die."

"Word of honor, I'll never tell."

"Charles, are you sure you understand? When you know the truth, you have to eat it."

"Agreed."

"Some of it's guesswork." Only two people knew the real story. One was a gifted liar, and the other was a dying whore with a scrambled brain. "Fifteen years ago, Sparrow did a drug deal with a really scurvy character. She was trading stolen VCRs for heroin."

"The VCRs that Kathy stole?"

"Yeah. So the hookers told you about the great truck robbery? Well, I'm guessing the drug dealer picked the location for the meet, a place with boarded-up windows and no back door. No neighbors either. The buildings on both sides were torn down, and this one was due for a midnight demolition."

"Pardon?"

"The owner was planning to torch the place for the insurance money. He had accelerants stashed on every floor, kerosene, paint thinner. But that came out later—after the fire."

"The fire that killed Kathy?"

"That's the one. I figure this dealer—"

"Frankie Delight?"

"Yeah." Riker wondered what else Charles had pieced together with the help of the Hooker Book Salon. "Frankie was gonna double-cross Sparrow. So he would've been the first one to draw a knife."

"The one that made that huge scar in Sparrow's side?"

Riker nodded. "And she won that fight, but she left her knife behind. I've got a witness who saw it buried in Frankie Delight's dead body. An ambulance picked up Sparrow three blocks away."

"And Kathy?"

"She saw the whole thing. Another whore can place the kid in Sparrow's hospital room the next day—one real tired little girl. And that's when

Kathy was sent back to the crime scene to get the murder weapon." This was the picture Riker wanted out of his head—that child pulling a knife from a corpse.

"Lou and me, we're in the car when we hear a call on the radio. A dispatcher's sending all available units to investigate a puddle of blood on Avenue B. We would've blown it off, but then another call placed a little blond girl at the same address—following a blood trail into an empty building. We got there just in time to see the flames. That's when Kathy came out the front door. One look at us and she runs back inside—back into the fire."

"But that's not—"

"Not *normal?* No, you wouldn't expect a kid to do that. But she was carrying a knife with Sparrow's initial on the hilt and probably a good set of prints. If the kid was caught near Frankie's body with the murder weapon, her favorite whore would go to jail."

"So she ran into a burning building, *knowing* she could die?"

"Naw, we never figured that—not for a second. This kid had a world-class survival instinct. Lou figured she was heading for the roof, maybe counting on a fire escape."

"Could Kathy have staged her own death?"

"That was one theory, and she was that smart. But there was no fire escape. That morning, the owner sold the iron for scrap. We tried to follow her into the building. Then the first explosion blew out the boards on the downstairs windows. Cans of kerosene and paint thinner were goin' off like bombs. And now there's no way in, no way out." He recalled the open doorway as a wall of fire. Flames had boiled out of the ground-floor windows like the tail burners of a rocket. "I thought the building was gonna take off and fly away. The back door was boarded up. The firemen didn't even try to break it down. All they could do was contain the blaze to one building."

Riker slapped his hand on the bar. "Bang, bang, bang! All the accelerants were blowing up in sympathetic explosions—all the way up to the top of the building. Then the roof went up in a ball of fire, and we knew the kid was dead. . . . Well, *I* did." It had taken more than Armageddon to convince Lou Markowitz.

"The fire marshal showed us the kid's shoes—proof that she made it up to the roof. They were still laced, blown off her feet in the final blast. One shoe was clean, thrown clear. The other one burnt black. The arson team figured she was at the center of the last explosion, and they didn't expect to find her in one piece."

"So Kathy was presumed dead?"

"Well, they didn't know her name. All they had was one of her books, half fried . . . and her shoes. Later, a snitch tied the western and the kid to Sparrow. Two cops showed up in Sparrow's hospital room and told her that Kathy was dead."

"Except that she wasn't." Charles ticked off the points on his fingers. "Boarded windows, no back door, no fire escape, no neighboring roof. How did she escape?"

"Kathy wouldn't tell. She *never* will. She *knows* it still drives me crazy. Damn kid never misses an opportunity to get even."

"With a concussion," said Charles, "she might not remember."

"But that won't explain how she got off the roof alive. Who knows? Maybe she flew. That was Sparrow's favorite theory."

"I like it. If a shoe can be thrown clear, why not a little girl? With something soft like garbage bags on another roof—"

"No, Charles, we checked. No soft landing. And remember, this building was an island—twenty feet to the next roof. We caught Kathy that same night—no cuts, no bruises, not a mark on her. If you think about it long enough, it'll give you a headache."

"All right." Charles covered his eyes with one hand. "You thought she was dead, but that was the night you found her—which suggests that you were still looking for her."

"Right." Riker slapped the mahogany. "We were in this same bar, me and Lou." He looked up at the television set mounted on the wall. "Watching TV. The lead story was a little girl with green eyes who loved westerns. The kid was famous for two minutes on the news." And she would have gotten more airtime if a city garbage strike had not stolen her thunder.

"Suddenly the place gets real quiet. I turn to the door, and there's Sparrow. Well, this is a cop bar, and she's lookin' every inch a hooker. Just begging for a twisted arm and a short flight through the front door. I tried to get rid of her. Junkies are always messing with your head, and Lou was in a bad way. I didn't think he could take anymore. But now I see the blood leaking through her clothes and a hospital bracelet on her wrist."

"And that's when you guessed she'd killed the drug dealer?"

"No, they hadn't even found his bones yet. It was the next day when they brought him in tagged for a John Doe. The autopsy turned up a thigh bone chipped twice by a blade. Dr. Slope figured the knife cut an artery and it bled out. He even diagrammed the angle of the strike. That put Sparrow on her knees when she sank her knife into Frankie Delight. And it fit with the wound in Sparrow's side. The shock would've brought her down."

"But *Kathy* was charged with the murder."

"Charles, you're gettin' ahead of the story. So we're in the bar with Sparrow, and we wanna take her back to the hospital. But the whore won't go. She's sweatin' and she's got the shakes real bad. Lou figures she's strung out from withdrawal pains. So he empties out his damn wallet. It was maybe eighty dollars, a fortune to a sick junkie. And he slides the money down the bar. Now Sparrow says, 'Her name is *Kathy*, and I'm tellin' you that kid is unnatural. She could be *alive*.' And Lou says, 'No, Sparrow—only if you believe in Superman comic books. Kathy was just a little girl. . . . She didn't fly away. . . . She *died*.'"

Riker held up his glass and stared at the last drops of liquid gold. "There's not much difference between me and a junkie. As long as I got my booze, I'm an okay guy. But take it away from me?" He shook his head. "Much as I like you, Charles, I'd slit your throat for the next drink. With Sparrow it was heroin. Well, she's too bloody to work the street. No money to score her next needle. She's dope sick, *dying* for a fix, but she pushes Lou's money back across the bar and says, 'You gotta find the kid. She might be hurt.'"

"So she *knew* Kathy was alive."

"No, she didn't. That's the kicker. Sparrow was going on faith. And *that's* what the whore was buying when she gave the money back. She had to make Lou believe in Kathy, too. Because the kid *might* be out there alone in the dark, maybe hurt real bad."

Riker drained his glass. "That night, Sparrow was more of a man than I was. Well, she's got our attention. She says this drag queen commissioned the kid to steal parts off a Jaguar. Sparrow only found out 'cause Kathy had to ask what a Jag was before she could rob one. Now this happened way before the dicks tell Sparrow the kid is dead. She's still in the hospital and thinkin' ahead to her next needle. She tells Kathy about this rich yuppie who trolls East Village clubs and whores every weekend. And *he's* got a Jag. Well, it's Saturday night. I'm three sheets to the wind when Lou grabs my arm. And off we go with Sparrow."

Three fools with absolute faith in comic-book heroes.

Riker could still see Lou Markowitz driving through the wet streets at a crawl of ten miles an hour, haunting every place where they had ever seen Kathy, chased her and lost her. It was insane to believe that the child had escaped from that fire. Yet they drove on through drizzling rain. "We knew she was dead, but we couldn't stop looking for her. How crazy was that?"

As if it were happening all over again, Riker watched his old friend tune the car radio. Rock 'n' roll did not suit him that night. Lou picked a station that played bluesy music from an earlier era. There were pauses between the sad notes and phrases, like a conversation with the sorry man behind the wheel. "And then we found the Jag. Lou pulls over to the curb and cuts the lights."

The three of them listened to a sweet ripple of ivory keys tapering off in the low notes. Three pairs of eyes were trained on the sports car parked across the street. Piano chords dropped into spaces of silence, like footsteps of a child. And then, as if Duke Ellington had orchestrated the moment— along came Kathy. The golden head was bobbing and dodging behind the garbage cans. Out on the open street now, barefooting down the pavement, homing in on the Jaguar's trademark hood ornament.

Baby needs new shoes.

In and out of the lamplight, her small wet face glistened through the rain and the smoky gray cover of steam hissing up through a subway grate. The child was coming closer. Sparrow sank low in the backseat. Lou Markowitz and Riker slumped down behind the dashboard and watched, fascinated, as a little girl worked bits of metal in a lock. No crude coat hangers or broken windows for this kid. She opened the door with the finesse of a pro.

Once the child was inside the Jaguar, the two policemen left their vehicle, moving quickly, silently. It was a fight not to laugh out loud—or cry.

When Markowitz bent down to the open door of the Jaguar, the little girl was sitting on the front seat, calmly dismantling the dashboard toys, tape deck and radio, using Sparrow's knife as a screwdriver. Lou leaned in close, saying, "Hey, kid, whatcha doin'?"

The little girl smelled of sulfur and smoke; that should have been a warning. How indignant she was, and so angry, pointing her knife and yelling, "Back off, old man, or I'll *cut* you."

Lou's right hand flashed out, and startled Kathy looked down to see that her tiny fist was empty.

"So then, Lou says to the kid, 'Pretty fast moves for a fat man, huh, Kathy?' He pulled her out of the car, but she got away from him. Ran straight into Sparrow's arms. And then, what happened next—well, the kid never saw that coming. It was brutal. The whore drags Kathy back to Lou, and she's saying, 'Baby, if you don't go with the man, how am I gonna get *paid?*' "

"So she did accept the—"

"Not one dime. At the end of the day, that whore showed a lotta class." The detective lifted his glass in a salute, not noticing that it was empty, for he was still looking at Kathy's face, the confusion in her eyes. Her world was collapsing all around her, above and beneath her. "The kid's survival was geared on running. Sparrow made sure she had no one to run to— no one who cared."

And *that* was the moment when the little girl died, her bones going to liquid as she was sliding to the ground, trying to save herself by grabbing Sparrow's skirt, then collapsing and crying at the whore's feet. "Kathy risked her life—and this was her payback. Sparrow just walked away. No good-bye, nothin'." Riker looked down at his glass for a moment. "So Kathy thinks she's been sold for money, right? That's all she's worth to the whore, another damn needle—and *still* she tried to run after Sparrow."

"Because she loved her?"

"Because that whore was all she had." Riker could hear the small needy voice crying, begging Sparrow to come back, *please, please.* So much pain— the child's and his own. Oh, the panic in Kathy's eyes when Sparrow turned a corner and disappeared.

"And then the kid went wild. All the guns and knives came out. I mean that literally. She drew on us with a damn pellet gun. God, how she hated

Lou. He'd run her ragged, took everything away from her—first her books and then her whore."

"Well, that explains the early animosity," said Charles. "Why she never called him anything but Markowitz."

"Yeah, she blamed him for turning Sparrow against her. He spent years paying for that. So did I. That brat never forgets, *never* forgives." Riker pushed his glass to the edge of the bar. "So now we're headin' for Brooklyn. I'm in the backseat, and the kid's up front with Lou." He recalled every detail of that drive, the smell of rain-washed air, the suburban lawns littered with bicycles and tricycles. The car radio was cranked up all the way, breaking the peace in a rock 'n' roll celebration. Dogs barked to the high notes, and the lights of fireflies winked in sync with the beat of a golden oldie by Buddy Holly.

And a feral child was manacled to the dashboard. Kathy was a hellmouth of obscenities, a small storm of energy fighting against her chains, though she must have known she could never break them.

"Now it gets a little spooky." And the music had changed to the Rolling Stones. "But it helps if you know that Lou's wife could hear lost children crying on other planets." The old green sedan pulled up to the curb in front of the house, where Helen Markowitz was framed in a square of yellow light—waiting. Suddenly, she was drawn away from the window and moving toward the front door with a sense of great urgency.

The car and the music should have reassured her that nothing was wrong. Bad news was so seldom announced by loud rock 'n' roll. And Lou's wife could not have seen the baby thief in the dark of the car nor heard one small angry voice above a chorus of wailing rockers, steel guitars and drums. Yet Helen was clearly on a mission when she burst through the front door, flew down the porch steps and ran across the wet grass.

The little girl was screaming death threats at the top of her tiny lungs while Lou Markowitz grinned broadly and foolishly. His life was complete. His wife was busy ripping the passenger door off its hinges, and Kathy was almost home.

TWENTY-FIVE

THE LONG SUMMER FEVER WAS OVER. THE HEAT WAS dying off in cool wet gusts of air and rain. The two men stepped out onto the sidewalk and stood beneath the awning.

"Louis must have told Mallory about the murder charge," said Charles. "When she joined the police department, he 'would've—"

"Yeah." Riker was on the lookout for a cab to carry him home. "He told her that much. Now she thinks it was Sparrow who pinned the murder on her. Lou couldn't set her straight. She would've wondered why he didn't make a case against the whore."

Charles kept silent for a moment and listened to the steady rain. "Mallory will never have any peace."

"Neither will you. . . . Me either."

Disregarding Riker's plans to take a cab, Charles opened the door of his Mercedes and guided him into the passenger seat, then politely looked the other way while the man wrestled with a drunk's problem of fastening a safety belt.

Charles started the engine, then pulled into traffic. "Did Sparrow tell you she was defending Kathy when she got stabbed?"

"No, we couldn't ask her anything about that night. Guilty knowledge. If you know about a murder, then you're part of the crime. But it wasn't hard to work out. Frankie Delight was outmatched, a real flyweight. But good as Sparrow was in a street fight, she was never the aggressor. She would've kicked off her high heels and run when that knife came out. But she's got the kid with her, and little legs can't run as fast as a barefoot whore. So we figured Frankie stabbed her while she was shielding Kathy. I know he made the first cut, 'cause the whore was on her knees when she put her shiv in his leg."

Charles vividly recalled the photograph of Sparrow's scar. He could see it now—not a slit, but a gaping hole dug into her side. Yet she had found the strength to drive a knife through a man's clothing and muscle.

Riker read his mind and said, "Sparrow's knife was razor sharp, and she got damn lucky when she hit that artery."

Charles nodded absently, listening to the rain on the roof. "Mallory's at the hospital now, isn't she? That's why you didn't go. She wouldn't allow it."

His friend wore a look of surprise, perhaps wondering what he might have said to give that away. One hand on the armrest, he tapped his fingers to the beat of the windshield wipers.

"So," said Charles, "you're planning to let her bludgeon a dying woman? Oh, not with her fists—but you know what's going on in that hospital room. You *know*."

"I can't tell her the truth. And neither can you. I had to pick a memory she could believe in. I'm gonna let her hold on to Lou."

So she would never discover that Louis had ripped out her ten-year-old heart with a conspiracy of lies. "And she goes on hating Sparrow until it's too late?"

"It won't be long now." Riker rolled down the window and sent his cigarette flying into the rain.

Charles sensed a door closing here, and he picked up the thread of the previous conversation. "Lucky the wound was in Frankie's thigh. I suppose that made it easy to blame a child."

"You make it sound like we framed the kid." Riker almost smiled. "It wasn't even our case. Two other detectives closed out the paperwork. The death was self-defense but connected to felony arson. Sparrow would've gone to prison."

"So you kept silent, and Kathy took the blame."

"Well, the kid was guilty on the arson charge. Kathy decided to get rid of *all* the evidence. She soaked the body with kerosene. Very thorough. All the medical examiner had to work with was some charcoaled meat and bone. So a nameless, dead kid took the blame for everything." Riker yawned. "Case closed." And then his eyes closed.

Twenty minutes passed in silence before Charles pulled up to the curb at Riker's address. Rather than disturb his sleep, Charles gathered the man into his arms, then carried him through the door and up the stairs to the apartment. He laid the detective down on an unmade bed, then removed the revolver and put it away in a drawer. After slipping the shoes from Riker's feet, Charles followed the last of Mallory's instructions. He entered the bathroom and flicked on the switch for a plastic Jesus night-light.

On the lonely ride home, he thought about Riker's version of events and then the way it had really happened. On one point, he and the detective agreed. The drug dealer had made the first strike before his artery became a fountain of spraying blood. Sparrow's wound had come first—but not while shielding a child. That woman had been laughing when Frankie Delight put his knife in her side—Mallory's own words, the testimony of an eyewitness.

Caught by surprise, Sparrow had fallen to her knees, crippled with blood loss and shock, then a sudden drop in blood pressure and the resulting lightness in head and chest—the weakness of limbs. He could see her hands trying to plug that hideous hole. Perhaps there had been time to pull a weapon, but no strength to drive it home. And the dealer would have been on his guard against reprisal.

There were *two* chips in the thigh bone of Frankie Delight, an act of violence powered by rage and fear. Only a ten-year-old girl could have taken him down by stealth and surprise. Charles could see the small thief stealing the knife from the hand of the fallen prostitute, then driving it into a man's thigh once—twice—getting even. How surprised the child must have been to see Frankie Delight fall and die, wondering then, *How could such a wound be mortal?*

The little girl had killed a man for Sparrow's sake, then risked her life in trial by fire, and Kathy's reward was not the ongoing love she needed so badly, but betrayal and desertion. That was the only scenario to fit every fact and explain why the prostitute remained unforgiven.

Charles knew what was happening in Sparrow's hospital room. The dying woman, though deep in coma dreams, had been defeating the death sentences of her doctors for days. And this will to live suggested the stuff of her dreams, unfinished business. All this time, Sparrow had been waiting for Mallory.

His car rolled to a stop, and he closed his eyes in pain, not wanting to imagine this reunion, a chanted litany of hateful acts and trespasses, music to die by.

And so he turned his mind to the last riddle, expecting to make short work of it: How had Kathy escaped the fire?

Logic could not carry him everywhere, but damned close. He liked Sparrow's theory best. The child must have been thrown clear in the explosion. He envisioned Kathy surrounded by fire and running past the corpse of Frankie Delight as it burned brightly head to toe. Kathy's feet barely touched ground, all but flying to gain that staircase before the flames could eat her. Behind her, the boards were awash in roiling liquid fire. He could hear her scream the only prayer a child knows to ask for pity and mercy, "Mama!" Or had she called out for Sparrow? The flames raced up the stairs with her, singeing hair as she climbed higher and higher. Bombs were going off on the floors below.

Bang! Bang! Bang!

Kathy pushed through the rooftop door and saw the sky and—then what? No fire escape, no way out. She raised her arms like thin white wings. And what happened next? The whole world exploded under her feet. She must have been thrown clear, but how to account for her lack of injuries? How far could one throw a child without harming her? Given the probable force of the blast, the speed of propulsion and the sudden impact—the child lay dead or badly broken in every logical scenario *all night long.*

Over the ensuing years, Charles would come to understand the persistence of whores, their book salon and the maddening quest for the end of a story. The problem of the escape would never be solved—unless one counted the last words he would write in his journal toward the end of a very long life. Because he had never betrayed his role as a keeper of secrets, an eater of sins, his children and grandchildren would be forever confounded by his homage to Sparrow's faith in comic-book heroes, a single line at the center of the page, "Kathy, can you fly?"

EPILOGUE

DETECTIVE MALLORY SHUDDERED SO SLIGHTLY THAT THE doctor beside her failed to notice. She dug her fingernails into her palms to bring on the pain—to stay awake and focused, to see this thing through.

Payback.

Rain drummed on the window of Sparrow's hospital room. The lights were low, and Father Rose hovered over the sickbed, armed with his magical rosary beads. Mallory watched him don his surplice to perform the sacrament of last rites—a waste of precious time.

The young intern affirmed this idea, saying, "I don't think she knows what's going on."

Mallory stared at the woman on the bed, eyes rolling, mouth drooling. Sparrow seemed smaller now, as houses do when children revisit them later in life. "How can you tell if she's awake?"

The doctor shrugged. "Does it matter? There's a big difference between awake and aware. She only has a few hours, I'm sure of that much. Her organs are shutting down."

And the physician did not want to be here at the end. Why linger over his failure? He left the room quickly—escaping. Mallory listened to his footsteps hurrying down the corridor, outrunning death. Only a priest would be attracted to Sparrow now.

"Do you heartily repent your sins?"

"Father, that would take years. She's a whore." Mallory opened the door as an invitation for the man to leave, and soon. The priest stared at her in surprise, as though her hint might have been too subtle. "Speed it up," she said. "I haven't got all night—and neither does Sparrow."

Father Rose bent over his parishioner. "Can you give me a sign of contrition?"

"She's sorry," said Mallory. "I saw her eyes move."

"You're heartless."

"I know that."

"She's dying. Why can't you leave her in peace?" The rest of his words to Sparrow were close to mime, inaudible and ending with the sign of the cross.

"You're done. Good." Mallory walked across the room and stood very close to the man. "Father, leave *now*." She held up her gold shield to remind him that she was the law. "I've got official business here. I'm not giving you a choice."

She would have liked him better if he had put up a fight, but he turned his eyes to Sparrow's, and every thought in his head was there to read when he shrugged. The priest was already writing off the whore as a corpse. What more damage could be done to her now? What comfort could his presence bring? *None.*

He left the room quietly, and Mallory shut the door behind him, then jammed a straight-back chair beneath the knob to keep it closed. There would be no more visitors tonight.

She walked back to her old enemy on the hospital bed, the woman who had betrayed her and, worse, *abandoned* her. Now the whore was the one who was utterly helpless, unable to lift one hand in defense. Her skin was as pale as the sheets.

"Sparrow? It's *me!*"

There was no response beyond ragged breathing and the endless demented motion of blue eyes that saw nothing. Could Sparrow hear? Could she understand the words? There was no way to tell. The only certainty in this room was death; it was coming.

The young detective leaned over the woman, bending low enough for her lips to lightly brush a tuft of hair near Sparrow's ear, then whispered, "It's Kathy."

And I'm lost.

Mallory settled into a chair beside the bed, then opened an old paperback book—the last western. Her head was bowed, eyes fixed on the page. "I'm going to read you a story," she said, as one blind hand reached out for the comfort of Sparrow's.